OXFORD WORLD'S CLASSICS

EMPIRE WRITING

THE short stories, poems, essays, travel writing, and memoirs in this anthology belong to that phase of British expansionist imperialism known as high empire (1870–1918). This was a time when an infectious excitement and conviction about world domination in ruling circles at home was beginning to be met by questioning voices from colonized territories. While statesmen, adventurers, and propagandists were envisioning and applauding imperial exploits, we see in this book how native and settler peoples at once undercut and strangely mimicked their rhetoric and most favoured images. By gathering together writings from India, Africa, the West Indies, Australia, New Zealand, Canada, Ireland, and Britain, this wide-ranging selection reveals the startling multiplicity and proliferation, the vivid contrasts and subtle shifts in responses to colonial experience, and embraces some of empire's key symbols and emblematic moments. Selected authors include Toru Dutt, Henry Lawson, Mary Kingsley, Hugh Clifford, J. E. Casely Hayford, Claude McKay, Katherine Mansfield, and Solomon Plaatje, as well as Anthony Trollope, John Ruskin, Rudyard Kipling, Flora Annie Steel, Robert Louis Stevenson, Olive Schreiner, Joseph Conrad, and Leonard Woolf.

ELLEKE BOEHMER is the author of *Colonial and Postcolonial Literature* (1995) and of two novels, *Screens Against the Sky* (1990) and *An Immaculate Figure* (1993). She has written widely on post-colonial writing and has co-edited *Altered State? Writing and South Africa* (1994). She is a lecturer in English at the University of Leeds.

OXFORD WORLD'S CLASSICS

*For almost 100 years Oxford World's Classics have brought
readers closer to the world's great literature. Now with over 700
titles—from the 4,000-year-old myths of Mesopotamia to the
twentieth century's greatest novels—the series makes available
lesser-known as well as celebrated writing.*

*The pocket-sized hardbacks of the early years contained
introductions by Virginia Woolf, T. S. Eliot, Graham Greene,
and other literary figures which enriched the experience of reading.
Today the series is recognized for its fine scholarship and
reliability in texts that span world literature, drama and poetry,
religion, philosophy and politics. Each edition includes perceptive
commentary and essential background information to meet the
changing needs of readers.*

OXFORD WORLD'S CLASSICS

Empire Writing

An Anthology of Colonial Literature
1870–1918

Edited with an Introduction and Notes by
ELLEKE BOEHMER

Oxford   New York
OXFORD UNIVERSITY PRESS
1998

Oxford University Press, Great Clarendon Street, Oxford OX2 6DP

Oxford New York

Athens Auckland Bangkok Bogota Bombay Buenos Aires
Calcutta Cape Town Dar es Salaam Delhi Florence Hong Kong Istanbul
Karachi Kuala Lumpur Madras Madrid Melbourne Mexico City
Nairobi Paris Singapore Taipei Tokyo Toronto Warsaw

and associated companies in
Berlin Ibadan

Oxford is a trade mark of Oxford University Press

British Library Cataloging in Publication Data
Data available

Library of Congress Cataloguing in Publication Data
Empire writing : an anthology of colonial literature, 1870-1918/
edited with an introduction and notes by Elleke Boehmer.
(Oxford world's classics)
Includes index.
1. Commonwealth countries—Literary collections. 2. Great Britain—
Colonies—Literary collections. 3. Commonwealth literature (English)
4. Imperialism—Literary collections. 5. English literature—19th century.
6. English literature—20th century. I. Boehmer, Elleke, 1961- .
II. Series: Oxford world's classics (Oxford University Press)
PR 9085.E46 1998   820.8'.09171241—dc21   98-10539
ISBN 0-19-283265-4 (pbk. : alk. paper)

1 3 5 7 9 10 8 6 4 2

Typeset by The Spartan Pres Limited
Printed in Great Britain by
Cox & Wyman Ltd.
Reading, Berkshire

for Thomas

CONTENTS

1880s AND 1890s CANADIAN POETRY

THE *BULLETIN* WRITERS OF THE 1890s

FIN DE SIÈCLE

ACKNOWLEDGEMENTS

Not long into the work on this anthology it became apparent that for anyone adequately to sift through the vast literature of the time of British Empire, even that of a circumscribed period, taking into account not only writing within Britain but also importantly literature from the 'colonies and dependencies', and the Indian *imperium in imperio*, would require Gargantuan capacities as well as the persistence of the tortoise. While any deficiencies in this collection are entirely my own responsibility, I am indebted to the following: for characteristically wide-ranging suggestions and advice, Shirley Chew; for breathtaking help with two sets of elusive allusions, Raymond Hargreaves and Alistair Stead; for enabling conversation about anthologies and anthologizing, Alison Donnell, David Fairer, Kate Flint, Vivien Jones, Judith Luna; for the loan of or procuring useful books and other material, Jean Cook, Anna Donald, Michael Anderson, Richard Drayton, Denis Flannery, Lynette Hunter, John McLeod, Sarah Nuttall, Nivedita Rama-krishnan; for, variously, indispensable hints, tips, notes, words, Chris Brooks, Fredrika Boehmer, Margaret Daymond, Liz Goodman, Claudia Gualtieri, Liz Gunner, Paul Hammond, Hugh Haughton, Hermione Lee, Boris Maksimov, David Mehnert, Helen Richman, Jon Stallworthy, Rajeswari Sunder Rajan, Senorina Wendoh, and the unnamed OUP adviser; for generous assistance with the background to individual authors, Edmund Candler's granddaughter, Rachael Corkill, P. J. Merrington (on Fairbridge), and Richard Sorabji. Thanks also to the staff of the Bodleian, Indian Institute, Rhodes House, and Brotherton Libraries for their help on many fronts. Above all, my gratitude is to Steven Matthews for hours of library searches, sustaining conversation, patience under pressure, gleaming yet concise advice, and wonderful unfailing support. And without Thomas's general tolerance and cheerfulness the work would have been a lot harder.

INTRODUCTION

The writings gathered together in this anthology belong to the phase of British high empire, embracing the years 1870 to 1918.[1] They reflect colonial experiences in India, Malaya, Australia, New Zealand, the West Indies, Canada, Ireland, Britain, and different regions in Africa, so suggesting the scale as well as the diversity and complexity of empire at this time.

What formally distinguished the period of high (also called new or forward) imperialism was, in particular, a more officially expansionist, assertive, and self-conscious approach to empire than had been expressed before. Under pressure of competition from other European nations, Britain was extending its colonial responsibilities, taking over more territory, and formalizing spheres of influence, especially in South East Asia, Africa, and the South Pacific. In jingoist effusions, this expansion was embodied in images of the British reveille or military waking-signal resounding continuously round the globe and of the Union Jack flying across the continents: this was the empire on which the sun never set. In fact, however, the geopolitical make-up of the British Empire at its height was a great deal more uneven and higgledy-piggledy than these images of continuity and worldwide spread allowed. In 1897, the year of Queen Victoria's Diamond Jubilee, the empire embraced not only the white self-governing colonies and British India, an empire in itself, but also Crown Colonies ruled from Britain like the West Indian islands; protectorates and protected states as in Egypt, Uganda, or Malaya, where indigenous rulers were made to co-operate with the Foreign Office or British Residents; and chartered territories like Rhodesia. It was in response to this picture of an apparently ramshackle empire that, in certain colonialist circles, federation was suggested as a way

---

[1] I have chosen a slightly more capacious period than that demarcated by Eric Hobsbawm, *The Age of Empire, 1875–1914* (Weidenfeld and Nicolson, 1987). As the Note on the Anthology also explains, these dates allow the inclusion of texts from the time of John Ruskin's influential Inaugural Lecture at the beginning of the period, and from the First World War at the end. Strictly speaking, empire in this book signifies the second phase of British imperialism, the first having ended with the loss of Britain's American empire at the end of the eighteenth century.

of welding the white colonies more firmly together. This interest in consolidation, too, characterized formal imperialism.

The beginning of the period of high empire is signalled by two significant events, the opening of the Suez Canal in 1869, which dramatically shortened communication links between Britain, India, and the Antipodes, and Benjamin Disraeli's 1872 Crystal Palace speech in which, by admonishing Britons to recognize and live up to their imperial responsibilities, he laid the groundwork for his time as pro-imperial Prime Minister. Within only a few years, as expansionist and defensive campaigns were being waged or were about to be waged in Afghanistan, Malaya, Egypt, and southern and West Africa, Victoria was proclaimed Empress of India (1877), a powerfully symbolic move which was designed to consolidate further the British Raj and prevent for all time rebellions of the kind traumatically witnessed there in 1857–8, or in Jamaica in 1865. However, within only a couple of decades, a mere fourteen years after the European carve-up of Africa at the Berlin Conference of 1885, and in the immediate aftermath of the triumphalist celebration of empire that was Victoria's Diamond Jubilee, British imperialist self-congratulation was severely jolted by the setbacks of the South African War in December 1899. Around the same time, Australian Federation (1901) had inspired a vociferous republican movement in that country, and the years following witnessed uprisings and resistance movements in both Natal and Bengal.

The course even of apparently unassailable formal empire never ran completely smoothly. It was not until the cataclysmic events of the First World War (1914–18), however, that serious questions were asked in Britain about the benefits and the propriety of ruling other people 'for their own good'. Up until that time, as we see marked in various large Edwardian colonial conferences, and in the magnificent Delhi Durbar of 1911, it was fairly confidently assumed that if Britain held the imperial upper hand, all was right with the world.

A muddle of confused interactions, or a model of global control? The stentorian voice of authority, or the hubbub of a colonial trading depot? The 'banner of England' fluttering defiantly on the topmost ramparts of the besieged Residency in Tennyson's 'The Defence of Lucknow', or the Indian sepoy rebels tunnelling under the fortifications in the same poem, threatening to undermine the entire edifice? Which of these might be taken as the representative sign of British Empire in the competitive, expansive years covered by this anthology? In what, according to the multiple texts it promiscuously produced, did empire consist?

For G. O. Trevelyan, whose 1864 comments on India appear as the Foreword to this anthology, English imperial conquest, its 'march of mind' across the 'boundless Eastern plains', is symbolized in the Indian railway, in its two 'thin strips of iron' branching across the subcontinent, its mighty viaducts and ubiquitous refreshment rooms imported, it seems, straight out of the English countryside. Of course, Trevelyan concedes, this could seem a rather commonplace representation. Rudyard Kipling, Flora Annie Steel, and Edmund Candler, as we see here, were certainly soon to reinforce it.[2] Images of engineering and technology in general—not only the railway but also canals and dams, as in John Beames's 'Memoirs', or the telegraph, as in Kipling's 'His Chance in Life'—bulked large in colonial writing as symbols of the advancement white men claimed to bring.

And yet, Trevelyan also observes, this colossal grid, this triumph of European civilization, as he sees it, has also become a local network of commerce and interaction to which 'Hindoos have taken most kindly'. Across the railway's lengths hawkers and pedlars conduct their trade, and dacoits allegedly use it to put distance between themselves and the scene of their assaults. Even to the eyes of a relative outsider, English imperial values, ideals, and structures are being rapidly adapted and creatively reinterpreted in the foreign colonial context. The Englishman himself may be viewed in a new light. The 'indefatigable, public-spirited, plain-spoken, beer-drinking, cigar-smoking, tiger-shooting collector', the agent of imperial conquest, Trevelyan later reflects, may well from the different vantage-point of, say, a devout Brahmin or local 'Maharaja', be perceived as a 'somewhat objectionable demon' of 'debased' habits.

This perception of the multiplicity and instability of meanings which existed at the very heart of the colonial project, informs the whole of this anthology of empire writing. We cannot, of course,

[2] And understandably so. The length of the Indian railway increased from 1,588 miles in 1861, to 24,760 by 1900. For Victorians this represented as magnificent an achievement as the building of imperial Rome. See Bernard Porter, *The Lion's Share: A Short History of British Imperialism* (Longman, 1984), 41.

deny that the word 'empire' continues for obvious reasons to carry a heavy freight of jingoist, Social Darwinist, and racist connotation. The literature of empire, readers might therefore understandably assume, must be largely preoccupied with ideas of European superiority and the 'enlightenment' of natives once seen as consequent upon that superiority. Yet it is often forgotten that millions of people, both colonized and colonizing, who were identified with or unconcerned about colonization, formed part of the British Empire, in the sense of responding to it, having to deal with it, and in many millions of cases surviving through it. Such vast differences of position had important implications also for writing. Even among convinced English imperialists there was no homogeneous or unquestioned approach to colonization. In her descriptions of the West African 'Fetish' which deeply interested her, the woman traveller Mary Kingsley, for example, warned her English readers that their 'superior culture-instincts' had to be put aside when approaching African cultures. And Hugh Clifford, the 'pacifier' of hinterland Malaya and several times colonial governor across the empire, expressed a sincere regard for the Malay people he also believed to be unregenerate and in need of civilizing. The 'grinding' of 'the heel of the white man' brought 'Trade, and Money . . . and Sanitation, and Drains, and a thousand other blessings', he wrote, yet he saw that grinding as at the same time a highly destructive process, undermining customs and breaking people's spirits.[3] If these writers expressed their uncertainties, how much more dubious about empire would be a West African intellectual such as J. E. Casely Hayford, highly educated within the British colonial system, but denied representation as an African, as his *Ethiopia Unbound* shows? Whether the texts which are gathered together here are read chronologically in the order in which they appear, or in the clusters formed by the reading pathways suggested at the end of each text (or, in some cases, each group of texts), and by the intertextual links drawn in the Explanatory Notes, together they trace out a matrix of values and experiences that is both broad and contrastive. The British Empire formed what was probably the most globally extensive system of oppositions the world has seen, but it was also seething with different yet intersecting lives and doings.

[3] See Hugh Clifford, 'At the Heels of the White Man', *Studies in Brown Humanity* (Grant Richards, 1898), 124–5; and 'The East Coast', *In Court and Kampong* (Grant Richards, 1897), 1–9.

Having underlined this vast variety, it should immediately be added that the remit of the anthology was in fact a wide representativeness—to juxtapose within the relatively short and arguably distinct time of high empire well-established and less well-known writers working in English on both sides of the often too-embedded colonial divide. As the Note on the Anthology also points out, the aim was to bring together not only metropolitan colonialists, but settler colonials, colonial natives, and peripatetic colonial administrators and teachers; not only the pro- and anti-imperial, but also those in-between, relatively indifferent to the ideas and aims of empire but, during imperial times, nonetheless affected by and responding to them. Difference, therefore, was a governing principle of selection.

On the same basis I have made a concerted attempt to cover different geographical spaces and definitive historical moments (moves towards imperial federation; the Boer War; the emergence of settler and native nationalisms, including Irish anti-colonialism[4]). Texts were chosen that could be seen as symptomatic or emblematic of key areas of colonial perception and imagining. These included assumptions of supremacy and hierarchy captured in images of work, 'improvement', and 'progress'; visual bafflement at 'impenetrable' and apparently featureless foreign landscapes; stories and poems of encounter, conflict, and connection; and also preoccupations with cultural difference, dislocation, and 'taint', as well as with the inventive hybridization of languages and social habits emerging out of contact with other cultures. Texts were also drawn from different discursive and cultural contexts—demonstrating the extent to which imperial rule 'elaborated' and 'consolidated' itself in a variety of kinds of writing.[5] The range extends from G. A. Henty's Indian Mutiny story, 'A Pipe of Mystery', in the *Boy's Own* style so central to imperial self-imagining; through Jubilee verse, 'pushful' colonial

[4] With regard to colonial and nationalist issues in Ireland, see for example: David Cairns and Shaun Richards, *Writing Ireland: Colonialism, Nationalism and Culture* (Manchester UP, 1988); Vincent Cheng, *Joyce, Race and Empire* (Cambridge UP, 1995); Declan Kiberd, *Inventing Ireland: The Literature of the Modern Nation* (Cape, 1995); David Lloyd, *Anomalous States: Irish Writing and the Post-Colonial Moment* (Lilliput Press, 1993); and Emer Nolan, *James Joyce and Nationalism* (Routledge, 1995). These texts have particular reference to the inclusion of James Joyce and W. B. Yeats in the anthology. Because long-standing, proximate to England, and therefore 'snarled', as Joyce suggests, the colonial situation in Ireland is often seen as presenting a special case.

[5] Edward Said, *Culture and Imperialism* (Chatto and Windus, 1993), 14.

speeches, ethnography, and travel writing; to protest journalism and lyrics by Indian poets like Toru Dutt and Sarojini Naidu which are apparently only tangentially concerned with empire.

And yet even had the emphasis not been on range across several levels, and on a time when empire was at its most triumphal but also its most anxious, the extent of diversity not only across but within texts would probably still have been noteworthy. In reading through this anthology, it soon becomes clear that colonial relations were not only textually excessive, but excessive in their suggestiveness, in the sense that those relations not only generated a wealth of texts but that the texts continually tug against, contradict, and balloon beyond the definitions which they impose, and which may be imposed upon them. Colonial discourse, as Bart Moore-Gilbert writes, involved a 'process of cultural negotiation in constant conflict and evolution'.[6] Or, as Hugh Clifford puts it somewhat more figuratively, the transplanted white man on the Malay Peninsula lived simultaneously in a Hell, that is, Malaya as perceived through European eyes, and a Heaven, a land that was 'very dear to him'.[7] Not merely his experiences but his identifications were ambivalent at root. Within a different constituency of writers we might compare this ambivalence with the unstable register of indignation and ingratiation—stern biblical exhortation laid alongside sentimental phrases originating in a mission education—which is used by the black nationalist Solomon Plaatje to indict the new South African Union's racial land law. Again, 'cultural negotiation in constant conflict'. Or, to take one further example of many, there is the at-once categorical and contradictory voice of Flora Annie Steel, the Anglo-Indian novelist versed in several Indian languages, whose reliance on and interest in collaborations between Indian and European (as captured in her transcriptions of oral tales and her own short stories, as we see here), coexist with her firm instruction to memsahibs to govern their households as the Indian empire is governed. 'Make a hold': treat the Indian servant as you would a naughty child. These various dissonances dramatize the ambiguities and the sheer messiness that were involved in the experience of empire, and in the implementation of imperial authority itself.

[6] Bart Moore-Gilbert, 'Introduction', *Writing India, 1757–1990* (Manchester UP, 1996), 23.

[7] In addition to the sketch collected here, see also Clifford's 'Preface', *Studies in Brown Humanity*, p. viii.

Far from resolving neatly into the oppositional categories of self/other, black/white, therefore, colonial relations, and also the texts used to articulate them, can rather be seen to form a network of complicated transactions of meaning and knowledge, as several colonial discourse theorists have recently pointed out.[8] To adapt remarks which have also been made in this regard by the historian Linda Colley, the study of imperial or colonial literature should, therefore, properly involve looking at a diversity of contacts, responses, and exchanges dispersed across the globe.[9] These contacts could be incongruous, improvised, botched, bizarre, and often cruel, but occasionally they were also mutually beneficial, the ruled reacting against but also interacting with the ruler. Imperial power, Anne McClintock has importantly pointed out, 'took haphazard shape from myriad encounters with alternative forms of authority, knowledge, and power'.[10] Whether expressed in the form of census, treaty, housekeeping manual, or *Boy's Own* story, the establishment and administration of empire everywhere ran up against and had to take account of different subjectivities and local histories, alternative culinary, religious, medical, and sexual practices, even where these were seemingly ignored.[11] A telling figure for the noise and movement not only surrounding but impinging on the colonial presence can be found in the 'multitudes' of brightly dressed, multilingual Africans and Arabs who form an intrinsic part of the famous Livingstone and Stanley meeting in both the accounts excerpted in the anthology. Therefore, quite contrary to the sanctioned model of dominant centre imposed upon periphery, and periphery responding to centre, which has in the past organized colonial studies, what we begin to see forming here is a world picture in which different regions and literatures conduct their own particular negotiations and accommodations of dominant meanings. In effect, to take a motto from the postcolonial writer Ben Okri's story 'Incidents at the

[8] Like Moore-Gilbert, Harish Trivedi, *Colonial Transactions: English Literature and India* (Manchester UP, 1995), 1, for example, underlines the complex cultural exchanges which imperial relations involved.

[9] Linda Colley, 'Clashes and Collaborations', *London Review of Books* (18 July 1996), 8–9.

[10] Anne McClintock, *Imperial Leather* (Routledge, 1995), 15–16. See also Robert Young, *Colonial Desire* (Routledge, 1995), 1–28, for a discussion of the hybridity fundamental to colonial relations.

[11] See Alan Lawson and Chris Tiffin (eds.), *De-scribing Empire* (Routledge, 1994), 233.

Shrine', these regions and literatures are, in so doing, forming 'centres' to themselves.[12]

It is admittedly the case that binary patterns offer convenient ways of thinking about the immensity of what colonialism involved. For, though the British Empire may have been an 'inexorably integrative', merging force, in the phrase of Edward Said,[13] yet we might also want paradoxically to agree with the following characterization of its expansive oddities given by the imperial pragmatist Benjamin Disraeli: 'No Caesar or Charlemagne ever presided over a dominion so peculiar. Its flag floats on many waters; it has provinces in every zone, they are inhabited by persons of different races, different religions, different laws, manners, customs.'[14] The broad organizing categories of West and East, the 'typical' African, Indian, or Imperialist, have been and are still used by colonial and postcolonial commentators in order to understand and explain the bewildering diversity of empire. The stereotyped end of the spectrum of such generalities would also include, as we find in the anthology, Trollope's 'altogether low' and 'perishable' Aboriginal, the bovinely 'good-natured' blacks in Froude's account of the West Indies (which is so incisively taken apart by the Trinidadian writer J. J. Thomas), and the resolutely superstitious mass of Indians in both Edmund Candler's and Cornelia Sorabji's writing. The latter group of formulations underlines the extent to which empire across its lengths and breadths relied on homogenizing negative categories for its operation. In this we also find an important reason why anti-colonial theorists like Frantz Fanon, Albert Memmi, and Walter Rodney themselves set up generalizing terms—self and other, white man and black—as part of their critique and analysis of those earlier categories.[15]

Despite the 'haphazard shape' of imperial power, therefore, it remains true that the West established its sovereignty by defining its

---

[12] 'The world is the shrine and the shrine is the world. Everything must have a centre.' Ben Okri, *Incidents and the Shrine* (Heinemann, 1986), 60.

[13] Said, *Culture and Imperialism*, 4.

[14] Benjamin Disraeli, 'Speech on Calling out Reserve Forces', *Selected Speeches of the Late Right Honourable the Earl of Beaconsfield*, vol. 1, ed. T. E. Kebbel (Longmans, Green and Co., 1882), 177. Compare Curzon's evocation of the heterogeneity of the empire in 'The British Empire'.

[15] Albert Memmi, *The Colonizer and the Colonized* (Boston: Beacon, 1965); Frantz Fanon, *Black Skin, White Masks*, trans. Charles Lam Markmann (1952; Pluto, 1986), and *The Wretched of the Earth*, trans. Constance Farrington (1961; Penguin, 1986); Walter Rodney, *How Europe Underdeveloped Africa* (Bogle L'Ouverture Publications, 1972).

colonies as 'others', with all the accompanying significations of lesser, effeminate, savage, unearthly, monstrous, expendable, which that concept bears.[16] So it would give serious cause for concern if, as a result of attending to the multiple textures of colonial writing, we ignored the coerciveness and oppression intended by empire—an oppression that depended on negative generalizations like those just cited, as well as on strategies of 'divide and rule'. Texts, too, aided in the implementation of this oppressive rule. It was not only the laws and treaties alienating people from their lands, as Casely Hayford and Plaatje eloquently describe, which inflicted long-lasting damage on societies and cultures. The disparaging remarks about other peoples made by literary and historical writers like Trollope or Froude in the apparently objective interests of colonial advancement also assumed and helped consolidate the brute force on which colonial possession depended. In *Trooper Peter Halket of Mashonaland*, a relentless parable-exposé of the white persecution of African 'rebels' in order to obtain 'lots of loot', Olive Schreiner shows searching awareness of this fact: how language might at once disguise and direct colonial violence. Or, as J. A. Hobson remarks towards the end of his still-often-cited *Imperialism* (from which an extract appears in this book): 'Imperialism is based upon a persistent misrepresentation of the facts and forces chiefly through a most refined process of selection, exaggeration, and attenuation, directed by interested cliques and persons so as to distort the face of history.'[17] In 'Pearls and Swine', the Afterword of the anthology, Leonard Woolf uses a cutting irony borrowed from Conrad to slice open such hypocrisies, peeling the sordid reality away from the inflated platitudes of empire.

But to turn the situation round yet again, in spite of coercive efforts to set up distinct categories and impose racial divisions, colonial territories always remained borderlines or 'intermediate' spaces (as Kipling and Trevelyan emphasize), contact zones criss-crossed by other cultural perceptions, multiple different histories and stories. The boundary between the colonizer and the colonized, Homi Bhabha has pointed out in an important group of essays, could never be fixed or impermeable.[18]

---

[16] See, for example, Gayatri Spivak, 'The Rani of Sirmur', *Europe and its Others*, ed. Francis Barker *et al.* (University of Essex, 1985).

[17] J. A. Hobson, *Imperialism: A Study* (James Nisbet and Co., 1902), 222–4.

[18] Homi Bhabha, *The Location of Culture* (Routledge, 1995). On how the imperial sense of self continually oscillated through aversion and attraction, see also Young, *Colonial Desire*, 1–28.

This may seem an obvious point, yet it is worth appreciating as a lived fact: colonial rule was exercised in proximity to the native, within sight of the compound, the market-place, the burial ground. Taking any position in such a situation involved at once a displacement of and a jostling against others. In this regard it is significant how many of the texts set in colonial spaces which appear in this anthology are concerned with encounters and moments of exchange between white and native, including that most intimate exchange of all, the mingling of 'bloods' in the veins of Michele D'Cruze in Kipling's 'His Chance in Life', or of Peter Halket's lost 'kid'. In all such situations, it would seem, official colonial perceptions and self-representations were being ceaselessly waylaid, sidetracked, interrupted, and unsettled by countervailing perceptions and impulses. Repulsion at peoples 'lapsed into the darkest barbarism' (to quote Haggard's Allan Quatermain) coexisted with attraction towards what that barbarity signified in terms of forbidden pleasure and delicious release (mingled bloods again), as well as, differently, spiritual freedom and mystical revelation (especially during Europe's religious explorations of the 1890s, represented here in the voices of Vivekananda and Yeats). In the physiognomy of the native, whites both feared and loved to recognize the lineaments of their own face. Mary Kingsley briskly acknowledges this fact of connection in the parallels she traces between European and African religious thought.

The ambivalence around which white colonial writing pivots—indeed, one might say through which it comes into being—has already been suggested with reference to Hugh Clifford. It is also brilliantly outlined by Conrad in the darkly ironic 'An Outpost of Progress', as the Belgian traders Kayerts and Carlier negotiate with their assistant Makola about the 'beautiful lot' of ivory that is both intensely desirable to them yet has been won by grossly corrupt means. Rather differently but also revealingly, while Alice Perrin's short story 'The Rise of Ram Din' might be read as an oblique lesson on how not to rule, the dishwasher Ram Din's fatal perfection of obedience to imperial authority ends up by neatly and disturbingly upending master–servant relations within the sahib's household.

As this satire of colonial circumstance or Conrad's withering insights into imperial hypocrisy show, concepts of European cultural superiority were always shadowed by self-contradiction and self-doubt. This could be true also for those writing at some distance from the benighted trading-posts of the Congo or the imprisoning *godowns* of North India. Even in the words of one as imperially ebullient as Joseph Chamberlain there are instants of fracture, momentary admissions that Britain's greatness may one day collapse, even in assertions to the contrary: 'There are in our present condition no visible signs of decrepitude and decay.' Similar moments of wavering can be discerned in Tennyson, in Ruskin's influential instruction that the English, a 'mingled' race, maintain their unregenerate status by founding colonies, or in Froude's worry about the neglect of the West Indies. Henley's querulous 'Who says that we shall pass?' in 'The Choice of the Will', too, admits to the transitoriness of empire even in the act of denying it. The preoccupation with imperial federation itself—'Greater Britain' as a worldwide federalist state or family firm, modelled on the United States[19]—developed as a stay against the dreaded fragmentation of the empire. Federation was a concern shared by Chamberlain, Froude, Ruskin, Seeley, and Tennyson, and endorsed by colonial settler writers such as Sara Jeannette Duncan and Stephen Leacock.

The stresses surrounding the empire's watchwords of civilization and superiority emerge prominently also in writers' continuing fascinated anxiety about the fragility of apparent imperial successes and the fatigues of toting the white man's burden. Where civilizing work slackened, it was feared, reversion, degeneration, and cultural disaster must surely follow. The irrevocable 'return into the savage' links Trollope's comments on Australia not only with Kipling's short story or Lady Mary Anne Barker's reflections on 'the strength of race instinct' (which transforms the 'comely' Zulu servant Maria in her Gainsborough hat into a half-naked 'savage'). It is also suggestively present in the reformist Cornelia Sorabji's representation not merely of the Indian masses, but of her own fictional *alter ego* submitting to the call of her kind. And yet if the slip back into the native state was a condition to work against or ultimately resign oneself to with regard to colonized peoples, a European's 'going native' represented a deeper crisis entirely, one that Kipling in the poem 'Giffen's Debt' handles with characteristic subtlety. Degenerating primitives clearly boded no good for advanced races, however arrogant: the veneer of

---

[19] Seeley's 'community of race, community of religion, community of interest', as he says in *The Expansion of England*, excerpted in this book.

'civilization' everywhere was perilously thin. No matter how strict the precautions taken, the fear of contamination by barbarous back-wardness was pervasive, often emerging, as in Barker, Sorabji, and Dorothea Fairbridge, in tropes of poisoning, infection, and disease.

It was with the outbreak of the Boer or South African War (1899–1902), however, more than at any other time up until 1914, that the fault-lines in imperial self-perceptions were most revealingly laid bare. As Britain's massed imperial forces struggled for almost three years to defeat the guerilla army of the two tiny Boer republics, the weaknesses of an over-extended and over-confident empire, which several writers and politicians had already suspected, could no longer be very easily masked. The texts clustered round this watershed imperial moment in the anthology dramatize the crisis in confidence —arrogant belligerence decaying into uncertainty—which mark the years which symbolically fell at the turn of the century, at the *fin* of a pessimistic *fin-de-siècle*. Placed at this emblematic time of turning, the Boer War poems form a point of particular focus in the anthology itself.

And yet, though events in South Africa had highlighted the effort needed to maintain British supremacy, imperial self-confidence was bruised but not permanently damaged. Relative to developments in both Germany and the United States, Britain's monopoly of world influence and economic power had, it was true, started to unravel as far back as the 1870s (this reason too underlies the anxieties already mentioned).[20] But doubts about the colonial project itself were hardly yet admissible, let alone conceivable, within the imperial metropolis. Though writing from native colonials significantly comes into greater prominence after 1902, it is noteworthy that Edmund Candler and Lady Barker, amongst others, continue to speak as knowing and confidently distanced observers of colonial scenes well into the twentieth century.

However, as the repetitiousness of imperialist bombast in the Boer War verse itself suggests, imperial power could never assume itself to be absolutely secure. There were always areas within colonial relations

[20] In the thirty years from 1880 Britain's proportion of the world's trade had shrunk by a drastic and unprecedented 6%. Those essential implements of British imperial campaigns, Gatling machine-guns, were now being manufactured in America. See Lawrence James, *The Rise and Fall of the British Empire* (Abacus, 1995), 202; Denis Judd, *Empire* (HarperCollins, 1996), esp. 130–70; and Porter, *The Lion's Share*, 117.

which could not be resolved into forms of straightforward domination and submission—which also implied, as I will shortly discuss, that colonized people were never merely abjectly oppressed and silent. Another key area of unresolvability emerged in the ranks of the colonialists or imperialists themselves, in the important and varying experiences of white women. Here we should bear in mind that, in the colonial context, though Western women may have shared the race and (generally speaking) the class of those officially in charge, they were in almost all cases differently positioned relative to colonial power on the basis of their gender. They also tended to be in the minority: it was men who ran the empire.

It is because of this predominance of men that colonialism is usually accurately represented as a male institutional practice, involving the feminization of colonized peoples, the sexual and economic subjection of native women, the employment of native men in the lower ranks of administration, and the reification of white women as symbols of race purity. As is widely acknowledged, the colonial project was also governed by unabashedly masculine public-school values emphasizing sportsmanship, hard selfless work, and military glory. Yet the bonding between men that imperial values took for granted could at times assume the subversive forms of homoerotic desire.[21] In A. E. Housman's Boer War poem 'Grenadier', for instance, the identification with the grenadier, whose life is otherwise seen as dispensable, is closely bound up with the poem's overall cynicism about imperial self-sacrifice.

However, even if men did hold sway over the imperial field, colonial women in the multiple roles not only of memsahibs, wives, and mistresses of households (the obvious example here is Flora Annie Steel), but also of travellers and ethnographers (like Isabella Bird and Mary Kingsley), social reformers and critics (like B. E. Baughan and Olive Schreiner), journalists, missionaries, settlers, and so on, did contribute to imperial projects, and did so from positions that inevitably did not coincide with those of their male colonial counterparts. Can such women then be heard to speak with a different voice? Despite colonialism, despite what might be called

[21] See Joseph Bristow, *Empire Boys: Adventures in a Man's World* (HarperCollins, 1991); Tony Davies and Nigel Woods (eds.), *A Passage to India* (Open University Press, 1994); and Christopher Lane, *The Ruling Passion: British Colonial Allegory and the Paradox of Homosexual Desire* (Duke University Press, 1995).

an imperious 'maternalism', an often convinced identification with colonial rhetoric, did women see the colonized differently, in more nuanced and identified ways, as Kumari Jayawardena proposes in her study of white women in India?[22] Did their different positions within colonial society impact on their writing?

As the critic Lisa Lowe suggests, white women's colonial discourse was probably complicated by their sense of sharing common experiences with colonized women, primarily their related positions of marginality.[23] Certainly Olive Schreiner in *Trooper Peter Halket* betrays a tacit approval when Peter tells of his 'supportive' black wife absconding with his ammunition and Martini-Henry rifle. And Mansfield's white child Pearl Button paradoxically finds a short-lived release from the regimented life of respectable bourgeois New Zealand when she is abducted by Maoris. Although B. E. Baughan's story of the meeting between the 'prowling' scavenger Pipi and the Pakeha women is often patronizing of the old Maori, their conversation does appear intentionally to exemplify a process of gradual accommodation–through–mutual–outwitting between these two representatives of different New Zealand cultures. It is also significant that the wilful Pipi is represented as evading the control of her daughter Miria, who is, we are told, a 'slavish advocate and copyist' of whites.

In those instances where women writers reproduce standard colonialist views, therefore, the accompanying language of racial discrimination seems to come under pressure, perhaps even to buckle and shift, at moments of identification, such as when the writer expresses a close interest in colonized individuals. The travel writer Isabella Bird (like Mary Kingsley a refugee from Victorian England) in her 'Letter from Sungei Ujong' expresses approval at the 'security and justice' of British rule at the same time as modifying her assumptions regarding the frenzied or *amok* behaviour of a 'tiger-like' Malay man. With regard to diversity within the ranks of colonialists, it is also interesting that Bird, the rough-and-ready wanderer, feels little identification with her ailing fellow travellers, the 'Misses Shaw'. Lady Barker similarly shares no sisterly feeling with the 'ignorant' English-born 'maid-servants' she employs in New Zealand and Natal, in this case for obvious reasons of class. Yet

[22] Kumari Jayawardena, *The White Woman's Other Burden* (Routledge, 1995).
[23] Lisa Lowe, *Critical Terrains* (Cornell UP, 1991).

in reminiscing about her experiences with native servants across the empire she shows considerable curiosity and even a passing respect for their particular skills and idiosyncrasies. Under empire white colonial women themselves formed a highly differentiated group.

Yet while such differences are perhaps more noticeable in women's discourses, male empire writing too can at moments slip and undercut itself, especially where it comes under pressure from lived experience, from particular subjective interests connected with specific colonial places. Significantly, this pressure is again most obvious at moments of close interaction or involvement with individuals from other cultures and regions, or with those other cultures and geographic regions more broadly. So, in Kipling's 'Mandalay' the yearning of the speaker for the 'Burma girl' and the way of life 'somewheres East of Suez' is surely more than simply Orientalist. By contrast, while Edwin Arnold's blank-verse rendition of the life of Buddha, *The Light of Asia*, *is* characteristically Orientalist in its attempt to transmit the religious teaching of the East to the West, his desire to 'indicate the philosophy of that noble hero and reformer . . . Prince Gautama' also reads as imaginatively committed, even as devoted. In a different realm of experience, what of the Mancunian engineer Faulkner in Beames's multifaceted portrait, infantilizing Indians and yet at home in India, the designer of bridges and canal systems, as well as delicate screens and croquet mallets, all made from local substances, ivory, ebony, and teak?

At such moments of involvement in several of the texts selected here, the received terms and stereotyped images no longer seem exactly to fit. The words sit lightly on the surface of the description or conversation; a different world of meaning glimmers in the interstices between. This is brilliantly demonstrated in the Irish poet W. B. Yeats's intense response to Rabindranath Tagore's devotional poetry in his 'Introduction to *Gitanjali*', in which he seems to strain against the information about the East which he has to hand. It is a telling sign of this strain, and of Yeats's sense of fellowship with the cultural nationalist Tagore, that the dreamy remoteness of the Bengali poet which Yeats at first outlines soon gives way to an attempt to find common ground. Despite its 'immeasurable strangeness', he says, Tagore's poetry moves us because we find in it 'our own image'.

Perhaps one of the most evocative examples of close colonial description scored by lived experience can be found in Robert Louis Stevenson's sketch of Tembinok', the King of Apemama, an individual whose relationships and interests are themselves criss-crossed by diverse influences. Stevenson's disapproval of Europe's 'world-enveloping dishonesty', and his respect for Tembinok''s sternly defended autonomy on his island, intersect in his account of the King's mania for collecting—his hoardings of clocks, musical boxes, blue spectacles, sewing machines, scented soap, goldfish, and so on—all the unique and desirable objects that he has been able to extract from traders, or that they have chosen to foist on him. Discernible in Tembinok''s mismatches of European commodities are the beginnings of that inventive mixing and appropriation of signs and meanings out of which native resistance to the white man's presence might start to emerge. Yet, at the same time, the King's dependency on the traders who feed his hoarding habit underlines the extent to which native self-expression was enclosed and compromised by the colonial presence virtually from its inception: 'the white man is everywhere', as Stevenson says.

Given this ubiquity, this white encirclement, how were native writers from places under colonial occupation to inscribe their own points of view, let alone threaten colonial authority? Especially where, as in the case of Toru Dutt, Sarojini Naidu, or Sri Aurobindo, they use English and appear to repeat accepted Western styles and Orientalist rhetoric, how were they to undercut the languages which presumed to categorize and describe them? How to talk across the silencing that James Joyce damningly evokes in 'Ireland at the Bar'? Could it be that by speaking from their own cultural points of view, but in ways cunningly acceptable to colonial culture, by adopting the colonial images of themselves as degenerate, inferior, barbaric, but subtly reworking them (acquiring Western commodities, like Tembinok', but making of them their own objects of desire)—that in these ways they undermined and refigured the dominant culture's claim to authority?

As a glance at the Contents pages of this anthology will show, even at the height of British Empire, when colonial hegemony was apparently at its most unassailable, African, West Indian, and Indian writers were declaring themselves, and doing so in powerful, transforming ways. As early as 1881 the Liberian educationalist Edmund Blyden was laying the groundwork for twentieth-century African nationalism, and for his protégé J. E. Casely Hayford's own work on African nationality, in his demand that where European training disparaged African cultural traditions, black men and women needed to 'carve out our own way'. Later in the same decade J. J. Thomas roundly (and successfully, according to the reviews of the time) attacked the conservative historian J. A. Froude's stereotyped account of political and economic prospects in the West Indies. And just a few years prior to Blyden's lecture, the precocious Bengali poet Toru Dutt was publishing poems so strikingly imitative of English and French verse forms that she drew attention in Europe. Yet these are poems whose images of transplanted flowers in decay and absent, deeply missed Calcutta trees seem also to reflect on her own sense of cultural displacement.

True, these voices were not emerging cleanly and fully formed out of native culture, as their adoption of English and classical allusion immediately shows, and Walter Jekyll's editorial work on Claude McKay's Creole further emphasizes.[24] What they had to say was heavily inflected by the speaking positions allowed within colonial culture: for Blyden or Plaatje, the persona of the middle-class intellectual respectful of the European civilizing mission; for Aurobindo, of the uniquely talented classicist, so polymathic as to be almost an honorary Englishman; for the Indian women poets, Dutt and Naidu, of a remarkable but tame 'nightingale'. In all these cases, the role the writers took up, or indeed that they were permitted to take up, was of spokesperson for their culture such as Europe saw it, or even, more patronizingly, of native prodigy ('brown gentleman', 'Babu', star colonial pupil, Woolf's 'Board School angel'), exceptional and hence mostly unthreatening. All of the writers were in one or other way native interpreters, 'Macaulay's children', the products, that is, of the globally influential Minute on Indian Education of 1835 in which the historian Thomas Babington Macaulay had advocated the formation of a Western-educated native elite to help govern the empire, to mediate between ruler and ruled.

And yet, though their language may have been borrowed and

---

[24] On the non-recovery of subaltern voices, see Gayatri Spivak, 'Can the Subaltern Speak?', in *Colonial Discourse and Post-Colonial Criticism: A Reader*, eds. Patrick Williams and Laura Chrisman (Harvester Wheatsheaf, 1993), and 'The Rani of Sirmur', *Europe and its Others*. See also the comments by Robert Young, *White Mythologies* (Routledge, 1990), 162–7.

vetted, their figures of speech second-hand, these native writers *were* giving utterance to their own experience, however obliquely. While Blyden and Thomas are obviously forthright in their criticism of Europe, others disguise what they have to say by copying the vocabulary and symbolism of imperialism. The resistance which they offer, therefore, can appear subtle to the point of being almost invisible, buried in understatement and irony, seemingly awkward juxtapositions, cunning echoes, partial repetitions, and telling silences. (Indeed, it is revealing to observe the extent to which native writing, whether in English or a vernacular, is interested in the *effects* of colonization—the railway, for instance—rather than in the presence of the colonial master as such.) Resistance also emerges, somewhat more prominently, in the at times intentional, at times accidental, intrusion of hybrid forms into the writers' texts—in the interleaved voices, mixed cultural allusions, and, probably most clearly (as we find in Claude McKay), the transliterated and creolized Englishes that are the betraying signs of their different perspective on colonial reality. Taking over European terms of description, native intellectuals in these ways refracted empire writing away from the mean and the acceptable, unsettling its careful discriminations sometimes simply by virtue of *where* they were speaking *from*. Their diligent mimicry *as natives* of Keats or Matthew Arnold, of the Shakespearean sonnet or of Orientalist scene-painting, produced a kind of warping or exaggeration, a half-unconscious excess that could become extravagant and therefore disruptive in its intensity. At the end of the day, after all—so the implacable logic of the civilizing mission insisted—no matter how precise their imitation, Anglicized natives could never be truly English; the colonized writer might speak 'almost the same' as the colonial master, 'but not quite'.[25]

A symptomatic case of extravagant mimicry offers itself in the work of Sarojini Naidu, the 'mockingbird with a vengeance' as the Victorian critic Edmund Gosse described her, who was also fiercely committed to freedom for India.[26] Having begun her poetic career somewhat like Toru Dutt by producing precisely turned pastiches of

[25] For his influential theorization of the native's subversive mimicry, see, in particular, Homi Bhabha, 'Of Mimicry and Man', *The Location of Culture*, 85–92.

[26] Edmund Gosse, 'Introduction', *The Bird of Time: Songs of Life, Death and the Spring* (William Heinemann, 1912).

English Romantic poetry, Naidu subsequently attempted, on advice from her English mentors, to make herself over into 'a genuine Indian poet of the Deccan'. Paradoxically, though predictably, this decision involved her in yet another act of westernizing translation, reproducing Orientalist images of a 'köil-haunted' and muskily sensuous India, in the exquisite and luxuriant language favoured by 1890s Symbolist poetry. As did Plaatje, as did the later Claude McKay, Naidu made heavy rhetorical concessions to the ruling elite in order to make herself heard.

Despite her deepening nationalist commitment throughout the period that she was working on *The Bird of Time* (1912), it may indeed seem that the sentimentality and silky textures of Naidu's verse resist a political reading. Even where she turns aside to invite India to lead the 'fettered' nations of the world into a significantly unspecific, but obviously sovereign new day, as in 'To India' and 'An Anthem of Love', she leans on the same weighty and Orientalizing archaisms as elsewhere. But if resistance seems lacking, the sheer extent of her copying, its conscientiousness and intensity, underlines the range of strictures she operated under not only as an Indian writer fêted in the West, but as both a woman poet and a woman nationalist. There is an unambiguous identification with the oppression of women in India wherever Naidu speaks of purdah (the same is true for Sorabji's work); in a poem such as 'Village Song', sentimental conventions are manipulated in order to warn against child marriage. The bizarre and disturbing force of Naidu's ventriloquism of an 'Easternized' poetic voice, therefore, is only fully heard in juxtaposition, when we read her poetry side-by-side with an awareness of her nationalist involvements—of, for example, her rousing 1920s speeches in favour of Home Rule. In this her work bears comparison with the writing of her compatriot Sri Aurobindo, the activist and mystic, though in his case the contrasts are perhaps even starker, and more manifest in the writing itself, as we see when, as here, his tersely worded journalism reviling British 'executive tyranny' over India is set against his orotund late Victorian poetry with its echoes from Keats, Matthew Arnold, and Tennyson.

In my attempt at once to address and to get away from the too-rigid divisions of colonizer and colonized, I have so far said little about the settler texts which also make up an important constituency in empire writing of the period, one which yet again blurs easy binary distinctions. That there is more writing from white colonial territories than non-white at the highpoint of empire, as reflected in the anthology, is to be explained by the racially exclusive encouragement and, later, official sanction, which settler nationalism received from London. (Self-governing white colonies were, it was thought, economical to an extent and could be expected to pay their own way.) However, like Indian, African, and West Indian writers, settlers also faced the problem of generating new self-images through the medium of aesthetic traditions inherited from Europe. In Australia, Marcus Clarke and (later) Henry Lawson, as we see, regret the lack of a perceptual framework through which to translate the 'subtle charms' of the Australian landscape, to read the 'hieroglyphs of haggard gum trees'. In 1886 in Canada, the journalist and novelist Sara Jeannette Duncan, too, laments the lack of a national literature, of an imaginative vehicle for the Confederation's vitality as a country —a lack which she attributes to feelings of cultural inferiority relative to England.

Evidently, in both Australia and Canada at this time—as well as in white South Africa, as we find in Dorothea Fairbridge's 1911 story—there was a strong desire to develop literary and cultural traditions that would give form and significance to newly emergent nationalist feelings. In almost all cases these efforts were marked by the characteristic colonial bifurcation of inclination (towards the local landscape) and influence (from elsewhere) that we again encounter in the 1890s Canadian poetry of Charles G. D. Roberts or Archibald Lampman. Yet paradoxically, it was out of this very dissonance that new settler literatures began to emerge. In their own sometimes pessimistic writing, Clarke and Lawson anticipate and lay the foundations of a symbolism that would be both adaptable and grounded enough to interpret Australia on its own terms. As we have already seen, a hybridization of different voices and vocabularies, perhaps salted by the addition of a local vernacular, provided fertile soil for new forms of self-expression. In the 1890s, 'Banjo' Paterson's literary adaptation of the 'bushman's' song and idiom was soon adopted by the newly self-conscious white community in Australia as their authentic folk voice.

Citing the example of the Eurasian poet Henry Derozio, Kipling, in 'His Chance in Life', looks forward to the days when 'a writer or a

poet' will spring from the 'Borderline folk' of the empire: 'and then
we shall know how they live and what they feel. In the meantime, any
stories about them cannot be absolutely correct in fact or inference.'
At the end of the twentieth century there is no doubt that the days of
'Borderline' writing have triumphantly arrived. Writers have for
some time now been speaking from and beyond the boundaries and
contact zones of what was once the empire. The question might then
well be asked, relative to the cultural interest and significance of this
wealth of work, how might the value of an anthology of empire
writing be justified? To this the answer must lie first and foremost in
the recognition of the ambivalence that has been the keynote of this
introduction. Postcolonial literatures may movingly dramatize the
contraries and contrariness that were central to colonial experience,
yet those shifts and indeterminacies can be discerned within the
writing of empire itself, even within the texts that lay at the heart of
imperial self-conception, like those of Kipling, Henty, or Steel.
Colonial textuality, whether white, black, or in-between, emerged
out of a thick live network of 'multiple encounters and negotiations of
differential meanings' that in many ways anticipated *avant la lettre*
the indeterminacies with which we are preoccupied in Third World,
migrant, and minority writings today.[27]

That said, there is another equally important but opposite way in
which we might encourage paying further attention to empire
writing. For it is through reading colonial literature as traditionally
defined—as white writing, in other words—that we begin to develop
a sense of the myths, tales, symbols, and self-representations that
sustained empire. These poems, short stories, and essays allow us to
take the measure of what anti-colonial literary resistance was up
against, or, putting it slightly differently, what the 'colonial' in the
term 'postcolonial' entailed. And in the presence of many of the same
(yet differently employed) symbols and self-representations in the
work of native writers at the time, we also see how powerful and
pervasive the effects of empire were, how they spread through
cultures and into psyches.

And finally, when we look at J. J. Thomas's deft counter-attack
upon an English historian of considerable status, or Claude McKay's
rendition of Jamaican street voices in Creole, we are reminded that

---

[27] Homi Bhabha, 'The Postcolonial and the Postmodern', *The Location of Culture*, 173.

the inventive energies and resistances we now value in postcolonial writing did not begin yesterday. Toru Dutt's praise for the lotus within a sonnet form derived from her European education creates a disruption of the accepted which may strike late-twentieth-century readers as oddly familiar. Is this incongruity not akin to what the Nigerian novelist Chinua Achebe described when he took it as his task as an African writer to teach that 'the palm tree is a fit subject for poetry'?[28] The 'width of the British Empire', as Derek Walcott has emphasized, eventually accommodated these kinds of recreative and exciting cultural 'cross-overs', like reading the classics 'at the same time as you're eating a mango'. That experience, as Walcott suggests, offers the opportunity of moving beyond the political wounding of empire, of enjoying two disparate but now interconnected 'sensualities'.[29]

[28] Chinua Achebe, 'The Novelist as Teacher', *Hopes and Impediments, 1965–1989* (Heinemann, 1988).

[29] Derek Walcott, 'Poet of the Island', *Arena* interview with Stuart Hall (BBC 2, 1993).

NOTE ON THE ANTHOLOGY

Principles of Ordering and Selection

The process of compiling an anthology which aimed to offer a representative selection of texts in English to do with the experience of colonization for the period of British 'high empire', 1870 to 1918, inevitably involved making difficult choices. For every reader there no doubt will be different gaping omissions, though, I would hope, rich concatenations and surprises also. This Note will attempt to give some account of the issues and decisions which eventually produced the shape and look of the anthology.

In order to create a viable historical frame for a potentially huge body of modern colonial writing, arguably ranging from William Jones's translations in late-eighteenth-century Bengal to the latest Raj fiction, the period 1870 to 1918 was chosen for what might be termed its coherence as a time of new or forward imperialism. Roughly corresponding to Eric Hobsbawm's 'Age of Empire', the period is widely recognized as marked by the rise of a more urgent, assertive, and officially directed attitude to empire in Britain, while it closes, cataclysmically, with the First World War and the beginning of the twentieth-century sea-change in European attitudes to colonialism. The year 1918 rather than 1914, however, was chosen as a cut-off point as it surely was the case that it took the duration of the war for the contradictions of empire as signifying progress and civilization to be fully exposed. (Formal colonialism—if not expansive imperialism—of course continued for several more decades.)

A chief intention behind the anthology—as discussed at more length in the Introduction—was to capture the multiplicity and proliferation of writing at the time of empire, and in particular to reflect responses from both within and without the British Empire's centres of power, and from mainstream and less well-known names. Texts were to cover a number of key areas of colonial perception, and would be drawn from a range of genres, primarily poems, novels, and short stories, but also the related and supporting discourses of essays, travel writing, published lectures, political pamphlets, economic analysis, memoirs, and a housekeeping manual. The 1870–1918 framework was broad enough to make it possible to find and embrace this kind of heterogeneity. The period included not only literature written in support of empire, or texts which give careful or coded voice to incipient doubts concerning the imperial mission, but also, importantly, writing which speaks of the different reality of colonized and settler people, and of their emergent nationalist self-regard, though in many cases they continued to accept the fact of British world power.

As this might suggest, attitudes and responses to empire during the period can be seen to form a wide spectrum of now starkly contrasting, now subtly varying perspectives. To bring this out, and to give some sense of shift and change across the period—of developments in opinion and emotion, collective reactions to key events, new interventions and departures, and emerging uncertainties—the anthology is arranged in chronological order based on the date of first book publication or, in the case of some lectures, of first delivery. In a few instances, where poems or stories were collected some time later or posthumously, the date of first periodical publication is given. In the exceptional case of Leonard Woolf, as I will explain, and more obviously of A. E. Housman's Boer War poem 'Grenadier', the time of composition is noted. Though several of the writings appeared earlier in fairly prominent magazines, as the Explanatory Notes show, the date of the first book edition was favoured because it reflected a text's entry into a wider readership, beyond the audience indicated by a particular periodical or society. As far as alternative arrangements were concerned, a chronology based on, say, the birth-dates of writers would have produced unhelpfully incongruous juxtapositions (Yeats alongside Toru Dutt, for instance). Theme-groupings were felt to be too directive, as was a binary pro- and anti-imperial division of texts. Though non-metropolitan writers are relatively well represented in the anthology, regional or geographic subsections would unavoidably have created an uneven distribution of writing (the greater number of published writers in English at this time were concentrated in England).

It might be pointed out that a publication time-line is a rather *flat* system of ordering, in several senses of the word. However, what quickly became apparent was that it also created interesting and sometimes unexpected pairings, contrasts, and strange attractions between texts. To give only two of many possible examples: immediately after Tennyson's mythologizing work on an episode of British imperial history in 'The Defence of Lucknow', we find Blyden describing the 'Negro' mind as revolting at white historical misrepresentation. Or, differently, McKay speaks of Jamaican experience in Creole at around the same time as Tagore's translations of Hindu mystic ideas reach the West.

In a few instances strict chronology was suspended or compacted where texts were responding to a specific imperial event—most notably the South African War (1899–1902), but also Queen Victoria's two Jubilee celebrations (1887 and 1897)—or where they were in some sense in dialogue with one another, as we see in the description of their famous meeting by both Livingstone and Stanley, and in J. J. Thomas's critique of J. A. Froude. Though he does not address the Indian situation as such, Curzon, the architect of Bengal Partition, speaking in 1906, stands beside one of the leading opponents of Partition, Sri Aurobindo, with his 1907 call for anti-imperial resistance. Boer War poetry forms a substantial cluster of texts around the middle point of the anthology, which seemed appropriate as the war represented an important watershed in British imperial self-perception.

Writings have also been gathered together where they formed part of a distinct literary development, specifically the emergence of a self-conscious nationalist literature in the settler societies of both Australia and Canada during the 1890s. Such groupings, like that around the Boer War, are opened and marked off in each instance by an introductory headnote. As far as their position within the overall chronology is concerned, the Canadians' poems, though published at different times in the 1880s and 1890s, are clustered around 1893, an important debut year for several of the poets. The Australian *Bulletin* texts, which appeared across the 1890s, follow immediately after the Canadian group.

At the end of individual texts, or of a group of linked texts, 'See also' pointers suggest further connections and intertextual links between writings, which are then backed up by the reference tags in the Explanatory Notes and the Biographical section, as well as in the headnotes where these occur. This system, it is hoped, will create alternative reading pathways and thematic juxtapositions within the seeming linearity of the chronological ordering.

Where more than one text by an author has been included, these are again usually grouped under the first date of publication. A few exceptions were made in the light of historical congruity, thematic connections, or other related textual considerations. So, for example, the first appearance by Flora Annie Steel is the introductory chapter to her *The Complete Indian Housekeeper and Cook* (1889) and not the transcribed oral tale 'Bopolûchî', first published in 1884. As the Notes explain, the latter text was the product of collective work, and though interesting precisely for that reason, was not thought to be sufficiently representative of Steel's own writing to stand first. As her three texts are spread across fourteen years, the intermediate date also gives a balance to her place in the collection. Within the Mansfield selection, the story of the abduction of a white child by Maori women, 'How Pearl Button was Kidnapped' (1912), appears before the 1910 poem 'To Stanislaw Wyspianski', in order to juxtapose the story with 'Pipi on the Prowl' (1913) by B. E. Baughan, which also features an encounter between Pakeha and Maori. The Boer War texts have been grouped in such a way as to give an impression of how feeling shifted across the period of the war, an arrangement which is in fact by and large chronological. W. E. Henley's war poems are dated 1900, when his collection *For England's Sake* came out, though some of the verses had appeared before this time.

As the previous paragraph suggests, an author's works for the most part stand alongside each other. Certain texts by Rudyard Kipling, A. E. Housman, and William Watson, however, appear at different points across the chronological frame in accordance with the occasions of their genesis. For Kipling in particular the exception was made, first because he wrote so prolifically and across a wide thematic and generic range about the empire—both the Indian Empire where he was born, and the wider empire which he supported. In addition, like Housman and Watson, he produced poems specifically about the Boer War and in commemoration of Queen Victoria's two Jubilees, which are therefore arranged according to chronology. With regard to the former imperial event, Kipling's poems first of *fin-de-siècle* foreboding ('Recessional' and 'The White Man's Burden', which appear under their pre-war dates of newspaper publication), and then of matter-of-fact admonishment ('The Lesson'), occur as brackets to the Boer War group of texts. On empire Kipling often had the first and the last word.

On the subject of brackets and last words, two texts in the anthology fall outside the period markers of 1870 and 1918, G. O. Trevelyan's *The Competition Wallah* (1864), and Leonard Woolf's 'Pearls and Swine' (1921), and have been placed in the collection in the positions of Fore- and Afterword. This was done not only because the texts serve as convenient matching bookends to the collection—both are about the form-giving 'Empire within an Empire' in India, both chart changes of political heart in the face of imperial prejudice—but also because both are transitional texts, reflecting on the past and (though implicitly in Woolf's case) seeking changes in the future. *The Competition Wallah* (a book Kipling won as a school prize) very clearly builds a bridge between the reformist empire of the first half of the century, whose passing it regrets, and the defensive, militarist imperialism of the last decades, in part a legacy of the Indian Mutiny or Sepoy Rebellion of 1857–8, which Trevelyan discusses. Written not long after 1857, this study of the impact of the Mutiny on Anglo-Indian society was, as Woolf himself said, 'extraordinary' for its time: courageous in its analysis of race prejudice, searching in its exploration of the gulf of cultural misunderstanding dividing people in India. At the same time, *The Competition Wallah* was very much within the Liberal imperialist camp in its reaffirmation of the English duty to spread well-being and justice, to educate and Christianize. The book is also noteworthy for containing the first full publication in the West of Macaulay's influential 1835 Minute on Indian Education, which Trevelyan strongly endorsed.

At the end of the anthology, Woolf's 'Pearls and Swine' expresses the deep disgust at the imperial mission which had crept upon him while working in the Ceylon Civil Service (1905–11). Begun not long after his return to England (and in this respect falling within the temporal framework of the anthology), the story gives some sense of the finally untenable colonial contradictions which were not only to turn Woolf into an anti-imperialist, but to set in motion, from about 1919, the decolonizing forces that produced the world map we have today. With its strong echoes of Conrad and touches of Kiplingesque macabre, 'Pearls and Swine' produces a fitting thematic and stylistic coda to the book.

In deciding on the final character of the anthology, preference was given to textual complexity and resonance, as well as to the

representativeness and diversity already mentioned. Throughout I
wanted to demonstrate that empire writing offers aesthetic value and
pleasure as well as political and historical significance. Emphasis was
also placed on the integrity and coherence of individual texts.
Extracts from novels and poems were avoided where possible, and in
most cases the continuity of a piece of writing was respected. In the
end excerpts were made from two novels only, Haggard's influentially mythopoeic and unmissable *King Solomon's Mines* (which had
therefore to stand in, as it were, for John Buchan's similarly iconographic fiction), and *Ethiopia Unbound* by J. E. Casely Hayford, a
loosely constructed novel which is itself made up of writing in
different generic forms.

Where extracts have been made from longer work, the wider
context is given in the headnotes to individual texts. Writers' own
notes have been retained throughout. On matters of form and writing
style, it perhaps goes without saying that because of the time-scale
and the overarching colonial remit of the anthology, it was not
possible in some cases to include a writer's most achieved work—
D. C. Scott's short stories form a case in point.

To impose some limit on what would otherwise have been an even
fatter and more miscellaneous collection, music-hall ballads and
jingoist poems and songs were excluded fairly early on. These were
composed and sung right the way across the empire, which meant
that authors were often unknown and dates of composition and
publication difficult to establish. Translated work was generally
avoided, again primarily in order to control the potential sprawl of
the anthology. Exceptions are the extract from Edwin Arnold's verse
translation of the life of the Buddha, an example of late-
nineteenth-century Orientalism, Flora Annie Steel's transcribed
oral tale, and James Joyce's self-translated article, as well as a translation into English from a famous Bengali nationalist song by Sri
Aurobindo, and Tagore's self-translations, which demonstrate the
range of Indian self-expression at this time and also (in the case of
Aurobindo) its accommodation to European verse forms.

At the end of the book the Biographies have been designed to give
substantial background on little-known writers, while sketching in
mainly salient details in the case of established names. This procedure has led in many instances to marked disparities of length
between individual biographies. This seemed justified as a symbolic

reversal, an overturning of the traditional distinctions made between metropolitan and so-called colonized writers appropriate for these postcolonial times.

The texts used have been those of the first book edition where relevant and possible. In some cases, because of inaccessibility either across time or place, the available English edition was taken instead of, say, the Australian or Indian first edition (Steel's *Complete Housekeeper* is an example). Three pieces, significantly all journalism by women (Duncan, Kingsley and Fairbridge), were not collected into books, and here the periodicals themselves were used as the basis for the anthology selection. In a majority of cases I drew the titles of texts from the works themselves, where they occur either as the book titles *tout court*, or as chapter or subheadings. In the interests of general readability, typographical errors (mostly fairly infrequent) have been silently corrected.

The term 'native', traditionally pejorative but subverted and reclaimed by postcolonial writers and theorists in recent years, has been used throughout.

SELECT BIBLIOGRAPHY

Unless otherwise stated, place of publication is London, and for University Presses is generally implied by the university's name.

For further historical, social, and cultural background on the texts of the period, readers may find the following useful:

Michael Adas, *Machines as the Measure of Man: Science, Technology, and Ideologies of Western Dominance* (New York: Cornell UP, 1989).

A. L. Basham, *The Wonder that was India* (Sidgwick and Jackson, 1954).

C. A. Bayly, *Imperial Meridian: The British Empire and the World, 1780–1831* (Harlow, Essex: Longman, 1989).

—— *Indian Society and the Making of the British Empire* (Cambridge UP, 1988).

Pat Barr, *The Memsahibs: The Women of Victorian India* (Secker and Warburg, 1976).

Christine Bolt, *Victorian Attitudes to Race* (Routledge and Kegan Paul, 1971).

David Burton, *The Raj at Table: A Culinary History of the British in India* (Faber, 1993).

P. J. Cain and A. G. Hopkins, *British Imperialism: Crisis and Deconstruction* (Harlow, Essex: Longman, 1993).

Helen Callaway, *Gender, Culture and Empire: European Women in Colonial Nigeria* (Urbana: University of Illinois Press, 1987).

C. E. Carrington, *The British Overseas: Exploits of a Nation of Shopkeepers* (Macmillan, 1955).

Nirad C. Chaudhuri, *Hinduism* (Oxford UP, 1979).

Neil Charlesworth, *British Rule and the Indian Economy, 1800–1914* (Macmillan, 1982).

Alfred Crosby, *Ecological Imperialism* (Cambridge UP, 1986).

Michael W. Doyle, *Empires* (Ithaca: Cornell UP, 1986).

John Eddy and Deryck Schreuder, *The Rise of Colonial Nationalism, 1850–1914* (Sydney: Allen and Unwin, 1988).

Ainslie Embree (ed.), *1857 in India: Mutiny or War of Independence* (Boston: Heath, 1963).

R. F. Foster, *Modern Ireland, 1600–1972* (Allen Lane, 1988).

Ranajit Guha (ed.), *Subaltern Studies: Writings on South Asian History and Culture*, 6 vols. (New Delhi: Oxford UP, 1988).

Jose Harris, *Private Lives, Public Spirit, 1870–1914* (Oxford UP, 1993).

Christopher Hibbert, *The Great Mutiny: India, 1857* (Allen Lane, 1978).

E. J. Hobsbawm, *The Age of Capital, 1848–1875* (Weidenfeld and Nicolson, 1975).

—— *The Age of Empire, 1875–1914* (Weidenfeld and Nicolson, 1987).

—— *Age of Extremes: The Short Twentieth Century, 1914–1991* (Michael Joseph, 1994).

—— and Terence Ranger (eds.), *The Invention of Tradition* (Cambridge UP, 1983).

Peter Hopkirk, *The Great Game: On Secret Service in High Asia* (Oxford UP, 1991).

Ronald Hyam, *Britain's Imperial Century, 1815–1914: A Study of Empire and Expansion* (Macmillan, 1993).

—— *Empire and Sexuality: The British Experience* (Manchester UP, 1990).

Samuel Hynes, *The Edwardian Turn of Mind* (Princeton UP, 1968).

Lawrence James, *The Rise and Fall of the British Empire* (Abacus, 1994).

Kumari Jayawardena, *The White Woman's Other Burden: Western Women and South Asia During British Rule* (Routledge, 1995).

Gordon Johnson, C. A. Bayly, and John F. Richards (eds.), *The New Cambridge History of India*, Parts III and IV (Cambridge UP, 1992–).

Denis Judd, *Empire: The British Imperial Experience, 1765 to the Present* (HarperCollins, 1996).

V. G. Kiernan, *European Empires from Conquest to Collapse* (Leicester UP and Fontana, 1982).

—— *The Lords of Human Kind: European Attitudes towards the Outside World in the Imperial Age* (Weidenfeld and Nicolson, 1969).

—— *Marxism and Imperialism* (Edward Arnold, 1974).

Richard Koebner and Helmut Dan Schmidt, *Imperialism: The Story and Significance of a Political Word, 1840–1960* (Cambridge UP, 1964).

Mary Ann Lind, *The Compassionate Memsahibs: Welfare Activities of British Women in India, 1900–1947* (New York: Greenwood Press, 1988).

P. J. Marshall, *The Cambridge Illustrated History of the British Empire* (Cambridge UP, 1996).

Frank McLynn, *Hearts of Darkness* (Hutchinson, 1992).

James Morris, *Farewell the Trumpets: An Imperial Retreat* (Faber, 1978).

—— *Heaven's Command* (Faber, 1973).

—— *Pax Britannica* (Faber, 1968).

Jan Morris, *The Spectacle of Empire: Style, Effect and Pax Britannica* (Faber, 1982).

Thomas Pakenham, *The Scramble for Africa, 1876–1912* (Weidenfeld and Nicholson, 1991).

—— The Boer War (Weidenfeld and Nicholson, 1979).

Bernard Porter, *The Lion's Share: A Short History of British Imperialism*, 2nd edn. (Harlow, Essex: Longman, 1984).

Brian Roberts, *Cecil Rhodes: Flawed Colossus* (Hamish Hamilton, 1987).

Portia Robinson, The Women of Botany Bay (1988; Ringwood: Penguin, 1993).

Ronald Robinson and John Gallagher, *Africa and the Victorians: The Official Mind of Imperialism* (Macmillan, 1961).

Walter Rodney, *How Europe Underdeveloped Africa* (Bogle L'Ouverture Publications, 1972).

Raphael Samuel (ed.), *The Making and Unmaking of British National Identity*, 3 vols. (Routledge, 1989).

Sumit Sarkar, *Modern India, 1885–1947* (1983; Macmillan, 1989).

Vinayek Savarkar, *The Indian War of Independence: 1857* (Bombay: Phoenix, 1947).

George Stocking, *Victorian Anthropology* (New York: The Free Press, 1987).

Eric Stokes, *The Peasant Armed: The Indian Revolt of 1857* (Oxford UP, 1986).

Anthony Thomas, *Rhodes* (BBC Books, 1996).

Joanna Trollope, *Britannia's Daughters: Women of the British Empire* (Hutchinson, 1983).

Vron Ware, *Beyond the Pale: White Women, Racism and History* (Verso, 1992).

Eric Wolf, *Europe and the People Without History* (Berkeley: University of California Press, 1982).

Stanley Wolpert, *A New History of British India*, 4th edn. (Oxford UP, 1993).

Also of interest in developing a sense of context are biographies and single-author studies, of which the following are a sampling:

Alison Blunt, *Travel, Gender and Imperialism: Mary Kingsley and West Africa* (Harlow, Essex: Longman, 1994).

C. E. Carrington, *Rudyard Kipling: His Life and Work* (Macmillan, 1955).

Vincent Cheng, *Joyce, Race and Empire* (Cambridge, 1995).

Cherry Clayton (ed.), *Olive Schreiner* (Johannesburg: McGraw-Hill, 1983).

Wayne Cooper, *Claude McKay: Rebel Sojourner* (Louisiana State UP, 1987).

Pamela Dunbar, *Radical Mansfield* (Macmillan, 1997).

Krishna Dutta and Andrew Robinson, *Rabindranath Tagore: The Myriad Minded Man* (Bloomsbury, 1995).

Brian Elliott, *Marcus Clarke* (Oxford: Clarendon Press, 1958).

Richard Ellmann, *The Identity of Yeats* (Faber, 1964).

—— *Yeats: The Man and the Masks* (1948; Penguin, 1988).

Peter Berresford Ellis, *Rider Haggard: A Voice from the Infinite* (Routledge and Kegan Paul, 1978).

Dorothy Farmiloe, *Isabella Valancy Crawford: The Life and Legends* (Ottawa: Tecumseh Press, 1983).

Ruth First and Ann Scott, *Olive Schreiner* (1980; Women's Press, 1989).

Roy Foster, *W. B. Yeats: A Life: I. The Apprentice Mage 1865–1914* (Oxford UP, 1997).

Christopher Fyfe, *Africanus Horton: West African Scientist and Patriot* (New York: Oxford UP, 1972).

Harry A. Gailey, *Clifford: Imperial Proconsul* (Rex Collings, 1982).

David Gilmour, *Curzon* (John Murray, 1994).

Ian A. Gordon (ed.), *Undiscovered Country: The New Zealand Stories of Katherine Mansfield* (Harlow, Essex: Longman, 1974).

Claire Hanson and Andrew Gurr, *Katherine Mansfield* (Macmillan, 1981).

Timothy Holmes, *Journey to Livingstone* (Edinburgh: Canongate Press, 1993).

K. R. Srinivasa Iyengar, *On the Mother* (Pondicherry: Sri Aurobindo Centre of Education, 1978).

—— *Swami Vivekananda* (Madras: Samata Books, 1988).

Denis Judd, *Radical Joe: A Life of Joseph Chamberlain* (Hamish Hamilton, 1977).

Peter Keating, *Kipling the Poet* (Secker and Warburg, 1994).

Sandra Kemp, *Kipling's Hidden Narratives* (Oxford: Basil Blackwell, 1988).

Krishna Kripalani, *Rabindranath Tagore: A Biography* (Oxford UP, 1962).

Robert Kubicek, *The Administration of Imperialism: Joseph Chamberlain at the Colonial Office* (Baltimore, NC: Duke UP, 1969).

Mary Lago, *Rabindranath Tagore* (Boston: Twayne Publishers, 1976).

Hollis R. Lynch, *Edward Wilmot Blyden: Pan-Negro Patriot, 1832–1912* (Oxford UP, 1967)

Jeffrey Meyers, *Joseph Conrad* (John Murray, 1991).

Frank McLynn, *Robert Louis Stevenson* (Hutchinson, 1993).

Muriel Miller, *Bliss Carman: Quest and Revolt* (St John's, Newfoundland: Jesperson Press, 1985).

Michael Millgate, *Thomas Hardy* (Oxford UP, 1982).

Theresa Moritz, *Stephen Leacock* (Toronto: Stoddard Press, 1995).

Henry Newbolt, *My World as in My Time: Memoirs of Henry Newbolt, 1862–1932* (Faber, 1932).

Sister Nivedita, *The Master as I Saw Him: Being Pages from the Life of the Swami Vivekananda* (Longmans, Green and Co., 1910).

Emer Nolan, *James Joyce and Nationalism* (Routledge, 1995).

L. H. Ofosu-Appiah, *Joseph Ephraim Casely Hayford: The Man of Vision and Faith* (Accra: Academy of Arts and Sciences, 1975).

Benita Parry, *Conrad and Imperialism* (Macmillan, 1983).

Tom Pocock, *Rider Haggard and the Lost Empire* (Weidenfeld and Nicolson, 1993).

Nicholas Rankin, *Dead Man's Chest: Travels After Robert Louis Stevenson* (Faber, 1987).

Colin Roderick, *Henry Lawson: A Life* (Sydney: Angus and Robertson, 1991).

Alan Sandison, *Robert Louis Stevenson and the Appearance of Modernism* (Macmillan, 1997).

Michael Schneider, *J. A. Hobson* (Macmillan, 1996).

George Seaver, *David Livingstone: His Life and Letters* (Lutterworth Press, 1957).

Clement Semmler, *The Banjo of the Bush: The Life and Times of A. B. Paterson*, 2nd edn. (1966; University of Queensland Press, 1974).

Norman Sherry, *Conrad's Eastern World* (Cambridge UP, 1966).

—— *Conrad's Western World* (Cambridge UP, 1971).

Zohrah T. Sullivan, *Narratives of Empire: The Fictions of Rudyard Kipling* (Cambridge UP, 1993).

Claire Tomalin, *Katherine Mansfield: A Secret Life* (Viking, 1987).

Jules Townshend, *J. A. Hobson* (Manchester UP, 1990).

George Macaulay Trevelyan, *Sir George Otto Trevelyan: A Memoir* (Longmans, Green and Co., 1932).

Michael Wilding (ed.), *Marcus Clarke: His Life and Stories* (Sydney: Hale and Ironmonger, 1983).

Ian Watt, *Conrad in the Nineteenth Century* (Berkeley: University of California Press, 1979).

Brian Willan, *Sol Plaatje: South African Nationalist, 1876–1932* (Heinemann, 1984).

Duncan Wilson, *Leonard Woolf: A Political Biography* (Hogarth, 1978).

Colonial discourse theory and literary criticism is an area that has burgeoned in recent years, offering different perspectives on the ideology and writing of empire. What is listed here reflects the range of readings on offer:

Aijaz Ahmad, *In Theory: Classes, Nations, Literatures* (Verso, 1992).

Syed Hussein Alatas, *The Myth of the Lazy Native* (Frank Cass, 1977).

Bill Ashcroft, Gareth Griffiths, and Helen Tiffin, *The Empire Writes Back: Theory and Practice in Post-Colonial Literatures* (Routledge, 1989).

Michael Banton, *Racial Theories* (Cambridge UP, 1987).

Francis Barker, Peter Hulme, Margaret Iversen, and Diana Loxley (eds.), *Europe and its Others: Proceedings of the Essex Conference*, 2 vols. (Colchester: University of Essex, 1985).

—— —— —— *Colonial Discourse/Postcolonial Theory* (Manchester UP, 1994).

Geoff Bennington, Rachel Bowlby, and Robert Young (eds.), *Oxford Literary Review: Colonialism and Other Essays*, 9:1–2 (1987).

Eugene Benson and L. W. Conolly (eds.), *Encyclopedia of Post-Colonial Literatures in English*, 2 vols. (Routledge, 1994).

Homi Bhabha, *The Location of Culture* (Routledge, 1994).

—— (ed.), *Nation and Narration* (Routledge, 1990).

Elleke Boehmer, *Colonial and Postcolonial Literature* (Oxford UP, 1995).

Chris Bongie, *Exotic Memories* (Stanford UP, 1991).

James A. Boon, *Other Tribes, Other Scribes: Symbolic Anthropology in the Comparative Study of Culture* (Cambridge UP, 1982).

Patrick Brantlinger, *Rule of Darkness: British Literature and Imperialism, 1830–1914* (Ithaca: Cornell UP, 1988).

Joseph Bristow, *Empire Boys: Adventures in a Man's World* (HarperCollins, 1991).

David Cairns and Shaun Richards, *Writing Ireland: Colonialism, Nationalism and Culture* (Manchester UP, 1988).

Paul Carter, *The Road to Botany Bay: An Essay in Spatial History* (Faber, 1987).

Aimé Césaire, *Discours sur le colonialisme* (Paris: Présence Africaine, 1955).

Suhash Chakravarty, *The Raj Syndrome: A Study in Imperial Perceptions* (New Delhi: Penguin, 1989).

Partha Chatterjee, *Nationalist Thought and the Colonial World* (Zed, 1986).

Gail Ching-Liang Low, *White Skins/Black Masks: Representation and Colonialism* (Routledge, 1996).

James Clifford, *The Predicament of Culture* (Cambridge, Mass.: Harvard UP, 1988).

J. M. Coetzee, *White Writing: On the Culture of Letters in South Africa* (Yale UP, 1989).

Robert Colls and Philip Dodd (eds.), *Englishness: Politics and Culture, 1880–1920* (Croom Helm, 1987).

Richard Cronin, *Imagining India* (Macmillan, 1989).

Kate Darian-Smith, Liz Gunner, and Sarah Nuttall (eds.), *Text, Theory, Space* (Routledge, 1996).

Tony Davies and Nigel Woods (eds.), *A Passage to India* (Buckingham: Open University Press, 1994).

John Drew, *India and the Romantic Imagination* (New Delhi: Oxford UP, 1987).

Terry Eagleton, Frederic Jameson, and Edward W. Said, *Nationalism, Colonialism and Literature* (Minneapolis: University of Minnesota Press, 1990).

Frantz Fanon, *Black Skin, White Masks*, trans. Charles Lam Markmann (1952; Pluto, 1986).

—— *Studies in a Dying Colonialism* (Earthscan Press, 1989).

—— *The Wretched of the Earth*, trans. Constance Farrington (1961; Harmondsworth: Penguin, 1986).

Henry Louis Gates (ed.), *'Race', Writing and Difference* (University of Chicago Press, 1986).

Sander Gilman, *Difference and Pathology: Stereotypes of Sexuality, Race and Madness* (New York: Cornell UP, 1985).

Paul Gilroy, *The Black Atlantic: Modernity and Double Consciousness* (Verso, 1993).

Martin Green, *Dreams of Adventure, Deeds of Empire* (Routledge and Kegan Paul, 1980).

Allen J. Greenberger, *The British Image of India: Studies in the Literature of British Imperialism, 1880–1960* (Oxford, 1969).

Dorothy Hammond and Alta Jablow, *The Africa that Never Was: Four Centuries of British Writing About Africa* (New York: Twayne, 1970).

Ronald Inden, *Imagining India* (Oxford: Basil Blackwell, 1990).

A. N. Joshi, *The West Looks at India* (New Delhi: Prakash Book Depot, 1969).

Rana Kabbani, *Europe's Myths of the Orient* (Macmillan, 1986).

Declan Kiberd, *Inventing Ireland* (Cape, 1995).

Peter Knox-Shaw, *The Explorer in English Literature* (Macmillan, 1986).

Dominic LaCapra, *The Bounds of Race* (Ithaca: Cornell UP, 1991).

Christopher Lane, *The Ruling Passion: British Colonial Allegory and the Paradox of Sexual Desire* (Baltimore, NC: Duke UP, 1995).

Reina Lewis, *Gendering Orientalism* (Routledge, 1997).

David Lloyd, *Anomalous States: Irish Writing and the Post-Colonial Moment* (Dublin: Lilliput Press, 1993).

Lisa Lowe, *Critical Terrains: French and British Orientalisms* (Ithaca: Cornell UP, 1991).

Anne McClintock, *Imperial Leather: Race, Gender and Sexuality in the Colonial Contest* (Routledge, 1995).

John A. McClure, *Kipling and Conrad: The Colonial Fiction* (Cambridge, Mass.: Harvard UP, 1981).

John MacKenzie, *Propaganda and Empire* (Manchester UP, 1984).

Albert Memmi, *The Colonizer and the Colonized* (Boston: Beacon, 1965).

Jeffrey Meyers, *Fiction and the Colonial Experience* (Ipswich: Boydell Press, 1973).

Clare Midgley (ed.), *Gender and Imperialism* (Manchester UP, 1998).

Christopher L. Miller, *Blank Darkness: Africanist Discourse in French* (University of Chicago Press, 1985).

Sara Mills, *Discourses of Difference: An Analysis of Women's Travel Writing and Colonialism* (Routledge, 1992).

Udayon Misra, *The Raj in Fiction: A Study of Nineteenth-Century British Attitudes Towards India* (New Delhi: BR Publishing, 1987).

B. J. Moore-Gilbert, *Kipling and 'Orientalism'* (Croom Helm, 1986).

—— *Postcolonial Theory: Contexts, Practices, Politics* (Verso, 1997).

—— (ed.), *Writing India, 1757–1990: The Literature of British India* (Manchester UP, 1996).

V. Y. Mudimbe, *The Invention of Africa: Gnosis, Philosophy and the Order of Knowledge* (James Currey, 1988).

M. K. Naik, *Perspectives on Indian Poetry in English* (New Delhi: Abhinav Publications, 1984).

Ashis Nandy, *The Intimate Enemy: Loss and Recovery of Self under Colonialism* (New Delhi: Oxford UP, 1983).

Benita Parry, *Conrad and Imperialism* (Macmillan, 1983).

—— *Delusions and Discoveries: Studies on India in the British Imagination, 1880–1930* (Allen Lane, 1972).

Mary Louise Pratt, *Imperial Eyes: Travel Writing and Transculturation* (Routledge, 1992).

David Richards, *Masks of Difference* (Cambridge UP, 1995).

Jeffrey Richards (ed.), *Imperialism and Juvenile Literature* (Manchester UP, 1989).

Hugh Ridley, *Images of Imperial Rule* (Croom Helm, 1983).

Edward Said, *Culture and Imperialism* (Chatto and Windus, 1993).

—— *Orientalism* (1978; Harmondsworth: Penguin, 1987).

Alan Sandison, *The Wheel of Empire: A Study of the Imperial Idea* (Macmillan, 1967).

Kumkum Sangari and Sudesh Vaid (eds.), *Recasting Women: Essays in Colonial History* (Delhi: Kali for Women, 1989).

Kay Schaffer, *Women and the Bush: Forces of Desire in the Australian Cultural Tradition* (Cambridge UP, 1989).

Jenny Sharpe, *Allegories of Empire: The Figure of the Woman in the Colonial Text* (Minneapolis: University of Minnesota Press, 1993).

Bhupal Singh, *A Survey of Anglo-Indian Fiction* (1934; Curzon, 1975).

Jyotsna Singh, *Colonial Narratives: 'Discoveries' of India in the Language of Colonialism* (Routledge, 1996).

Rashna Singh, *The Imperishable Empire: A Study of British Fiction on India* (Washington DC: Three Continents Press, 1988).

R. P. N. Sinha, *Indo-Anglian Poetry: Its Birth and Growth* (New Delhi: Reliance Publishing House, 1987).

Gayatri Spivak, *In Other Worlds* (Methuen, 1987).

—— *The Post-colonial Critic: Interviews, Strategies, Dialogues*, ed. Sarah Harasym (Routledge, 1990).

David Spurr, *The Rhetoric of Empire: Colonial Discourse in Journalism, Travel Writing and Imperial Administration* (Baltimore, NC: Duke UP, 1993).

Nancy Stepan, *The Idea of Race in Science: Great Britain, 1800–1960* (Macmillan, 1982).

Brian Street, *The Savage in Literature: Representatives of the 'Primitive' in English Fiction, 1858–1920* (Routledge and Kegan Paul, 1975).

Sara Suleri, *The Rhetoric of English India* (University of Chicago Press, 1992).

Ngugi wa Thiong'o, *Decolonising the Mind* (Heinemann, 1986).

Chris Tiffin and Alan Lawson (eds.), *De-scribing Empire* (Routledge, 1994).

Mariana Torgovnik, *Gone Primitive: Savage Intellects, Modern Lives* (University of Chicago Press, 1992).

Harish Trivedi, *Colonial Transactions: English Literature and India* (1993; Manchester UP, 1995).

Gauri Viswanathan, *Masks of Conquest: Literary Study and British Rule in India* (Faber, 1990).

Shearer West (ed.), *The Victorians and Race* (Aldershot: Ashgate, 1996).

Patrick Williams and Laura Chrisman (eds.), *Colonial Discourse and Post-Colonial Criticism* (Brighton: Harvester Wheatsheaf, 1993).

Malvern van Wyk Smith, *Drummer Hodge: The Poetry of the Anglo-Boer War (1899–1902)* (Oxford: Clarendon Press, 1978).

Robert Young, *White Mythologies: Writing History and the West* (Routledge, 1990).

—— *Colonial Desire: Hybridity in Theory, Race and Culture* (Routledge, 1995).

Related anthologies in the field of colonial literature include:

Michael Ackland (ed.), *The Penguin Book of 19th Century Australian Literature* (Ringwood, Australia: Penguin, 1993).

Margaret Atwood (ed.), *The Oxford Anthology of Canadian Short Stories* (Oxford UP, 1986).

Charles Allen (ed.), *Plain Tales from the Raj* (Newton Abbot: Readers Union, 1976).

Chris Brooks and Peter Faulkner (eds.), *The White Man's Burdens: An Anthology of British Poetry of the Empire* (Exeter UP, 1996).

Paula Burnett (ed.), *The Penguin Book of Caribbean Verse in English* (Harmondsworth: Penguin, 1986).

Saros Cowasjee (ed.), *Stories from the Raj: from Kipling to Independence* (Bodley Head, 1982).

—— (ed.), *More Stories from the Raj and After: From Kipling to the Present Day* (Grafton, 1986).

Alison Donnell and Sarah Lawson Welsh (eds.), *Reader in Caribbean Literature* (Routledge, 1995).

Lucy Frost, *No Place for a Nervous Lady: Voices from the Australian Bush* (St Lucia: University of Queensland Press, 1984).

Andrew Hassan (ed.), *Sailing to Australia: Shipboard Diaries by Nineteenth-Century British Emigrants* (Manchester UP, 1994).

Susan Lever (ed.), *The Oxford Book of Australian Women's Verse* (Melbourne: Oxford UP, 1995).

Dale Spender (ed.), *The Penguin Anthology of Australian Women's Writing* (Ringwood: Penguin, 1988).

Susie Tharu and K. Lalita (eds.), *Women Writing in India: 600 B.C. to the Present*, vol. 1 (Delhi: Oxford UP, 1991).

John Thieme (ed.), *The Arnold Anthology of Post-Colonial Literatures in English* (Arnold, 1997).

CHRONOLOGY OF KEY EVENTS

This chronology of key events in British colonial history during the period of the anthology, is intended to provide a basic context for the literary chronology formed by the arrangement of texts.

1858 Following the Sepoy Rebellion or Indian Mutiny (1857), the British government assumes control over India.

1860 Maori resistance to British land-ownership leads to the Second Maori War (–1863).

1865 Rebellion in Jamaica led by G. W. Gordon, harshly repressed by Governor Eyre.

1867 British North America Act establishes the Dominion of Canada.

1869 Suez Canal formally opened.

1872 Benjamin Disraeli gives rousing pro-empire Crystal Palace speech.

1873 Asante Expedition (–1874) leads to the creation of the Gold Coast Crown Colony.

1874 Disraeli becomes Prime Minister. Britain establishes Residencies in the Malay States.

1876 Truganini, the last full-blooded Tasmanian Aboriginal, dies.

1877 Queen Victoria proclaimed Empress of India. Britain annexes the Transvaal.

1878 Second Afghanistan campaign launched.

1879 The British–Zulu War. Zulu victory at Isandhlwana. *Boy's Own Paper* established.

1880 First Boer War in South Africa. Transvaal independence follows British humiliation at Majuba (1881).

1882 British military intervention in Egypt.

1884 Imperial Federation League founded.

1885 Berlin Conference regulating the Partition of Africa among European nations. The Congo Free State declares the personal fealty of the Belgian King Leopold II. The Mahdi captures Khartoum in the Sudan and General Gordon is killed. The Indian National Congress meets for the first time. After the Second Métis Rebellion in Canada the leader, Louis Riel, is hanged.

1886 Following the annexation of Upper Burma, Burma becomes a province of British India. British government split over Irish Home Rule.

1887 Queen Victoria's Golden Jubilee. First Colonial Conference held in London.

1889 Cecil John Rhodes launches his Chartered British South Africa Company for the conquest of Mashonaland and development of mining in the region.

1891 Death of Parnell, finally shattering hopes for Irish Home Rule.

1893 Gaelic League founded in Ireland.

1895 The Jameson Raid into the Transvaal Republic. Cecil John Rhodes and Joseph Chamberlain implicated.

1896 Boxer Rebellion in China. British 99-year lease of the New Territories adjacent to Hong Kong. Launch of the *Daily Mail* creates a popular jingoist press. Ndebele and Shona Rebellions in Rhodesia.

1897 Queen Victoria's Diamond Jubilee.

1898 Kitchener fights against the Mahdists at Omdurman to avenge Gordon's death. Fashoda Incident on the Upper Nile between the British and the French.

1899 Outbreak of the Second Anglo-Boer or South African War (October).

1900 Nigeria becomes a British protectorate. Relief of the besieged cities of Ladysmith and Mafeking in South Africa.

1901 Australian federation (Aboriginals not counted in the federal census). Queen Victoria dies. In India 1.25 million have died from famine since 1899. Britain annexes the Asante Kingdom as part of the Gold Coast.

1902 South African War ends.

1904 Japanese victorious in Russo-Japanese War.

1905 Partition of Bengal, initiated by Curzon. Swadeshi movement of resistance follows (–1908).

1906 Zulu uprising in Natal. Liberal Party sweeps to victory in British general election over opposition to Imperial Tariff Reform.

1907 The self-governing (white) colonies are declared Dominions.

1909 Morley–Minto reforms in India.

1911 Imperial Conference attempts to rationalize Britain's relationship with the white Dominions.

1912 Formation of the South African Natives National Congress (later the ANC).

1914 Outbreak of the First World War. Northern and Southern Nigeria united. Mohandas Gandhi returns to India from South Africa.

1916 Easter Rising in Ireland. Battle of the Somme.

1917 Bolshevik October Revolution.

1918 The Allies and Germany sign Armistice. Declaration of the Irish Republic.

1919 Montagu–Chelmsford reforms (permitting partial self-government), Rowlatt Acts (devised to suppress public protest and opposition), and Amritsar Massacre in India. Peace Conference at

Versailles. Despite Britain's steady economic decline, the empire attains its widest extent with the acquisition of the mandated territories. The Dominions obtain greater autonomy within the British Commonwealth. Division of the Austro-Hungarian Empire. Outbreak of Anglo-Irish War (–1921).

EMPIRE WRITING

FOREWORD

GEORGE OTTO TREVELYAN
(1838–1928)

from *The Competition Wallah* (1864)

While working in India during 1862 Trevelyan experienced a 'gradual but complete' change of political heart which he recorded in the letters written for Macmillan's Magazine *which became* The Competition Wallah. *It was a change from 'rabid Anglo-Saxonism' and 'nigger' hatred, as he said in the Preface to the book, to a deeper recognition of cultural relativity, and, accompanying this, an affirmation of the imperialist's duty to govern 'for the benefit of the inhabitants of India'. The* Competition Wallah *is a series of fictionalized 'letters home' from Henry Broughton, a Cambridge hearty who has surprised everyone by passing the competitive examination for the Indian Civil Service, to his stay-at-home friend Charles Simkins. Trevelyan was no competition wallah himself but, following the success of the book, the term became a catchphrase to distinguish those who had sat the competitive examinations to the Civil Service (instituted from 1856) from those who had proceeded by nomination (such as John Beames (q.v.)).*

An Indian Railway

Bankipore, alias Patna,
Feb. 7, 1863.

Towards the end of last month I applied for, and obtained, six weeks' leave, after passing in the first of my two languages.* It is a fact worthy of note, that the men who fail are very generally dissatisfied with the manner in which this examination is conducted, while the men who succeed seem, on the whole, inclined to think that there is not much amiss. On the evening of the 31st I left Calcutta by train, with the intention of living a week at Patna with Major Ratcliffe, who is on special duty there, and then passing the rest of my leave with my cousin, Tom Goddard, at Mofussilpore.* Ratcliffe is a Bengal Club acquaintance, who gave me first a general, and then a most particular invitation to stay with him up country. There is something stupendous in the hospitality of India. It appears to be the ordinary thing, five minutes after a first introduction for people to ask you to come and spend a month with them. And yet there is a general complaint that the old good-fellowship is going out fast; that there are so many Europeans about of questionable position and most unquestionable breeding that it is necessary to know something of a man besides the colour of his skin before admitting him into the bosom of a family.

There is something very interesting in a first railway journey in Bengal. Never was I so impressed with the triumphs of progress, the march of mind. In fact, all the usual common-places genuinely filled my soul. Those two thin strips of iron, representing as they do the mightiest and the most fruitful conquest of science, stretch hundreds and hundreds of miles across the boundless Eastern plains—rich, indeed, in material products, but tilled by a race far below the most barbarous of Europeans in all the qualities that give good hope for the future of a nation—through the wild hills of Rajmahal, swarming with savage beasts, and men more savage than they; past Mussulman shrines and Hindoo temples; along the bank of the great river* that cannot be bridged, whose crocodiles fatten on the corpses which superstition still supplies to them by hundreds daily. Keep to the lines, and you see everywhere the unmistakable signs of England's handiwork. There are the colossal viaducts, spanning wide tracts of pool and sandbank, which the first rains will convert into vast torrents. There are the long rows of iron sheds, with huge engines running in and out of them with that indefiniteness of purpose which seems to characterise locomotives all over the world. There is the true British stationmaster, grand but civil on ordinary occasions, but bursting into excitement and ferocity when things go wrong, or when his will is disputed; who fears nothing human or divine, except the daily press. There is the refreshment-room, with its half-crown dinner that practically always costs five and ninepence. Stroll a hundred yards from the embankment, and all symptoms of civilization have vanished. You find yourself in the midst of scenes that Arrian* might have witnessed; among manners unchanged by thousands of years—unchangeable, perhaps, by thousands more.

The gay bullock-litter bearing to her wedding the bride of four years old; the train of pilgrims, their turbans and cummerbunds stained with pink, carrying back the water of the sacred stream to their distant homes; the filthy, debauched beggar, whom all the neighbourhood pamper like a bacon-hog, and revere as a Saint Simeon*—these are sights which have very little in common with Didcot or Crewe Junction.

A station on an Indian line affords much that is amusing to a curious observer. Long before the hour at which the train is expected, a dense crowd of natives collects outside the glass-doors, dressed in their brightest colours, and in a wild state of excitement. The Hindoos have taken most kindly to railway-travelling. It is a species of locomotion which pre-eminently suits their lazy habits; and it likewise appeals to their love of turning a penny. To them every journey is a petty speculation. If they can sell their goods at a distance for a price which will cover the double fare, and leave a few pice* over, they infinitely prefer sitting still in a truck to earning a much larger sum by genuine labour. A less estimable class of men of business, who are said to make great use of the railway, are the dacoits,* who travel often sixty or seventy miles to commit their villainies, in order to escape the observation of the police in their own district. Every native carries a parcel of some sort of kind, and it often happens that a man brings a bundle so large that it cannot be got in at the door.

At length the barrier is opened, and the passengers are admitted in small parties by a policeman, who treats them with almost as little courtesy as is shown to Cook's tourists by a Scotch railway official. When his turn comes to buy a ticket, your true Hindoo generally attempts to make a bargain with the clerk, but is very summarily snubbed by that gentleman, and, after an unsuccessful effort to conceal a copper coin, he is shoved by a second policeman on to the platform, where he and his companions discuss the whole proceeding at great length and with extraordinary warmth.

Natives almost invariably travel third-class. At one time a train used to run consisting entirely of first and third-class carriages. Every first-class passenger was entitled to take two servants at third-class prices. It was no uncommon thing for well-to-do natives to entreat an English traveller to let them call themselves his servants for the sake of the difference in the fares. The most wealthy Hindoos would probably go first-class if it were not for a well-founded fear of the Sahibs, and therefore they share the second-class with our poorer countrymen. In fact, in spite of the fraternity and equality which exists in theory between the subjects of our beloved Queen, the incompatibility of manners is such that English ladies could not use the railway at all if native gentlemen were in the constant habit of travelling in the same compartment. If you ask how our country-men manage to appropriate to themselves the first-class carriages without a special regulation to that effect, I ask you in return, How is it that there are no tradesmen's sons at Eton and Harrow? There is no law, written or unwritten, which excludes them from those schools, and yet the boys take good care that if one comes he shall not stay there very long.

To return to our scene at the station. Suddenly, in the rear of the crowd, without the gates, there arises a great hubbub, amidst which, from time to time, may be distinguished an imperious, sharp-cut voice, the owner of which appears to show the most lordly indifference to the remarks and answers made around him. A few moments more, after some quarrelling and shoving about, the throng divides, and down the lane thus formed stalks the Sahib of the period, in all the glory of an old flannel shirt and trousers, a dirty alpaca coat, no collar, no waistcoat, white canvas shoes, and a vast pith helmet. Behind him comes his chief bearer, with a cash-box, a loading-rod, two copies of the *Saturday Review* of six months back, and three bottles of soda-water. Then follows a long team of coolies, carrying on their heads a huge quantity of shabby and nondescript luggage, including at least one gun-case and a vast shapeless parcel of bedding. On the portmanteau you may still read, in very faint letters, 'Calcutta-Cabin.' The Sahib, with the freedom and easy insolence of a member of the Imperial race, walks straight into the sacred enclosure of the clerk's office, and takes a ticket, at five times the price paid by his native brethren. Meanwhile, his bearer disposes the luggage in a heap, rewards the coolies on a scale which seems to give them profound discontent, and receives a third-class ticket from his master's hands with every mark of the most heartfelt gratitude. If there happens to be another Sahib on the platform, the two fall to talking on the extreme badness of the road in the district made by the Supreme Government, as opposed to those constructed by the local authorities. If he is alone, our Sahib contemplates the statement of offence committed against the railway rules and regulations, and the penalties inflicted, and sees with satisfaction that his own country-men enjoy the privilege of being placed at the head of the list, which generally runs somewhat thus:-

'John Spinks, formerly private in the ——th Foot, was charged, before the magistrate of Howrah, with being drunk and disorderly on the Company's premises, in which state he desired the station-master to run a special train for him, and, on this being refused, he assaulted that official, and grievously wounded three native police-men. On conviction, he was sentenced to three months' impris-onment.'

'David Wilkins, who described himself as a professional man, was charged with being drunk and disorderly, and with refusing to leave a railway carriage when requested to do so. He was reprimanded and discharged.'

Then comes a long series of native misdemeanours, chiefly con-sisting in riding with intent to defraud.

At length the train arrives. As the traffic is very large, and there is only a single line (though the bridges and viaducts have been built for a double line), the trains are necessarily composed of a great number of trucks. First, perhaps, come eight or ten second-class carriages, full of pale panting English soldiers, in their shirt-sleeves. Then one first-class, of which the *coupé* is occupied by a young couple going to an appointment up-country. They have become acquainted during the balls and tiffins* of the cold season at Calcutta, and were married at the end of it. Perhaps they may never see it again until the bridegroom, who seems a likely young fellow, is brought down from the Mofussil to be put into the Secretariat. They have got a happy time before them. India is a delightful country for the first few years of married life. Lovers are left very much to themselves, and are able to enjoy to the full that charmingly selfish concentration of affection which is sometimes a little out of place in general society. When the eldest child must positively go home before the next hot season, and ought to have gone home before the last—when aunts, and grandmothers, and schoolmistresses at Brighton, and agents in London, have to be corresponded with—then troubles begin to come thick. The next compartment is filled by a family party—a languid, bilious, mother; a sickly, kindly, indefatigable nurse; and three little ones sprawling on the cushions in different stages of undress. In the netting overhead are plentiful stores of bottles of milk, bread and butter, and toys. Poor things! What an age a journey from Calcutta to Benares must seem at four years old! In the third compartment are two Sahibs smoking, who have filled every corner of the carriage with their bags and trunks, the charge for luggage in the van being preposterously high out here. Our Sahib, who is too good-natured to disturb the lovers, and who has no great fancy for children as fellow-travellers through the dust and glare of a journey in India, determines to take up his quarters with the last-mentioned party. The two gentlemen object very strongly to being crowded, although there is full room for eight passengers; but our Sahib is a determined man, and he soon establishes himself, with all his belongings, as comfortably as circumstances will admit, and before very long the trio have fraternized over Manilla cheroots and the Indigo question.* Behind the first-class carriage come an interminable row of third-class, packed to overflowing with natives in high exhilaration, stripped to the waist, chattering, smoking hubble-bubbles, chewing betel-nut, and endeavouring to curry favour with the guard—for your true native never loses an opportunity of conciliating a man in authority. Though there does not appear to be an inch of room available, the crowd of newcomers are pushed and heaved in by the station-master and his subordinates, and left to settle down by the force of gravity. In an incredibly short space of time the platform is cleared; the guard bawls out something that might once have borne a dim resemblance to 'all right behind,' the whistle sounds, and the train moves on at the rate of twenty-five miles an hour, including stoppages.

The Gulf Between Us

[. . .] When but seven years have passed since such a mine [the Mutiny of 1857] lay beneath our feet unheeded and unknown, we should be slow to affirm that we understand the feelings and character of the people of India. Their inner life still remains a sealed book to us. Certain it is that we have a very vague notion of the estimation in which they hold us. It is hardly possible for a man brought up amidst European scenes and associations to realize the idea conceived of him and his countrymen by a thorough-bred

Hindoo. On the one hand, the natives must acknowledge our vast superiority in the arts of war and government. Our railways, and steamships, and Armstrong guns are tangible facts which cannot be slighted. They must be perfectly aware that we have conquered them, and are governing them in a more systematic and downright manner than they have ever been governed before. But, on the other hand, many of our usages must in their eyes appear most debased and revolting. Imagine the horror with which a punctilious and devout Brahmin cannot but regard a people who eat the flesh of cow and pig, and drink various sorts of strong liquors from morning till night. It is at least as hard for such a man to look up to us as his betters, morally and socially, as it would be for us to place amongst the most civilized nations of the world a population which was in the habit of dining on human flesh, and intoxicating itself daily with laudanum and sal-volatile. The peculiar qualities which mark the Englishman are singularly distasteful to the Oriental, and are sure to be strangely distorted when seen from his point of view. Our energy and earnestness appear oppressive and importunate to the languid voluptuous aristocracy of the East. Our very honesty seems ostentatious and contemptible to the wily and tortuous Hindoo mind. That magnificent disregard of *les convenances*, which has rendered our countrymen so justly beloved by all the continental nations, is inexplicable and hateful to a race who consider external pomp and reticent solemnity to be the necessary accompaniments of rank, worth, or power. The Maharaja of Kishnagur once described to me his disgust and surprise at seeing an English magistrate, during a shooting excursion, bathe in the tank near which the tents were pitched. Europeans who have resided many years in the East seldom fail to acquire some of these so-called Oriental prejudices. Some of my Anglo-Indian friends have told me that nothing would persuade them to strip themselves in a public swimming-bath; and I have seen a high official unable to conceal his horror when a sucking-pig, which by that time was a sucking-pig only in name, was placed on the table directly under his nose.

It is noteworthy that the free and hardy customs of the ancient Greeks produced much the same effect upon the effeminate subjects of Darius and Artaxerxes.* The Persian, whose every action was dictated by a spirit of intense decorum and self-respect, could not appreciate the lordly indifference to appearances displayed by the

Spartan, accustomed to box, and run, and wrestle without a shred of clothing, in the presence of myriads of his brother Hellenes. Herodotus tells his countrymen, as a remarkable piece of information, that, 'among the Lydians, and, speaking loosely, among barbarians in general, it is held to be a great disgrace to be seen naked, even for a man.'

Add the mysterious awe by which we are shrouded in the eyes of the native population, which very generally attributes to magic our uniform success in everything we take in hand, and you will have some conception of the picture presented to the Hindoo mind by an indefatigable, public-spirited, plain-spoken, beer-drinking, cigar-smoking, tiger-shooting collector. We should not be far wrong if we were content to allow that we are regarded by our Eastern subjects as a species of quaint and somewhat objectionable demons, with a rare aptitude for fighting and administration; foul and degraded in our habits, though with reference to those habits not to be judged by the same standard as ordinary men; not malevolent withal (that is to say, the official fiends), but entirely wayward and unaccountable; a race of demi-devils: neither quite human, nor quite supernatural; not wholly bad, yet far from perfectly beneficent; who have been settled down in the country by the will of fate, and seem very much inclined to stay there by our own. If this is not the idea entertained of us by an average Bengalee rustic, it is something very near it.

Such is the incompatibility of sentiment and custom between the European and the native, that even the firmest friends of the latter allow that a complete amalgamation is quite hopeless. The wide and radical difference between the views held by the respective races with regard to the weaker sex alone, forms a bar, at present insuperable, to any very familiar intercourse. We, who still live among the recollections and records of chivalry, horrify utilitarians by persisting in regarding women as goddesses. The Hindoos, who allow their sisters and daughters few or no personal rights—the Mahommedans, who do not even allow them souls—cannot bring themselves to look upon women as better than playthings. The pride of a Mussulman servant is terribly wounded by a scolding from the lady of the house. He takes every opportunity of showing contempt for his mistress by various childish impertinences when the Sahib and his horsewhip are well out of the way. Among the numberless symptoms of our national eccentricity, that which seems most extraordinary to a native is our submitting to be governed by a woman. For a long time they accounted for the presence of the Queen's effigy on the rupee by setting her down as the wife of John Kumpani.* Now they probably imagine that John Kumpani is dead, and that she has come into possession as residuary legatee. The free and unrestrained life of an English lady excites the strangest and most unjust ideas in the mind of an Hindoo. To see women riding in public, driving about in open carriages, dining and talking and dancing with men connected with them neither by blood nor marriage, never fails to produce upon him a most false and unfortunate impression. Many gentlemen who are intimately acquainted with native ways of thought are not often very ready to take their wives and daughters to balls where the guests are of mixed nationality. I was present lately at an entertainment given by the Maharaja of Nilpore. The dancing went on in a sort of atrium in the centre of the palace, while the host, in a blaze of diamonds from head to foot, inspected the scene through a lorgnette, from the gallery, turning from time to time to make a remark to a circle of his friends and hangers-on. He resembled Lord Steyne at the opera, surrounded by his Wenhams and Waggs,* rather than the received notion of 'the man of the house' of a Belgravian ball-room. His bearing aroused the most lively indignation among the older Anglo-Indians. Suggestions to 'turn him out,' and 'throw him over' were bandied about in an audible key. One old campaigner sighed for the halcyon days of the mutiny. 'Hang him! I should like to loot him. He must be worth a quarter of a crore of rupees as he stands. His cap alone would be a good two lacs.'*

The longer a man lives in this country the more firmly convinced does he become that the amalgamation of the conquerors and the conquered is an idea impracticable, and, to use an odious word, Utopian. But this does not imply that, as time goes on, as the native becomes civilized, and the European humane and equitable, the two races should not live side by side with mutual sympathy and self-respect, and work together heartily for the same great ends. But this consummation is simply impossible until there is a marked improvement in the tone of the European settlers. That intense Anglo-Saxon spirit of self-approbation, which, though dormant at home, is unpleasantly perceptible among vulgar Englishmen on the Continent, becomes rampant in India. It is painful, indeed, to observe the deep pride and insolence of race which is engrained in our nature, and which yields only to the highest degree of education and enlightenment. The lower in the scale of society, the more marked become the symptoms of that baneful sentiment. A native of rank, whom men like Sir John Lawrence or Sir Herbert Edwardes* treat with the courtesy due to an equal, will be flouted and kicked about by any planter's assistant or sub-deputy railway contractor whose path he may chance to cross. On such a question as this, one fact is worth volumes of declamation; and facts of grave import may be gathered by the bushel by any one who spends three days in the country with his mouth shut and his eyes wide open.

Sonepore, the point at which the Gunduck* runs into the Ganges, is the most sacred spot in the North of India. Thither, time out of mind, at a certain phase of the moon during the late autumn, devout Hindoos have been wont to repair from hundreds of miles round, for the purpose of washing away their sins. Men discovered that ex-piatory bathing was not incompatible with business, and a great fair began to be held yearly during the festival, principally for dealings in elephant and horse-flesh. The Anglo-Indians, who attended for the purpose of buying nags, soon took to running their purchases one against another; and the attractions of a European race-meeting were thus added to those which Sonepore already possessed during the sacred week. The whole of Bahar society now makes holiday in that week, and a more pleasant reunion it is difficult to imagine. Men rejoice in the annual opportunity of renewing Haileybury and Addiscombe* friendships with old companions from whom they have been separated throughout the remainder of the year by vast distances and vile roads. The complicated family connexions, so general in the Civil Service, render this periodical gathering peculiarly pleasant. The wife of the Judge of Boglipore looks forward for months to meeting her sister, the Collectrix of Gya;* and the Commissioner of Benares, like a good cousin, has promised to bring her brother in his train, though that promising but susceptible Assistant-Magistrate has exceeded his privilege leave by ten days' extra philandering at Simla. The desirable young ladies come to Sonepore already engaged to local partners for every dance during the meeting—a circumstance extremely discouraging to casual swells who may have been attracted from Calcutta by the glowing accounts of the doings at the races put about by Bahar members of the Secretariat. Beneath a vast circular grove stretches a camp more than a mile in extent, where croquet and betting go on briskly by day, and waltzing and flirtation by night. The tents of each set of friends cluster round a large open pavilion, belonging to some liberal planter or magistrate, where covers are laid three times a day for every one who can be cajoled into joining the party. I could talk on for ever about Sonepore; such dear associations does it conjure up of open-handed Indian hospitality and open-hearted Indian friends, from my feeling for whom neither time, nor absence, nor opposed sentiments, nor divided interests, can ever, shall ever, abate one atom of affection and gratitude.

It was there, during one of the principal races, that I was standing at the Judge's posts, divided by the breadth of the course from a platform occupied by some dozen Englishmen. Close up to this platform crowded a number of well-dressed, well-to-do natives —respectable shopkeepers from Chupra;* warm men of business from Patna; gentlemen of rank from Benares and Lucknow. I saw— with my own eyes I saw—a tall raw-boned brute of a planter, whose name I should not hesitate to publish if it were worth the publishing, rush at these men, who had as good a right to be there as the Governor-General himself, and flog them with a double-thonged hunting-whip, until he had driven them in humiliating confusion and terror for the distance of many yards. One or two civilians present said to each other that it was a 'shame;' but no one seemed astounded or horrified; no one interposed; no one prosecuted; no one objected to meet the blackguard at dinner, or to take the odds from him at the ordinary.

A Judge of the High Court at Calcutta informed me that he had himself witnessed the following scene, while travelling on the East Indian Railway between Benares and Howrah. When the train stopped at a certain station, a Bengalee attempted to get into a second-class carriage. Some Europeans, who were comfortably settled down for a long sleep, told him to go about his business. He appealed to the officials, stating himself to be a native gentleman. A person in authority told him he must be contented to travel third-class—to which he replied that he preferred to be left behind. By this time he was surrounded by a circle of bullying English travellers; whom *the guard of the train* convulsed with delight by holding up his lantern to the poor man's face, and in a strong Irish brogue bidding the bystanders look at 'a specimen of a native gentleman.'

If I could think that the interest with which you read these stories could be one-tenth as deep as the pain with which I write them, you should have enough to keep you in indignation for the next twelvemonth. But things which, when acted, set the teeth chattering and the fingers twitching, seem childish enough when turned into sentences and divided with commas and colons. Heaven knows I would give a month's pay or a year's pension to have my will of some ruffians for what I have heard them say with applause, and seen them to do with impunity. Fearful symptoms these of what must be seething below! However kind he might be to his native servants, however just to his native tenants, there is not a single non-official person in India, with whom I have conversed on public questions, who would not consider the sentiment that we hold India for the benefit of the inhabitants of India a loathsome un-English piece of cant. Hence comes the paramount necessity that opinion at home should keep a close watch upon the conduct of the affairs of India. It is not enough that we send her out able and high-minded rulers. While there, they must never be allowed to forget that the eyes of England are upon them. Lord Canning* was as brave a man and as good a man as could well be found within our isles. Such he proved himself to be at a crisis when virtue was useless without courage, and when courage without virtue was far worse than useless. Yet even he succumbed at last to the ravening clamour of the friends of indigo. If Lord Canning had been left to himself, the ryot would have been delivered over to his tyrants bound hand and foot by a law illogical, inhumane, and inexpedient in all the highest senses.

What is the meaning of the Anglo-Saxon outcry? We cannot exterminate a wealthy and ancient community of a hundred and fifty millions of human beings, like so many Maories or Cherokees; and, if we do not exterminate them, we cannot continue to humble and to wrong them. If this state of things is disregarded at home, most serious evils must ensue. If it should ever come to pass that for a single period of five years India should be governed under the auspices of a Secretary of State of anti-native tendencies, the certain result would be a wide-spread system of social oppression, degrading and cruel to the native, shameful and demoralizing to us. The apathy of Englishmen to the affairs of India would be venial if our interests alone were thereby placed in peril; but, when the consequences fall on the innocent children of the soil, that apathy becomes nothing less than criminal. While honest men doze, bad men are hard at work. The people of Hindostan, if they be wise, will make it their prayer that they may gain the ear of England; for, if they succeed in obtaining her attention, they are secure of her humanity and her justice.

See also: Candler; Kipling; Perrin; Steel; Woolf.

EARLY DECADES

JOHN RUSKIN
(1819–1900)

John Ruskin delivered his Inaugural Lecture as Slade Professor of Fine Art at Oxford on 8 February 1870. The following paragraphs (27 to 30), with their message of mutually reinforcing aesthetic, moral, and patriotic responsibility, form the rousing conclusion to that lecture. He himself called the passage beginning at paragraph three of this extract 'the most pregnant and essential' of all his teaching. The lecture, said the imperialist Cecil John Rhodes, 'made a forceful entry into my mind': its idealism about empire matched his own far-reaching visions. Ruskin's series of lectures as Slade Professor, published as Lectures on Art *(1870), represented a distillation of his ideas on art and its relation to human life. As he put it in the main part of the Inaugural Lecture, art education, and cultural work in general, should be practical, 'worthy', and in sympathy with national character. It was on this basis that he went on to expound his idea that a nation's (specifically Britain's) moral fibre, on which its progress in commerce and the arts depended, was strengthened by colonial leadership. He therefore supported imperial expansion in so far as it was spiritually elevating for the English. Colonization was justified by honourable rule and by maintaining strong cross-empire links, 'a fixed fleet of colonies'. The audience for Ruskin's lectures was so large that the venue had to be shifted from the University Museum to the Sheldonian Theatre.*

Conclusion to Inaugural Lecture (1870)

[. . .] But if either our work, or our enquiries, are to be indeed successful in their own field, they must be connected with others of a sterner character. Now listen to me, if I have in these past details lost or burdened your attention; for this is what I have chiefly to say to you. The art of any country *is the exponent of its social and political virtues.** I will show you that it is so in some detail, in the second of my subsequent course of lectures; meantime accept this as one of the things, and the most important of all things, I can positively declare to you. The art, or general productive and formative energy, of any country, is an exact exponent of its ethical life. You can have noble art only from noble persons, associated under laws fitted to their time and circumstances. And the best skill that any teacher of art could spend here in your help, would not end in enabling you even so much as rightly to draw the water-lilies in the Cherwell* (and though it did, the work when done would not be worth the lilies themselves) unless both he and you were seeking, as I trust we shall together seek, in the laws which regulate the finest industries, the clue to the laws which regulate *all* industries, and in better obedience to which we shall actually have henceforward to live: not merely in compliance with our own sense of what is right, but under the weight of quite literal necessity. For the trades by which the British people has believed it to be the highest of destinies to maintain itself, cannot now long remain undisputed in its hands; its unemployed poor are daily becoming more violently criminal; and a certain distress in the middle classes, arising, *partly from their vanity in living always up to their incomes, and partly from their folly in imagining that they can subsist in idleness upon usury*, will at last compel the sons and daughters of English families to acquaint themselves with the principles of providential economy; and to learn that food can only be got out of the ground, and competence only secured by frugality; and that although it is not possible for all to be occupied in the highest arts, nor for any, guiltlessly, to pass their days in a succession of pleasures, the most perfect mental culture possible to men is founded on their useful energies, and their best arts and brightest happiness are consistent, and consistent only, with their virtue.

This, I repeat, gentlemen, will soon become manifest to those among us, and there are yet many, who are honest-hearted. And the future fate of England depends upon the position they then take, and on their courage in maintaining it.

There is a destiny now possible to us—the highest ever set before a nation to be accepted or refused. We are still undegenerate in race; a race mingled of the best northern blood. We are not yet dissolute in temper, but still have the firmness to govern, and the grace to obey. We have been taught a religion of pure mercy, which we must either now betray, or learn to defend by fulfilling. And we are rich in an inheritance of honour, bequeathed to us through a thousand years of noble history, which it should be our daily thirst to increase with splendid avarice, so that Englishmen, if it be a sin to covet honour, should be the most offending souls alive.* Within the last few years we have had the laws of natural science opened to us with a rapidity which has been blinding by its brightness; and means of transit and communication given to us, which have made but one kingdom of the habitable globe. One kingdom;—but who is to be its king? Is there to be no king in it, think you, and every man to do that which is right in his own eyes?* Or only kings of terror, and the obscene empires of Mammon and Belial? Or will you, youths of England, make your country again a royal throne of kings; a sceptred isle,* for all the world a source of light, a centre of peace; mistress of Learning and of the Arts;—faithful guardian of great memories in the midst of irreverent and ephemeral visions;—faithful servant of time-tried principles, under temptation from fond experiments and licentious desires; and amidst the cruel and clamorous jealousies of the nations, worshipped in her strange valour of goodwill towards men?*

'Vexilla regis prodeunt.'* Yes, but of which king? There are the two oriflammes; which shall we plant on the farthest islands—the one that floats in heavenly fire, or that hangs heavy with foul tissue of terrestrial gold? There is indeed a course of beneficent glory open to us, such as never was yet offered to any poor group of mortal souls. But it must be—it *is* with us, now, 'Reign or Die.' And if it shall be said of this country, 'Fece per viltate, il gran rifiuto,'* that refusal of the crown will be, of all yet recorded in history, the shamefullest and most untimely.

And this is what she must either do, or perish: she must found colonies as fast and as far as she is able, formed of her most energetic and worthiest men;—seizing every piece of fruitful waste ground she can set her foot on, and there teaching these her colonists that their chief virtue is to be fidelity to their country, and that their first aim is to be to advance the power of England by land and sea: and that, though they live on a distant plot of ground, they are no more to consider themselves therefore disfranchised from their native land, than the sailors of her fleets do, because they float on distant waves. So that literally, these colonies must be fastened fleets; and every man of them must be under authority of captains and officers, whose better command is to be over fields and streets instead of ships of the line; and England, in these her motionless navies (or, in the true and mightiest sense, motionless *churches*, ruled by pilots on the Galilean lake* of all the world), is to 'expect every man to do his duty';* recognizing that duty is indeed possible no less in peace than war; and that if we can get men, for little pay, to cast themselves against cannon-mouths for love of England, we may find men also who will plough and sow for her, who will behave kindly and righteously for her, who will bring up their children to love her, and who will gladden themselves in the brightness of her glory, more than in all the light of tropic skies.

But that they may be able to do this, she must make her own majesty stainless; she must give them thoughts of their home of which they can be proud. The England who is to be mistress of half the earth, cannot remain herself a heap of cinders, trampled by contending and miserable crowds; she must yet again become the England she was once, and in all beautiful ways,—more: so happy, so secluded, and so pure, that in her sky—polluted by no unholy clouds—she may be able to spell rightly of every star that heaven doth show; and in her fields, ordered and wide and fair, of every herb that sips the dew;* and under the green avenues of her enchanted garden, a sacred Circe,* true Daughter of the Sun, she must guide the human arts, and gather the divine knowledge, of distant nations, transformed from savageness to manhood, and redeemed from despairing into peace.

You think that an impossible ideal. Be it so; refuse to accept it if you will; but see that you form your own in its stead. All that I ask of you is to have a fixed purpose of some kind for your country and yourselves; no matter how restricted, so that it be fixed and unselfish. I know what stout hearts are in you, to answer acknowledged need: but it is the fatallest form of error in English youths to hide their hardihood till it fades for lack of sunshine, and to act in disdain of purpose, till all purpose is vain. It is not by deliberate, but by careless selfishness; not by compromise with evil, but by dull following of good, that the weight of national evil increases upon us daily. Break through at least this pretence of existence; determine what you will be, and what you would win. You will not decide wrongly if you will resolve to decide at all. Were even the choice between lawless pleasure and loyal suffering, you would not, I believe, choose basely. But your trial is not so sharp. It is between drifting in confused wreck among the castaways of Fortune, who condemns to assured ruin those who know not either how to resist her, or obey; between this, I say, and the taking of your appointed part in the heroism of Rest; the resolving to share in the victory which is to the weak rather than the strong; and the binding yourselves by that law, which, thought on through lingering night and labouring day, makes a man's life to be as a tree planted by the water-side, that bringeth forth his fruit in his season;—

ET FOLIUM EJUS NON DEFLUET,
ET OMNIA, QUÆCUNQUE FACIET, PROSPERABUNTUR.*

See also: Chamberlain; Beames; Blyden; Seeley; Tennyson; Trollope.

ANTHONY TROLLOPE
(1815–1882)

As comparison with Froude's writing (q.v.) will show, Trollope's thinking on race was of a piece with imperialist ideology of his time. His brusque conviction concerning the inevitable extinction of the Aborigines fits in with social evolutionist ideas based on the concept of a ladder of being on which some progressed and others were doomed to drop away. Trollope's fierce antipathy to philanthropic ventures also deepened his race pessimism. Elsewhere in his book Australia, *in which this chapter appears, and in* South Africa *(1878), he emphasizes that the black man cannot be civilized except by learning how to work. Complicating this racial work ethic, however, is his concession that the Aborigines were in possession of Australia before the white man came.*

Aboriginals (1873)

From Rockhampton I returned to Maryborough, with the intention of returning thence overland by Gympie to Brisbane;*—and I did so. I had touched at Maryborough on my way northwards, and as I saw a greater cluster of Australian black men at Maryborough than elsewhere, and as the question of the treatment of the black men is at present more important in Queensland than in the other colonies, I may as well say here what has to be said on this very disagreeable subject. There is an island—Frazer's Island—at the mouth of the Mary River, in which they are allowed to live without molestation,—no doubt because the place can be converted to no use by white settlers,—and here they seem to be almost amphibious. They live on fish, opossums, iguanas, and whatever can be filched from or may be given to them by their neighbours on the main land. As the steamers run up the river they swim off, thirty or forty of them coming together. A rope is flung out, and the captain generally allows one or two to come on board. These are taken up to Maryborough, where they loaf about, begging for money and tobacco, and return by the same boat on its downward journey. They are not admitted without some article of clothes, and this they bring tied on to their heads. When seen in the water, they are very picturesque,—an effect which is lost altogether on terra firma. I have heard many speak of a certain dignity of deportment which is natural to them. I cannot say that I have seen it. To my eyes the deportment of the dignified aboriginal is that of a sapient monkey imitating the gait and manners of a do-nothing white dandy.

It will be as well to call the race by the name officially given to it. The government styles them 'aboriginals'. We saw 'Aboriginal Boney'* on the police-sheet, when he was standing his trial in respect of the bit of tobacco which he had not succeeded in stealing. This is more necessary to be understood, as the word native is almost universally applied to white colonists born in Australia. We have some slight account given to us of these aboriginals by Dampier, the buccaneer, who made acquaintance with them on the western coast of Australia in 1688, and again in 1699. He tried to make friends with them; but they attacked his men with spears, wounding some of the party; and at last he shot one of them,—a circumstance which he mentions with great regret. He was good to them, and thought to make them work, but in vain, for, as he says, 'they stood like statues, without motion, but grinned like so many monkeys . . . so we were forced to carry our water ourselves.' This we can imagine very well, remembering that these Australians had never been called upon for an hour's work in their lives. Dampier tried to clothe some of them, but they preferred being naked. But the chiefs were painted. He tells us of one young warrior who was daubed with white paint;—'not for beauty or for ornament, one would think, but, as some wild Indian warriors are said to do, he seemed thereby to design the looking more terrible. This, his painting, added very much to his natural deformity; for they all of them have the most unpleasant looks and worst features of any people I ever saw,—though I have seen great variety of savages.'*

A hundred years afterwards, in 1770, Cook encountered them at Botany Bay, on the eastern coast, and he endeavoured to make friends with them, and to trade with them,—but in vain. He observes in reference to their nudity, 'We thought it remarkable that of all the people we had yet seen, not one had the least appearance of clothing, the old woman herself being destitute even of a fig-leaf.' But then Adam and Eve went equally naked till sin had convinced them of shame. Cook, however, certainly endeavoured to treat them well, but without effect. 'They did not appear to be numerous,' he says, 'nor to live in societies, but like other animals, were scattered about along the coasts, and in the woods. Of their manner of life, however, we could know but little, as we were never able to form the least connection with them. After the first contest at our landing they would never come near enough to parley; nor did they touch a single article of all that we had left at their huts and places they frequented, on purpose for them to take away.'*

When Governor Phillip,—the first governor,—arrived on Cook's foot-tracks in 1788, he fared a little better with the blacks. He found them still naked,—as a matter of course,—but they took the presents he offered them, and they were at first tractable with him and courteous. When the white men came to settle in numbers round the grand inlet of the sea, which is now Sydney Harbour, the kangaroo ran away, and the fish became scarce in the waters, and the black men lost their usual food. They began to perish from starvation, and of course were not fond of their visitors. They could not depart inland because other tribes would not have them;—for it seems that though no man owned individual property, inland tribes were very jealous of their confines.

Captain Hunter, who was with Governor Phillip, and was afterwards himself governor, took great pains with them, and seems to have succeeded in conciliating them for awhile; but quarrels arose, as was so natural when everything that the black man had was taken away from him,—and white men were killed. Many of the blacks were starved, their accustomed food having been driven away, and others were slaughtered in return for injuries done by them,—which injuries were the natural result of wrongs done to them. And so the quarrel began,—with what result between civilized and savage it is almost needless to say. In 1788 'the aborigines were rendered so desperate by hunger,'—I am quoting Bennet's history* of Australian discovery and colonization,—'that on the 21st of August a large party of them landed near the Observatory, attacked the people who were employed there, and killed a goat and carried it off in triumph. This was the boldest attempt yet made and caused the governor himself to go in pursuit. The live stock were so few in number that even the loss of a single goat was looked upon as a public misfortune. The governor, however, neither succeeded in recovering the carcass of the goat, nor in overtaking the sable cattle stealers. In the following month the natives made another attempt on the stock. On this occasion those who had charge of the sheep and goats were prepared for the attack, and the blacks were beaten off without the loss of a single animal. From this a chronic state of hostilities may be said to have existed between the two races, and lives were sacrificed almost daily on one side or the other.' Thus, with the goat which Governor Phillip, with great but futile energy, endeavoured to redeem for his puny settlement, commenced that system of cattle-stealing which, on the part of the black men, has been so natural,—we may almost say, so innocent,—but which it has been essential that the white man should stamp out and make to cease, unless he made up his mind to abandon his purpose of peopling Australia.

Philanthropical advocates for the black man,—who seem, by reason of their negro-philanthropy, to be called upon to constitute themselves the enemies of the white settler,—talk of the bloody revenge which is taken for petty pilferings. This, I think, is unfair, and I am quite sure that no unfairness either on one side or other can lead to good results. The Australian grazier cannot live unless he defend his cattle. The pilferings have not been petty, and in many districts, I believe in all districts, would have absolutely destroyed the flocks and made grazing in Australia impossible, had not the squatter defended himself either with a red hand,—or with a hand prepared to be red if occasion required. The stealing of cattle by tribes of black men,—or rather the slaughter of cattle, for the black man never has an idea of taking away the cattle and making them his own, and desires to appropriate no more than he can eat at the time, but, nevertheless, will kill as many as he can muster,—has in many cases been accompanied by preconcerted attacks upon the stations; and these attacks are made in the absence of the owner, when his wife and children are there almost unguarded. It is not difficult to imagine that the squatter, in such circumstances, should choose to be regarded by his black neighbours as a man who was prone to be red-handed on occasions. Of course there arises, as the result of this, much rough justice,—perhaps also much rough injustice. When white men steal cattle the individual thief can be traced and brought to punishment;—but this cannot be done with a tribe of Australian aborigines. The execution must be of the Jedburgh kind,* or there must be none, and if none, then the squatter must vanish. No doubt there have been dreadful instances of indiscriminate and perfectly unjustifiable slaughter;—but then it must be remembered also that the law has interfered when evidence has been attainable, and that white men have been hung for their barbarity. There seems to be an idea prevalent with many that the black man is not defended by the law. This is an erroneous idea. The black man has been treated with all possible tenderness by the law;—but his life is such that the law can hardly reach him either to defend or to punish.

The promiscuous slaughter of the races by each other was continued through Governor Hunter's time, which lasted from 1795 till 1800. This took place still in the Sydney district of New South Wales, that being the only district then colonized;—but similar circumstances have produced similar results throughout Australia. It is difficult, 'if not impossible,' says the authority I have quoted before,*—and I believe there is none more impartial or trustworthy,—'to arrive at anything like a correct estimate of the number of settlers killed by the blacks, but there is every reason to believe that it was scarcely a tithe of the number of aborigines whose lives were sacrificed in return.' He again says, quoting the words of Colonel Collins, the judge-advocate, 'These people, when spoken to or censured for robbing the maize grounds, to be revenged, were accustomed to assemble in large bodies and burn the houses of the settlers if they stood in lonely situations, frequently attempting to take their lives. . . . The governor also signified his determination, if any of the natives were taken in the act of robbing the settlers, to hang them in chains near the spot as an example to others. Could it have been foreseen that this was their natural temper, it would have been wiser to have kept them at a distance, and in fear.' Of course it was their natural temper. The land was theirs and the fulness thereof, or emptiness as it might be. The white man was catching all their fish, driving away their kangaroos, taking up their land, domineering over them, and hanging them in chains when they did that which to them was only natural and right. The white man, of course, felt that he was introducing civilisation; but the black man did not want civilisation. He wanted fish, kangaroos, and liberty. And yet is there any one bold enough to go back to the first truth and say that the white man should not have taken the land because it belonged to the black man;—or that if, since the beginning of things, similar justice had prevailed throughout the world, the world would now have been nearer the truth and honesty in its ways than it is?

These people were in total ignorance of the use of metals, they went naked, they ill-used their women, they had no houses, they produced nothing from the soil. They had not even flint arrow-heads. They practised infanticide. In some circumstances of life they practised cannibalism. They were and are savages of the lowest kind. With reference to their cannibal propensities I heard many varying stories, but I never heard one which accused them of eating white people. When they do devour human flesh, it is the flesh of their own people. They have laws which they obey,—or at least used to obey,— most rigidly. In reference to these two propensities, that of eating each other and obeying the laws, Mr Bennet gives the following details. 'A very painful and striking proof of the stringent nature of their laws, the fixed character of their institutions, and the great pressure upon their means of existence under ordinary conditions, is afforded by circumstances which have taken place in the Bunya-Bunya district of Queensland. The district in which the bunya-bunya tree bears fruit is very restricted, and it bears in profusion only once in about three years. When this occurs the supply is vastly larger than can be consumed by the tribes within whose territory the trees are found. Consequently, large numbers of strangers visit the district, some of them coming from very great distances, and all are welcome to consume as much as they desire; for there is enough and to spare during the few months while the season lasts. The fruit is of a richly farinaceous kind, and the blacks quickly fatten upon it. But after a short indulgence on an exclusive vegetable diet, having previously been accustomed to live almost entirely upon animal food, they experience an irresistible longing for flesh. This desire they dare not indulge by killing any of the wild animals of the district. Kangaroos, opossums, and bandicoot are alike sacred from their touch, because they are absolutely necessary for the existence of the friendly tribe whose hospitality they are partaking. In this condition some of the stranger tribes resort to the horrible practice of cannibalism, and sacrifice one of their own number to provide the longed-for feast of flesh. It is not the disgusting cruelty, the frightful inhumanity, or the curious physiological question involved, that is now under consideration; but the remarkable fact educed of an unhesitating obedience, under circumstances of extraordinary temptation, to laws arising out of the necessities of their existence, and the indirect proof afforded of the severe pressure on the supply of food which, under ordinary circumstances, must have prevailed among the aboriginal tribes. The strangers dared not, in their utmost longing, touch the wild animals, because they were absolutely necessary for the existence of the tribes to which the district belonged. They might eat their fill with the bunya-bunya, because that was in profusion, and prescription had given them the right to it. Such a singular condition of things could never have arisen but in an old, over-populated country, the laws of which had acquired that immutable character which is conferred only by immemorial custom.' I myself believe this story of the bunya-bunya feast, having heard it corroborated by various persons in Queensland; but I do not believe that cannibalism has ever been general among the Australian blacks.*

Their laws, especially with regard to marriage, are complex and wonderful. Their corroborees, or festival dances, are very wonderful. Their sagacity, especially on the tracking of men or cattle, is very wonderful. The skill with which they use the small appliances of life which they possess is very wonderful. But for years, probably for many centuries, they have made no progress, and the coming of the white man among them has had no tendency to civilise,—only a tendency to exterminate them.

The question I am now endeavouring to discuss is that of the white man's duty in respect to these blacks,—and also the further question whether the white Englishman in Australia has done his duty. There is a strong sect of men in England,—a sect with whom I fully sympathize in their aspirations, though I have sometimes found myself compelled to doubt their information,—who think that the English settler abroad is not to be trusted, except under severe control, with the fate of the poor creatures of inferior races with whom he comes in contact on the distant shores to which his search for wealth may lead him. The settler, as a matter of course, is in quest of fortune, and is one who, living among rough things, is apt to become rough and less scrupulous than his dainty brother at home. When this philanthropy first became loud in its expression in England, we were ourselves the owners of slaves in our own colonies, and the great and glorious task of abolishing that horror for ourselves, so that other nations might afterwards follow in our steps, had to be achieved. Wilberforce, Clarkson, Buxton, Brougham, and others, did achieve it, and it is natural that their spirit should be defended and protected. Some years since I ventured to express my opinion on that matter.* Of all the absurdities in political economy which I ever encountered, that of protecting the labour of the negroes in Jamaica from competition was to my eyes the most gross. And it appeared to me that the idea of training negroes to be magistrates, members of parliament, statesmen, or even merchants, was one destined to failure by the very nature of the man. That a race should have been created so low in its gifts as to be necessarily fit only for savage life or for the life of servants among civilised men was a fact on which I could only speculate,—or hardly speculate; but I could not on that account abstain from forming the opinion. Since that time negroes, many more in number and certainly upon the whole more handy in the use of such gifts as they possessed than those in the West Indies, have been made free in the United States, and have then been put in possession of all the privileges belonging to white men. The more I see of the experiment the more convinced I am that the negro cannot live on equal terms with the white man, and that any land, state or district in which the negro is empowered for awhile to have ascend- ency over the white man by number of suffrages or other causes, will have but a woeful destiny till such a condition of things be made to cease. White men will quit such land in disgust,—or the white minority will turn, and rend, and trample into dust the black majority. This allusion to the African negro in the western hemi- sphere would be out of place here, were it not that the mantle of which I have spoken, resting still on most worthy shoulders, is now used,—or a skirt of it is used,—to cover up the nakedness of the poor

Australian aboriginal. The idea prevails that he also may be a member of parliament, minister of state, a man and a brother, or what not. That he is infinitely lower in his gifts than the African negro there can be no doubt. Civilisation among the African tribes is not very high, and our knowledge as to the point which it has reached is still defective. But where he has come within the compass of the white man's power, he has been taught to work for his bread,—which of all teaching is the most important. The Australian black man has not been so taught, and, in spite of a few instances to the contrary, I think I am justified in saying that he cannot be so taught. Individual instances are adduced,—instances which are doubtless true,—of continued service having been rendered by aboriginals; but they are so few,—so contrary to the life of the tribes as any traveller may see it,—that they do but prove the rule. That dignity of black deportment of which one hears not unfrequently is simply the dignity of idleness. The aboriginal walks along erect through the streets of the little town, or more frequently in the forest outskirt, followed at humble distance by his gin, and does evince something of that pride with which wealthy idleness in civilised life is able to encounter obligatory toil. His sinews are never tired and torn and stunted by burdens, and he can go erect. He does in his heart despise the working white man, and he shows in his countenance the fact that he has resolved to beg, or steal, or eat opossum,—and at any rate to be free from toil. This so-called dignity has to me been the most odious part of his altogether low physiognomy. When he has mixed much among white men, and has learned that he is quite safe in numerous communities from the raids which would be made upon him and his tribe if he employed himself on cattle-stealing at a distance, he exchanges his ferocity for a cunning good-humoured impudence which is more revolting than his native savagery, and would be more dangerous were it not that he ceases to be prolific in this begging, slouching life, with trailing gins and dignity of deportment.

Our friends at home with the philanthropic mantle tell the Australian colonist repeatedly that he has taught the black man nothing but his vices,—and they mean the charge to contain the bitterest reproach. A man going out among other men gets taught what he will learn. The aboriginals have become drunkards and thieves; and it is said of them, that they sell their women to white men. That there are white drunkards and white thieves in Australia is certainly true; and no doubt there is immorality in regard to women,—though in new colonies and thinly inhabited countries such vice is always less prominent than in the large towns of an old country. But good qualities of living,—the finer characteristics of manhood,—are at any rate as prominent in the Australian colonies as the bad qualities. Men are energetic, independent, and good to their wives. Women are kindly, unexacting, and careful. Why have not the black men learned also some of the virtues? I assert that every effort has been made to teach them the lessons,—as will be evident to any one who will reflect of how great value would have been their thews and sinews if only they could have been induced to work. But how can you teach any good lesson to a man who will only hold his head erect as he grins and asks you for sixpence, or a glass of grog, or a bit of tobacco, or a pair of old trousers? If he gets the sixpence, no doubt he will drink it;—with some little difficulty, for the law in its endeavour to save the poor aboriginal from learning the bad lessons, makes it illegal for the publican to sell him liquor. Of course a virtuous publican obeys the law. But all publicans are not virtuous, and so far it may be said with truth that we teach the black man our vices. So far as the law can protect the black man from the learning of vice it has striven to do so;—but no law in any country was ever efficacious to such purpose.

It is difficult to make intelligible to those who know nothing of Australia the strange condition of these people,—the mixture of servility and impudence, of ferocity and good-humour, which prevails among them. I heard of a gentleman who trained one to be his gamekeeper,—for they learn to shoot with skill, and are quick in the pursuit of game. At last, confiding in his black gamekeeper as he would in one at home, he gave the man his flask to carry. When he shot till he was thirsty, he asked for his bottle. 'Es massa,' said the grinning nigger, handing over the empty flask. 'Here him is; no noting in it.' He was not a bit afraid of his master because he had stolen all the drink;—nor in such circumstances could there be any idea of punishing him; you would as soon think of punishing a dog for eating a mutton chop you had put in his mouth. It might be possible to teach a dog to carry a mutton chop without eating it;—and perhaps an aboriginal might be found who after many lessons would not swallow all the wine.

Children of mixed breed,—of white fathers and black mothers are found, but do not become a race as they have done in the western world. I have seen and heard of instances in which girls so born have been brought up as domestic servants. But it seems that they always return to the bush and become some black man's gin,—or strive to do so. I heard of one girl who had been trained to take care of children till she was fourteen. She had never known savage life, and had become docile and affectionate. But at fourteen she vanished into the bush. In another house I saw a girl about fourteen waiting at table, and was told that she had made repeated attempts at escape. I ventured to ask the lady by what right she was retained, and how caught when she had fled. The lady laughed at my scruples as to retention, and told me with a boast that she could always put a black fellow on the girl's track if she made an attempt. Here at any rate was something like slavery,—for the girl was not apprenticed, nor her position re-cognised by any legal transfer of service. She had been picked up, and bred, and fed, and used kindly,—and was now the possession of the lady. When a little older no doubt she will escape and become a gin.

I once asked a member of parliament in one of the colonies and a magistrate what he would do,—or rather what he would recommend me to do,—if stress of circumstances compelled me to shoot a black man in the bush. Should I go to some nearest police station, as any one would do who in self-defence had shot a white man;—or should I go on rejoicing as though I had shot a tiger or killed a deadly snake? His advice was clear and explicit. 'No one but a fool would say anything about it.' The aboriginal therefore whom you are called on to kill,—lest he should kill you or your wife, or because he spears your cattle,—is to be to you the same as a tiger or a snake. But this would be in the back districts, far away from towns, in which the black man has not yet learned to be a fine gentleman with dignified deportment, barely taking the trouble to open his mouth as he asks for sixpence and tobacco.

There can be no doubt that the law does hardly reach him in those distant districts for purposes either of punishment or protection. He cannot be numbered up and classified. If he disappears his absence is known only to his tribe, who do not recognise our law, and will not ask for its interference. He cannot be traced. The very hue of his face prevents evidence as to his identity. He cannot be found, and he is never missed. The distant squatter, whom he attacks or whose beasts he kills, knows that he must be redhanded himself, or that the black man will go unpunished;—and he knows too that unless some black man be punished, life for him on his distant run will be impossible. It is not for petty pilferings that he is concerned;—but for life and the means of living. The black men in his neighbourhood have determined to be his enemies, and as enemies he feels himself bound to treat them. No doubt he is unscrupulous,—but scruples won't serve his turn. He has come to a country in which savage life prevails,—and he finds it necessary to be, not savage, but ruthless.

In saying so much I have endeavoured to state the case fairly between the squatter and the aboriginal; for the real question at issue now lies between them. And I find that it resolves itself to this;—had the first English settlers any right to take the country from the black men who were its owners, and have the progressing colonists who still go westward and northward in search of fresh lands the right to drive the black men back, seeing as they do that they cannot live together? If they have no such right,—that is, if they be morally wrong to do it,—then has the whole colonizing system of Great Britain been wrong, not only in Australia, but in every portion of the globe? And had Britain abstained from colonizing under the conviction of conscientious scruples, would it have been better for the human race? Four nations struggled for the possession of Australia, the Portuguese, the Dutch, the French, and ourselves. It fell into our hands, chiefly through the enterprise and skill of Captain Cook. Should we have abstained when we found that it was peopled,—and, so to say, already possessed? And had we done so should we have served the cause of humanity? I doubt whether any philanthropist will say that we should have abstained;—or will think that had we done so the Australian aborigines would at the present moment have fared better with Dutch or French masters than they are now faring with us. It is their fate to be abolished; and they are already vanishing. Nothing short of abstaining from encroaching upon their lands, —abstaining that is from taking possession of Australia could be of any service to them. They have been treated, I think, almost invariably with proffered kindness when first met,—but they have not wanted and have not understood the kindness. For a time they would not submit at all, and now their submission is partial. In 1864 an expedition was made to take cattle from Rockhampton overland to Cape York, the northern extremity of Queensland, by two brothers, Frank and Alexander Jardine. The cattle were then driven up to save

the lives of the occupants of a new settlement. The enterprise was
carried through with admirable spirit and final success after terrible
difficulties. But their progress was one continued battle with black
tribes, who knew nothing of them, and who of course regarded them
as enemies. Which party was to blame for this bloodshed,—the
Messrs. Jardine who were risking their own lives to save the
inhabitants of a distant settlement,—or the poor blacks who were
struggling against unknown and encroaching enemies? In this case
there was certainly no cruelty, no thoughtless arrogance, no white
man's indifference to the lives of black men. The Messrs. Jardine
would have been glad enough to have made their progress without
fighting battles, and fought when they did fight simply in self-
protection. And yet the blacks were invaded,—most unjustly and
cruelly as they must have felt.

Of the Australian black man we may certainly say that he has to
go.* That he should perish without unnecessary suffering should be
the aim of all who are concerned in the matter. But no good can be
done by giving to the aboriginal a character which he does not
deserve, or by speaking of the treatment which he receives in
language which the facts do not warrant.

See also: Clarke; Kingsley; McKay, 'Cudjoe Fresh From de Lecture';
Woolf.

JOHN BEAMES
(1837–1902)

*John Beames's Memoirs of his thirty-five-year career in the Indian Civil
Service gives a clear impression of the daily office routine—'the day's
work' in Kipling's phrase—on which the empire rested, not only in India,
but also in the many other more recently established native colonies where
administration was generally modelled on the Indian system. Work, as
Beames points out, is rule; and rule is processing petitions, making
grammars, working efficiently and on time. As Leonard Woolf (q.v.)
would find out more than thirty years later in Ceylon, through 'utmost
punctuality and strictness' a young Englishman fresh from Oxbridge could
rapidly gain promotion to the position of minor despot of an entire district.*

Civilian Memoirs (1873)

[. . .] It seems unnecessary to enter into a detailed account of the work I had to do in Cuttack.* It did not very much differ from what has already been described in previous districts, though it was heavier and more varied. In fact the great charm of the work of Civil officers in India is its variety. One has no fear of getting wearied by a monotonous routine, or by perpetually hammering away at one unchanging task. In the course of one day's work one has a dozen or more different things to do, each presenting some new feature of interest, so that if one goes to bed very tired at night, it is not the depressing weariness of sameness or drudgery, but the healthy fatigue of keeping mind and body on the stretch with a multitude of ever-varying calls on one's attention, and the joy (than which I know no greater—and which I sigh for now in my unemployed old age) of feeling that one is working and ruling and making oneself useful in God's world. A brief outline of an ordinary day's work may be given once for all. We got up at five or thereabouts, drank a cup of tea while our horses were being brought, and went for a ride. If I had official work to do, I went alone, but mostly my wife and I went together. On our ride we met friends and rode with them, or stopped to talk and rode on. Returning about six-thirty we had our regular chota haziri* in the veranda; our little girls, who had been for a ride on their ponies, played around us. Then we went round our beautiful garden and gave orders, or showed our roses and other plants to friends who dropped in. About seven the post came in and we read the paper, the *Englishman*—the leading journal in Bengal in those days—looked at our letters, discussed any matters requiring arrangement, and by eight I was settled in my study for two hours' work at my big book, my *Comparative Grammar*.* At ten, bath and breakfast and off to cutcherry* in my brougham, a drive of three miles, during which I read official letters or thought over the day's business. On reaching office about eleven, the first thing was to take the Faujdari or Magistrate's work. The public crowded into my large court-room and presented many petitions, each of which was read to me by a clerk and orders passed thereon. Most of them were plaints in criminal cases, which were made over to the various subordinate Magistrates for disposal. Then came the great police charge-book, in which were entered all the criminal cases sent up that day from the

various police stations in the district—murders, robberies, burg-
laries, thefts and the like. Some of these cases I took myself, but the
greater part of them was made over to the Joint Magistrate and
others. On this followed a large number of miscellaneous petitions
and reports about all sorts of things—ferries, cattle-pounds, jail
matters, recovery of fines and forfeitures, arrangement of records;
also punishments, rewards and promotions of officials and other
matters. By the time all these things were disposed of it would be
about twelve-thirty, and if I had no criminal cases to try—and I could
but seldom find time to try any—the Magisterial officials were sent
away to issue the orders I had passed and carry out those which it fell
to them to do. Now followed interviews with the Head Clerks of
each department—Magistrate's Office, Excise, Stamps, Treasury,
Customs, Salt, Road Cess, Municipal, Education, Registration, Land
Revenue. Each man brought those papers on which orders were
required, took his orders and departed. Of course, the whole of them
did not come every day, but only those who had something to report,
or something which required orders. When they had gone I wrote
replies to letters from the Commissioner, Board and other officials,
and was usually a good deal hindered and interrupted by Deputy
Collectors and other officers coming in to speak to me about this or
that. Generally, however, by two o'clock the correspondence was
finished. Whether it was or not, at two we had tiffin*—and we
wanted it. At this meal, served in a quiet room at the end of the
terrace overlooking the broad river and the blue hills beyond, the
Joint Magistrate, Stevens, and the District Superintendent of police
joined me, and while we ate we talked shop and got through a good
deal of business. At half past two I returned to my office and finished
any correspondence that remained. At three the Collectorate officers
came with a pile of reports and other business, sometimes with a case
to try. A little before four I called for petitions on the Collectorate
side; these were not so numerous as those on the Magisterial side, and
while hearing them and passing orders on them, I was busy signing all
the orders and letters I had issued during the day. By four o'clock the
work was done and I went home. It was, of course, only by the utmost
punctuality and strictness that so much work could be got through,
but each clerk and official knew exactly what he had to do and at what
hour he was to come to me for orders and reports. When once you
establish a 'dastúr' (a custom or fixed routine) with natives they are

all right, there is nothing they love so much as dastúr; they make themselves into machines and work admirably. There were never any arrears in the Cuttack office during the four years of my incumbency, and this was due not to any superior merit or cleverness on my part but simply to the introduction of a regular routine of work.

When I got home I had a cup of tea, and then received any native Rajas or other gentlemen. This was a tedious and tiresome business, but before six I had generally got rid of them and drove with my wife. We had a pretty Victoria and pair of grey Arabs. Our drive generally ended at the club in the Fort, where we met nearly everyone in the station, both men and women. Here there were sports of many kinds; some played lawn-tennis, others billiards or whist, others—mostly the chiefs—sat in the veranda round old Ravenshaw* and talked—a good deal of 'shop' I fear—but many other things besides. About seven-thirty we drove home to dinner and were generally in bed and asleep soon after nine.

Then we had mornings at Jobra. Jobra was a suburb of Cuttack, a green, woody little village on the bank of the great river Mahanadi. Just above it the river was dammed by an anicut, a mighty wall of stone more than a mile in length, and at one end of it stood the great range of Canal workshops, under the management of George Faulkner. Faulkner was a man of a type perhaps little known in England, but far from uncommon in India; the Englishman to whom India has become a second mother-country, and who would be unhappy and totally misunderstood and out of place in England. Thoroughly English in manners and feelings, so much so that though he had been forty years in India he could not speak a dozen words of any Indian language, he had no wish to return to his native land, and though he spoke of it with pride and affection he preferred India as a place to live in.

A native of Manchester, bred up as a mechanical engineer in one of the big engineering works in Lancashire, he had come out to India at the age of twenty or thereabouts in the service of the Irrigation Company.[1] This company, formed for the purpose of making canals, had constructed several on the Godavery river in the Madras presidency, and had then extended its operations to Orissa where it

[1] On second thoughts I am not sure of this. I think he came out to Madras in some other employ and joined the Irrigation Company later. But his yarns and reminiscences were, as usual with such men, apt to be a little confused, especially after dinner.

had constructed three canals, of which I shall have much to say hereafter. Eventually the Company was dissolved and its works, plant and employees taken over by Government. Thus Faulkner and a number of others became Government servants.

In person he was a tall, stout, powerfully-built man with a ruddy face, a huge shock of flaxen hair turning white, and an immense white beard which hung down over his broad chest and floated all round his face. He looked like an old lion, a grand, jovial, coarse, hard-drinking old Viking, full of songs and jokes and highly improper stories. Utterly reckless and wild about money matters, always in debt, always full of wild schemes, and yet this rough old creature had the most exquisitely delicate taste as a designer, and the greatest skill and fineness of touch as an artisan. He painted, he carved, he moulded; he designed buildings, boats, bridges; he grew the most beautiful flowers, planned and laid out the most lovely gardens, and could use a chisel or any other tool as well as his best workman. He had four stalwart sons, three of whom were engineers and the fourth a doctor, all of them artists and skilful men with their hands. And the strange thing was that all these big, coarse, athletic men, father as well as sons, were fond of reading, read extensively and remembered what they read; had a fine taste in literature, loved their Ruskin and could quote and argue and talk admirably. The boys had, of course, been born in Madras and sent home to be educated. There were also three handsome daughters who had been educated partly in England, partly in Paris, and were very accomplished, speaking French in particular with a pure Parisian accent and playing and singing well. They were, in fact, a very interesting family and we became great friends with them all. Old Mrs Faulkner, the wife of the Viking, was as such men's wives generally are for some reason, a small, delicate, feeble-looking woman, very much better bred than her husband; but feeble as she looked, she had much determination and courage in her frail little body, and it was by her principally that their brilliant, reckless, rollicking family was kept going. She slaved for them and got them out of their scrapes and was always cheerful and helpful though she confessed to my wife that they were a sore burden to her.

Jobra was Faulkner's glory and the despair of the Public Works Department. Both by nature and by his irregular training Faulkner was quite incapable of red-tape or of following a decorous official routine. He was perpetually harrowing the souls of his official superiors and the Heads of the Department in Calcutta by doing the most unheard of and irregular things. He ruled Jobra in a way of his own, and could by no means be brought to understand or follow the official way of doing things. But he was tolerated because they could not well do without him. Among other things he was a most ingenious inventor, and if ever in the extensive and complicated canal works that were going on all over Cuttack district any hitch occurred, Faulkner was safe to invent some machine or device which solved the difficulty. His shutters for the sluices, his valves, screws, self-acting locks and other contrivances would have made the fortune of anyone else. He had a large number of Telugu artisans who had followed him from the Godavery. There were both men and women; the former were carpenters, smiths and the like, while the latter worked as coolies. Among these people, foreigners in Orissa crowded together in a small settlement near the workshops, there was at first much promiscuous intercourse and the chaplain complained to Faulkner, as a certain number of them were native Christians. So Faulkner assembled them all, Christians and heathens alike, and told them that he was not going to have any immorality in his works, and to stop it he ordered each man to select one woman as his wife. This being done he had the names entered in a book, made them a curious address in which scraps of the Church of England marriage service were mixed up, and then, to clench the matter, made each man pay one rupee. Then he solemnly informed them that they were all married! Of course they did not understand much of what he said as he spoke in English, and did not wait to have it all translated to them. But the ceremony and especially the payments were clear enough to them. It was indeed suggested to Faulkner that some, probably most, of them were married already, but he said that didn't matter. He gave them all a big feast, and spent the money they had paid in relieving widows and orphans among them. This strange plan answered admirably. Each man henceforth kept strictly to his so-called wife, and new-comers were made to come before Faulkner to be solemnly married and have their names entered in the big book. Immorality ceased and the little settlement became peaceful and orderly. If any man went away, he divorced his wife by the simple process of having his name scratched out of the book, and she was promptly married to someone else. A school was established for the children who were taken on to the works when old enough.

A morning's stroll through the long lines of workshops at Jobra was very interesting. The great Nasmyth's steam hammer* would be made to beat a huge mass of red-hot iron, or crack a nut, other machines shaved iron like so much soap, or sawed big logs into planks in a few seconds. Then Faulkner would make the most beautiful ivory and ebony croquet mallets for the ladies, or exhibit his portfolios of lovely designs, his fretwork brackets and screens, stained-glass windows, designs in plaster or stone, a bewildering variety of beautiful things. He made for my wife two lovely screens of teak wood, perforated, which he had designed himself; I have them still. Many other things the old man made for us all, and he was always ready to put to rights anything in the way of machinery that went wrong in our houses. It used to be said with truth, 'Give old Faulkner a cheroot and a whisky peg[1] and there is nothing he cannot do.' Among other peculiarities of speech he totally ignored the letter 'h': saying, ''ead,' ''and,' ''igh,' ''eavy,' ''ot,' for 'head', 'hand', etc. He did not seem to be conscious of the omission. Some people said it was a characteristic of the Lancashire dialect. In other respects he spoke quite correct English.

---

[1] 'Peg'. This is an expression universal in India. It means a big tumbler of brandy or whisky and soda water. It does not seem to be known in England.

See also: Clifford; Kipling; Steel.

DAVID LIVINGSTONE
(1813–1873)

In this account from Livingstone's Last Journals, *and the following extract from an 1886 lecture by Henry Morton Stanley, the mythologized moment of their meeting—white man confronting white in the heart of Africa—is told in their own words. Immediately noticeable in both accounts is the village setting and the moving crowds of non-white men and women involved as participants in and spectators to the greeting. This is in direct contrast to the popular lithograph of the time showing the two men meeting against a background of open savannah. Both driven, fanatical, and ambitious, Livingstone and Stanley did in effect become each other's spiritual brothers for the few months they spent together on the shores of Lake Tanganyika. Certainly Stanley's visit temporarily renewed Livingstone's vigour and enabled him to go on travelling, though again hampered by illness and bad weather, until his death around midnight on 30 April 1873.*

The Meeting with Stanley (1874)

23rd September. [1871]—We now passed through the country of mixed Barua and Baguha, crossed the River Loñgumba* twice and then came near the great mountain mass on west of Tanganyika. From Mokwaniwa's to Tanganyika is about ten good marches through open forest. The Guha people are not very friendly; they know strangers too well to show kindness: like Manyuema, they are also keen traders. I was sorely knocked up by this march from Nyañgwé* back to Ujiji. In the latter part of it, I felt as if dying on my feet. Almost every step was in pain, the appetite failed and a little bit of meat caused violent diarrhœa, whilst the mind, sorely depressed, reacted on the body. All the traders were returning successful: I alone had failed and experienced worry, thwarting, baffling, when almost in sight of the end towards which I strained.*

3rd October.—I read the whole Bible through four times whilst I was in Manyuema.

8th October.—The road covered with angular fragments of quartz was very sore to my feet, which are crammed into ill-made French shoes. How the bare feet of the men and women stood out, I don't know; it was hard enough on mine though protected by the shoes. We marched in the afternoons where water at this season was scarce. The dust of the march caused ophthalmia, like that which afflicted Speke:* this was my first touch of it in Africa. We now came to the Lobumba River, which flows into Tanganyika, and then to the village Loanda and sent to Kasanga, the Guha chief, for canoes. The Loñgumba rises, like the Lobumba, in the mountains called Kabogo West. We heard great noises, as if thunder, as far as twelve days off, which were ascribed to Kabogo, as if it had subterranean caves into which the waves rushed with great noise, and it may be that the Loñgumba is the outlet of Tanganyika: it becomes the Luassé further down, and then the Luamo before it joins the Lualaba: the country slopes that way, but I was too ill to examine its source.

9*th October*.—On to islet Kasengé.* After much delay got a good canoe for three dotis,* and on 15*th October* went to the islet Kabiziwa.

18*th October*.—Start for Kabogo East, and 19*th* reach it 8 A.M.

20*th October*.—Rest men.

22*nd October*.—To Rombola.

23*rd October*.—At dawn, off and go to Ujiji. Welcomed by all the Arabs, particularly by Moenyegheré. I was now reduced to a skeleton, but the market being held daily, and all kinds of native food brought to it, I hoped that food and rest would soon restore me, but in the evening my people came and told me that Shereef* had sold off all my goods, and Moenyegheré confirmed it by saying, 'We protested, but he did not leave a single yard of calico out of 3000, nor a string of beads out of 700 lbs.' This was distressing. I had made up my mind, if I could not get people at Ujiji, to wait till men should come from the coast, but to wait in beggary was what I never contemplated, and I now felt miserable. Shereef was evidently a moral idiot, for he came without shame to shake hands with me, and when I refused, assumed an air of displeasure, as having been badly treated; and afterwards came with his 'Balghere,' good-luck salutation, twice a day, and on leaving said, 'I am going to pray,' till I told him that were I an Arab, his hand and both ears would be cut off for thieving, as he knew, and I wanted no salutations from him. In my distress it was annoying to see Shereef's slaves passing from the market with all the good things that my goods had bought.

24*th October*.—My property had been sold to Shereef's friends at merely nominal prices. Syed bin Majid, a good man, proposed that they should be returned, and the ivory be taken from Shereef; but they would not restore stolen property, though they knew it to be stolen. Christians would have acted differently, even those of the lowest classes. I felt in my destitution as if I were the man who went down from Jerusalem to Jericho, and fell among thieves; but I could not hope for Priest, Levite, or good Samaritan to come by on either side, but one morning Syed bin Majid said to me, 'Now this is the first time we have been alone together; I have no goods, but I have ivory; let me, I pray you, sell some ivory, and give the goods to you.' This was encouraging; but I said, 'Not yet, but by-and-bye.' I had still a few barter goods left, which I had taken the precaution to deposit with Mohamad bin Saleh before going to Manyuema, in case of returning in extreme need. But when my spirits were at their lowest ebb, the good Samaritan was close at hand, for one morning Susi came running at the top of his speed and gasped out, 'An Englishman! I see him!' and off he darted to meet him. The American flag at the head of a caravan told of the nationality of the stranger. Bales of goods, baths of tin, huge kettles, cooking pots, tents, &c., made me think 'This must be a luxurious traveller, and not one at his wits' end like me.' (28*th October*.) It was Henry Moreland Stanley,* the travelling correspondent of the *New York Herald*, sent by James iGordon Bennett, junior, at an expense of more than 4000*l.*, to obtain accurate information about Dr Livingstone if living, and if dead to bring home my bones. The news he had to tell to one who had been two full years without any tidings from Europe made my whole frame thrill. The terrible fate that had befallen France,* the telegraphic cables successfully laid in the Atlantic, the election of General Grant,* the death of good Lord Clarendon*—my constant friend, the proof that Her Majesty's Government had not forgotten me in voting 1000*l.* for supplies, and many other points of interest, revived emotions that had lain dormant in Manyuema. Appetite returned, and instead of the spare, tasteless, two meals a day, I ate four times daily, and in a week began to feel strong. I am not of a demonstrative turn; as cold, indeed, as we islanders are usually reputed to be, but this disinterested kindness of Mr Bennett, so nobly carried into effect by Mr Stanley, was simply overwhelming. I really do feel extremely grateful, and at the same time I am a little ashamed at not being more worthy of the generosity. Mr Stanley has done his part with untiring energy; good judgment in the teeth of very serious obstacles. His helpmates turned out depraved blackguards, who, by their excesses at Zanzibar and elsewhere, had ruined their constitutions, and prepared their systems to be fit provender for the grave. They had used up their strength by wickedness, and were of next to no service, but rather downdrafts and unbearable drags to progress.

16*th November*, 1871.—As Tanganyika explorations are said by Mr Stanley to be an object of interest to Sir Roderick,* we go at his expense and by his men to the north of the Lake.

HENRY MORTON STANLEY
(1841–1904)

The Meeting with Livingstone (1886)

[. . .] Up to that date* Livingstone had been fifty-eight months in the interior of Africa, and during nearly fifty months of which no news had been received of him. Now cast your eyes over that huge configuration called Africa, or take the Equatorial portion of it. I knew he had entered it near S. lat. 10° on the East Coast; that he intended, after arriving at Nyassa Lake, to turn north-westerly. In fifty-eight months one might travel far; for even at a mile per day one could march 1,750 miles. Measure about 1,600 miles north-west, even from the south end of Nyassa Lake,* and you will find a prong of your compasses resting on a point somewhere near 10° N. lat. But supposing that the traveller had marched at an average of two miles per day within the same period, he would have traversed as many degrees as he had been months away from the sea. Now fifty-eight degrees in a north-westerly direction from the southern end of Nyassa would take one near the desert frontier of Algeria or Morocco, and the time I might occupy getting within a decent distance inland, he might utilise in reaching the Mediterranean Sea or some port on the North Atlantic Ocean.

Probably this method of describing the difficulty that now confronted me will suffice to bring the matter vividly home to your minds. I should also tell you that, before arriving at Zanzibar, it had not impressed itself sufficiently on my mind that I should have to travel for many months, perhaps years, through lands inhabited by people whose complexion was of an alarming blackness, that the cream-coloured man would be more of a rarity with them than a coal-black man would be with us in England.

Nor had I thought to any great extent that all these black men were in a manner lawless; that many of them were savage; that some might be ferocious as wild dogs; that Africa possessed no theatres, newspapers, or agreeable society; and that a wheaten loaf could not be purchased with Rothschild's wealth. When I came face to face with the semi-naked blacks of Zanzibar, these horrors flashed upon me like a revelation. I felt I had been betrayed by rashness into a perilous as well as most disagreeable undertaking. Yet it was impossible to retire without making an effort. There was also some consolation in the thought that if my heart became too feeble in resolution, that I could return the way I went without anyone being able to accuse me of returning from mere cowardice.

In due time the expedition was organised, and we soon began our march into the interior. Despite the strangeness of the land and our surroundings, we soon adjusted ourselves to our condition, and, after a manner, were content that fate had fixed us where it had. Very quickly the glamour that high and romantic expectations had cast over the country wore away. Game was not so plentiful as it might have been; the forests and jungles were lovely to look at from the plain, but within they were full of creeping things and abominable insects, scorpions and centipedes, ants and pismires, cobras and pythons. A luxuriance of dank tropical vegetation distilled continually great drops of dew, which dripped on the road; the road became miry and slippery with the tread of many feet. Our bodies perspired intolerably in the warm suffocating air; our clothes galled us; our boots became limp and shapeless in the continual and everlasting mud. As we emerged from the jungle, and looked over the rolling plains, nothing could be more inviting than the prospect. We called it 'park land' as we viewed it from a distance. But as we trod the too narrow path, meandering like a tortuous stream, and became hemmed in by tall coarse grass, with the fervid sun scorching our heads with its intolerable heat, attacked by gadflies and hordes of persistent tsetse, our admiration of park land was not increased by our experience of its many discomforts; nor during the night, when with aching limbs, and half parboiled bodies, we sought well-earned repose, were we deprived of our quota of miseries, for red-water ants infested our bedding, an incredible number of mosquitos hung to our faces, crickets uttered their exasperatingly monotonous cricks, wood-ticks fastened on our bodies like vampires, wild animals haunted the neighbourhood of our camp, hyænas laughed diabolically outdoors, the nitrous earth exhaled its mephitic vapours, until the night seemed to us to rival the day in producing mortifying incidents.

Added to these were hourly troubles with our carriers and animals. The stubborn pack-donkeys continually contrived to upset the loads of cloth in the mud; they sprawled over the greasy, slippery roads as though they were demented; the rain showered on us daily, either soon after commencing a march, or just before we could house ourselves and goods; the porters threw away their packs and deserted;* the native chiefs took occasion at every stage to exact toll and irritate us, and neither animate nor inanimate nature appeared to favour our wanderings.

On the 8th May, 1871, we began to ascend the Usagara range, and in eight marches we arrived on the verge of the dry rolling, mostly wooded, plateau which continues almost without change for nearly 600 miles westward. We soon after entered Ugogo, inhabited by a bumptious, full-chested, square-shouldered people, who exact heavy tribute on all caravans. Nine marches took us through their country, and when we finally shook the dust of its red soil off our feet, we were rich in the experience of native manners and arrogance, but considerably poorer in means.

Beyond Ugogo undulated the Land of the Moon, or Unyamwezi, inhabited by a turbulent and combative race, who are as ready to work for those who can afford to pay as they are to fight those they consider unduly aggressive. Towards the middle of this land we came to a colony of Arab settlers and traders. Some of these have built excellent and spacious houses of sun-dried brick, and cultivate extensive gardens. The Arabs located here were great travellers. Every region round about the colony had been diligently searched by them for ivory. If Livingstone was anywhere within reach, some of these people ought surely to have known. But although I questioned eagerly all whom I became acquainted with, no one could give me definite information of the missing man.

We were preparing to leave the Arab colony in Unyanyembe* when war broke out between the settlers and a native chief named Mirambo, and a series of sanguinary contests followed. In the hope that by adding my force to that of the Arabs a route west might be opened I foolishly enough joined them. We did not succeed, however, in our enterprise, and a disastrous retreat followed. The country became more and more disturbed; bandits infested every road leading from the colony; cruel massacres, destruction of villages, raids by predatory Watuta were daily reported to us, until it seemed to us that there was neither means for advance nor retreat left. As our expedition had become thoroughly disorganized during our flight with the Arabs from the fatal campaign against Mirambo, I turned my attention first to form another which, whether we should continue our search for the lost traveller, or abandon it and turn our faces homeward, would be equally necessary; and as during such an unquiet period it would be a task requiring much time and patience, I meanwhile consulted my charts and the best-informed natives as to the possibility of evading the hostile bands of Mirambo by taking a circuitous route round the disturbed territory.

September 20th, we resumed our journey with a new expedition, much smaller in numbers, but stronger in discipline and means of defence. We had weeded out all the incapables, as well as all the ordinary unarmed porters, and instead of them we had men accustomed to travel, and to the vicissitudes of an African journey. I had also changed for the better. The raw youth who left the coast with a straggling caravan of 192 men of many tribes, willing to be guided by every hint the veteran porters had been pleased to give him, had, through bitter experience, been taught to lead his own force, and to exact ready and immediate obedience. Discipline over such a lawless mob as I had gathered from among the wilder spirits of Unyanyembe could not be enforced, of course, without a few tempestuous scenes, but by exhibiting liberality to the deserving, and severity to the more turbulent, long before we arrived at Lake Tanganika our expedition was a trained force, able to cope with the varied difficulties which beset a traveller in such wild regions.

Lake Tanganika, and the Arab colony on its eastern shore around the port of Ujiji, were the objective point of this second journey. The distance from the sea to this lake-port by the circuitous route we adopted was 975 miles, which occupied us about 8 months, inclusive of marches and halts.

But all this time we had heard nothing definite about the object of our search, until a few days from the Lake, when we met a native caravan which stated that a white man had appeared at Ujiji from the westward of the Tanganika.

At cock-crow of the last day of the journey—the 10th day of November, 1871—we awoke and strengthened ourselves with a substantial meal against the fatigues of a long march. With the clear dawn we were in full swing on the road. Two hours later we obtained our first view of Lake Tanganika, stretched out wide and long like a broad sea-arm between two rows of mountains, and made luminous as a mirror by a bright morning sun. From our conspicuous elevation the land sloped, tree-covered and green, to a wooded terrace, then subsided into a valley, and beyond the valley it waved in succeeding swells westward until it finally dipped, as it seemed to us, into the sheeny Lake. Beyond the great Lake, which was between 30 and 40 miles wide, rose a lengthy range of mountains, dimly outlined, a faint purple-blue in colour, its summits half-buried in masses of sunny-edged clouds.

The admiring people grouped around me gave a shout of joy at the view of the bright and grand beauty, and because they knew that on the shores of the Lake was the haven of their hopes—Ujiji, the terminus of their daily mileage, and the place of the holiday life they were soon to live.

We continue the march, descending the slope of the uplands, thread our way between depths of umbrageous forest, plunge through tunnels of cane grass, emerge on the crests of grassy hills, dip down again into cultivated vales, striding eagerly, pressingly onward, crossing many a babbling brook or muddy creek, skirting past plots of sugar cane, winding among oil palms, laughing and chatting gaily with the villagers, who come out of their huts to hail us, making light of the miles which every half-hour diminish in number, until at last the goal is well-nigh won. We have, as it draws near noon, climbed up the last grassy ridge, have strode across its crest, and have drawn near its westernmost edge, when the Lake appears suddenly only about half-a-mile distant from our feet, and we halt to breathe and rest.

The Lake appears to be about 150 feet below us, to which the road descends gradually through a long straggling town, the northern portions of which are half-buried in palms and other trees.

The people are almost breathless from their rapid marching; they point to the town below us and cry 'Ujiji!' and then each man throws himself on the ground to rest and enjoy the scene. The march has been long, the heat of the day great, and the stragglers from the caravan are many. Meantime, while these are arriving and collecting, the veterans who have been here before act as interpreters of the various views around to the younger men.

After a sufficient rest, and the laggards and weaklings are once more with us, a general movement to somewhat smarten their personal appearance is made. Fine white cotton shirts are brought out, and bright or clean headdresses are wound around their heads. They are then told to load their muskets with plentiful charges of powder to waken up the drowsy and sleepy townspeople of Ujiji, and announce by volleys the arrival of friends. When the flags are unfurled and everything is ready the word is given to fire, and fifty well-loaded muskets sound the news of our arrival to Ujiji. Again and again the loud signal was given, and then the caravan began its slow descent towards the town.

The people of Ujiji experienced a shock of surprise at this sudden announcement, for they were slow to venture out. I was told afterwards they had taken us for the dreaded Mirambo, for at the earliest firing hasty consultations had taken place as to what was best to be done. However, the head of the column was barely a hundred yards below the brow of the hill when by every pathway multitudes of people were seen rushing up with muskets, spears, bows and arrows. The steady march of the caravan with its loads, and the flag-bearers clad in scarlet in the front, satisfied everyone instantly that by some strange chance the advancing strangers were friends from Zanzibar.

We were soon surrounded by hundreds of friendly townspeople, who exchanged their welcomes with our people in many languages, and escorted us down the hill with gladsome shouts. Though a great crowd paid particular attention to me, and made walking difficult by their numbers and inordinate curiosity, I had as yet heard no remark that I understood, except the Zanzibari hail and greeting, 'Yambo!'

But presently, to my astonishment, an extremely black man, neatly clad in a snowy shirt, pressed forward impulsively, and delivered the unmistakable English greeting—

'Good morning, sir.'

'Hallo!' I replied; 'who in the mischief are you?'

His face lighted up with a broad smile as he answered, 'I am Susi, the servant of Dr Livingstone.'

'What! is Dr Livingstone here?'

'Yes, sir.'

'In this village? In Ujiji?'

'Yes, sir.'

'But, are you sure?'

'Sure, sure, sir. Why, I leave him just now, sir.'

Before any more remarks could be uttered expressive of my wonderment, a younger man, dressed in the same manner, pressed forward, and cried out hurriedly—

'Good morning, sir.'

'Hallo!' said I; 'is this another of Dr Livingstone's servants?'

'Yes, sir.'

'And what is your name?'

'Chumah, sir,' he answered.

'Oh, Chumah, the friend of Wekotani?'*

'Yes, sir.'

'And how is the Doctor?'

'Not very well,' they both replied.

'But where has he been so long?'

'We just come from Manyema.'

'Well, I think one of you had better run and tell the Doctor you have seen me, and that I am coming to see him.'

Susi seemed to be of the same opinion, as he darted through the crowd, regardless of whom he pushed against, and, once clear of the mass, was observed speeding away downhill with his loose white dress streaming behind like a pennant.

Meanwhile we had arrived near the outskirts of the town, the ivory horn of our gigantic guide sounding its mellow and clear notes far above the murmur of the multitude. For the tidings had quickly spread abroad that it was another white man who had come from the eastward with a caravan, and while many were anxious to learn the news from Unyanyembe, many were curious to see the second white man, who had dropped amongst them as suddenly as though he had come from the clouds.

The scene was also rendered more animated by the great number of flags and streamers that floated and rippled over the heads of the dense mass. Important Arabs and head men came forward and delivered their welcomes impressively and fervently, and the cordial shakings of the hand I received communicated something of the excitement around to myself, for they seemed to say by their manner that we belonged to them, for had we not come from Zanzibar and Unyanyembe? It was a wondering question with many of them —However did we come from Unyanyembe, at a time when all the country was disturbed by war?

Before I could explain Susi again presented himself as suddenly as he had disappeared, and brusquely asked—

'What is your name, sir? The Doctor will not believe me when I say a white man is coming.'

I gave him the desired information, and again Susi vanished

quickly from view. But while Susi had been hastening to make amends for his lack of ability to give the Doctor my name, others had hastened to the traveller to congratulate him upon the arrival of a white man—a friend—who knows? perhaps a relative, please God; and though he had ridiculed Susi, his servant, for his extraordinary tale, the reiteration of the same news had at last wrought conviction in his mind that the news must be true, and he had permitted himself to be persuaded to accompany the Arab magnates to the market-place, which was but a few paces from his dwelling, to publicly welcome the stranger.

In a few minutes, for so great was the crowd that our progress had been slow, the market-place of Ujiji was reached by the head of the Expedition, which halted there to await instructions, and as fast as the members arrived at the place where the flags were streaming aloft, they naturally formed two equal groups around the central figures—the great traveller, and his Arab neighbours; and as the rearguard arrived and separated on each side they disclosed to my view the object of my search, Dr David Livingstone.

When I caught my first view of him I may have been fifty paces off, and in that one glance whatever of doubts about his identity still clung to my mind vanished.

I saw an elderly man, dressed in cloth cap, red blouse, and grey tweed pants. His frame was large, but shrunken, as the unspeakable miseries of African travel might well reduce it. His years had not aged him so much as one might have supposed, for his face was compara-tively unwrinkled. It was sad and grave from long distress of body and mind, pinched and meagre through lack of nourishment, sunken and hollow through privations, pale through dolour, wan and wearied from long-lasting troubles, and withered by much sickness. As he described himself, he was 'a mere ruckle of bones,' but within the casket was an undaunted soul. I could see it in the now animated face, in the bright and piercing eyes gazing into mine. The general impression I received was that, under favourable conditions, his recuperation would be easy, and that speedy restoration to health and strength was possible.

Conscious that I was observed by hundreds of strangers, who had no conception of the emotions that filled me, and doubtful of my reception by the old traveller himself, I simply doffed my helmet, bowed, and gravely said—

'Dr Livingstone, I presume?'

'Yes,' he answered with a cordial smile, as he lifted his cap in salute.

With mutual goodwill we grasped each other's hands, and I said:

'I thank God, Doctor, I have been permitted to see you.'

To which he replied: 'I feel very thankful that I am here to welcome you.'

When about an hour later Livingstone and myself sat down to an improvised banquet, and warmly toasted one another in champagne that had been carried by me into Central Africa for such an interesting occasion, we both heard the Doctor's cook expressing the general sense of the native community of Ujiji with admirable fitness, upon the sudden meeting that had just taken place.

'It is true—yes, by Allah it is true, and there is no lie in it. There are two white men to-day, where only one sat yesterday. One comes from across the Lake, the other comes from across the sea. I wonder whether there are any more white men in this world?'

See also: Bird; Blyden; Haggard; Kingsley; Plaatje.

MARCUS CLARKE
(1846–1881)

Clarke's Preface, and the poem by 'Australie' immediately following, offer early responses from Australian settler writers to the question of how to comprehend and represent the land's apparent oddities and excesses —lushness in winter, bare monotony, 'Weird Melancholy'.

from Preface to Adam Lindsay Gordon's *Poems* (1876)

[. . .] The student of these unpretending volumes will be repaid for his labour. He will find in them something very like the beginnings of a national school of Australian poetry. In historic Europe, where every rood of ground is hallowed in legend and in song, the least imaginative can find food for sad and sweet reflection. When strolling at noon down an English country lane, lounging at sunset by some ruined chapel on the margin of an Irish lake, or watching the mists of morning unveil Ben Lomond, we feel all the charm which springs from association with the past. Soothed, saddened, and cheered by turns, we partake of the varied moods which belong not so much to ourselves as to the dead men who, in old days, sung, suffered, or conquered in the scenes which we survey. But this our native or adopted land has no past, no story. No poet speaks to us. Do we need a poet to interpret Nature's teachings, we must look into our own hearts, if perchance we may find a poet there.

What is the dominant note of Australian scenery? That which is the dominant note of Edgar Allan Poe's poetry—Weird Melancholy. A poem like 'L'Allegro'* could never be written by an Australian. It is too airy, too sweet, too freshly happy. The Australian mountain forests are funereal, secret, stern. Their solitude is desolation. They seem to stifle, in their black gorges, a story of sullen despair. No tender sentiment is nourished in their shade. In other lands the dying year is mourned, the falling leaves drop lightly on his bier. In the Australian forests no leaves fall. The savage winds shout among the rock clefts. From the melancholy gum strips of white bark hang and rustle. The very animal life of these frowning hills is either grotesque or ghostly. Great grey kangaroos hop noiselessly over the coarse grass. Flights of white cockatoos stream out, shrieking like evil souls. The sun suddenly sinks, and the mopokes burst out into horrible peals of semi-human laughter. The natives aver that, when night comes, from out the bottomless depth of some lagoon the Bunyip* rises, and, in form like monstrous sea calf, drags his loathsome length from out the ooze. From a corner of the silent forest rises a dismal chant, and around a fire dance natives painted like skeletons. All is fear-inspiring and gloomy. No bright fancies are linked with the memories of the mountains. Hopeless explorers have named them out of their sufferings—Mount Misery, Mount Dreadful, Mount Despair. As when among sylvan scenes in places

> Made green with the running of rivers,
> And gracious with temperate air,*

the soul is soothed and satisfied, so, placed before the frightful grandeur of these barren hills, it drinks in their sentiment of defiant ferocity, and is steeped in bitterness.

Australia has rightly been named the Land of the Dawning.

Wrapped in the mist of early morning, her history looms vague and gigantic. The lonely horseman riding between the moonlight and the day sees vast shadows creeping across the shelterless and silent plains, hears strange noises in the primeval forest where flourishes a vegetation long dead in other lands, and feels, despite his fortune, that the trim utilitarian civilisation which bred him shrinks into insignificance beside the contemptuous grandeur of forest and ranges coeval with an age in which European scientists have cradled his own race.

There is a poem in every form of tree or flower, but the poetry which lives in the trees and flowers of Australia differs from those of other countries. Europe is the home of knightly song, of bright deeds and clear morning thought. Asia sinks beneath the weighty recollections of her past magnificence, as the Suttee sinks, jewel-burdened, upon the corpse of dead grandeur, destructive even in its death. America swiftly hurries on her way, rapid, glittering, insatiable even as one of her own giant waterfalls. From the jungles of Africa, and the creeper-tangled groves of the islands of the South, arise, from the glowing hearts of a thousand flowers, heavy and intoxicating odours —the Upas-poison* which dwells in barbaric sensuality. In Australia alone is to be found the Grotesque, the Weird, the strange scribblings of nature learning how to write. Some see no beauty in our trees without shade, our flowers without perfume, our birds who cannot fly, and our beasts who have not yet learned to walk on all fours. But the dweller in the wilderness acknowledges the subtle charm of this fantastic land of monstrosities. He becomes familiar with the beauty of loneliness. Whispered to by the myriad tongues of the wilderness, he learns the language of the barren and the uncouth, and can read the hieroglyphs of haggard gum trees, blown into odd shapes, distorted with fierce hot winds, or cramped with cold nights, when the Southern Cross freezes in a cloudless sky of icy blue. The phantasmagoria of that wild dreamland termed the Bush interprets itself, and the Poet of our desolation begins to comprehend why free Esau loved his heritage of desert sand better than all the bountiful richness of Egypt.

See also: Crawford; Lampman; Lawson; Paterson; Roberts; Stephens.

'AUSTRALIE' (EMILY MANNING)
(1845–1890)

From the Clyde to Braidwood (1877)

A winter morn. The blue Clyde river winds
'Mid sombre slopes, reflecting in clear depths
The tree-clad banks or grassy meadow flats
Now white with hoary frost, each jewell'd blade
With myriad crystals glistening in the sun.

Thus smiles the Vale of Clyde, as through the air
So keen and fresh three travellers upward ride
Toward the Braidwood heights. Quickly they pass
The rustic dwellings on the hamlet's verge,
Winding sometimes beside the glassy depths
Of Nelligen Creek, where with the murmuring bass
Of running water sounds the sighing wail
Of dark swamp-oaks, that shiver on each bank;
Then winding through a shady-bower'd lane,
With the flickering streaks of sunlight beaming through
The feathery leaves and pendant tassels green
Of bright mimosa, whose wee furry balls
Promise to greet with golden glow of joy
The coming spring-tide.

                              Now a barren length
Of tall straight eucalyptus, till again
A babbling voice is heard, and through green banks
Of emerald fern and mossy boulder rocks,
The Currawong dances o'er a pebbly bed,
In rippling clearness, or with cresting foam
Splashes and leaps in snowy cascade steps.
Then every feature changes—up and down,
O'er endless ranges like great waves of earth,
Each weary steed must climb, e'en like a ship
Now rising high upon some billowy ridge
But to plunge down to mount once more, again
And still again.

                              Naught on the road to see
Save sullen trees, white arm'd, with naked trunks,
And hanging bark, like tatter'd clothes thrown off,
An undergrowth of glossy zamia palms*
Bearing their winter store of coral fruit,
And here and there some early clematis,
Like starry jasmine, or a purple wreath
Of dark kennedea,* blooming o'er their time,
As if in pity they would add one joy
Unto the barren landscape.

                              But at last
A clearer point is reach'd, and all around
The loftier ranges loom in contour blue,
With indigo shadows and light veiling mist
Rising from steaming valleys. Straight in front
Towers the Sugarloaf, pyramidal King
Of Braidwood peaks.

                              Impossible it seems
To scale that nature–rampart, but where man
Would go he must and will; so hewn from out
The mountain's side, in gradual ascent
Of league and half of engineering skill
There winds the Weber Pass.

                              A glorious ride!
Fresher and clearer grows the breezy air,
Lighter and freer beats the quickening pulse
As each fair height is gain'd. Stern, strong, above
Rises the wall of mountain; far beneath,
In sheer precipitancy, gullies deep
Gloom in dark shadow, on their shelter'd breast
Cherishing wealth of leafage richly dight
With tropic hues of green.

                              No sound is heard
Save the deep soughing of the wind amid
The swaying leaves and harp–like stems, so like
A mighty breathing of great mother earth,

That half they seem to see her bosom heave
With each pulsation as she living sleeps.
And now and then to cadence of these throbs
There drops the bell-bird's knell, the coach-whip's crack,
The wonga-pigeon's coo, or echoing notes
Of lyre-tail'd pheasants in their own rich tones,
Mocking the song of every forest bird.

Higher the travellers rise—at every turn
Gaining through avenued vista some new glimpse
Of undulating hills, the Pigeon-house
Standing against the sky like eyrie nest
Of some great dove or eagle. On each side
Of rock-hewn road, the fern trees cluster green,
Now and then lighted by a silver star
Of white immortelle flower, or overhung
By crimson peals of bright epacris bells.

Another bend, a shelter'd deepening rift,
And in the mountain's very heart they plunge—
So dark the shade, the sun is lost to view.
Great silver wattles tremble o'er the path,
Which overlooks a glen one varying mass
Of exquisite foliage, full-green sassafras,*
The bright-leaf'd myrtle, dark-hued Kurrajong
And lavender, musk-plant, scenting all the air,
Entwined with clematis or bignonia vines,
And raspberry tendrils hung with scarlet fruit.

The riders pause some moments, gazing down,
Then upward look. Far as the peeping sky
The dell-like gully yawns into the heights;
A tiny cascade drips o'er mossy rocks,
And through an aisle of over-arching trees,
Whose stems are dight with lichen, creeping vines,
A line of sunlight pierces, lighting up
A wealth of fern trees; filling every nook
With glorious circles of voluptuous green,
Such as, unview'd, once clothed the silent earth
Long milliards past in Carboniferous Age.

A mighty nature-rockery! Each spot
Of fertile ground is rich with endless joys
Of leaf and fern; now here a velvet moss,
And there a broad asplenium's shining frond
With red-black veinings or a hart's-tongue point,
Contrasting with a pale-hued tender brake
Or creeping lion's-foot. See where the hand
Of ruthless man hath cleft the rock, each wound
Is hidden by thick verdure, leaving not
One unclothed spot, save on the yellow road.

Reluctant the travellers leave the luscious shade
To mount once more. But now another joy—
An open view is here! Before them spreads
A waving field of ranges, purple grey,
In haze of distance with black lines of shade
Marking the valleys, bound by a line
Of ocean-blue, o'er whose horizon verge
The morning mist-cloud hangs. The distant bay
Is clear defined. The headland's dark arms stretch
(Each finger-point white-lit with dashing foam)
In azure circlet, studded with rugged isles—
A picturesque trio, whose gold rock sides glow
In noonday sunlight, and round which the surf
Gleams like a silvery girdle.

                              The grand Pass
Is traversed now, the inland plateau reach'd,
The last sweet glimpse of violet peaks is lost,
An upland rocky stream is pass'd and naught
But same same gum-trees vex the wearied eye
Till Braidwood plain is reach'd.

                              A township like
All others, with its houses, church, and school—
Bare, bald, prosaic—no quaint wild tower,
Nor ancient hall to add poetic touch,
As in the dear old land—no legend old
Adds softening beauty to the Buddawong Peak,
Or near-home ranges with too barbarous names.

But everything is cold, new, new, too new
To foster poesy; and famish'd thought
Looks back with longing to the mountain dream.

See also: as for Clarke, but, in particular, Crawford; Stephens.

EDWIN ARNOLD
(1832–1904)

*This extract from Arnold's blank-verse rendition of the life of the Buddha,
presents the reunion between Prince Siddhartha (or the Buddha) and his
father, King Suddhohana, after the visionary's long period of retreat and
meditation.*

from *The Light of Asia* (1879)

[. . .] But when the King heard how Siddârtha came
Shorn, with the mendicant's sad-coloured cloth,
And stretching out a bowl to gather orts
From base-borns' leavings, wrathful sorrow drove
Love from his heart. Thrice on the ground he spat,
Plucked at his silvered beard, and strode straight forth
Lackeyed by trembling lords. Frowning he clomb
Upon his war-horse, drove the spurs, and dashed,
Angered, through wondering streets and lanes of folk,
Scarce finding breath to say, 'The King! bow down!'
Ere the loud cavalcade had clattered by:
Which—at the turning by the Temple-wall
Where the south gate was seen—encountered full
A mighty crowd; to every edge of it
Poured fast more people, till the roads were lost,
Blotted by that huge company which thronged
And grew, close following him whose look serene
Met the old King's. Nor lived the father's wrath
Longer than while the gentle eyes of Buddha
Lingered in worship on his troubled brows,

Then downcast sank, with his true knee, to earth
In proud humility. So dear it seemed
To see the Prince, to know him whole, to mark
That glory greater than of earthly state
Crowning his head, that majesty which brought
All men, so awed and silent, in his steps.
Nathless the King broke forth, 'Ends it in this
That great Siddârtha steals into his realm,
Wrapped in a clout, shorn, sandalled, craving food
Of low-borns, he whose life was as a God's?
My son! heir of this spacious power, and heir
Of Kings who did but clap their palms to have
What earth could give or eager service bring?
Thou should'st have come apparelled in thy rank,
With shining spears and tramp of horse and foot.
Lo! all my soldiers camped upon the road,
And all my city waited at the gates;
Where hast thou sojourned through these evil years
Whilst thy crowned father mourned? and she,* too, there
Lived as the widows use, foregoing joys;
Never once hearing sound of song or string,
Nor wearing once the festal robe, till now
When in her cloth of gold she welcomes home
A beggar-spouse in yellow remnants clad.
Son! why is this?'

      'My Father!' came reply,
'It is the custom of my race.'

        'Thy race,'
Answered the King 'counteth a hundred thrones
From Maha Sammât, but no deed like this.'

  'Not of a mortal line,' the Master said,
'I spake, but of descent invisible,
The Buddhas who have been and who shall be:
Of these am I, and what they did I do,
And this which now befalls so fell before
That at his gate a King in warrior-mail
Should meet his son, a Prince in hermit-weeds;

And that, by love and self-control, being more
Than mightiest Kings in all their puissance,
The appointed Helper of the Worlds should bow—
As now do I—and with all lowly love
Proffer, where it is owed for tender debts,
The first-fruits of the treasure* he hath brought;
Which now I proffer.' [. . .]

See also: Aurobindo; McKay; Naidu; Tagore; Vivekananda.

ALFRED, LORD TENNYSON
(1809–1892)

The Defence of Lucknow (1880)

I

Banner of England, not for a season, O banner of Britain, hast thou
Floated in conquering battle or flapt to the battle-cry!
Never with mightier glory than when we had reared thee on high
Flying at top of the roofs in the ghastly siege of Lucknow—*
Shot through the staff or the halyard, but ever we raised thee anew,
And ever upon the topmost roof our banner of England blew.

II

Frail were the works that defended the hold that we held with our
    lives—
Women and children among us, God help them, our children and
    wives!
Hold it we might—and for fifteen days or for twenty at most.
'Never surrender, I charge you, but every man die at his post!'
Voice of the dead whom we loved, our Lawrence* the best of the
    brave:
Cold were his brows when we kissed him—we laid him that night in
    his grave.
'Every man die at his post!' and there hailed on our houses and halls
Death from their rifle-bullets, and death from their cannon-balls,

Death in our innermost chamber, and death at our slight barricade,
Death while we stood with the musket, and death while we stoopt to
the spade,
Death to the dying, and wounds to the wounded, for often there fell,
Striking the hospital wall, crashing through it, their shot and their
shell,
Death—for their spies were among us, their marksmen were told of
our best,
So that the brute bullet broke through the brain that could think for
the rest;
Bullets would sing by our foreheads, and bullets would rain at our
feet—
Fire from ten thousand at once of the rebels that girdled us round—
Death at the glimpse of a finger from over the breadth of a street,
Death from the heights of the mosque and the palace, and death in
the ground!
Mine? yes, a mine! Countermine! down, down! and creep through
the hole!
Keep the revolver in hand! you can hear him—the murderous mole!
Quiet, ah! quiet—wait till the point of the pickaxe be through!
Click with the pick, coming nearer and nearer again than before—
Now let it speak, and you fire, and the dark pioneer is no more;
And ever upon the topmost roof our banner of England blew!

III

Ay, but the foe sprung his mine many times, and it chanced on a day
Soon as the blast of that underground thunderclap echoed away,
Dark through the smoke and the sulphur like so many fiends in their
hell—
Cannon-shot, musket-shot, volley on volley, and yell upon yell—
Fiercely on all the defences our myriad enemy fell.
What have they done? where is it? Out yonder. Guard the Redan!
Storm at the Water-gate! storm at the Bailey-gate! storm, and it ran
Surging and swaying all round us, as ocean on every side
Plunges and heaves at a bank that is daily devoured by the tide—
So many thousands that if they be bold enough, who shall escape?
Kill or be killed, live or die, they shall know we are soldiers and men!
Ready! take aim at their leaders—their masses are gapped with our
grape—

Backward they reel like the wave, like the wave flinging forward
    again,
Flying and foiled at the last by the handful they could not subdue;
And ever upon the topmost roof our banner of England blew.

IV

Handful of men as we were, we were English in heart and in limb,
Strong with the strength of the race to command, to obey, to endure,
Each of us fought as if hope for the garrison hung but on him;
Still—could we watch at all points? we were every day fewer and
    fewer.
There was a whisper among us, but only a whisper that past:
'Children and wives—if the tigers* leap into the fold unawares—
Every man die at his post—and the foe may outlive us at last—
Better to fall by the hands that they love, than to fall into theirs!'
Roar upon roar in a moment two mines by the enemy sprung
Clove into perilous chasms our walls and our poor palisades.
Rifleman, true is your heart, but be sure that your hand be as true!
Sharp is the fire of assault, better aimed are your flank fusillades—
Twice do we hurl them to earth from the ladders to which they had
    clung,
Twice from the ditch where they shelter we drive them with hand-
    grenades;
And ever upon the topmost roof our banner of England blew.

V

Then on another wild morning another wild earthquake out-tore
Clean from our lines of defence ten or twelve good paces or more.
Rifleman, high on the roof, hidden there from the light of the sun—
One has leapt up on the breach, crying out: 'Follow me, follow
    me!'—
Mark him—he falls! then another, and *him* too, and down goes he.
Had they been bold enough then, who can tell but the traitors had
    won?
Boardings and rafters and doors—an embrasure! make way for the
    gun!
Now double-charge it with grape! It is charged and we fire, and they
    run.
Praise to our Indian brothers, and let the dark face have his due!

Thanks to the kindly dark faces who fought with us, faithful and few,
Fought with the bravest among us, and drove them, and smote them,
 and slew,
That ever upon the topmost roof our banner in India blew.

VI

Men will forget what we suffer and not what we do. We can fight!
But to be soldier all day and be sentinel all through the night—
Ever the mine and assault, our sallies, their lying alarms,
Bugles and drums in the darkness, and shoutings and soundings to
 arms,
Ever the labour of fifty that had to be done by five,
Ever the marvel among us that one should be left alive,
Ever the day with its traitorous death from the loop-holes around,
Ever the night with its coffinless corpse to be laid in the ground,
Heat like the mouth of a hell, or a deluge of cataract skies,
Stench of old offal decaying, and infinite torment of flies,
Thoughts of the breezes of May blowing over an English field,
Cholera, scurvy, and fever, the wound that *would* not be healed,
Lopping away of the limb by the pitiful-pitiless knife,—
Torture and trouble in vain,—for it never could save us a life.
Valour of delicate women who tended the hospital bed,
Horror of women in travail among the dying and dead,
Grief for our perishing children, and never a moment for grief,
Toil and ineffable weariness, faltering hopes of relief,
Havelock* baffled, or beaten, or butchered for all that we knew—
Then day and night, day and night, coming down on the still-
 shattered walls
Millions of musket-bullets, and thousands of cannon-balls—
But ever upon the topmost roof our banner of England blew.

VII

Hark cannonade, fusillade! is it true what was told by the scout,
Outram and Havelock breaking their way through the fell
 mutineers?
Surely the pibroch of Europe is ringing again in our ears!
All on a sudden the garrison utter a jubilant shout,
Havelock's glorious Highlanders answer with conquering cheers,
Sick from the hospital echo them, women and children come out,

Blessing the wholesome white faces of Havelock's good fusileers,
Kissing the war-hardened hand of the Highlander wet with their
    tears!
Dance to the pibroch!—saved! we are saved!—is it you? is it you?
Saved by the valour of Havelock, saved by the blessing of Heaven!
'Hold it for fifteen days!' we have held it for eighty-seven!
And ever aloft on the palace roof the old banner of England blew.

Opening of the Indian and Colonial Exhibition
by the Queen (1886)

Written at the Request of the Prince of Wales

I

Welcome, welcome with one voice!
In your welfare we rejoice,
Sons and brothers that have sent,
From isle and cape and continent,
Produce of your field and flood,
Mount and mine, and primal wood;
Works of subtle brain and hand,
And splendours of the morning land,
Gifts from every British zone;
    Britons, hold your own!*

II

May we find, as ages run,
The mother featured in the son;
And may yours for ever be
That old strength and constancy
Which has made your fathers great
In our ancient island State,
And wherever her flag fly,
Glorying between sea and sky,
Makes the might of Britain known;
    Britons, hold your own!

III

Britain fought her sons of yore—
Britain failed; and never more,
Careless of our growing kin,
Shall we sin our fathers' sin,
Men that in a narrower day—
Unprophetic rulers they –
Drove from out the mother's nest
That young eagle of the West
To forage for herself alone;
    Britons, hold your own!

IV

Sharers of our glorious past,
Brothers, must we part at last?
Shall we not through good and ill
Cleave to one another still?
Britain's myriad voices call,
'Sons, be welded each and all,
Into one imperial whole,
One with Britain, heart and soul!
One life, one flag, one fleet, one Throne!'
    Britons, hold your own!

See also: Chamberlain; Henty; Seeley; Trevelyan.

EDWARD WILMOT BLYDEN
(1835–1883)

from The Aims and Methods of a Liberal Education for Africans (1881)

[. . .] To a certain extent, perhaps to a very important extent, Negroes trained on the soil of Africa have the advantage of those trained in foreign countries; but in all, as a rule, the intellectual and moral results thus far have been far from satisfactory. There are many men of book-learning, but few, very few, of any *capability* —even few who have that amount or that sort of culture which produces self-respect, confidence in one's self, and efficiency in work. Now why is this? The evil, it is considered, lies in the system and method of European training, to which Negroes are everywhere in Christian lands subjected, and which everywhere affects them unfavorably. Of a different race, different susceptibility, different bent of character from that of the European, they have been trained under influences in many respects adapted only to the Caucasian race. Nearly all the books they read, the very instruments of their culture, have been such as to force them from the groove which is natural to them, where they would be strong and effective, without furnishing them with any avenue through which they may move naturally and free from obstruction. Christian and so-called civilized Negroes live for the most part in foreign countries, where they are only passive spectators of the deeds of a foreign race; and where, with other impressions which they receive from without, an element of doubt as to their own capacity and their own destiny is fastened upon them and inheres in their intellectual and social constitution. They depreciate their own individuality, and would escape from it if they could. And in countries like this, where they are free from the hampering surroundings of an alien race, they still read and study the books of foreigners, and form their idea of everything that man may do, or ought to do, according to the standard held up in those teachings. Hence without the physical or mental aptitude for the enterprises which they are taught to admire and revere, they attempt to copy and imitate them, and share the fate of all copyists and imitators. Bound to move on a lower level, they acquire and retain a practical inferiority, transcribing very often the faults rather than the virtues of their models.

Besides this result of involuntary impressions, they often receive direct teachings which are not only incompatible with but destructive of their self-respect.

In all English-speaking countries the mind of the intelligent Negro child revolts against the descriptions given in elementary books —geographies, travels, histories—of the Negro; but, though he experiences an instinctive revulsion from these caricatures and misrepresentations, he is obliged to continue, as he grows in years, to study such pernicious teachings. After leaving school he finds the same things in newspapers, in reviews, in novels, in *quasi* scientific works; and after a while—*saepe cadendo**—they begin to seem to him the proper things to say and to feel about his race, and he accepts what at first his fresh and unbiased feelings naturally and indignantly repelled. Such is the effect of repetition.

Having embraced or at least assented to these errors and falsehoods about himself, he concludes that his only hope of rising in the scale of respectable manhood is to strive after whatever is most unlike himself and most alien to his peculiar tastes. And whatever his literary attainments or acquired ability, he fancies that he must grind at the mill which is provided for him, putting in the material furnished to his hands, bringing no contribution from his own field; and of course nothing comes out but what is put in. Thus he can never bring any real assistance to the European. He can never attain to that essence of progress which Mr Herbert Spencer describes as *difference*:* and therefore, he never acquires the self-respect or self-reliance of an independent contributor. He is not an independent help, only a subject help; so that the European feels that he owes him no debt, and moves on in contemptuous indifference of the Negro, teaching him to contemn himself.

Those who have lived in civilized communities, where there are different races, know the disparaging views which are entertained of the blacks by their neighbors and (often, alas!) by themselves. The standard of all physical and intellectual excellencies in the present civilization being the white complexion, whatever deviates from that favored color is proportionally depreciated, until the black, which is the opposite, becomes not only the most unpopular but the most unprofitable color. Black men, and especially black women, in such communities experience the greatest imaginable inconvenience. They never feel at home. In the depth of their being they always feel themselves strangers in the land of their exile, and the only escape from this feeling is to escape from themselves. And this feeling of self-depreciation is not diminished, as I have intimated above, by the books they read. Women, especially, are fond of reading novels and light literature; and it is in these writings that flippant and eulogistic reference is constantly made to the superior physical and mental characteristics of the Caucasian race, which by contrast suggests the inferiority of other races—especially of that race which is furthest removed from it in appearance.

It is painful in America to see the efforts which are made by Negroes to secure outward conformity to the appearance of the dominant race.

This is by no means surprising; but what is surprising is that, under the circumstances, any Negro has retained a particle of self-respect. Now in Africa, where the color of the majority is black, the fashion in personal matters is naturally suggested by the personal characteristics of the race, and we are free from the necessity of submitting to the use of 'incongruous feathers awkwardly stuck on.' Still, we are held in bondage by our indiscriminate and injudicious use of a foreign literature; and we strive to advance by the methods of a foreign race. In this effort we struggle with the odds against us. We fight at the disadvantage which David would have experienced in Saul's armor. The African must advance by methods of his own. He must possess a power distinct from that of the European. It has been proven that he knows how to take advantage of European culture, and that he can be benefited by it. This proof was perhaps necessary, but it is not sufficient. We must show that we are able to go alone, to carve out our own way. We must not be satisfied that in this nation European influence shapes our polity, makes our laws, rules in our tribunals, and impregnates our social atmosphere. We must not suppose that the Anglo-Saxon methods are final, that there is nothing for us to find out for our own guidance, and that we have nothing to teach the world. There is inspiration for us also. We must study our brethren in the interior, who know better than we do the laws of growth for the race. We see among them the rudiments of that which, with fair play and opportunity, will develop into important and effective agencies for our work. We look too much to foreigners, and are dazzled almost to blindness by their exploits—so as to fancy that they have exhausted the possibilities of humanity. In our estimation they, like Longfellow's Iagoo,* have done and can do everything better than anybody else.

'Never heard he an adventure
But himself had made a greater;
Never any deed of daring,
But himself had done a bolder;
Never any marvelous story
But himself could tell a stranger.
No one ever shot an arrow
Half so far and high as he had,

Ever caught so many fishes,
Ever killed so many reindeer,
Ever trapped so many beaver.
None could run so fast as he could;
None could dive so deep as he could;
None could swim so far as he could;
None had made so many journeys;
None had seen so many wonders,
As this wonderful Iagoo.'

But there are possibilities before us not yet dreamed of by the Iagoos of civilization. Dr Alexander Winchell, professor in one of the American universities,—who has lately written a book, in the name of science, in which he reproduces all the old slanders against the Negro, and writes of the African at home as if Livingstone, Barth, Stanley, and Cameron* had never written,—mentions it, as one of the evidences of Negro inferiority, that 'in Liberia he is indifferent to the benefits of civilization.'[1] I stand here to-day to justify and commend the Negro of Liberia—and of everywhere else in Africa—for rejecting with scorn, 'always and every time,' the 'benefits' of a civilization whose theories are to degrade him in the scale of humanity, and of which such sciolists as Dr Winchell are the exponents and representative elements. We recommend all Africans to treat such 'benefits' with even more decided 'indifference' than that with which the guide in Dante treated the despicable herd,—

'Non ragionam di lor, ma guarda, e passa.'*

Those of us who have traveled in foreign countries and who witness the general results of European influence along this coast, have many reasons for misgivings and reserves and anxieties about European civilization for this country. Things which have been of great advantage to Europe may work ruin to us; and there is often such a striking resemblance, or such a close connection between the nocuous and the beneficial, that we are not always able to discriminate. I have heard of a native in one of the settlements on the coast who, having grown up in the use of the simple but efficient remedies of the country doctors, and having prospered in business, conceived the idea that he must avail himself of the medicines he saw used by the European traders. Suffering from sleeplessness he was advised to

[1] Pre-Adamite Man, p. 265.*

take Dover's powders,* but in his inexperience took instead an overdose of morphine, and next morning he was a corpse. So we have reason to apprehend that in our indiscriminate appropriations of European agencies or methods in our political, educational, and social life, we are often imbibing overdoses of morphine when we fancy we are only taking Dover's powders.

See also: Aurobindo; Casely Hayford; Joyce; McKay; Plaatje; Ruskin.

TORU DUTT
(1856–1877)

Ancient Ballads and Legends of Hindustan (1882), in which three of the following four poems appeared, is particularly noteworthy for being the first collection of Indian poetry in English to be published by a woman.

À mon Père (1876)

The flowers look loveliest in their native soil
Amid their kindred branches; plucked, they fade,
And lose the colours Nature on them laid,
Though bound in garlands with assiduous toil.
Pleasant it was, afar from all turmoil,
To wander through the valley, now in shade
And now in sunshine, where these blossoms made
A Paradise, and gather in my spoil.
But better than myself no man can know
How tarnished have become their tender hues
E'en in the gathering, and how dimmed their glow!
Wouldst thou again new life in them infuse,
Thou who hast seen them where they brightly blow?
Ask Memory. She shall help my stammering Muse.

Sonnet—Baugmaree* (1882)

A sea of foliage girds our garden round,
   But not a sea of dull unvaried green,
   Sharp contrasts of all colours here are seen;
The light-green graceful tamarinds abound
Amid the mangoe clumps of green profound,
   And palms arise, like pillars gray, between;
And o'er the quiet pools the seemuls* lean,
Red,—red, and startling like a trumpet's sound.
But nothing can be lovelier than the ranges
   Of bamboos to the eastward, when the moon
Looks through their gaps, and the white lotus changes
Into a cup of silver. One might swoon
   Drunken with beauty then, or gaze and gaze
On a primeval Eden, in amaze.

Sonnet—The Lotus

Love came to Flora* asking for a flower
   That would of flowers be undisputed queen,
   The lily and the rose, long, long had been
Rivals for that high honour. Bards of power
Had sung their claims. 'The rose can never tower
   Like the pale lily with her Juno* mien'—
   'But is the lily lovelier?' Thus between
Flower-factions rang the strife in Psyche's* bower.
'Give me a flower delicious as the rose
   And stately as the lily in her pride'—
'But of what colour?'—'Rose-red,' Love first chose,
   Then prayed,—'No, lily-white,—or, both provide;'
   And Flora gave the lotus, 'rose red' dyed,
And 'lily-white,' queenliest flower that blows.

Our Casuarina Tree*

Like a huge Python, winding round and round
   The rugged trunk, indented deep with scars
   Up to its very summit near the stars,
A creeper climbs, in whose embraces bound
   No other tree could live. But gallantly
The giant wears the scarf, and flowers are hung
In crimson clusters all the boughs among,
   Whereon all day are gathered bird and bee;
And oft at nights the garden overflows
With one sweet song that seems to have no close,
Sung darkling from our tree, while men repose.

When first my casement is wide open thrown*
   At dawn, my eyes delighted on it rest;
   Sometimes, and most in winter,—on its crest
A gray baboon sits statue-like alone
   Watching the sunrise; while on lower boughs
His puny offspring leap about and play;
And far and near *kokilas** hail the day;
   And to their pastures wend our sleepy cows;
And in the shadow, on the broad tank cast
By that hoar tree, so beautiful and vast,
The water-lilies spring, like snow enmassed.

But not because of its magnificence
   Dear is the Casuarina to my soul:
   Beneath it we have played; though years may roll,
O sweet companions,* loved with love intense,
   For your sakes shall the tree be ever dear!
Blent with your images, it shall arise
In memory, till the hot tears blind mine eyes!
   What is that dirge-like murmur that I hear
Like the sea breaking on a shingle-beach?
It is the tree's lament, an eerie speech,
That haply to the unknown land may reach.

Unknown, yet well-known to the eye of faith!
   Ah, I have heard that wail far, far away
   In distant lands, by many a sheltered bay,
When slumbered in his cave the water-wraith
   And the waves gently kissed the classic shore
Of France or Italy, beneath the moon,
When earth lay trancéd in a dreamless swoon:
   And every time the music rose,—before
Mine inner vision rose a form sublime,
Thy form, O Tree, as in my happy prime
I saw thee, in my own loved native clime.

Therefore I fain would consecrate a lay
   Unto thy honour, Tree, beloved of those
   Who now in blessed sleep for aye repose,
Dearer than life to me, alas! were they!
Mayst thou be numbered when my days are done
With deathless trees—like those in Borrowdale,*
Under whose awful branches lingered pale
   'Fear, trembling Hope, and Death, the skeleton,
And Time the shadow;'* and though weak the verse
That would thy beauty fain, oh fain rehearse,
May Love defend thee from Oblivion's curse.

See also: Crawford; Naidu; Tagore.

JOHN SEELEY
(1834–1895)

These paragraphs from Seeley's history, The Expansion of England, *form the origin of that well-known description of British imperialism as having been accomplished in 'a fit of absence of mind'. Throughout the lecture series on which the book is based, Seeley argued from the premiss that history, in particular the period 1688–1815 covering the rise of British colonial power, offered object lessons for the present. As soon becomes apparent, his image of the empire is of the family of white colonies, with the anomalous attachment of an unfree India. (Unlike*

Hobson (q.v.), he was sure that the carefully controlled autocracy of the Raj would not have a deleterious influence on British democracy.) Seeley was in agreement with his fellow-historian J. A. Froude (q.v.) that Greater Britain would best function as an enlargement of the English state organized on federal lines. The key to imperial success, as he explains in the rest of the series, was responsibility and organization: the vastness of the empire was no excuse for slipshod administration. Seeley's book became popular as a kind of colonialist primer, remaining in print until 1956.

from *The Expansion of England* (1883)

[. . .] The English State then, in what direction and towards what goal has that been advancing? The words which jump to our lips in answer are Liberty, Democracy! They are words which want a great deal of defining. Liberty has of course been a leading characteristic of England as compared with continental countries, but in the main liberty is not so much an end to which we have been tending as a possession which we have long enjoyed. The struggles of the seventeenth century secured it—even if they did not first acquire it—for us. In later times there has been a movement towards something which is often called liberty, but not so correctly. We may, if we like, call it democracy; and I suppose the current opinion is that if any large tendency is discernible in the more recent part of English history, it is this tendency, by which first the middle class and then gradually the lower classes have been admitted to a share of influence in public affairs.

Discernible enough no doubt this tendency is, at least in the nineteenth century, for in the eighteenth century only the first beginnings of it can be traced. It strikes our attention most, because it has made for a long time past the staple of political talk and controversy. But history ought to look at things from a greater distance and more comprehensively. If we stand aloof a little and follow with our eyes the progress of the English State, the great governed society of English people, in recent centuries, we shall be much more struck by another change, which is not only far greater but even more conspicuous, though it has always been less discussed, partly because it proceeded more gradually, partly because it excited less opposition. I mean the simple obvious fact of the extension of the English name into other countries of the globe, the foundation of Greater Britain.

There is something very characteristic in the indifference which we show towards this mighty phenomenon of the diffusion of our race and the expansion of our state. We seem, as it were, to have conquered and peopled half the world in a fit of absence of mind. While we were doing it, that is in the eighteenth century, we did not allow it to affect our imaginations or in any degree to change our ways of thinking; nor have we even now ceased to think of ourselves as simply a race inhabiting an island off the northern coast of the Continent of Europe. We constantly betray by our modes of speech that we do not reckon our colonies as really belonging to us; thus if we are asked what the English population is, it does not occur to us to reckon-in the population of Canada and Australia. This fixed way of thinking has influenced our historians. It causes them, I think, to miss the true point of view in describing the eighteenth century. They make too much of the mere parliamentary wrangle and the agitations about liberty, in all which matters the eighteenth century of England was but a pale reflexion of the seventeenth. They do not perceive that in that century the history of England is not in England but in America and Asia. In like manner I believe that when we look at the present state of affairs, and still more at the future, we ought to beware of putting England alone in the foreground and suffering what we call the English possessions to escape our view in the background of the picture.

Let me describe with some exactness the change that has taken place. In the last years of Queen Elizabeth England had absolutely no possessions outside Europe, for all schemes of settlement, from that of Hore in Henry VIII's reign to those of Gilbert and Raleigh, had failed alike. Great Britain did not yet exist; Scotland was a separate kingdom, and in Ireland the English were but a colony in the midst of an alien population still in the tribal stage. With the accession of the Stuart family commenced at the same time two processes, one of which was brought to completion under the last Stuart, Queen Anne, while the other has continued without interruption ever since. Of these the first is the internal union of the three kingdoms, which, though technically it was not completed till much later, may be said to be substantially the work of the seventeenth century and the Stuart dynasty. The second was the creation of a still larger Britain comprehending vast possessions beyond the sea. This process began with the first Charter given to Virginia in 1606. It made a great advance in the seventeenth century; but not till the eighteenth did Greater Britain in its gigantic dimensions and with its vast politics first stand clearly before the world. Let us consider what this Greater Britain at the present day precisely is.

Excluding certain small possessions, which are chiefly of the nature of naval or military stations, it consists besides the United Kingdom of four great groups of territory, inhabited either chiefly or to a large extent by Englishmen and subject to the Crown, and a fifth great territory also subject to the Crown and ruled by English officials, but inhabited by a completely foreign race. The first four are the Dominion of Canada, the West Indian Islands, among which I include some territories on the continent of Central and Southern America, the mass of South African possessions of which Cape Colony is the most considerable, and fourthly the Australian group, to which, simply for convenience, I must here add New Zealand. The dependency is India.

Now what is the extent and value of these possessions? First let us look at their population, which, the territory being as yet newly settled, is in many cases thin. The Dominion of Canada with Newfoundland had in 1881 a population of rather more than four millions and a half, that is, about equal to the population of Sweden; the West Indian group rather more than a million and a half, about equal to the population at the same time of Greece; the South African group about a million and three quarters, but of these much less than a half are of European blood; the Australian group about three millions, rather more than the population of Switzerland. This makes a total of ten millions and three quarters, or about ten millions of English subjects of European and mainly English blood outside the British Islands.

The population of the great dependency India was nearly a hundred and ninety-eight millions, and the native states in India which look up to England as the paramount Power had about fifty-seven millions in addition. The total makes a population roughly equal to that of all Europe excluding Russia.

But of course it strikes us at once that this enormous Indian population does not make part of Greater Britain in the same sense as those ten millions of Englishmen who live outside of the British Islands. The latter are of our own blood, and are therefore united with us by the strongest tie. The former are of alien race and religion, and are bound to us only by the tie of conquest. It may be fairly questioned whether the possession of India does or ever can increase our power or our security, while there is no doubt that it vastly increases our dangers and responsibilities. Our colonial Empire stands on quite a different footing; it has some of the fundamental conditions of stability. There are in general three ties by which states are held together, community of race, community of religion, community of interest. By the first two our colonies are evidently bound to us, and this fact by itself makes the connexion strong. It will grow indissolubly firm if we come to recognise also that interest bids us maintain the connexion, and this conviction seems to gain ground. When we inquire then into the Greater Britain of the future we ought to think much more of our Colonial than of our Indian Empire.

This is an important consideration when we come to estimate the Empire not by population but by territorial area. Ten millions of Englishmen beyond the sea,—this is something; but it is absolutely nothing compared with what will ultimately, nay with what will speedily, be seen. For those millions are scattered over an enormous area, which fills up with a rapidity quite unlike the increase of population in England. That you may measure the importance of this consideration, I give you one fact. The density of population in Great Britain is two hundred and ninety-one to the square mile, in Canada it is not much more than one to the square mile. Suppose for a moment the Dominion of Canada peopled as fully as Great Britain, its population would actually be more than a thousand millions. That state of things is no doubt very remote, but an immense increase is not remote. In not much more than half a century the Englishmen beyond the sea—supposing the Empire to hold together—will be equal in number to the Englishmen at home, and the total will be much more than a hundred millions.

These figures may perhaps strike you as rather overwhelming than interesting. You may make it a question whether we ought to be glad of this vast increase of our race, whether it would not be better for us to advance morally and intellectually than in mere population and possessions, whether the great things have not for the most part been done by the small nations, and so on. But I do not quote these figures in order to gratify our national pride. I leave it an open question whether our increase is matter for exultation or for regret. It is not yet time to consider that. What is clear in the mean time is the immense importance of this increase. Good or bad, it is evidently the great fact of modern English history. And it would be the greatest mistake to imagine that it is a merely material fact, or that it carries no moral and intellectual consequences. People cannot change their abodes, pass from an island to a continent, from the 50th degree of north latitude to the tropics or the Southern Hemisphere, from an ancient community to a new colony, from vast manufacturing cities to sugar plantations, or to lonely sheepwalks in countries where aboriginal savage tribes still wander, without changing their ideas and habits and ways of thinking, nay without somewhat modifying in the course of a few generations their physical type. We know already that the Canadian and the Victorian are not quite like the Englishman; do we suppose then that in the next century, if the colonial population has become as numerous as that of the mother country, assuming that the connexion has been maintained and has become closer, England itself will not be very much modified and transformed? Whether good or bad then, the growth of Greater Britain is an event of enormous magnitude.

Evidently as regards the future it is the greatest event. But an event may be very great, and yet be so simple that there is not much to be said about it, that it has scarcely any history. It is thus that the great English Exodus is commonly regarded, as if it had happened in the most simple, inevitable manner, as if it were merely the unopposed occupation of empty countries by the nation which happened to have the greatest surplus population and the greatest maritime power. I shall show this to be a great mistake. I shall show that this Exodus makes a most ample and a most full and interesting chapter in English history. I shall venture to assert that during the eighteenth century it determines the whole course of affairs, that the main struggle of England from the time of Louis XIV to the time of Napoleon was for the possession of the New World, and that it is for want of perceiving this that most of us find that century of English history uninteresting.

The great central fact in this chapter of history is that we have had at different times two such Empires. So decided is the drift of our destiny towards the occupation of the New World that after we had created one Empire and lost it, a second grew up almost in our own despite. The figures I gave you refer exclusively to our second Empire, to that which we still possess. When I spoke of the ten millions of English subjects who live beyond the sea, I did not pause to mention that a hundred years ago we had another set of colonies which had already a population of three millions, that these colonies broke off from us and formed a federal state, of which the population has in a century multiplied more than sixteenfold, and is now equal to that of the mother country and its colonies taken together. It is an event of prodigious magnitude, not only that this Empire should have been lost to us, but that a new state, English in race and character, should have sprung up, and that this state should have grown in a century to be greater in population than every European state except Russia. But the loss we suffered in the secession of the American colonies has left in the English mind a doubt, a misgiving, which affects our whole forecast of the future of England.

For if this English Exodus has been the greatest English event of the eighteenth and nineteenth centuries, the greatest English question of the future must be, what is to become of our second Empire, and whether or no it may be expected to go the way of the first. In the solution of this question lies that moral which I said ought to result from the study of English history.

It is an old saying, to which Turgot* gave utterance a quarter of a century before the Declaration of Independence, 'Colonies are like fruits which cling to the tree only till they ripen.' He added, 'As soon as America can take care of herself, she will do what Carthage did.' What wonder that when this prediction was so signally fulfilled, the proposition from which it had been deduced rose, especially in the minds of the English, to the rank of a demonstrated principle! This no doubt is the reason why we have regarded the growth of a second Empire with very little interest or satisfaction. 'What matters,' we have said, 'its vastness or its rapid growth? It does not grow for us.' And to the notion that we cannot keep it we have added the notion that we need not wish to keep it, because, with that curious kind of optimistic fatalism to which historians are liable, the historians of our American war have generally felt bound to make out that the loss of our colonies was not only inevitable, but was even a fortunate thing for us.

Whether these views are sound, I do not inquire now. I merely point out that two alternatives are before us, and that the question, incomparably the greatest question which we can discuss, refers to the choice between them. The four groups of colonies may become four independent states, and in that case two of them, the Dominion of Canada and the West Indian group, will have to consider the question whether admission into the United States will not be better for them than independence. In any case the English name and English institutions will have a vast predominance in the New World, and the separation may be so managed that the mother-country may continue always to be regarded with friendly feelings. Such a separation would leave England on the same level as the states nearest to us on the Continent, populous, but less so than Germany and scarcely equal to France. But two states, Russia and the United States would be on an altogether higher scale of magnitude, Russia having at once, and the United States perhaps before very long, twice our population. Our trade too would be exposed to wholly new risks.

The other alternative is, that England may prove able to do what the United States does so easily, that is, hold together in a federal union countries very remote from each other. In that case England will take rank with Russia and the United States in the first rank of state, measured by population and area, and in a higher rank than the states of the Continent. We ought by no means to take for granted that this is desirable. Bigness is not necessarily greatness; if by remaining in the second rank of magnitude we can hold the first rank morally and intellectually, let us sacrifice mere material magnitude. But though we must not prejudge the question whether we ought to retain our Empire, we may fairly assume that it is desirable after due consideration to judge it. [. . .]

See also: Chamberlain; Curzon; Ruskin; Tennyson, 'Opening of the Indian and Colonial Exhibition'.

ISABELLA BIRD
(1831–1904)

Letter from Sungei Ujong, Malay Peninsula (1883)

SEMPANG POLICE STATION.
(At the junction of the Loboh-Chena, and Linggi rivers),
Territory of the Datu Klana of Sungei Ujong,* Malay
Peninsula.

Jan. 24. 1 P.M. Mercury, 87°.

We left Malacca at seven this morning in the small, unseaworthy,
untrustworthy, unrigged steam-launch *Moosmee*, and after crawling
for some hours at a speed of about five miles an hour along brown and
yellow shores with a broad, dark belt of palms above them, we left the
waveless, burning sea behind, and after a few miles of tortuous
steaming through the mangrove swamps of the Linggi river, landed
here to wait for sufficient water for the rest of our journey.

This is a promontory covered with coco-palms, bananas, and small
jungle growths. On either side are small rivers densely bordered by
mangrove swamps. The first sight of a real mangrove swamp is an
event. This *mangi-mangi* of the Malays (the *Rhizophera mangil* of
botanists) has no beauty. All along this coast within access of tidal
waters there is a belt of it many miles in breadth, dense, impenetrable, from forty to fifty feet high, as nearly level as may be, and of a
dark, dull green. At low water the mangroves are seen standing close
packed along the shallow and muddy shores on cradles or erections of
their own roots five or six feet high, but when these are covered at
high tide they appear to be growing out of the water. They send down
roots from their branches, and all too quickly cover a large space.
Crabs and other shellfish attach themselves to them, and aquatic
birds haunt their slimy shades. They form huge breeding grounds for
alligators and mosquitos, and usually for malarial fevers, but from the
latter the Peninsula is very free. The seeds germinate while still
attached to the branch. A long root pierces the covering and grows
rapidly downwards from the heavy end of the fruit, which arrangement secures that when the fruit falls off the root shall at once
become embedded in the mud. Nature has taken abundant trouble to

ensure the propagation of this tree, nearly worthless as timber. Strange to say, its fruit is sweet and eatable, and from its fermented juice wine can be made. The mangrove swamp is to me an evil mystery.

Behind, the jungle stretches out—who can say how far, for no European has ever penetrated it?—and out of it rise, jungle-covered, the Rumbow hills. The elephant, the rhinoceros, the royal tiger, the black panther, the boar, the leopard, and many other beasts, roam in its tangled, twilight depths, but in this fierce heat they must be all asleep in their lairs. The Argus-pheasant too, one of the loveliest birds of a region whose islands are the home of the Bird of Paradise, haunts the shade, and the shade alone. In the jungle too is the beautiful bantam fowl, the possible progenitor of all that useful race. The cobra, the python (?), the boa-constrictor, the viper, and at least fourteen other ophidians, are winding their loathsome and lissome forms through slimy jungle recesses; and large and small apes and monkeys, flying foxes, iguanas, lizards, peacocks, frogs, turtles, tortoises, alligators, besides tapirs, rarely seen, and the palandok or chevrotin,* the hog deer, the spotted deer, and the sambre, may not be far off. I think that this part of the country, intersected by small, shallow, muddy rivers, running up through slimy mangrove swamps into a vast and impenetrable jungle, must be like many parts of Western Africa.

One cannot walk three hundred yards from this station, for there are no tracks. We are beyond the little territory of Malacca, but this bit of land was ceded to England after the 'Malay disturbances' in 1875, and on it has been placed the Sempang police station, a four-roomed shelter, roofed with *attap*, a thatch made of the fronds of the *nipah* palm, supported on high posts,—an idea perhaps borrowed from the mangrove,—and reached by a ladder. In this four Malay policemen and a corporal have dwelt for three years to keep down piracy. 'Piracy,' by which these rivers were said to be infested, is a very ugly word, suggestive of ugly deeds, bloody attacks, black flags, and no quarter; but here it meant, in our use of the word at least, a particular mode of raising revenue, and no boat could go up or down the Linggi without paying black mail to one or more river rajahs.

Our wretched little launch, moored to a coco-palm, flies a blue ensign, and the Malay policemen wear an imperial crown upon their caps,—both representing somewhat touchingly in this equatorial jungle the might of the small island lying far off amidst the fogs of the northern seas, and in this instance at least not her might only, but the security and justice of her rule.*

Two or three canoes hollowed out of tree trunks have gone up and down the river since we landed, each of the inward bound being paddled by four men, who ply their paddles facing forwards, which always has an aboriginal look, those going down being propelled by single, square sails made of very coarse matting. It is very hot and silent. The only sounds are the rustle of the palm fronds and the sharp din of the cicada, abruptly ceasing at intervals.

In this primitive police station the notices are in both Tamil and Arabic, but the reports are written in Arabic only. Soon after we sat down to drink fresh coco-nut milk, the great beverage of the country, a Malay bounded up the ladder and passed through us with the most rapid and feline movements I have ever seen in a man. His large, prominent eyes were fixed, tiger-like, on a rifle which hung on the wall, at which he darted, clutched it, and, with a feline leap, sprang through us again. I have heard much of *amok** running lately, and have even seen the two-pronged fork which was used for pinning a desperate *amok* runner to the wall, so that for a second I thought that this Malay was 'running amuck;' but he ran down towards Mr Hayward, our escort, and I ran after him, just in time to see a large alligator plunge from the bank into the water. Mr Hayward took a steady aim at the remaining one, and hit him, when he sprang partly up as if badly wounded, and then plunged into the river after his companion, staining the muddy water with his blood for some distance.

Police Station, Permatang Pasir. Sungei Ujong, 5 P.M.—We are now in a native state, in the territory of the friendly Datu Klana, Syed Abdulrahman,* and the policemen wear on their caps not an imperial crown, but a crescent, with a star between its horns.

This is a far more adventurous expedition than we expected. Things are not going altogether as straight as could be desired, considering that we have the Governor's daughters* with us, who, besides being very precious, are utterly unseasoned and inexperienced travellers, quite unfit for 'roughing it.' For one thing, it turns out to be an absolute necessity for us to be out all night, which I am very sorry for, as one of the girls is suffering from the effects of exposure to the intense heat of the sun.

We left Sempang at two, the Misses Shaw reeling rather than walking to the launch. I cannot imagine what the mercury was in the sun, but the copper sheathing of the gunwale was too hot to be touched. Above Sempang the river narrows and shoals rapidly, and we had to crawl, taking soundings incessantly, and occasionally dragging heavily over mud banks. We saw a large alligator sleeping in the sun in the mud, with a mouth, I should think, a third of the length of his body; and as he did not wake as we panted past him, a rifle was loaded and we backed up close to him; but Babu,* who had the weapon, and had looked quite swaggering and belligerent so long as it was unloaded, was too frightened to fire, the saurian awoke, and his hideous form and corrugated hide plunged into the water so close under the stern as to splash us. After this alligators were so common, singly or in groups or in families, that they ceased to be exciting. It is difficult for anything to produce continuous excitement under this fierce sun, and conversation, which had been flagging before noon, ceased altogether. It was awfully hot in the launch, between fire and boiler heat and solar fury. I tried to keep cool by thinking of Mull, and powdery snow and frosty stars, but it would not do. It was a solemn afternoon, as the white, unwinking sun looked down upon our silent party, on the narrow turbid river, silent too, except for the occasional plunge of an alligator or other water monster,—on mangrove swamps and *nipah* palms dense along the river side, on the blue gleam of countless kingfishers, on slimy creeks arched over to within a few feet of their surface by grand trees with festoons of lianas, on an infinite variety of foliage, on an abundance of slender shafted palms, on great fruits brilliantly coloured, on wonderful flowers on the trees, on the *hoya carnosa* and other waxen-leaved trailers matting the forest together and hanging down in great festoons, the fiery tropic sun-blaze stimulating all this over production into perennial activity, and vivifying the very mud itself.

Occasionally we passed a canoe with a 'savage' crouching in it fishing, but saw no other trace of man, till an hour ago we came upon large coco groves, a considerable clearing in the jungle, and a very large Malayan-Chinese village with mosques, one on either side of the river, houses built on platforms over the water, large and small native boats covered and thatched with *attap*, roofed platforms on stilts answering the purpose of piers, bathing-houses on stilts carefully secluded, all forming the (relatively) important village of Permatang Pasir.

Up to this time we had expected to find perfectly smooth sailing, as a runner was sent from Malacca to the Resident yesterday. We supposed that we should be carried in chairs six miles through the jungle to a point where a gharrie* could meet us, and that we should reach the Residency by nine to-night at the latest. On arriving at Sempang Mr Hayward had sent a canoe to this place with instructions to send another runner to the Resident; but

'The best laid schemes of men and mice gang aft agee.'*

The messenger seemed to have served no other purpose than to assemble the whole male population of Permatang Pasir on the shore—a sombre-faced throng, with an aloofness of manner and expression far from pleasing. The thatched piers were crowded with turbaned Mussulmen in their *bajus* or short jackets, full white trousers, and red *sarongs* or pleatless kilts—the boys dressed in silver fig-leaves and silver bangles only. All looked at our unveiled faces silently, and, as I thought, disapprovingly.

After being hauled up the pier with great difficulty, owing to the lowness of the water, we were met by two of the Datu Klana's policemen, who threw cold water on the idea of our getting on at all unless Captain Murray sent for us. These men escorted us to this police station,—a long walk through a lane of much decorated shops, exclusively Chinese, succeeded by a lane of detached Malay houses, each standing in its own fenced and neatly-sanded compound under the shade of coco-palms and bananas. The village paths are carefully sanded and very clean. We emerged upon the neatly sanded open space on which this barrack stands, glad to obtain shelter, for the sun is still fierce. It is a genuine Malay house on stilts; but where there should be an approach of eight steps there is only a steep ladder of three round rungs, up which it is not easy to climb in boots! There is a deep veranda under an *attap* roof of steep slope, and at either end a low bed for a constable, with the usual very hard, circular Malay bolsters, with red silk ends, ornamented with gold and silk embroidery.

Besides this verandah there is only a sort of inner room, with just space enough for a table and four chairs. The wall is hung with rifles, *krises*,* and handcuffs, with which a 'Sam Slick' clock,* an engraving from the *Graphic*, and some curious Turkish pictures of Stamboul, are oddly mixed up. Babu, the Hadji, having recovered from a sulk into which he fell in consequence of Mr Hayward having quizzed him for cowardice about an alligator, has made everything (our very limited everything) quite comfortable, and, with as imposing an air as if we were in Government House, asks us when we will have dinner! One policeman has brought us fresh coco-nut milk, another sits outside pulling a small punkah, and two more have mounted guard over us. This stilted house is the barrack of eleven Malay constables. Under it are four guns of light calibre, mounted on carriages, and outside is a gong on which the policemen beat the hours.

At the river we were told that the natives would not go up the shallow rapid stream by night, and now the corporal says that no man will carry us through the jungle; that trees are lying across the track; that there are dangerous swamp holes; that though the tigers which infest the jungle never attack a party, we might chance to see their glaring eyeballs; that even if men could be bribed to undertake to carry us, they would fall with us, or put us down and run away, for no better reason than that they caught sight of the 'spectre bird' (the owl); and he adds, with a gallantry remarkable in a Mohammedan, that he should not care about Mr Hayward, but 'it would not do for the ladies.' So we are apparently stuck fast, the chief cause for anxiety and embarrassment being that the youngest Miss Shaw is lying huddled up and shivering on one of the beds, completely prostrated by a violent sick headache brought on by the heat of the sun in the launch. She declares that she cannot move; but our experienced escort, who much fears bilious fever for her, is resolved that she shall as soon as any means of transit can be procured. Heretofore I have always travelled 'without encumbrance.' Is it treasonable to feel at this moment that these fair girls are one?

See also: Barker; Clifford; Kingsley; Livingstone and Stanley.

H. RIDER HAGGARD
(1856–1925)

Using the device of an ancient map, 'The Legend of Solomon's Mines', chapter 2 of King Solomon's Mines, *traces the legendary and symbolic background of this most iconic of Victorian adventure tales. The opening chapter has brought together the three central characters, Sir Henry Curtis, a gentleman, Captain John Good, a retired Royal Naval officer, and the big-game hunter and narrator of the tale, Allan Quatermain. On board ship from Cape Town to Durban, Sir Henry has explained his mission to find his estranged brother, George, or 'Neville', who was last sighted, by Quatermain himself, heading in the direction of 'Suliman's country'. In Quatermain's story of what he knows of this fatal country and its fabulous wealth, Haggard gathers together the central heady ingredients of his mythically charged romance: the quest for long-buried treasure; the African land as prone female body; blacks 'lapsed into the darkest barbarism'; the death and disappearance of other white (but non-English) colonial adventurers; and the contemporary, racially skewed rumour of King Solomon's Ophir mines, the fabled source of his riches, being located somewhere in the heart of Africa, and having been built by whites.*

The Legend of Solomon's Mines (1885)

'What was it that you heard about my brother's journey at Bamangwato?'* said Sir Henry, as I paused to fill my pipe before answering Captain Good.

'I heard this,' I answered, 'and I have never mentioned it to a soul till to-day. I heard that he was starting for Solomon's Mines.'*

'Solomon's Mines!' ejaculated both my hearers at once. 'Where are they?'

'I don't know,' I said; 'I know where they are said to be. I once saw the peaks of the mountains that border them, but there was a hundred and thirty miles of desert between me and them, and I am not aware that any white man ever got across it save one. But perhaps the best thing I can do is to tell you the legend of Solomon's Mines as I know it, you passing your word not to reveal anything I tell you without my permission. Do you agree to that? I have my reasons for asking it.'

Sir Henry nodded, and Captain Good replied, 'Certainly, certainly.'

'Well,' I began, 'as you may guess, in a general way, elephant hunters are a rough set of men, and don't trouble themselves with much beyond the facts of life and the ways of Kafirs.* But here and there you meet a man who takes the trouble to collect traditions from the natives, and tries to make out a little piece of the history of this dark land. It was such a man as this who first told me the legend of Solomon's Mines, now a matter of nearly thirty years ago. It was when I was on my first elephant hunt in the Matabele country. His name was Evans, and he was killed next year, poor fellow, by a wounded buffalo, and lies buried near the Zambesi Falls. I was telling Evans one night, I remember, of some wonderful workings I had found whilst hunting koodoo* and eland in what is now the Lydenburg district of the Transvaal. I see they have come across these workings again lately in prospecting for gold, but I knew of them years ago. There is a great wide waggon road cut out of the solid rock, and leading to the mouth of the working or gallery. Inside the mouth of this gallery are stacks of gold quartz piled up ready for crushing, which shows that the workers, whoever they were, must have left in a hurry, and about twenty paces in the gallery is built across, and a beautiful bit of masonry it is.

'"Ay," said Evans, "but I will tell you a queerer thing than that;" and he went on to tell me how he had found in the far interior a ruined city, which he believed to be the Ophir of the Bible,* and, by the way, other more learned men have said the same long since poor Evans' time. I was, I remember, listening open-eared to all these wonders, for I was young at the time, and this story of an ancient civilisation and of the treasure which those old Jewish or Phœnician adventurers used to extract from a country long since lapsed into the darkest barbarism took a great hold upon my imagination, when suddenly he said to me, "Lad, did you ever hear of the Suliman Mountains up to the north-west of the Mashukulumbwe country?" I told him I never had. "Ah, well," he said, "that was where Solomon really had his mines, his diamond mines, I mean."

'"How do you know that?" I asked.

'"Know it; why what is 'Suliman' but a corruption of Solomon!¹ and, besides, an old Isanusi* (witch doctor) up in the Manica country told me all about it. She said that the people who lived across those mountains were a branch of the Zulus, speaking a dialect of Zulu, but finer and bigger men even; that there lived among them great wizards, who had learnt their art from white men when 'all the world

---

¹ Suliman is the Arabic form of Solomon.—EDITOR.

was dark,' and who had the secret of a wonderful mine of 'bright stones.'"

'Well, I laughed at this story at the time, though it interested me, for the diamond fields were not discovered then, and poor Evans went off and got killed, and for twenty years I never thought any more of the matter. But just twenty years afterwards—and that is a long time, gentlemen, an elephant hunter does not often live for twenty years at his business—I heard something more definite about Suliman's Mountains and the country which lies beyond it. I was up beyond the Manica country at a place called Sitanda's Kraal, and a miserable place it was, for one could get nothing to eat there, and there was but little game about. I had an attack of fever, and was in a bad way generally, when one day a Portugee arrived with a single companion—a half-breed. Now I know your Delagoa Portugee* well. There is no greater devil unhung in a general way, battening as he does upon human agony and flesh in the shape of slaves. But this was quite a different type of man to the low fellows I had been accustomed to meet; he reminded me more of the polite dons I have read about. He was tall and thin, with large dark eyes and curling grey moustachios. We talked together a little, for he could speak broken English, and I understood a little Portugee, and he told me that his name was José Silvestre, and that he had a place near Delagoa Bay; and when he went on next day with his half-breed companion, he said, "Good-bye," taking off his hat quite in the old style. "Good-bye, senor," he said; "if ever we meet again I shall be the richest man in the world, and I will remember you." I laughed a little—I was too weak to laugh much—and watched him strike out for the great desert to the west, wondering if he was mad, or what he thought he was going to find there.

'A week passed, and I got the better of my fever. One evening I was sitting on the ground in front of the little tent I had with me, chewing the last leg of a miserable fowl I had bought from a native for a bit of cloth worth twenty fowls, and staring at the hot red sun sinking down into the desert, when suddenly I saw a figure, apparently that of a European, for it wore a coat, on the slope of the rising ground opposite to me, about three hundred yards away. The figure crept along on its hands and knees, then it got up and staggered along a few yards on its legs, only to fall and crawl along again. Seeing that it must be somebody in distress, I sent one of my hunters to help him, and presently he arrived, and who do you suppose it turned out to be?'

'José Silvestre, of course,' said Captain Good.

'Yes, José Silvestre, or rather his skeleton and a little skin. His face was bright yellow with bilious fever, and his large, dark eyes stood nearly out of his head, for all his flesh had gone. There was nothing but yellow parchment-like skin, white hair, and the gaunt bones sticking up beneath.

'"Water! for the sake of Christ, water!" he moaned. I saw that his lips were cracked, and his tongue, which protruded between them, swollen and blackish.

'I gave him water with a little milk in it, and he drank it in great gulps, two quarts or more, without stopping. I would not let him have any more. Then the fever took him again, and he fell down and began to rave about Suliman's Mountains, and the diamonds, and the desert. I took him into the tent and did what I could for him, which was little enough; but I saw how it must end. About eleven o'clock he got quieter, and I lay down for a little rest and went to sleep. At dawn I woke again, and saw him in the half light sitting up, a strange, gaunt form, and gazing out towards the desert. Presently the first ray of the sun shot right across the wide plain before us till it reached the far-away crest of one of the tallest of the Suliman Mountains more than a hundred miles away.

'"There it is!" cried the dying man in Portuguese, stretching out his long, thin arm, "but I shall never reach it, never. No one will ever reach it!"

'Suddenly he paused, and seemed to take a resolution. "Friend," he said, turning towards me, "are you there? My eyes grow dark."

'"Yes," I said; "yes, lie down now, and rest."

'"Ay," he answered, "I shall rest soon, I have time to rest—all eternity. Listen, I am dying! You have been good to me. I will give you the paper. Perhaps you will get there if you can live through the desert, which has killed my poor servant and me."

'Then he groped in his shirt and brought out what I thought was a Boer tobacco pouch of the skin of the Swart-vet-pens (sable antelope). It was fastened with a little strip of hide, what we call a rimpi,* and this he tried to untie, but could not. He handed it to me. "Untie it," he said. I did so, and extracted a bit of torn yellow linen, on which something was written in rusty letters. Inside was a paper.

'Then he went on feebly, for he was growing weak: "The paper has it all, that is on the rag. It took me years to read. Listen: my ancestor, a political refugee from Lisbon, and one of the first Portuguese who landed on these shores, wrote that when he was dying on those mountains which no white foot ever pressed before or since. His name was José da Silvestra, and he lived three hundred years ago. His slave, who waited for him on this side the mountains, found him dead, and brought the writing home to Delagoa. It has been in the family ever since, but none have cared to read it till at last I did. And I have lost my life over it, but another may succeed, and become the richest man in the world—the richest man in the world. Only give it to no one; go yourself!" Then he began to wander again, and in an hour it was all over.

'God rest him! he died very quietly, and I buried him deep, with big boulders on his breast; so I do not think that the jackals can have dug him up. And then I came away.'

'Ay, but the document,' said Sir Henry, in a tone of deep interest.

'Yes, the document; what was in it?' added the captain.

'Well, gentlemen, if you like I will tell you. I have never showed it to anybody yet except my dear wife, who is dead, and she thought it was all nonsense, and a drunken old Portuguese trader who translated it for me, and had forgotten all about it next morning. The original rag is at my home in Durban, together with poor Dom José's translation, but I have the English rendering in my pocket-book, and a fac-simile of the map, if it can be called a map. Here it is.'

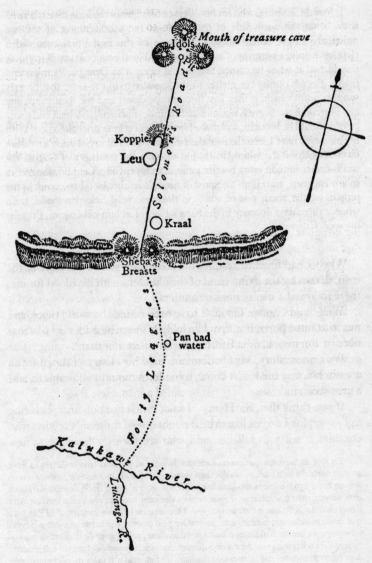

Idols **Mouth of treasure cave**

Pit

Solomon's Road

Koppie

Leu

Kraal

Sheba's
Breasts

Forty Leagues

**Pan bad
water**

Kalukawe River

Lukanga R.

MAP.

'I, José da Silvestra, who am now dying of hunger in the little cave where no snow is on the north side of the nipple of the southernmost of the two mountains I have named Sheba's Breasts, write this in the year 1590 with a cleft bone upon a remnant of my raiment, my blood being the ink. If my slave should find it when he comes, and should bring it to Delagoa, let my friend (name illegible) bring the matter to the knowledge of the king, that he may send an army which, if they live through the desert and the mountains, and can overcome the brave Kukuanes and their devilish arts, to which end many priests should be brought, will make him the richest king since Solomon. With my own eyes have I seen the countless diamonds stored in Solomon's treasure chamber behind the white Death; but through the treachery of Gagool the witch-finder I might bring nought away, scarcely my life. Let him who comes follow the map, and climb the snow of Sheba's left breast till he comes to the nipple, on the north side of which is the great road Solomon made, from whence three days' journey to the King's Place. Let him kill Gagool. Pray for my soul. Farewell.

'José da Silvestra.'[1]

When I had finished reading the above and shewn the copy of the map, drawn by the dying hand of the old Dom with his blood for ink, there followed a silence of astonishment.

'Well,' said Captain Good, 'I have been round the world twice, and put in at most ports, but may I be hung if I ever heard a yarn like that out of a story book, or in it either, for the matter of that.'

'It's a queer story, Mr Quatermain,' said Sir Henry. 'I suppose you are not hoaxing us? It is, I know, sometimes thought allowable to take a greenhorn in.'

'If you think that, Sir Henry,' I said, much put out, and pocketing my paper, for I do not like to be thought one of those silly fellows who consider it witty to tell lies, and who are for ever boasting to new

---

[1] Eu José da Silvestra que estou morrendo de fome ná pequena cova onde não ha neve ao lado norte do bico mais ao sul das duas montanhas que chamei seio de Sheba; escrevo isto no anno 1590; escrevo isto com um pedaço d' ôsso n' um farrapo de minha roupa e com sangue meu por tinta; se o meu escravo dér com isto quando venha as levar para Lourenzo Marquez, que o meu amigo (——) leve a cousa ao conhecimento d' El Rei, para que possa mandar um exercito que, se desfiler pelo deserto e pelas montanhas e mesmo sobrepujar os bravos Kukuanes e suas artes diabolicas, pelo que se deviam trazer muitos padres Fara o Rei mais rico depois de Salomão. Com meus proprios olhos vé os di amantes sem conto guardados nas camaras do thesouro de Salomão a traz da morte branca, mas pela traição de Gagoal a feiticeira achadora, nada poderia levar, e apenas a minha vida. Quem vier siga o mappa e trepe pela neve de Sheba peito à esquerda até chegar ao bico, do lado norte do qual está a grande estrada do Salomão por elle feita, donde ha tres dias de jornada até ao Palacio do Rei. Mate Gagoal. Reze por minha alma. Adeos.

José da Silvestra.

comers of extraordinary hunting adventures which never happened, 'why there is an end of the matter,' and I rose to go.

Sir Henry laid his large hand upon my shoulder. 'Sit down, Mr Quatermain,' he said, 'I beg your pardon; I see very well you do not wish to deceive us, but the story sounded so extraordinary that I could hardly believe it.'

'You shall see the original map and writing when we reach Durban,' I said, somewhat mollified, for really when I came to consider the matter it was scarcely wonderful that he should doubt my good faith. 'But I have not told you about your brother. I knew the man Jim who was with him. He was a Bechuana by birth, a good hunter, and for a native a very clever man. The morning Mr Neville was starting, I saw Jim standing by my waggon and cutting up tobacco on the disselboom.*

'"Jim," said I, "where are you off to this trip? Is it elephants?"

'"No, Baas," he answered, "we are after something worth more than ivory."

'"And what might that be?" I said, for I was curious. "Is it gold?"

'"No, Baas, something worth more than gold," and he grinned.

'I did not ask any more questions, for I did not like to lower my dignity by seeming curious, but I was puzzled. Presently Jim finished cutting his tobacco.

'"Baas," said he.

'I took no notice.

'"Baas," said he again.

'"Eh, boy, what is it?" said I.

'"Baas, we are going after diamonds."

'"Diamonds! why, then, you are going in the wrong direction; you should head for the Fields."

'"Baas, have you ever heard of Suliman's Berg?" (Solomon's Mountains).

'"Ay!"

'"Have you ever heard of the diamonds there?"

'"I have heard a foolish story, Jim."

'"It is no story, Baas. I once knew a woman who came from there, and got to Natal with her child, she told me:—she is dead now."

'"Your master will feed the aasvogels (vultures), Jim, if he tries to reach Suliman's country, and so will you if they can get any pickings off your worthless old carcass," said I.

'He grinned. "Mayhap, Baas. Man must die; I'd rather like to try a new country myself; the elephants are getting worked out about here."

'"Ah! my boy," I said, "you wait till the 'pale old man' (death) gets a grip of your yellow throat, and then we'll hear what sort of a tune you sing."

'Half an hour after that I saw Neville's waggon move off. Presently Jim came running back. "Goodbye, Baas," he said. "I didn't like to start without bidding you good-bye, for I daresay you are right, and we shall never come back again."

'"Is your master really going to Suliman's Berg, Jim, or are you lying?"

'"No," says he; "he is going. He told me he was bound to make his fortune somehow, or try to; so he might as well try the diamonds."

'"Oh!" said I; "wait a bit, Jim; will you take a note to your master, Jim, and promise not to give it to him till you reach Inyati?" (which was some hundred miles off).

'"Yes," said he.

'So I took a scrap of paper, and wrote on it, "Let him who comes . . . climb the snow of Sheba's left breast, till he comes to the nipple, on the north side of which is Solomon's great road."

'"Now, Jim," I said, "when you give this to your master, tell him he had better follow the advice implicitly. You are not to give it to him now, because I don't want him back asking me questions which I won't answer. Now be off, you idle fellow, the waggon is nearly out of sight."

'Jim took the note and went, and that is all I know about your brother, Sir Henry; but I am much afraid——'

'Mr Quatermain,' said Sir Henry, 'I am going to look for my brother; I am going to trace him to Suliman's Mountains, and over them if necessary, till I find him, or till I know that he is dead. Will you come with me?'

I am, as I think I have said, a cautious man, indeed a timid one, and I shrunk from such an idea. It seemed to me that to start on such a journey would be to go to certain death, and putting other things aside, as I had a son to support, I could not afford to die just then.

'No, thank you, Sir Henry, I think I had rather not,' I answered. 'I am too old for wild-goose chases of that sort, and we should only end up like my poor friend Silvestre. I have a son dependent on me, so cannot afford to risk my life.'

Both Sir Henry and Captain Good looked very disappointed.

'Mr Quatermain,' said the former, 'I am well off, and I am bent upon this business. You may put the remuneration for your services at whatever figure you like in reason, and it shall be paid over to you before we start. Moreover, I will, before we start, arrange that in the event of anything happening to us or to you, that your son shall be suitably provided for. You will see from this how necessary I think your presence. Also if by any chance we should reach this place, and find diamonds, they shall belong to you and Good equally. I do not want them. But of course the chance is as good as nothing, though the same thing would apply to any ivory we might get. You may pretty well make your own terms with me, Mr Quatermain; and of course I shall pay all expenses.'

'Sir Henry,' said I, 'this is the most liberal offer I ever had, and one not to be sneezed at by a poor hunter and trader. But the job is the biggest I ever came across, and I must take time to think it over. I will give you my answer before we get to Durban.'

'Very good,' answered Sir Henry, and then I said good-night and turned in, and dreamt about poor long-dead Silvestre and the diamonds.

See also: Conrad; Henty; Kingsley; Livingstone and Stanley.

SARA JEANNETTE DUNCAN
(1861–1922)

Colonials and Literature (1886)

We are still an eminently unliterary people.

Another Canadian summer has waxed and waned; mysterious in our forests, idyllic in our gardens, ineffably gracious upon our mountains. Another year of our national existence has rounded into the golden fulness of its harvest time. The yellow leaves of another September are blowing about our streets; since last we watched their harlequin dance to dusty death a cycle has come and gone. And still the exercise of hope and faith—charity we never had—continue to constitute the sum of our literary endeavour. We are conscious of not having been born in time to produce an epic poet or a dramatist; but still in vain do we scan the west for the lyrist, the east for the novelist whose appearing we may not unreasonably expect. Our bard is still loath to leave his Olympian pleasures; our artisan in fiction is busy with the human product of some other sphere.

And we look blankly at each other at every new and vain adjustment of the telescope to the barren literary horizon, and question 'Why?' And our American cousins with an indifferent wonder, and a curious glance at our census returns, make the same interrogatory; whereupon one of them tarries in Montreal for three days, ascertains, and prints in *Harper's Magazine* that it is our arctic temperature! And in England, if our sterile national library excites any comment at all, it is only a semi-contemptuous opinion that it is all that might be expected of 'colonials.'

Mr Warner's idea that the Canadian climate reduces the Canadian brain to a condition of torpor during the six months of the year may be dismissed with something of the irritation which it inspired in every Canadian who read it, that a writer who observes so keenly in his own country could be led to such an absurd and superficial conclusion in ours. One would naturally suppose that climatic influences which produce the bodily results to be found in the average Canadian, at least conduce toward giving him an active mind as well. Physically, Canadians compare with Americans to the great disadvantage of the latter; that they do not intellectually, alas! is not the fault of the climate.

Nor can we place the slightest responsibility for our literary short-comings upon our educational system. On the contrary, our colleges and public schools are our pride and glory. We point boastfully to the opportunities for intellectual elevation Ontario offers to the children of her navvies and farm labourers; and the ease with which Canadian graduates obtain all sorts of American degrees testifies to the thoroughness of our university training. So great indeed are our facilities for education that our farm lands lie untilled while our offices are filled to unprofitable repletion, and grave protest is arising in many quarters against the State's present liberal abetment of this false adjustment of national energy to national needs. Clearly, Nature and the Hon. G. W. Ross can do no more for us. We are a well-developed and well-educated people; but we do not write books.

'No, for we are not rich enough,' you say. 'The cultivation of letters demands wealth and a leisure class. We have a professional market in view for our hard-bought college training. We cannot afford to offer it up in unremunerative libations to the muses. We choose between the rustic homespun and the academic bombasin, but there the alternative ends. It is hard work thenceforward in either case. For Canadians to "sport with Amaryllis in the shade, or with the tangles of Neraea's hair"* is an idyllic occupation which, for financial reasons, must be sternly ignored.'

This is a comfortable way of relegating the responsibility for our literary inactivity to an economic dispensation of an overruling Providence which finds favour with a great many people. The disabilities of poverty are so easy to assume! But the theory is too plausible to be tenable. A wealthy public is necessary perhaps to the existence of authors who shall also be capitalists. A leisure class is a valuable stimulus to literary production. But money and the moneyed can neither command nor forbid the divine afflatus. The literary work produced solely by hope of gain is not much of an honour to any country. While authorship is a profession with pecuniary rewards like any other, those who are truly called to it obey a law far higher than that of demand and supply. Genius has always worked in poverty and obscurity; but we never find it withdrawing from its divinely appointed labour, and taking to law or merchandise on that account. When the great Canadian *litterateur* recognises himself he will not pause to weigh the possibilities of Canada's literary market before he writes the novel or the poem that is to redeem our literary reputation. Let genius be declared amongst us, and the market may be relied upon to adjust itself to the marvellous circumstance, for a great deal of the talk of Canadian poverty is the veriest nonsense. Riches are relative. We have no bonanza kings; but our railroad magnates are comfortably, not to say luxuriously, housed and horsed and apparelled. We work hard, but the soil is grateful; we are not compelled to struggle for existence. The privations of our Loyalist forefathers do not survive in us. We are well fed, well clad, well read. Why should we not buy our own books!

We would buy them if they were written. That they are not written is partly our own fault and partly that of circumstances. We cannot compel the divine afflatus; but we can place ourselves in an attitude to receive that psychical subtlety should the gods deign to bestow it upon us. But the Olympians, bending Canada-ward, hear no prayer for their great guerdons. We are indifferent; we go about our business and boast of the practical nature of our aspirations; we have neither time nor the inclination for star-gazing, we say. The Province of Ontario is one great camp of the Philistines.

Apart from the necessarily untrustworthy testimony of one's own more or less limited acquaintance, there is but one proof of this—the newspapers; and in a free and enlightened country there is no better exponent of the character of the people than the character of its press. The influence of the daily newspaper is not greater than the influence of public opinion upon the daily newspaper. In a very great measure we dictate what manner of editorial we shall take with our coffee; and either of our great morning dailies is eloquent of our tastes. Politics and vituperation, temperance and vituperation,- religion and vituperation; these three dietetic articles, the vituperative sauce invariably accompanying, form the exclusive journalistic pabulum of three-quarters of the people of Ontario. No social topics of other than a merely local interest, no scientific, artistic, or literary discussions, no broad consideration of matters of national interest—nothing but perpetual jeering, misconstruction, and misrepresentation for party ends of matters within an almost inconceivably narrow range.

'Why do you print no book reviews?' I asked the editor of a leading journal recently.

'People don't care about them, and it interfered with advertising,' was his truly Philistinish response. And the first reason must have a certain amount of truth in it; for if it were not so, public spirit would never tolerate the withholding of such matter for the contemptible—in this connection—consideration of 'advertising.' Our French compatriots have not this spirit. But they have their Frechette and their Garneau.*

A spirit of depreciation of such faint stirrings of literary life as we have amongst us at present has often been remarked in Canadians, a tendency to nip forth-putting buds by contemptuous comparison with the full blown production of other lands, where conditions are more favourable to literary efflorescence. This is a distinctly colonial trait; and in our character as colonists we find the root of all our sins of omission in letters. 'In the political life of a colony,' writes one of us in the New York *Critic*, 'there is nothing to fire the imagination, nothing to arouse enthusiasm, nothing to appeal to national pride.' Our enforced political humility is the distinguishing characteristic of every phase of our national life. We are ignored, and we ignore ourselves. A nation's development is like a plant's, unattractive under ground. So long as Canada remains in political obscurity, content to thrive only at the roots, so long will the leaves and blossoms of art and literature be scanty and stunted products of our national energy. We are swayed by no patriotic sentiment that might unite our diverse provincial interests in the common cause of our country. Our politics are a game of grab. At stated intervals our school children sing with great gusto, 'The Maple Leaf Forever!' but before reaching man's estate, they discover that it is only the provincial variety of maple leaf vegetation that they may reasonably be expected to toast. Even civil bloodshed in Canada has no dignity, but takes the form of inter-provincial squabbling. A national literature cannot be looked for as an outcome of anything less than a complete national existence.

Of course we have done something since we received our present imperfect autonomy in 1867. We have our historians, our essayists, and our chirping poets.* And in due time, we are told, if we have but faith and patience, Canadian literature will shine as a star in the firmament. Meanwhile, however, we are uncomfortably reminded of that ancient and undisputed truism, 'Faith without works is dead.'*

See also: 1880s and 1890s Canadian poetry; Clarke; Fairbridge; Leacock; Stephens.

RUDYARD KIPLING
(1865–1936)

His Chance in Life (1888)

Then a pile of heads he laid—
Thirty thousands heaped on high—
All to please the Kafir* maid,
Where the Oxus ripples by.
Grimly spake Atulla Khan:–
'Love hath made this thing a Man.'

Oatta's Story.

If you go straight away from Levées and Government House Lists, past Trades' Balls—far beyond everything and everybody you ever knew in your respectable life—you cross, in time, the Borderline where the last drop of White blood ends and the full tide of Black sets in. It would be easier to talk to a new-made Duchess on the spur of the moment than to the Borderline folk without violating some of their conventions or hurting their feelings. The Black and the White mix very quaintly in their ways. Sometimes the White shows in spurts of fierce, childish pride—which is Pride of Race run crooked —and sometimes the Black in still fiercer abasement and humility, half-heathenish customs and strange, unaccountable impulses to crime. One of these days, this people—understand they are far lower than the class whence Derozio,* the man who imitated Byron, sprung—will turn out a writer or a poet; and then we shall know how they live and what they feel. In the meantime, any stories about them cannot be absolutely correct in fact or inference.

Miss Vezzis came from across the Borderline to look after some children who belonged to a lady until a regularly ordained nurse could come out. The lady said Miss Vezzis was a bad, dirty nurse and inattentive. It never struck her that Miss Vezzis had her own life to lead and her own affairs to worry over, or that these affairs were the most important things in the world to Miss Vezzis. Very few mistresses admit this sort of reasoning. Miss Vezzis was as black as a boot, and, to our standard of taste, hideously ugly. She wore cotton-print gowns and bulgy shoes; and when she lost her temper with the children, she abused them in the language of the Borderline—which is part English, part Portuguese, and part Native. She was not attractive; but she had her pride, and she preferred being called 'Miss Vezzis.'

Every Sunday she dressed herself wonderfully and went to see her Mamma, who lived, for the most part, on an old cane chair in a greasy *tussur*-silk* dressing-gown and a big rabbit-warren of a house full of Vezzises, Pereiras, Ribieras, Lisboas, and Gonsalveses, and a floating population of loafers; besides fragments of the day's market, garlic, stale incense, clothes thrown on the floor, petticoats hung on strings for screens, old bottles, pewter crucifixes, dried *immortelles*, pariah puppies, plaster images of the Virgin, and hats without crowns. Miss Vezzis drew twenty rupees a month for acting as nurse, and she squabbled weekly with her Mamma as to the percentage to be given towards housekeeping. When the quarrel was over, Michele D'Cruze used to shamble across the low mud wall of the compound and make love to Miss Vezzis after the fashion of the Borderline, which is hedged about with much ceremony. Michele was a poor, sickly weed and very black; but he had his pride. He would not be seen smoking a *huqa** for anything; and he looked down on natives as only a man with seven-eighths native blood in his veins can. The Vezzis Family had their pride too. They traced their descent from a mythical platelayer who had worked on the Sone Bridge when railways were new in India, and they valued their English origin. Michele was a Telegraph Signaller on Rs.35 a month. The fact that he was in Government employ made Mrs Vezzis lenient to the shortcomings of his ancestors.

There was a compromising legend—Dom Anna the tailor brought it from Poonani—that a black Jew of Cochin* had once married into the D'Cruze family; while it was an open secret that an uncle of Mrs D'Cruze was, at that very time, doing menial work, connected with cooking, for a Club in Southern India! He sent Mrs D'Cruze seven rupees eight annas a month; but she felt the disgrace to the family very keenly all the same.

However, in the course of a few Sundays, Mrs Vezzis brought herself to overlook these blemishes, and gave her consent to the marriage of her daughter with Michele, on condition that Michele should have at least fifty rupees a month to start married life upon. This wonderful prudence must have been a lingering touch of the mythical platelayer's Yorkshire blood; for across the Borderline people take a pride in marrying when they please—not when they can.

Having regard to his departmental prospects, Mrs Vezzis might as well have asked Michele to go away and come back with the Moon in his pocket. But Michele was deeply in love with Miss Vezzis, and that helped him to endure. He accompanied Miss Vezzis to Mass one Sunday, and after Mass, walking home through the hot stale dust with her hand in his, he swore by several Saints, whose names would not interest you, never to forget Miss Vezzis; and she swore by her Honour and the Saints—the oath runs rather curiously; '*In nomine Sanctissimae**—' (whatever the name of the she-Saint is) and so forth, ending with a kiss on the forehead, a kiss on the left cheek, and a kiss on the mouth—never to forget Michele.

Next week Michele was transferred, and Miss Vezzis dropped

tears upon the window-sash of the 'Intermediate'* compartment as he left the Station.

If you look at the telegraph-map of India you will see a long line skirting the coast from Backergunge to Madras. Michele was ordered to Tibasu, a little Sub-office one-third down this line, to send messages on from Berhampur to Chicacola,* and to think of Miss Vezzis and his chances of getting fifty rupees a month out of office-hours. He had the noise of the Bay of Bengal and a Bengali Babu* for company; nothing more. He sent foolish letters, with crosses tucked inside the flaps of the envelopes, to Miss Vezzis.

When he had been at Tibasu for nearly three weeks his chance came.

Never forget that unless the outward and visible signs of Our Authority are always before a native he is as incapable as a child of understanding what authority means, or where is the danger of disobeying it. Tibasu was a forgotten little place with a few Orissa* Mahommedans in it. These, hearing nothing of the Collector-*Sahib* for some time, and heartily despising the Hindu Sub-Judge, arranged to start a little Mohurrum* riot of their own. But the Hindus turned out and broke their heads; when, finding lawlessness pleasant, Hindus and Mahommedans together raised an aimless sort of Donnybrook* just to see how far they could go. They looted each other's shops, and paid off private grudges in the regular way. It was a nasty little riot, but not worth putting in the newspapers.

Michele was working in his office when he heard the sound that a man never forgets all his life—the '*ah-yah*' of an angry crowd. (When that sound drops about three tones, and changes to a thick, droning *ut*, the man who hears it had better go away if he is alone.) The Native Police Inspector ran in and told Michele that the town was in an uproar and coming to wreck the Telegraph Office. The Babu put on his cap and quietly dropped out of the window; while the Police Inspector, afraid, but obeying the old race-instinct which recognises a drop of White blood as far as it can be diluted, said, 'What orders does the *Sahib* give?'

The '*Sahib*' decided Michele. Though horribly frightened, he felt that, for the hour, he, the man with the Cochin Jew and the menial uncle in his pedigree, was the only representative of English author-ity in the place. Then he thought of Miss Vezzis and the fifty rupees, and took the situation on himself. There were seven native policemen in Tibasu, and four crazy smooth-bore muskets among them. All the men were gray with fear, but not beyond leading. Michele dropped the key of the telegraph instrument, and went out, at the head of his army, to meet the mob. As the shouting crew came round a corner of the road, he dropped and fired; the men behind him loosing off instinctively at the same time.

The whole crowd—curs to the back-bone—yelled and ran, leaving one man dead and another dying in the road. Michele was sweating with fear; but he kept his weakness under, and went down into the town, past the house where the Sub-Judge had barricaded himself. The streets were empty. Tibasu was more frightened than Michele, for the mob had been taken at the right time.

Michele returned to the Telegraph-Office, and sent a message to Chicacola asking for help. Before an answer came, he received a deputation of the elders of Tibasu, telling him that the Sub-Judge said his actions generally were 'unconstitutional,' and trying to bully him. But the heart of Michele D'Cruze was big and white in his breast, because of his love for Miss Vezzis, the nurse-girl, and because he had tasted for the first time Responsibility and Success. Those two make an intoxicating drink, and have ruined more men than ever has Whisky. Michele answered that the Sub-Judge might say what he pleased, but, until the Assistant Collector came, he, the Telegraph Signaller, was the Government of India in Tibasu, and the elders of the town would be held accountable for further rioting. Then they bowed their heads and said, 'Show mercy!' or words to that effect, and went back in great fear; each accusing the other of having begun the rioting.

Early in the dawn, after a night's patrol with his seven policemen, Michele went down the road, musket in hand, to meet the Assistant Collector who had ridden in to quell Tibasu. But, in the presence of this young Englishman, Michele felt himself slipping back more and more into the native; and the tale of the Tibasu Riots ended, with the strain on the teller, in an hysterical outburst of tears, bred by sorrow that he had killed a man, shame that he could not feel as uplifted as he had felt through the night, and childish anger that his tongue could not do justice to his great deeds. It was the White drop in Michele's veins dying out, though he did not know it.

But the Englishman understood; and, after he had schooled those men of Tibasu, and had conferred with the Sub-Judge till that excellent official turned green, he found time to draft an official letter describing the conduct of Michele. Which letter filtered through the Proper Channels, and ended in the transfer of Michele up-country once more, on the Imperial salary of sixty-six rupees a month.

So he and Miss Vezzis were married with great state and ancientry; and now there are several little D'Cruzes sprawling about the verandahs of the Central Telegraph Office.

But, if the whole revenue of the Department he serves were to be his reward, Michele could never, never repeat what he did at Tibasu for the sake of Miss Vezzis the nurse-girl.

Which proves that, when a man does good work out of all proportion to his pay, in seven cases out of nine there is a woman at the back of the virtue.

The two exceptions must have suffered from sunstroke.

Christmas in India (1888)

Dim dawn behind the tamarisks—the sky is saffron-yellow—
   As the women in the village grind the corn,
And the parrots seek the river-side, each calling to his fellow
   That the Day, the staring Eastern Day, is born.
     O the white dust on the highway! O the stenches in the byway!
      O the clammy fog that hovers over earth!
     And at Home they're making merry 'neath the white and scarlet
      berry—
      What part have India's exiles in their mirth?

Full day behind the tamarisks—the sky is blue and staring—
   As the cattle crawl afield beneath the yoke,
And they bear One o'er the field-path, who is past all hope or caring,
   To the ghat below the curling wreaths of smoke.
     Call on Rama, going slowly, as ye bear a brother lowly—
      Call on Rama—he may hear, perhaps, your voice!
     With our hymn-books and our psalters we appeal to other altars,
      And to-day we bid 'good Christian men rejoice!'

High noon behind the tamarisks—the sun is hot above us—
   As at Home the Christmas Day is breaking wan.

They will drink our healths at dinner—those who tell us how they
    love us,
  And forget us till another year be gone!
      O the toil that knows no breaking! O the *Heimweh*,* ceaseless,
        aching!
        O the black dividing Sea* and alien Plain!
      Youth was cheap—wherefore we sold it. Gold was good—we
        hoped to hold it.
        And to-day we know the fulness of our gain!

Grey dusk behind the tamarisks—the parrots fly together—
  As the Sun is sinking slowly over Home;
And his last ray seems to mock us shackled in a lifelong tether
  That drags us back howe'er so far we roam.
      Hard her service, poor her payment—she in ancient, tattered
        raiment—
        India, she the grim Stepmother of our kind.
      If a year of life be lent her, if her temple's shrine we enter,
        The door is shut—we may not look behind.

Black night behind the tamarisks—the owls begin their chorus—
  As the conches from the temple scream and bray.
With the fruitless years behind us and the hopeless years before us,
  Let us honour, O my brothers, Christmas Day!
      Call a truce, then, to our labours—let us feast with friends and
        neighbours,
        And be merry as the custom of our caste;
      For, if 'faint and forced the laughter,' and if sadness follow after,
        We are richer by one mocking Christmas past.

Giffen's Debt (1886)

*Imprimis** he was 'broke.' Thereafter left
His Regiment and, later, took to drink;
Then, having lost the balance of his friends,
'Went Fantee'*—joined the people of the land,
Turned three parts Mussulman and one Hindu,
And lived among the Gauri* villagers,

Who gave him shelter and a wife or twain,
And boasted that a thorough, full-blood *sahib*
Had come among them. Thus he spent his time,
Deeply indebted to the village *shroff*[1]
(Who never asked for payment), always drunk,
Unclean, abominable, out-at-heels;
Forgetting that he was an Englishman.

You know they dammed the Gauri with a dam,
And all the good contractors scamped their work
And all the bad material at hand
Was used to dam the Gauri—which was cheap,
And, therefore, proper. Then the Gauri burst,
And several hundred thousand cubic tons
Of water dropped into the valley, *flop*,
And drowned some five-and-twenty villagers,
And did a lakh or two of detriment
To crops and cattle. When the flood went down
We found him dead, beneath an old dead horse
Full six miles down the valley. So we said
He was a victim to the Demon Drink,
And moralised upon him for a week,
And then forgot him. Which was natural.

But, in the valley of the Gauri, men
Beneath the shadow of the big new dam,
Relate a foolish legend of the flood,
Accounting for the little loss of life
(Only those five-and-twenty villagers)
In this wise:—On the evening of the flood,
They heard the groaning of the rotten dam,
And voices of the Mountain Devils. Then
An incarnation of the local God,
Mounted upon a monster-neighing horse,
And flourishing a flail-like whip, came down,
Breathing ambrosia, to the villages,
And fell upon the simple villagers
With yells beyond the power of mortal throat,
And blows beyond the power of mortal hand,

And smote them with his flail-like whip, and drove
Them clamorous with terror up the hill,
And scattered, with the monster-neighing steed,
Their crazy cottages about their ears,
And generally cleared those villages.
Then came the water, and the local God,
Breathing ambrosia, flourishing his whip,
And mounted on his monster-neighing steed,
Went down the valley with the flying trees
And residue of homesteads, while they watched
Safe on the mountain-side these wondrous things,
And knew that they were much beloved of Heaven.

Wherefore, and when the dam was newly built,
They raised a temple to the local God,
And burnt all manner of unsavoury things
Upon his altar, and created priests,
And blew into a conch and banged a bell,
And told the story of the Gauri flood
With circumstance and much embroidery . . .
So he, the whiskified Objectionable,
Unclean, abominable, out-at-heels,
Became the Tutelary Deity
Of all the Gauri valley villages,
And may in time become a Solar Myth.*

¹ Money-lender.

Mandalay (1892)

By the old Moulmein* Pagoda, lookin' lazy at the sea,
There's a Burma girl a-settin', and I know she thinks o' me;
For the wind is in the palm-trees, and the temple-bells they say:
'Come you back, you British soldier; come you back to Mandalay!*
      Come you back to Mandalay,
      Where the old Flotilla lay:
      Can't you 'ear their paddles chunkin' from Rangoon to
        Mandalay?

On the road to Mandalay,
Where the flyin'-fishes play,
An' the dawn comes up like thunder outer China 'crost the
　　Bay!

'Er petticoat was yaller an' 'er little cap was green,
An' 'er name was Supi-yaw-lat—jes' the same as Theebaw's Queen,*
An' I seed her first a-smokin' of a whackin' white cheroot,
An' a-wastin' Christian kisses on an 'eathen idol's foot:
　　　　Bloomin' idol made o' mud—
　　　　Wot they called the Great Gawd Budd—
　　　　Plucky lot she cared for idols when I kissed 'er where she
　　　　　　stud!
　　　　On the road to Mandalay . . .

When the mist was on the rice-fields an' the sun was droppin' slow,
She'd git 'er little banjo an' she'd sing '*Kulla-lo-lo!*'
With 'er arm upon my shoulder an' 'er cheek agin my cheek
We useter watch the steamers an' the *hathis** pilin' teak.
　　　　Elephints a-pilin' teak
　　　　In the sludgy, squdgy creek,
　　　　Where the silence 'ung that 'eavy you was 'arf afraid to
　　　　　　speak!
　　　　On the road to Mandalay . . .

But that's all shove be'ind me—long ago an' fur away,
An' there ain't no 'buses runnin' from the Bank to Mandalay;
An' I'm learnin' 'ere in London what the ten-year soldier tells:
'If you've 'eard the East a-callin', you won't never 'eed naught else.'
　　　　No! you won't 'eed nothin' else
　　　　But them spicy garlic smells,
　　　　An' the sunshine an' the palm-trees an' the tinkly
　　　　　　temple-bells;
　　　　On the road to Mandalay . . .

I am sick o' wastin' leather on these gritty pavin'-stones,
An' the blasted English drizzle wakes the fever in my bones;
Tho' I walks with fifty 'ousemaids outer Chelsea to the Strand,
An' they talks a lot o' lovin', but wot do they understand?

Beefy face an' grubby 'and—
Law! wot do they understand?
I've a neater, sweeter maiden in a cleaner, greener land!
On the road to Mandalay . . .

Ship me somewheres east of Suez, where the best is like the worst,
Where there aren't no Ten Commandments an' a man can raise a
       thirst;
For the temple-bells are callin', an' it's there that I would be—
By the old Moulmein Pagoda, looking lazy at the sea;
      On the road to Mandalay,
      Where the old Flotilla lay,
      With our sick beneath the awnings when we went to
         Mandalay!
      On the road to Mandalay,
      Where the flyin'-fishes play,
      An' the dawn comes up like thunder outer China 'crost the
         Bay!

What the People Said

Queen Victoria's Jubilee
JUNE 21ST, 1887

By the well, where the bullocks go
Silent and blind and slow—
By the field, where the young corn dies
In the face of the sultry skies,
They have heard, as the dull Earth hears
The voice of the wind of an hour,
The sound of the Great Queen's voice:—
'My God hath given me years,
Hath granted dominion and power:
And I bid you, O Land, rejoice.'

And the Ploughman settles the share
More deep in the grudging clod;
For he saith:—'The wheat is my care,
And the rest is the will of God.

He sent the Mahratta spear
As He sendeth the rain,
And the *Mlech*,[1] in the fated year,
Broke the spear in twain,
And was broken in turn. Who knows
How our Lords make strife?
It is good that the young wheat grows,
For the bread is Life.'

Then, far and near, as the twilight drew,
    Hissed up to the scornful dark
Great serpents, blazing, of red and blue,
That rose and faded, and rose anew,
    That the Land might wonder and mark.
'To-day is a day of days,' they said,
'Make merry, O People, all!'
And the Ploughman listened and bowed his head.
'To-day and to-morrow God's will,' he said,
As he trimmed the lamps on the wall.

'He sendeth us years that are good,
As He sendeth the dearth.
He giveth to each man his food,
Or Her food to the Earth.
Our Kings and our Queens are afar—
On their peoples be peace—
God bringeth the rain to the Bar,
That our cattle increase.'

And the Ploughman settled the share
More deep in the sun-dried clod:—
'Mogul, Mahratta, and *Mlech* from the North,
And White Queen over the Seas—
God raiseth them up and driveth them forth
As the dust of the ploughshare flies in the breeze;
But the wheat and the cattle are all my care,
And the rest is the will of God.'

[1] The foreigner.

See also: Candler; Clifford; Conrad; Perrin; Steel; Trevelyan; Woolf.

A. E. HOUSMAN
(1859–1936)

1887 (1896)

From Clee to heaven the beacon burns,
    The shires have seen it plain,
From north and south the sign returns
    And beacons burn again.

Look left, look right, the hills are bright,
    The dales are light between,
Because 'tis fifty years to-night
    That God has saved the Queen.

Now, when the flame they watch not towers
    About the soil they trod,
Lads, we'll remember friends of ours
    Who shared the work with God.

To skies that knit their heartstrings right,
    To fields that bred them brave,
The saviours come not home to-night:
    Themselves they could not save.

It dawns in Asia, tombstones show
    And Shropshire names are read;
And the Nile spills his overflow
    Beside the Severn's dead.

We pledge in peace by farm and town
    The Queen they served in war,
And fire the beacons up and down
    The land they perished for.

'God save the Queen' we living sing,
    From height to height 'tis heard;
And with the rest your voices ring,
    Lads of the Fifty-third.

Oh, God will save her, fear you not:
    Be you the men you've been,
Get you the sons your fathers got,
    And God will save the Queen.

See also: Kipling, 'Recessional' and 'What the People Said'; Watson, 'Jubilee Night in Westmorland'.

J. A. FROUDE
(1818–1894)

The historian J. A. Froude's The English in the West Indies, *a travelogue interspersed with political and social commentary, offers his response to the topical issue of constitutional government for the islands. Whereas white colonial autonomy would lead to the formation of closer links on the basis of common blood, as Froude saw it, self-government—'Dark Parliament'—for black West Indians could bring only racial conflict, a white exodus, the betrayal of imperial trust, and the dissolution of this portion of a once-glorious empire. 'Managing one's own affairs' was suitable for no people other than the pure-blood descendants of Englishmen, 'in their special capacity of leaders and governors of men'. In J. J. Thomas's important riposte to Froude,* Froudacity, *which appeared a year later, we find embodied the first written exchange between a West Indian black colonial and an English imperialist. A 'small man' from a small colony, Thomas in answering back to the world-renowned historian set a pattern of oppositional retort which others, in the West Indies and beyond, would follow over the next century of anti-imperial writing. By 'Froudacity' Thomas meant the 'injurious' 'negrophobia' and 'reckless invention' with which the historian had represented West Indian history and society in an attempt to thwart emergent political aspirations in the Antilles. Such injustice and 'skin-dominancy' had to be strongly resisted. Thomas's critique of Froude is*

*captured here by setting his comments on the historian's account of
Barbados, St Vincent, and Grenada alongside a corresponding section in
Froude (specifically on St Vincent and Grenada). As we see, Thomas's
vindication of his people and their ambitions proceeded by close reading,
alternating quoted statement and counter-statement, in order to expose
one by one Froude's inaccuracies, prejudices, and 'hard and fast' views of
West Indian society as comprising 'white-master' against 'Black-slave'.
'No one', Thomas wrote in a later section of* Froudacity, *'can deserve to
govern simply because he is white, and no one is bound to be subject simply
because he is black.'*

from *The English in the West Indies; or, the Bow of Ulysses*
(1888)

West Indian civilisation is old-fashioned, and has none of the pushing
manners which belong to younger and perhaps more thriving communities. The West Indians* themselves, though they may be
deficient in energy, are uniformly ladies and gentlemen, and all their
arrangements take their complexion from the general tone of society.
There is a refinement visible at once in the subsidiary vessels of the
mail service which ply among the islands. They are almost as large as
those which cross the Atlantic, and never on any line in the world
have I met with officers so courteous and cultivated. The cabins were
spacious and as cool as a temperature of 80°, gradually rising as
we went south, would permit. Punkahs waved over us at dinner. In
our berths a single sheet was all that was provided for us, and this was
one more than we needed. A sea was running when we cleared out
from under the land. Among the cabin passengers was a coloured
family in good circumstances moving about with nurses and children. The little things, who had never been at sea before, sat on the
floor, staring out of their large helpless black eyes, not knowing what
was the matter with them. Forward there were perhaps two or three
hundred coloured people going from one island to another, singing,
dancing, and chattering all night long, as radiant and happy as
carelessness and content could make them. Sick or not sick made no
difference. Nothing could disturb the imperturbable good humour
and good spirits.

It was too hot to sleep; we sat several of us smoking on deck, and I learnt the first authentic particulars of the present manner of life of these much misunderstood people. Evidently they belonged to a race far inferior to the Zulus and Caffres,* whom I had known in South Africa. They were more coarsely formed in limb and feature. They would have been slaves in their own country if they had not been brought to ours, and at the worst had lost nothing by the change. They were good-natured, innocent, harmless, lazy perhaps, but not more lazy than is perfectly natural when even Europeans must be roused to activity by cocktail.

In the Antilles generally, Barbadoes being the only exception, negro families have each their cabin, their garden ground, their grazing for a cow. They live surrounded by most of the fruits which grew in Adam's paradise—oranges and plantains, bread-fruit, and cocoa-nuts, though not apples. Their yams and cassava grow without effort, for the soil is easily worked and inexhaustibly fertile. The curse is taken off from nature, and like Adam again they are under the covenant of innocence. Morals in the technical sense they have none, but they cannot be said to sin, because they have no knowledge of a law, and therefore they can commit no breach of the law. They are naked and not ashamed. They are *married* as they call it, but not *parsoned*. The woman prefers a looser tie that she may be able to leave a man if he treats her unkindly. Yet they are not licentious. I never saw an immodest look in one of their faces, and never heard of any venal profligacy. The system is strange, but it answers. A missionary told me that a connection rarely turns out well which begins with a legal marriage. The children scramble up anyhow, and shift for themselves like chickens as soon as they are able to peck. Many die in this way by eating unwholesome food, but also many live, and those who do live grow up exactly like their parents. It is a very peculiar state of things, not to be understood, as priest and missionary agree, without long acquaintance. There is evil, but there is not the demoralising effect of evil. They sin, but they sin only as animals, without shame, because there is no sense of doing wrong. They eat the forbidden fruit, but it brings with it no knowledge of the difference between good and evil. They steal, but if detected they fall back upon the Lord. It was de will of de Lord that they should do this or that. De Lord forbid that they should go against his holy pleasure. In fact these poor children of darkness have escaped the conse-quences of the Fall, and must come of another stock after all.

Meanwhile they are perfectly happy. In no part of the globe is there any peasantry whose every want is so completely satisfied as her Majesty's black subjects in these West Indian islands. They have no aspirations to make them restless. They have no guilt upon their consciences. They have food for the picking up. Clothes they need not, and lodging in such a climate need not be elaborate. They have perfect liberty, and are safe from dangers, to which if left to themselves they would be exposed, for the English rule prevents the strong from oppressing the weak. In their own country they would have remained slaves to more warlike races. In the West Indies their fathers underwent a bondage of a century or two, lighter at its worst than the easiest form of it in Africa; their descendants in return have nothing now to do save to laugh and sing and enjoy existence. Their quarrels, if they have any, begin and end in words. If happiness is the be all and end all of life, and those who have most of it have most completely attained the object of their being, the 'nigger'* who now basks among the ruins of the West Indian plantations is the supremest specimen of present humanity.

We retired to our berths at last. At waking we were at anchor off St Vincent, an island of volcanic mountains robed in forest from shore to crest. Till late in the last century it was the headquarters of the Caribs, who kept up a savage independence there, recruited by runaway slaves from Barbadoes or elsewhere. Brandy and Sir Ralph Abercrombie* reduced them to obedience in 1796, and St Vincent throve tolerably down to the days of free trade. Even now when I saw it, Kingston, the principal town, looked pretty and well to do, reminding me, strange to say, of towns in Norway, the houses stretching along the shore painted in the same tints of blue or yellow or pink, with the same red-tiled roofs, the trees coming down the hill sides to the water's edge, villas of modest pretensions shining through the foliage, with the patches of cane fields, the equivalent in the landscape of the brilliant Norwegian grass. The prosperity has for the last forty years waned and waned. There are now two thousand white people there, and forty thousand coloured people, and the proportion alters annually to our disadvantage. The usual remedies have been tried. The constitution has been altered a dozen times. Just now I believe the Crown is trying to do without one, having found the results of the elective principle not encouraging, but we shall perhaps revert to it before long; any way, the tables show that each year the trade of the island decreases, and will continue to decrease while the expenditure increases and will increase.

I did not land, for the time was short, and as a beautiful picture the island was best seen from the deck. The characteristics of the people are the same in all the Antilles, and could be studied elsewhere. The bustle and confusion in the ship, the crowd of boats round the ladder, the clamour of negro men's tongues, and the blaze of colours from the negro women's dresses, made up together a scene sufficiently entertaining for the hour which we remained. In the middle of it the Governor, Mr S——,* came on board with another official. They were going on in the steamer to Tobago, which formed part of his dominions.

Leaving St Vincent, we were all the forenoon passing the Grenadines, a string of small islands fitting into their proper place in the Antilles semicircle, but as if Nature had forgotten to put them together or else had broken some large island to pieces and scattered them along the line. Some were large enough to have once carried sugar plantations, and are now made over wholly to the blacks; others were fishing stations, droves of whales during certain months frequenting these waters; others were mere rocks, amidst which the white-sailed American coasting schooners were beating up against the north-east trade. There was a stiff breeze, and the sea was white with short curling waves, but we were running before it and the wind kept the deck fresh. At Grenada, the next island, we were to go on shore.

Grenada was, like St Vincent, the home for centuries of man-eating Caribs, French for a century and a half, and finally, after many desperate struggles for it, was ceded to England at the peace of Versailles. It is larger than St Vincent, though in its main features it has the same character. There are lakes in the hills, and a volcanic crater not wholly quiescent; but the especial value of Grenada, which made us fight so hardly to win it, is the deep and landlocked harbour, the finest in all the Antilles.

Père Labat,* to whose countrymen it belonged at the time of his own visit there, says that 'if Barbadoes had such a harbour as Grenada it would be an island without a rival in the world. If Grenada belonged to the English, who knew how to turn to profit natural advantages, it would be a rich and powerful colony. In itself it was all that man could desire. To live there was to live in paradise.' Labat found the island occupied by countrymen of his own, '*paisans aisez*,'* he calls them, growing their tobacco, their indigo and scarlet rocou,* their pigs and their poultry, and contented to be without sugar, without slaves, and without trade. The change of hands from which he expected so much had actually come about. Grenada did belong to the English, and had belonged to us ever since Rodney's peace.* I was anxious to see how far Labat's prophecy had been fulfilled.

St George's, the 'capital,' stands on the neck of a peninsula a mile in length, which forms one side of the harbour. Of the houses, some look out to sea, some inwards upon the *carenage*, as the harbour is called. At the point there was a fort, apparently of some strength, on which the British flag was flying. We signalled that we had the Governor on board, and the fort replied with a puff of smoke. Sound there was none or next to none, but we presumed that it had come from a gun of some kind. We anchored outside. Mr S—— landed in an official boat, with two flags, to distinguish it from a missionary's boat, which had only one. The crews of a dozen other boats then clambered up the gangway to dispute possession of the rest of us, shouting, swearing, lying, tearing us this way and that way as if we were carcases and they wild beasts wanting to dine upon us. We engaged a boat for ourselves as we supposed; we had no sooner entered it than the scandalous boatman proceeded to take in as many more passengers as it would hold. Remonstrance being vain, we settled the matter by stepping into the boat next adjoining, and amidst howls and execrations we were borne triumphantly off and were pulled in to the land.

Labat had not exaggerated the beauty of the landlocked basin into which we entered on rounding the point. On three sides wooded hills rose high till they passed into mountains; on the fourth was the castle with its slopes and batteries, the church and town beyond it, and everywhere luxuriant tropical forest trees overhanging the violet-coloured water. I could well understand the Frenchman's delight when he saw it, and also the satisfaction with which he would now acknowledge that he had been a shortsighted prophet. The English had obtained Grenada, and this is what they had made of it. The forts which had been erected by his countrymen had been deserted and dismantled; the castle on which we had seen our flag flying was a ruin; the walls were crumbling and in many places had fallen down. One solitary gun was left, but that was honeycombed and could be fired only with half a charge to salute with. It was true that the forts had ceased to be of use, but that was because there was nothing left to defend. The harbour is, as I said, the best in the West Indies. There was not a vessel in it, nor so much as a boat-yard where a spar could be replaced or a broken rivet mended. Once there had been a line of wharves, but the piles had been eaten by worms and the platforms had fallen through. Round us when we landed were unroofed warehouses, weed-choked courtyards, doors gone, and window frames fallen in or out. Such a scene of desolation and desertion I never saw in my life save once, a few weeks later at Jamaica. An English lady with her children had come to the landing place to meet my friends. They, too, were more like wandering ghosts than human beings with warm blood in them. All their thoughts were on going home—home out of so miserable an exile.

Nature had been simply allowed by us to resume possession of the island. Here, where the cannon had roared, and ships and armies had fought, and the enterprising English had entered into occupancy, under which, as we are proud to fancy, the waste places of the earth grow green, and industry and civilisation follow as its inevitable fruit, all was now silence. Not Babylon itself, with its bats and owls, was more dreary and desolate. And this was an English Crown colony, as rich in resources as any area of soil of equal size in the world. England had demanded and seized the responsibility of managing it—this was the result.

A gentleman, who for some purpose was a passing resident in the island, had asked us to dine with him. His house was three or four miles inland. A good road remained as a legacy from other times, and a pair of horses and a phaeton carried us swiftly to his door. The town of St George's had once been populous, and even now there seemed no want of people, if mere numbers sufficed. We passed for half a mile through a straggling street, where the houses were evidently occupied though unconscious for many a year of paint or repair. They were squalid and dilapidated, but the luxuriant bananas and orange trees in the gardens relieved the ugliness of their appearance. The road when we left the town was overshadowed with gigantic mangoes planted long ago, with almond trees and cedar trees, no relations of our almonds or our cedars, but the most splendid ornaments of the West Indian forest. The valley up which we drove was beautiful, and the house, when we reached it, showed taste and culture. Mr—— had rare trees, rare flowers, and was taking advantage of his temporary residence in the tropics to make experiments in horticulture. He had been brought there, I believe, by some necessities of business. He told us that Grenada was now the ideal country of modern social reformers. It had become an island of pure peasant proprietors. The settlers, who had once been a thriving and wealthy community, had melted away. Not more than six hundred English were left, and these were clearing out at their best speed. They had sold their estates for anything which they could get. The free blacks had bought them, and about 8,000 negro families, say 40,000 black souls in all, now shared the soil between them. Each family lived independently, growing coffee and cocoa and oranges, and all were doing very well. The possession of property had brought a sense of its rights with it. They were as litigious as Irish peasants; everyone was at law with his neighbour, and the island was a gold mine to the Attorney-General; otherwise they were quiet harmless fellows, and if the politicians would only let them alone, they would be perfectly contented, and might eventually, if wisely managed, come to some good. To set up a constitution in such a place was a ridiculous mockery, and would only be another name for swindling and jobbery. Black the island was, and black it would remain. The conditions were never likely to arise which would bring back a European population; but a governor who was a sensible man, who would reside and use his natural influence, could manage it with perfect ease. The island belonged to England; we were responsible for what we made of it, and for the blacks' own sakes we ought not to try experiments upon them. They knew their own deficiencies, and would infinitely prefer a wise English ruler to any constitution which could be offered them. If left entirely to themselves, they would in a generation or two relapse into savages; there were but two alternatives before not Grenada only, but all the English West Indies—either an English administration pure and simple like the East Indian, or a falling eventually into a state like that of Hayti,* where they eat the babies, and no white man can own a yard of land.

It was dark night when we drove back to the port. The houses along the road, which had looked so miserable on the outside, were now lighted with paraffin lamps. I could see into them, and was astonished to observe signs of comfort and even signs of taste—arm-chairs, sofas, side-boards with cut glass upon them, engravings and coloured prints upon the walls. The old state of things is gone, but a new state of things is rising which may have a worth of its own. The plant of civilisation as yet has taken but feeble root, and is only beginning to grow. It may thrive yet if those who have troubled all the earth will consent for another century to take their industry elsewhere.

The ship's galley was waiting at the wharf when we reached it. The captain also had been dining with a friend on shore, and we had to wait for him. The offshore night breeze had not yet risen. The harbour was smooth as a looking glass, and the stars shone double in the sky and on the water. The silence was only broken by the whistle of the lizards or the cry of some far-off marsh frog. The air was warmer than we ever feel it in the depth of an English summer, yet pure and delicious and charged with the perfume of a thousand flowers. One felt it strange that with so beautiful a possession lying at our doors, we should have allowed it to slide out of our hands. I could say for myself, like Père Labat, the island was all that man could desire. 'En un mot, la vie y est délicieuse.'* [. . .]

See also: Chamberlain; Seeley; Trollope.

J. J. THOMAS
(1840–1889)

from *Froudacity* (1889)

Like the ancient hero, one of whose warlike equipments furnishes the complementary title of his book, the author of 'The English in the West Indies; or, The Bow of Ulysses,' sallied forth from his home to study, if not cities, at least men (especially *black* men), and their manners in the British Antilles.

James Anthony Froude is, beyond any doubt whatever, a very considerable figure in modern English literature. It has, however, for some time ceased to be a question whether his acceptability, to the extent which it reaches, has not been due rather to the verbal attractiveness than to the intrinsic value and trustworthiness of his opinions and teachings. In fact, so far as a judgment can be formed from examined specimens of his writings, it appears that our author is the bond-slave of his own phrases. To secure an artistic perfection of style, he disregards all obstacles, not only those presented by the requirements of verity, but such as spring from any other kind of consideration whatsoever. The doubt may safely be entertained whether, among modern British men of letters, there be one of equal capability who, in the interest of the happiness of his sentences, so cynically sacrifices what is due not only to himself as a public instructor, but also to that public whom he professes to instruct. Yet, as the too evident plaything of an over-permeable moral constitution, he might set up some plea in explanation of his ethical vagaries. He might urge, for instance, that the high culture of which his books are all so redolent has utterly failed to imbue him with the *nil admirari**sentiment, which Horace commends as the sole specific for making men happy and keeping them so. For, as a matter of fact, and with special reference to the work we have undertaken to discuss, Mr Froude, though cynical in his general utterances regarding Ne-groes—of the male sex, be it noted—is, in the main, all extravagance and self-abandonment whenever he brings an object of his arbitrary likes or dislikes under discussion. At such times he is no ob-server, much less worshipper, of proportion in his delineations. Thorough-paced, scarcely controllable, his enthusiasm for or against admits no degree in its expression, save and except the superlative. Hence Mr Froude's statement of facts or description of phenomena, whenever his feelings are enlisted either way, must be taken with the proverbial 'grain of salt' by all when enjoying the luxury of perusing his books. [. . .]

Barbados

Our distinguished voyager visited many of the British West Indies, landing first at Barbados, his social experience whereof is set forth in a very agreeable account. Our immediate business, however, is not with what West Indian hospitality, especially among the well-to-do classes, can and does accomplish for the entertainment of visitors, and particularly visitors so eminent as Mr Froude. We are concerned with what Mr Froude has to say concerning our dusky brethren and sisters in those Colonies. We have, thus, much pleasure in being able at the outset to extract the following favourable verdict of his respecting them—premising, at the same time, that the balcony from which Mr Froude surveyed the teeming multitude in Bridgetown was that of a grand hotel at which he had, on invitation, partaken of the refreshing beverage mentioned in the citation:—*

'Cocktail over, and walking in the heat of the sun being a thing not to be thought of, I sat for two hours in the balcony, watching the people, who were as thick as bees in swarming time. Nine-tenths of them were pure black. You rarely saw a white face, but still less would you see a discontented one, imperturbable good humour and self-satisfaction being written on the features of every one. The women struck me especially. They were smartly dressed in white calico, scrupulously clean, and tricked out with ribands and feathers; but their figures were so good, and they carried themselves so well and gracefully, that although they might make themselves absurd, they could not look vulgar. Like the Greek and Etruscan women, they are trained from childhood to carry weights on their heads. They are thus perfectly upright, and plant their feet firmly and naturally on the ground. They might serve for sculptors' models, and are well aware of it.'

Regarding the other sex, Mr Froude says:—

'The men were active enough, driving carts, wheeling barrows, and selling flying-fish,' &c.

He also speaks with candour of the entire absence of drunkenness and quarrelling, and the agreeable prevalence of good humour and light-heartedness among them. Some critic might, on reading the above extract from our author's account of the men, be tempted to ask— 'But what is the meaning of that little word "enough" occurring therein?' We should be disposed to hazard a suggestion that Mr Froude, being fair-minded and loyal to truth, as far as is compatible with his sympathy for his hapless 'Anglo-West Indians,' could not give an entirely ungrudging testimony in favour of the possible, nay probable, voters by whose suffrages the supremacy of the Dark Parliament will be ensured, and the relapse into obeahism, devil-worship, and children-eating be inaugurated. Nevertheless, *Si sic omnia dixisset*—if he had said all things thus! Yes, if Mr Froude had, throughout his volume, spoken in this strain, his occasional want of patience and fairness with regard to our male kindred might have found condonation in his even more than chivalrous appreciation of our womankind. But it has been otherwise. So we are

forced to try conclusions with him in the arena of his own selection
—unreflecting spokesman that he is of British colonialism, which, we
grieve to learn through Mr Froude's pages, has, like the Bourbon
family, not only forgotten nothing, but, unfortunately for its own
peace, learnt nothing also.

St Vincent

The following are the words in which our traveller embodies the
main motive and purpose of his voyage:—

'My own chief desire was to see the human inhabitants, to learn
what they were doing, how they were living, and what they were
thinking about . . .'

But, alas, with the mercurialism of temperament in which he has
thought proper to indulge when only Negroes and Europeans not of
'Anglo-West Indian' tendencies were concerned, he jauntily threw to
the winds all the scruples and cautious minuteness which were
essential to the proper execution of his project. At Barbados, as we
have seen, he satisfies himself with sitting aloft, at a balcony-window,
to contemplate the movements of the sable throng below, of whose
character, moral and political, he nevertheless professes to have
become a trustworthy delineator. From the above-quoted account of
his impressions of the external traits and deportment of the Ethiopic
folk thus superficially gazed at, our author passes on to an analysis of
their mental and moral idiosyncrasies, and other intimate matters,
which the very silence of the book as to his method of ascertaining
them is a sufficient proof that his knowledge in their regard has not
been acquired directly and at first hand. Nor need we say that the
generally adverse cast of his verdicts on what he had been at no pains
to study for himself points to the 'hostileness' of the witnesses whose
testimony alone has formed the basis of his conclusions. Throughout
Mr Froude's tour in the British Colonies his intercourse was
exclusively with 'Anglo-West Indians,' whose aversion to the Blacks
he has himself, perhaps they would think indiscreetly, placed on
record. In no instance do we find that he condescended to visit the
abode of any Negro, whether it was the mansion of a gentleman or the
hut of a peasant of that race. The whole tenor of the book indicates his
rigid adherence to this onesided course, and suggests also that, as a
traveller, Mr Froude considers maligning on hearsay to be just as

convenient as reporting facts elicited by personal investigation. Proceed we, however, to strengthen our statement regarding his definitive abandonment, and that without any apparent reason, of the plan he had professedly laid down for himself at starting, and failing which no trustworthy data could have been obtained concerning the character and disposition of the people about whom he undertakes to thoroughly enlighten his readers. Speaking of St Vincent, where he arrived immediately after leaving Barbados, our author says:—

'I did not land, for the time was short, and as a beautiful picture the island was best seen from the deck. The characteristics of the people are the same in all the Antilles, and could be studied elsewhere.'

Now, it is a fact, patent and notorious, that 'the characteristics of the people are' *not* 'the same in all the Antilles.' A man of Mr Froude's attainments, whose studies have made him familiar with ethnological facts, must be aware that difference of local surroundings and influences does, in the course of time, inevitably create difference of characteristic and deportment. Hence there is in nearly every Colony a marked dissimilarity of native qualities amongst the Negro inhabitants, arising not only from the causes above indicated, but largely also from the great diversity of their African ancestry. We might as well be told that because the nations of Europe are generally white and descended from Japhet, they could be studied one by the light derived from acquaintance with another. We venture to declare that, unless a common education from youth has been shared by them, the Hamitic inhabitants of one island have very little in common with those of another, beyond the dusky skin and woolly hair. In speech, character, and deportment, a coloured native of Trinidad differs as much from one of Barbados as a North American black does from either, in all the above respects.

Grenada

In Grenada, the next island he arrived at, our traveller's procedure with regard to the inhabitants was very similar. There he landed in the afternoon, drove three or four miles inland to dine at the house of a 'gentleman who was a passing resident,' returned in the dark to his ship, and started for Trinidad. In the course of this journey back, however, as he sped along in the carriage, Mr Froude found opportunity to look into the people's houses along the way, where, he tells us, he 'could see and was astonished to observe signs of comfort, and even signs of taste—armchairs, sofas, side-boards with cut-glass upon them, engravings and coloured prints upon the walls.' As a result of this nocturnal examination, *à vol d'oiseau,** he has written paragraph upon paragraph about the people's character and prospects in the island of Grenada. To read the patronizing terms in which our historian-traveller has seen fit to comment on Grenada and its people, one would believe that his account is of some half-civilized, out-of-the-way region under British sway, and inhabited chiefly by a horde of semi-barbarian ignoramuses of African descent. If the world had not by this time thoroughly assessed the intrinsic value of Mr Froude's utterances, one who knows Grenada might have felt inclined to resent his causeless depreciation of the intellectual capacity of its inhabitants; but consider-ing the estimate which has been pretty generally formed of his historical judgment, Mr Froude may be dismissed, as regards Grenada and its people, with a certain degree of scepticism. Such scepticism, though lost upon himself, is unquestionably needful to protect his readers from the hallucination which the author's singular contempt for accuracy is but too liable to induce.

Those who know Grenada and its affairs are perfectly familiar with the fact that all of its chief intellectual business, whether official (even in the highest degree, such as temporary administration of the govern-ment), legal, commercial, municipal, educational, or journalistic, has been for years upon years carried on by men of colour. And what, as a consequence of this fact, has the world ever heard in disparagement of Grenada throughout this long series of years? Assuredly not a syllable. On the contrary, she has been the theme of praise, not only for the admirable foresight with which she avoided the sugar crisis, so disast-rous to her sister islands, but also for the pluck and persistence shown in sustaining herself through an agricultural emergency brought about by commercial reverses, whereby the steady march of her sons in self-advancement was only checked for a time, but never definitively arrested. In fine, as regards every branch of civilized employment pursued there, the good people of Grenada hold their own so well and worthily that any show of patronage, even from a source more entitled to confidence, would simply be a piece of obtrusive kindness, not accept-able to any, seeing that it is required by none.

See also: Aurobindo; McKay; Plaatje; Schreiner.

FLORA ANNIE STEEL
(1847–1929)

A writer of diverse aptitudes and contradictory insights, the redoubtable
Flora Annie Steel is here represented by three different texts, each relating
to a key aspect of imperial experience: domestic work and the memsahib's
rule of her household; the collection of local knowledge in the form of a
transcribed oral tale; and a story about building the Indian railway, that
vast network seen as both instrument and symbol of imperial rule.

The Duties of the Mistress (1889)

Housekeeping in India, when once the first strangeness has worn off,
is a far easier task in many ways than it is in England, though it none
the less requires time, and, in this present transitional period, an
almost phenomenal patience; for, while one mistress enforces
cleanliness according to European methods, the next may belong to
the opposite faction, who, so long as the dinner is nicely served,
thinks nothing of it being cooked in a kitchen which is also used as a
latrine; the result being that the servants who serve one, and then the
other stamp of mistress, look on the desire for decency as a mere
personal and distinctly disagreeable attribute of their employer,
which, like a bad temper or stinginess, may be resented or evaded.

And, first, it must be distinctly understood, that it is not necessary,
or in the least degree desirable, that an educated woman should waste
the best years of her life in scolding and petty supervision. Life holds
higher duties, and it is indubitable that friction and over-zeal is a sure
sign of a bad housekeeper. But there is an appreciable difference
between the careworn Martha vexed with many things, and the
absolute indifference displayed by many Indian mistresses, who put
up with a degree of slovenliness and dirt which would disgrace a den
in St Giles,* on the principle that it is no use attempting to teach the
natives.

They never go into their kitchens, for the simple reason that their
appetite for breakfast might be marred by seeing the khitmatghar*
using his toes as an efficient toast-rack (*fact*); or their desire for
dinner weakened by seeing the soup strained through a greasy pagri.*

The ostrich, who, according to the showman, '*'ides 'is head in the sand, and thinks as 'e can't see no one, as nobody can't see 'e,'** has, fortunately, an exceptional faculty of digestion. With this remark we will leave a very unpleasant subject.

Easy, however, as the actual housekeeping is in India, the personal attention of the mistress is infinitely more needed here than at home. There, once the machine is well oiled and set in motion, the mistress may rely on fairly even and regular working; here, a few days of absence, or neglect to keep her eyes open, and she will find the servants fall into their old habits with the inherited conservatism of dirt. This is, of course, disheartening, but it has to be faced as a necessary condition of life, until a few generations of training shall have started the Indian servant on a new inheritance of habit. It must never be forgotten that at present those mistresses who aim at anything beyond keeping a good table are in the minority, and that pioneering is always arduous work.

The first duty of a mistress is, of course, to be able to give intelligible orders to her servants, therefore it is necessary she should learn to speak Hindustani. No sane Englishwoman would dream of living, say, for twenty years, in Germany, Italy, or France, without making the *attempt*, at any rate, to learn the language. She would, in fact, feel that by neglecting to do so she would '*write herself down an ass.*' It would be well, therefore, if ladies in India were to ask themselves if a difference in longitude increases the latitude allowed in judging of a woman's intellect.

The next duty is obviously to insist on her orders being carried out. And here we come to the burning question, 'How is this to be done?' Certainly, there is at present very little to which we can appeal in the average Indian servant, but then, until it is implanted by training, there is very little sense of duty in a child; yet in some well-regulated nurseries obedience is a foregone conclusion. The secret lies in making rules, and *keeping to them*. The Indian servant is a child in everything save age, and should be treated as a child; that is to say, kindly, but with the greatest firmness. The laws of the household should be those of the Medes and Persians,* and first faults should never go unpunished. By overlooking a first offence, we lose the only opportunity we have of preventing it becoming a habit.

But it will be asked, How are we to punish our servants when we have no hold either on their minds or bodies?—when cutting their pay is illegal, and few, if any, have any sense of shame.

The answer is obvious. Make a hold.

In their own experience the authors have found a system of rewards and punishments perfectly easy of attainment. One of them has for years adopted the plan of engaging her servants at so much a month—the lowest rate at which such servant is obtainable—and so much extra as *bakshish*, conditional on good service. For instance, a khitmatghar is engaged permanently on Rs.9 a month, but the additional rupee which makes the wage up to that usually demanded by good servants is a fluctuating assessment! From it small fines are levied, beginning with one pice for forgetfulness, and running up, through degrees of culpability, to one rupee for lying. The money thus returned to imperial coffers may very well be spent on giving small rewards; so that each servant knows that by good service he can get back his own fines. That plan has never been objected to, and such a thing as a servant giving up his place has never been known in the author's experience. On the contrary, the household quite enters into the spirit of the idea, infinitely preferring it to volcanic eruptions of faultfinding.

To show what absolute children Indian servants are, the same author has for years adopted castor oil as an ultimatum in all obstinate cases, on the ground that there must be some physical cause for inability to learn or to remember. This is considered a great joke, and exposes the offender to much ridicule from his fellow-servants; so much so, that the words, '*Mem Sahib tum ko zarur kaster ile pila dena hoga*' (*The Mem Sahib will have to give you castor oil*), is often heard in the mouths of the upper servants when new-comers give trouble. In short, without kindly and reasonable devices of this kind, the usual complaint of a want of hold over servants *must* remain true until they are educated into some sense of duty. Of course, common sense is required to adjust the balance of rewards and punishments, for here again Indian servants are like children, in that they have an acute sense of justice. A very good plan for securing a certain amount of truthfulness in a servant is to insist that any one who has been caught out in a distinct falsehood should invariably bring witnesses to prove the truth of the smallest detail. It is a great disgrace and worry, generally producing a request to be given another chance after a few days.

To turn to the minor duties of a mistress, it may be remarked that she is primarily responsible for the decency and health of all persons living in her service or compound. With this object, she should insist upon her servants living in their quarters, and not in the bazaar; but this, on the other hand, is no reason why they should turn your domain into a caravanserai for their relations to the third and fourth generation. As a rule, it is well to draw a very sharp line in this respect, and if it be possible to draw it on the other side of the mothers-in-law, so much the better for peace and quietness.

Of course, if the rule that all servants shall live in quarters be enforced, it becomes the mistress's duty to see that they are decently housed, and have proper sanitary conveniences. The bearer should have strict orders to report any illness of any kind amongst the servants or their belongings; indeed, it is advisable for the mistress to inquire every day on this point, and as often as possible—once or twice a week at least—she should go a regular inspection round the compound, not forgetting the stables, fowl-houses, etc.

With regard to the kitchen, every mistress, worthy the name, will insist on having a building suitable for this use, and will not put up with a dog-kennel. On this point the authors cannot refrain from expressing their regret, that where the power exists of forcing landlords into keeping their houses in repair, and supplying sanitary arrangements as in cantonments, this power has not been exercised in regard to the most important thing of all, that is, to the procuring of kitchens, where the refuse and offal of ages cannot percolate through the mud floors, and where the drain water does not most effectually apply sewage to a large surrounding area. With existing arrangements many and many an attack of typhoid might be traced to children playing near the kitchen and pantry drain, and as in large stations the compounds narrow from lessening room, the evil will grow greater.

In regard to actual housekeeping, the authors emphatically deny the common assertion that it must necessarily run on different lines to what it does in England. Economy, prudence, efficiency are the same all over the world, and because butcher meat is cheap, that is no excuse for its being wasted. There is no reason whatever why the ordinary European routine should not be observed; indeed, the more everything is assimilated to English ways, the better and more economical will be the result. Some modification, of course, there must be, *but as little as possible*. It is, for instance, most desirable that the mistress should keep a regular storeroom, containing not merely an assortment of tins, as is usually the case, but rice, sugar, flour, potatoes, etc.; everything, in short, which, under the common custom, comes into the khansamah's* daily account, and helps more than larger items to swell the monthly bills. For it is *absolutely impossible* for the khansamah to give a true account of consumption of these things daily, without descending to cowries, and the item is, it may be safely said in every case, a nominal charge far above actual expenditure. With regard to the best plan for keeping this storeroom, the next chapter must be consulted.

A good mistress in India will try to set a good example to her servants in routine, method, and tidiness. Half an hour after breakfast should be sufficient for the whole arrangements for the day; but that half hour should be given as punctually as possible. An untidy mistress invariably has *untidy*, a weak one, *idle* servants. It should never be forgotten that—although it is most true in India—if you want a thing done, you should do it yourself; still, having to do it is a distinct confession of failure in your original intention. Anxious housewives are too apt to accept defeat in this way; the result being that the lives of educated women are wasted in doing the work of lazy servants.

The author's advice is therefore—

'*Never do work which an ordinarily good servant ought to be able to do. If the one you have will not or cannot do it, get another who can.*'

In regard to engaging new servants, written certificates to character are for the most part of no use whatever, except in respect to length of service, and its implied testimony to honesty. A man who has been six or seven years in one place is not likely to be a thief, though the authors regret to say the fact is no safeguard as far as qualifications go. The best plan is to catch your servants young, promoting them to more experienced wages on the *bakshish* theory above-mentioned. They generally learn fast enough if it is made worth their while in this way. On the other hand, it is, as a rule, a mistake to keep servants *too long* in India. Officials should be especially careful on this point, as the Oriental mind connects a confidential servant with corruption.

To return to written certificates. Their total abolition is impossible in India where the society is so fluctuating, but it would certainly be advantageous if a stand against them was made, except in certain cases. There is no reason whatever why further personal reference should not be requested in every '*chit*.'* In the majority of cases this request *could* be complied with, to the great benefit of distracted housekeepers who, having engaged a cook adorned apparently by the seven cardinal virtues, find that the only merit he possesses is being the son of a father who, having died in the odour of sanctity, left his certificates to be divided amongst his children. But in this, as in all the difficulties besetting Indian housekeeping, *combined* effort is wanting. It may safely be said that if Indian servants found cleanliness necessary in every service they took, the present abominations would soon disappear.

It is always advisable to give neat, durable, livery coats for wearing when on actual duty in the house. Broadcloth is a mistake, being hard to keep clean, and apt to get fusty. Good washing serge is best, made to fit well, but loosely, with sleeves of proper length and width. These coats, in the case of table servants, should hang on pegs in the pantry, and only be put on for actual attendance. If carefully brushed and put away as the warm season comes on, they will last for two years. For camp work, etc., a commoner washing suit may be given, and in the hot weather cotton liveries of dark blue may be given and washed regularly every week. Any little extra expense is better than having a servant behind your chair who reeks of dirt and smoke; or what is worse, in the cold season a whited sepulchre whose outside snowiness conceals warm clothes which have been slept in for months.

Finally, when all is said and done, the whole duty of an Indian mistress towards her servants is neither more or less than it is in England. Here, as there, a little reasonable human sympathy is the best oil for the household machine. Here, as there, the end and object is not merely personal comfort, but the formation of a home—that unit of civilisation where father and children, master and servant, employer and employed, can learn their several duties. [. . .]

The great object is to secure two things—smooth working, quick ordering, and subsequent peace and leisure to the mistress. It is as well, therefore, with a view to the preservation of temper, to eat your breakfast in peace before venturing into the pantry and cook-room; it is besides a mistake to be constantly on the worry.

Inspection parade should begin, then, immediately after breakfast, or as near ten o'clock as circumstances will allow. The cook should be waiting—in clean raiment—with a pile of plates, and his viands for the day spread out on a table. With everything *en evidence*, it will not take five minutes to decide on what is best, while a very constant occurrence at Indian tables—the serving up of stale, sour, and unwholesome food—will be avoided. It is perhaps *not* pleasant to go into such details, but a good mistress will remember the breadwinner who requires blood-forming nourishment, and the children whose constitutions are being built up day by day, sickly or healthy, according to the food given them; and bear in mind the fact that, in India especially, half the comfort of life depends on clean, wholesome, digestible food.

Luncheon and dinner ordered, the mistress should proceed to the storeroom, when both the bearer and the khitmatghar should be in attendance. Another five minutes will suffice to give out everything required for the day's consumption. The accounts, writing of orders, etc., will follow, and then the mistress (with a sinking heart) may begin the daily inspection of pantry, scullery, and kitchen. But before she sets foot in the back purlieus, let her remember that if a mistress will not give proper appliances, she cannot expect cleanliness. If, however, this excuse is not valid, the authors' advice is—notice the *least* dirt, *quietly*, with the order that before going for his midday recess the servant in fault shall come personally and report its removal. Let the mistress then send another servant to see if this be true; but let her guard against giving herself the least trouble in the matter. For here, again, Indian servants are like children, gaining a certain satisfaction in the idea that at any rate they have been *troublesome*.

We do not wish to advocate an unholy haughtiness; but an Indian household can no more be governed peacefully, without dignity and prestige, than an Indian Empire. For instance, if the mistress wishes to teach the cook a new dish, let her give the order for everything, down to charcoal, to be ready at a given time, and the cook in attendance; and let her do nothing herself that the servants can do, if only for this reason, that the only way of teaching is to *see* things done, not to let others see you do them. [. . .]

Bopolûchî[1] (1884)

Once upon a time a number of young girls went to draw water at the village well, and while they were filling their jars, fell a-talking of their betrothals and weddings.

Said one—'My uncle[2] will soon be coming with the bridal presents, and he is to bring the finest clothes imaginable.'

Said a second—'And my uncle-in-law is coming, I know, bringing the most delicious sweetmeats you could think of.'

Said a third—'Oh, my uncle will be here in no time, with the rarest jewels in the world.'

But Bopolûchî, the prettiest girl of them all, looked sad, for she was an orphan, and had no one to arrange a marriage for her. Nevertheless she was too proud to remain silent, so she said gaily—'And my uncle is coming also, bringing me fine dresses, fine food, and fine jewels.'

Now a wandering pedlar,[3] who sold sweet scents and cosmetics of all sorts to the country women, happened to be sitting near the well, and heard what Bopolûchî said. Being much struck by her beauty and spirit, he determined to marry her himself, and the very next day, disguised as a well-to-do farmer, he came to Bopolûchî's house laden with trays upon trays full of fine dresses, fine food, and fine jewels; for he was not a real pedlar, but a wicked robber,[4] ever so rich.

Bopolûchî would hardly believe her eyes, for everything was just as she had foretold, and the robber said he was her father's brother, who had been away in the world for years, and had now come back to arrange her marriage with one of his sons, her cousin.

Hearing this, Bopolûchî of course believed it all, and was ever so much pleased; so she packed up the few things she possessed in a bundle, and set off with the robber in high spirits.

But as they went along the road, a crow sitting on a branch croaked——

---

[1] *Bopolûcht*—Means Trickster.

[2] *Uncle: uncle-in-law*—The words used were *mâmû*, mother's brother, and *patiauhrâ*, husband's (or father-in-law's) younger brother.

[3] *Pedlar*—*Wanjârâ* or *banjârâ* (from *wanaj* or *banaj*, a bargain), a class of wandering pedlars who sell spices, etc.

[4] *Robber*—The word used was *thag, lit.* a deceiver. The *Thags* are a class but too well known in India as those who make their living by deceiving and strangling travellers. Meadows Taylor's somewhat sensational book, *The Confessions of a Thug*, has made their doings familiar enough, too, in England. In the Indian Penal Code a *thag* is defined as a person habitually associated with others for the purpose of committing robbery or child-stealing by means of murder.

> 'Bopolûchî, 'tis a pity!
> You have lost your wits, my pretty!
> 'Tis no uncle that relieves you,
> But a robber who deceives you!'[1]

'Uncle!' said Bopolûchî, 'that crow croaks funnily. What does it say?'

'Pooh!' returned the robber, 'all the crows in this country croak like that.'

A little farther on they met a peacock, which, as soon as it caught sight of the pretty little maiden, began to scream——

> 'Bopolûchî, 'tis a pity!
> You have lost your wits, my pretty!
> 'Tis no uncle that relieves you,
> But a robber who deceives you!'

'Uncle!' said the girl, 'that peacock screams funnily. What does it say?'

'Pooh!' returned the robber, 'all peacocks scream like that in this country.'

By and by a jackal slunk across the road; the moment it saw poor pretty Bopolûchî it began to howl——

> 'Bopolûchî, 'tis a pity!
> You have lost your wits, my pretty!
> 'Tis no uncle that relieves you,
> But a robber who deceives you!'

'Uncle!' said the maiden, 'that jackal howls funnily. What does it say?'

'Pooh!' returned the robber, 'all jackals howl like that in this country.'

---

[1] *Crow's, etc., verses*—The original words were—
> *Bopo Lûchî!*
> *Aqloṅ ghutî,*
> *Thag nâl ṭhagî gaî.*
> Bopo Lûchî!
> You have lost your wits,
> And have been deceived by a *ṭhag.*

So poor pretty Bopolûchî journeyed on till they reached the robber's house. Then he told her who he was, and how he intended to marry her himself. She wept and cried bitterly, but the robber had no pity, and left her in charge of his old, oh! ever so old mother, while he went out to make arrangements for the marriage feast.

Now Bopolûchî had such beautiful hair that it reached right down to her ankles, but the old mother hadn't a hair on her old bald head.

'Daughter!' said the old, ever so old mother, as she was putting the bridal dress on Bopolûchî, 'how did you manage to get such beautiful hair?'

'Well,' replied Bopolûchî, 'my mother made it grow by pounding my head in the big mortar for husking rice. At every stroke of the pestle my hair grew longer and longer. I assure you it is a plan that never fails.'

'Perhaps it would make *my* hair grow!' said the old woman eagerly.

'Perhaps it would!' quoth cunning Bopolûchî.

So the old, ever so old mother put her head in the mortar, and Bopolûchî pounded away with such a will that the old lady died.

Then Bopolûchî dressed the dead body in the scarlet bridal dress,[1] seated it on the low bridal chair, drew the veil well over the face, and put the spinning-wheel in front of it, so that when the robber came home he might think it was the bride. Then she put on the old mother's clothes, and seizing her own bundle, stepped out of the house as quickly as possible.

On her way home she met the robber, who was returning with a stolen millstone, to grind the corn for the wedding feast, on his head. She was dreadfully frightened, and slipped behind the hedge, so as not to be seen. But the robber, not recognising her in the old mother's dress, thought she was some strange woman from a neighbouring village, and so to avoid being seen he slipped behind the other hedge. Thus Bopolûchî reached home in safety.

Meanwhile, the robber, having come to his house, saw the figure in bridal scarlet sitting on the bridal chair, spinning, and of course thought it was Bopolûchî. So he called to her to help him down with the millstone, but she didn't answer. He called again, but still she didn't answer. Then he fell into a rage, and threw the millstone at her

[1] *Bridal scarlet*—Every Panjâbî bride, however poor, wears a dress of scarlet and gold for six months, and if rich, for two years.

head. The figure toppled over, and lo and behold! it was not Bopolûchî at all, but his old, ever so old mother! Whereupon the robber wept, and beat his breast, thinking he had killed her; but when he discovered pretty Bopolûchî had run away, he became wild with rage, and determined to bring her back somehow.

Now Bopolûchî was convinced that the robber would try to carry her off, so every night she begged a new lodging in some friend's house, leaving her own little bed in her own little house quite empty; but after a month or so she had come to the end of her friends, and did not like to ask any of them to give her shelter a second time. So she determined to brave it out and sleep at home, whatever happened; but she took a bill-hook to bed with her. Sure enough, in the very middle of the night four men crept in, and each seizing a leg of the bed, lifted it up and walked off, the robber himself having hold of the leg close behind her head. Bopolûchî was wide awake, but pretended to be fast asleep, until she came to a wild deserted spot, where the thieves were off their guard; then she whipped out the bill-hook, and in a twinkling cut off the heads of the two thieves at the foot of the bed. Turning round quickly, she did the same to the other thief at the head, but the robber himself ran away in a terrible fright, and scrambled like a wild cat up a tree close by before she could reach him.

'Come down!' cried brave Bopolûchî, brandishing the bill-hook, 'and fight it out!'

But the robber would not come down; so Bopolûchî gathered all the sticks she could find, piled them round the tree, and set fire to them. Of course the tree caught fire also, and the robber, half stifled with the smoke, tried to jump down, and was killed.

After that, Bopolûchî went to the robber's house and carried off all the gold and silver, jewels and clothes, that were hidden there, coming back to the village so rich that she could marry any one she pleased. And that was the end of Bopolûchî's adventures.

In the Permanent Way (1898)

I heard this story in a rail-trolly on the Pind-Dadur line, so I always think of it with a running accompaniment; a rhythmic whir of wheels in which, despite its steadiness, you feel the propelling impulse of the unseen coolies behind, then the swift skimming as they set their feet on the trolly for the brief rest which merges at the first hint of lessened speed into the old racing measure. Whir and slide, racing and resting!—while the wheels spin like bobbins and the brick rubble in the permanent way slips under your feet giddily, until you could almost fancy yourself sitting on a stationary engine, engaged in winding up an endless red ribbon. A ribbon edged, as if with tinsel, by steel rails stretching away in ever narrowing lines to the level horizon. Stretching straight as a die across a sandy desert, rippled and waved by wrinkled sand-hills into the semblance of a sandy sea.

And that, from its size, must be a seventh wave. I was just thinking this when the buzz of the brake jarred me through to the marrow of my bones.

'What's up? A train?' I asked of my companion who was giving me a lift across his section of the desert.

'No!' he replied laconically. 'Now, then! hurry up, men.'

Nothing in the wide world comes to pieces in the hand like a trolly. It was dismembered and off the line in a moment; only however, much to my surprise, to be replaced upon the rails some half a dozen yards further along them. I was opening my lips for one question when something I saw at my feet among the brick rubble made me change it for another.

'Hullo! what the dickens is that?'

To the carnal eye it was two small squares of smooth stucco, the one with an oval black stone set in it perpendicularly, the other with a round purplish one—curiously ringed with darker circles—set in it horizontally. On the stucco of one were a few dried *tulsi*[1] leaves and grains of rice; on the other suspicious-looking splashes of dark red.

'What's what?' echoed my friend, climbing up to his seat again.

'Why, man, that thing!—that thing in the permanent way!' I replied, nettled at his manner.

He gave an odd little laugh, just audible above the first whir of the wheels as we started again.

'That's about it. In the permanent way—considerably.' He paused, and I thought he was going to relapse into the silence for which he was famous; but he suddenly seemed to change his mind.

'Look here,' he said, 'it's a fifteen-mile run to the first curve, and no trains due, so if you like I'll tell you why we left the track.'

[1] Marjoram.

And he did.

When they were aligning this section I was put on to it—preliminary survey work under an R.E. man* who wore boiled shirts in the wilderness, and was great on 'Departmental Discipline.' He is in Simla* now, of course. Well, we were driving a straight line through the whole solar system and planting it out with little red flags, when one afternoon, just behind that big wave of a sand-hill, we came upon something in the way. It was a man. For further description I should say it was a thin man. There is nothing more to be said. He may have been old, he may have been young, he may have been tall, he may have been short, he may have been halt and maimed, he may have been blind, deaf, or dumb, or any or all of these. The only thing I know for *certain* is that he was thin. The *kalassies*¹ said he was some kind of a Hindu saint, and they fell at his feet promptly. I shall never forget the R.E.'s face as he stood trying to classify the creature according to Wilson's *Hindu Sects*,* or his indignation at the *kalassies'* ignorant worship of a man who, for all they knew, might be a follower of Shiva,* while they were bound to Vishnu,* or *vice versâ*. He was very learned over the *Vaishnavas* and the *Saivas*;* and all the time that bronze image with its hands on its knees squatted in the sand staring into space perfectly unmoved. Perhaps the man saw us, perhaps he didn't. I don't know; as I said before, he was thin.

So after a time we stuck a little red flag in the ground close to the small of his back, and went on our way rejoicing until we came to our camp, a mile further on. It doesn't look like it, but there is a brackish well and a sort of a village away there to the right, and of course we always took advantage of water when we could.

It must have been a week later, just as we came to the edge of the sand-hills, and could see a landmark or two, that I noticed the R.E. come up from his prismatic compass looking rather pale. Then he fussed over to me at the plane table.

'We're out,' he said, 'there is a want of Departmental Discipline in this party, and we are out.' I forget how many fractions he said, but some infinitesimal curve would have been required to bring us plumb on the next station, and as that would have ruined the R.E.'s professional reputation, we harked back to rectify the error. We

---

¹ Tent-pitchers—men employed in measuring land.

found the bronze image still sitting on the sand with its hands on its knees; but apparently it had shifted its position some three feet or so to the right, for the flag was fully that distance to the left of it. That night the R.E. came to my tent with his hands full of maps and his mind of suspicions.

'It seems incredible,' he said, 'but I am almost convinced that *byragi* or *jogi*, or *gosain* or *sunyasi*,* whichever he may be, has had the unparalleled effrontery to move my flag. I can't be sure, but if I were, I would have him arrested on the spot.'

I suggested he was that already; but it is sometimes difficult to make an R.E. see a Cooper's Hill joke,* especially when he is your superior officer. So we did that bit over again. As it happened, my chief was laid up with sun fever when we came to the bronze image, and I had charge of the party. I don't know why, exactly, but it seemed to me rough on the thin man to stick a red flag at the small of his back, as a threat that we meant to annex the only atom of things earthly to which he still clung; time enough for that when the line was actually under construction. So I told the *kalassies* to let him do duty as a survey mark; for, from what I had heard, I knew that once a man of that sort fixes on a place in which to gain immortality by penance, he sticks to it till the mortality, at any rate, comes to an end. And this one, I found out from the villagers, had been there for ten years. Of course they said he never ate, nor drank, nor moved, but that, equally of course, was absurd.

A year after this I came along again in charge of a construction party, with an overseer called Craddock, a big yellow-headed Saxon who couldn't keep off the drink, and who had in consequence been going down steadily in one department or another for years. As good a fellow as ever stepped when he was sober. Well, we came right on the thin one again, plump in the very middle of the permanent way. We dug round him and levelled up to him for some time, and then one day Craddock gave a nod at me and walked over to where that image squatted staring into space. I can see the two now, Craddock in his navvy's dress, his blue eyes keen yet kind in the red face shaded by the dirty pith hat, and the thin man without a rag of any sort to hide his bronze anatomy.

'Look here, sonny,' said Craddock, stooping over the other, 'you're in the way—in the permanent way.'

Then he just lifted him right up, gently, as if he had been a child, and set him down about four feet to the left. It was to be a metre gauge, so that was enough for safety. There he sat after we had propped him up again with his *byraga* or cleft stick under the left arm, as if he were quite satisfied with the change. But next day he was in the old place. It was no use arguing with him. The only thing to be done was to move him out of the way when we wanted it. Of course when the earthwork was finished there was the plate-laying and ballasting and what not to be done, so it came to be part of the big Saxon's regular business to say in his Oxfordshire drawl—

'Sonny, yo're in the waiy—in the permanent waiy.'

Craddock, it must be mentioned, was in a peculiarly sober, virtuous mood, owing, no doubt, to the desolation of the desert; in which, by the way, I found him quite a godsend as a companion, for when he was on the talk the quaintness of his ideas was infinitely amusing, and his knowledge of the natives, picked up as a loafer in many a bazaar and *serai*,* was surprisingly wide, if appallingly inaccurate.

'There is something, savin' yo're presence, sir, blamed wrong in the whole blamed business,' he said to me, with a mild remonstrance in his blue eyes, one evening after he had removed the obstruction to progress. 'That pore fellar, sir, 'e's a meditatin' on the word *Hom—Hommipuddenhome*[1] it is, sir, I've bin told—an' doin' 'is little level to make the spiritooal man subdoo 'is fleshly hinstinckts. And I, Nathaniel James Craddock, so called in Holy Baptism, I do assure you, a-eatin' and a-drinkin' 'early, catches 'im right up like a babby, and sets 'im on one side, as if I was born to it. And so I will—an' willin', too—so as to keep 'im from 'arm's way; for 'eathin or Christian, sir, 'e's an eggsample to the spiritooal part of me which, savin' your presence, sir, is most ways drink.'

Poor Craddock! He went on the spree hopelessly the day after we returned to civilisation, and it was with the greatest difficulty that I succeeded in getting him a trial as driver to the material train which commenced running up and down the section. The first time I went with it on business I had an inspection carriage tacked on behind the truck-loads of coolies and ballast, so that I could not make out why on earth we let loose a danger whistle and slowed down to full stop in the very middle of the desert until I jumped down and ran forward. Even

---

[1] *Om mi pudmi houm.** The Buddhist invocation.

then I was only in time to see Craddock coming back to his engine with a redder face than ever.

'It's only old Meditations, sir,' he said apologetically, as I climbed in beside him. 'It don't take a minute; no longer nor a cow, and them's in the reg'lations. You see, sir, I wouldn't 'ave 'arm come to the pore soul afore 'is spiritooal nater 'ad the straight tip hoäm. Neither would none of us, sir, coolie nor driver, sir, on the section. We all likes old *Hommipuddenhome*; 'e sticks to it so stiddy, that's where it is.'

'Do you mean to say that you always have to get out and lift him off the line?' I asked, wondering rather at the patience required for the task.

'That's so, sir,' he replied slowly, in the same apologetic tones. 'It don't take no time you see, sir, that's where it is. P'r'aps you may 'ave thought, like as I did first time, that 'e'd save 'is bacon when the engine come along. Lordy! the cold sweat broke out on me that time. I brought 'er up, sir, with the buffers at the back of 'is 'ed like them things the photographers jiminy you straight with. But 'e ain't that sort, ain't Meditations.' Here Craddock asked leave to light his pipe, and in the interval I looked ahead along the narrowing red ribbon with its tinsel edge, thinking how odd it must have been to see it barred by that bronze image.

'No! that ain't his sort,' continued Craddock meditatively, 'though wot 'is sort may be, sir, is not my part to say. I've arst, and arst, and arst them pundits, but there ain't one of them can really tell, sir, 'cos he ain't got any marks about him. You see, sir, it's by their marks, like cattle, as you tell 'em. Some says he worships bloody *Shivers*[1]—'im 'oos wife you know, sir, they calls *Martha Davy*[2]—a Christian sort o' name, ain't it, sir, for a 'eathin idol?—and some says 'e worships *Wishnyou Lucksmi*[3] an' that lot, an' *Holy*[4] too, though, savin' your presence, sir, it ain't much holiness I see at them times, but mostly drink. It makes me feel quite 'omesick, I do assure you, sir, more as if they was humans like me, likewise.'

'And which belief do you incline to?' I asked, for the sake of prolonging the conversation.

He drew his rough hand over his corn-coloured beard, and quite a grave look came to the blue eyes. 'I inclines to *Shiver*,' he said

---

[1] *Shiva.*
[2] *Mata devi.**
[3] *Vishnu Lukshmi.**
[4] *Holi*, the Indian Saturnalia.*

decisively, 'and I'll tell you why, sir. *Shiver*'s bloody; but 'e's dead on death. They calls 'im the Destroyer. 'E don't care a damn for the body; 'e's all for the spiritooal nater, like old Meditations there. Now *Wishnyou Lucksmi* an' that lot is the Preservers. They eats an' drinks 'earty, like me. So it stands to reason, sir, don't it? that 'e's a *Shiver*, and I'm a *Wishnyou Lucksmi*.' He stood up under pretence of giving a wipe round a valve with the oily rag he held, and looked out to the horizon where the sun was setting, like a huge red signal right on the narrowing line. 'So,' he went on after a pause, 'that's why I wouldn't 'ave 'arm come to old Meditations. 'E's a *Shiver*, I'm a *Wishnyou Lucksmi*. That's what *I* am.'

His meaning was quite clear, and I am not ashamed to say that it touched me.

'Look here,' I said, 'take care you don't run over that old chap some day when you are drunk, that's all.'

He bent over another valve, burnishing it. 'I hope to God I don't,' he said in a low voice. 'That'd about finish me altogether, I expect.'

We returned the next morning before daybreak; but I went on the engine, being determined to see how that bronze image looked on the permanent way when you were steaming up to it.

'You ketch sight of 'im clear this side,' said Craddock, 'a good two mile or more; ef you had a telescope ten for that matter. It ain't so easy t'other side with the sun a-shining bang inter the eyes. And there ain't no big wave as a signal over there. But Lordy! there ain't no fear of my missin' old Meditations.'

Certainly, none that morning. He showed clear, first against the rosy flush of dawn, afterwards like a dark stain on the red ribbon.

'I'll run up close to him to-day, sir,' said Craddock, 'so as you shall see wot 'e's made of.'

The whistle rang shrill over the desert of sand, which lay empty of all save that streak of red with the dark stain upon it; but the stain never moved, never stirred, though the snorting demon from the west came racing up to it full speed.

'Have a care, man! Have a care!' I shouted; but my words were almost lost in the jar of the brake put on to the utmost. Even then I could only crane round the cab with my eyes fixed on that bronze image straight ahead of us. Could we stop in time—would it move? Yes! no! yes! Slower and slower—how many turns of the fly-wheel to so many yards?—I felt as if I were working the sum frantically in my head, when, with a little backward shiver, the great circle of steel stopped dead, and Craddock's voice came in cheerful triumph—

'There! didn't I tell you, sir? Ain't 'e stiddy? Ain't 'e a-subdooin' of mortality beautiful?' The next instant he was out, and as he stooped to his task he flung me back a look.

'Now, sonny, you'll 'ave to move. You're in the way—the permanent way, my dear.'

That was the last I saw of him for some time, for I fell sick and went home. When I returned to work I found, much to my surprise, that Craddock was in the same appointment; in fact, he had been promoted to drive the solitary passenger train which now ran daily across the desert. He had not been on the spree once, I was told; indeed, the R.E., who was of the Methodist division of that gallant regiment, took great pride in a reformation which, he informed me, was largely due to his religious teaching combined with Departmental Discipline.

'And how is Meditations?' I asked, when the great rough hand had shaken mine vehemently.

Craddock's face seemed to me to grow redder than ever. ''E's very well, sir, thanking you kindly. There's a native driver on the Goods now. 'E's a *Shiver-Martha Davy* lot, so I pays 'im five rupee a month to nip out sharp with the stoker an' shovel 'is old saint to one side. I'm gettin' good pay now, you know, sir.'

I told him there was no reason to apologise for the fact, and that I hoped it might long continue; whereat he gave a sheepish kind of laugh, and said he hoped so too.

Christmas came and went uneventfully without an outbreak, and I could not refrain from congratulating Craddock on one temptation safely over.

He smiled broadly.

'Lor' bless you, sir,' he said, 'you didn't never think, did you, that Nathaniel James Craddock, which his name was given to 'im in Holy Baptism, I do assure you, was going to knuckle down that way to old *Hommipuddenhome*? 'Twouldn't be fair on Christmas noways, sir, and though I don't set the store 'e does on 'is spiritooal nater, I was born and bred in a Christyan country, I do assure you.'

I congratulated him warmly on his sentiments, and hoped again that they would last; to which he replied as before that he hoped so too.

And then *Holi* time came round, and, as luck would have it, the place was full of riff-raff low whites going on to look for work in a further section. I had to drive through the bazaar on my way to the railway station, and it beat anything I had ever seen in various vice. East and West were outbidding each other in iniquity, and to make matters worse, an electrical dust-storm was blowing hard. You never saw such a scene; it was pandemonium, background and all. I thought I caught a glimpse of a corn-coloured beard and a pair of blue eyes in a wooden balcony among tinkling *sútáras** and jasmin chaplets, but I wasn't sure. However, as I was stepping into the inspection carriage, which, as usual, was the last in the train, I saw Craddock crossing the platform to his engine. His white coat was all splashed with the red dye they had been throwing at each other, *Holi* fashion, in the bazaar; his walk, to my eyes, had a lilt in it, and finally, the neck of a black bottle showed from one pocket.

Obedient to one of those sudden impulses which come, Heaven knows why, I took my foot off the step and followed him to the engine.

'Comin' aboard, sir,' he said quite collectedly. 'You'd be better be'ind to-night, for it's blowin' grit fit to make me a walkin' sandpaper inside and out.' And before I could stop him the black bottle was at his mouth. This decided me. Perhaps my face showed my thoughts, for as I climbed into the cab he gave an uneasy laugh. 'Don't be afraid, sir: it's black as pitch, but I knows where old Meditations comes by instinck, I do assure you. One hour an' seventeen minutes from the distance signal with pressure as it oughter be. Hillo! there's the whistle and the baboo a-waving. Off we goes!'

As we flashed past a red light I looked at my watch.

'Don't you be afraid, sir,' he said, again looking at his. 'It's ten to ten now, and in one hour an' seventeen minutes on goes the brake. That's the ticket for *Shivers* and *Martha Davy*; though I *am* a *Wishnyou Lucksmi*.' He paused a moment, and as he stood put his hand on a stanchion to steady himself.

'Very much of a *Wishnyou Lucksmi*,' he went on with a shake of the head. 'I've 'ad a drop too much, and I know it; but it ain't fair on a fellar like me, 'aving so many names to them, when they're all the same—a eatin' an' drinkin' lot like me. There's Christen[1]—you'd

---

[1] *Kristna.*

'ave thought he'd 'ave been a decent chap by 'is name, but 'e went on orful with them *Gopis*—that's Hindu for milkmaids, sir. And Harry[1]—well, he wasn't no better than some other Harrys I've heard on. And Canyer,[2] I expect he could just about. To say nothin' of *Gopi-naughty*;[3] and naughty he were, as no doubt you've heard tell, sir. There's too many on them for a pore fellar who don't set store by 'is spiritooal nater; especially when they mixes themselves up with *Angcore*[4] whisky, an' ginger ale.'

His blue eyes had a far-away look in them, and his words were fast losing independence, but I understood what he meant perfectly. In that brief glimpse of the big bazaar I had seen the rows of Western bottles standing cheek by jowl with the bowls of *dolee* dye, the sour curds and sweetmeats of *Holi*-tide.

'You had better sit down, Craddock,' I said severely, for I saw that the fresh air was having its usual effect. 'Perhaps if you sleep a bit you'll be more fit for work. I'll look out and wake you when you're wanted.'

He gave a silly laugh, let go the stanchion, and drew out his watch.

'Don't you be afraid, sir! One hour and seventeen minutes from the distance signal. I'll keep 'im out o' 'arm's way, an' willing, to the end of the chapter.'

He gave a lurch forward to the seat, stumbled, and the watch dropped from his hand. For a moment I thought he might go overboard, and I clutched at him frantically; but with another lurch and an indistinct admonition to me not to be afraid, he sank into the corner of the bench and was asleep in a second. Then I stooped to pick up the watch, and, rather to my surprise, found it uninjured and still going.

Craddock's words, 'ten minutes to ten,'* recurred to me. Then it would be twenty-seven minutes past eleven before he was wanted. I sat down to wait, bidding the native stoker keep up the fire as usual. The wind was simply shrieking round us, and the sand drifted thick on Craddock's still, upturned face. More than once I wiped it off, feeling he might suffocate. It was the noisiest, and at the same time the most silent journey I ever undertook. Pandemonium, with seventy times seven of its devils let loose outside the cab; inside

---

[1] *Hari.*   [2] *Kaniya.*
[3] *Gopi-nath.* These are all names of Vishnu in his various Avatars.*   [4] *Encore.*

Craddock asleep, or dead—he might have been the latter from his stillness. It became oppressive after a time, as I remembered that other still figure, miles down the track, which was so strangely bound to this one beside me. The minutes seemed hours, and I felt a distinct relief when the watch, which I had held in my hand most of the time, told me it was seventeen minutes past eleven. Only ten minutes before the brake should be put on; and Craddock would require all that time to get his senses about him.

I might as well have tried to awaken a corpse, and it was three minutes to the twenty-seven when I gave up the idea as hopeless. Not that it mattered, since I could drive an engine as well as he; still the sense of responsibility weighed heavily upon me. My hand on the brake valve trembled visibly as I stood watching the minute-hand of the watch. Thirty seconds before the time I put the brake on hard, determining to be on the safe side. And then when I had taken this precaution a perfectly unreasoning anxiety seized on me. I stepped on to the footboard and craned forward into the darkness which, even without the wind and the driving dust, was blinding. The lights in front shot slantways, showing an angle of red ballast, barred by gleaming steel; beyond that a formless void of sand. But the centre of the permanent way, where that figure would be sitting, was dark as death itself. What a fool I was, when the great circle of the fly-wheel was slackening, slackening, every second! And yet the fear grew lest I should have been too late, lest I should have made some mistake. To appease my own folly I drew out my watch in confirmation of the time. Great God! a difference of two minutes!—two whole minutes!—yet the watches had been the same at the distance signal?—the fall, of course! the fall!

I seemed unable to do anything but watch that slackening wheel, even though I became conscious of a hand on my shoulder, of some one standing beside me on the footboard. No! not standing, swaying, lurching——

'Don't!' I cried. 'Don't! it's madness!' But that some one was out in the darkness. Then I saw a big white figure dash across the angle of light with outspread arms.

'Now then, sonny! yo're in the way—the permanent way.'

The inspector paused, and I seemed to come back to the sliding whir of the trolly wheels. In the distance a semaphore was dropping its red arm, and a pointsman, like a speck on the ribbon, was at work shunting us into a siding.

'Well?' I asked.

'There isn't anything more. When a whole train goes over two men who are locked in each other's arms it is hard—hard to tell—well, which is *Shivers Martha Davy*, and which is *Wishnyou Lucksmi*. It was right out in the desert in the hot weather, no parsons or people to object; so I buried them there in the permanent way.'

'And those are tombstones, I suppose?'

He laughed. 'No; altars. The native *employés* put them up to their saint. The oval black upright stone is Shiva, the Destroyer's *lingam*,* those splashes are blood. The flat one, decorated with flowers, is the *salagrama*,[1] sacred to Vishnu the Preserver. You see nobody really knew whether old Meditations was a *Saiva* or a *Vaishnava*; so I suggested this arrangement* as the men were making a sectarian quarrel out of the question.' He paused again and added—

'You see it does for both of them.'

The jar of the points prevented me from replying.

See also: Barker; Baughan; Clifford; Conrad; Kingsley; Kipling; Perrin; Trevelyan.

G. A. HENTY
(1832–1902)

A Pipe of Mystery (1890)

A jovial party were gathered round a blazing fire in an old grange near Warwick. The hour was getting late; the very little ones had, after dancing round the Christmas-tree, enjoying the snapdragon,* and playing a variety of games, gone off to bed; and the elder boys and girls now gathered round their uncle, Colonel Harley, and asked him for a story—above all, a ghost story.

'But I have never seen any ghosts,' the colonel said, laughing; 'and, moreover, I don't believe in them one bit. I have travelled pretty well

---

[1] A fossil ammonite.

all over the world, I have slept in houses said to be haunted, but nothing have I seen—no noises that could not be accounted for by rats or the wind have I ever heard. I have never'—and here he paused—'never but once met with any circumstances or occurrence that could not be accounted for by the light of reason, and I know you prefer hearing stories of my own adventures to mere invention.'

'Yes, uncle. But what was the "once" when circumstances happened that you could not explain?'

'It's rather a long story,' the colonel said, 'and it's getting late.'

'Oh! no, no, uncle; it does not matter a bit how late we sit up on Christmas Eve, and the longer the story is, the better; and if you don't believe in ghosts, how can it be a story of something you could not account for by the light of nature?'

'You will see when I have done,' the colonel said. 'It is rather a story of what the Scotch call second sight, than one of ghosts. As to accounting for it, you shall form your own opinion when you have heard me to the end.

'I landed in India in '50, and after going through the regular drill work, marched with a detachment up country to join my regiment, which was stationed at Jubbalpore,* in the very heart of India. It has become an important place since; the railroad across India passes through it, and no end of changes have taken place; but at that time it was one of the most out-of-the-way stations in India, and, I may say, one of the most pleasant. It lay high, there was capital boating on the Nerbudda, and, above all, it was a grand place for sport, for it lay at the foot of the hill country, an immense district, then but little known, covered with forests and jungle, and abounding with big game of all kinds.

'My great friend there was a man named Simmonds. He was just of my own standing; we had come out in the same ship, had marched up the country together, and were almost like brothers. He was an old Etonian, I an old Westminster, and we were both fond of boating, and, indeed, of sport of all kinds. But I am not going to tell you of that now. The people in these hills are called Gonds, a true hill tribe —that is to say, aborigines, somewhat of the negro type. The chiefs are of mixed blood, but the people are almost black. They are supposed to accept the religion of the Hindus, but are in reality deplorably ignorant and superstitious. Their priests are a sort of compound of a Brahmin priest and a negro fetish man, and among their principal duties is that of charming away tigers from the villages by means of incantations. There, as in other parts of India, were a few wandering fakirs, who enjoyed an immense reputation for holiness and wisdom. The people would go to them from great distances for charms or predictions, and believed in their power with implicit faith.

'At the time when we were at Jubbalpore, there was one of these fellows, whose reputation altogether eclipsed that of his rivals, and nothing could be done until his permission had been asked and his blessing obtained. All sorts of marvellous stories were constantly coming to our ears of the unerring foresight with which he predicted the termination of diseases, both in men and animals; and so generally was he believed in that the colonel ordered that no one connected with the regiment should consult him, for these predictions very frequently brought about their own fulfilment; for those who were told that an illness would terminate fatally, lost all hope, and literally lay down to die.

'However, many of the stories that we heard could not be explained on these grounds, and the fakir and his doings were often talked over at mess, some of the officers scoffing at the whole business, others maintaining that some of these fakirs had, in some way or another, the power of foretelling the future, citing many well authenticated anecdotes upon the subject.

'The older officers were the believers, we young fellows were the scoffers. But for the well-known fact that it is very seldom indeed that these fakirs will utter any of their predictions to Europeans, some of us would have gone to him, to test his powers. As it was, none of us had ever seen him.

'He lived in an old ruined temple, in the middle of a large patch of jungle at the foot of the hills, some ten or twelve miles away.

'I had been at Jubbalpore about a year, when I was woke up one night by a native, who came in to say that at about eight o'clock a tiger had killed a man in his village, and had dragged off the body.

'Simmonds and I were constantly out after tigers,* and the people in all the villages within twenty miles knew that we were always ready to pay for early information. This tiger had been doing great damage, and had carried off about thirty men, women, and children. So great was the fear of him, indeed, that the people in the neighbourhood he frequented scarcely dared stir out of doors, except in parties of five or six. We had had several hunts after him, but, like all man-eaters, he was old and awfully crafty; and although we got several snap shots at him, he had always managed to save his skin.

'In a quarter of an hour after the receipt of the message, Charley Simmonds and I were on the back of an elephant, which was our joint property; our shekarry,* a capital fellow, was on foot beside us, and with the native trotting on ahead as guide we went off at the best pace of old Begaum, for that was the elephant's name. The village was fifteen miles away, but we got there soon after daybreak, and were received with delight by the population. In half an hour the hunt was organized; all the male population turned out as beaters, with sticks, guns, tom-toms, and other instruments for making a noise.

'The trail was not difficult to find. A broad path, with occasional smears of blood, showed where he had dragged his victim through the long grass to a cluster of trees a couple of hundred yards from the village.

'We scarcely expected to find him there, but the villagers held back, while we went forward with cocked rifles. We found, however, nothing but a few bones and a quantity of blood. The tiger had made off at the approach of daylight into the jungle, which was about two miles distant. We traced him easily enough, and found that he had entered a large ravine, from which several smaller ones branched off.

'It was an awkward place, as it was next to impossible to surround it with the number of people at our command. We posted them at last all along the upper ground, and told them to make up in noise what they wanted in numbers. At last all was ready, and we gave the signal. However, I am not telling you a hunting story, and need only say that we could neither find nor disturb him. In vain we pushed Begaum through the thickest of the jungle which clothed the sides and bottom of the ravine, while the men shouted, beat their tom-toms, and showered imprecations against the tiger himself and his ancestors up to the remotest generations.

'The day was tremendously hot, and, after three hours' march, we gave it up for a time, and lay down in the shade, while the shekarries made a long examination of the ground all round the hillside, to be sure that he had not left the ravine. They came back with the news that no traces could be discovered, and that, beyond a doubt, he was still there. A tiger will crouch up in an exceedingly small clump of grass or bush, and will sometimes almost allow himself to be trodden on before moving. However, we determined to have one more search, and if that should prove unsuccessful, to send off to Jubbalpore for some more of the men to come out with elephants, while we kept up a circle of fires, and of noises of all descriptions, so as to keep him a prisoner until the arrival of the reinforcements. Our next search was no more successful than our first had been; and having, as we imagined, examined every clump and crevice in which he could have been concealed, we had just reached the upper end of the ravine, when we heard a tremendous roar, followed by a perfect babel of yells and screams from the natives.

'The outburst came from the mouth of the ravine, and we felt at once that he had escaped. We hurried back to find, as we had expected, that the tiger was gone. He had burst out suddenly from his hiding-place, had seized a native, torn him horribly, and had made across the open plain.

'This was terribly provoking, but we had nothing to do but follow him. This was easy enough, and we traced him to a detached patch of wood and jungle, two miles distant. This wood was four or five hundred yards across, and the exclamations of the people at once told us that it was the one in which stood the ruined temple of the fakir of whom I have been telling you. I forgot to say, that as the tiger broke out one of the village shekarries had fired at, and, he declared, wounded him.

'It was already getting late in the afternoon, and it was hopeless to attempt to beat the jungle that night. We therefore sent off a runner with a note to the colonel, asking him to send the work-elephants, and to allow a party of volunteers to march over at night, to help surround the jungle when we commenced beating it in the morning.

'We based our request upon the fact that the tiger was a notorious man-eater, and had been doing immense damage. We then had a talk with our shekarry, sent a man off to bring provisions for the people out with us, and then set them to work cutting sticks and grass to make a circle of fires.

'We both felt much uneasiness respecting the fakir, who might be seized at any moment by the enraged tiger. The natives would not allow that there was any cause for fear, as the tiger would not dare to touch so holy a man. Our belief in the respect of the tiger for sanctity was by no means strong, and we determined to go in and warn him of the presence of the brute in the wood. It was a mission which we could not intrust to anyone else, for no native would have entered the jungle for untold gold; so we mounted the Begaum again, and started. The path leading towards the temple was pretty wide, and as we went along almost noiselessly, for the elephant was too well trained to tread upon fallen sticks, it was just possible we might come upon the tiger suddenly, so we kept our rifles in readiness in our hands.

'Presently we came in sight of the ruins. No one was at first visible; but at that very moment the fakir came out from the temple. He did not see or hear us, for we were rather behind him and still among the trees, but at once proceeded in a high voice to break into a sing-song prayer. He had not said two words before his voice was drowned in a terrific roar, and in an instant the tiger had sprung upon him, struck him to the ground, seized him as a cat would a mouse, and started off with him at a trot. The brute evidently had not detected our presence, for he came right towards us. We halted the Begaum, and with our fingers on the triggers, awaited the favourable moment. He was a hundred yards from us when he struck down his victim; he was not more than fifty when he caught sight of us. He stopped for an instant in surprise. Charley muttered, "Both barrels, Harley," and as the beast turned to plunge into the jungle, and so showed us his side, we sent four bullets crashing into him, and he rolled over lifeless.

'We went up to the spot, made the Begaum give him a kick, to be sure that he was dead, and then got down to examine the unfortunate fakir. The tiger had seized him by the shoulder, which was terribly torn, and the bone broken. He was still perfectly conscious.

'We at once fired three shots, our usual signal that the tiger was dead, and in a few minutes were surrounded by the villagers, who hardly knew whether to be delighted at the death of their enemy, or to grieve over the injury to the fakir. We proposed taking the latter to our hospital at Jubbalpore, but this he positively refused to listen to. However we finally persuaded him to allow his arm to be set and the wounds dressed in the first place by our regimental surgeon, after which he could go to one of the native villages and have his arm dressed in accordance with his own notions. A litter was soon improvised, and away we went to Jubbalpore, which we reached about eight in the evening.

'The fakir refused to enter the hospital, so we brought out a couple of trestles, laid the litter upon them, and the surgeon set his arm and dressed his wounds by torch-light, when he was lifted into a dhoolie,* and his bearers again prepared to start for the village.

'Hitherto he had only spoken a few words; but he now briefly expressed his deep gratitude to Simmonds and myself. We told him that we would ride over to see him shortly, and hoped to find him getting on rapidly. Another minute and he was gone.

'It happened that we had three or four fellows away on leave or on staff duty, and several others knocked up with fever just about this time, so that the duty fell very heavily upon the rest of us, and it was over a month before we had time to ride over to see the fakir.

'We had heard he was going on well; but we were surprised, on reaching the village, to find that he had already returned to his old abode in the jungle. However, we had made up our minds to see him, especially as we had agreed that we would endeavour to persuade him to do a prediction for us; so we turned our horses' heads towards the jungle. We found the fakir sitting on a rock in front of the temple, just where he had been seized by the tiger. He rose as we rode up.

'"I knew that you would come to-day, sahibs, and was joyful in the thought of seeing those who have preserved my life."

'"We are glad to see you looking pretty strong again, though your arm is still in a sling," I said, for Simmonds was not strong in Hindustani.

'"How did you know that we were coming?" I asked, when we had tied up our horses.

'"Siva* has given to his servant to know many things," he said quietly.

'"Did you know beforehand that the tiger was going to seize you?" I asked.

'"I knew that a great danger threatened, and that Siva would not let me die before my time had come."

'"Could you see into our future?" I asked.

'The fakir hesitated, looked at me for a moment earnestly to see if I was speaking in mockery, and then said:

'"The sahibs do not believe in the power of Siva or of his servants. They call his messengers impostors, and scoff at them when they speak of the events of the future."

'"No, indeed," I said. "My friend and I have no idea of scoffing. We have heard of so many of your predictions coming true, that we are really anxious that you should tell us something of the future."

'The fakir nodded his head, went into the temple, and returned in a minute or two with two small pipes used by the natives for opium-smoking, and a brazier of burning charcoal. The pipes were already charged. He made signs to us to sit down, and took his place in front of us. Then he began singing in a low voice, rocking himself to and fro, and waving a staff which he held in his hand. Gradually his voice rose, and his gesticulations and actions became more violent. So far as I could make out, it was a prayer to Siva that he would give some glimpse of the future which might benefit the sahibs who had saved the life of his servant. Presently he darted forward, gave us each a pipe, took two pieces of red-hot charcoal from the brazier in his fingers, without seeming to know that they were warm, and placed them in the pipes; then he recommenced his singing and gesticulations.

'A glance at Charley, to see if, like myself, he was ready to carry the thing through, and then I put the pipe to my lips. I felt at once that it was opium, of which I had before made experiment, but mixed with some other substance, which was, I imagine, haschish, a preparation of hemp. A few puffs, and I felt a drowsiness creeping over me. I saw, as through a mist, the fakir swaying himself backwards and forwards, his arms waving, and his face distorted. Another minute, and the pipe slipped from my fingers, and I fell back insensible.

'How long I lay there I do not know. I woke with a strange and not unpleasant sensation, and presently became conscious that the fakir was gently pressing, with a sort of shampooing action, my temples and head. When he saw that I opened my eyes he left me, and performed the same process upon Charley. In a few minutes he rose from his stooping position, waved his hand in token of adieu, and walked slowly back into the temple.

'As he disappeared I sat up; Charley did the same.

'We stared at each other for a minute without speaking, and then Charley said:

'"This is a rum go, and no mistake, old man."

'"You're right, Charley. My opinion is, we've made fools of ourselves. Let's be off out of this."

'We staggered to our feet, for we both felt like drunken men, made our way to our horses, poured a mussuk* of water over our heads, took a drink of brandy from our flasks, and then feeling more like ourselves, mounted and rode out of the jungle.

'"Well, Harley, if the glimpse of futurity which I had is true, all I can say is that it was extremely unpleasant."

'"That was just my case, Charley."

'"My dream, or whatever you like to call it, was about a mutiny of the men."

'"You don't say so, Charley; so was mine. This is monstrously strange, to say the least of it. However, you tell your story first, and then I will tell mine."

'"It was very short," Charley said. "We were at mess—not in our present mess-room—we were dining with the fellows of some other regiment. Suddenly, without any warning, the windows were filled with a crowd of Sepoys, who opened fire right and left into us. Half the fellows were shot down at once; the rest of us made a rush to our swords just as the niggers came swarming into the room. There was a desperate fight for a moment. I remember that Subadar Pirán—one of the best native officers in the regiment, by the way—made a rush at me, and I shot him through the head with a revolver. At the same moment a ball hit me, and down I went. At the moment a Sepoy fell dead across me, hiding me partly from sight. The fight lasted a minute or two longer. I fancy a few fellows escaped, for I heard shots outside. Then the place became quiet. In another minute I heard a crackling, and saw that the devils had set the mess-room on fire. One of our men, who was lying close by me, got up and crawled to the window, but he was shot down the moment he showed himself. I was hesitating whether to do the same or to lie still and be smothered, when suddenly I rolled the dead sepoy off, crawled into the ante-room half-suffocated by smoke, raised the lid of a very heavy trap-door, and stumbled down some steps into a place, half store-house half cellar, under the mess-room. How I knew about it being there I don't know. The trap closed over my head with a bang. That is all I remember."

'"Well, Charley, curiously enough my dream was also about an extraordinary escape from danger, lasting, like yours, only a minute or two. The first thing I remember—there seems to have been something before, but what, I don't know—I was on horseback, holding a very pretty but awfully pale girl in front of me. We were pursued by a whole troop of Sepoy cavalry, who were firing pistol-shots at us. We were not more than seventy or eighty yards in front, and they were gaining fast, just as I rode into a large deserted temple. In the centre was a huge stone figure. I jumped off my horse with the lady, and as I did so she said, 'Blow out my brains, Edward; don't let me fall alive into their hands.'

'"Instead of answering, I hurried her round behind the idol, pushed against one of the leaves of a flower in the carving, and the stone swung back, and showed a hole just large enough to get through, with a stone staircase inside the body of the idol, made no doubt for the priest to go up and give responses through the mouth. I hurried the girl through, crept in after her, and closed the stone, just as our pursuers came clattering into the courtyard. That is all I remember."

'"Well, it is monstrously rum," Charley said, after a pause. "Did you understand what the old fellow was singing about before he gave us the pipes?"

'"Yes; I caught the general drift. It was an entreaty to Siva to give us some glimpse of futurity which might benefit us."

'We lit our cheroots and rode for some miles at a brisk canter without remark. When we were within a short distance of home we reined up.

'"I feel ever so much better," Charley said. "We have got that opium out of our heads now. How do you account for it all, Harley?"

'"I account for it in this way, Charley. The opium naturally had the effect of making us both dream, and as we took similar doses of the same mixture, under similar circumstances, it is scarcely extraordinary that it should have affected the same portion of the brain, and caused a certain similarity in our dreams. In all nightmares something terrible happens, or is on the point of happening; and so it was here. Not unnaturally in both our cases, our thoughts turned to soldiers. If you remember there was a talk at mess some little time since, as to what would happen in the extremely unlikely event of the sepoys mutinying in a body. I have no doubt that was the foundation of both our dreams. It is all natural enough when we come to think it over calmly. I think, by the way, we had better agree to say nothing at all about it in the regiment."

'"I should think not," Charley said. "We should never hear the end of it; they would chaff us out of our lives."

'We kept our secret, and came at last to laugh over it heartily when we were together. Then the subject dropped, and by the end of a year had as much escaped our minds as any other dream would have done. Three months after the affair the regiment was ordered down to Allahabad, and the change of place no doubt helped to erase all memory of the dream. Four years after we had left Jubbalpore we went to Beerapore. The time is very marked in my memory, because the very week we arrived there, your aunt, then Miss Gardiner, came out from England, to her father, our colonel. The instant I saw her I was impressed with the idea that I knew her intimately. I recollected her face, her figure, and the very tone of her voice, but wherever I had met her I could not conceive. Upon the occasion of my first introduction to her, I could not help telling her that I was convinced that we had met, and asking her if she did not remember it. No, she did not remember, but very likely she might have done so, and she suggested the names of several people at whose houses we might have met. I did not know any of them. Presently she asked how long I had been out in India?

'"Six years," I said.

'"And how old, Mr Harley," she said, "do you take me to be?"

'I saw in one instant my stupidity, and was stammering out an apology, when she went on,—

'"I am very little over eighteen, Mr Harley, although I evidently look ever so many years older; but papa can certify to my age; so I was only twelve when you left England."

'I tried in vain to clear matters up. Your aunt would insist that I took her to be forty, and the fun that my blunder made rather drew us together, and gave me a start over the other fellows at the station, half of whom fell straightaway in love with her. Some months went on, and when the mutiny broke out we were engaged to be married. It is a proof of how completely the opium-dreams had passed out of the minds of both Simmonds and myself, that even when rumours of general disaffection among the Sepoys began to be current, they never once recurred to us; and even when the news of the actual mutiny reached us, we were just as confident as were the others of the fidelity of our own regiment. It was the old story, foolish confidence and black treachery. As at very many other stations, the mutiny broke out when we were at mess. Our regiment was dining with the 34th Bengalees. Suddenly, just as dinner was over, the window was opened, and a tremendous fire poured in. Four or five men fell dead at once, and the poor colonel, who was next to me, was shot right through the head. Every one rushed to his sword and drew his pistol—for we had been ordered to carry pistols as part of our uniform. I was next to Charley Simmonds as the Sepoys of both regiments, headed by Subadar Pirán, poured in at the windows.

'"I have it now," Charley said; "it is the scene I dreamed."'

'As he spoke he fired his revolver at the subadar, who fell dead in his tracks.

'A Sepoy close by levelled his musket and fired. Charley fell, and the fellow rushed forward to bayonet him. As he did so I sent a bullet through his head, and he fell across Charley. It was a wild fight for a minute or two, and then a few of us made a sudden rush together, cut our way through the mutineers, and darted through an open window on to the parade. There were shouts, shots, and screams from the officers' bungalows, and in several places flames were already rising. What became of the other men I knew not; I made as hard as I could tear for the colonel's bungalow. Suddenly I came upon a sowar* sitting on his horse watching the rising flames. Before he saw me I was on him, and ran him through. I leapt on his horse and galloped down to Gardiner's compound. I saw lots of Sepoys in and around the bungalow, all engaged in looting. I dashed into the compound.

'"May! May!" I shouted. "Where are you?"

'I had scarcely spoken before a dark figure rushed out of a clump of bushes close by with a scream of delight.

'In an instant she was on the horse before me, and shooting down a couple of fellows who made a rush at my reins, I dashed out again. Stray shots were fired after us. But fortunately the Sepoys were all busy looting, most of them had laid down their muskets, and no one really took up the pursuit. I turned off from the parade-ground, dashed down between the hedges of two compounds, and in another minute we were in the open country.

'Fortunately, the cavalry were all down looting their own lines, or we must have been overtaken at once. May happily had fainted as I lifted her on to my horse—happily, because the fearful screams that we heard from the various bungalows almost drove me mad, and would probably have killed her, for the poor ladies were all her intimate friends.

'I rode on for some hours, till I felt quite safe from any immediate pursuit, and then we halted in the shelter of a clump of trees.

'By this time I had heard May's story. She had felt uneasy at being alone, but had laughed at herself for being so, until upon her speaking to one of the servants he had answered in a tone of gross insolence, which had astonished her. She at once guessed that there was danger, and the moment that she was alone caught up a large, dark carriage rug, wrapped it round her so as to conceal her white dress, and stole out into the verandah. The night was dark, and scarcely had she left the house than she heard a burst of firing across at the mess-house. She at once ran in among the bushes and crouched there, as she heard the rush of men into the room she had just left. She heard them searching for her, but they were looking for a white dress, and her dark rug saved her. What she must have suffered in the five minutes between the firing of the first shots and my arrival, she only knows. May had spoken but very little since we started. I believe that she was certain that her father was dead, although I had given an evasive answer when she asked me; and her terrible sense of loss, added to the horror of that time of suspense in the garden, had completely stunned her. We waited in the tope until the afternoon, and then set out again.

'We had gone but a short distance when we saw a body of the rebel cavalry in pursuit. They had no doubt been scouring the country generally, and the discovery was accidental. For a short time we kept away from them, but this could not be for long, as our horse was carrying double. I made for a sort of ruin I saw at the foot of a hill half a mile away. I did so with no idea of the possibility of concealment. My intention was simply to get my back to a rock and to sell my life as dearly as I could, keeping the last two barrels of the revolver for ourselves. Certainly no remembrance of my dream influenced me in any way, and in the wild whirl of excitement I had not given a second thought to Charley Simmonds' exclamation. As we rode up to the ruins only a hundred yards ahead of us, May said,—

'"Blow out my brains, Edward; don't let me fall alive into their hands."

'A shock of remembrance shot across me. The chase, her pale face, the words, the temple—all my dream rushed into my mind.

'"We are saved," I cried, to her amazement, as we rode into the courtyard, in whose centre a great figure was sitting.

'I leapt from the horse, snatched the mussuk of water from the saddle, and then hurried May round the idol, between which and the rock behind, there was but just room to get along.

'Not a doubt entered my mind but that I should find the spring as I had dreamed. Sure enough there was the carving, fresh upon my memory as if I had seen it but the day before. I placed my hand on the leaflet without hesitation, a solid stone moved back, I hurried my amazed companion in, and shut to the stone. I found, and shot to, a massive bolt, evidently placed to prevent the door being opened by accident or design when anyone was in the idol.

'At first it seemed quite dark, but a faint light streamed in from above; we made our way up the stairs, and found that the light came through a number of small holes pierced in the upper part of the head, and through still smaller holes lower down, not much larger than a good-sized knitting-needle could pass through. These holes, we afterwards found, were in the ornaments round the idol's neck. The holes enlarged inside, and enabled us to have a view all round.

'The mutineers were furious at our disappearance, and for hours searched about. Then, saying that we must be hidden somewhere, and that they would wait till we came out, they proceeded to bivouac in the courtyard of the temple.

'We passed four terrible days, but on the morning of the fifth a scout came in to tell the rebels that a column of British troops marching on Delhi would pass close by the temple. They therefore hastily mounted and galloped off.

'Three quarters of an hour later we were safe among our own people. A fortnight afterwards your aunt and I were married. It was no time for ceremony then; there were no means of sending her away; no place where she could have waited until the time for her mourning for her father was over. So we were married quietly by one of the chaplains of the troops, and, as your story-books say, have lived very happily ever after.'

'And how about Mr Simmonds, uncle? Did he get safe off too?'

'Yes, his dream came as vividly to his mind as mine had done. He crawled to the place where he knew the trap-door would be, and got into the cellar. Fortunately for him there were plenty of eatables there, and he lived there in concealment for a fortnight. After that he crawled out, and found the mutineers had marched for Delhi. He went through a lot, but at last joined us before that city. We often talked over our dreams together, and there was no question that we owed our lives to them. Even then we did not talk much to other people about them, for there would have been a lot of talk, and inquiry, and questions, and you know fellows hate that sort of thing. So we held our tongues. Poor Charley's silence was sealed a year later at Lucknow, for on the advance with Lord Clyde* he was killed.

'And now, boys and girls, you must run off to bed. Five minutes more and it will be Christmas-day. So you see, Frank, that although I don't believe in ghosts, I have yet met with a circumstance which I cannot account for.'

'It is very curious anyhow, uncle, and beats ghost stories into fits.'

'I like it better, certainly,' one of the girls said, 'for we can go to bed without being afraid of dreaming about it.'

'Well, you must not talk any more now. Off to bed, off to bed,' Colonel Harley said, 'or I shall get into terrible disgrace with your fathers and mothers, who have been looking very gravely at me for the last three quarters of an hour.'

See also: Haggard; Tennyson; Trevelyan.

1880s AND 1890s CANADIAN POETRY

In the 1880s and, especially, the 1890s Canadian poets were beginning to write out of a shared sense of new national identity. In so doing they helped build a framework for an autonomous Canadian literary tradition, grounded in a Canadian context, even though the borrowed forms and Tennysonian idiom with which they continued to work rarely matched that context. The four foremost male poets of this group—Roberts, Carman, Lampman, and D. C. Scott—have conventionally been called the Confederation poets because they were all born around the same time during the decade of Canadian Confederation (1867). In recent years it has been increasingly recognized that the woman poet Isabella Valancy Crawford also made a significant contribution during the early part of this period. More concertedly than the Confederationists, Crawford experimented with poetic form and voice in order to find appropriate ways of giving expression to her Canadian experience (compare the grim anti-imperial criticism of 'War' with the nature-based lyricism of 'Said the Canoe').

ISABELLA VALANCY CRAWFORD
(1850–1887)

War (1879)

Shake, shake the earth with giant tread,
  Thou red-maned Titan bold;
For every step a man lies dead,
  A cottage hearth is cold.
Take up the babes with mailèd hands,
  Transfix them with thy spears,
Spare not the chaste young virgin-bands,
  Tho' blood may be their tears.

Beat down the corn, tear up the vine,
    The waters turn to blood;
And if the wretch for bread doth whine,
    Give him his kin for food.
Ay, strew the dead to saddle-girth,
    They make so rich a mold,
Thou wilt enrich the wasted earth—
    They'll turn to yellow gold.

On with thy thunders! Shot and shell
    Send screaming, featly hurled—
Science has made them in her cell
    To *civilize* the world.
Not, not alone where Christian men
    Pant in the well-armed strife,
But seek the jungle-throttled glen—
    The savage has a life!

He has a soul—so priests will say—
    Go, save it with thy sword!
Thro' his rank forests force thy way,
    Thy war cry, 'For the Lord!'
Rip up his mines, and from his strands
    Wash out the gold with blood—
Religion raises blessing hands,
    'War's evil worketh good!'

When striding o'er the conquered land
    Silence thy rolling drum,
And, led by white-robed choiring band,
    With loud '*Te Deum*' come.
Seek the grim chancel, on its wall
    Thy blood-stiff banner hang;
They lie who say thy blood is gall,
    Thy tooth the serpent's fang.

See, the white Christ is lifted high,
    Thy conquering sword to bless!
Smiles the pure Monarch of the sky—
    Thy king can do no less.

Drink deep with him the festal wine,
    Drink with him drop for drop;
If like the sun his throne doth shine,
    Of it *thou* art the prop.

If spectres wait upon the bowl,
    Thou needst not be afraid;
Grin hell-hounds for thy bold, black soul,
    His purple be thy shade.
Go, feast with Commerce, be her spouse!
    She loves thee, thou art hers;
For thee she decks her board and house,
    Then how may others curse.

If she, mild-seeming matron, leans
    Upon thine iron neck,
And leaves with thee her household scenes
    To follow at thy beck?
Bastard in brotherhood of kings,
    Their blood runs in thy veins;
For them the crowns; the sword that swings
    For thee, to hew their chains.

For thee the rending of the prey;
    They, jackals to the lion,
Tread after in the gory way
    Trod by the mightier scion.
O slave, that slayest other slaves,
    O'er vassals crowned a king,
O War, build high thy throne with graves,
    High as the vulture's wing!

Said the Canoe (1905)

My masters twain made me a bed
    Of pine-boughs resinous, and cedar;
Of moss, a soft and gentle breeder
    Of dreams of rest; and me they spread

With furry skins and, laughing, said:
'Now she shall lay her polished sides
As queens do rest, or dainty brides,
Our slender lady of the tides!'

My masters twain their camp-soul lit;
Streamed incense from the hissing cones;
Large crimson flashes grew and whirled;
Thin golden nerves of sly light curled
Round the dun camp; and rose faint zones,
Half way about each grim bole knit,
Like a shy child that would bedeck
With its soft clasp a Brave's red neck,
Yet sees the rough shield on his breast,
The awful plumes shake on his crest,
And, fearful, drops his timid face,
Nor dares complete the sweet embrace.

Into the hollow hearts of brakes—
Yet warm from sides of does and stags
Passed to the crisp, dark river-flags—
Sinuous, red as copper-snakes,
Sharp-headed serpents, made of light,
Glided and hid themselves in night.

My masters twain the slaughtered deer
Hung on forked boughs with thongs of leather:
Bound were his stiff, slim feet together,
His eyes like dead stars cold and drear.
The wandering firelight drew near
And laid its wide palm, red and anxious,
On the sharp splendour of his branches,
On the white foam grown hard and sere
  On flank and shoulder.
Death—hard as breast of granite boulder—
  Under his lashes
Peered thro' his eyes at his life's grey ashes.

My masters twain sang songs that wove—
As they burnished hunting-blade and rifle—
A golden thread with a cobweb trifle,
Loud of the chase and low of love:

'O Love! art thou a silver fish,
Shy of the line and shy of gaffing,
Which we do follow, fierce, yet laughing,
Casting at thee the light-winged wish?
And at the last shall we bring thee up
From the crystal darkness, under the cup
   Of lily folden
   On broad leaves golden?

'O Love! art thou a silver deer
With feet as swift as wing of swallow,
While we with rushing arrows follow?
And at the last shall we draw near
And o'er thy velvet neck cast thongs
Woven of roses, stars and songs—
   New chains all moulden
   Of rare gems olden?'

They hung the slaughtered fish like swords
   On saplings slender; like scimitars,
   Bright, and ruddied from new-dead wars,
Blazed in the light the scaly hordes.

They piled up boughs beneath the trees,
   Of cedar web and green fir tassel.
   Low did the pointed pine tops rustle,
The camp-fire blushed to the tender breeze.

The hounds laid dewlaps on the ground
   With needles of pine, sweet, soft and rusty,
   Dreamed of the dead stag stout and lusty;
A bat by the red flames wove its round.

The darkness built its wigwam walls
　　Close round the camp, and at its curtain
　　Pressed shapes, thin, woven and uncertain
As white locks of tall waterfalls.

BLISS CARMAN
(1861–1929)

Low Tide on Grand Pré (1893)

The sun goes down, and over all
　　These barren reaches by the tide
Such unelusive glories fall,
　　I almost dream they yet will bide
　　Until the coming of the tide.

And yet I know that not for us,
　　By any ecstasy of dream,
He lingers to keep luminous
　　A little while the grievous stream,
　　Which frets, uncomforted of dream—

A grievous stream, that to and fro
　　Athrough the fields of Acadie
Goes wandering, as if to know
　　Why one beloved face should be
　　So long from home and Acadie.

Was it a year or lives ago
　　We took the grasses in our hands,
And caught the summer flying low
　　Over the waving meadow lands,
　　And held it there between our hands?

The while the river at our feet—
    A drowsy inland meadow stream—
At set of sun the after-heat
    Made running gold, and in the gleam
    We freed our birch upon the stream.

There down along the elms at dusk
    We lifted blade to drift,
Through twilight scented fine like musk,
    Where night and gloom awhile uplift.
    Nor sunder soul and soul adrift.

And that we took into our hands
    Spirit of life or subtler thing—
Breathed on us there, and loosed the bands
    Of death, and taught us, whispering,
    The secret of some wonder-thing.

Then all your face grew light, and seemed
    To hold the shadow of the sun;
The evening faltered, and I deemed
    That time was ripe, and years had done
    Their wheeling underneath the sun.

So all desire and all regret,
    And fear and memory, were naught;
One to remember or forget
    The keen delight our hands had caught;
    Morrow and yesterday were naught.

The night has fallen, and the tide . . .
    Now and again comes drifting home,
Across these aching barrens wide,
    A sigh like driven wind or foam:
    In grief the flood is bursting home.

A Vagabond Song (1896)

There is something in the autumn that is native to my blood—
Touch of manner, hint of mood;
And my heart is like a rhyme,
With the yellow and the purple and the crimson keeping time.

The scarlet of the maples can shake me like a cry
Of bugles going by.
And my lonely spirit thrills
To see the frosty asters like a smoke upon the hills.

There is something in October sets the gypsy blood astir;
We must rise and follow her,
When from every hill of flame
She calls and calls each vagabond by name.

CHARLES G. D. ROBERTS
(1860–1943)

The Pea-Fields (1893)

These are the fields of light, and laughing air,
    And yellow butterflies, and foraging bees,
    And whitish, wayward blossoms winged as these,
And pale green tangles like a seamaid's hair.
Pale, pale the blue, but pure beyond compare,
    And pale the sparkle of the far-off seas,
    A-shimmer like these fluttering slopes of peas,
And pale the open landscape everywhere.

From fence to fence a perfumed breath exhales
    O'er the bright pallor of the well-loved fields,—
My fields of Tantramar* in summer-time;
    And, scorning the poor feed their pasture yields,
Up from the bushy lots the cattle climb,
    To gaze with longing through the grey, mossed rails.

My Trees (1893)

At evening, when the winds are still,
　　And wide the yellowing landscape glows,
My firwoods on the lonely hill
　　Are crowned with sun and loud with crows.
Their flocks throng down the open sky
　　From far salt flats and sedgy seas;
Then dusk and dewfall quench the cry,—
　　So calm a home is in my trees.

At morning, when the young wind swings
　　The green slim tops and branches high,
Out puffs a noisy whirl of wings,
　　Dispersing up the empty sky.
In this dear refuge no roof stops
　　The skyward pinion winnowing through.
My trees shut out the world;—their tops
　　Are open to the infinite blue.

ARCHIBALD LAMPMAN
(1861–1899)

Late November (1888)

The hills and leafless forests slowly yield
　　To the thick-driving snow. A little while
　　And night shall darken down. In shouting file
The woodmen's carts go by me homeward-wheeled,
Past the thin fading stubbles, half concealed,
　　Now golden-gray, sowed softly through with snow,
　　Where the last ploughman follows still his row,
Turning black furrows through the whitening field.
Far off the village lamps begin to gleam,
　　Fast drives the snow, and no man comes this way;
　　　The hills grow wintry white, and bleak winds moan
　　　About the naked uplands. I alone
　　Am neither sad, nor shelterless, nor gray,
Wrapped round with thought, content to watch and dream.

Among the Orchards (1899)

Already in the dew-wrapped vineyards dry
Dense weights of wheat press down. The large bright drops
Shrink in the leaves. From dark acacia tops
The nut-hatch flings his short reiterate cry;
As ever the sun mounts hot and high
Thin voices crowd the grass. In soft long strokes
The wind goes murmuring through the mountain oaks.
Faint wefts creep out along the blue and die.
I hear far in among the motionless trees—
Shadows that sleep upon the shaven sod—
The thud of dropping apples. Reach on reach
Stretch plots of perfumed orchard, where the bees
Murmur among the full-fringed goldenrod
Or cling half-drunken to the rotting peach.

DUNCAN CAMPBELL SCOTT
(1862–1947)

The Onondaga Madonna (1898)

She stands full-throated and with careless pose,
This woman of a weird and waning race,
The tragic savage lurking in her face,
Where all her pagan passion burns and glows;
Her blood is mingled with her ancient foes,
And thrills with war and wildness in her veins;
Her rebel lips are dabbled with the stains
Of feuds and forays and her father's woes.

And closer in the shawl about her breast,
The latest promise of her nation's doom,
Paler than she her baby clings and lies,
The primal warrior gleaming from his eyes;
He sulks, and burdened with his infant gloom,
He draws his heavy brows and will not rest.

See also: the *Bulletin* Writers of the 1890s; Clarke; Duncan.

THE *BULLETIN* WRITERS OF THE 1890s

In the 1890s writers clustered around the Sydney republican paper the Bulletin *began to articulate a newly emergent Australian self-awareness and a distinctive national voice. Here, in the sere vision and colloquial language of A. B. Paterson, Henry Lawson, Barbara Baynton, and others, was an assured response to Marcus Clarke's (q.v.) earlier call for writers to learn the 'language' of the Australian landscape. Though he was otherwise hostile to his representation of the country, the* Bulletin's *literary editor A. G. Stephens echoed Clarke's anticipations in his Introduction to* The Bulletin Story Book *(1901), an extract from which rounds off this grouping of Australian writers. As these texts make clear, while they were all seeking to give utterance to Australian realities, there were marked differences between the writers of the 1890s. This is perhaps most obvious in Barbara Baynton's rewriting of Lawson's paradigmatic story of the besieged bushwoman. Against the predominant masculinity of the nationalist tradition, Baynton underlines how mateship ignored—even while depending on—the brutalizing hardship of women.*

A. B. ('BANJO') PATERSON
(1864–1941)

Clancy of the Overflow (1895)

I had written him a letter which I had, for want of better
   Knowledge, sent to where I met him down the Lachlan years ago;
He was shearing when I knew him, so I sent the letter to him,
   Just on spec, addressed as follows, 'Clancy, of The Overflow'.

And an answer came directed in a writing unexpected
   (And I think the same was written with a thumb-nail dipped in
     tar);
'Twas his shearing mate who wrote it, and *verbatim* I will quote it:

'Clancy's gone to Queensland droving, and we don't know where
 he are.'

. . . . .

In my wild erratic fancy visions come to me of Clancy
  Gone a-droving 'down the Cooper' where the Western drovers go;
As the stock are slowly stringing, Clancy rides behind them singing,
  For the drover's life has pleasures that the townsfolk never know.

And the bush has friends to meet him, and their kindly voices greet
  him
  In the murmur of the breezes and the river on its bars,
And he sees the vision splendid of the sunlit plains extended,
  And at night the wondrous glory of the everlasting stars.

. . . . .

I am sitting in my dingy little office, where a stingy
  Ray of sunlight struggles feebly down between the houses tall,
And the foetid air and gritty of the dusty, dirty city,
  Through the open window floating, spreads its foulness over all.

And in place of lowing cattle, I can hear the fiendish rattle
  Of the tramways and the buses making hurry down the street;
And the language uninviting of the gutter children fighting
  Comes fitfully and faintly through the ceaseless tramp of feet.

And the hurrying people daunt me, and their pallid faces haunt me
  As they shoulder one another in their rush and nervous haste,
With their eager eyes and greedy, and their stunted forms and weedy,
  For townsfolk have no time to grow, they have no time to waste.

And I somehow rather fancy that I'd like to change with Clancy,
  Like to take a turn at droving where the seasons come and go,
While he faced the round eternal of the cash-book and the journal—
  But I doubt he'd suit the office, Clancy, of The Overflow.

The Travelling Post Office (1895)

The roving breezes come and go, the reed-beds sweep and sway,
The sleepy river murmurs low, and loiters on its way,
It is the land of lots o' time along the Castlereagh.

.　　.　　.　　.　　.

The old man's son had left the farm, he found it dull and slow,
He drifted to the great North-west, where all the rovers go.
'He's gone so long,' the old man said, 'he's dropped right out of mind,
But if you'd write a line to him I'd take it very kind;
He's shearing here and fencing there, a kind of waif and stray—
He's droving now with Convoy's sheep along the Castlereagh.

'The sheep are travelling for the grass, and travelling very slow;
They may be at Mundooran now, or past the Overflow,
Or tramping down the black-soil flats across by Waddiwong
But all those little country towns would send the letter wrong.
The mailman, if he's extra tired, would pass them in his sleep;
It's safest to address the note to "Care of Conroy's sheep",
For five and twenty thousand head can scarcely go astray,
You write to "Care of Conroy's sheep along the Castlereagh".'

.　　.　　.　　.　　.

By rock and ridge and riverside the western mail has gone
Across the great Blue Mountain Range to take that letter on.
A moment on the topmost grade, while open fire-doors glare,
She pauses like a living thing to breathe the mountain air,
Then launches down the other side across the plains away
To bear that note to 'Conroy's sheep along the Castlereagh'.

And now by coach and mailman's bag it goes from town to town,
And Conroy's Gap and Conroy's Creek have marked it 'Further
　　　down'.
Beneath a sky of deepest blue, where never cloud abides,
A speck upon the waste of plain the lonely mailman rides.
Where fierce hot winds have set the pine and myall boughs asweep
He hails the shearers passing by for news of Conroy's sheep.

By big lagoons where wildfowl play and crested pigeons flock,
By camp-fires where the drovers ride around their restless stock,
And past the teamster toiling down to fetch the wool away
My letter chases Conroy's sheep along the Castlereagh.

Old Australian Ways (1902)

The London lights are far abeam
    Behind a bank of cloud,
Along the shore the gaslights gleam,
    The gale is piping loud;
And down the Channel, groping blind,
    We drive her through the haze
Towards the land we left behind—
The good old land of 'never mind',
    And old Australian ways.

The narrow ways of English folk
    Are not for such as we;
They bear the long-accustomed yoke
    Of staid conservancy:
But all our roads are new and strange,
    And through our blood there runs
The vagabonding love of change
That drove us westward of the range
    And westward of the suns.

The city folk go to and fro
    Behind a prison's bars,
They never feel the breezes blow
    And never see the stars;
They never hear in blossomed trees
    The music low and sweet
Of wild birds making melodies,
Nor catch the little laughing breeze
    That whispers in the wheat.

Our fathers came of roving stock
    That could not fixed abide:
And we have followed field and flock
    Since e'er we learnt to ride;
By miner's camp and shearing shed,
    In land of heat and drought,
We followed where our fortunes led,
With fortune always on ahead
    And always farther out.

The wind is in the barley-grass,
    The wattles are in bloom;
The breezes greet us as they pass
    With honey-sweet perfume;
The parakeets go screaming by
    With flash of golden wing,
And from the swamp the wild-ducks cry
Their long-drawn note of revelry,
    Rejoicing at the Spring.*

So throw the weary pen aside
    And let the papers rest,
For we must saddle up and ride
    Towards the blue hill's breast:
And we must travel far and fast
    Across their rugged maze,
To find the Spring of Youth at last,
And call back from the buried past
    The old Australian ways.

When Clancy took the drover's track
    In years of long ago,
He drifted to the outer back
    Beyond the Overflow;
By rolling plain and rocky shelf,
    With stockwhip in his hand,
He reached at last (oh, lucky elf!)*
The Town of Come-and-Help-Yourself
    In Rough-and-Ready Land.

And if it be that you would know
    The tracks he used to ride,
Then you must saddle up and go
    Beyond the Queensland side,
Beyond the reach of rule or law,
    To ride the long day through,
In Nature's homestead—filled with awe,
You then might see what Clancy saw
    And know what Clancy knew.

HENRY LAWSON
(1867–1922)

The Drover's Wife (1894)

The two-roomed house is built of round timber, slabs, and stringy bark, and floored with split slabs. A big bark kitchen standing at one end is larger than the house itself, verandah included.

Bush all round—bush with no horizon, for the country is flat. No ranges in the distance. The bush consists of stunted, rotten native apple trees. No undergrowth. Nothing to relieve the eye save the darker green of a few sheoaks which are sighing above the narrow, almost waterless creek. Nineteen miles to the nearest sign of civilization—a shanty on the main road.

The drover, an ex-squatter,* is away with sheep. His wife and children are left here alone.

Four ragged, dried-up-looking children are playing about the house. Suddenly one of them yells: 'Snake! Mother, here's a snake!'

The gaunt, sun-browned bushwoman dashes from the kitchen, snatches her baby from the ground, holds it on her left hip, and reaches for a stick.

'Where is it?'

'Here! gone into the wood-heap!' yells the eldest boy—a sharp-faced, excited urchin of eleven. 'Stop there, mother! I'll have him. Stand back! I'll have the beggar!'

'Tommy, come here, or you'll be bit. Come here at once when I tell you, you little wretch!'

The youngster comes reluctantly, carrying a stick bigger than himself. Then he yells, triumphantly:

'There it goes—under the house!' and darts away with club uplifted. At the same time the big, black, yellow-eyed dog-of-all-breeds, who has shown the wildest interest in the proceedings, breaks his chain and rushes after that snake. He is a moment late, however, and his nose reaches the crack in the slabs just as the end of its tail disappears. Almost at the same moment the boy's club comes down and skins the aforesaid nose. Alligator takes small notice of this, and proceeds to undermine the building; but he is subdued after a struggle and chained up. They cannot afford to lose him.

The drover's wife makes the children stand together near the dog-house while she watches for the snake. She gets two small dishes of milk and sets them down near the wall to tempt it to come out; but an hour goes by and it does not show itself.

It is near sunset, and a thunderstorm is coming. The children must be brought inside. She will not take them into the house, for she knows the snake is there, and may at any moment come up through the cracks in the rough slab floor; so she carries several armfuls of firewood into the kitchen, and then takes the children there. The kitchen has no floor—or, rather, an earthen one—called a 'ground floor' in this part of the bush. There is a large, roughly made table in the centre of the place. She brings the children in, and makes them get on this table. They are two boys and two girls—mere babies. She gives them some supper, and then, before it gets dark, she goes into the house, and snatches up some pillows and bedclothes—expecting to see or lay her hand on the snake any minute. She makes a bed on the kitchen table for the children, and sits down beside it to watch all night.

She has an eye on the corner, and a green sapling club laid in readiness on the dresser by her side, together with her sewing basket and a copy of the *Young Ladies' Journal*. She has brought the dog into the room.

Tommy turns in, under protest, but says he'll lie awake all night and smash that blinded snake.

His mother asks him how many times she has told him not to swear.

He has his club with him under the bedclothes, and Jacky protests:

'Mummy! Tommy's skinnin' me alive wif his club. Make him take it out.'

Tommy: 'Shet up, you little——! D'yer want to be bit with the snake?'

Jacky shuts up.

'If yer bit,' says Tommy, after a pause, 'you'll swell up, an' smell, an' turn red an' green an' blue all over till yer bust. Won't he, mother?'

'Now then, don't frighten the child. Go to sleep,' she says.

The two younger children go to sleep, and now and then Jacky complains of being 'skeezed'. More room is made for him. Presently Tommy says: 'Mother! listen to them (adjective) little 'possums. I'd like to screw their blanky necks.'

And Jacky protests drowsily:

'But they don't hurt us, the little blanks!'

Mother: 'There, I told you you'd teach Jacky to swear.' But the remark makes her smile. Jacky goes to sleep.

Presently Tommy asks:

'Mother! Do you think they'll ever extricate the (adjective) kangaroo?'

'Lord! How am I to know, child? Go to sleep.'

'Will you wake me if the snake comes out?'

'Yes. Go to sleep.'

Near midnight. The children are all asleep and she sits there still, sewing and reading by turns. From time to time she glances round the floor and wall-plate, and whenever she hears a noise she reaches for the stick. The thunderstorm comes on, and the wind, rushing through the cracks in the slab wall, threatens to blow out her candle. She places it on a sheltered part of the dresser and fixes up a newspaper to protect it. At every flash of lightning, the cracks between the slabs gleam like polished silver. The thunder rolls, and the rain comes down in torrents.

Alligator lies at full length on the floor, with his eyes turned towards the partition. She knows by this that the snake is there. There are large cracks in that wall opening under the floor of the dwelling-house.

She is not a coward, but recent events have shaken her nerves. A little son of her brother-in-law was lately bitten by a snake, and died. Besides, she has not heard from her husband for six months, and is anxious about him.

He was a drover, and started squatting here when they were

married. The drought of 18— ruined him. He had to sacrifice the remnant of his flock and go droving again. He intends to move his family into the nearest town when he comes back, and, in the meantime, his brother, who keeps a shanty on the main road, comes over about once a month with provisions. The wife has still a couple of cows, one horse, and a few sheep. The brother-in-law kills one of the sheep occasionally, gives her what she needs of it, and takes the rest in return for other provisions.

She is used to being left alone. She once lived like this for eighteen months. As a girl she built the usual castles in the air; but all her girlish hopes and aspirations have long been dead. She finds all the excitement and recreation she needs in the *Young Ladies' Journal*, and, Heaven help her! takes a pleasure in the fashion-plates.

Her husband is an Australian, and so is she. He is careless, but a good enough husband. If he had the means he would take her to the city and keep her there like a princess. They are used to being apart, or at least she is. 'No use fretting,' she says. He may forget sometimes that he is married; but if he has a good cheque when he comes back he will give most of it to her. When he had money he took her to the city several times—hired a railway sleeping compartment, and put up at the best hotels. He also bought her a buggy, but they had to sacrifice that along with the rest.

The last two children were born in the bush—one while her husband was bringing a drunken doctor, by force, to attend to her. She was alone on this occasion, and very weak. She had been ill with a fever. She prayed to God to send her assistance. God sent Black Mary—the 'whitest' gin in all the land. Or, at least, God sent 'King Jimmy' first, and he sent Black Mary. He put his black face round the door-post, took in the situation at a glance, and said cheerfully: 'All right, Missis—I bring my old woman, she down alonga creek.'

One of her children died while she was here alone. She rode nineteen miles for assistance, carrying the dead child.

It must be near one or two o'clock. The fire is burning low. Alligator lies with his head resting on his paws, and watches the wall. He is not a very beautiful dog to look at, and the light shows numerous old wounds where the hair will not grow. He is afraid of nothing on the face of the earth or under it. He will tackle a bullock as readily as he will tackle a flea. He hates all other dogs—except kangaroo-dogs

—and has a marked dislike to friends or relations of the family. They seldom call, however. He sometimes makes friends with strangers. He hates snakes and has killed many, but he will be bitten some day and die; most snake-dogs end that way.

Now and then the bushwoman lays down her work and watches, and listens, and thinks. She thinks of things in her own life, for there is little else to think about.

The rain will make the grass grow, and this reminds her how she fought a bush fire once while her husband was away. The grass was long, and very dry, and the fire threatened to burn her out. She put on an old pair of her husband's trousers and beat out the flames with a green bough, till great drops of sooty perspiration stood out on her forehead and ran in streaks down her blackened arms. The sight of his mother in trousers greatly amused Tommy, who worked like a little hero by her side, but the terrified baby howled lustily for his 'mummy'. The fire would have mastered her but for four excited bushmen who arrived in the nick of time. It was a mixed-up affair all round; when she went to take up the baby he screamed and struggled convulsively, thinking it was a 'black man'; and Alligator, trusting more to the child's sense than his own instinct, charged furiously, and (being old and slightly deaf) did not in his excitement at first recognize his mistress's voice, but continued to hang on to the moleskins until choked off by Tommy with a saddle-strap. The dog's sorrow for his blunder, and his anxiety to let it be known that it was all a mistake, was as evident as his ragged tail and a twelve-inch grin could make it. It was a glorious time for the boys; a day to look back to, and talk about, and laugh over for many years.

She thinks how she fought a flood during her husband's absence. She stood for hours in the drenching downpour, and dug an overflow gutter to save the dam across the creek. But she could not save it. There are things that a bushwoman cannot do. Next morning the dam was broken, and her heart was nearly broken too, for she thought how her husband would feel when he came home and saw the result of years of labour swept away. She cried then.

She also fought the *pleuro-pneumonia*—dosed and bled the few remaining cattle, and wept again when her two best cows died.

Again, she fought a mad bullock that besieged the house for a day. She made bullets and fired at him through cracks in the slabs with an old shotgun. He was dead in the morning. She skinned him and got seventeen-and-six for the hide.

She also fights the crows and eagles that have designs on her chickens. Her plan of campaign is very original. The children cry 'Crows, mother!' and she rushes out and aims a broomstick at the birds as though it were a gun, and says, 'Bung!' The crows leave in a hurry; they are cunning, but a woman's cunning is greater.

Occasionally a bushman in the horrors, or a villainous-looking sundowner, comes and nearly scares the life out of her. She generally tells the suspicious-looking stranger that her husband and two sons are at work below the dam, or over at the yard, for he always cunningly inquires for the boss.

Only last week a gallows-faced swagman—having satisfied himself that there were no men on the place—threw his swag down on the verandah, and demanded tucker. She gave him something to eat; then he expressed his intention of staying for the night. It was sundown then. She got a batten from the sofa, loosened the dog, and confronted the stranger, holding the batten in one hand and the dog's collar with the other. 'Now you go!' she said. He looked at her and at the dog, said 'All right, mum,' in a cringing tone, and left. She was a determined-looking woman, and Alligator's yellow eyes glared un-pleasantly—besides, the dog's chawing-up apparatus greatly re-sembled that of the reptile he was named after.

She has few pleasures to think of as she sits here alone by the fire, on guard against a snake. All days are much the same to her; but on Sunday afternoon she dresses herself, tidies the children, smartens up baby, and goes for a lonely walk along the bush-track, pushing an old perambulator in front of her. She does this every Sunday. She takes as much care to make herself and the children look smart as she would if she were going to do the block in the city. There is nothing to see, however, and not a soul to meet. You might walk for twenty miles along this track without being able to fix a point in your mind, unless you are a bushman. This is because of the everlasting, maddening sameness of the stunted trees—that monotony which makes a man long to break away and travel as far as trains can go, and sail as far as ships can sail—and further.

But this bushwoman is used to the loneliness of it. As a girl-wife she hated it, but now she would feel strange away from it.

She is glad when her husband returns, but she does not gush or make a fuss about it. She gets him something good to eat, and tidies up the children.

She seems contented with her lot. She loves her children, but has no time to show it. She seems harsh to them. Her surroundings are not favourable to the development of the 'womanly' or sentimental side of nature.

It must be near morning now; but the clock is in the dwelling-house. Her candle is nearly done; she forgot that she was out of candles. Some more wood must be got to keep the fire up, and so she shuts the dog inside and hurries round to the wood-heap. The rain has cleared off. She seizes a stick, pulls it out, and—crash! the whole pile collapses.

Yesterday she bargained with a stray blackfellow to bring her some wood, and while he was at work she went in search of a missing cow. She was absent an hour or so, and the native black made good use of his time. On her return she was so astonished to see a good heap of wood by the chimney, that she gave him an extra fig of tobacco, and praised him for not being lazy. He thanked her, and left with head erect and chest well out. He was the last of his tribe and a King; but he had built that wood-heap hollow.

She is hurt now, and tears spring to her eyes as she sits down again by the table. She takes up a handkerchief to wipe the tears away, but pokes her eyes with her bare fingers instead. The handkerchief is full of holes, and she finds that she has put her thumb through one, and her forefinger through another.

This makes her laugh, to the surprise of the dog. She has a keen, very keen, sense of the ridiculous; and some time or other she will amuse bushmen with the story.

She has been amused before like that. One day she sat down 'to have a good cry,' as she said—and the old cat rubbed against her dress and 'cried too.' Then she had to laugh.

It must be near daylight. The room is very close and hot because of the fire. Alligator still watches the wall from time to time. Suddenly he becomes greatly interested; he draws himself a few inches nearer the partition, and a thrill runs through his body. The hair on the back of his neck begins to bristle, and the battle-light is in his yellow eyes. She knows what this means, and lays her hand on the stick. The lower end of one of the partition slabs has a large crack on both sides. An evil pair of small, bright, bead-like eyes glisten at one of these holes. The snake—a black one—comes slowly out, about a foot, and moves its head up and down. The dog lies still, and the woman sits as one fascinated. The snake comes out a foot further. She lifts her stick, and the reptile, as though suddenly aware of danger, sticks his head in through the crack on the other side of the slab, and hurries to get his tail round after him. Alligator springs, and his jaws come together with a snap. He misses, for his nose is large and the snake's body down in the angle formed by the slabs and the floor. He snaps again as the tail comes round. He has the snake now, and tugs it out eighteen inches. Thud, thud comes the woman's club on the ground. Alligator pulls again. Thud, thud Alligator gives another pull and he has the snake out—a black brute, five feet long. The head rises to dart about, but the dog has the enemy close to the neck. He is a big, heavy dog, but quick as a terrier. He shakes the snake as though he felt the original curse in common with mankind. The eldest boy wakes up, seizes his stick, and tries to get out of bed, but his mother forces him back with a grip of iron. Thud, thud—the snake's back is broken in several places. Thud, thud—its head is crushed, and Alligator's nose skinned again.

She lifts the mangled reptile on the point of her stick, carries it to the fire, and throws it in; then piles on the wood, and watches the snake burn. The boy and dog watch, too. She lays her hand on the dog's head, and all the fierce, angry light dies out of his yellow eyes. The younger children are quieted, and presently go to sleep. The dirty-legged boy stands for a moment in his shirt, watching the fire. Presently he looks up at her, sees the tears in her eyes, and, throwing his arms round her neck, exclaims:

'Mother, I won't never go drovin'; blast me if I do!'

And she hugs him to her worn-out breast and kisses him; and they sit thus together while the sickly daylight breaks over the bush.

BARBARA BAYNTON
(1857–1929)

The Tramp (1901)

She laid the stick and her baby on the grass while she untied the rope
that tethered the calf. The length of the rope separated them. The
cow was near the calf, and both were lying down. Every day she
found a fresh place to tether it—since tether it she must, for there
was no one to go after it but herself. She had plenty of time, but then
there was baby; and if the cow turned on her out on the plains, and
she with baby—— She was afraid of the cow; she had been a town
girl, only she did not want the cow to know it. She used to run at first
when the cow bellowed its protest against the penning-up of its calf.
This suited the cow, also the calf, but the woman's husband was
wroth, and called her—the noun was cur. It was he who forced her to
run and meet the advancing cow, brandishing a stick and uttering
threatening words till the enemy turned tail and ran. 'That's the way!'
the man said, laughing at her white face. In many things he was worse
than the cow, and she wondered if the same rule would apply to the
man, but she was not one to provoke skirmishes, even with the cow.

It was early for the calf to go 'to bed'—nearly an hour earlier than
usual; but she felt so weirdly lonely. Partly because it was Monday,
and her husband had been home for Saturday night and Sunday. He
had gone off before daylight this morning; he was a shearer, and
fifteen miles as the crow flies separated them. She knew of no one
nearer, unless the tramp. Ah! that was why she had penned the calf
up so early. She feared more from the look of his eyes, and the gleam
of his teeth, as he watched her newly-awakened baby beat its
impatient fists upon her covered breasts, than from the knife that was
sheathed in the belt at his waist.

Her husband, she had told him, was sick. She always said that
when she was alone and a tramp came—and she had gone in from the
kitchen to the bedroom and asked questions and replied to them in
the best man's voice she could assume. But this tramp had walked
round and round the house, and there were cracks in some
places,—and after the last time he had asked for tobacco. She had

none to give, and he had grinned, because there was a broken clay pipe near the wood-heap where he stood, and if there were a man inside there ought to have been tobacco. Then he asked for money, but women in the bush never have money.

At last he was gone, and she, watching through the cracks inside, saw him when about a quarter of a mile away turn and look back at the house. Then he went further in the direction that she would have him go; but he paused again, turned and looked behind him, and, apparently satisfied, moved to the left towards the creek. The creek made a bow round the house, and when he came to it she lost sight of him. Hours after, watching intently in that direction for signs of smoke, she saw the man's dog chasing some sheep that had gone to the creek for water, and saw it slink back suddenly, as if the man had called it.

More than once she thought of taking her baby and going to her husband, but as yet she had not set her will against his as with the cow, and so dared not. Long before nightfall she placed food in the kitchen, and a big brooch that had been her mother's she put upon the table, because, if the man did come back and robbery were his object, it was the only thing valuable that she had. And she left the kitchen door open—wide open; but this was not wise.

How she fastened the doors inside! Beside the bolt in the back one she drove in the steel and the scissors; against it she piled the stools and the table. Beside the lock on the front door she forced the handle of the spade, under the middle bar, and the blade between the cracks in the flooring boards. Then the prop-stick, cut into lengths, held the top as the spade held the middle. The windows were little more than port-holes; she had nothing to fear through them.

She ate a few mouthfuls of food and drank a cup of cold milk, for she lighted no fire, and when night came no candle, but crept with her baby to bed.

What woke her? The wonder was that she had slept: she had not meant to, but she was young, very young. Perhaps the shrinking of the galvanised roof—yet hardly, that was too usual. Something had set her heart beating wildly, and the very air she breathed seemed fraught with terrible danger, but she lay quite still—only she put her other arm over her baby. Then she had both round it, and she prayed: 'Little baby—little baby—don't wake!'

She saw one of the open cracks, quite close to where she lay, darken with a shadow—for the moon's rays shone on that side. Then a protesting growl reached her; and she could fancy she heard the man turn hastily: she plainly heard the thud of something striking the dog's ribs, and the long, flying strides of the animal as it howled and ran. Still watching, she saw the shadow darken every crack along the wall: she knew by the sounds that the man was trying every position that might help him to see in; but how much he saw she could not tell. She thought of doing many things that might deceive him into the idea that she was not alone, but the sound of her voice would wake baby, and, as though that were the only danger that threatened her, she dreaded it. If baby cried she felt as if she, in turn, must betray her weakness, and instinctively cry to her protector, fifteen miles away. So she prayed: 'Little baby, don't wake! don't cry!'

Very stealthily the man crept about. She knew he had his boots off, because of the vibration that his feet caused as he walked along the verandah, gauging the width of the little window in her room and the resistance of the front door. Then he went to the other end, and the uncertainty of what he might be doing was fearful: she had felt safer, far safer, while he was close, and she could watch and listen. But now! Oh, God! it was terrible. She felt she must watch, and again the great fear of wakening baby assailed her. And there was another thing: on that side of the house one of the slabs had shrunk in length as well as in width, and had once fallen out. It was held in position only by a wedge of wood underneath. What if he should discover that! The uncertainty increased her terror. She felt she must rise: and now, how she prayed as she gently raised herself with her little one in her arms, held tightly to her breast!

The vital parts in her child's body she tried to shield with her hands and arms as she thought of the knife: even its little feet she covered with its white gown, and baby never murmured—it liked to be held so. Noiselessly she crossed to the other side, and stood where she could see and hear, but not be seen. He was trying every slab, and was very near to that with the wedge under it. Then, even while hoping, she saw him find it; and heard the sound of the knife as bit by bit he began to cut away the wooden barrier.

She waited still, with her baby pressed tightly to her; though she knew that in another few minutes this man with the cruel eyes, lascivious mouth and gleaming knife would be able to enter. One side of the slab tilted; there was nothing to do now but cut away the remaining little end, when the slab, unless he held it, would fall inside or out; and then——

She heard his jerked breathing as it kept time with the cuts of the knife, and heard the brush of his clothes as they rubbed the walls with his movements, for she was so still and quiet that she did not even tremble. And she knew when he ceased, and wondered why. She stood well concealed; she knew he could not see her and that he would not fear if he did; yet she heard him move cautiously away. Perhaps he expected the slab to fall. Still, his motive puzzled her: his retreat was a pretence, she felt sure; and she moved even closer and bent her body the better to listen. Ah! what sound was that? 'Listen! Listen!' she bade her heart—her heart that had kept so still hitherto, but now bounded with tumultuous throbs that dulled her ears. Nearer and nearer came the sounds, till the welcome thud of horse's hoofs rang out clearly.

'Oh, God! Oh, God! Oh, God!' she cried; for they were very close before she could make sure, and then there was the door so locked and barred with many bars. The age it took to tear away its fastenings!

Out she darted at last, and, tearing madly along, saw the horseman far beyond her in the distance. She called to him in Christ's name, in her babe's name, still flying like the wind with the speed that deadly peril sends; but the distance grew greater and greater between them, and when she reached the creek her prayers turned to wild shrieks, for there crouched the man she feared, with outstretched hands that had caught her ere she saw him. She knew he was offering terms if she ceased to struggle and cry for help, though louder and louder did she cry for it; but it was only when the man's hand gripped her throat that the cry of 'Murder!' came from her lips; and when she fell the startled curlews took up the awful sound, and flew over the horseman's head shrieking 'M-u-r-d-e-r! M-u-r-d-e-r! M-u-r-d-e-r!'

'By God!' said the boundary-rider, 'it's been a dingo right enough. Eight killed up here, and there's more down in the creek—a ewe and lamb, I'll bet; and the lamb's alive.' And he shut out the sky with his hand and watched the crows that were circling round and round, nearing the earth one moment and the next shooting skyward. By that he knew the lamb must be alive. Even a dingo will spare a lamb sometimes.

Yes, the lamb was alive, and after the manner of lambs of its age did not know its mother when the light came. It had sucked the still-warm breasts and laid its little head on her bosom and slept till morn; then, when the wee one looked at the swollen, disfigured face with the starting eyes, and clenched teeth that had bitten through the tongue and stained the bodice crimson, it wept and would have crept away but for the hand that still clutched its little gown. Sleep was nodding its golden head and swaying its small body, and the crows were close, so close, to the other's wide-open eyes, when the boundary-rider galloped down. He reeled in his saddle when he saw the two, and, covering his eyes, cried, 'Jesus Christ!' And he told afterwards how the little child held out its arms to him, and how he was forced to cut the portion of its gown that the dead hand held.

A few miles further down the creek a man kept throwing an old cap into the water. The dog would bring it out and lay it on the opposite side from where the man stood, but would not allow the man to catch him, though it was only to wash the blood of the sheep from his mouth and throat, for the sight of blood made the man tremble.

But the dog also was guilty.

A. G. STEPHENS
(1865–1933)

from Introductory to *The Bulletin Story Book* (1901)

[. . .] The grotesque English prejudice against things Australian, founded on no better reason than that they are unlike English things, still remains to vitiate the local sense of local beauty;* but every year is teaching us wisdom. We have learnt to laugh at the ridiculous and reiterated fiction that our flowers have no scent and our birds no song. Why, the whole Bush is scented; in no land is there a greater wealth of aromatic perfume from tree and shrub and blossom —making the daisied meadows of England, as honest Henry Kingsley suggests,* tame and suburban by comparison. And when you go up beyond the tropic-line, and walk out of your tent at dawn, the air in many places is literally weighed down with the fragrance of a hundred brilliant flowers. What would they not give in England for ten acres of wattle-blossom on Wimbledon Common? and how many nightingales would they exchange for a flight of crimson lories at sunset?—a shower of flaming rubies. Did Marcus Clarke never hear the fluting of an Australian magpie?—so mellow, so round, so sweet. If the little brown English birds sing better than our vari-plumaged parrakeets, is not the strife at least equal? Does not fine colour yield as much pleasure to the artist eye as fine song to the artist ear? When will Englified city critics realise that Australia is a country which extends through forty degrees of latitude and thirty-five of longitude, and comprehends all climates, all scenery—snow-capped mountain and torrid desert, placid lake and winding river, torrent and brook, charm as well as grandeur, garden and homely field as well as barren solitude?

It is heredity and custom which again betray us. The rose is a beautiful flower, but the most beautiful only because thousands of years of care and cultivation have been lavished to bring it to perfection, because thousands of lovers have breathed its perfume, thousands of poets have apostrophised its exquisite form. Give the same care and cultivation to a hundred modest bush flowers, draw them from obscurity as the rose has been drawn from the parent wilderness, let them be worshipped and adored through centuries of sentiment—and we have here the rivals of the rose herself. Cluster the associations of the oak and yew around the yarran or the cedar (all the cedars of Lebanon were not more stately than those of the Herberton scrub), and the oak and yew will shrink, not indeed into insignificance, but into their proper proportion as regarded from Australia. In a word, let us look at our country and its fauna and flora, its trees and streams and mountains, through clear Australian eyes, not through bias-bleared English spectacles; and there is no more beautiful country in the world.

It will be the fault of the writers, not of the land, if Australian literature does not by-and-by become memorable. In the field of the short sketch or story, for example,—the field which includes this book,—what country can offer to writers better material than Australia? We are not yet snug in cities and hamlets, moulded by routine, regimented to a pattern. Every man who roams the Australian wilderness is a potential knight of Romance; every man who grapples with the Australian desert for a livelihood might sing a Homeric chant of victory, or listen, baffled and beaten, to an Æschylean dirge of defeat. The marvels of the adventurous are our daily common-places. The drama of the conflict between Man and Destiny is played here in a scenic setting whose novelty is full of vital suggestion for the literary artist. In the twilit labour of the timber-getter in a Richmond scrub; in the spectacle of the Westralian prospector tramping across his mirage-haunted waste; in the tropic glimpse of the Thursday Island pearling fleet, manned by men of a dozen turbulent races,—the luggers floating so calmly above a search so furious;—here, and in a hundred places besides, there is wealth of novel inspiration for the writers who will live Australia's life and utter her message. And when those writers come, let us tell them that we will never rest contented until Australian authors reach the highest standards set in literature, in order that we may set the standards higher and preach discontent anew.

See also: Duncan; Fairbridge; 1880s and 1890s Canadian Poetry.

FIN DE SIÈCLE

SWAMI VIVEKANANDA
(1863–1902)

Towards the end of the nineteenth century, belief in the underlying connectedness of all religions seemed to some to offer a powerful alternative to the idea of a world linked through loyalty to, and domination by, the British flag. In speeches given in Chicago, New York, and London during the mid-1890s, including that from which the extract here is taken, the Swami Vivekananda of Calcutta stood out as an important spokesman for the unity of world faiths. Numbers of Westerners were stirred by his spiritual but also implicitly political message that 'the Many and the One are the same Reality': there were no hierarchies and no overlords in the world of the spirit. It was paradoxical, however, that the dissemination of such ideas was made possible by the networks of communication which empire had laid down.

from The Ideal of a Universal Religion (1896)

[. . .] Is it possible that there should ever reign unbroken harmony in this plane of mighty religious struggle? The world is exercised in the latter part of this century by the question of harmony; in society, various plans are being proposed, and attempts are made to carry them into practice; but we know how difficult it is to do so. People find that it is almost impossible to mitigate the fury of the struggle of life, to tone down the tremendous nervous tension that is in man. Now, if it is so difficult to bring harmony and peace to the physical plane of life—the external, gross, and outward side of it—then a thousand times more difficult is it to bring peace and harmony to rule over the internal nature of man. I would ask you for the time being to come out of the network of words. We have all been hearing from childhood of such things as love, peace, charity, equality, and universal brotherhood; but they have become to us mere words without meaning, words which we repeat like parrots, and it has become quite natural for us to do so. We cannot help it. Great souls, who first felt these great ideas in their hearts, manufactured these words; and at that time many understood their meaning. Later on, ignorant people have taken up those words to play with them and made religion a mere play upon words, and not a thing to be carried into practice. It becomes 'my father's religion,' 'our nation's religion,' 'our country's religion,' and so forth. It becomes only a phase of patriotism to profess any religion, and patriotism is always partial. To bring harmony into religion must always be difficult. Yet we will consider this problem of the harmony of religions.

We see that in every religion there are three parts—I mean in every great and recognised religion. First, there is the philosophy which presents the whole scope of that religion, setting forth its basic principles, the goal and the means of reaching it. The second part is mythology, which is philosophy made concrete. It consists of legends relating to the lives of men, or of supernatural beings, and so forth. It is the abstractions of philosophy concretised in the more or less imaginary lives of men and supernatural beings. The third part is the ritual. This is still more concrete and is made up of forms and ceremonies, various physical attitudes, flowers and incense, and many other things that appeal to the senses. In these consists the ritual. You will find that all recognised religions have these three elements. Some lay more stress on one, some on another. Let us now take into consideration the first part, philosophy. Is there one universal philosophy? Not yet. Each religion brings out its own doctrines and insists upon them as being the only true ones. And not only does it do that, but it thinks that he who does not believe in them must go to some horrible place. Some will even draw the sword to compel others to believe as they do. This is not through wickedness, but through a particular disease of the human brain called fanaticism. They are very sincere, these fanatics, the most sincere of human beings; but they are quite as irresponsible as other lunatics in the world. This disease of fanaticism is one of the most dangerous of all diseases. All the wickedness of human nature is roused by it. Anger is stirred up, nerves are strung high, and human beings become like tigers.

Is there any mythological similarity, is there any mythological harmony, any universal mythology accepted by all religions? Certainly not. All religions have their own mythology, only each of them says: 'My stories are not mere myths.' Let us try to understand the question by illustration. I simply mean to illustrate, I do not mean criticism of any religion. The Christian believes that God took the shape of a dove and came down to earth; to him this is history, and not mythology. The Hindu believes that God is manifested in the cow. Christians say that to believe so is mere mythology, and not history, that it is superstition. The Jews think if an image be made in the form of a box, or a chest, with an angel on either side, then it may be placed in the Holy of Holies; it is sacred to Jehovah; but if the image be made in the form of a beautiful man or woman, they say, 'This is a horrible idol; break it down!' This is our unity in mythology! If a man stands up and says, 'My prophet did such and such a wonderful thing,' others will say, 'That is only superstition,' but at the same time they say that their own prophet did still more wonderful things, which they hold to be historical. Nobody in the world, as far as I have seen, is able to make out the fine distinction between history and mythology, as it exists in the brains of these persons. All such stories, to whatever religion they may belong, are really mythological, mixed up occasionally, it may be, with a little history.

Next come the rituals. One sect has one particular form of ritual and thinks that that is holy, while the rituals of another sect are simply arrant superstition. If one sect worships a peculiar sort of symbol, another sect says, 'Oh, it is horrible.' Take for instance a general form of symbol. The Phallus symbol* is certainly a sexual symbol, but gradually that aspect of it has been forgotten, and it stands now as a symbol of the Creator. Those nations which have this as their symbol never think of it as the phallus; it is just a symbol, and there it ends. But a man from another race or creed sees in it nothing but the phallus, and begins to condemn it; yet at the same time he may be doing something which to the so-called phallic worshippers appears most horrible. Let me take two points for illustration, the phallus symbol and the sacrament of the Christians. To the Christians the phallus is horrible, and to the Hindus the Christian sacrament is horrible. They say that the Christian sacrament, the killing of a man and the eating of his flesh and the drinking of his blood to get the good qualities of that man, is cannibalism. This is what some of the savage tribes do; if a man is brave, they kill him and eat his heart, because they think it will give them the qualities of courage and bravery possessed by that man. Even such a devout Christian as Sir John Lubbock* admits this and says that the origin of this Christian symbol is in this savage idea. The Christians, of course, do not admit this view of its origin; and what it may imply never comes to their mind. It stands for holy things, and that is all they want to know. So even in rituals there is no universal symbol, which can command general recognition and acceptance. Where then is any universality? How is it possible then to have a universal form of religion? That, however, already exists. And let us see what it is.

We all hear about universal brotherhood, and how societies stand up especially to preach this. I remember an old story. In India, taking wine is considered very bad. There were two brothers who wished, one night, to drink wine secretly; and their uncle, who was a very orthodox man, was sleeping in a room quite close to theirs. So, before they began to drink, they said to each other, 'We must be very silent, or uncle will wake up.' When they were drinking, they continued repeating to each other 'Silence! Uncle will wake up,' each trying to shout the other down. And, as the shouting increased, the uncle woke up, came into the room, and discovered the whole thing. Now, we all shout like these drunken men, 'Universal brotherhood! We are all equal, therefore let us make a sect.' As soon as you make a sect you protest against equality, and equality is no more. Mohammedans talk of universal brotherhood, but what comes out of that in reality? Why, anybody who is not a Mohammedan will not be admitted into the brotherhood; he will more likely have his throat cut. Christians talk of universal brotherhood; but anyone who is not a Christian must go to that place where he will be eternally barbecued.

And so we go on in this world in our search after universal brotherhood and equality. When you hear such talk in the world I would ask you to be a little reticent, to take care of yourselves, for, behind all this talk is often the intensest selfishness. 'In the winter sometimes a thunder-cloud comes up; it roars, but it does not rain; but in the rainy season the clouds speak not, but deluge the world with water.' So those who are *really* workers, and *really* feel at heart the universal brotherhood of man, do not talk much, do not make little sects for universal brotherhood; but their acts, their movements, their whole life, show out clearly that they in truth possess the feeling of brotherhood for mankind, that they have love and sympathy for all. They do not speak, they *do* and they *live*. This world is too full of blustering talk. We want a little more earnest work, and less talk.

So far we see that it is hard to find any universal features in regard to religion, and yet we know that they exist. We are all human beings, but are we all equal? Certainly not. Who says we are equal? Only the lunatic. Are we all equal in our brains, in our powers, in our bodies? One man is stronger than another, one man has more brain power than another. If we are all equal, why is there this inequality? Who made it? We. Because we have more or less powers, more or less brain, more or less physical strength, it must make a difference between us. Yet we know that the doctrine of equality appeals to our heart. We are all human beings; but some are men, and some are women. Here is a black man, there is a white man; but all are men, all belong to one humanity. Various are our faces; I see no two alike, yet we are all human beings. Where is this one humanity? I find a man or a woman, either dark or fair; and among all these faces, I know that there is an abstract humanity which is common to all. I may not find it when I try to grasp it, to sense it, and to actualise it, yet I know for certain that it is there. If I am sure of anything, it is of this humanity which is common to us all. It is through this generalised entity that I see you as a man or a woman. So it is with this universal religion, which runs through all the various religions of the world in the form of God; it must and does exist through eternity. 'I am the thread that runs through all these pearls,'* and each pearl is a religion or even a sect thereof. Such are the different pearls, and the Lord is the thread that runs through all of them; only the majority of mankind are entirely unconscious of it.

Unity in variety is the plan of the universe. We are all men, and yet we are all distinct from one another. As a part of humanity, I am one with you, and as Mr So-and-so I am different from you. As a man you are separate from the woman; as a human being you are one with the woman. As a man you are separate from the animal, but as living beings, man, woman, animal, and plant are all one; and as existence, you are one with the whole universe. That universal existence is God, the ultimate Unity in the universe. In Him we are all one. At the same time, in manifestation, these differences must always remain. In our work, in our energies, as they are being manifested outside, these differences must always remain. We find then that if by the idea of a universal religion it is meant that one set of doctrines should be believed in by all mankind, it is wholly impossible. It can never be, there can never be a time when all faces will be the same. Again, if we expect that there will be one universal mythology, that is also impossible; it cannot be. Neither can there be one universal ritual. Such a state of things can never come into existence; if it ever did, the world would be destroyed, because variety is the first principle of life. What makes us formed beings? Differentiation. Perfect balance would be our destruction. Suppose the amount of heat in this room, the tendency of which is towards equal and perfect diffusion, gets that kind of diffusion, then for all practical purpose that heat will cease to be. What makes motion possible in this universal? Lost balance. The unity of sameness can come only when this universe is destroyed, otherwise such a thing is impossible. Not only so, it would be dangerous to have it. We must not wish that all of us should think alike. There would then be no thought to think. We should be all alike, as the Egyptian mummies in a museum, looking at each other without a thought to think. It is this difference, this differentiation, this losing of the balance between us, which is the very soul of our progress, the soul of all our thought. This must always be.

What then do I mean by the ideal of a universal religion? I do not mean any one universal philosophy, or any one universal mythology, or any one universal ritual held alike by all; for I know that this world must go on working, wheel within wheel, this intricate mass of machinery, most complex, most wonderful. What can we do then? We can make it run smoothly, we can lessen the friction, we can grease the wheels, as it were. How? By recognising the natural necessity of variation. Just as we have recognised unity by our very nature, so we must also recognise variation. We must learn that truth may be expressed in a hundred thousand ways, and that each of these ways is true as far as it goes. We must learn that the same thing can be viewed from a hundred different standpoints, and yet be the same thing. Take for instance the sun. Suppose a man standing on the earth looks at the sun when it rises in the morning; he sees a big ball. Suppose he starts on a journey towards the sun and takes a camera with him, taking photographs at every stage of his journey, until he reaches the sun. The photographs of each stage will be seen to be different from those of the other stages; in fact, when he gets back, he brings with him so many photographs of so many different stages of his progress. Even so is it with the Lord. Through high philosophy or low, through the most exalted mythology or the grossest, through the most refined ritualism or arrant fetishism, every sect, every soul, every nation, every religion, consciously or unconsciously, is struggling upward, towards God; every vision of truth that man has, is a vision of Him and of none else. Suppose we all go with vessels in our hands to fetch water from a lake. One has a cup, another a jar, another a bucket, and so forth, and we all fill our vessels. The water in each case naturally takes the form of the vessel carried by each of us. He who brought the cup has the water in the form of a cup; he who brought the jar—his water is in the shape of a jar, and so forth; but, in every case, water, and nothing but water, is in the vessel. So it is in the case of religion; our minds are like these vessels, and each one of us is trying to arrive at the realisation of God. God is like that water filling these different vessels, and in each vessel the vision of God comes in the form of the vessel. Yet He is One. He is God in every case. This is the only recognition of universality that we can get. [. . .]

See also: Aurobindo; Blyden; Kingsley; Schreiner; Tagore; Yeats.

ROBERT LOUIS STEVENSON
(1850–1894)

The King of Apemama: The Royal Trader (1896)

There is one great personage in the Gilberts: Tembinok' of Apemama: solely conspicuous, the hero of song, the butt of gossip. Through the rest of the group the kings are slain or fallen in tutelage: Tembinok' alone remains, the last tyrant, the last erect vestige of a dead society. The white man is everywhere else, building his houses, drinking his gin, getting in and out of trouble with the weak native governments. There is only one white on Apemama, and he on sufferance, living far from court, and hearkening and watching his conduct like a mouse in a cat's ear. Through all the other islands a stream of native visitors comes and goes, travelling by families, spending years on the grand tour. Apemama alone is left upon one side, the tourist dreading to risk himself within the clutch of

Tembinok'. And fear of the same Gorgon follows and troubles them at home. Maiana once paid him tribute; he once fell upon and seized Nonuti:* first steps to the empire of the archipelago. A British warship coming on the scene, the conqueror was driven to disgorge, his career checked in the outset, his dear-bought armoury sunk in his own lagoon. But the impression had been made: periodical fear of him still shakes the islands; rumour depicts him mustering his canoes for a fresh onfall; rumour can name his destination; and Tembinok' figures in the patriotic war-songs of the Gilberts like Napoleon in those of our grandfathers.

We were at sea, bound from Mariki to Nonuti and Tapituea, when the wind came suddenly fair for Apemama. The course was at once changed; all hands were turned-to to clean ship, the decks holy-stoned, the cabin washed, the trade-room overhauled. In all our cruising we never saw the *Equator* so smart as she was made for Tembinok'. Nor was Captain Reid alone in these coquetries; for, another schooner chancing to arrive during my stay in Apemama, I found that she also was dandified for the occasion. And the two cases stand alone in my experience of South Sea traders.

We had on board a family of native tourists, from the grandsire to the babe in arms, trying (against an extraordinary series of ill-luck) to regain their native island of Peru.[1] Five times already they had paid their fare and taken ship; five times they had been disappointed, dropped penniless upon strange islands, or carried back to Butaritari, whence they sailed. This last attempt had been no better-starred; their provisions were exhausted. Peru was beyond hope, and they had cheerfully made up their mind to a fresh stage of exile in Tapituea or Nonuti. With this slant of wind their random destination became once more changed; and like the Calendar's pilot,* when the 'black mountains' hove in view, they changed colour and beat upon their breasts. Their camp, which was on deck in the ship's waist, re-sounded with complaint. They would be set to work, they must become slaves, escape was hopeless, they must live and toil and die in Apemama, in the tyrant's den. With this sort of talk they so greatly terrified their children, that one (a big hulking boy) must at last be torn screaming from the schooner's side. And their fears were wholly groundless. I have little doubt they were not suffered to be idle; but I

---

[1] In the Gilbert group.

can vouch for it that they were kindly and generously used. For, the matter of a year later, I was once more shipmate with these inconsistent wanderers on board the *Janet Nicoll*. Their fare was paid by Tembinok'; they who had gone ashore from the *Equator* destitute, reappeared upon the *Janet* with new clothes, laden with mats and presents, and bringing with them a magazine of food, on which they lived like fighting-cocks throughout the voyage; I saw them at length repatriated, and I must say they showed more concern on quitting Apemama than delight at reaching home.

We entered by the north passage (Sunday, September 1st),* dodging among shoals. It was a day of fierce equatorial sunshine; but the breeze was strong and chill; and the mate, who conned the schooner from the cross-trees, returned shivering to the deck. The lagoon was thick with many-tinted wavelets; a continuous roaring of the outer sea overhung the anchorage; and the long, hollow crescent of palm ruffled and sparkled in the wind. Opposite our berth the beach was seen to be surmounted for some distance by a terrace of white coral, seven or eight feet high and crowned in turn by the scattered and incongruous buildings of the palace. The village adjoins on the south, a cluster of high-roofed maniap's.* And village and palace seemed deserted.

We were scarce yet moored, however, before distant and busy figures appeared upon the beach, a boat was launched, and a crew pulled out to us bringing the king's ladder. Tembinok' had once an accident; has feared ever since to intrust his person to the rotten chandlery of South Sea traders; and devised in consequence a frame of wood, which is brought on board a ship as soon as she appears, and remains lashed to her side until she leave. The boat's crew, having applied this engine, returned at once to shore. They might not come on board; neither might we land, or not without danger of offence; the king giving pratique in person. An interval followed, during which dinner was delayed for the great man; the prelude of the ladder, giving us some notion of his weighty body and sensible, ingenious character, had highly whetted our curiosity; and it was with something like excitement that we saw the beach and terrace suddenly blacken with attendant vassals, the king and party embark, the boat (a man-of-war gig) come flying towards us dead before the wind, and the royal coxswain lay us cleverly aboard, mount the ladder with a jealous diffidence, and descend heavily on deck.

Not long ago he was overgrown with fat, obscured to view, and a burthen to himself. Captains visiting the Island advised him to walk; and though it broke the habits of a life and the traditions of his rank, he practised the remedy with benefit. His corpulence is now portable; you would call him lusty rather than fat; but his gait is still dull, stumbling, and elephantine. He neither stops nor hastens, but goes about his business with an implacable deliberation. We could never see him and not be struck with his extraordinary natural means for the theatre: a beaked profile like Dante's in the mask, a mane of long black hair, the eye brilliant, imperious, and inquiring: for certain parts, and to one who could have used it, the face was a fortune. His voice matched it well, being shrill, powerful, and uncanny, with a note like a sea-bird's. Where there are no fashions, none to set them, few to follow them if they were set, and none to criticise, he dresses—as Sir Charles Grandison lived—'to his own heart.'* Now he wears a woman's frock, now a naval uniform; now (and more usually) figures in a masquerade costume of his own design: trousers and a singular jacket with shirt tails, the cut and fit wonderful for island workmanship, the material always handsome, sometimes green velvet, sometimes cardinal red silk. This masquerade becomes him admirably. In the woman's frock he looks ominous and weird beyond belief. I see him now come pacing towards me in the cruel sun, solitary, a figure out of Hoffmann.*

A visit on board ship, such as that at which we now assisted, makes a chief part and by far the chief diversion of the life of Tembinok'. He is not only the sole ruler, he is the sole merchant of his triple kingdom, Apemama, Aranuka, and Kuria, well-planted islands. The taro* goes to the chiefs, who divide as they please among their immediate adherents; but certain fish, turtles—which abound in Kuria,—and the whole produce of the coco-palm, belong exclusively to Tembinok'. 'A' cobra[1] berong me,' observed his majesty with a wave of his hand; and he counts and sells it by the houseful. 'You got copra, king?' I have heard a trader ask. 'I got two, three outches,'[2] his majesty replied: 'I think three.' Hence the commercial importance of Apemama, the trade of three islands being centred there in a single hand; hence it is that so many whites have tried in vain to gain or to

---

[1] Copra: the dried kernel of the cocoa-nut, the chief article of commerce throughout the Pacific Islands.
[2] Houses.

preserve a footing; hence ships are adorned, cooks have special orders, and captains array themselves in smiles, to greet the king. If he be pleased with his welcome and the fare he may pass days on board, and every day, and sometimes every hour, will be of profit to the ship. He oscillates between the cabin, where he is entertained with strange meats, and the trade-room, where he enjoys the pleasures of shopping on a scale to match his person. A few obsequious attendants squat by the house door, awaiting his least signal. In the boat, which has been suffered to drop astern, one or two of his wives lie covered from the sun under mats, tossed by the short sea of the lagoon, and enduring agonies of heat and tedium. This severity is now and then relaxed and the wives allowed on board. Three or four were thus favoured on the day of our arrival: substantial ladies airily attired in *ridis*.* Each had a share of copra, her *peculium*, to dispose of for herself. The display in the trade-room —hats, ribbons, dresses, scents, tins of salmon—the pride of the eye and the lust of the flesh—tempted them in vain. They had but the one idea—tobacco, the island currency, tantamount to minted gold; returned to shore with it, burthened but rejoicing; and late into the night, on the royal terrace, were to be seen counting the sticks by lamplight in the open air.

The king is no such economist. He is greedy of things new and foreign. House after house, chest after chest, in the palace precinct, is already crammed with clocks, musical boxes, blue spectacles, umbrellas, knitted waistcoats, bolts of stuff, tools, rifles, fowling-pieces, medicines, European foods, sewing-machines, and, what is more extraordinary, stoves: all that ever caught his eye, tickled his appetite, pleased him for its use, or puzzled him with its apparent inutility. And still his lust is unabated. He is possessed by the seven devils of the collector. He hears a thing spoken of, and a shadow comes on his face. 'I think I no got him,' he will say; and the treasures he has seem worthless in comparison. If a ship be bound for Apemama, the merchant racks his brain to hit upon some novelty. This he leaves carelessly in the main cabin or partly conceals in his own berth, so that the king shall spy it for himself. 'How much you want?' inquires Tembinok', passing and pointing. 'No, king; that too dear,' returns the trader. 'I think I like him,' says the king. This was a bowl of gold-fish. On another occasion it was scented soap. 'No, king; that cost too much,' said the trader; 'too good for a Kanaka.' 'How much you got? I take him all,' replied his majesty, and became the lord of seventeen boxes at two dollars a cake. Or again, the merchant feigns the article is not for sale, is private property, an heirloom or a gift; and the trick infallibly succeeds. Thwart the king and you hold him. His autocratic nature rears at the affront of opposition. He accepts it for a challenge; sets his teeth like a hunter going at a fence; and with no mark of emotion, scarce even of interest, stolidly piles up the price. Thus, for our sins, he took a fancy to my wife's dressing-bag, a thing entirely useless to the man, and sadly battered by years of service. Early one forenoon he came to our house, sat down, and abruptly offered to purchase it. I told him I sold nothing, and the bag at any rate was a present from a friend; but he was acquainted with these pretexts from of old, and knew what they were worth and how to meet them. Adopting what I believe is called 'the object method,' he drew out a bag of English gold, sovereigns and half-sovereigns, and began to lay them one by one in silence on the table; at each fresh piece reading our faces with a look. In vain I continued to protest I was no trader; he deigned not to reply. There must have been twenty pounds on the table, he was still going on, and irritation had begun to mingle with our embarrassment, when a happy idea came to our delivery. Since his majesty thought so much of the bag, we said, we must beg him to accept it as a present. It was the most surprising turn in Tembinok's experience. He perceived too late that his persistence was unmannerly; hung his head a while in silence: then, lifting up a sheepish countenance, 'I 'shamed,' said the tyrant. It was the first and the last time we heard him own to a flaw in his behaviour. Half an hour after he sent us a camphor-wood chest, worth only a few dollars—but then heaven knows what Tembinok' had paid for it.

Cunning by nature, and versed for forty years in the government of men, it must not be supposed that he is cheated blindly, or has resigned himself without resistance to be the milch-cow of the passing trader. His efforts have been even heroic. Like Nakaeia of Makin, he has owned schooners. More fortunate than Nakaeia, he has found captains. Ships of his have sailed as far as to the colonies. He has trafficked direct, in his own bottoms, with New Zealand. And even so, even there, the world-enveloping dishonesty of the white man prevented him; his profit melted, his ship returned in debt, the money for the insurance was embezzled, and when the *Coronet* came to be lost, he was astonished to find he had lost all. At this he dropped his weapons; owned he might as hopefully wrestle with the winds of heaven; and like an experienced sheep, submitted his fleece thenceforward to the shearers. He is the last man in the world to waste anger on the incurable; accepts it with cynical composure; asks no more in those he deals with than a certain decency of moderation; drives as good a bargain as he can; and when he considers he is more than usually swindled, writes it in his memory against the merchant's name. He once ran over to me a list of captains and supercargoes with whom he had done business, classing them under three heads: 'He cheat a litty'—'He cheat plenty'—and 'I think he cheat too much.' For the first two classes he expressed perfect toleration; sometimes, but not always, for the third. I was present when a certain merchant was turned about his business, and was the means (having a considerable influence ever since the bag) of patching up the dispute. Even on the day of our arrival there was like to have been a hitch with Captain Reid: the ground of which is perhaps worth recital. Among goods exported specially for Tembinok' there is a beverage known (and labelled) as Hennessy's brandy. It is neither Hennessy, nor even brandy; it is about the colour of sherry, but is not sherry; tastes of kirsch, and yet neither is it kirsch. The king, at least, has grown used to this amazing brand, and rather prides himself upon the taste; and any substitution is a double offence, being at once to cheat him and to cast a doubt upon his palate. A similar weakness is to be observed in all connoisseurs. Now, the last case sold by the *Equator* was found to contain a different and I would fondly fancy a superior distillation; and the conversation opened very black for Captain Reid. But Tembinok' is a moderate man. He was reminded and admitted that all men were liable to error, even himself; accepted the principle that a fault handsomely acknowledged should be condoned; and wound the matter up with this proposal: 'Tuppoti[1] I mi'take, you 'peakee me. Tuppoti you mi'take, I 'peakee you. Mo' betta.'

After dinner and supper in the cabin, a glass or two of 'Hennetti'—the genuine article this time, with the kirsch bouquet, —and five hours' lounging on the trade-room counter, royalty embarked for home. Three tacks grounded the boat before the palace; the wives were carried ashore on the backs of vassals; Tembinok' stepped on a railed platform like a steamer's gangway,

---

[1] Suppose.

and was borne shoulder-high through the shallows, up the beach, and by an inclined plane, paved with pebbles, to the glaring terrace where he dwells.

See also: Baughan; Bird; Clifford; Conrad; Mansfield; Schreiner.

HUGH CLIFFORD
(1866–1941)

Up Country (1897)

The days are hot and damp, and my legs are stiff with cramp,
    And the office punkahs creak!
And I'd give my tired soul, for the life that makes man whole,
    And a whiff of the jungle reek!
Ha' done with the tents of Shem, dear boys,
    With office stool and pew,
For it's time to turn to the lone Trail, our own Trail, the far Trail,
    Dig out, dig out on the old trail—
    The trail that is always new.

*A Parody.**

It has been said that a white man, who has lived twelve consecutive months in complete isolation, among the people of an alien Asiatic race, is never wholly sane again for the remainder of his days. This, in a measure, is true; for the life he then learns to live, and the discoveries he makes in that unmapped land, the gates of which are closed, locked, barred, and chained against all but a very few of his countrymen, teach him to love many things which all right-minded people very properly detest. The free, queer, utterly unconventional life has a fascination which is all its own. Each day brings a little added knowledge of the hopes and fears, longings and desires, joys and sorrows, pains and agonies of the people among whom his lot is cast. Each hour brings fresh insight into the mysterious workings of the minds and hearts of that very human section of our race, which ignorant Europeans calmly class as 'niggers.' All these things come to possess a charm for him, the power of which grows apace, and eats into the very marrow of the bones of the man who has once tasted this particular fruit of the great Tree of Knowledge. Just as the old smugglers, in the Isle of Man, were wont to hear the sea calling to them; go where he may, do what he will, the voice of the jungle, and of the people who dwell in those untrodden places, sounds in the ears of one who has lived the life. Ever and anon it cries to him to come back, come back to the scenes, the people, the life which he knows and understands, and which, in spite of all its hardships, he has learned to love.

The great wheel of progress, like some vast snowball, rolls steadily along, gathering to itself all manner of weird and unlikely places and people, filling up the hollows, laying the high hills low. Rays of searching garish light reflected from its surface are pitilessly flashed into the dark places of the earth, which have been wrapped around by the old-time dim religious light, since first the world began. The people in whose eyes these rays beat so mercilessly, reel and stumble blindly on in their march through life, taking wrong turnings at every step, and going woefully astray. Let us hope that succeeding generations will become used to the new conditions, and will fight their way back to a truer path; for there is no blinking the fact that the first, immediate, and obvious effects of our spirit of progress upon the weaker races, tend towards degeneration.

Ten years ago the Peninsula was very different from what it has since become, and many places where the steam-engine now shrieks to the church bells, and the shirt-collar galls the perspiring neck, were but recently part and parcel of that vast 'up country,' which is so little known but to the few who dwell in it, curse it,—and love it.

> I sent my soul through the invisible,
> Some Letter of the After-Life to spell,
> And Presently my Soul returned to me
> And whispered 'Thou thyself are Heaven or Hell.'*

So sings the old Persian poet, lying in his rose garden, by the wine-cup that robbed him of his Robe of Honour, and his words are true; though not quite in the sense in which he wrote them. For this wisdom the far-away jungles also teach a man who has to rely solely upon himself, and upon his own resources, for the manner of his life, and the form which it is to take. To all dwellers in the desolate solitude, which every white man experiences, who is cast alone among natives, there are two 'up countries'—his Heaven and Hell, and both are of his own making. The latter is the one of which he speaks to his fellow race-mates—if he speaks at all about his solitary life. The former lies at the back of his heart, and is only known to himself, and then but dimly known till the time comes for a return to the Tents of Shem. Englishmen, above all other men, revel in their privilege of being allowed to grumble and 'grouse' over the lives which the Fates have allotted to them. They speak briefly, roughly, and gruffly of the hardships they endure, making but little of them perhaps, and talking as though their lives, as a matter of course, were made up of these things only. The instinct of the race is to see life through the national pea-soup fog, which makes all things dingy, unlovely, and ugly. Nothing is more difficult than to induce men of our race to confess that in their lives—hard though they may have been—good things have not held aloof, and that they have often been quite happy under the most unlikely circumstances, and in spite of the many horrors and privations which have long encompassed them about.

Let us take the Hell first. We often have to do so, making a virtue of necessity, and a habit is a habit; moreover, our pains are always more interesting than our pleasures—to our neighbours. Therefore, let us take the dark view of up-country life to start upon. In the beginning, when first a man turns from his own people, and dwells in isolation among an alien race, he suffers many things. The solitude of soul— that terrible solitude which is only to be experienced in a crowd—the dead monotony, without hope of change; the severance from all the pleasant things of life, and the want of any substitutes for them, eat into the heart and brain of him as a corrosive acid eats into iron. He longs for the fellowship of his own people with an exceeding great longing, till it becomes a burden too grievous to bear; he yearns to find comradeship among the people of the land, but he knows not yet the manner by which their confidence may be won, and they, on their side, know him for a stranger within their gates, view him with keen suspicion, and hold him at arm's length. His ideas, his prejudices, his modes of thought, his views on every conceivable subject differ too widely from their own, for immediate sympathy to be possible between him and them. His habits are the habits of a white man, and many little things, to which he has not yet learned to attach importance, are as revolting to the natives, as the pleasant custom of spitting on the carpet, which some old-world *Rajas* still affect, is to

Europeans. His manners, too, from the native point of view, are as bad as his habits are unclean. He is respected for his wisdom, hated for his airs of superiority, pitied for his ignorance of many things, feared for what he represents, laughed at for his eccentric habits and customs, despised for his infidelity to the Faith, abhorred for his want of beauty, according to native standards of taste, and loved not at all. The men disguise their feelings, skilfully as only Orientals can, but the women and the little children do not scruple to show what their sentiments really are. When he goes abroad, the old women snarl at him as he passes, and spit ostentatiously, after the native manner when some unclean thing is at hand. The mothers snatch up their little ones and carry them hurriedly away, casting a look of hate and fear over their shoulders as they run. The children scream and yell, clutch their mothers' garments, or trip and fall, howling dismally the while, in their frantic efforts to fly his presence. He is Frankenstein's monster,* yearning for love and fellowship with his kind, longing to feel the hand of a friend in his, and yet knowing, by the unmistakable signs which a sight of him causes, that he is indescribably repulsive to the people among whom he lives. Add to all this that he is cut off from all the things which, to educated Europeans, make life lovely, and you will realise that his is indeed a sorry case. The privations of the body, if he has sufficient grit to justify his existence, count for little. He can live on any kind of food, sleep on the hardest of hard mats, or on the bare ground, with his head and feet in a puddle, if needs must. He can turn night into day, and sleep through the sunlight, or sleep not at all, as the case may be, if any useful purpose is to be served thereby. These are not things to trouble him, though the fleshpots of Egypt are very good when duty allows him to turn his back for a space upon the desert. Privations all these things are called in ordinary parlance, but they are of little moment, and are good for his liver. The real privations are of quite another sort. He never hears music; never sees a lovely picture; never joins in the talk and listens lovingly to conversation which strikes the answering sparks from his sodden brain. Above all, he never encounters the softening influence of the society of ladies of his own race. His few books are for a while his companions, but he reads them through and through, and cons them o'er and o'er, till the best sayings of the best authors ring flat on his sated ears like the echo of a twice-told tale. He has not yet learned that there is a great and marvellous book lying beneath his hand, a book in which all may read if they find but the means of opening the clasp which locks it, a book in which a man may read for years and never know satiety, which, though older than the hills, is ever new, and which, though studied for a lifetime, is never exhausted, and is never completely understood. This knowledge comes later; and it is then that the Chapter of the Great Book of Human Nature, which deals with natives, engrosses his attention and, touching the grayness of his life, like the rising sun, turns it into gold and purple.

Many other things he has to endure. Educated white men have inherited an infinite capacity for feeling bored; and a hot climate, which fries us all over a slow fire, grills boredom into irritability. The study of oriental human nature requires endless patience; and this is the hardest virtue for a young, energetic white man, with the irritable brain of his race, to acquire. Without it life is a misery—for

> It is not good for the Christian's health
> To hurry the Aryan brown,
> For the Christian riles and the Aryan smiles,
> And he weareth the Christian down;
> And the end of that fight is a tombstone white,
> With the name of the late deceased,
> And the epitaph clear, A fool lies here
> Who tried to hustle the East.*

Then gradually, very gradually, and by how slow degrees he shudders in after days to recall, a change comes o'er the spirit of his nightmare. Almost unconsciously, he begins to perceive that he is sundered from the people of the land by a gulf which *they* can never hope to bridge over. If he is ever to gain their confidence the work must be of his own doing. They cannot come up to this level, he must go down to the plains in which they dwell. He must put off many of the things of the white man, must forget his airs of superiority, and must be content to be merely a native Chief among natives. His pride rebels, his prejudices cry out and will not be silenced, he knows that he will be misunderstood by his race-mates, should they see him among the people of his adoption, but the aching solitude beats down one and all of these things; and, like that eminently sensible man, the Prophet Mohammed, he gets him to the Mountain, since it is immovable and will not come to him.

Then begins a new life. He must start by learning the language of his fellows, as perfectly as it is given to a stranger to learn it. That is but the first step in a long and often a weary march. Next, he must study, with the eagerness of Browning's Grammarian,* every native custom, every native conventionality, every one of the ten thousand ceremonial observances to which natives attach so vast an importance. He must grow to understand each one of the hints and *doubles ententes*, of which Malays make such frequent use, every little mannerism, sign and token, and, most difficult of all, every motion of the hearts, and every turn of thought, of those whom he is beginning to call his own people. He must become conscious of native Public Opinion, which is often diametrically opposed to the opinion of his race-mates on one and the same subject. He must be able to unerringly predict how the slightest of his actions will be regarded by the natives, and he must shape his course accordingly, if he is to maintain his influence with them, and to win their sympathy and their confidence. He must be able to place himself in imagination in all manner of unlikely places, and thence to instinctively feel the native Point of View. That is really the whole secret of governing natives. A quick perception of their Point of View, under all conceivable circumstances, a rapid process by which a European places himself in the position of the native, with whom he is dealing, an instinctive and instantaneous apprehension of the precise manner in which he will be affected, and a clear vision of the man, his feelings, his surroundings, his hopes, his desires, and his sorrows,—these, and these alone, mean that complete sympathy, without which the white man among Malays, is but as a sounding brass and as a tinkling cymbal.*

It does not all come at once. Months, perhaps years, pass before the exile begins to feel that he is getting any grip upon the natives, and even when he thinks that he knows as much about them as is good for any man, the oriental soul shakes itself in its brown casing, and comes out in some totally unexpected and unlooked-for place, to his no small mortification and discouragement. But, when he has got thus far, discouragement matters little, for he has become bitten with the love of his discoveries, and he can no more quit them than the dipsomaniac can abandon the drams which are killing him.

Then he gets deep into a groove and is happy. His fingers are between the leaves of the Book of Human Nature, and his eager eyes are scanning the lines of the chapter which in time he hopes to make his own. The advent of another white man is a weariness of the flesh.

The natives about him have learned to look upon him as one of their own people. His speech is their speech, he can think as they do, can feel as they feel, rejoice in their joys, and sorrow in their pains. He can tell them wonderful things, and a philosophy of which they had not dreamed. He never offends their susceptibilities, never wounds their self-respect, never sins against their numerous conventionalities. He has feasted with them at their weddings, doctored their pains, healed their sick, protected them from oppression, stood their friend in time of need, done them a thousand kindnesses, and has helped their dying through the strait and awful pass of death. Above all, he *understands*, and, in a manner, they love him. A new white man, speaking to him in an unknown tongue, seems to lift him for the time out of their lives. The stranger jars on the natives, who are the exile's people, and he, looking through the native eyes which are no longer strange to him, sees where his race-mate offends, and in his turn is jarred, until he begins to hate his own countrymen. Coming out of the groove hurts badly, and going back into it is almost worse, but when a man is once well set in the rut of native life, these do not disturb him, for he is happy, and has no need of other and higher things. This is the exile's Heaven.

As years go on the up-country life of which I write will become less and less common in this Peninsula of ours, and the Malays will be governed wholly by men, who, never having lived their lives, cannot expect to have more than a surface knowledge of the people whose destinies are in their hands. The Native States will, I fancy, be none the better governed, and those who rule them will miss much which has tended to widen the lives of the men who came before them, and who dwelt among the people while they were still as God made them.

And those who led these lives? The years will dim the memories of all they once learned and knew and experienced; and as they indite the caustic minute to the suffering subordinate, and strangle with swaddlings of red-tape the tender babe of prosperity, they will perchance look back with wonder at the men they once were, and thinking of their experiences in the days of long ago will marvel that each one of them as he left the desert experienced the pang of Chillon's prisoner:—

Even I
Regained my freedom with a sigh.*

See also: Candler; Conrad; Kingsley; Kipling; Woolf.

JOSEPH CHAMBERLAIN
(1836–1914)

The True Conception of Empire (1897)

[. . .] It seems to me that there are three distinct stages in our Imperial history. We began to be, and we ultimately became, a great Imperial Power in the eighteenth century, but, during the greater part of that time, the colonies were regarded, not only by us, but by every European Power that possessed them, as possessions valuable in proportion to the pecuniary advantage which they brought to the mother country, which, under that order of ideas was not truly a mother at all, but appeared rather in the light of a grasping and absentee landlord desiring to take from his tenants the utmost rents he could exact. The colonies were valued and maintained because it was thought that they would be a source of profit—of direct profit—to the mother country.

That was the first stage, and when we were rudely awakened by the War of Independence in America from this dream, that the colonies could be held for our profit alone, the second chapter was entered upon, and public opinion seems then to have drifted to the opposite extreme; and, because the colonies were no longer a source of revenue, it seems to have been believed and argued by many people that their separation from us was only a matter of time, and that that separation should be desired and encouraged lest haply they might prove an encumbrance and a source of weakness.

It was while those views were still entertained, while the little Englanders were in their full career, that this [Royal Colonial] Institute was founded to protest against doctrines so injurious to our interests and so derogatory to our honour; and I rejoice that what was then, as it were, 'a voice crying in the wilderness' is now the expressed and determined will of the overwhelming majority of the British people. Partly by the efforts of this Institute and similar organisations, partly by the writing of such men as Froude and Seeley, but mainly by the instinctive good sense and patriotism of the people at large, we have now reached the third stage in our history, and the true conception of our Empire.

What is that conception? As regards the self-governing colonies we no longer talk of them as dependencies. The sense of possession has given place to the sentiment of kinship. We think and speak of them as part of ourselves, as part of the British Empire, united to us, although they may be dispersed throughout the world, by ties of kindred, of religion, of history, and of language, and joined to us by the seas that formerly seemed to divide us.

But the British Empire is not confined to the self-governing colonies and the United Kingdom. It includes a much greater area, a much more numerous population in tropical climes, where no considerable European settlement is possible, and where the native population must always vastly outnumber the white inhabitants; and in these cases also the same change has come over the Imperial idea. Here also the sense of possession has given place to a different sentiment—the sense of obligation. We feel now that our rule over these territories can only be justified if we can show that it adds to the happiness and prosperity of the people, and I maintain that our rule does, and has, brought security and peace and comparative prosperity to countries that never knew these blessings before.

In carrying out this work of civilisation we are fulfilling what I believe to be our national mission, and we are finding scope for the exercise of the faculties and qualities which have made of us a great governing race. I do not say that our success has been perfect in every case, I do not say that all our methods have been beyond reproach; but I do say that in almost every instance in which the rule of the Queen has been established and the great *Pax Britannica* has been enforced, there has come with it greater security to life and property, and a material improvement in the condition of the bulk of the population. No doubt, in the first instance, when these conquests have been made, there has been bloodshed, there has been loss of life among the native populations, loss of still more precious lives among those who have been sent out to bring these countries into some kind of disciplined order, but it must be remembered that that is the condition of the mission we have to fulfil. There are, of course, among us—there always are among us, I think—a very small minority of men who are ready to be the advocates of the most detestable tyrants, provided their skin is black—men who sympathise with the sorrows of Prempeh and Lobengula,* and who denounce as murderers those of their country-men who have gone forth at the command of the Queen, and who have redeemed districts as large as Europe from the barbarism and the superstition in which they have been steeped for centuries. I remember a picture by Mr Selous* of a philanthropist—an imaginary philanthropist, I will hope—sitting cosily by his fireside and denouncing the methods by which British civilisation was promoted. This philanthropist complained of the use of Maxim guns and other instruments of warfare, and asked why we could not proceed by more conciliatory methods, and why the impis of Lobengula could not be brought before a magistrate, fined five shillings, and bound over to keep the peace.

No doubt there is humorous exaggeration in this picture, but there is gross exaggeration in the frame of mind against which it was directed. You cannot have omelettes without breaking eggs;* you cannot destroy the practices of barbarism, of slavery, of superstition, which for centuries have desolated the interior of Africa, without the use of force; but if you will fairly contrast the gain to humanity with the price which we are bound to pay for it, I think you may well rejoice in the result of such expeditions as those which have recently been conducted with such signal success—in Nyassaland, Ashanti, Benin, and Nupe—expeditions which may have, and indeed have, cost valuable lives, but as to which we may rest assured that for one life lost a hundred will be gained, and the cause of civilisation and the prosperity of the people will in the long run be eminently advanced. But no doubt such a state of things, such a mission as I have described, involve heavy responsibility. In the wide dominions of the Queen the doors of the temple of Janus* are never closed, and it is a gigantic task that we have undertaken when we have determined to wield the sceptre of empire. Great is the task, great is the responsibility, but great is the honour; and I am convinced that the conscience and the spirit of the country will rise to the height of its obligations, and that we shall have the strength to fulfil the mission which our history and our national character have imposed upon us.

In regard to the self-governing colonies our task is much lighter. We have undertaken, it is true, to protect them with all the strength at our command against foreign aggression, although I hope that the need for our intervention may never arise. But there remains what then will be our chief duty—that is, to give effect to that sentiment of kinship to which I have referred and which I believe is deep in the heart of every Briton. We want to promote a closer and a firmer union between all members of the great British race, and in this respect we have in recent years made great progress—so great that I think sometimes some of our friends are apt to be a little hasty, and to expect even a miracle to be accomplished. I would like to ask them to remember that time and patience are essential elements in the development of all great ideas. Let us, gentlemen, keep our ideal always before us. For my own part, I believe in the practical possibility of a federation of the British race, but I know that it will come, if it does come, not by pressure, not by anything in the nature of dictation from this country, but it will come as the realisation of a universal desire, as the expression of the dearest wish of our colonial fellow-subjects themselves.

That such a result would be desirable, would be in the interest of all of our colonies as well as of ourselves, I do not believe any sensible man will doubt. It seems to me that the tendency of the time is to throw all power into the hands of the greater Empire, and the minor kingdoms—those which are non-progressive—seem to be destined to fall into a secondary and subordinate place. But, if Greater Britain remains united, no empire in the world can ever surpass it in area, in population, in wealth, or in the diversity of its resources.

Let us, then, have confidence in the future. I do not ask you to anticipate with Lord Macaulay the time when the New Zealander will come here to gaze upon the ruins of a great dead city.* There are in our present condition no visible signs of decrepitude and decay. The mother country is still vigorous and fruitful, is still able to send forth troops of stalwart sons to people and to occupy the waste spaces of the earth; but yet it may well be that some of these sister nations whose love and affection we eagerly desire may in the future equal and even surpass our greatness. A trans-oceanic capital may arise across the seas, which will throw into shade the glories of London itself; but in the years that must intervene let it be our endeavour, let it be our task, to keep alight the torch of Imperial patriotism, to hold fast the affection and the confidence of our kinsmen across the seas, that so in every vicissitude of fortune the British Empire may present an unbroken front to all her foes, and may carry on even to distant ages the glorious traditions of the British flag.

See also: Curzon; Froude; Hobson; Ruskin; Schreiner; Seeley.

OLIVE SCHREINER
(1855–1920)

*This two-part 'allegory-story' was Olive Schreiner's J'Accuse aimed at
the capitalist exploiters of southern African black people, in particular
Cecil John Rhodes (1853–1902), the mining magnate, imperialist, and
Cape Colony Prime Minister. Rhodes's ambition was to develop a new
Johannesburg in the north that would rival the power and wealth of the
Transvaal, a Boer Republic. In Schreiner's story, Trooper Peter, a young
Englishman who idolizes Rhodes, is working as a scout in the forces of the
British South African Company. They are engaged in putting down the
1896 Ndebele and Shona rebellions (which resisted white attempts to
annex the land that would eventually be named Rhodesia). Lost on the
veld one night, Peter Halket is visited by a Christ-like stranger who in a
series of parables convinces him of the injustice of these operations. In the
second half of the story he questions the decision of his troop captain to
shoot a black prisoner suspected of being a spy, arguing that the man is
fighting for his freedom. Halket is shot in an attempt to release the man. In
later years Schreiner would see* Trooper Peter *as marking her greatest
moral and political achievement as a writer.*

from *Trooper Halket of Mashonaland* (1897)

[. . .] Peter Halket looked into the fire completely absorbed in his
calculations.—Peter Halket, Esq., Director of the Peter Halket Gold
Mining Company, Limited. Then, when he had got thousands, Peter
Halket, Esq., MP. Then, when he had millions, Sir Peter Halket,
Privy Councillor!

He reflected deeply, looking into the blaze. If you had five or six
millions you could go where you liked and do what you liked. You
could go to Sandringham. You could marry anyone. No one would
ask what your mother had been; it wouldn't matter.

A curious dull sinking sensation came over Peter Halket; and he
drew in his broad leathern belt two holes tighter.

Even if you had only two millions you could have a cook and a
valet, to go with you when you went into the veld or to the wars; and
you could have as much champagne and other things as you liked. At

that moment that seemed to Peter more important than going to Sandringham.

He took out his flask of Cape Smoke,[1] and drew a tiny draught from it.

Other men had come to South Africa with nothing, and had made everything! Why should not he?

He stuck small branches under the two great logs, and a glorious flame burst out. Then he listened again intently. The wind was falling and the night was becoming very still. It was a quarter to twelve now. His back ached, and he would have liked to lie down; but he dared not, for fear he should drop asleep. He leaned forward with his hands between his crossed knees, and watched the blaze he had made.

Then, after a while, Peter Halket's thoughts became less clear: they became at last, rather, a chain of disconnected pictures, painting themselves in irrelevant order on his brain, than a line of connected ideas. Now, as he looked into the crackling blaze, it seemed to be one of the fires they had made to burn the natives' grain by, and they were throwing in all they could not carry away: then, he seemed to see his mother's fat ducks waddling down the little path with the green grass on each side. Then, he seemed to see his huts where he lived with the prospectors, and the native women who used to live with him; and he wondered where the women were. Then—he saw the skull of an old Mashona blown off at the top, the hands still moving. He heard the loud cry of the native women and children as they turned the maxims on to the kraal; and then he heard the dynamite explode that blew up a cave. Then again he was working a maxim gun, but it seemed to him it was more like the reaping machine he used to work in England, and that what was going down before it was not yellow corn, but black men's heads; and he thought when he looked back they lay behind him in rows, like the corn in sheaves.

The logs sent up a flame clear and high, and, where they split, showed a burning core inside: the cracking and spluttering sounded in his brain like the discharge of a battery of artillery. Then he thought suddenly of a black woman he and another man caught alone in the bush, her baby on her back, but young and pretty. Well, they didn't shoot her!—and a black woman wasn't white! His mother

---

[1] Cape Smoke, a very inferior brandy made in Cape Colony.

didn't understand these things; it was all so different in England from South Africa. You couldn't be expected to do the same sort of things here as there. He had an unpleasant feeling that he was justifying himself to his mother, and that he didn't know how to.

He leaned further and further forward: so far at last, that the little white lock of his hair which hung out under his cap was almost singed by the fire. His eyes were still open, but the lids drooped over them, and his hands hung lower and lower between his knees. There was no picture left on his brain now, but simply an impress of the blazing logs before him.

Then, Trooper Peter Halket started. He sat up and listened. The wind had gone; there was not a sound: but he listened intently. The fire burnt up into the still air, two clear red tongues of flame.

Then, on the other side of the koppje* he heard the sound of footsteps ascending; the slow even tread of bare feet coming up.

The hair on Trooper Peter Halket's forehead slowly stiffened itself. He had no thought of escaping; he was paralyzed with dread. He took up his gun. A deadly coldness crept from his feet to his head. He had worked a maxim gun in a fight when some hundred natives fell and only one white man had been wounded; and he had never known fear; but to-night his fingers were stiff on the lock of his gun. He knelt low, tending a little to one side of the fire, with his gun ready. A stone half sheltered him from anyone coming up from the other side of the koppje, and the instant the figure appeared over the edge he intended to fire.

Then, the thought flashed on him; what, and if it were one of his own comrades come in search of him, and no bare-footed enemy! The anguish of suspense wrung his heart; for an instant he hesitated. Then, in a cold agony of terror, he cried out, 'Who is there?'

And a voice replied in clear, slow English, 'A friend.'

Peter Halket almost let his gun drop, in the revulsion of feeling. The cold sweat which anguish had restrained burst out in large drops on his forehead; but he still knelt holding his gun.

'What do you want?' he cried out quiveringly.

From the darkness at the edge of the koppje a figure stepped out into the full blaze of the fire-light.

Trooper Peter Halket looked up at it.

It was the tall figure of a man, clad in one loose linen garment, reaching lower than his knees, and which clung close about him. His head, arms, and feet were bare. He carried no weapon of any kind; and on his shoulders hung heavy locks of dark hair.*

Peter Halket looked up at him with astonishment. 'Are you alone?' he asked.

'Yes, I am alone.'

Peter Halket lowered his gun and knelt up.

'Lost your way, I suppose?' he said, still holding his weapon loosely.

'No; I have come to ask whether I may sit beside your fire for a while.'

'Certainly, certainly!' said Peter, eyeing the stranger's dress carefully, still holding his gun, but with the hand off the lock. 'I'm confoundedly glad of any company. It's a beastly night for anyone to be out alone. Wonder you find your way. Sit down! sit down!' Peter looked intently at the stranger; then he put his gun down at his side.

The stranger sat down on the opposite side of the fire. His complexion was dark; his arms and feet were bronzed; but his aquiline features, and the domed forehead, were not of any South African race.

'One of the Soudanese Rhodes brought with him from the north, I suppose?' said Peter, still eyeing him curiously.

'No; Cecil Rhodes* has had nothing to do with my coming here,' said the stranger.

'Oh——' said Peter. 'You didn't perhaps happen to come across a company of men to-day, twelve white men and seven coloured, with three cart loads of provisions? We were taking them to the big camp, and I got parted from my troop this morning. I've not been able to find them, though I've been seeking for them ever since.'

The stranger warmed his hands slowly at the fire; then he raised his head:—'They are camped at the foot of those hills to-night,' he said, pointing with his hand into the darkness at the left. 'To-morrow early they will be here, before the sun has risen.'

'Oh, you've met them, have you!' said Peter joyfully; 'that's why you weren't surprised at finding me here. Take a drop!' He took the small flask from his pocket and held it out. 'I'm sorry there's so little, but a drop will keep the cold out.'

The stranger bowed his head; but thanked and declined.

Peter raised the flask to his lips and took a small draught; then returned it to his pocket. The stranger folded his arms about his knees, and looked into the fire.

'Are you a Jew?' asked Peter, suddenly; as the firelight fell full on the stranger's face.

'Yes; I am a Jew.'

'Ah,' said Peter, 'that's why I wasn't able to make out at first what nation you could be of; your dress, you know——' Then he stopped, and said, 'Trading here, I suppose? Which country do you come from; are you a Spanish Jew?'

'I am a Jew of Palestine.'

'Ah!' said Peter; 'I haven't seen many from that part yet. I came out with a lot on board ship; and I've seen Barnato and Beit;* but they're not very much like you. I suppose it's coming from Palestine makes the difference.'

All fear of the stranger had now left Peter Halket. 'Come a little nearer the fire,' he said, 'you must be cold, you haven't too much wraps. I'm chill in this big coat.' Peter Halket pushed his gun a little further away from him; and threw another large log on the fire. 'I'm sorry I haven't anything to eat to offer you; but I haven't had anything myself since last night. It's beastly sickening, being out like this with nothing to eat. Wouldn't have thought a fellow'd feel so bad after only a day of it. Have you ever been out without grub?' said Peter cheerfully, warming his hands at the blaze.

'Forty days and nights,' said the stranger.

'Forty days! Phe—e—w!' said Peter. 'You must have had a lot to drink, or you wouldn't have stood it. I was feeling blue enough when you turned up, but I'm better now, warmer.'

Peter Halket re-arranged the logs on the fire.

'In the employ of the Chartered Company,* I suppose?' said Peter, looking into the fire he had made.

'No,' said the stranger; 'I have nothing to do with the Chartered Company.'

'Oh,' said Peter, 'I don't wonder, then, that things aren't looking very smart with you! There's not too much cakes and ale up here for those that do belong to it, if they're not big-wigs, and none at all for those who don't. I tried it when I first came up here. I was with a prospector who was hooked on to the Company somehow, but I worked on my own account for the prospector by the day. I tell you what, it's not the men who work up here who make the money; it's the big-wigs who get the concessions!'

Peter felt exhilarated by the presence of the stranger. That one unarmed man had robbed him of all fear.

Seeing that the stranger did not take up the thread of conversation, he went on after a time: 'It wasn't such a bad life, though. I only wish I was back there again. I had two huts to myself, and a couple of nigger girls. It's better fun,' said Peter, after a while, 'having these black women than whites. The whites you've got to support, but the niggers support you! And when you've done with them you can just get rid of them. I'm all for the nigger gals.' Peter laughed. But the stranger sat motionless with his arms about his knees.

'You got any girls?' said Peter. 'Care for niggers?'

'I love *all* women,' said the stranger, refolding his arms about his knees.

'Oh, you do, do you?' said Peter. 'Well, I'm pretty sick of them. I had bother enough with mine,' he said genially, warming his hands by the fire, and then interlocking the fingers and turning the palms towards the blaze as one who prepares to enjoy a good talk. 'One girl was only fifteen; I got her cheap from a policeman who was living with her, and she wasn't much. But the other, by Gad! I never saw another nigger like her; well set up, I tell you, and as straight as that——' said Peter, holding up his finger in the firelight. 'She was thirty if she was a day. Fellows don't generally fancy women that age; they like slips of girls. But I set my heart on her the day I saw her. She belonged to the chap I was with. He got her up north. There was a devil of a row about his getting her, too; she'd got a nigger husband and two children; didn't want to leave them, or some nonsense of that sort: you know what these niggers are? Well, I tried to get the other fellow to let me have her, but the devil a bit he would. I'd only got the other girl, and I didn't much fancy her; she was only a child. Well, I went down Umtali way and got a lot of liquor and stuff, and when I got back to camp I found them clean dried out. They hadn't had a drop of liquor in camp for ten days, and the rainy season coming on and no knowing when they'd get any. Well, I'd a "vatje" of Old Dop[1] as high as that——,' indicating with his hand an object about two feet high, 'and the other fellow wanted to buy it from me. I knew two of

---

[1] Vatje of Old Dop, a little cask of Cape brandy.

that. I said I wanted it for myself. He offered me this, and he offered me that. At last I said, "Well, just to oblige you, I give you the 'vatje' and you give me the girl!" And so he did. Most people wouldn't have fancied a nigger girl who'd had two nigger children, but I didn't mind; it's all the same to me. And I tell you she worked. She made a garden, and she and the other girl worked in it; I tell you I didn't need to buy a sixpence of food for them in six months, and I used to sell green mealies[1] and pumpkins to all the fellows about. There weren't many flies on her, I tell you. She picked up English quicker than I picked up her lingo, and took to wearing a dress and shawl.'

The stranger still sat motionless, looking into the fire.

Peter Halket reseated himself more comfortably before the fire. 'Well, I came home to the huts one day, rather suddenly, you know, to fetch something; and what did I find? She, talking at the hut door with a nigger man. Now it was my strict orders they were neither to speak a word to a nigger man at all; so I asked what it was. And she answers, as cool as can be, that he was a stranger going past on the road, and asked her to give him a drink of water. Well, I just ordered him off. I didn't think anything more about it. But I remember now. I saw him hanging about the camp the day after. Well, she came to me the next day and asked me for a lot of cartridges. She'd never asked me for anything before. I asked her what the devil a woman wanted with cartridges, and she said the old nigger woman who helped carry in water to the garden said she couldn't stay and help her any more unless she got some cartridges to give her son who was going up north hunting elephants. The woman got over me to give her the cartridges because she was going to have a kid, and she said she couldn't do the watering without help. So I gave them her. I never put two and two together.

'Well, when I heard that the Company was going to have a row with the Matabele, I thought I'd volunteer. They said there was lots of loot to be got, and land to be given out, and that sort of thing, and I thought I'd only be gone about three months. So I went. I left those women there, and a lot of stuff in the garden and some sugar and rice, and I told them not to leave till I came back; and I asked the other man to keep an eye on them. Both those women were Mashonas. They always said the Mashonas didn't love the Matabele; but, by God, it

---

[1] Mealies, maize.

turned out that they loved them better than they loved us. They've got the damned impertinence to say, that the Matabele oppressed them sometimes, but the white man oppresses them all the time!

'Well, I left those women there,' said Peter, dropping his hands on his knees. 'Mind you, I'd treated those women really well. I'd never given either of them one touch all the time I had them. I was the talk of all the fellows round, the way I treated them. Well, I hadn't been gone a month, when I got a letter from the man I worked with, the one who had the woman first—he's dead now, poor fellow; they found him at his hut door with his throat cut—and what do you think he said to me? Why, I hadn't been gone six hours when those two women skooted! It was all the big one. What do you think she did? She took every ounce of ball and cartridge she could find in that hut, and my old Martini-Henry,* and even the lid off the tea-box to melt into bullets for the old muzzle-loaders they have; and off she went, and took the young one too. The fellow wrote me they didn't touch another thing: they left the shawls and dresses I gave them kicking about the huts, and went off naked with only their blankets and the ammunition on their heads. A nigger man met them twenty miles off, and he said they were skooting up for Lo-Magundi's country as fast as they could go.

'And do you know,' said Peter, striking his knee, and looking impressively across the fire at the stranger; 'what I'm as sure of as that I'm sitting here? It's that that nigger I caught at my hut, that day, was her nigger husband! He'd come to fetch her that time; and when she saw she couldn't get away without our catching her, she got the cartridges for *him!*' Peter paused impressively between the words. 'And now she's gone back to him. It's for him she's taken that ammunition!'

Peter looked across the fire at the stranger, to see what impression his story was making.

'I tell you what,' said Peter, 'if I'd had any idea that day who that bloody nigger was, the day I saw him standing at my door, I'd have given him one cartridge in the back of his head more than ever he reckoned for!' Peter looked triumphantly at the stranger. This was his only story; and he had told it a score of times round the camp fire for the benefit of some new-comer. When this point was reached, a low murmur of applause and sympathy always ran round the group: tonight there was quiet; the stranger's large dark eyes watched the fire almost as though he heard nothing.

'I shouldn't have minded so much,' said Peter after a while, 'though no man likes to have his woman taken away from him; but she was going to have a kid in a month or two—and so was the little one for anything I know; she looked like it! I expect they did away with it before it came; they've no hearts, these niggers; they'd think nothing of doing that with a white man's child. They've no hearts; they'd rather go back to a black man, however well you've treated them. It's all right if you get them quite young and keep them away from their own people; but if once a nigger woman's had a nigger man and had children by him, you might as well try to hold a she-devil! they'll always go back. If ever I'm shot, it's as likely as not it'll be by my own gun, with my own cartridges. And she'd stand by and watch it, and cheer them on; though I never gave her a blow all the time she was with me. But I tell you what—if ever I come across that bloody nigger, I'll take it out of him. He won't count many days to his year, after I've spotted him!' Peter Halket paused. It seemed to him that the eyes under their heavy, curled lashes, were looking at something beyond him with an infinite sadness, almost as of eyes that wept.

'You look awfully tired,' said Peter; 'wouldn't you like to lie down and sleep? You could put your head down on that stone, and I'd keep watch.'

'I have no need of sleep,' the stranger said; 'I will watch with you.'

'You've been in the wars, too, I see,' said Peter, bending forward a little, and looking at the stranger's feet. 'By God! Both of them!— And right through! You must have had a bad time of it?'

'It was very long ago,' said the stranger.

Peter Halket threw two more logs on the fire. 'Do you know,' he said, 'I've been wondering ever since you came, who it was you reminded me of. It's my mother! You're not like her in the face, but when your eyes look at me it seems to me as if it was she looking at me. Curious, isn't it? I don't know you from Adam, and you've hardly spoken a word since you came; and yet I seem as if I'd known you all my life.' Peter moved a little nearer him. 'I was awfully afraid of you when you first came; even when I first saw you;—you aren't dressed as most of us dress, you know. But the minute the fire shone on your face I said, "It's all right." Curious, isn't it?' said Peter. 'I don't know you from Adam, but if you were to take up my gun and point it at me, I wouldn't move! I'd lie down here and go to sleep with my head at your feet; curious, isn't it, when I don't know you from Adam? My name's Peter Halket. What's yours?'

But the stranger was arranging the logs on the fire. The flames shot up bright and high, and almost hid him from Peter Halket's view.

'By gad! how they burn when you arrange them!' said Peter.

They sat quiet in the blaze for a while.

Then Peter said, 'Did you see any niggers about yesterday? I haven't come across any in this part.'

'There is,' said the stranger, raising himself, 'an old woman in a cave over yonder, and there is one man in the bush, ten miles from this spot. He has lived there six weeks, since you destroyed the kraal, living on roots or herbs. He was wounded in the thigh, and left for dead. He is waiting till you have all left this part of the country that he may set out to follow his own people. His leg is not yet so strong that he may walk fast.'

'Did you speak to him?' said Peter.

'I took him down to the water where a large pool was. The bank was too high for the man to descend alone.'

'It's a lucky thing for you our fellows didn't catch you,' said Peter 'Our captain's a regular little martinet. He'd shoot you as soon as look at you, if he saw you fooling round with a wounded nigger. It's lucky you kept out of his way.'

'The young ravens have meat given to them,' said the stranger, lifting himself up; 'and the lions go down to the streams to drink.'

'Ah—yes—' said Peter; 'but that's because we can't help it!'

They were silent again for a little while. Then Peter, seeing that the stranger showed no inclination to speak, said, 'Did you hear of the spree they had up Bulawayo way, hanging those three niggers for spies? I wasn't there myself, but a fellow who was told me they made the niggers jump down from the tree and hang themselves; one fellow wouldn't bally jump, till they gave him a charge of buckshot in the back: and then he caught hold of a branch with his hands and they had to shoot 'em loose. He didn't like hanging. I don't know if it's true, of course; I wasn't there myself, but a fellow who was told me. Another fellow who was at Bulawayo, but who wasn't there when they were hung, said they fired at them just after they jumped, to kill 'em. I——'

'I was there,' said the stranger.

'Oh, you were?' said Peter. 'I saw a photograph of the niggers hanging, and our fellows standing round smoking; but I didn't see you in it. I suppose you'd just gone away?'

'I was beside the men when they were hung,' said the stranger.

'Oh, you were, were you?' said Peter. 'I don't much care about seeing that sort of thing myself. Some fellows think it's the best fun out to see the niggers kick; but I can't stand it: it turns my stomach. It's not liver-heartedness,' said Peter, quickly, anxious to remove any adverse impression as to his courage which the stranger might form; 'if it's shooting or fighting, I'm there. I've potted as many niggers as any man in our troop, I bet. It's floggings and hangings I'm off. It's the way one's brought up, you know. My mother never even would kill our ducks; she let them die of old age, and we had the feathers and the eggs: and she was always drumming into me;—don't hit a fellow smaller than yourself; don't hit a fellow weaker than yourself; don't hit a fellow unless he can hit you back as good again. When you've always had that sort of thing drummed into you, you can't get rid of it, somehow. Now there was that other nigger they shot. They say he sat as still as if he was cut out of stone, with his arms round his legs; and some of the fellows gave him blows about the head and face before they took him off to shoot him. Now, that's the sort of thing I can't do. It makes me sick here, somehow.' Peter put his hand rather low down over the pit of his stomach. 'I'll shoot as many as you like if they'll run, but they mustn't be tied up.'

'I was there when that man was shot,' said the stranger.

'Why, you seem to have been everywhere,' said Peter. 'Have you seen Cecil Rhodes?'

'Yes, I have seen him,' said the stranger.

'Now *he's* death on niggers,' said Peter Halket, warming his hands by the fire; 'they say when he was Prime Minister down in the Colony* he tried to pass a law that would give masters and mistresses the right to have their servants flogged whenever they did anything they didn't like; but the other Englishmen wouldn't let him pass it. But *here* he can do what he likes. That's the reason some fellows don't want him to be sent away. They say, "If we get the British Government here,* they'll be giving the niggers land to live on; and let them have the vote, and get civilised and educated, and all that sort of thing; but Cecil Rhodes, he'll keep their noses to the grindstone." *I prefer land to niggers*, he says. They say he's going to parcel them out, and make them work on our lands whether they like it or not—just as good as having slaves, you know: and you haven't the bother of looking after them when they're old. Now, there I'm with Rhodes; I think it's an awfully good move. We don't come out here to work; it's all very well in England; but we've come here to make money, and how are we to make it, unless you get niggers to work for you, or start a syndicate? He's death on niggers, is Rhodes!' said Peter, meditating; 'they say if we had the British Government here and you were thrashing a nigger and something happened, there'd be an investigation, and all that sort of thing. But, with Cecil, it's all right, you can do what you like with the niggers, provided you don't get *him* into trouble.'

The stranger watched the clear flame as it burnt up high in the still night air; then suddenly he started.

'What is it?' said Peter; 'do you hear anything?'

'I hear far off,' said the stranger, 'the sound of weeping, and the sound of blows. And I hear the voices of men and women calling to me.'

Peter listened intently. 'I don't hear anything!' he said. 'It must be in your head. I sometimes get a noise in mine.' He listened intently. 'No, there's nothing. It's all so deadly still.'

They sat silent for a while.

'Peter Simon Halket,' said the stranger suddenly—Peter started; he had not told him his second name—'if it should come to pass that you should obtain those lands you have desired, and you should obtain black men to labour on them and make to yourself great wealth; or should you create that company'—Peter started—'and fools should buy from you, so that you became the richest man in the land; and if you should take to yourself wide lands, and raise to yourself great palaces, so that princes and great men of earth crept up to you and laid their hands against yours, so that you might slip gold into them—what would it profit you?'

'Profit!' Peter Halket stared: 'Why, it would profit everything. What makes Beit and Rhodes and Barnato so great? If you've got eight millions——'

'Peter Simon Halket, which of those souls you have seen on earth is to you greatest?' said the stranger, 'Which soul is to you fairest?'

'Ah,' said Peter, 'but we weren't talking of souls at all; we were talking of money. Of course if it comes to souls, my mother's the best person I've ever seen. But what does it help her? She's got to stand washing clothes for those stuck-up nincompoops of fine ladies! Wait till I've got money! It'll be somebody else then, who——'

'Peter Halket,' said the stranger, 'who is the greatest; he who serves or he who is served?' Peter looked at the stranger: then it flashed on him that he was mad.

'Oh,' he said, 'if it comes to that, what's anything! You might as well say, sitting there in your old linen shirt, that you were as great as Rhodes or Beit or Barnato, or a king. Of course a man's just the same whatever he's got on or whatever he has; but he isn't the same to other people.'

'There have been kings born in stables,' said the stranger.

Then Peter saw that he was joking, and laughed. 'It must have been a long time ago; they don't get born there now,' he said. 'Why, if God Almighty came to this country, and hadn't half-a-million in shares, they wouldn't think much of Him.'

Peter built up his fire. Suddenly he felt the stranger's eyes were fixed on him.

'Who gave you your land?' the stranger asked.

'Mine! Why, the Chartered Company,' said Peter.

The stranger looked back into the fire. 'And who gave it to them?' he asked softly.

'Why, England, of course. She gave them the land to far beyond the Zambesi to do what they liked with, and make as much money out of as they could, and she'd back 'em.'

'Who gave the land to the men and women of England?' asked the stranger softly.

'Why, the devil! They said it was theirs, and of course it was,' said Peter.

'And the people of the land: did England give you the people also?'

Peter looked a little doubtfully at the stranger. 'Yes, of course, she gave us the people; what use would the land have been to us otherwise?'

'And who gave her the people, the living flesh and blood, that she might give them away, into the hands of others?' asked the stranger, raising himself.

Peter looked at him and was half afeared. 'Well, what could she do with a lot of miserable niggers, if she didn't give them to us? A lot of good-for-nothing rebels they are, too,' said Peter.

'What is a rebel?' asked the stranger.

'My Gawd!' said Peter, 'you must have lived out of the world if you don't know what a rebel is! A rebel is a man who fights against his king and his country. These bloody niggers here are rebels because they are fighting against us. They don't want the Chartered Company to have them. But they'll have to. We'll teach them a lesson,' said Peter Halket, the pugilistic spirit rising, firmly reseating himself on the South African earth, which two years before he had never heard of, and eighteen months before he had never seen, as if it had been his mother earth, and the land in which he first saw light.

The stranger watched the fire; then he said musingly, 'I have seen a land far from here. In that land are men of two kinds who live side by side. Well nigh a thousand years ago one conquered the other; they have lived together since. To-day the one people seeks to drive forth the other who conquered them.* Are these men rebels, too?'

'Well,' said Peter, pleased at being deferred to, 'that all depends who they are, you know!'

'They call the one nation Turks, and the other Armenians,' said the stranger.

'Oh, the Armenians aren't rebels,' said Peter; 'they are on our side! The papers are all full of it,' said Peter, pleased to show his knowledge. 'Those bloody Turks! What right had they to conquer the Armenians? Who gave them their land? I'd like to have a shot at them myself!'

'*Why* are Armenians not rebels?' asked the stranger, gently.

'Oh, you do ask such curious questions,' said Peter. 'If they don't like the Turks, why should they have 'em? If the French came now and conquered us, and we tried to drive them out first chance we had; you wouldn't call *us* rebels! Why shouldn't they try to turn those bloody Turks out? Besides,' said Peter, bending over and talking in the manner of one who imparts secret and important information; 'you see, if we don't help the Armenians the Russians would; and we,' said Peter, looking exceedingly knowing, 'we've got to prevent that: they'd get the land; and it's on the road to India. And we don't mean them to. I suppose you don't know much about politics in Palestine?' said Peter, looking kindly and patronisingly at the stranger.

'If these men,' said the stranger, 'would rather be free, or be under the British Government, than under the Chartered Company, why, when they resist the Chartered Company, are they more rebels than the Armenians when they resist the Turk? Is the Chartered Company God, that every knee should bow before it, and before it every head be bent? Would you, the white men of England, submit to its rule for one day?'

'Ah,' said Peter, 'no, of course we shouldn't, but we are white men, and so are the Armenians—almost——' Then he glanced at the stranger's dark face, and added quickly, 'At least, it's not the colour that matters, you know. I rather like a dark face, my mother's eyes are brown—but the Armenians, you know, they've got long hair like us.'

'Oh, it is the hair, then, that matters,' said the stranger softly.

'Oh, well,' said Peter, 'it's not altogether, of course. But it's quite a different thing, the Armenians wanting to get rid of the Turks, and these bloody niggers wanting to get rid of the Chartered Company. Besides, the Armenians are Christians, like us!'

'Are *you* Christians?' A strange storm broke across the stranger's features; he rose to his feet.

'Why, of course, we are!' said Peter. 'We're all Christians, we English. Perhaps you don't like Christians, though? Some Jews don't, I know,' said Peter, looking up soothingly at him.

'I neither love nor hate any man for that which it is called,' said the stranger; 'the name boots nothing.'

The stranger sat down again beside the fire, and folded his hands.

'Is the Chartered Company Christian also?' he asked.

'Yes, oh yes,' said Peter.

'What is a Christian?' asked the stranger.

'Well, now, you really do ask such curious questions. A Christian is a man who believes in Heaven and Hell, and God and the Bible, and in Jesus Christ, that he'll save him from going to Hell, and if he believes he'll be saved, he *will* be saved.'

'But here, in this world, what is a Christian?'

'Why,' said Peter, 'I'm a Christian—we're all Christians.'

The stranger looked into the fire; and Peter thought he would change the subject. 'It's curious how like my mother you are; I mean, your ways. She was always saying to me, "Don't be too anxious to make money, Peter. Too much wealth is as bad as too much poverty." You're very like her.'

After a while Peter said, bending over a little towards the stranger, 'If you don't want to make money, what did you come to this land for? No one comes here for anything else. Are you in with the Portuguese?'

'I am not more with one people than with another,' said the

stranger. 'The Frenchman is not more to me than the Englishman, the Englishman than the Kaffir, the Kaffir than the Chinaman. I have heard,' said the stranger, 'the black infant cry as it crept on its mother's body and sought for her breast as she lay dead in the roadway. I have heard also the rich man's child wail in the palace. I hear all cries.'

Peter looked intently at him. 'Why, who are you?' he said; then, bending nearer to the stranger and looking up, he added, 'What is it that you are doing here?'

'I belong,' said the stranger, 'to the strongest company on earth.' [. . .]

Peter moved nearer, so that he almost knelt at the stranger's feet: his gun lay on the ground at the other side of the fire.

'I would like to be one of your men,' he said. 'I am tired of belonging to the Chartered Company.'

The stranger looked down gently. 'Peter Simon Halket,' he said, 'can you bear the weight?'

And Peter said, 'Give me work, that I may try.'

There was silence for a time; then the stranger said, 'Peter Simon Halket, take a message to England'—Peter Halket started—'Go to that great people and cry aloud to it: "Where is the sword was given into your hand, that with it you might enforce justice and deal out mercy? How came you to give it up into the hands of men whose search is gold, whose thirst is wealth, to whom men's souls and bodies are counters in a game? How came you to give up the folk that were given into your hands, into the hand of the speculator and the gamester; as though they were dumb beasts who might be bought or sold?

'"Take back your sword, Great People—but wipe it first, lest some of the gold and blood stick to your hand.

'"What is this, I see!—the sword of the Great People, transformed to burrow earth for gold, as the snouts of swine for earth nuts! Have you no other use for it, Great Folk?

'"Take back your sword; and, when you have thoroughly cleansed it and wiped it of the blood and mire, then raise it to set free the oppressed of other climes.

'"Great Prince's Daughter, take heed! You put your sword into the hands of recreant knights; they will dull its edge and mar its brightness, and, when your hour of need comes and you would put it into other hands, you will find its edge chipped and its point broken. Take heed! Take heed!"

'Cry to the wise men of England: "You, who in peace and calm in shaded chambers ponder on all things in heaven and earth, and take all knowledge for your province, have you no time to think of this? To whom has England given her power? How do the men wield it who have filched it from her? Say not, What have we to do with folk across the waters; have we not matter enough for thought in our own land? Where the brain of a nation has no time to go, there should its hands never be sent to labour: where the power of a people goes, there must its intellect and knowledge go, to guide it. Oh, you who sit at ease, studying past and future—and forget the present—you have no right to sit at ease knowing nothing of the working of the powers you have armed and sent to work on men afar. Where is your nation's sword—you men of thought?"

'Cry to the women of England: "You, who repose in sumptuous houses, with children on your knees; think not it is only the rustling of the soft draped curtains, or the whistling of the wind, you hear. Listen! May it not be the far off cry of those your sword governs, creeping towards you across wide oceans till it pierces even into your inmost sanctuary? Listen!

'"For the womanhood of a dominant people has not accomplished all its labour when it has borne its children and fed them at its breast: there cries to it also from over seas and across continents the voice of the child-peoples—'Mother-heart, stand for us!' It would be better for you that your wombs should be barren and that your race should die out; than that you should listen, and give no answer."'

The stranger lifted his hands upwards as he spoke, and Peter saw there were the marks of old wounds in both.

'Cry aloud to the working men and women of England: "You, who for ages cried out because the heel of your masters was heavy on you; and who have said, 'We curse the kings that sit at ease, and care not who oppresses the folk, so their coffers be full and their bellies satisfied, and they be not troubled with the trouble of rule'; you, who have taken the king's rule from him and sit enthroned within his seat; is his sin not yours to-day? If men should add but one hour to your day's labour, or make but one fraction dearer the bread you eat, would you not rise up as one man? Yet, what is dealt out to men beyond seas whom you rule wounds you not. Nay, have you not sometimes said, as kings of old: 'It matters not who holds out our sword, marauder or speculator, so he calls it ours, we must cloak up the evil it has done!' Think you, no other curses rise to heaven but yours? Where is your sword? Into whose hand has it fallen? Take it quickly and cleanse it!"'

Peter Halket crouched, looking upwards; then he cried: 'Master, I cannot give that message, I am a poor unlearn'd man. And if I should go to England and cry aloud, they would say, "Who is this, who comes preaching to a great people? Is not his mother with us, and a washerwoman; and was not his father a day labourer at two shillings a day?" and they would laugh me to scorn. And, in truth, the message is so long I could not well remember it; give me other work to do.'

And the stranger said, 'Take a message to the men and women of this land. Go, from the Zambesi to the sea, and cry to its white men and women, and say: "I saw a wide field, and in it were two fair beasts. Wide was the field about them and rich was the earth with sweet scented herbs, and so abundant was the pasturage that hardly might they consume all that grew about them: and the two were like one to another, for they were the sons of one mother.* And as I looked, I saw, far off to the northward, a speck within the sky, so small it was, and so high it was, that the eye scarce might mark it. Then it came nearer and hovered over the spot where the two beasts fed:—and its neck was bare, and its beak was hooked, and its talons were long, and its wings strong. And it hovered over the field where the two beasts were; and I saw it settle down upon a great white stone; and it waited. And I saw more specks to the northward, and more and more came onward to join him who sat upon the stone. And some hovered over the beasts, and some sharpened their beaks on the stones; and some walked in and out between the beasts' legs. And I saw that they were waiting for something.

'"Then he who first came flew from one of the beasts to the other, and sat upon their necks, and put his beak within their ears. And he flew from one to the other and flapped his wings in their faces till the beasts were blinded, and each believed it was his fellow who attacked him. And they fell to, and fought; they gored one another's sides till the field was red with blood and the ground shook beneath them. The birds sat by and watched; and when the blood flowed they walked round and round. And when the strength of the two beasts was exhausted they fell to earth. Then the birds settled down upon them, and feasted; till their maws were full, and their long bare necks were wet; and they stood with their beaks deep in the entrails of the two dead beasts; and looked out with their keen bright eyes from above them. And he who was king of all plucked out the eyes, and fed on the hearts of the dead beasts. And when his maw was full, so that he could eat no more, he sat on his stone hard by and flapped his great wings."

'Peter Simon Halket, cry to the white men and women of South Africa: "You have a goodly land; you and your children's children shall scarce fill it; though you should stretch out your arms to welcome each stranger who comes to live and labour with you. You are the twin branches of one tree; you are the sons of one mother. Is this goodly land not wide enough for you, that you should rend each other's flesh at the bidding of those who will wet their beaks within both your vitals?—Look up, see, they circle in the air above you!"'

Almost Peter Halket started and looked upward; but there was only the black sky of Mashonaland over his head.

The stranger stood silent looking downward into the fire. Peter Halket half clasped his arms about his knees.

'My master,' he cried, 'how can I take this message? The Dutchmen of South Africa will not listen to me, they will say I am an Englishman. And the Englishmen will say: "Who is this fellow who comes preaching peace, peace, peace? Has he not been a year in the country and he has not a share in a single company? Can anything he says be worth hearing? If he were a man of any sense he would have made five thousand pounds at least." And they will not listen to me. Give me another labour!' [. . .]

See also: Aurobindo; Conrad; Hobson; Joyce; Plaatje; Woolf.

MARY KINGSLEY
(1862–1900)

Black Ghosts (1897)

My own feelings regarding ghosts are those of Dr Johnson's dear old lady. I do not believe in them, but I am very much afraid of them; particularly am I afraid of them when they are not ghosts but something else. No, I do not mean devils—perhaps I had better give an explanatory instance, as I feel I am becoming complicated in expression.

I do not intend to give names in the affair, because some of the actors in it are still living, and the house wherein it took place is still a source of livelihood, for it is an inn. So let it suffice that this said inn is situate on the South Coast of England, facing the harbour of a town which kills half a bullock a week with a neighbouring town. In my days we had no railway, and you went, wind and weather permitting, to it on a steam-packet; but although it has got a railway now, I am told, the old inn is unaltered, and so you may take it that it still smells strongly of straw, rotten apples, manure, and stale beer, and still has its bedrooms in long rows opening out of narrow one-sided passages, which, by an occasional window, give the visitor a commanding view of the stable-yard with a pump in it; being desirous of being careful, I will not swear the pump will be in working order. Well, to this humble scene, wind and weather having permitted, arrive three ladies—the other side of forty—lashings of luggage and a swarm of children, on what happened to be market day. A scene of some confusion ensued, but, at last, after a most unsatisfactory meal, all the party retired to their rooms, save one lady, who had to sit up until the local gentlemen had done with the billiard-room, for she had to pass through this to her passage.

The rooms left much to be desired; one was, we still believe, a chamber in a chimney, formerly used for smoking bacon, because, when the landlady was communicated with and told the house was on fire, she said, 'No, it was all right; smoke always came up through the floor like that,' and 'was always a bit hot.' But, in spite of the simple carolling of the intoxicated villagers in the tap-room below, and the presence of some fine specimens of *aphaniptera* and *acanthia lectularia*,* exhausted nature claimed her due and the whole party slept, including the estimable lady, when she had safely reached her room *viâ* the deserted billiard saloon. This room was at the extreme end of one of the afore-mentioned passages overlooking the stable yard, and she had congratulated herself, she subsequently remarked, on finding none of the other rooms in her passage were occupied.

About 2.30 A.M. she was aroused by a sound, and while she was drowsily deliberating whether the sound was a real sound, or a dream sound, it was repeated, and, after a short interval, it came again. It was a queer, dragging sound, and a flump. She sat up in bed and listened intently, and she decided two things regarding it; one was that it was in her passage, the other was that the intervals between the noise were growing gradually greater, but whatever was making them was approaching her door. The correctness of this surmise was soon demonstrated, for whatever it was that dragged and flumped was now fumbling at the door-handle, and, after a few minutes, fumbled successfully, and then flumped, and there was silence for a few minutes. The lady's whole attention was now concentrated —spell-bound—on a patch of utter darkness on the floor. She saw a flicker of light on the wall of the passage, that came in from the end window thereof, but what was on the floor she could not see. Presently it started again—making its way towards the bed; twice more it dragged, and flumped, and paused, and then she felt its hands, or something, grasping and twining in the bed-clothes, dragging them off. Then she gave a shriek that was a credit to the sex, and very wisely fainted. Everyone on that side of the house heard the shriek, and rising up grasped a candle—candlesticks were rare in that inn—and went with all haste in the direction the shriek had come from, expecting to hear more, but no more came. So the billiard-room door opening into the passage was cautiously opened. The appearance of the passage was anything but reassuring; the strip of narrow stair-carpeting which was spread along it was dragged up and twisted, and over it, and on the bare boards, lay a stream of blood straight to the lady's door; there were little pools of it every here and there, but it was in continuous line, you understand. On following this trail up, and into the room, the lady was found safe, dead off in a swoon, and hanging on to her bed-clothes the dead body of a man who had, it turned out, gone into his room at the billiard-room end of the passage after she had retired, then cut his throat, so that he could not speak, and, apparently knowing there was someone at the other end of the passage, started off to get assistance.

This affair made such an impression on my youthful mind that for many years after I said, 'Give me real ghosts;' but of late years I have been on the West African coast, where real ghosts fairly swarm, and I have found them such a dreadful hindrance and nuisance that I really feel I cannot tell you whether they were any safer or pleasanter to deal with than repentant suicides.

This immense number of ghosts arises partly from everyone

having four separate souls: three of these souls expire with life, and only one survives after death, and it is not generally held that this survives in a state of immortality; but, when it does survive, it is a great nuisance and a considerable expense to its living relations, more particularly when it is the soul of the father of a family, for then it is a perfect curse to its many widows, and 'a very dangerous wild-fowl' to their suitors. The other three strictly mortal souls are mainly a cause of apprehension and alarm to their individual owner, but a source of general trouble and expense as well.

The study of the ramifications of spiritual beings is about as complex as that of the genealogy of the Emperor of China, and although not so dull is far more dangerous; and, as I feel a conviction this study will lead me to an unknown tomb before my book on Fetish, in seventeen volumes, folio size, written mostly in cuneiform or early Welsh—for Latin every young lady knows nowadays—can come out, I will give you a few rough notes on ghosts properly so called. There is great trouble in correcting and classifying the spirit fauna of West Africa, owing to your having to hunt the specimens through the labyrinths of the Ethiopian with-thick-fog-overhung mind,* as a German would say. For some time I thought four Families would do, each containing, of course, many genera and varieties, not to mention individual freaks, but now I have been obliged to enlarge the number of Families to nine. I will here only refer to the spirits of human origin, and we will first take the conduct of the souls of the living, and classify them.

1. The soul that survives. 2. The bush soul. 3. The dream soul. 4. The shadow on the path.

1. We will leave this soul out of the affair at present, merely remarking that it does not leave the body during life, but it soon withers if its companion souls are taken away from it. It grows up with its owner, taking its image from him, and therefore it is no good in dealing with life as it comes on—no more good than the photograph of an eminent lawyer, for example, would be to deal with a law case, even if the photograph were taken immediately before the case came on.

2. The bush soul. This is, I think, confined to negroes, and not possessed by Bantu.* This soul is always in the form of an animal, never in that of a plant, and it is a wild animal in the forest. If a man sickens it is because his bush soul is angry at being neglected, and a

witch doctor is called in, who diagnoses the case, and advises the administration of some kind of sedative, in the shape of an offering, to his bush soul. When you walk in the Calabar forests you will see little dwarf huts with these offerings under them. You must be careful not to confuse these little huts with those, looking very like them, that you will see in the plantations, or near roads, which refer to other things entirely.

These offerings are put in the place in the forest where your bush soul was last seen. Unfortunately the witch doctor has to be called in to determine the spot (which is expensive, for there is no free medical black advice in Africa), because you cannot see your own bush soul unless you are an 'Ebum tup,' which is a rare occurrence. If his offering acts well on the bush soul you get better, but occasionally the bush soul gives great trouble. This arises from the bush soul not knowing that, by exposing itself to danger recklessly, it injures itself, and if you die it dies. A man may be a quiet and respectable citizen, devoted to caution in his diet, &c., and devoted to a whole skin, yet that same man may have a sadly flighty, disreputable bush soul, which from its recklessness gets itself injured or killed, and causes you sickness or death. From this notion regarding the soul arises a good deal of the respect in which old people were held among the Calabar tribes; for, however wicked their record may have been, their longevity demonstrates the possession of a powerful bush soul whom it would be unwise to offend. When the man dies, the animal of the soul 'can no longer find a good place,' and goes mad, rushing wildly to and fro; if it sees a fire, it rushes into it; if it sees a lot of people, it rushes into them, until it gets itself killed, and when it is killed —'finish,' as M. Pichault* would say.

3. The dream soul. This is undoubtedly the greatest nuisance a man possesses. It seems an utter idiot, and, as soon as you go to sleep, off it ganders, playing with other souls, making dreams. While it is away you are exposed to three dangers: first, it may get caught by a witch, who sets a trap for it, usually a pot half full of some stuff attractive to the dream soul, with a knife or hook of iron concealed in it which the soul gets caught on, but I have seen soul traps made of string, &c.; anyhow, when the soul is caught it is tied up, usually over the canoe fire, which withers it up, and its original owner is out of his mind, or, I should perhaps say, his mind's out of him, until medical advice restores the truant. I have the greatest veneration for the

medical profession, but I must say I have had grave reason to suspect some practitioners of having had the soul in their own possession all the time; and I do think if the treatment administered by a certain Red Indian tribe to a doctor, who is supposed to have accidentally swallowed a patient's soul, were administered to these African doctors who first steal the soul, and then pretend to have had to send one of their own souls out to fetch it from the topmost branches of a silk cotton tree, or some such place—whereas they had it all the time in a basket at their side—and they were held upside down over a calabash, and had emetic remedies administered as is done to their poor unintentionally offending Red Indian professional brethren, this disgraceful practice would be suppressed. Many Africans have complained to me of their local medical man. 'Why do you call him in then?' I say. 'Well, one must, you see; he is very clever, but totally unprincipled; we shall really have to kill him off one day.' The second danger that overhangs a sleeping man is that, during the absence of his dream soul, one of that tiresome pauper class of souls, 'insisa,'[1] may whip in and take its place, and the original soul, when it comes back, finds no room for it. Certain kindly witch doctors keep a sort of asylums for these ousted dream souls, and I have often seen baskets-ful of them hanging up among the other strange things in their houses; they keep them and supply them to people who have lost, or had stolen from them a soul, and although, from being out of a body some time they are weakly, they are far better than having an insisa in, for insisa are never healthy; they are the souls of people who have died before their time, or of twin children,* or of people whose friends have not thought them worth burying properly, and they frequently have blood stains on them. It is true they are very careful how they leave their new-found body, but the blood on them is very likely to attract all sorts of devils. Blood on a soul devils always smell out and go for, and then the unfortunate, innocent man who has housed one, gets epileptic fits, general convulsions, or the twitches, and has to go to great expense, and endure some rigorous treatment to get all the devils, and the carrion soul they have come after, cast out of him. I once saw this operation performed, I was told, successfully, and a new dream soul blown into his mouth and nose, but the poor fellow was a wreck for days. This danger of getting invaded by a

[1] Fantee.

disagreeable spirit is thought to be best guarded against by sleeping on the face, the usual African sleep attitude; if you cannot do this, it is wise to put a piece of cloth over the mouth and nose. The third danger is that you may get awakened suddenly before your dream soul, who may be sky-larking off fishing or hunting, can get back.

4. The shadow on the path. This is a soul, because it is your own property. 'No man can cast the same shadow as his brother,' says the West African proverb; and as it is intangible, of course it is a soul. It has other forms of existence besides being a shadow. It is your photographic image, and you can lose it by being measured with a tape, or piece of string, for it goes into the string, and when that rots, it rots. It is, however, not so tiresome to look after as your other three souls, because it is less easily detached from you, and gets refreshed every night by the darkness, which a Bakele once told me was the shadow of the Great God. The chief danger to it is at high noon, in open ground, when it dwindles and may disappear, and this is why you often see a good jujuist circumnavigate an open yard, keeping in the shadow of the huts, instead of crossing it. It is, like other souls, of a delicate texture, and may be injured by being trodden on, &c. It is a great insult to a man to tread or spit on his shadow; to do so is an excellent recipe for making a quarrel, I once saw a dramatic scene in Qua Town.—A man was talking to some other men and his shadow fell strong on the ground; a woman went softly towards it and drove into the head a long darning needle. Both the stealth and rapidity with which the thing was done was wonderful, and it was murder—in intent. I was sitting in her house waiting for her to come in, and she did not know anyone was there to see her.

I cannot go into the subject of the diseases of the living soul here, because that would necessitate my writing an introductory monograph on Devils, particularly the red devil variety, which would run to the size of a monograph on the Medusæ or the Crustacea, and I will pass on to the consideration of the soul after death. The death-scene, when the dying man or woman is free, and has dependent on him or her many human beings, is peculiarly dreadful. The fetid atmosphere of the hut, crowded by human beings, beside themselves with grief and anxiety about their own fate, and quivering with hate against the person they think is in some vile sorcerous way stealing the life away that is so dear to them, make a never to be obliterated impression. I have many burnt into my mind. It is, of course, sad when the person dying is a slave or a woman of no importance, but one knows then that there will not follow to such an extent the misery and danger to the survivors.

When the person seems about to die, a perfect madness seizes those round him. Red pepper is forced into his nose and eyes, those near him stoop down to call his name into his ears, with the high-intoned voice used for calling people away in the bush. 'Come back! Come back! Where are you going to? This is your house! This is your house! Come back!' and their calling is taken up by all the bystanders; and when it is at last evident it is of no avail, the soul has gone, there is a breathless momentary pause, and then rises from every man and woman there that awful, wild, despairing death-wail that never loses its power to chill the white man's heart, even though he soon learns it does not mean the utter heart-broken grief it so superbly represents. But we will leave the survivors to their complicated and awful rites, and follow the soul.

The soul does not leave its old haunts until it is buried in a suitable and proper manner, no matter how long a time may elapse before the ceremony is carried out by the relations. Frequently a long time, may be a year or more, elapses before—for various financial and social reasons—this can be done. The soul during the whole of this period is a fearful domestic trial, particularly to its widows, who have to remain in a state of abomination and abasement as long as it is about.

In the Upper Calabar districts they have to take it turn and turn about to keep lights burning at night over where the body is buried, under the floor of the house, and entertain at their own expense all the people who come to pay their respects to the deceased. The house where the death took place may in no way be swept or tidied up, because the soul may be clinging on to the things, or lying on the floor, and get damaged. Indeed, what those poor women have to go through—those who are not killed for having bewitched it, or to be companions to it in the underworld, or representative of its earthly wealth—is beyond description all along the entire coast; but in every district the customs vary. Thus, in Togoland, where the ladies seem to be a little strong-minded, the widow has a rare good stout stick given her, wherewith to whack her deceased lord's soul if it gets beyond bearing with during the first six weeks' mourning, during which time she keeps in the hut. For six months after this the ghost remains in his old haunts and she has to be very careful.

The customs and ideas vary so much with each locality that it is unwise to generalise about them. There is a great division line between Calabar and Cameroon—that is to say, between the true negroes and Bantu; but some general ideas are common to the inhabitants north and south of this division line, such as the plurality of souls, &c., and the habit of the soul to haunt its hut, or place where it left its body, until such time as it is buried, *i.e.* sent off to the spirit-world, either for re-incarnation, as in the Calabar regions, or for permanent residence, as in the Windward Coast regions, *i.e.* the Gold, Slave, Grain, and Ivory Coasts.

South of Calabar you are among the Bantu, whose ideas on spiritual matters are nothing like so definite as those of the negroes. They always gave me the impression of having once known the things the negroes know, but to have partially forgotten them, only keeping the witchcraft proceedings fresh and green in their memories. I hasten to say I have no intention of starting rocking a common cradle for these two races away in the north-east. I will, therefore, only attempt now to follow a Windward Coast soul when it starts to leave this world for that of Srahmandazi.* I do not think you will find this region, a most important region though it is, even in the 'Times New Atlas,' so I will give you hastily a few notes on its geography, physiognomy, fauna, and flora. If you look in the atlas you will see to the east of Accra the Volta river down. Well, a good way up, and on the eastern bank, lies the entrance to Srahmandazi, and when the sun sets on this world it rises on Srahmandazi. There is everything there that there is in the world: men, women, children, animals, trees, plants, insects, reptiles, fish, houses, markets, towns, &c., but—and this is a 'but' that refers, I fear, to all of the spirit-worlds of we poor human beings, when it comes to the final test—a day in this world of ours is worth a whole year over there; for, after all, these are only the shadows of things, their souls, in this spirit world, and in the African underworld, as in the Christian heaven, there is no marriage. The African, however, thinks this evil can be provided against by taking a supply of wives with him; hence arises his killing of wives, sometimes wrongly called sacrificing at funerals.

A man takes the same rank there, if he has been properly buried, that he has had in this world, but the state of health he arrives in varies much on his arrival. You see, each soul has a certain definite earthly existence allotted to it. Say, for example, a soul has thirty years' existence in a body on earth, and its body gets killed off at twenty-five years, the remaining five years it has to spend knocking about its old haunts, homes, and wives. In this state it is a public curse, and is called a 'sisa.'[1] It will cause sickness, it will throw stones, it will rip off the thatch from roofs, and it will play what Mr Kipling calls 'the cat and banjo'* with husband Number 2 in all directions; all because, not having reached its allotted span, it has not been able to learn its way down the dark and difficult road to Srahmandazi, a knowledge that grows on a soul gradually.

A troublesome sisa can, by skilful witch doctors, be sent off before its time is up. In such a case, on its arrival in Srahmandazi, it is feeble from the difficulties and damages it has sustained during its journey. I find a certain amount of difference of opinion regarding the condition of the soul during the early days of its existence; some informants saying that a soul sent hence before its time, and in the vigour of its early years, although exhausted by its hardships on the road, recovers health in a month or so, while one that has run its allotted span and dies, say, of disease, is as feeble as a new-born child, and takes years to pull round. Others do not pretend to a knowledge of these details, and say the only difference that they know of between the souls of killed men and others is that the soul of a murdered man can always come back, and therefore the safest way of disposing of a troublesome sisa is by spells and incantations to get it to enter the sleeping body of a new-born child, when it can live its time out. This method is not difficult, because, as I have said anent the dream soul, a sisa is always on the look out to get into a body. But getting a sisa into a new-born baby is a mean thing to do, for this method is supposed by many parents of deceased children to have been the cause of their affliction; if it is not this, it is either a witch sucking the child's blood, or a wanderer soul having got into the family. This latter soul is a terrible plague. One child dies; the next child born to the same father or mother dies; and then a third child arrives, puts its parents to the usual trouble and expense, lives a couple of months or so, and then it dies;* but at this juncture the worm—the father, I mean—turns and, before burying his child's body, breaks one of its legs, or chops the whole body up into small pieces, and scatters them far and wide. The first method is followed

---

[1] Fantee.

by parents who are anxious for more children, the second by those who are heartily sick of the bother of their squalling and crying about the place. The parent's action is rational in both cases, his opinion being that by cutting up the body the soul gets destroyed, and by breaking the leg the soul will be warned that, if it really wants to come into the family, it must leave off its roaming habits and settle down, though he knows if it comes back again the child that it comes in will limp; but the wanderer soul must be made of utter foolishness to want to go through repeated courses of black babyhood—for remember, although the negro baby has neither pap, nor pins to poison the joy of its life-dawn, yet, on the other hand, it has no paregoric, no bassinettes, nor warm flannels, nor toys, and it leads a melancholy existence you can see by its great sad eyes, that seem to say, 'Here's a pretty mess! Why did I come to Africa?'

Even when ghosts have been properly buried they still preserve an interest in human affairs, for not only do they have local palavers, but try over again palavers left outstanding from their earthly lives; so when there is an outbreak of sickness in a Fantee village, and several inhabitants die off, the opinion is held that there is a big palaver down below, and that the ghosts have sent up for witnesses, subpœnaed them as it were. The medicine men, or priests, are called in to find out what particular earthly grievance can be the subject of this ghostly case. When they have ascertained this, they take the evidence, on commission as it were, of everyone who knows anything about the case in the town, and then transmit the information to the Court sitting in Srahmandazi, thereby saving the witnesses from the inconvenience of a personal journey thither.

It is impossible within the limits of this article to even touch upon the immense variety of ceremonial surrounding soul affairs in this West Coast 'land of the living that's thronged with the dead;' and you must remember that, of the throng of spirits, these dead men's souls are only a very small section, for almost everything in West Africa has a soul, trees, rivers, weapons, &c., and that it is mainly by this soul they act. Thus, among the Congo-Française tribes, it is held that, in the matter of medicine, the soul of the medicine combats with the soul of the disease, and so on. Neither are human souls the one and only cause of harm. There is that wretch Tando—I beg his majesty's pardon—the great god of Ashantee, who is still worshipped, though his cult is not what it was before the defeat his favourite people sustained at the hands of the English in 1874,* and after this present defeat it may still further fall into neglect, and he will probably end in the mere pauper state of sheer devildom. For, say the Ashantee, he was either too weak to defend them, or he was not inclined to exert his power on their behalf; in either case he was unsatisfactory. His priests say he was disinclined, for some reasons arising from breaches of sacrificial observances; but the Ashantee laity know that the land simply reeked with human blood for his delectation, young boys having been sacrificed in the path of each English line of advance, besides the ample sacrifices in the towns. There is absolutely no trick too venomous or mean for Tando, the Hater; for example, he has a way of wandering about near a village he has a grudge against, in the form of a male child, and crying bitterly until some kind-hearted, unsuspecting person comes and takes him in and feeds him; then he develops a contagious disease which clears that village out.

And an enormous quantity of hauntings arise from manifestations of that awful genus of devils grouped under the name of Sasahbomsum and Shramantin. It is little use giving you directions regarding the recognition of a Sasahbomsum manifestation, because if you meet him he kills and eats you, except in Apollonia, where he sucks your blood, but usually to such an extent that if you do drag yourself home you die then of exhaustion. He is said, by people who have seen him, to be of enormous size and a red colour; his hair, which is straight, he wears long. It is generally regarded as unadvisable to make camp near a silk-cotton tree which has red earth round its roots, because that earth has got stained that colour by the blood which it has whipped off a Sasahbomsum as he has gone down through it to his underworld home after a night's carnage, in the morning time. Shramantin, I may remark, is the female form of this demon; she is not so bad, for she only detains her prisoners for three or four months in the forest, teaching them what herbs are good to eat, where the game come down to drink, and what the animals and plants say to each other. Her appearance is against her, however, though she is white, and, like her lord, she is of colossal size.

The ghosts of what we Europeans call inanimate things also cause inconvenience, and like most things, living or dead, in West Africa, they cause delay. I and my black companions had once to sit down and wait two and a half hours at a place on a fairly open forest path, because across it, in front of us, about that time in the afternoon, the ghost of a spear flew, and a touch from it was necessarily fatal. And there is a spring I know of, in the Kacongo district, where, when you go to fill your pitcher, you see a very handsome pitcher standing ready filled. Many a lady, seeing no one about to whom the pitcher belongs, has picked this up and left her own; but as soon as she has got it within sight of the village it crumbles into earth, and the water is spilt on the ground. On returning for her own discarded one, that is always found broken.

Then there are that very varied and widely diffused set of phenomena connected with living people sending one of their souls into some animal, such as a crocodile, or leopard, to work vengeance on enemies; but this comes under the head of witchcraft, so I will conclude by giving you the description of a peculiar haunt, interesting chiefly to me because I have heard of it occurring to two people, one a Negro lady, one a Bantu. I give you the Bantu version, because I heard the details of it in full, immediately after its occurrence. She had been down river to the factory,* on trade business, and returned home after dark to her house, well satisfied with the result of a day's haggling with the trader. There was a miserably small fire burning in the cook-house, by which her slave girls were trying to cook her evening meal. She blew them up for not having a larger fire, and they said the wood was wet and would not burn. She said they lied, and she would see to them later on, and went into her living house, treading, on the way there, into some wet on the ground. 'Those good-for-nothing hussies of girls have been spilling some water,' she thought, and when she got into her room she found the hanging palm-oil lamp was not alight; she sat down on her wood bed, and found there was a lot of nastiness there. This was not to be stood; so, dismissing from her mind the commercial considerations with which it was full when she came home, she rose up, and went to the door and called for 'Ingimina' and others, in a state of high rage. She is a notable housewife, and keeps her house extremely neat and clean, and her slaves in good order; so these young ladies came 'one time,' and cuffing their heads, she asked them how they dared forget to light her lamp; they swore they had lit it, but it must have gone out like all the other lamps had, after burning down and spluttering. They had been sitting round the fire and not bothering about it till she came in. So she whacked and pulled the ears of all she could—she is not very active, weighing, I fancy, some sixteen stone—and then she went to her room and got out her beautiful, English paraffin lamp, bringing it out to the sizzling fire to light it with a bit of burning stick, which, when she lifted it up, she found coated with the damp, sticky stuff that she had got into before, and it smelt of the same faint smell she had noticed as oppressive when she entered her yard. As soon as the lamp was alight she saw what it was, *i.e.* blood. Blood was everywhere, the rest of the fire sticks were covered with it, it sizzled at their lighted ends, and it oozed from their other ends. There were pools of it on the clean, sandy yard; her own room was reeking—the bed, the floor, and the stools. It ran and hung in coagulated gouts down the door-posts, and lay on the lintel. She herself was smeared with it from having come in contact with it in the dark. She picked a plate up off the shelf, and its impression was there on the shelf in a rim of the blood. She looked in her skillet—more there. The palm-oil in the lamps had got a film of it floating on top of the oil, and investigation of the whole of the rest of the house demonstrated that things were similarly afflicted throughout.

The slave girls were utterly scared when the light showed with what they had been surrounded. Their mistress called in some influential friends and relations; they could make nothing out of it, but they said they thought something must be going to happen, and suggested, in the kind, helpful, cheering way friends and relations have in such matters, that they should fancy it was a prophecy that she was going to die without shedding blood, and that this was the blood come before. This view irritated her, as she is an uncommonly common-sense woman, so she sent them about their business, and started the slaves house-cleaning. The blood, she said, cleaned up all right, but reappeared as soon as you left off. She cleaned on, however, till about 10 A.M., 'before noon time,' when it gradually faded off, but the smell remained about the house for days.

I hope that the readers of this incomplete sketch of the African's views concerning souls will not hastily write the African down an ass, but will remember the words of the greatest of ethnologists, E. B. Tylor,* of Oxford, saying:—'Few who will give their minds to master the general principles of savage religion will ever again think it ridiculous, or the knowledge of it superfluous to the rest of mankind. Far from its beliefs and practices being a rubbish heap of miscellaneous forms, they are consistent and logical in so high a degree as to begin, as soon as even roughly classified, to display the principles of their formation and development, and these principles prove to be essentially rational, although working in a mental condition of intense and inveterate ignorance.'

And also the African idea of the continuity of the individualism of the soul is the same as our own.

> Eternal form shall still divide
> The Eternal Soul from all beside,
> And I shall know him when we meet.
> ('In Memoriam.')*

See also: Bird; Casely Hayford; Clifford; Conrad; Kipling.

JOSEPH CONRAD
(1857–1924)

An Outpost of Progress (1898)

I

There were two white men in charge of the trading station. Kayerts, the chief, was short and fat; Carlier, the assistant, was tall, with a large head and a very broad trunk perched upon a long pair of thin legs. The third man on the staff was a Sierra Leone nigger, who maintained that his name was Henry Price. However, for some reason or other, the natives down the river had given him the name of Makola, and it stuck to him through all his wanderings about the country. He spoke English and French with a warbling accent, wrote a beautiful hand, understood bookkeeping, and cherished in his innermost heart the worship of evil spirits. His wife was a negress from Loanda,* very large and very noisy. Three children rolled about in sunshine before the door of his low, shed-like dwelling. Makola, taciturn and impenetrable, despised the two white men. He had charge of a small clay storehouse with a dried-grass roof, and pretended to keep a correct account of beads, cotton cloth, red kerchiefs, brass wire, and other trade goods it contained. Besides the storehouse and Makola's hut, there was only one large building in the cleared ground of the station. It was built neatly of reeds, with a verandah on all the four sides. There were three rooms in it. The one in the middle was the living-room, and had two rough tables and a few stools in it. The other two were the bedrooms for the white men. Each had a bedstead and a mosquito net for all furniture. The plank floor was littered with the belongings of the white men; open half-empty boxes, town wearing apparel, old boots; all the things dirty, and all the things broken, that accumulate mysteriously round untidy men. There was also another dwelling-place some distance away from the buildings. In it, under a tall cross much out of the perpendicular, slept the man who had seen the beginning of all this; who had planned and had watched the construction of this outpost of progress. He had been, at home, an unsuccessful painter who, weary of pursuing fame on an empty stomach, had gone out there through high protections. He had been the first chief of that station. Makola had watched the energetic artist die of fever in the just finished house with his usual kind of 'I told you so' indifference. Then, for a time, he dwelt alone with his family, his account books, and the Evil Spirit that rules the lands under the equator. He got on very well with his god. Perhaps he had propitiated him by a promise of more white men to play with, by and by. At any rate the director of the Great Trading Company, coming up in a steamer that resembled an enormous sardine box with a flat-roofed shed erected on it, found the station in good order, and Makola as usual quietly diligent. The director had the cross put up over the first agent's grave, and appointed Kayerts to the post. Carlier was told off as second in charge. The director was a man ruthless and efficient, who at times, but very imperceptibly, indulged in grim humour. He made a speech to Kayerts and Carlier, pointing out to them the promising aspect of their station. The nearest trading-post was about three hundred miles away. It was an exceptional opportunity for them to distinguish themselves and to earn percentages on the trade. This appointment was a favour done to beginners. Kayerts was moved almost to tears by his director's kindness. He would, he said, by doing his best, try to justify the flattering confidence, &c., &c. Kayerts had been in the Administration of the Telegraphs, and knew how to express himself correctly. Carlier, an ex-non-commissioned officer of cavalry in an army guaranteed from harm by several European Powers, was less impressed. If there were commissions to get, so much the better; and, trailing a sulky glance over the river, the forests, the impenetrable bush that seemed to cut off the station from the rest of the world, he muttered between his teeth, 'We shall see, very soon.'

Next day, some bales of cotton goods and a few cases of provisions having been thrown on shore, the sardine-box steamer went off, not to return for another six months. On the deck the director touched his cap to the two agents, who stood on the bank waving their hats, and turning to an old servant of the Company on his passage to headquarters, said, 'Look at those two imbeciles. They must be mad at home to send me such specimens. I told those fellows to plant a vegetable garden, build new storehouses and fences, and construct a landing-stage. I bet nothing will be done! They won't know how to begin. I always thought the station on this river useless, and they just fit the station!'

'They will form themselves there,' said the old stager with a quiet smile.

'At any rate, I am rid of them for six months,' retorted the director.

The two men watched the steamer round the bend, then, ascending arm in arm the slope of the bank, returned to the station. They had been in this vast and dark country only a very short time, and as yet always in the midst of other white men, under the eye and guidance of their superiors. And now, dull as they were to the subtle influences of surroundings, they felt themselves very much alone, when suddenly left unassisted to face the wilderness; a wilderness rendered more strange, more incomprehensible by the mysterious glimpses of the vigorous life it contained. They were two perfectly insignificant and incapable individuals, whose existence is only rendered possible through the high organization of civilized crowds. Few men realize that their life, the very essence of their character, their capabilities and their audacities, are only the expression of their belief in the safety of their surroundings. The courage, the composure, the confidence; the emotions and principles; every great and every insignificant thought belongs not to the individual but to the crowd: to the crowd that believes blindly in the irresistible force of its institutions and of its morals, in the power of its police and of its opinion.* But the contact with pure unmitigated savagery, with primitive nature and primitive man, brings sudden and profound trouble into the heart. To the sentiment of being alone of one's kind, to the clear perception of the loneliness of one's thoughts, of one's sensations—to the negation of the habitual, which is safe, there is added the affirmation of the unusual, which is dangerous; a suggestion of things vague, uncontrollable, and repulsive, whose discomposing intrusion excites the imagination and tries the civilized nerves of the foolish and the wise alike.

Kayerts and Carlier walked arm in arm, drawing close to one another as children do in the dark; and they had the same, not altogether unpleasant, sense of danger which one half suspects to be imaginary. They chatted persistently in familiar tones. 'Our station is prettily situated,' said one. The other assented with enthusiasm, enlarging volubly on the beauties of the situation. Then they passed near the grave. 'Poor devil!' said Kayerts. 'He died of fever, didn't he?' muttered Carlier, stopping short. 'Why,' retorted Kayerts, with indignation, 'I've been told that the fellow exposed himself recklessly to the sun. The climate here, everybody says, is not at all worse than at home, as long as you keep out of the sun. Do you hear that, Carlier? I am chief here, and my orders are that you should not expose yourself to the sun!' He assumed his superiority jocularly, but his meaning was serious. The idea that he would, perhaps, have to bury Carlier and remain alone, gave him an inward shiver. He felt suddenly that this Carlier was more precious to him here, in the centre of Africa, than a brother could be anywhere else. Carlier, entering into the spirit of the thing, made a military salute and answered in a brisk tone, 'Your orders shall be attended to, chief!' Then he burst out laughing, slapped Kayerts on the back and shouted, 'We shall let life run easily here! Just sit still and gather in the ivory those savages will bring. This country has its good points, after all!' They both laughed loudly while Carlier thought: That poor Kayerts; he is so fat and unhealthy. It would be awful if I had to bury him here. He is a man I respect . . . Before they reached the verandah of their house they called one another 'my dear fellow'.

The first day they were very active, pottering about with hammers and nails and red calico, to put up curtains, make their house habitable and pretty; resolved to settle down comfortably to their new life. For them an impossible task. To grapple effectually with even purely material problems requires more serenity of mind and more lofty courage than people generally imagine. No two beings could have been more unfitted for such a struggle. Society, not from any tenderness, but because of its strange needs, had taken care of those two men, forbidding them all independent thought, all initiative, all departure from routine; and forbidding it under pain of death. They could only live on condition of being machines. And now, released from the fostering care of men with pens behind the ears, or of men with gold lace on the sleeves, they were like those lifelong prisoners who, liberated after many years, do not know what use to make of their freedom. They did not know what use to make of their faculties, being both, through want of practice, incapable of independent thought.

At the end of two months Kayerts often would say, 'If it was not for my Melie, you wouldn't catch me here.' Melie was his daughter. He had thrown up his post in the Administration of the Telegraphs, though he had been for seventeen years perfectly happy there, to earn a dowry for his girl. His wife was dead, and the child was being brought up by his sisters. He regretted the streets, the pavements, the cafés, his friends of many years; all the things he used to see, day after day; all the thoughts suggested by familiar things—the thoughts effortless, monotonous, and soothing of a Government clerk; he regretted all the gossip, the small enmities, the mild venom, and the little jokes of Government offices. 'If I had had a decent brother-in-law,' Carlier would remark, 'a fellow with a heart, I would not be here.' He had left the army and had made himself so obnoxious to his family by his laziness and impudence, that an exasperated brother-in-law had made superhuman efforts to procure him an appointment in the Company as a second-class agent. Having not a penny in the world he was compelled to accept this means of livelihood as soon as it became quite clear to him that there was nothing more to squeeze out of his relations. He, like Kayerts, regretted his old life. He regretted the clink of sabre and spurs on a fine afternoon, the barrack-room witticisms, the girls of garrison towns; but, besides, he had also a sense of grievance. He was evidently a much ill-used man. This made him moody, at times. But the two men got on well together in the fellowship of their stupidity and laziness. Together they did nothing, absolutely nothing, and enjoyed the sense of idleness for which they were paid. And in time they came to feel something resembling affection for one another.

They lived like blind men in a large room, aware only of what came in contact with them (and of that only imperfectly), but unable to see the general aspect of things. The river, the forest, all the great land throbbing with life, were like a great emptiness.* Even the brilliant sunshine disclosed nothing intelligible. Things appeared and disappeared before their eyes in an unconnected and aimless kind of way. The river seemed to come from nowhere and flow nowhither. It flowed through a void. Out of that void, at times, came canoes, and men with spears in their hands would suddenly crowd the yard of the station. They were naked, glossy black, ornamented with snowy shells and glistening brass wire, perfect of limb. They made an uncouth babbling noise when they spoke, moved in a stately manner, and sent quick, wild glances out of their startled, never-resting eyes. Those warriors would squat in long rows, four or more deep, before the verandah, while their chiefs bargained for hours with Makola over an elephant tusk. Kayerts sat on his chair and looked down on the proceedings, understanding nothing. He stared at them with his round blue eyes, called out to Carlier, 'Here, look! look at that fellow there—and that other one, to the left. Did you ever see such a face? Oh, the funny brute!'

Carlier, smoking native tobacco in a short wooden pipe, would swagger up twirling his moustaches, and surveying the warriors with haughty indulgence, would say—

'Fine animals. Brought any bone? Yes? It's not any too soon. Look at the muscles of that fellow—third from the end. I wouldn't care to get a punch on the nose from him. Fine arms, but legs no good below the knee. Couldn't make cavalry men of them.' And after glancing down complacently at his own shanks, he always concluded: 'Pah! Don't they stink! You, Makola! Take that herd over to the fetish! (the storehouse was in every station called the fetish,* perhaps because of the spirit of civilization it contained) 'and give them up some of the rubbish you keep there. I'd rather see it full of bone than full of rags.'

Kayerts approved.

'Yes, yes! Go and finish that palaver over there, Mr Makola. I will come round when you are ready, to weigh the tusk. We must be careful.' Then turning to his companion: 'This is the tribe that lives down the river; they are rather aromatic. I remember, they had been once before here. D'ye hear that row? What a fellow has got to put up with in this dog of a country! My head is split.'

Such profitable visits were rare. For days the two pioneers of trade and progress would look on their empty courtyard in the vibrating brilliance of vertical sunshine. Below the high bank, the silent river flowed on glittering and steady. On the sands in the middle of the stream, hippos and alligators sunned themselves side by side. And stretching away in all directions, surrounding the insignificant cleared spot of the trading post, immense forests, hiding fateful complications of fantastic life, lay in the eloquent silence of mute greatness. The two men understood nothing, cared for nothing but for the passage of days that separated them from the steamer's return. Their predecessor had left some torn books. They took up these wrecks of novels, and, as they had never read anything of the kind before, they were surprised and amused. Then during long days there were interminable and silly discussions about plots and personages. In the centre of Africa they made acquaintance of Richelieu and of d'Artagnan, of Hawk's Eye and of Father Goriot,* and of many other people. All these imaginary personages became subjects for gossip as if they had been living friends. They discounted their virtues, suspected their motives, decried their successes; were scandalized at their duplicity or were doubtful about their courage. The accounts of crimes filled them with indignation, while tender or pathetic passages moved them deeply. Carlier cleared his throat and said in a soldierly voice, 'What nonsense!' Kayerts, his round eyes suffused with tears, his fat cheeks quivering, rubbed his bald head, and declared, 'This is a splendid book. I had no idea there were such clever fellows in the world.' They also found some old copies of a home paper. That print discussed what it was pleased to call 'Our Colonial Expansion' in high-flown language. It spoke much of the rights and duties of civilization, of the sacredness of the civilizing work, and extolled the merits of those who went about bringing light, and faith and commerce to the dark places of the earth. Carlier and Kayerts read, wondered, and began to think better of themselves. Carlier said one evening, waving his hand about, 'In a hundred years, there will be perhaps a town here. Quays, and warehouses, and barracks, and—and—billiard-rooms. Civilization, my boy, and virtue—and all. And then, chaps will read that two good fellows, Kayerts and Carlier, were the first civilized men to live in this very spot!' Kayerts nodded, 'Yes, it is a consolation to think of that.' They seemed to forget their dead predecessor; but, early one day, Carlier went out and replanted the cross firmly. 'It used to make me squint whenever I walked that way,' he explained to Kayerts over the morning coffee. 'It made me squint, leaning over so much. So I just planted it upright. And solid, I promise you! I suspended myself with both hands to the cross-piece. Not a move. Oh, I did that properly.'

At times Gobila came to see them. Gobila was the chief of the neighbouring villages. He was a grey-headed savage, thin and black, with a white cloth round his loins and a mangy panther skin hanging over his back. He came up with long strides of his skeleton legs, swinging a staff as tall as himself, and, entering the common room of the station, would squat on his heels to the left of the door. There he sat, watching Kayerts, and now and then making a speech which the other did not understand. Kayerts, without interrupting his occupation, would from time to time say in a friendly manner: 'How goes it, you old image?' and they would smile at one another. The two whites had a liking for that old and incomprehensible creature, and called him Father Gobila. Gobila's manner was paternal, and he seemed really to love all white men. They all appeared to him very young, indistinguishably alike (except for stature), and he knew that they were all brothers, and also immortal. The death of the artist, who was the first white man whom he knew intimately, did not disturb this belief, because he was firmly convinced that the white stranger had pretended to die and got himself buried for some mysterious purpose of his own, into which it was useless to inquire. Perhaps it was his way of going home to his own country? At any rate, these were his brothers, and he transferred his absurd affection to them. They returned it in a way. Carlier slapped him on the back, and recklessly struck off matches for his amusement. Kayerts was always ready to let him have a sniff at the ammonia bottle. In short, they behaved just like that other white creature that had hidden itself in a hole in the ground. Gobila considered them attentively. Perhaps they were the same being with the other—or one of them was. He couldn't decide—clear up that mystery; but he remained always very friendly. In consequence of that friendship the women of Gobila's village walked in single file through the reedy grass, bringing every morning to the station, fowls, and sweet potatoes, and palm wine, and sometimes a goat. The Company never provisions the stations fully, and the agents required those local supplies to live. They had them through the good-will of Gobila, and lived well. Now and then one of them had a bout of fever, and the other nursed him with gentle devotion. They did not think much of it. It left them weaker, and their appearance changed for the worse. Carlier was hollow-eyed and irritable. Kayerts showed a drawn, flabby face above the rotundity of his stomach, which gave him a weird aspect. But being constantly together, they did not notice the change that took place gradually in their appearance, and also in their dispositions.

Five months passed in that way.

Then, one morning, as Kayerts and Carlier, lounging in their chairs under the verandah, talked about the approaching visit of the steamer, a knot of armed men came out of the forest and advanced towards the station. They were strangers to that part of the country. They were tall, slight, draped classically from neck to heel in blue fringed cloths, and carried percussion muskets over their bare right shoulders. Makola showed signs of excitement, and ran out of the storehouse (where he spent all his days) to meet these visitors. They came into the courtyard and looked about them with steady, scornful glances. Their leader, a powerful and determined-looking negro with bloodshot eyes, stood in front of the verandah and made a long speech. He gesticulated much, and ceased very suddenly.

There was something in his intonation, in the sounds of the long sentences he used, that startled the two whites. It was like a reminiscence of something not exactly familiar, and yet resembling the speech of civilized men. It sounded like one of those impossible languages which sometimes we hear in our dreams.

'What lingo is that?' said the amazed Carlier. 'In the first moment I fancied the fellow was going to speak French. Anyway, it is a different kind of gibberish to what we ever heard.'

'Yes,' replied Kayerts. 'Hey, Makola, what does he say? Where do they come from? Who are they?'

But Makola, who seemed to be standing on hot bricks, answered hurriedly, 'I don't know. They come from very far. Perhaps Mrs Price will understand. They are perhaps bad men.'

The leader, after waiting for a while, said something sharply to Makola, who shook his head. Then the man, after looking round, noticed Makola's hut and walked over there. The next moment Mrs Makola was heard speaking with great volubility. The other strangers—they were six in all—strolled about with an air of ease, put their heads through the door of the storeroom, congregated round the grave, pointed understandingly at the cross, and generally made themselves at home.

'I don't like those chaps—and, I say, Kayerts, they must be from the coast; they've got firearms,' observed the sagacious Carlier.

Kayerts also did not like those chaps. They both, for the first time, became aware that they lived in conditions where the unusual may be dangerous, and that there was no power on earth outside of themselves to stand between them and the unusual. They became uneasy, went in and loaded their revolvers. Kayerts said, 'We must order Makola to tell them to go away before dark.'

The strangers left in the afternoon, after eating a meal prepared for them by Mrs Makola. The immense woman was excited, and talked much with the visitors. She rattled away shrilly, pointing here and there at the forests and at the river. Makola sat apart and watched. At times he got up and whispered to his wife. He accompanied the strangers across the ravine at the back of the station-ground, and returned slowly looking very thoughtful. When questioned by the white men he was very strange, seemed not to understand, seemed to have forgotten French —seemed to have forgotten how to speak altogether. Kayerts and Carlier agreed that the nigger had had too much palm wine.

There was some talk about keeping a watch in turn, but in the evening everything seemed so quiet and peaceful that they retired as usual. All night they were disturbed by a lot of drumming in the villages. A deep, rapid roll near by would be followed by another far off—then all ceased. Soon short appeals would rattle out here and there, then all mingle together, increase, become vigorous and sustained, would spread out over the forest, roll through the night, unbroken and ceaseless, near and far, as if the whole land had been one immense drum booming out steadily an appeal to heaven. And through the deep and tremendous noise sudden yells that resembled snatches of songs from a madhouse darted shrill and high in discordant jets of sound which seemed to rush far above the earth and drive all peace from under the stars.

Carlier and Kayerts slept badly. They both thought they had heard shots fired during the night—but they could not agree as to the direction. In the morning Makola was gone somewhere. He returned about noon with one of yesterday's strangers, and eluded all Kayerts' attempts to close with him: had become deaf apparently. Kayerts wondered. Carlier, who had been fishing off the bank, came back and remarked while he showed his catch, 'The niggers seem to be in a deuce of a stir; I wonder what's up. I saw about fifteen canoes cross the river during the two hours I was there fishing.' Kayerts, worried, said, 'Isn't this Makola very queer today?' Carlier advised, 'Keep all our men together in case of some trouble.'

2

There were ten station men who had been left by the Director. Those fellows, having engaged themselves to the Company for six months (without having any idea of a month in particular and only a very faint notion of time in general), had been serving the cause of progress for upwards of two years. Belonging to a tribe from a very distant part of the land of darkness and sorrow, they did not run away, naturally supposing that as wandering strangers they would be killed by the inhabitants of the country; in which they were right. They lived in straw huts on the slope of a ravine overgrown with reedy grass, just behind the station buildings. They were not happy, regretting the festive incantations, the sorceries, the human sacrifices of their own land; where they also had parents, brothers, sisters, admired chiefs, respected magicians, loved friends, and other ties supposed generally to be human. Besides, the rice rations served out by the Company did not agree with them, being a food unknown to their land, and to which they could not get used. Consequently they were unhealthy and miserable. Had they been of any other tribe they would have made up their minds to die—for nothing is easier to certain savages than suicide—and so have escaped from the puzzling difficulties of existence. But belonging, as they did, to a warlike tribe with filed teeth, they had more grit, and went on stupidly living through disease and sorrow. They did very little work, and had lost their splendid physique. Carlier and Kayerts doctored them assiduously without being able to bring them back into condition again. They were mustered every morning and told off to different tasks—grass-cutting, fence-building, tree-felling, &c., &c., which no power on earth could induce them to execute efficiently. The two whites had practically very little control over them.

In the afternoon Makola came over to the big house and found Kayerts watching three heavy columns of smoke rising above the forests. 'What is that?' asked Kayerts. 'Some villages burn,' answered Makola, who seemed to have regained his wits. Then he said abruptly: 'We have got very little ivory; bad six months' trading. Do you like get a little more ivory?'

'Yes,' said Kayerts, eagerly. He thought of percentages which were low.

'Those men who came yesterday are traders from Loanda who have got more ivory than they can carry home. Shall I buy? I know their camp.'

'Certainly,' said Kayerts. 'What are those traders?'

'Bad fellows,' said Makola, indifferently. 'They fight with people, and catch women and children. They are bad men, and got guns. There is a great disturbance in the country. Do you want ivory?'

'Yes,' said Kayerts. Makola said nothing for a while. Then: 'Those workmen of ours are no good at all,' he muttered, looking round. 'Station in very bad order, sir. Director will growl. Better get a fine lot of ivory, then he say nothing.'

'I can't help it; the men won't work,' said Kayerts. 'When will you get that ivory?'

'Very soon,' said Makola. 'Perhaps tonight. You leave it to me, and keep indoors, sir. I think you had better give some palm wine to our men to make a dance this evening. Enjoy themselves. Work better tomorrow. There's plenty palm wine—gone a little sour.'

Kayerts said yes, and Makola, with his own hands, carried big calabashes to the door of his hut. They stood there till the evening, and Mrs Makola looked into every one. The men got them at sunset. When Kayerts and Carlier retired, a big bonfire was flaring before the men's huts. They could hear their shouts and drumming. Some men from Gobila's village had joined the station hands, and the entertainment was a great success.

In the middle of the night, Carlier waking suddenly, heard a man shout loudly; then a shot was fired. Only one. Carlier ran out and met Kayerts on the verandah. They were both startled. As they went across the yard to call Makola, they saw shadows moving in the night. One of them cried, 'Don't shoot! It's me, Price.' Then Makola appeared close to them. 'Go back, go back, please,' he urged, 'you spoil all.' 'There are strange men about,' said Carlier. 'Never mind; I know,' said Makola. Then he whispered, 'All right. Bring ivory. Say nothing! I know my business.' The two white men reluctantly went back to the house, but did not sleep. They heard footsteps, whispers, some groans. It seemed as if a lot of men came in, dumped heavy things on the ground, squabbled a long time, then went away. They lay on their hard beds and thought: 'This Makola is invaluable.' In the morning Carlier came out, very sleepy, and pulled at the cord of the big bell. The station hands mustered every morning to the sound of the bell. That morning nobody came. Kayerts turned out also, yawning. Across the yard they saw Makola come out of his hut, a tin basin of soapy water in his hand. Makola, a civilized nigger, was very neat in his person. He threw the soapsuds skilfully over a wretched little yellow cur he had, then turning his face to the agent's house, he shouted from the distance, 'All the men gone last night!'

They heard him plainly, but in their surprise they both yelled out together: 'What!' Then they stared at one another. 'We are in a proper fix now,' growled Carlier. 'It's incredible!' muttered Kayerts. 'I will go to the huts and see,' said Carlier, striding off. Makola coming up found Kayerts standing alone.

'I can hardly believe it', said Kayerts, tearfully. 'We took care of them as if they had been our children.'

'They went with the coast people,' said Makola after a moment of hesitation.

'What do I care with whom they went—the ungrateful brutes!' exclaimed the other. Then with sudden suspicion, and looking hard at Makola, he added: 'What do you know about it?'

Makola moved his shoulders, looking down on the ground. 'What do I know? I think only. Will you come and look at the ivory I've got there? It is a fine lot. You never saw such.'

He moved towards the store. Kayerts followed him mechanically, thinking about the incredible desertion of the men. On the ground before the door of the fetish lay six splendid tusks.

'What did you give for it?' asked Kayerts, after surveying the lot with satisfaction.

'No regular trade,' said Makola. 'They brought the ivory and gave it to me. I told them to take what they most wanted in the station. It is a beautiful lot. No station can show such tusks. Those traders wanted carriers badly, and our men were no good here. No trade, no entry in books; all correct.'

Kayerts nearly burst with indignation. 'Why!' he shouted, 'I believe you have sold our men for these tusks!' Makola stood impassive and silent. 'I—I—will—I', stuttered Kayerts. 'You fiend!' he yelled out.

'I did the best for you and the Company,' said Makola imperturbably. 'Why you shout so much? Look at this tusk.'

'I dismiss you! I will report you—I won't look at the tusk. I forbid you to touch them. I order you to throw them into the river. You—you!'

'You very red, Mr Kayerts. If you are so irritable in the sun, you will get fever and die—like the first chief!' pronounced Makola impressively.

They stood still, contemplating one another with intense eyes, as if they had been looking with effort across immense distances. Kayerts shivered. Makola had meant no more than he said, but his words seemed to Kayerts full of ominous menace! He turned sharply and went away to the house. Makola retired into the bosom of his family; and the tusks, left lying before the store, looked very large and valuable in the sunshine.

Carlier came back on the verandah. 'They're all gone, hey?' asked Kayerts from the far end of the common room in a muffled voice. 'You did not find anybody?'

'Oh yes,' said Carlier, 'I found one of Gobila's people lying dead before the huts—shot through the body. We heard that shot last night.'

Kayerts came out quickly. He found his companion staring grimly over the yard at the tusks, away by the store. They both sat in silence for a while. Then Kayerts related his conversation with Makola. Carlier said nothing. At the midday meal they ate very little. They hardly exchanged a word that day. A great silence seemed to lie heavily over the station and press on their lips. Makola did not open the store; he spent the day playing with his children. He lay full-length on a mat outside his door, and the youngsters sat on his chest and clambered all over him. It was a touching picture. Mrs Makola was busy cooking all day as usual. The white men made a somewhat better meal in the evening. Afterwards, Carlier smoking his pipe strolled over to the store; he stood for a long time over the tusks, touched one or two with his foot, even tried to lift the largest one by its small end. He came back to his chief, who had not stirred from the verandah, threw himself in the chair and said—

'I can see it! They were pounced upon while they slept heavily after drinking all that palm wine you've allowed Makola to give them. A put-up job! See? The worst is, some of Gobila's people were there, and got carried off too, no doubt. The least drunk woke up, and got shot for his sobriety. This is a funny country. What will you do now?'

'We can't touch it, of course,' said Kayerts.

'Of course not,' assented Carlier.

'Slavery is an awful thing,' stammered out Kayerts in an unsteady voice.

'Frightful—the sufferings,' grunted Carlier with conviction.

They believed their words. Everybody shows a respectful deference to certain sounds that he and his fellows can make. But about feelings people really know nothing. We talk with indignation or enthusiasm; we talk about oppression, cruelty, crime, devotion, self-sacrifice, virtue, and we know nothing real beyond the words. Nobody knows what suffering or sacrifice mean—except, perhaps the victims of the mysterious purpose of these illusions.

Next morning they saw Makola very busy setting up in the yard the big scales used for weighing ivory. By and by Carlier said: 'What's that filthy scoundrel up to?' and lounged out into the yard. Kayerts followed. They stood watching. Makola took no notice. When the balance was swung true, he tried to lift a tusk into the scale. It was too heavy. He looked up helplessly without a word, and for a minute they stood round that balance as mute and still as three statues. Suddenly Carlier said: 'Catch hold of the other end, Makola—you beast!' and together they swung the tusk up. Kayerts trembled in every limb. He muttered, 'I say! O! I say!' and putting his hand in his pocket found there a dirty bit of paper and the stump of a pencil. He turned his back on the others, as if about to do something tricky, and noted stealthily the weights which Carlier shouted out to him with unnecessary loudness. When all was over Makola whispered to himself: 'The sun's very strong here for the tusks.' Carlier said to Kayerts in a careless tone: 'I say, chief, I might just as well give him a lift with this lot into the store.'

As they were going back to the house Kayerts observed with a sigh: 'It had to be done.' And Carlier said: 'It's deplorable, but, the men being Company's men the ivory is Company's ivory. We must look after it.' 'I will report to the Director, of course,' said Kayerts. 'Of course; let him decide,' approved Carlier.

At midday they made a hearty meal. Kayerts sighed from time to time. Whenever they mentioned Makola's name they always added to it an opprobrious epithet. It eased their conscience. Makola gave himself a half-holiday, and bathed his children in the river. No one from Gobila's villages came near the station that day. No one came the next day, and the next, nor for a whole week. Gobila's people might have been dead and buried for any sign of life they gave. But they were only mourning for those they had lost by the witchcraft of white men, who had brought wicked people into their country. The wicked people were gone, but fear remained. Fear always remains. A man may destroy everything within himself, love and hate and belief, and even doubt; but as long as he clings to life he cannot destroy fear: the fear, subtle, indestructible, and terrible, that pervades his being; that tinges his thoughts; that lurks in his heart; that watches on his lips the struggle of his last breath. In his fear, the mild old Gobila offered extra human sacrifices to all the Evil Spirits that had taken possession of his white friends. His heart was heavy. Some warriors spoke about burning and killing, but the cautious old savage dissuaded them. Who could foresee the woe those mysterious creatures, if irritated, might bring? They should be left alone. Perhaps in time they would disappear into the earth as the first one had disappeared. His people must keep away from them, and hope for the best.

Kayerts and Carlier did not disappear, but remained above on this earth, that, somehow, they fancied had become bigger and very empty. It was not the absolute and dumb solitude of the post that impressed them so much as an inarticulate feeling that something from within them was gone, something that worked for their safety, and had kept the wilderness from interfering with their hearts. The images of home; the memory of people like them, of men that thought and felt as they used to think and feel, receded into distances made indistinct by the glare of unclouded sunshine. And out of the great silence of the surrounding wilderness, its very hopelessness and savagery seemed to approach them nearer, to draw them gently, to look upon them, to envelop them with a solicitude irresistible, familiar, and disgusting.*

Days lengthened into weeks, then into months. Gobila's people drummed and yelled to every new moon, as of yore, but kept away from the station. Makola and Carlier tried once in a canoe to open communications, but were received with a shower of arrows, and had to fly back to the station for dear life. That attempt set the country up and down the river into an uproar that could be very distinctly heard for days. The steamer was late. At first they spoke of delay jauntily, then anxiously, then gloomily. The matter was becoming serious. Stores were running short. Carlier cast his lines off the bank, but the river was low, and the fish kept out in the stream. The dared not stroll far away from the station to shoot. Moreover, there was no game in the impenetrable forest. Once Carlier shot a hippo in the river. They had no boat to secure it, and it sank. When it floated up it drifted away, and Gobila's people secured the carcase. It was the occasion for a national holiday, but Carlier had a fit of rage over it and talked about the necessity of exterminating all the niggers before the country could be made habitable. Kayerts mooned about silently; spent hours looking at the portrait of his Melie. It represented a little girl with long bleached tresses and a rather sour face. His legs were much swollen, and he could hardly walk. Carlier, undermined by fever, could not swagger any more, but kept tottering about, still with a devil-may-care air, as became a man who remembered his crack regiment. He had become hoarse, sarcastic, and inclined to say unpleasant things. He called it 'being frank with you'. They had long ago reckoned their percentages on trade, including in them that last deal of 'this infamous Makola'. They had also concluded not to say anything about it. Kayerts hesitated at first—was afraid of the Director.

'He has seen worse things done on the quiet,' maintained Carlier, with a hoarse laugh. 'Trust him! He won't thank you if you blab. He is no better than you or me. Who will talk if we hold our tongues? There is nobody here.'

That was the root of the trouble! There was nobody there; and being left there alone with their weakness, they became daily more like a pair of accomplices than like a couple of devoted friends. They had heard nothing from home for eight months. Every evening they said, 'Tomorrow we shall see the steamer.' But one of the Company's steamers had been wrecked, and the Director was busy with the other, relieving very distant and important stations on the main river. He thought that the useless station, and the useless men, could wait. Meantime Kayerts and Carlier lived on rice boiled without salt, and cursed the Company, all Africa, and the day they were born. One must have lived on such diet to discover what ghastly trouble the necessity of swallowing one's food may become. There was literally nothing else in the station but rice and coffee; they drank the coffee without sugar. The last fifteen lumps Kayerts had solemnly locked away in his box, together with a half-bottle of Cognâc, 'in case of sickness,' he explained. Carlier approved. 'When one is sick,' he said, 'any little extra like that is cheering.'

They waited. Rank grass began to sprout over the courtyard. The bell never rang now. Days passed, silent, exasperating, and slow. When the two men spoke, they snarled; and their silences were bitter, as if tinged by the bitterness of their thoughts.

One day after a lunch of boiled rice, Carlier put down his cup untasted, and said: 'Hang it all! Let's have a decent cup of coffee for once. Bring out that sugar, Kayerts!'

'For the sick,' muttered Kayerts, without looking up.

'For the sick,' mocked Carlier. 'Bosh! . . . Well! I am sick.'

'You are no more sick than I am, and I go without,' said Kayerts in a peaceful tone.

'Come! out with that sugar, you stingy old slave dealer.'

Kayerts looked up quickly. Carlier was smiling with marked insolence. And suddenly it seemed to Kayerts that he had never seen that man before. Who was he? He knew nothing about him. What was he capable of? There was a surprising flash of violent emotion within him, as if in the presence of something undreamt-of, dangerous, and final. But he managed to pronounce with composure—

'That joke is in very bad taste. Don't repeat it.'

'Joke!' said Carlier, hitching himself forward on his seat. 'I am hungry—I am sick—I don't joke! I hate hypocrites. You are a hypocrite. You are a slave-dealer. I am a slave-dealer. There's nothing but slave-dealers in this cursed country. I mean to have sugar in my coffee today, anyhow!'

'I forbid you to speak to me in that way,' said Kayerts with a fair show of resolution.

'You!—What?' shouted Carlier, jumping up.

Kayerts stood up also. 'I am your chief,' he began, trying to master the shakiness of his voice.

'What?' yelled the other. 'Who's chief? There's no chief here. There's nothing here: there's nothing but you and I. Fetch the sugar—you pot-bellied ass.'

'Hold your tongue. Go out of this room,' screamed Kayerts. 'I dismiss you—you scoundrel!'

Carlier swung a stool. All at once he looked dangerously in earnest. 'You flabby, good-for-nothing civilian—take that!' he howled.

Kayerts dropped under the table, and the stool struck the grass inner wall of the room. Then, as Carlier was trying to upset the table, Kayerts in desperation made a blind rush, head low, like a cornered pig would do, and over-turning his friend, bolted along the verandah, and into his room. He locked the door, snatched his revolver, and stood panting. In less than a minute Carlier was kicking at the door furiously, howling, 'If you don't bring out that sugar, I will shoot you at sight, like a dog. Now then—one—two—three. You won't? I will show you who's the master.'

Kayerts thought the door would fall in, and scrambled through the square hole that served for a window in his room. There was then the whole breadth of the house between them. But the other was apparently not strong enough to break in the door, and Kayerts heard him running round. Then he also began to run laboriously on his swollen legs. He ran as quickly as he could, grasping the revolver, and unable yet to understand what was happening to him. He saw in succession Makola's house, the store, the river, the ravine, and the low bushes; and he saw all those things again as he ran for the second time round the house. Then again they flashed past him. That morning he could not have walked a yard without a groan.

And now he ran. He ran fast enough to keep out of sight of the other man.

Then as, weak and desperate, he thought, 'Before I finish the next round I shall die,' he heard the other man stumble heavily, then stop. He stopped also. He had the back and Carlier the front of the house, as before. He heard him drop into a chair cursing, and suddenly his own legs gave way, and he slid down into a sitting posture with his back to the wall. His mouth was as dry as a cinder, and his face was wet with perspiration—and tears. What was it all about? He thought it must be a horrible illusion; he thought he was dreaming; he thought he was going mad! After a while he collected his senses. What did they quarrel about? That sugar! How absurd! He would give it to him—didn't want it himself. And he began scrambling to his feet with a sudden feeling of security. But before he had fairly stood upright, a common-sense reflection occurred to him and drove him back into despair. He thought: If I give way now to that brute of a soldier, he will begin this horror again tomorrow—and the day after—every day—raise other pretensions, trample on me, torture me, make me his slave—and I will be lost! Lost! The steamer may not come for days—may never come. He shook so that he had to sit down on the floor again. He shivered forlornly. He felt he could not, would not move any more. He was completely distracted by the sudden perception that the position was without issue—that death and life had in a moment become equally difficult and terrible.

All at once he heard the other push his chair back; and he leaped to his feet with extreme facility. He listened and got confused. Must run again! Right or left? He heard footsteps. He darted to the left, grasping his revolver, and at the very same instant, as it seemed to him, they came into violent collision. Both shouted with surprise. A loud explosion took place between them; a roar of red fire, thick smoke; and Kayerts, deafened and blinded, rushed back thinking: I am hit—it's all over. He expected the other to come round—to gloat over his agony. He caught hold of an upright of the roof—'All over!' Then he heard a crashing fall on the other side of the house, as if somebody had tumbled headlong over a chair—then silence. Nothing more happened. He did not die. Only his shoulder felt as if it had been badly wrenched, and he had lost his revolver. He was disarmed and helpless! He waited for his fate. The other man made no sound. It was a stratagem. He was stalking him now! Along what side? Perhaps he was taking aim this very minute!

After a few moments of an agony frightful and absurd, he decided to go and meet his doom. He was prepared for every surrender. He turned the corner, steadying himself with one hand on the wall; made a few paces, and nearly swooned. He had seen on the floor, protruding past the other corner, a pair of turned-up feet. A pair of white naked feet in red slippers. He felt deadly sick, and stood for a time in profound darkness. Then Makola appeared before him, saying quietly: 'Come along, Mr Kayerts. He is dead.' He burst into tears of gratitude; a loud, sobbing fit of crying. After a time he found himself sitting in a chair and looking at Carlier, who lay stretched on his back. Makola was kneeling over the body.

'Is this your revolver?' asked Makola, getting up.

'Yes,' said Kayerts; then he added very quickly, 'He ran after me to shoot me—you saw!'

'Yes, I saw,' said Makola. 'There is only one revolver; where's his?'

'Don't know,' whispered Kayerts in a voice that had become suddenly very faint.

'I will go and look for it,' said the other, gently. He made the round along the verandah, while Kayerts sat still and looked at the corpse. Makola came back empty-handed, stood in deep thought, then stepped quietly into the dead man's room, and came out directly with a revolver, which he held up before Kayerts. Kayerts shut his eyes. Everything was going round. He found life more terrible and difficult than death. He had shot an unarmed man.

After meditating for a while, Makola said softly, pointing at the dead man who lay there with his right eye blown out—

'He died of fever.' Kayerts looked at him with a stony stare. 'Yes,' repeated Makola, thoughtfully, stepping over the corpse, 'I think he died of fever. Bury him tomorrow.'

And he went away slowly to his expectant wife, leaving the two white men alone on the verandah.

Night came, and Kayerts sat unmoving on his chair. He sat quiet as if he had taken a dose of opium. The violence of the emotions he had passed through produced a feeling of exhausted serenity. He had plumbed in one short afternoon the depths of horror and despair, and now found repose in the conviction that life had no more secrets for him: neither had death! He sat by the corpse thinking; thinking very actively, thinking very new thoughts. He seemed to have broken loose from himself altogether. His old thoughts, convictions, likes and dislikes, things he respected and things he abhorred, appeared in their true light at last! Appeared contemptible and childish, false and ridiculous. He revelled in his new wisdom while he sat by the man he had killed. He argued with himself about all things under heaven with that kind of wrong-headed lucidity which may be observed in some lunatics. Incidentally he reflected that the fellow dead there had been a noxious beast anyway; that men died every day in thousands; perhaps in hundreds of thousands—who could tell?—and that in the number, that one death could not possibly make any difference; couldn't have any importance, at least to a thinking creature. He, Kayerts, was a thinking creature. He had been all his life, till that moment, a believer in a lot of nonsense like the rest of mankind—who are fools; but now he thought! He knew! He was at peace; he was familiar with the highest wisdom! Then he tried to imagine himself dead, and Carlier sitting in his chair watching him; and his attempt met with such unexpected success, that in a very few moments he became not at all sure who was dead and who was alive. This extraordinary achievement of his fancy startled him, however, and by a clever and timely effort of mind he saved himself just in time from becoming Carlier. His heart thumped, and he felt hot all over at the thought of that danger. Carlier! What a beastly thing! To compose his now disturbed nerves—and no wonder!—he tried to whistle a little. Then, suddenly, he fell asleep, or thought he had slept; but at any rate there was a fog, and somebody had whistled in the fog.

He stood up. The day had come, and a heavy mist had descended upon the land: the mist penetrating, enveloping, and silent; the morning mist of tropical lands; the mist that clings and kills; the mist white and deadly, immaculate and poisonous. He stood up, saw the body, and threw his arms above his head with a cry like that of a man who, waking from a trance, finds himself immured forever in a tomb. '*Help! . . . My God!*'

A shriek inhuman, vibrating and sudden, pierced like a sharp dart the white shroud of that land of sorrow. Three short, impatient screeches followed, and then, for a time, the fog-wreaths rolled on, undisturbed, through a formidable silence. Then many more shrieks, rapid and piercing, like the yells of some exasperated and ruthless creature, rent the air. Progress was calling to Kayerts from the river. Progress and civilization and all the virtues. Society was calling to its accomplished child to come, to be taken care of, to be instructed, to be judged, to be condemned; it called him to return to that rubbish heap from which he had wandered away, so that justice could be done.

Kayerts heard and understood. He stumbled out of the verandah, leaving the other man quite alone for the first time since they had been thrown there together. He groped his way through the fog, calling in his ignorance upon the invisible heaven to undo its work. Makola flitted by in the mist, shouting as he ran—

'Steamer! Steamer! They can't see. They whistle for the station. I go ring the bell. Go down to the landing, sir. I ring.'

He disappeared. Kayerts stood still. He looked upwards; the fog rolled low over his head. He looked round like a man who has lost his way; and he saw a dark smudge, a cross-shaped stain, upon the shifting purity of the mist. As he began to stumble towards it, the station bell rang in a tumultuous peal its answer to the impatient clamour of the steamer.

The Managing Director of the Great Civilizing Company (since we know that civilization follows trade) landed first, and incontinently lost sight of the steamer. The fog down by the river was exceedingly dense; above, at the station, the bell rang unceasing and brazen.

The Director shouted loudly to the steamer:

'There is nobody down to meet us; there may be something wrong, though they are ringing. You had better come, too!'

And he began to toil up the steep bank. The captain and the engine-driver of the boat followed behind. As they scrambled up the fog thinned, and they could see their Director a good way ahead. Suddenly they saw him start forward, calling to them over his shoulder:—'Run! Run to the house! I've found one of them. Run, look for the other!'

He had found one of them! And even he, the man of varied and startling experience, was somewhat discomposed by the manner of this finding. He stood and fumbled in his pockets (for a knife) while he faced Kayerts, who was hanging by a leather strap from the cross. He had evidently climbed the grave, which was high and narrow, and after tying the end of the strap to the arm, had swung himself off. His toes were only a couple of inches above the ground; his arms hung stiffly down; he seemed to be standing rigidly at attention, but with one purple cheek playfully posed on the shoulder. And, irreverently, he was putting out a swollen tongue at his Managing Director.

See also: Clifford; Kingsley; Schreiner; Stevenson; Woolf.

WILLIAM WATSON
(1858–1935)

Jubilee Night in Westmorland (1898)

Through that majestic and sonorous day,
When London was one gaze on her own joy,
I walked where yet is silence undeflowered,
In the lone places of the fells and meres;
And afterward ascended, night being come,
To where, high on a salient coign of crag,
Fuel was heaped, as on some altar old,
Whose immemorial priests propitiated,
With unrecorded rites, forgotten gods.

Darkly along the ridge the village folk
Had gathered, waiting till the unborn fire
Should, from its durance in the mother pine,
Leap; and anon was given the signal: thrice
A mimic meteor hissed aloft, and fell
All jewels, while the wondering hound that couched
Beside me lifted up his head and bayed
At the strange portent, with a voice that called
Far echoes forth, out of the hollow vales.

Then the piled timber blazed against the clouds,
Roaring, and oft, a monstrous madcap, shook
Hilarious sides, and showered ephemeral gold.

And one by one the mountain peaks forswore
Their vowed impassiveness, the mountain peaks
Confessed emotion, and I saw these kings
Doing perfervid homage to a Queen.

Long watched I, and at last to the sweet dale
Went down, with thoughts of two great women, thoughts
Of two great women who have ruled this land;
Of her, that mirrored a fantastic age,
The imperious, vehement, abounding Spirit,
Mightily made, but gusty as those winds,
Her wild allies that broke the spell of Spain;
And her who sways, how silently! a world
Dwarfing the glorious Tudor's queenliest dreams;
Who, to her wellnigh more than mortal task,
Hath brought the strength-in-sweetness that prevails,
The regal will that royally can yield:
Mistress of many peoples, heritress
Of many thrones, wardress of many seas;
But destined, more melodiously than thus,
To be hereafter and for ever hailed,
When our imperial legend shall have fired
The lips of sage and poet, and when these
Shall, to an undispersing audience, sound
No sceptred name so winningly august
As Thine, my Queen, Victoria the Beloved!

See also: Housman, '1887'; Kipling, 'Recessional'.

RUDYARD KIPLING
(1865–1936)

Recessional (1897)

God of our fathers, known of old,
   Lord of our far-flung battle-line,
Beneath whose awful Hand we hold
   Dominion over palm and pine—
Lord God of Hosts, be with us yet,
Lest we forget—lest we forget!

The tumult and the shouting dies;
   The Captains and the Kings depart:
Still stands Thine ancient sacrifice,
   An humble and a contrite heart.
Lord God of Hosts, be with us yet,
Lest we forget—lest we forget!

Far-called, our navies melt away;
   On dune and headland sinks the fire:
Lo, all our pomp of yesterday
   Is one with Nineveh and Tyre!
Judge of the Nations, spare us yet,
Lest we forget—lest we forget!

If, drunk with sight of power, we loose
   Wild tongues that have not Thee in awe,
Such boastings as the Gentiles use,
   Or lesser breeds without the Law—
Lord God of Hosts, be with us yet,
Lest we forget—lest we forget!

For heathen heart that puts her trust
   In reeking tube and iron shard,
All valiant dust that builds on dust,
   And guarding, calls not Thee to guard,
For frantic boast and foolish word—
Thy mercy on Thy People, Lord!

The White Man's Burden (1899)

(*The United States and the Philippine Islands*)*

Take up the White Man's burden—
    Send forth the best ye breed—
Go bind your sons to exile
    To serve your captives' need;
To wait in heavy harness
    On fluttered folk and wild—
Your new-caught, sullen peoples,
    Half devil and half child.

Take up the White Man's Burden—
    In patience to abide,
To veil the threat of terror
    And check the show of pride;
By open speech and simple,
    An hundred times made plain,
To seek another's profit,
    And work another's gain.

Take up the White Man's burden—
    The savage wars of peace—
Fill full the mouth of Famine
    And bid the sickness cease;
And when your goal is nearest
    The end for others sought,
Watch Sloth and heathen Folly
    Bring all your hope to nought.

Take up the White Man's burden—
    No tawdry rule of kings,
But toil of serf and sweeper—
    The tale of common things.
The ports ye shall not enter,
    The roads ye shall not tread,
Go make them with your living,
    And mark them with your dead!

Take up the White Man's burden—
    And reap his old reward:
The blame of those ye better,
    The hate of those ye guard—
The cry of hosts ye humour
    (Ah, slowly!) toward the light:—
'Why brought ye us from bondage,
    Our loved Egyptian night?'

Take up the White Man's burden—
    Ye dare not stoop to less—
Nor call too loud on Freedom
    To cloak your weariness;
By all ye cry or whisper,
    By all ye leave or do,
The silent, sullen peoples
    Shall weigh your Gods and you.

Take up the White Man's burden—
    Have done with childish days—
The lightly proffered laurel,
    The easy, ungrudged praise.
Comes now, to search your manhood
    Through all the thankless years,
Cold-edged with dear-bought wisdom,
    The judgment of your peers!

See also: Chamberlain; South African War verse; Watson, 'Jubilee Night in Westmorland'.

THE SOUTH AFRICAN WAR (1899–1902)

Following not long after the triumphalist celebration of Queen Victoria's Diamond Jubilee in 1897, the South African or Anglo-Boer War produced an outburst of strenuous jingoism in the British press not witnessed on this scale before. Both poets of imperialist persuasion, like Austin, Henley, and Newbolt, and those not usually moved to speak directly about empire, like Swinburne and Hardy, felt themselves buffeted by the wave of belligerent nationalism sweeping through the country. But the level of sentiment generated, expressed also in Mrs Ames's ABC, betrayed profound insecurities about Britain's supposed invincibility, as captured in Henley's defensive question, 'Who says that we shall pass?' Already before the outbreak of hostilities, at the time of the Jubilee, Kipling's 'Recessional' had presciently given expression to the anxieties fuelling the imperial war machine that lumbered so creakily to South Africa. Indeed, within the first few months of war it became apparent that the Boers were not to be easily defeated, even by the largest force that Britain had sent overseas since the Crimea. The national uncertainties, questions, and disillusionment that followed mark the late war poems of Housman, Watson, and Kipling.

ALGERNON CHARLES SWINBURNE
(1837–1909)

The Transvaal (1899)

Patience, long sick to death, is dead. Too long
    Have sloth and doubt and treason bidden us be
    What Cromwell's England was not, when the sea
To him bore witness given of Blake* how strong
She stood, a commonweal that brooked no wrong
    From foes less vile than men like wolves set free
    Whose war is waged where none may fight or flee—
With women and with weanlings. Speech and song
Lack utterance now for loathing. Scarce we hear

Foul tongues that blacken God's dishonoured name
With prayers turned curses and with praise found shame
Defy the truth whose witness now draws near
To scourge these dogs, agape with jaws afoam,
Down out of life. Strike, England, and strike home.

ALFRED AUSTIN
(1835–1913)

To Arms! (1899)

I

Now let the cry, 'To Arms! To Arms!'
    Go ringing round the world;
And swift a wave-wide Empire swarms
    Round Battleflag unfurled!
Wherever glitters Britain's might,
    Or Britain's banner flies,
Leap up mailed myriads with the light
    Of manhood in their eyes;
Calling from farmstead, mart, and strand,
    'We come! And we! And we!
That British steel may hold the land,
    And British keels the sea!'

II

From English hamlet, Irish hill,
    Welsh hearths, and Scottish byres,
They throng to show that they are still
    Sons worthy of their sires:
That what these did, we still can do,
    That what they were, we are,
Whose fathers fought at Waterloo,
    And died at Trafalgar!
Shoulder to shoulder see them stand,
    Wherever menace be,
To guard the lordship of the land
    And the Trident of the sea.

III

Nor in the parent Isle alone
  Spring squadrons from the ground;
Canadian shore and Austral zone
  With kindred cry resound:
'From shimmering plain and snow-fed stream,
  Across the deep we come,
Seeing the British bayonets gleam,
  Hearing the British drum.
Foot in the stirrup, hilt in hand,
  Free men, to keep men free,
All, all will help to hold the land
  While England guards the sea!'

IV

Comrades in arms, from every shore
  Where thundereth the main,
On to the front they press and pour
  To face the rifles' rain;
To force the foe from covert crag,
  And chase them till they fall,
Then plant for ever England's Flag*
  Upon the rebel wall!
What! Wrench the Sceptre from her hand,
  And bid her bow the knee!
Not while her Yeomen guard the land,
  And her ironclads the sea!

MRS ERNEST AMES
(*fl.* late-1880s)

An ABC, for Baby Patriots (1899)

A is the Army
    That dies for the Queen;
It's the very best Army
    That ever was seen.

B stands for Battles
　By which England's name
Has for ever been covered
　With glory and fame.

C is for Colonies
　Rightly we boast,
That of all the great nations
　Great Britain has most.

D is the Daring
　We show on the Field
Which makes every enemy
　Vanish or yield.

E is our Empire
　Where sun never sets;
The larger we make it
　The bigger it gets.

F is the flag
　Which wherever you see
You know that beneath it
　You're happy and free.

G is the Game
　We preserve with such care
To shoot, as it gracefully
　Flies through the air.

H is for Hunting,
　For this you've a box,
A thoro bred Hunter,
　Some hounds and a fox.

I is for India,
　Our land in the East
Where everyone goes
　To shoot tigers and feast.

J's for our Judges
    Who sit in a row
And send folks to prison
    When naughty you know!

K is for Kings;
    Once warlike and haughty,
Great Britain subdued them
    Because they'd been naughty.*

L is the Lion
    Who fights for the Crown
His smile when he's worried
    Is changed to a frown.*

M is for Magnates
    So great and so good,
They sit on gold chairs
    And eat Turtle for food.

N is the Navy
    We keep at Spithead,
It's a sight that makes foreigners
    Wish they were dead.*

O is the Ocean
    Where none but a fool
Would ever dare question
    Our title to rule.

P is our Parliament,
    Commons and Peers,
They will talk if permitted
    For months—nay for years.

Q is our Queen!
    It fills us with pride
To see the Queen's coach
    When the Queen is inside!

R is the Roast Beef
  That has made England great;
You see it here pictured
  Each piece on a plate.

S is for Scotland
  The home of the Scot!
It's wetter than England
  And isn't so hot.

T is the Tub
  That an Englishman takes
As a matter of course
  Just as soon as he wakes.*

U is our Unicorn,
  Such a nice beast
His home is here now
  Though he comes from the East.

V's Volunteers
  Who can shoot very straight;
They are drilled now and then
  Between seven and eight.

W is the Word
  Of an Englishman true;
When given, it means
  What he says, he will do.*

X as a rule means
  The London Police
Who are paid by the Country
  For keeping the peace.*

Y is for youngsters
  Gilded and gay,
The newspapers call them
  The 'Jeunesse dorée.'

Z is the Zeal
  Which is everywhere seen
When a family practises
  'God Save the Queen.'

THOMAS HARDY
(1840–1928)

Departure

(*Southampton Docks: October 1899*)

While the far farewell music thins and fails,
And the broad bottoms rip the bearing brine—
All smalling slowly to the gray sea-line—
And each significant red smoke-shaft pales,

Keen sense of severance everywhere prevails,
Which shapes the late long tramp of mounting men
To seeming words that ask and ask again:
'How long, O striving Teutons, Slavs, and Gaels
Must your wroth reasonings trade on lives like these,
That are as puppets in a playing hand?—
When shall the saner softer polities
Whereof we dream, have sway in each proud land
And patriotism, grown Godlike, scorn to stand
Bondslave to realms, but circle earth and seas?'

A Christmas Ghost-Story (1899)

South of the Line, inland from far Durban,
A mouldering soldier lies—your countryman.
Awry and doubled up are his gray bones,
And on the breeze his puzzled phantom moans
Nightly to clear Canopus: 'I would know
By whom and when the All-Earth-gladdening Law

Of Peace, brought in by that Man Crucified,
Was ruled to be inept, and set aside?
And what of logic or of truth appears
In tacking 'Anno Domini' to the years?
Near twenty-hunded liveried thus have hied,
But tarries yet the Cause for which He died.'

Drummer Hodge (1899)

I

They throw in Drummer Hodge, to rest
    Uncoffined—just as found:
His landmark is a kopje-crest*
    That breaks the veldt* around;
And foreign constellations west
    Each night above his mound.

II

Young Hodge the Drummer never knew—
    Fresh from his Wessex home—
The meaning of the broad Karoo,
    The Bush, the dusty loam,
And why uprose to nightly view
    Strange stars amid the gloam.

III

Yet portion of that unknown plain
    Will Hodge for ever be;
His homely Northern breast and brain
    Grow to some Southern tree,
And strange-eyed constellations reign
    His stars eternally.

W. E. HENLEY
(1849–1903)

from *For England's Sake* (1900)

Remonstrance

Hitch, blunder, check—
   Each is *a new disaster*,
And it is who shall bleat and scrawl
   The feebler and the faster.
Where is our ancient pride of heart?
   Our faith in blood and star?
Who but would marvel how we came
   If this were all we are?

Ours is the race
   That tore the Spaniard's ruff,
That flung the Dutchman by the breech,
   The Frenchman by the scruff;
Through his diurnal round of dawns
   Our drum-tap squires the sun;
And yet, an old mad burgher-man
   Can put us on the run!

Rise, England, rise!
   But in that calm of pride,
That hardy and high serenity,
   That none may dare abide;
So front the realms, your point abashed;
   So mark them chafe and foam;
And, if they challenge, so, by God,
   Strike, England, and strike home!*

Pro Rege Nostro

What have I done for you,
  England, my England?
What is there I would not do,
  England, my own?
With your glorious eyes austere,
As the Lord were walking near,
Whispering terrible things and dear
    As the Song on your bugles blown,
        England—
    Round the world on your bugles blown!

Where shall the watchful Sun,
  England, my England,
Match the master-work you've done,
  England, my own?
When shall he rejoice agen
Such a breed of mighty men
As come forward, one to ten,
    To the Song on your bugles blown,
        England—
    Down the years on your bugles blown?

Ever the faith endures,
  England, my England:—
'Take and break us: we are yours,
  England, my own!
Life is good, and joy runs high
Between English earth and sky:
Death is death; but we shall die
    To the Song on your bugles blown,
        England—
    To the stars on your bugles blown!'

They call you proud and hard,
  England, my England:
You with worlds to watch and ward,
  England, my own!

You whose mailed hand keeps the keys
Of such teeming destinies,
You could know nor dread nor ease,
    Were the Song on your bugles blown,
      England—
    Round the Pit on your bugles blown!

Mother of Ships whose might,
   England, my England,
Is the fierce old Sea's delight,
   England, my own,
Chosen daughter of the Lord,
Spouse-in-Chief of the ancient Sword,
There's the menace of the Word
    In the Song on your bugles blown,
      England—
    Out of heaven on your bugles blown!

The Choice of the Will

We are the Choice of the Will: God, when He gave the word
That called us into line, set at our hand a sword;

Set us a sword to wield none else could lift and draw,
And bade us forth to the sound of the trumpet of the Law.

East and West and North, wherever the battle grew,
As men to a feast we fared, the work of the Will to do.

Bent upon vast beginnings, bidding anarchy cease—
(Had we hacked it to the Pit, we had left it a place of peace!)—

Marching, building, sailing, pillar of cloud or fire,
Sons of the Will, we fought the fight of the Will, our sire.

Road was never so rough that we left its purpose dark;
Stark was ever the sea, but our ships were yet more stark;

We tracked the winds of the world to the steps of their very thrones;
The secret parts of the world were salted with our bones;

Till now the Name of Names, England, the name of might,
Flames from the austral fires to the deeps of the boreal night;

And the call of her morning drum goes in a girdle of sound,
Like the voice of the sun in song, the great globe round and round;*

And the shadow of her flag, when it shouts to the mother-breeze,
Floats from shore to shore of the universal seas;

And the loneliest death is fair with a memory of her flowers,
And the end of the road to Hell with the sense of her dews and
    showers!

Who says that we shall pass, or the fame of us fade and die,
While the living stars fulfil their round in the living sky?

For the sire lives in his sons, and they pay their father's debt,
And the Lion has left a whelp wherever his claw was set;

And the Lion in his whelps, his whelps that none shall brave,
Is but less strong than Time and the great, all-whelming Grave.

A. E. HOUSMAN
(1859–1936)

Grenadier (composed *c*.1900; 1922)

The Queen she sent to look for me,
    The sergeant he did say,
'Young man, a soldier will you be
    For thirteen pence a day?'

For thirteen pence a day did I
    Take off the things I wore,
And I have marched to where I lie,
    And I shall march no more.

My mouth is dry, my shirt is wet,
    My blood runs all away,
So now I shall not die in debt
    For thirteen pence a day.

To-morrow after new young men
    The sergeant he must see,
For things will all be over then
    Between the Queen and me.

And I shall have to bate my price,
    For in the grave, they say,
Is neither knowledge nor device
    Nor thirteen pence a day.

HENRY NEWBOLT
(1862–1938)

Vitaï Lampada (1897)

There's a breathless hush in the Close to-night—
    Ten to make and the match to win—
A bumping pitch and a blinding light,
    An hour to play and the last man in.
And it's not for the sake of a ribboned coat,
    Or the selfish hope of a season's fame,
But his Captain's hand on his shoulder smote—
    'Play up! play up! and play the game!'

The sand of the desert is sodden red,—
    Red with the wreck of a square that broke;—
The Gatling's jammed and the Colonel dead,
    And the regiment blind with dust and smoke.*
The river of death has brimmed his banks,
    And England's far, and Honour a name,
But the voice of a schoolboy rallies the ranks:
    'Play up! play up! and play the game!'

This is the word that year by year,
    While in her place the School is set,
Every one of her sons must hear,
    And none that hears it dare forget.
This they all with a joyful mind
    Bear through life like a torch in flame,
And falling fling to the host behind—
    'Play up! play up! and play the game!'

Peace (1902)

No more to watch by Night's eternal shore,
    With England's chivalry at dawn to ride;
No more defeat, faith, victory—O! no more
    A cause on earth for which we might have died.

April on Waggon Hill (1903)

Lad, and can you rest now,
    There beneath your hill?
Your hands are on your breast now,
    But is your heart so still?
'Twas the right death to die, lad,
    A gift without regret,
But unless truth's a lie, lad,
    You dream of Devon yet.

Ay, ay, the year's awaking,
    The fire's among the ling,*
The beechen hedge is breaking,
    The curlew's on the wing;
Primroses are out, lad,
    On the high banks of Lee,
And the sun stirs the trout, lad,
    From Brendon to the sea.

I know what's in your heart, lad,—
    The mare he used to hunt—
And her blue market-cart, lad,
    With posies tied in front—
We miss them from the moor road,
    They're getting old to roam,
The road they're on's a sure road
    And nearer, lad, to home.

Your name, the name they cherish?
    'Twill fade, lad, 'tis true:
But stone and all may perish
    With little loss to you.
While fame's fame you're Devon, lad,
    The Glory of the West;
Till the roll's called in heaven, lad,
    You may well take your rest.

Sráhmandázi (1902)

Deep embowered beside the forest river,
    Where the flame of sunset only falls,
Lapped in silence lies the House of Dying,
    House of them to whom the twilight calls.

There within when day was near to ending,
    By her lord a woman young and strong,
By his chief a songman old and stricken
    Watched together till the hour of song.

'O my songman, now the bow is broken,
    Now the arrows one by one are sped,
Sing to me the song of Sráhmandázi,[1]
    Sráhmandázi, home of all the dead.'

---

[1] *Sráhmandázi.*—This ballad is founded on materials given to the author by the late Miss Mary Kingsley on her return from her last visit to the Bantu peoples of West Africa. The song-net, as described by her, resembles a long piece of fishing-net folded, and is carried by the Songman over his shoulder. When opened and laid before an audience, it is

Then the songman, flinging wide his songnet,
  On the last token laid his master's hand,
While he sang the song of Sráhmandázi,
  None but dying men can understand.

'Yonder sun that fierce and fiery-hearted
  Marches down the sky to vanish soon,
At the self-same hour in Sráhmandázi
  Rises pallid like the rainy moon.

'There he sees the heroes by their river,
  Where the great fish daily upward swim;
Yet they are but shadows hunting shadows,
  Phantom fish in waters drear and dim.

'There he sees the kings among their headmen,
  Women weaving, children playing games;
Yet they are but shadows ruling shadows,
  Phantom folk with dim forgotten names.

'Bid farewell to all that most thou lovest,
  Tell thy heart thy living life is done;
All the days and deeds of Sráhmandázi
  Are not worth an hour of yonder sun.'

Dreamily the chief from out the songnet
  Drew his hand and touched the woman's head:
'Know they not, then, love in Sráhmandázi?
  Has a king no bride among the dead?'

seen to contain 'tokens'—such as a leopard's paw, a child's hair, a necklet, or a dried
fish—sewn firmly to the meshes of the net. These form a kind of symbolical index to the
Songman's repertory: the audience make their choice by laying a hand upon any token
which appears desirable. The last of the tokens is that which represents the Song of
Dying or Song of Sráhmandázi. It is a shapeless piece of any substance, and is recognized
only by its position in the net. The song, being unintelligible to the living, is never asked
for until the moment of death.

Then the songman answered, 'O my master,
    Love they know, but none may learn it there;
Only souls that reach that land together
    Keep their troth and find the twilight fair.

'Thou art still a king, and at thy passing
    By thy latest word must all abide:
If thou willest, here am I, thy songman;
    If thou lovest, here is she, thy bride.'

Hushed and dreamy lay the House of Dying,
    Dreamily the sunlight upward failed,
Dreamily the chief on eyes that loved him
    Looked with eyes the coming twilight veiled.

Then he cried, 'My songman, I am passing;
    Let her live, her life is but begun;
All the days and nights of Sráhmandázi
    Are not worth an hour of yonder sun.'

Yet, when there within the House of Dying
    The last silence held the sunset air,
Not alone he came to Sráhmandázi,
    Not alone she found the twilight fair:

While the songman, far beneath the forest
    Sang of Sráhmandázi all night through,
'Lovely be thy name, O Land of shadows,
    Land of meeting, Land of all the true!'

WILLIAM WATSON
(1858–1935)

from *For England* (1903)

Rome and Another

She asked for all things, and dominion such
    As never man had known,
The gods first gave; then lightly, touch by touch,
    O'erthrew her seven-hilled throne.

Imperial Power, that hungerest for the globe,
    Restrain thy conquering feet,
Lest the same Fates that spun thy purple robe
    Should weave thy winding-sheet.

The Inexorable Law

We too shall pass, we too shall disappear,
Ev'n as the mighty nations that have waned
And perished. Not more surely are ordained
The crescence and the cadence of the year,
High-hearted June, October spent and sere,
Than this gray consummation. We have reigned
Augustly; let our part be so sustained
That Time, far hence, shall hold our memory dear!
Let it be said: 'This Mistress of the sword
And conquering prow, this Empire swoln with spoils,
Yet served the human cause, yet strove for Man;
Hers was the purest greatness we record;
We whose ingathered sheaves her tilth foreran,
Whose peace comes of her tempests and her toils.'

The True Imperialism

Here, while the tide of conquest rolls
    Against the distant golden shore,
The starved and stunted human souls
    Are with us more and more.

Vain is your Science, vain your Art,
    Your triumphs and your glories vain,
To feed the hunger of their heart
    And famine of their brain.

Your savage deserts howling near,
    Your wastes of ignorance, vice, and shame,—
Is there no room for victories here,
    No field for deeds of fame?

Arise and conquer while ye can
    The foe that in your midst resides,
And build within the mind of Man
    The Empire that abides.

RUDYARD KIPLING
(1865–1936)

The Lesson (1903)

1899–1902
(Boer War)

Let us admit it fairly, as a business people should,
We have had no end of a lesson: it will do us no end of good.

Not on a single issue, or in one direction or twain,
But conclusively, comprehensively, and several times and again,
Were all our most holy illusions knocked higher than Gilderoy's
    kite.*
We have had a jolly good lesson, and it serves us jolly well right!

This was not bestowèd us under the trees, nor yet in the shade of a
  tent,
But swingingly, over eleven degrees of a bare brown continent.
From Lamberts to Delagoa Bay, and from Pietersburg to Sutherland,
Fell the phenomenal lesson we learned—with a fulness accorded no
  other land.

It was our fault, and our very great fault, and *not* the judgment of
  Heaven.
We made an Army in our own image, on an island nine by seven,
Which faithfully mirrored its makers' ideals, equipment, and mental
  attitude—
And so we got our lesson: and we ought to accept it with gratitude.

We have spent two hundred million pounds to prove the fact once more,
That horses are quicker than men afoot, since two and two make four;
And horses have four legs, and men have two legs, and two into four
  goes twice,
And nothing over except our lesson—and very cheap at the price.

For remember (this our children shall know: we are too near for that
  knowledge)
Not our mere astonied camps, but Council and Creed and College—
All the obese, unchallenged old things that stifle and overlie us—
Have felt the effects of the lesson we got—an advantage no money
  could buy us!

Then let us develop this marvellous asset which we alone command,
And which, it may subsequently transpire, will be worth as much as
  the Rand.
Let us approach this pivotal fact in a humble yet hopeful mood—
We have had no end of a lesson. It will do us no end of good!

It was our fault, and our very great fault—and now we must turn it to
  use.
We have forty million reasons for failure, but not a single excuse.
So the more we work and the less we talk the better results we shall
  get.
We have had an Imperial lesson. It may make us an Empire yet!

J. A. HOBSON
(1858–1940)

The widespread influence of Hobson's end-of-war book Imperialism *rested on the force and exhaustiveness of its anti-imperial arguments. Hobson's main aim was to show that empire was not profitable and therefore not necessary for national progress or welfare. Quite contrary to what was commonly claimed, trade did not follow the flag. Imperial activity, an 'unsound business', did not in any way increase Britain's income, instead benefiting only a tiny elite of international financiers. As the recent experience of war had brought home, imperialism was therefore antithetical to democracy, peace, and social reform, a blight on a free society.*

The Political Significance of Imperialism (1902)

Imperialism and popular government have nothing in common: they differ in spirit, in policy, in method. Of policy and method I have already spoken; it remains to point out how the spirit of Imperialism poisons the springs of democracy in the mind and character of the people. As our free self-governing colonies have furnished hope, encouragement, and leading to the popular aspiration in Great Britain, not merely by practical successes in the arts of popular government, but by the wafting of a spirit of freedom and equality, so our despotically ruled dependencies have ever served to damage the character of our people by feeding the habits of snobbish subservience, the admiration of wealth and rank, the corrupt survivals of the inequalities of feudalism. This process began with the advent of the East Indian Nabob* and the West Indian planter into English society and politics, bringing back with his plunders of the slave trade and the gains of corrupt and extortionate officialism the acts of vulgar ostentation, domineering demeanour and corrupting largesse to dazzle and degrade the life of our people. Cobden, writing in 1860 of our Indian Empire, put this pithy question: 'Is it not just possible that we may become corrupted at home by the reaction of arbitrary political maxims in the East upon our domestic politics, just as Greece and Rome were demoralised by their contact with Asia?'[1]

[1] Morley, 'Life of Cobden,' vol. ii, p. 361.*

Not merely is the reaction possible, it is inevitable. As the despotic portion of our Empire has grown in area, a larger and larger number of men, trained in the temper and methods of autocracy as soldiers and civil officials in our Crown colonies, protectorates, and Indian Empire, reinforced by numbers of merchants, planters, engineers, and overseers, whose lives have been those of a superior caste living an artificial life removed from all the healthy restraints of ordinary European society, have returned to this country, bringing back the characters, sentiments, and ideas imposed by this foreign environment. The South and South-West of England is richly sprinkled with these men, many of them wealthy, most of them endowed with leisure, men openly contemptuous of democracy, devoted to material luxury, social display, and the shallower arts of intellectual life. The wealthier among them discover political ambitions, introducing into our Houses of Parliament the coarsest and most selfish spirit of 'Imperialism,' using their imperial experience and connections to push profitable companies and concessions for their private benefits, and posing as authorities so as to keep the yoke of Imperialism firmly fixed upon the shoulders of the 'nigger.' The South African millionaire* is the brand most in evidence: his methods are the most barefaced, and his success, social and political, the most redoubtable. But the practices which are writ large in Rhodes, Beit, and their parliamentary confederates are widespread on a smaller scale; the South of England is full of men of local influence in politics and society whose character has been formed in our despotic Empire, and whose incomes are chiefly derived from the maintenance and furtherance of this despotic rule. Not a few enter our local councils, or take posts in our constabulary or our prisons: everywhere they stand for coercion and for resistance to reform. Could the incomes expended in the Home Counties and other large districts of Southern Britain be traced to their sources, it would be found that they were in large measure wrung from the enforced toil of vast multitudes of black, brown, or yellow natives, by arts not differing essentially from those which supported in idleness and luxury imperial Rome.

It is, indeed, a nemesis of Imperialism that the arts and crafts of tyranny, acquired and exercised in our unfree Empire, should be turned against our liberties at home. Those who have felt surprise at the total disregard or the open contempt displayed by the aristocracy and the plutocracy of this land for infringements of the liberties of the subject and for the abrogation of constitutional rights and usages have not taken sufficiently into account the steady reflux of this poison* of irresponsible autocracy from our 'unfree, intolerant, aggressive' Empire.

The political effects, actual and necessary, of the new Imperialism, as illustrated in the case of the greatest imperialist Powers, may be thus summarised.* It is a constant menace to peace, by furnishing continual temptations to further aggression upon lands occupied by lower races, and by embroiling our nation with other nations of rival imperial ambitions; to the sharp peril of war it adds the chronic danger and degradation of militarism, which not merely wastes the current physical and moral resources of the nations, but checks the very course of civilisation. It consumes to an illimitable and incalculable extent the financial resources of a nation by military preparation, estopping the expenditure of the current income of the State upon productive public purposes and burdening posterity with heavy loads of debt. Absorbing the public money, time, interest and energy on costly and unprofitable work of territorial aggrandisement, it thus wastes those energies of public life in the governing classes and the nations which are needed for internal reforms and for the cultivation of the arts of material and intellectual progress at home. Finally, the spirit, the policy, and the methods of Imperialism are hostile to institutions of popular self-government, favouring forms of political tyranny and social authority which are the deadly enemies of effective liberty and equality.

In relation to this group of South African War texts, see also: Chamberlain; Curzon; Schreiner; Woolf.

In relation specifically to Hobson, see also: Seeley; Froude.

LATER DECADES

CORNELIA SORABJI
(1866–1954)

Love and Death (1901)

'I tell you, Stewart, it's playing the very deuce with a man's life to treat him as I've been treated.'

'I thought that had been uncommonly well: by Fate certainly, in the way of fulfilled desires; and by your father, also undoubtedly, in the way of allowance. And what more can a man want?'

'Nothing—unless he's a married man.'

'Ah! an indiscretion. You have my condolences, old chap: our follies always do vex us more than our sins, I know.'

'Yes! and the offence is aggravated when you consider that it was someone else's folly. Listen, Stewart, and I'll tell you—I'm feeling communicative to-night, and this weed draws nicely.'

The two men stood on the forward deck of the P. & O. s.s. *Khartoum*, bound for India, and now in harbour off Brindisi, awaiting the mails.

A bright moon looked down on the squalid town and the great expanse of sea, on the farther shore with its Turkish gardens and its tale of handsome brigands, and on the lithe Indian sailors, bending their supple bodies under the precious weight of the post-office consignments. One after another they crossed the bridge in well-trained rapidity. Pity the night was so brilliant! What thrill might not the darkness have lent to that scene of swift, noiseless activity!

Presently the foreigner spoke— 'I was but seven years old,' said he, 'when my grandfather sent me to England, and, as you know, I have had no other home ever since. But there still linger with me Indian sights and sounds—music, and bright colours, and the scent of roses. I remember her, who must have been my mother, surrounded by chattering serving-women, who fed me with sweets, and flattered and spoilt me. But the memories all grow out of a noisy procession on a glaring day in midsummer. Dressed in garments of some startling hue, and smothered under the combined weight of heavy necklets and sickly odorous flowers, I rode gaily on a prancing nag, while the singers went before and the minstrels followed after. In the midst, however, was a single damsel, only—and she was not playing on a timbrel, but drumming two small henna-dyed hands on the horse's neck, as she sat astride in front of me . . . They tell me now that *that* meant my marriage! . . . It must, I think, have been almost immediately afterwards that I was packed away to the dear old dame's at Summerton, where we first met, you know, Stewart; for my memory comes to its *finis* about India when I have worried the past so far. And not a word, it's odd, has my father said on the subject all this long while; but in his last letter he tells me placidly, that both a welcome *and a wife* await me, in the land of my birth! I tell you, Stewart, it is infamous! She has most likely been kept a semi-prisoner all her life, knowing certainly nothing of the world, either as God or man has made it, and probably also nothing of books, even in her vernacular. I daresay she can cook a palatable Indian dinner, and scour the cooking-pans—but, well! it has not been fair to me at all. Systems cannot alter in a day, you will say. Exactly so! But why alter them at all in this one-sided way? Why create a false position for a pair of innocent children—Oh yes! I know it's hard on her too. Everything is a huge mistake: new patches can never mean aught but worsened rents to an old garment!'

'Poor old fellow!' said Stewart. 'I never guessed such a complication. However, there'll be your work, you know, and perhaps she's not impossible, after all. You may even be able to educate her.'

The conversation was not renewed through the voyage, and, on landing, the young Indian doctor and his friend found that stress of plague-work claimed their immediate presence. The welcome and the wife had alike to wait. 'Incidental freedom,' said the Indian grimly; but indeed there was scant time for reflection, whether congratulatory or self-compassionate. He was on search duty, and hunting the dread infection from street to street demanded the exercise of every nerve and faculty. Ah, the sadness of it all! The feeble subterfuges, the brave fight against the most patent symptoms, the gasping attempt to propitiate the microbe—and finally, the sullen submission to Fate! The hearts of the two young doctors were heavy within them. Disease and death were sufficiently appalling—but with superstition for ally!—

Only this morning they had passed a mad procession carrying the dead plague-infected rats on spikes, while broken-hearted mothers and anxious wives wailed a propitiatory serenade, ghastly in its pathos! 'We can't hold out any longer,' said the Indian one morning after breakfast. 'Write to headquarters, Stewart, and beg for a lady-doctor and a nurse.* They must spare them to us. The poor women whom we find in the bazaar have to submit to our ministrations. What alternative is there? But the better classes, as you see, choose death rather than be looked upon by a man; and indeed I must confess that I greatly dislike having to search their houses. Don't you yourself agree with me, that it is our inability to deal with this class of patient which fosters the microbe?'

'Yes,' said Stewart, 'I do, and I'll write this very moment. The fear of the microbe is the mother of virtue.'

'I wish it were the mother of sanitation,' growled the Indian. 'That's the kind of offspring I'm seeking just now.'

In a week came the answer. The request was only just in time. An Indian lady with European qualifications was temporarily at the disposal of the chief medical officer. He had meant to send her elsewhere, but, as this was so sacred and orthodox a town, and as she knew the vernacular of the district, Stewart might have her for six months. They might expect her and a nurse in a fortnight.

'That's well done,' said the Indian. 'Now we'll get the thing under!'

She was tall and slender, intelligent and eager in face rather than pretty; and she carried herself with the ease and freedom of her race. Indeed her attraction lay in grace of movement, in fineness of proportion, and in a certain delicate sensitiveness, which could hardly escape even the least observant. For such work as fell to her she was pre-eminently suited—tactful, gentle, persuasive; and if she gave out so largely of her sympathising self to each sufferer, was that a fault? Her masculine colleagues thought that it was certainly so. 'You'll break down,' they said. 'Besides, it's not professional!' And they devised common recreation to relieve the tension—golf, on the brown *maidan** to westward, clear of the temples and the odours; and tennis in the garden of the civil engineer, whose wife and the wife of the padre were indeed the only other ladies in the station, and both were ready to do everything that was hospitable and kindly. Such patches of sunlight were those afternoons!

Suffering and death and all ugliness were forgotten in congenial and healthful companionship. The girl had evidently been responsive to all the best influences of her Western training, while losing nothing of her own charming individuality. The effect was that of brilliant colouring under the brush of a master-painter. Even the women loved her. What of the men? Well! as to one of them, you must have guessed. That which happened was hopelessly inevitable. Could it be avoided between two young people of similar tastes, doing the same work, bearing the same sad burden, seeing the best and most unselfish side of each other, day after day, amid scenes which excited the keenest of sympathies? That it was a surprise to both, made the remedy no easier. The ludicrous side of it all was the similarity of experience. The obstacle was double-barrelled. There was a baby-husband as there had been a baby-wife!

'I always thought it very nice of him to allow me an English education,' she said; 'and I have often built him up round that one kind fact. But I begged a year's freedom on coming to India—and now, how ever am I to face that inevitable introduction? "Where is he?" Ah! that I cannot tell; but I expect you would find him in his native village, a pampered only son, too orthodox to cross the waters* himself, and managing the family property, in ignorant and comfortable self-satisfaction. What I cannot understand is my own liberty! There must be some third person acting a reformed up-to-date Providence, I'm sure! Till lately I've been so curious about it all, but now curiosity is swallowed up in loathing!'

'Pity we can't marry those two!' said the man.

It was the festival of the fire-god.* 'Though thou passest through the fire, thou shalt not be burned!' Who would make good the promise of the deity and face the ordeal? Through long months of prayer and fasting, certain rapt fanatics, and of good women not a few, had been preparing themselves to answer that question. And here was the very day at last! Down the heights into the hollows came the crowds of pilgrims—intending victims and applauding gallery all huddled together—one chattering, rattling, rumbling, seething mass, like to some mountain torrent seeking the level, and, when found, glittering light-imprisoned under the brilliant rays of a lingering sun.

By their dress shall ye know them—many-hued, many-fashioned —and also by their equipages.* That long, low, wicker cart, likest to a racing-boat on lumbering wheels, has had other geographical genesis than that flat cradle-shaped construction of wooden poles and bambus.

The great milk-white, soft-eyed bulls, easing tired necks with a graceful sweep of hoary tongue, have not before known as neighbour the small, perky, wiry cattle, tossing impertinent heads to the jingle of aggressive bells, and bellowing staccato inquiries.

But the crowd has one manner of encamping. Under each cart is tied a primitive hammock, and into this are thrown the squalling babies, safely out of the way, while their parents water the beasts and cook the evening meal. Secure are they here from intrusion. Do not the mountains stand sentinel? And are not the very clouds frowning a watchful '*cave*'?* Yet it behoved them to do quickly that which they were purposing, for a wise Government approved not of the rash sacrifice of life; and even now some message of prohibition may be travelling from the camp of the nearest collector.

'In the blackest watch of the night—the inrush!' said the priestly herald, beating a muffled drum among the *al fresco* cooking-pots.

Gradually, like a long, stealthy shadow, silence creeps over the face of the valley, and out of the wordless darkness arises a great lurid fiery furnace. It shows the mass of onlookers, earnest, fanatic—ringing the sacred enclosure—a phalanx strong enough to withstand any band of venturesome intruders; and, at a sanctified distance, the knot of priests and white-robed devotees.

The head priest was speaking—'To the holy,' said he, 'this is no wanton sacrifice of life, but merely a hymn to the praise of the Deity—the rhythm of your bodies to the accompaniment of that angry roar. The *evil* do indeed take hurt, but is that not the just reward of their offences?'

'Let us go and see the festival,' had said the doctor-girl to her friend. 'My mother belonged to these hill-folk, and something stirs within me at thought of the great ordeal. I believe the instincts of the savage still survive. Do let us go, and I will—yes, I shall appear in the white garments of the devotee.'

So they went, man and woman, in high spirits at the dubious adventure.

They arrived in time to hear the introductory address. The drums were growling now, and quaint pathetic incantations rose and fell on the midnight air. The first rush was just about to be made. One poor candidate has fainted. Carry her aside. *Now!*

They are through, unsinged, and a great shout of enthusiasm greets the semi-deities—canonisation dearly bought!

But more stirring matters still are afoot. For now a group of young girls stand hand in hand, gladly responsive to the heavenly call, thrilling with the joy of martyrdom. But a moment, and the priest will give the signal for the fresh inrush!

'The gods will stay the plague,' declares their messenger, 'for the willing sacrifice of a band of virgins. Who will come, who will be the brides of death, to buy life for the millions? Who? *Who?* One short black moment for you, brave virgins. For others, years of glad happiness. See! the corn is ready to harvest, but the hand which would gather it is stiff; the grain is garnered, but the arm which would grind it is withered; the meal is prepared, but they who would eat it are dead! dead *and defiled*! with no sacred rites to buy them the best eternity. . . . Buy *you* it for them, O virgins! *You!* Buy life now, and life hereafter—a double gift—and your own the hand to bestow it. Virgin life-givers!' . . .

In the silence one can almost hear life pulse! Then there is a sudden quick, convulsive sob—for, carried past all self-control, the doctor-girl has joined the band of vestal virgins. The word is given, and there they are, the white-robed seven, treading the flames.*

'O Agni! do not burn them altogether,' chanted the priests. 'Let the eye go to the sun, and the breath to the wind! Go to sky or earth, as is right; or to the waters, if it is good to be there. But the immortal, the unborn part, warm it with thy heat and flame! Carry them in thy kindliest shape to the world of those who have done well!'

'*Peste!** Why sings he the death chant!' murmured the crowd. 'It is ill luck!' And then—no one knew how it happened . . . '*The doctor-lady!*' they shrieked.

'She was tainted with infidel observances!' said the didactic priest; 'the gods were angry!'

'She was not quick enough,' said her companions. 'Hi! hi!

mourned the multitude. Her friend alone said not a word. And she, poor girl, lay terribly scarred in the accident ward of her own hospital.

The end was not long in coming. 'The decision of the gods,' she murmured, and so slept, her hand in his.

Postscriptum.—It was a month later, and the doctor sat in his consulting room. His face wore the look of the man to whom life has proved a resented discipline. There were arrears of correspondence clamouring for attention, and he settled wearily to the pile of multifarious envelopes.

Presently his eye flashed, and the sensitive mouth quivered, as he read a letter longer than the rest.

'Son,' wrote, after much circumlocution, the father of whom he knew so little, 'forgive the deception. It was part of your fate. The girl who worked in the hospital was your wife. We experimented for your good; but we were wrong. The gods resent experiments. In the path of orthodox monotony alone lieth safety. So perish all reform!'

But the man thought otherwise.

See also: Barker; Fairbridge; Kipling; Naidu.

LADY MARY ANNE BARKER
(1831–1911)

from Colonial Servants (1904)

My very first experience of the eccentricities of colonial servants dates a good deal more than half a century ago, and the scene was laid in Jamaica, where my father then held the office of 'Island Secretary' under Sir Charles—afterwards Lord Metcalfe—the Governor. It was Christmas day, and I had been promised as a great treat that my little sister and I should sit up to late dinner. But the morning began with an alarm, for just at breakfast-time an orderly from one of the West Indian regiments, then stationed in Spanish Town, had brought a letter to my father which had been sent upstairs to him. I was curled up in a deep window-seat in the shady breakfast-room, enjoying a brand-new story-book and the first puffs of the daily sea-breeze, when I heard a guttural voice close to my ear whispering, 'Kiss, missy, kiss.' There stood what seemed a real black giant compared with my childish stature, clad in gorgeous Turkish-looking uniform with a big white turban and a most benignant expression of face, holding his hand out, palm upwards.

I gazed at this apparition—for I had only just returned to Jamaica —with paralysed terror, while the smiling ogre came a step nearer and repeated his formula in still more persuasive tones. At this moment, however, my father appeared and said, 'Oh yes, all right; he wants you to give him a Christmas-box. Here is something for him.' It required even then a certain amount of faith as well as courage to put the silver dollar into the outstretched palm, but the man's joy and gratitude showed the interpretation had been quite right. I did not dare to say what my alarm had conjured up as the meaning of his request, for fear of being laughed at.

As well as I remember, at that Christmas dinner-party—and it was a large one—the food was distinctly eccentric, edibles usually boiled appearing as roasts and *vice versâ*. The service also was of a jerky and spasmodic character, and the authorities wore an air of anxiety, which, however, only added to the deep interest I took in the situation. But things came to a climax when the plum-pudding, which was to have been the great feature of the entertainment, did not appear at its proper time and place, and a tragic whisper from the butler suggested complications in the background. My father said laughingly, 'I am sorry to say the cook is drunk and will not part with the plum-pudding,' so we went on with the dinner without it. But just as the dessert was being put on the table there was a sound as of ineffectual scrimmaging outside, and the cook—a huge black man clad in spotless white—rushed in bearing triumphantly a large dish, which he banged down in front of my father, saying, 'Dere, my good massa, dere your pudding,' and immediately flung himself into the butler's arms with a burst of weeping. I shall always see that pudding as long as I live. It was about the size of an orange and as black as coal. Every attempt to cut it resulted in its bounding off the dish, for it was as hard as a stone. Though not exactly an object of mirth in itself, it certainly was 'a cause that mirth was in others,' and so achieved a success denied to many a better pudding.

Several years passed before I again came across black servants, and the next time was in India. I was not there long enough, nor did I lead a sufficiently settled life, to be able to judge of the Indian servant of that day. Half my stay in Bengal was spent under canvas, and certainly the way in which the servants arranged for one's comfort under those conditions was marvellous. The camp was a very large one, for we were making a sort of military promenade from Lucknow up to Lahore—my husband being the Commanding Officer of Royal Artillery in Bengal—but I only went as far as the foot of the Hills and then up to Simla. It was amazing the way in which nothing was ever forgotten or left behind during four months' continuous camp-life. All my possessions had to be divided, and, where necessary, duplicated, for what one used on Monday would not be get-at-able until Wednesday, and so on all through the week. No matter how interesting my book was, I could not go on with it for thirty-six hours—*i.e.* from, say Monday night till breakfast-time on Wednesday morning. I could have a new volume for Tuesday, but the interest of that had also to remain in abeyance until Thursday. Still, I would find the book precisely where I laid it down, and if I had put a mark, even a flower, it would be found exactly in the right place.

I always wondered when and how the servants rested, for they seemed to me to be packing and starting all night long, and yet when the new camping-ground was reached the head-servants would always be there in snowy garments, as fresh and trim as if they came out of a box. There were two sets of under-servants, but the head ones never seemed to be off duty.

We started with the first streak of daylight, and there was no choice about the matter, for if you did not get up when the first bugle blew, your plight would be a sorry one when the canvas walls of the large double tent fell flat at the sound of the second bugle, half-an-hour later. The roof of the tent was left a few moments longer, so one had time for hot fragrant coffee and bread and butter before starting either on horse or elephant back. I generally rode on a pad on the *hathi's** back for the first few miles while it was still dark, and mounted my little Arab some six or eight miles further on. The marches were as near twenty-five miles daily, as could be arranged to suit the Commander-in-Chief's convenience as to inspections, &c.

Everything was fresh and amusing, but I think I most delighted in seeing the modes of progression adopted by the various cooks. Our head-cook generally requisitioned a sort of gig, in which he sat in state and dignity, with many bundles heaped around him. Part of his cavalcade consisted of two or three very small ponies laden with paniers, on top of which invariably stood a chicken or two, apparently without any fastenings, who balanced themselves in a precarious manner according to the pony's gait. No one seemed to walk except those who led the animals, and as the camp numbered some 5000 soldiers and quite as many camp-followers the supply-train appeared endless.

Just as we neared the foot of the Himalayan range, where the camp was to divide, some of us going up to Simla, leaving a greatly lessened force to proceed to Lahore, smallpox appeared among our servants. I wonder it did not spread much more, but it was vigorously dealt with at the outset. I had as narrow an escape as anybody, for one morning, while I was drinking my early coffee and standing quite ready to start on our daily march, one of the servants, a very clever, useful Madras 'boy' whom I had missed from his duties for several days, suddenly appeared and cast himself at my feet, clutching my riding-habit and begging for some tea. He was quite unrecognisable, so swollen and disfigured was his poor face, and I had no idea what was the matter with him. He was delirious and apparently half-mad with thirst. The doctor had to be fetched to induce him to let me go, and as more than once the poor lad had seized my hands and kissed them in gratitude for the tea I at once gave him, I suppose I really ran some risks, for it turned out to be a very bad case of confluent smallpox. However, all the same, he had to be carried along with us in a dhooly* until we reached a station where he could be put into a hospital.

But certainly the strangest phase of colonial domestics within my experience were the New Zealand maid-servants of some thirty-five years ago. Perhaps by this time they are 'home-made,' and consequently less eccentric; but in my day they were all immigrants, and seemed drawn almost entirely from the ranks of factory girls. They were respectable girls apparently, but with very free and easy manners. However, that did not matter. What seriously inconvenienced me at the far up-country station where my husband and I had made ourselves a very pretty and comfortable home was the absolute and profound ignorance of these damsels. They took any sort of place which they fancied, at enormous wages, and when they had at great cost and trouble been fetched up to their new home I invariably discovered that the cook, who demanded and received the wages of a *chef*, knew nothing whatever of any sort of cooking and the housemaid had never seen a broom. They did not know how to thread a needle or wash a pocket-handkerchief, and, as I thought, must have been waited on all their lives. Indeed, one of my great difficulties was to get them away from the rapt admiration with which they regarded the most ordinary helps to labour. One day I heard peals of laughter from the wash-house, and found the fun consisted in the magical way in which the little cottage-mangle smoothed the aprons of the last couple of damsels. So I—who was extremely ignorant myself, and had no idea how the very beginnings of things should be taught—had to impart my slender store of knowledge as best I could. The little establishment would have collapsed entirely had it not been for my Scotch shepherd's wife, a dear woman with the manners of a lady and the knowledge of a thorough practical housewife. What broke our hearts was that we had to begin this elementary course of instruction over and over again, as my damsels could not endure the monotony of their country life longer than three or four months, in spite of the many suitors who came a-wooing with strictly honourable intentions. But the young ladies had no idea of giving up their liberty, and turned a deaf ear to all matrimonial suggestions, even when one athletic suitor put another into the water-barrel to get him out of the way, and urged that this step must be taken as a proof of his devotion.

After the New Zealand experiences came a period of English life, and I felt much more experienced in domestic matters by the time my wandering star led me forth once more and landed me in Natal. In spite, however, of this experience, I fell into the mistake of taking out three English servants, whom I had to get rid of as soon as possible after my arrival. They had all been with me some time in England; and I thought I knew them perfectly; but the voyage evidently 'wrought a sea change'* on them, for they were quite different people by the time Durban was reached. Two developed tempers for which the little Maritzburg house was much too small, and when it came to carving-knives hurtling through the air I felt it was more than my nerves could stand. The third only broke out in folly, and showed an amount of personal vanity which seemed almost to border on insanity. However, I gradually replaced them with Zulu servants, in whom I was really very fortunate. They learned so easily, and were so good-tempered and docile, their only serious fault being the in-eradicable tendency to return for a while—after a very few 'moons' of service—to their kraals. At first I thought it was family affection which impelled this constant homing, but it was really the desire to get back to the savage life, with its gorges of half-raw meat and native beer, and its freedom from clothes. It is true I had an occasional very bad quarter of an hour with some of my experiments, as, for instance, when I found an embryo valet blacking his master's socks as well as his boots, or detected the nurse-boy who was trusted to wheel the perambulator about the garden stuffing a half-fledged little bird into the baby's mouth, assuring me it was a diet calculated to make 'the little chieftain brave and strong.'

I think, however, quite the most curious instance of the thinness of surface civilisation among these people came to me in the case of a young Zulu girl who had been early left an orphan and had been carefully trained in a clergyman's family. She was about sixteen years old when she came as my nursemaid, and was very plump and comely, with a beaming countenance, and the sweetest voice and prettiest manners possible. She had a great love of music, and performed harmoniously enough on an accordion as well as on several queer little pipes and reeds. She could speak, read, and write Dutch perfectly, as well as Zulu, and was nearly as proficient in English. She carried a little Bible always in her pocket, and often tried my gravity by dropping on one knee by my side whenever she caught me sitting down and alone, and beginning to read aloud from it. It was quite a new possession, and she had not got beyond the opening chapters of Genesis and delighted in the story of 'Dam and Eva,' as she called our first parents. She proved an excellent nurse and thoroughly trustworthy; the children were devoted to her, especially the baby, who learned to speak Zulu before English, and to throw a reed assegai as soon as he could stand firmly on his little fat legs. I brought her to England after she had been about a year with me, and she adapted herself marvellously and unhesitatingly to the conditions of a civilisation far beyond what she had ever dreamed of. After she had got over her surprise at the ship knowing its way across the ocean, she proved a capital sailor. She took to London life and London ways as if she had never known anything else. The only serious mistake she made was once in yielding to the blandishments of a persuasive Italian image-man and promising to buy his whole tray of statues. I found the hall filled with these works of art, and 'Malia' tendering, with sweetest smiles, a few pence in exchange for them. It was a disagreeable job to have to persuade the man to depart in peace with all his images, even with a little money to console him. A friend of mine chanced to be returning to Natal, and proposed that I should spare my Zulu nurse to her. Her husband's magistracy being close to where Maria's tribe dwelt, it seemed a good opportunity for 'Malia' to return to her own country; so of course I let her go, begging my friend to tell me how the girl got on. The parting from the little boys was a heart-breaking scene, nor was Malia at all comforted by the fine clothes all my friends insisted on giving her. Not even a huge Gainsborough hat garnished with giant poppies could console her for leaving her 'little chieftain'; but it was at all events something to send her off so comfortably provided for, and with two large boxes of good clothes.

In the course of a few months I received a letter from my friend, who was then settled in her up-country home, but her story of Maria's doings seemed well-nigh incredible, though perfectly true.

All had gone well on the voyage and so long as they remained at Durban and Maritzburg; but as soon as the distant settlement was reached, Maria's kinsmen came around her and began to claim some share in her prosperity. Free fights were of constant occurrence, and in one of them Maria, using the skull of an ox as a weapon, broke her sister's leg. Soon after that she returned to the savage life she had not known since her infancy, and took to it with delight. I don't know what became of her clothes, but she had presented herself before my friend clad in an old sack and with necklaces of wild animals' teeth, and proudly announced she had just been married 'with cows'—thus showing how completely her Christianity had fallen away from her, and she had practically returned, on the first opportunity, to the depth of that savagery from which she had been taken before she could even remember it. I soon lost all trace of her, but Malia's story has always remained in my mind as an amazing instance of the strength of race-instinct. [. . .]

See also: Baughan; Clifford; Perrin; Sorabji; Steel.

SAROJINI NAIDU
(1876–1949)

from *The Golden Threshold* (1905)

Village-Song

Honey, child, honey, child, whither are you going?
Would you cast your jewels all to the breezes blowing?
Would you leave the mother who on golden grain has fed you?
Would you grieve the lover who is riding forth to wed you?

Mother mine, to the wild forest I am going,
Where upon the champa boughs the champa buds* are blowing;
To the köil-haunted* river-isles where lotus lilies glisten,
The voices of the fairy-folk are calling me: O listen!

Honey, child, honey, child, the world is full of pleasure,
Of bridal-songs and cradle-songs and sandal-scented leisure.
Your bridal robes are in the loom, silver and saffron glowing,
Your bridal cakes are on the hearth: O whither are you going?

The bridal-songs and cradle-songs have cadences of sorrow,
The laughter of the sun to-day, the wind of death to-morrow.
Far sweeter sound the forest-notes where forest-streams are falling;
O mother mine, I cannot stay, the fairy-folk are calling.

Humayun to Zobeida*

(*From the Urdu*)

You flaunt your beauty in the rose, your glory in the dawn,
Your sweetness in the nightingale, your whiteness in the swan.

You haunt my waking like a dream, my slumber like a moon,
Pervade me like a musky scent, possess me like a tune.

Yet, when I crave of you, my sweet, one tender moment's grace,
You cry, '*I sit behind the veil, I cannot show my face.*'

Shall any foolish veil divide my longing from my bliss?
Shall any fragile curtain hide your beauty from my kiss?

What war is this of *Thee* and *Me*? Give o'er the wanton strife,
You are the heart within my heart, the life within my life.

Ode to H.H. the Nizam of Hyderabad

(*Presented at the Ramzan Durbar*)

Deign, Prince, my tribute to receive,*
This lyric offering to your name,
Who round your jewelled sceptre bind
The lilies of a poet's fame;
Beneath whose sway concordant dwell
The peoples whom your laws embrace,
In brotherhood of diverse creeds,
And harmony of diverse race:

The votaries of the Prophet's faith,
Of whom you are the crown and chief;
And they, who bear on Vedic brows
Their mystic symbols of belief;
And they, who worshipping the sun,
Fled o'er the old Iranian sea;
And they, who bow to Him who trod
The midnight waves of Galilee.*

Sweet, sumptuous fables of Baghdad
The splendours of your court recall,
The torches of a *Thousand Nights*
Blaze through a single festival;
And Saki-singers down the streets,
Pour for us, in a stream divine,
From goblets of your love-*ghazals**
The rapture of your Sufi wine.

Prince, where your radiant cities smile,
Grim hills their sombre vigils keep,
Your ancient forests hoard and hold
The legends of their centuried sleep;
Your birds of peace white-pinioned float
O'er ruined fort and storied plain,
Your faithful stewards sleepless guard
The harvests of your gold and grain.

God give you joy, God give you grace
To shield the truth and smite the wrong,
To honour Virtue, Valour, Worth,
To cherish faith and foster song.
So may the lustre of your days
Outshine the deeds Firdusi* sung,
Your name within a nation's prayer,
Your music on a nation's tongue.

To India

O young through all thy immemorial years!
Rise, Mother,* rise, regenerate from thy gloom,
And, like a bride high-mated with the spheres,
Beget new glories from thine ageless womb!

The nations that in fettered darkness weep
Crave thee to lead them where great mornings break. . . .
Mother, O Mother, wherefore dost thou sleep?
Arise and answer for thy children's sake!

Thy Future calls thee with a manifold sound
To crescent honours, splendours, victories vast;
Waken, O slumbering Mother and be crowned,
Who once wert empress of the sovereign Past.

from *The Bird of Time* (1912)

Songs of my City

I. In a Latticed Balcony

How shall I feed thee, Beloved?
On golden-red honey and fruit.
How shall I please thee, Beloved?
With th' voice of the cymbal and lute.

How shall I garland thy tresses?
With pearls from the jessamine close.
How shall I perfume thy fingers?
With th' soul of the keora* and rose.

How shall I deck thee, O Dearest?
In hues of the peacock and dove.
How shall I woo thee, O Dearest?
With the delicate silence of love.

II. In the Bazaars of Hyderabad

To a tune of the Bazaars

What do you sell, O ye merchants?
Richly your wares are displayed.
Turbans of crimson and silver,
Tunics of purple brocade,
Mirrors with panels of amber,
Daggers with handles of jade.

What do you weigh, O ye vendors?
Saffron and lentil and rice.
What do you grind, O ye maidens?
Sandalwood, henna, and spice.
What do you call, O ye pedlars?
Chessmen and ivory dice.

What do you make, O ye goldsmiths?
Wristlet and anklet and ring,
Bells for the feet of blue pigeons,
Frail as a dragon-fly's wing,
Girdles of gold for the dancers,
Scabbards of gold for the king.

What do you cry, O ye fruitmen?
Citron, pomegranate, and plum.
What do you play, O musicians?
Cithār, sarangī, and drum.
What do you chant, O magicians?
Spells for the æons to come.

What do you weave, O ye flower-girls
With tassels of azure and red?
Crowns for the brow of a bridegroom,
Chaplets to garland his bed,
Sheets of white blossoms new-gathered
To perfume the sleep of the dead.

Song of Radha the Milkmaid*

I carried my curds to the Mathura fair[1]. . . .
How softly the heifers were lowing. . . .
I wanted to cry 'Who will buy, who will buy
These curds that are white as the clouds in the sky
When the breezes of *Shrawan* are blowing?'
But my heart was so full of your beauty, Beloved,
They laughed as I cried without knowing:
     Govinda! Govinda!
     Govinda! Govinda! . . .
How softly the river was flowing!

I carried my pots to the Mathura tide. . . .
How gaily the rowers were rowing! . . .

[1] Mathura is the chief centre of the mystic worship of Khrishna, the Divine Cowherd and Musician—the 'Divine Beloved' of every Hindu heart. He is also called Govinda.

My comrades called 'Ho! let us dance, let us sing
And wear saffron garments to welcome the spring,
And pluck the new buds that are blowing.'
But my heart was so full of your music, Beloved,
They mocked when I cried without knowing:
>   *Govinda! Govinda!*
>   *Govinda! Govinda! . . .*
How gaily the river was flowing!

I carried my gifts to the Mathura shrine. . . .
How brightly the torches were glowing! . . .
I folded my hands at the altars to pray
'O shining Ones guard us by night and by day'—
And loudly the conch shells were blowing.
But my heart was so lost in your worship, Beloved,
They were wroth when I cried without knowing:
>   *Govinda! Govinda!*
>   *Govinda! Govinda! . . .*
How brightly the river was flowing!

An Anthem of Love

Two hands are we to serve thee, O our Mother,
To strive and succour, cherish and unite;
Two feet are we to cleave the waning darkness,
And gain the pathways of the dawning light.

Two ears are we to catch the nearing echo,
The sounding cheer of Time's prophetic horn;
Two eyes are we to reap the crescent glory,
The radiant promise of renascent morn.

One heart are we to love thee, O our Mother,
One undivided, indivisible soul,
Bound by one hope, one purpose, one devotion
Towards a great, divinely-destined goal.

See also: Aurobindo; Dutt; McKay; Sorabji; Tagore; Yeats.

GEORGE NATHANIEL, MARQUESS CURZON
(1859–1925)

The British Empire (1906)

Our principal object in meeting here to-night has been to do honour to Lord Milner,* and that object, after the speech of our Chairman* and the magnificent reception that you have accorded to our guest, we may claim to have successfully attained. But on an occasion like this, when so many representative persons are present, and on a day like this, which is consecrated to the name and conception of Empire, it was thought by the organizers of this meeting that the opportunity should not be lost of proposing the toast of 'Our Dominions Beyond the Seas,' those dominions which have grown and spread by the self-sacrificing and often ill-requited labours of such men as Lord Milner, and which have never had a more brilliant or more devoted servant than he. That is the explanation of the toast which I have been instructed to propose.

No man can propose this toast—least of all any man who has borne a part in the task of governing the Empire—without a sense of great responsibility and almost of awe. For think of what this toast means. It embraces in a single formula more than one-fourth of the entire human race. It is a toast to no inconsiderable portion of the inhabited and civilized globe. The British Dominions Beyond the Seas include every colony and possession of the Crown, from the Federated Commonwealth of Australia, that great experiment so rich in promise, and the Dominion of Canada, with its heritage of glory and its future of hope, down to the smallest rocky island or coral reef over which the Union Jack may have been hoisted on the bosom of some distant ocean. It includes great self-governing communities who have left us far behind in experiments of government and economics, but whose heart still warms and whose pulse beats more quickly at the thought of the Mother Land. It includes the small but not uninteresting Crown Colonies* to which we have given what is, in my judgment, one of the best forms of government in the world. It includes all those vantage-points and places of arms with which we guard the ocean highways and of which we have been told that the drumbeat echoes round the world.* It includes the undeveloped Protectorates, which in backward continents are the first step towards higher forms of political evolution in the future. And lastly it includes India, that Empire within an Empire, that supreme test of our dominion and race, the successful government of which is by itself sufficient to differentiate the British Empire from anything that has preceded it. All this, and much more than this, is involved in the toast which I am allowed to place before you. I hope that no one will do me the injustice of thinking that in making this brief enumeration I have been actuated by any spirit of pride of possession, still less by any suggestion of increase. Believe me, it is not those who know most of the Empire who make broad its phylacteries. It is not from their lips that you hear about painting the map of the world red. I doubt if in the mind of any of them—and there are many here to-night—expansion ever figures as an object of ambition, though it may sometimes present itself to them, as it has often presented itself in the past, as an obligation of duty.

No, the Empire is to them, first and foremost, a great historical and political and sociological fact, which is one of the guiding factors in the development of mankind. Secondly, it is part of the dispensation of a higher Power which for some good purpose—it cannot possibly be for an evil one—has committed the fortunes of all these hundreds of millions of human beings to the custody of a single branch of the human family. And thirdly, it is a call to duty, to personal as well as national duty, more inspiring than has ever before sounded in the ears of a dominant people. The cynics may scoff at Empire. The doctrinaires may denounce it from the benches of the House of Commons or elsewhere, and the rhapsodists may sometimes conspire almost to render it ridiculous. But it is with us. It is part of us. It is bone of our bone and flesh of our flesh. We cannot get away from it. We cannot deny our own progeny. We cannot disown our own handiwork. The voyage which our predecessors commenced we have to continue. We have to answer our helm, and it is an Imperial helm, down all the tides of Time.

On an occasion like this, and with a subject like this, there are scores, I might say hundreds, of reflections which crowd on the mind of a man entrusted with the task of proposing such a toast. But there are only two to which I will venture to allude to-night. The first is this. Surely it is well and right that we should remember that the interest of the Empire is commensurate with its whole extent, and is equally shared by all its members. It is not greater in one part and less in another. It is the monopoly of no class or party or Government within the Empire. There can be no greater mistake than to regard the Empire as the peculiar property or the particular concern of those who are fortunate enough to administer it, whether from Downing Street or from the Governor's chair of authority in any part of the world. They are only the instruments and mouthpieces of a power outside of themselves, and the constituency they represent is co-extensive with the Empire itself, because it includes every one of its citizens. They may enjoy for a time the pride of place and the privilege of responsibility, and very great, I assure you, those chances and opportunities are; but only in proportion as they recognize the existence of something larger than themselves, only in proportion as they are obedient—as I think our guest of this evening was obedi-ent—to the higher laws and deeper principles which do not confuse the unit with the aggregate, but regard the effect produced upon the welfare of the Empire as a whole, only so far are they entitled to share in the credit.

Again, the Empire is not the interest of the Mother Country only, though we are sometimes disposed to talk as though it were. By the way of that fallacy, as history has too often shown, lies the path of disruption and ruin. But neither is it the interest of the Colonies alone, though we may allow them a prudent liberty sometimes to stand up and lecture their parents. Still, the Empire was not made for them, but they for the Empire; and my point is that the Empire is equally the interest of every land and island within it, of every man who inhabits it—in fact, of every subject of the King. Wherever he may be and whoever he may be, be he rich or poor, be he a dark-skinned man or a white-skinned man, he is equally concerned in the purity of our administration and in the results of our rule. Unless the Empire means something to him—I do not say always the same thing, but something of beneficence and advantage and profit in his life, whether he be a coolie in India, or a squatter in Tasmania, or a fisherman in Newfoundland—the Empire is not justifying itself, and there is something wrong about it. I do not say that, as long as they do good, Empires necessarily continue to wax, but I do say that, when they have ceased to do good to their citizens, they must inevitably tend to wane.

And this brings me to my second and concluding reflection. If this great Empire of ours has not been built up without courage and endurance—and those who know its history best know well through what travail it has passed to its greatness—it is also not without a spirit of self-sacrifice that it can be maintained. We cannot have a world-wide Empire, with all that that means, without paying a price for it, a price in effort, in labour, sometimes in danger, but always in duty. Unless every individual citizen of the Empire is prepared to accept that particular form of sacrifice, be it great or small—and in ninety-nine cases out of a hundred it is small rather than great—which he may be called on to perform, then our Empire is not a reality, but only a name. It is because I believe that the Empire is still an ideal to the best spirits within it, that it has a place in the consciences as well as on the lips of the majority of its peoples, and is a source of blessing to the world, that on Empire Day I think that any assemblage of Englishmen such as this may, not merely without compunction but with pride and satisfaction, be called on to drink the toast, which I now give you, of 'The British Dominions Beyond the Seas.'

See also: Chamberlain; Hobson; Kipling, 'The White Man's Burden'; Ruskin; Seeley.

SRI AUROBINDO
(1872–1950)

The widespread Swadeshi (self-help) protests against the Partition of Bengal in 1905–8 revealed to many Indians the immense possibilities of mass action. Using the upsurge as both an inspiration and an example, Sri Aurobindo elaborated a programme of large-scale passive resistance against British authority that anticipated yet also went further towards outright confrontation than Mohandas Gandhi's later did. In so doing he became at this time of upheaval one of the foremost Indian counter-voices to Curzon (q.v.), the Viceroy who propagated Partition. 'The Object of Passive Resistance' is the second in a series of articles published in 1907 in which Aurobindo looked forward to the ideal of national liberty secured through the 'new and mighty weapon' of an organized popular outburst. Despite his political radicalism, however, Aurobindo himself exhibited some of the 'fixed ideas' of the English-educated 'native' that he here criticizes, as the marked contrast between his ardent activist prose and his classically influenced poetry clearly demonstrates.

The Object of Passive Resistance (1907)

Organized resistance to an existing form of government may be undertaken either for the vindication of national liberty, or in order to substitute one form of government for another, or to remove particular objectionable features in the existing system without any entire or radical alteration of the whole, or simply for the redress of particular grievances. Our political agitation in the nineteenth century was entirely confined to the smaller and narrower objects. To replace an oppressive land revenue system by the security of a Permanent Settlement,* to mitigate executive tyranny by the separation of judicial from executive functions, to diminish the drain on the country naturally resulting from foreign rule by more liberal employment of Indians in the services—to these half-way houses our wise men and political seers directed our steps,—with this limited ideal they confined the rising hopes and imaginations of a mighty people re-awakening after a great downfall. Their political inexperience prevented them from realising that these measures on which we have mis-spent half a century of unavailing effort, were not only paltry and partial in their scope but in their nature ineffective. A Permanent Settlement can always be evaded by a spendthrift Government bent on increasing its resources and unchecked by any system of popular control; there is no limit to the possible number of cesses and local taxes by which the Settlement could be practically violated without any direct infringement of its provisions. The mere deprivation of judicial functions will not disarm executive tyranny so long as both executive and judiciary are mainly white and subservient to a central authority irresponsible, alien and bureaucratic; for the central authority can always tighten its grip on the judiciary of which it is the controller and paymaster and habituate it to a consistent support of executive action. Nor will Simultaneous Examinations* and the liberal appointment of Indians mend the matter; for an Englishman serves the Government as a member of the same ruling race and can afford to be occasionally independent; but the Indian civilian is a serf masquerading as a heaven-born and can only deserve favour and promotion by his zeal in fastening the yoke heavier upon his fellow-countrymen. As a rule the foreign Government can rely on the 'native' civilian to be more zealously oppressive than even the average Anglo-Indian official. Neither would the panacea of Simultaneous Examinations really put an end to the burden of the drain. The Congress insistence on the Home Charges* for a long time obscured the real accusation against British rule; for it substituted a particular grievance for a radical and congenital evil implied in the very existence of British control. The huge price India has to pay England for the inestimable privilege of being ruled by Englishmen is a small thing compared with the murderous drain by which we purchase the more exquisite privilege of being exploited by British capital. The diminution of Home Charges will not prevent the gradual death by bleeding of which exploitation is the true and abiding cause. Thus, even for the partial objects they were intended to secure, the measures for which we petitioned and clamoured in the last century were hopelessly ineffective. So was it with all the Congress nostrums; they were palliatives which could not even be counted upon to palliate; the radical evil, uncured, would only be driven from one seat in the body politic to take refuge in others where it would soon declare its presence by equally troublesome symptoms. The only true cure for a bad and oppressive financial system is to give the control over taxation to the people whose money pays for the needs of Government. The only effective way of putting an end to executive tyranny is to make the people and not an irresponsible Government the controller and paymaster of both executive and judiciary. The only possible method of stopping the drain is to establish a popular government which may be relied on to foster and protect Indian commerce and Indian industry conducted by Indian capital and employing Indian labour. This is the object which the new politics, the politics of the twentieth century, places before the people of India in their resistance to the present system of Government,—not tinkerings and palliatives but the substitution for the autocratic bureaucracy, which at present misgoverns us, of a free constitutional and democratic system of government and the entire removal of foreign control in order to make way for perfect national liberty.

The redress of particular grievances and the reformation of

particular objectionable features in a system of Government are sufficient objects for organized resistance only when the Government is indigenous and all classes have a recognized place in the political scheme of the State. They are not and cannot be a sufficient object in countries like Russia and India where the laws are made and administered by a handful of men, and a vast population, educated and uneducated alike, have no political right or duty except the duty of obedience and the right to assist in confirming their own servitude. They are still less a sufficient object when the despotic oligarchy is alien by race and has not even a permanent home in the country, for in that case the Government cannot be relied on to look after the general interest of the country, as in nations ruled by indigenous despotism; on the contrary, they are bound to place the interests of their own country and their own race first and foremost. Organized resistance in subject nations which mean to live and not to die, can have no less an object than an entire and radical change of the system of Government; only by becoming responsible to the people and drawn from the people can the Government be turned into a protector instead of an oppressor. But if the subject nation desires not a provincial existence and a maimed development but the full, vigorous and noble realisation of its national existence, even a change in the system of Government will not be enough, it must aim not only at a national Government responsible to the people but a free national Government unhampered even in the least degree by foreign control.

It is not surprising that our politicians of the nineteenth century could not realize these elementary truths of modern politics. They had no national experience behind them of politics under modern conditions; they had no teachers except English books and English liberal 'sympathisers' and 'friends of India'. Schooled by British patrons, trained to the fixed idea of English superiority and Indian inferiority, their imaginations could not embrace the idea of national liberty, and perhaps they did not even desire it at heart preferring the comfortable ease, which at that time still seemed possible in a servitude under British protection, to the struggles and sacrifices of a hard and difficult independence. Taught to take their political lessons solely from the example of England and ignoring or not valuing the historical experience of the rest of the world, they could not even conceive of a truly popular and democratic Government in India except as the slow result of the development of centuries, progress broadening down from precedent to precedent. They could not then understand that the experience of an independent nation is not valid to guide a subject nation, unless and until the subject nation throws off the yoke and itself becomes independent. They could not realize that the slow, painful and ultra-cautious development, necessary in mediaeval and semi-mediaeval conditions when no experience of a stable popular Government had been gained, need not be repeated in the days of the steamship, railway and telegraph, when stable democratic systems are part of the world's secured and permanent heritage. The instructive spectacle of Asiatic nations* demanding and receiving constitutional and parliamentary government as the price of a few years' struggle and civil turmoil, had not then been offered to the world. But even if the idea of such happenings had occurred to the more sanguine spirits, they would have been prevented from putting it into words by their inability to discover any means towards its fulfilment. Their whole political outlook was bounded by the lessons of English history,* and in English history they found only two methods of politics,—the slow method of agitation and the swift decisive method of open struggle and revolt. Unaccustomed to independent political thinking, they did not notice the significant fact that the method of agitation only became effective in England when the people had already gained powerful voice in the Government. In order to secure that voice they had been compelled to resort no less than three several times to the method of open struggle and revolt. Blind to the significance of this fact, our nineteenth-century politicians clung to the method of agitation, obstinately hoping against all experience and reason that it would somehow serve their purpose. From any idea of open struggle with the bureaucracy they shrank with terror and a sense of paralysis. Dominated by the idea of the overwhelming might of Britain and the abject weakness of India, their want of courage and faith in the nation, their rooted distrust of the national character, disbelief in Indian patriotism and blindness to the possibility of true political strength and virtue in the people, precluded them from discovering the rough and narrow way to salvation. Herein lies the superiority of the new school,* that they have an indomitable courage and faith in the nation and the people. By the strength of that courage and faith they have not only been able to enforce on the mind of the country a higher ideal but perceived an effective means to the realization of that ideal. By the strength of that courage and faith they have made such immense strides in the course of a few months. By the strength of that courage and faith they will dominate the future.

The new methods were first tried in the great Swadeshi outburst of the last two years,—blindly, crudely, without leading and organization, but still with amazing results. The moving cause was a particular grievance, the Partition of Bengal; and to the removal of that grievance, pettiest and narrowest of all political objects, our old leaders strove hard to confine the use of this new and mighty weapon. But the popular instinct was true to itself and would have none of it. At a bound we passed therefore from mere particular grievances, however serious and intolerable, to the use of passive resistance as a means of cure for the basest and evilest feature of the present system,—the bleeding to death of a country by foreign exploitation. And from that stage we are steadily advancing, under the guidance of such able political thinking as modern India has not before seen and with the rising tide of popular opinion at our back, to the one true object of all resistance, passive or active, aggressive or defensive,— the creation of a free popular Government and the vindication of Indian liberty.

Charles Stewart Parnell, 1891 (1895)

O pale and guiding light, now star unsphered,
Deliverer lately hailed, since by our lords
Most feared, most hated, hated because feared,
Who smot'st them with an edge surpassing swords!
Thou too wert then a child of tragic earth,
Since vainly filled thy luminous doom of birth.

Transiit, Non Periit (1909)

[*My grandfather, Rajnarayan Bose, died September 1899*]

Not in annihilation lost, nor given
To darkness art thou fled from us and light,
O strong and sentient spirit; no mere heaven
Of ancient joys, no silence eremite

Received thee; but the omnipresent Thought
Of which thou wast a part and earthly hour,
Took back its gift. Into that splendour caught
Thou hast not lost thy special brightness. Power
Remains with thee and the old genial force
Unseen for blinding light, not darkly lurks:
As when a sacred river in its course
Dives into ocean, there its strength abides
Not less because with vastness wed and works
Unnoticed in the grandeur of the tides.

Hymn to the Mother: Bandemataram (1909)

Mother,* I bow to thee!
Rich with thy hurrying streams,
Bright with thy orchard gleams,
Cool with thy winds of delight,
Dark fields waving, Mother of might,
Mother free.
Glory of moonlight dreams
Over thy branches and lordly streams,—
Clad in thy blossoming trees,
Mother, giver of ease,
Laughing low and sweet!
Mother, I kiss thy feet,
Speaker sweet and low!
Mother, to thee I bow.
Who hath said thou art weak in thy lands,
When the swords flash out in seventy million hands
And seventy million voices roar
Thy dreadful name from shore to shore?
With many strengths who art mighty and stored,
To thee I call, Mother and Lord!
Thou who savest, arise and save!
To her I cry who ever her foemen drave
Back from plain and sea
And shook herself free.

Thou art wisdom, thou art law,
Thou our heart, our soul, our breath,
Thou the love divine, the awe
In our hearts that conquers death.
Thine the strength that nerves the arm,
Thine the beauty, thine the charm.
Every image made divine
In our temples is but thine.
Thou art Durga,* Lady and Queen,
With her hands that strike and her swords of sheen,
Thou art Lakshmi lotus-throned,
And the Muse a hundred-toned.
Pure and perfect without peer,
Mother, lend thine ear.
Rich with thy hurrying streams,
Bright with thy orchard gleams,
Dark of hue, O candid-fair
In thy soul, with jewelled hair
And thy glorious smile divine,
Loveliest of all earthly lands,
Showering wealth from well-stored hands!
Mother, mother mine!
Mother sweet, I bow to thee
Mother great and free!

Revelation (1915)

Someone leaping from the rocks
Past me ran with wind-blown locks
Like a startled bright surmise
Visible to mortal eyes,—
Just a cheek of frightened rose
That with sudden beauty glows,
Just a footstep like the wind
And a hurried glance behind,
And then nothing,—as a thought
Escapes the mind ere it is caught.
Someone of the heavenly rout
From behind the veil ran out.

Rebirth (1915)

Not soon is God's delight in us completed,
    Nor with one life we end;
Termlessly in us are our spirits seated
    And termless joy intend.

Our souls and heaven are of an equal stature
    And have a dateless birth;
The unending seed, the infinite mould of Nature,
    They were not made on earth,

Nor to the earth do they bequeath their ashes,
    But in themselves they last.
An endless future brims beneath thy lashes,
    Child of an endless past.

Old memories come to us, old dreams invade us,
    Lost people we have known,
Fictions and pictures; but their frames evade us,—
    They stand out bare, alone.

Yet all we dream and hope are memories treasured,
    Are forecasts we misspell,
But of what life or scene he who has measured
    The boundless heavens can tell.

Time is a strong convention; future and present
    Were living in the past;
They are one image that our wills complaisant
    Into three schemes have cast.

Our past that we forget, is with us deathless,
    Our births and later end
Already accomplished. To a summit breathless
    Sometimes our souls ascend,

Whence the mind comes back helped; for there emerges
  The ocean vast of Time
Spread out before us with its infinite surges,
  Its symphonies sublime;

And even from this veil of mind the spirit
  Looks out sometimes and sees
The bygone æons that our lives inherit,
  The unborn centuries:

It sees wave-trampled realms expel the Ocean,—
  From the vague depths uphurled
Where now Himaloy stands, the flood's huge motion
  Sees measuring half the world;

Or else the web behind us is unravelled
  And on its threads we gaze,—
Past motions of the stars, scenes long since travelled
  In Time's far-backward days.

See also: Conrad; Naidu; Plaatje; Schreiner; Tagore; Thomas; Yeats.

ALICE PERRIN
(1867–1934)

The Rise of Ram Din (1906)

It was in the year of the famine when my father, Ram Bux of Kansrao in the Mathura district,* bade me make ready to go with him to the City of Kings—which is two days' journey by road from the village—that I might there obtain employment as dish-washer in the service of a sahib; for there were many of us in my father's house, and his crops had failed for want of rain, so that there was not enough food to fill our stomachs.

In his youth my father, Ram Bux, had himself served the Fering-hees*, and having heard him speak much of those days I felt that I should learn my duties with the greater ease; and as we journeyed through the dry, empty fields in the early morning time, he also told me many more things concerning the ways of the sahibs, which are not the ways of the dark people. I was but a stripling, and knew little of what happened beyond the village of my birth where I worked in the fields and tended the cattle until the day came of which I now speak; and I learned from my father that it is well to obey the orders of the master without thought or question, even when it might be hard to understand the reason of his wishes.

'Thou art somewhat of an owl,' my father told me, 'and not so sharp or clever as was I, who rose to be head-servant in my master's house. But thou hast enough sense to understand an order, and maybe with diligence and obedience thou mayest rise from dish-washer to table-servant, and from table-servant to *khansamah*,* and then will it be easy with the bazaar accounts in thy keeping, and power in the establishment, to gather rupees till thou canst return to thy home a person of wealth and importance, even as I did.'

'And what if the sahib beats me for no fault, as thou sayest will happen on occasions?'

'Take thy beating and say nothing. Above all things, do not run away. The Feringhees themselves are brave, though they are dogs and sons of dogs, and when they behold courage in others do they respect it. A beating does little harm. I lived once with a colonel-sahib who gave medicine as a punishment, and that was bad. There are certain sahibs who neither drink, nor beat, nor swear, but it is hard for a new-comer without recommendations or experience to obtain service with such, and the sahibs whom I served in the old days have now all died or gone back across the black water many years since. Thou must be content at first with what thou canst get; only remember this—obey orders without question, quarrel not with thy fellow-servants, and squander not thy wages in the bazaar.'

I pondered over the wise words of my father and laid them up in my heart, and I resolved that I would rise, even as he had done, to be the headservant of a sahib's household, that in time I might return to my village with riches and influence.

When we reached the city, we stayed for the night in the *serai*,* and until dawn I could not sleep for the strange sights and sounds, and the crowd that came and went; never before had I seen so many men together. In the morning sunshine we went through the streets, and I stared at the glittering vessels in the brass-shops, at the display of sweetmeats, toys, and jewels, and the gay materials shown by the cloth-merchants. My father bought me a white muslin coat, a pair of calico trousers tight below the knee, and a new *puggaree*;* and we took seats in the *ekka** and drove out to the part where the sahibs dwell beyond the city. Here it was all open space and broad roads, with trees of mango, teak, and tamarind, and the gardens were very beautiful. My father told me that, though the native city was wide and full of people, there were now but few sahibs, and no regiments at all; whereas he remembered that before the Mutiny there had been a large cantonment and many sepoys.

There was no service to be had at the house of the magistrate-sahib, or with the colonel-sahib of police, nor with the doctor-sahib, so we went to the bungalow of the engineer-sahib who looked after the roads and buildings of the district. There we heard that a dish-washer was needed, and the *khansamah-jee* said that if my father gave him a *backsheesh*, and I promised him a percentage of my pay, he could get me the place without any recommendation. He also said that the engineer-sahib was a good sahib, and the service to be desired, and that I should be well treated. So after some argument my father paid the *khansamah*, who was named Kullan, and I gave the promise. My father told me again to obey orders and answer not to abuse, and then he left me and went back to his village.

But after he had gone I learned from the bearer, who was also a follower of the Prophet, that no servant ever stayed long with the engineer-sahib. 'For,' he said, 'the sahib is truly a devil, and when I am near him my fear of him is such that my liver melts. Sometimes for weeks will he be quiet, and then he will drink too much whisky, and for days we go in fear of our lives.'

I felt angered that Kullan should have told my father naught of this, and though I said nothing I determined that, should the chance arise to do him an evil in return, I would remember how he had lied and taken my father's money, and bound me to give him percentage on my pay.

When I beheld my master I could well believe that what the bearer had told me was true, for the sahib had hair that was the colour of a polished copper cooking-vessel, and the flesh of his face was like unto raw meat; he ate his food with haste like a pariah dog, and looked about him as though he feared an enemy. Nevertheless, I stayed in his service, for was I not more or less in bondage to the *khansamah-jee*?

and also for the first few weeks matters went well. The sahib sometimes beat and abused the other servants, but not badly, and me he never noticed. I took care to be diligent over my work, I learned the ways of the compound, Kullan taught me how to cook (for this spared him trouble when he wished to stay late in the bazaar), and I helped the bearer to brush the sahib's clothes and to keep the rooms tidy.

But the peace did not continue. The sahib began to drink much whisky, and one evening, when some matter displeased him during dinner he sprang at the bearer, who was also table-servant, and smote him heavily, using words that burned mine ears as I sat in the pantry washing the dishes. The bearer cried out that he was hurt unto death; his *puggaree* came off, and the sahib kicked it through the open door and across the veranda into the bushes; then he shook the man as a dog will shake vermin, and all the time he smote and kicked him, and roared abuse.

For some hours afterwards the bearer lay in his outhouse groaning, and later in the night-time he rose and took his belongings and ran away without his arrears of wages or a written recommendation. Thus was the *khansamah* forced to do the bearer's work as well as his own, whereat he grumbled sorely; and my duties were doubled also, for I now helped to wait at table; and all the time I watched for a chance of letting the sahib see that I feared him not, for I remembered my father's words.

Two days later, when the sahib was sitting at breakfast eating but little and drinking whisky, the *khansamah* spilt some sauce on the tablecloth, and my knees shook as the sahib rose slowly from his seat, and, looking at Kullan with eyes like those of a tiger, walked towards him just as the striped-one approaches its victim. Kullan knelt and prayed for mercy, but the sahib dragged him over the floor till his coat came off in the sahib's hand, and he kicked the man along the ground like a game ball, driving him into the veranda. Kullan rose quickly, looking like a beast that is hunted, but before he could flee the sahib caught him and pushed him into the lamp-closet that led from the veranda, and locked the door. He laughed as he put the padlock key in his pocket, and heard Kullan crying and smiting at the door from the darkness within the go-down.* When he turned and saw me looking, he shook his fist at me, and told me to go to my work.

Then the sahib went to his room and lay on the bed and slept, and I cleared away the breakfast and washed up everything; afterwards I went to the kitchen and found it empty; the servants' houses were also empty, and none answered to my call. They had all fled in fear, having doubtless heard the noise of the sahib's rage, and there was no one left save I, Ram Din the dish-washer, and Kullan the *khansamah*, who was crying and calling in the lamp go-down.

Towards sundown a telegram came for the sahib, and not without misgiving in my heart I took it to his room. He awoke and read the telegram, and then arose in haste, speaking of trouble concerning a bridge in the district, and bidding me pack his bag with clothes sufficient for a day and night, and order his trap to be got ready, and bring him whisky.

I packed the bag and brought the whisky, and I said, 'Your highness, there is no syce* in the stables, they have all run away. But thy slave can harness the horse.'

I went straightaway, and with trouble and patience I put the horse to the cart and brought it to the door. The sahib did not beat me, though from want of knowledge I had done it badly, and when I told him there were no servants left at all he cursed their souls to hell, and bade me stay and take care of everything till he should return.

I asked him, 'What are the orders concerning Kullan *khansamah* who is imprisoned within the lamp go-down?'

He laughed, and the sound was like the cry of the hyena round the walls of the village at dusk. 'The order is that he stay there till I return. Dost thou understand?'

I salaamed, and he drove away.

Then did my heart glow within me, for now had my time come, and the sahib should see that I was of use, and could obey. All that evening was I alone in the kitchen, and Kullan cried in the go-down. I fed the horses and the fowls, and after locking up the house at night I took my bed and placed it in the veranda that I might guard against thieves. But I could not sleep by reason of the noise made by the *khansamah*, and I answered him not, for I feared he might persuade me to disobey orders and break open the padlock, and I remembered my father's words. Also did I rejoice that Kullan was in trouble, for had he not deceived my father and taken money under false pretences, and did he not exact percentage from my miserable pay as dishwasher? So I smiled when I heard him beating on the door and calling, and I only feared that when the sahib returned and let him out Kullan might kill me for heeding not his entreaties.

But the sahib did not return the next evening nor the next, and I was forced to move my bed from the front veranda to the back of the house on account of the howling of Kullan in the go-down. I slept the other side of the house, and I kept away from the front veranda, but still could I hear him wailing and calling, and I refrained from bursting open the padlock on the door because of the orders of the sahib.

On the fourth day the sahib had not returned; and the voice of Kullan was hoarse and faint. By the sixth day it was altogether silent, and I thought, 'Now shall I rise to be chief servant, and I shall appoint and have dominion over the other servants; also now will the household accounts be in my hands, and I shall amass wealth.'

When the sahib came back on the morning of the seventh day he looked weary, and as though he had suffered much care and anxiety; he took no notice of me nor did he ask me any questions. I led his horse and trap to the stables, I got his bath and laid out his clean clothes, and brought his breakfast. All the time he was deep in thought and was making figures with a pencil on a piece of paper. I wished to speak, and remind him about Kullan, but it was hard to attract his attention. I coughed and walked about the room, and moved the plates on the breakfast-table, and I took a fly-trap and killed flies with some noise.

At last, when the sahib began to light a big cheroot, I craved permission to speak, and he told me to say what I had to say quickly and not to disturb him.

'Sahib,' I said, with humility, 'concerning the matter of Kullan *khansamah* who is in the go-down, it is necessary to get out the lamp oil.'

He stared at me maybe for one minute, and then he dropped his cheroot, and his red face became white as my clean muslin coat. He rose and pushed me aside, saying no word, and strode into the veranda, I following him. He searched for the key of the padlock in his pockets, but found it not: so he wrenched the chain from the woodwork of the door with great force, and the dead body of Kullan *khansamah* fell out of the go-down face downwards on the veranda floor.

Then the sahib caught me by the shoulder and shook me backwards and forwards, shouting in mine ear and calling me names, and his voice sounded as though his throat were filled with dust. He cried out that he had meant to return in a day and a night, but that the damage to the bridge had delayed him, and he had forgotten all about Kullan the *khansamah*. He cursed me for a fool because I had not broken open the padlock.

'Sahib,' I said, and bowed my head before him, 'the order was that Kullan should stay in the go-down until the day of thine honour's return. This slave did but obey thy commands.'

Then the face of the sahib grew purple, and he choked and gasped, and fell at my feet with foam on his lips; and with much effort I got him into the house, and laid him on his bed.

Afterwards he was ill for many days; but no one, not even the doctor-sahib, or the nurse-mem who came to take care of him, ever knew what had happened, for before I fetched the doctor-sahib I pushed the body of Kullan *khansamah* back into the go-down and left it there till the night-time, when I buried it in a corner of the compound with all precaution.

There were none to witness the burial or to ask any question, for he was a down-country man, and I said in the bazaar that he had departed to his home.

While the sahib lay sick I made for him jelly, soup and custard, for I had learned from Kullan how to cook. I took my turn in watching by his bedside, and when his health returned I told him privately of what I had done.

For many years after this was I the sahib's head servant on thirty rupees a month, and he was as wax in the hands of his slave, Ram Din. I it was who had charge of the sahib's keys and kept his money. It was I appointed the other servants, and exacted percentage from their wages. It was I who made payments and gave the orders, and the sahib ever settled my accounts without argument. I had authority in the compound. I grew prosperous, and had a large stomach, and a watch and chain.

Now has the sahib retired from the service of the Government and has gone to England, and I, Ram Din, have bought land in mine own district and have married four wives and am a person of importance in the village.

So is it true what my father had told me: that by obeying orders and being fearless may a man rise in the service of the sahib people, and gain wealth and honour.

See also: Barker; Baughan; Beames; Kipling; Steel; Stevenson.

JAMES JOYCE
(1882–1941)

Ireland at the Bar (1907)

Several years ago a sensational trial was held in Ireland. In a lonely place in a western province, called Maamtrasna, a murder was committed.* Four or five townsmen, all belonging to the ancient tribe of the Joyces, were arrested. The oldest of them, the seventy year old Myles Joyce, was the prime suspect. Public opinion at the time thought him innocent and today considers him a martyr. Neither the old man nor the others accused knew English. The court had to resort to the services of an interpreter. The questioning, conducted through the interpreter, was at times comic and at times tragic. On one side was the excessively ceremonious interpreter, on the other the patriarch of a miserable tribe unused to civilized customs, who seemed stupefied by all the judicial ceremony. The magistrate said:

'Ask the accused if he saw the lady that night.' The question was referred to him in Irish, and the old man broke out into an involved explanation, gesticulating, appealing to the others accused and to heaven. Then he quieted down, worn out by his effort, and the interpreter turned to the magistrate and said:

'He says no, "your worship".'

'Ask him if he was in that neighbourhood at that hour.' The old man again began to talk, to protest, to shout, almost beside himself with the anguish of being unable to understand or to make himself understood, weeping in anger and terror. And the interpreter, again, dryly:

'He says no, "your worship".'

When the questioning was over, the guilt of the poor old man was declared proved, and he was remanded to a superior court which condemned him to the noose. On the day the sentence was executed, the square in front of the prison was jammed full of kneeling people shouting prayers in Irish for the repose of Myles Joyce's soul. The story was told that the executioner, unable to make the victim understand him, kicked at the miserable man's head in anger to shove it into the noose.

The figure of this dumbfounded old man, a remnant of a civilization not ours, deaf and dumb before his judge, is a symbol of the Irish nation at the bar of public opinion. Like him, she is unable to appeal to the modern conscience of England and other countries. The English journalists act as interpreters between Ireland and the English electorate, which gives them ear from time to time and ends up being vexed by the endless complaints of the Nationalist representatives who have entered her House, as she believes, to disrupt its order and extort money. Abroad there is no talk of Ireland except when uprisings break out, like those which made the telegraph office hop these last few days.* Skimming over the dispatches from London (which, though they lack pungency, have something of the laconic quality of the interpreter mentioned above), the public conceives of the Irish as highwaymen with distorted faces, roaming the night with the object of taking the hide of every Unionist. And by the real sovereign of Ireland, the Pope, such news is received like so many dogs in church. Already weakened by their long journey, the cries are nearly spent when they arrive at the bronze door. The messengers of the people who never in the past have renounced the Holy See, the only Catholic people to whom faith also means the exercise of faith, are rejected in favour of messengers of a monarch, descended from apostates, who solemnly apostasized himself on the day of his coronation, declaring in the presence of his nobles and commons that the rites of the Roman Catholic Church are 'superstition and idolatry'.

There are twenty million Irishmen scattered all over the world. The Emerald Isle contains only a small part of them. But, reflecting that, while England makes the Irish question the centre of all her internal politics she proceeds with a wealth of good judgment in quickly disposing of the more complex questions of colonial politics, the observer can do no less than ask himself why St George's Channel makes an abyss deeper than the ocean between Ireland and her proud dominator. In fact, the Irish question is not solved even today, after six centuries of armed occupation and more than a hundred years of English legislation, which has reduced the population of the unhappy island from eight to four million, quadrupled the taxes, and twisted the agrarian problem into many more knots.

In truth there is no problem more snarled than this one. The Irish themselves understand little about it, the English even less. For other people it is a black plague. But on the other hand the Irish know that it is the cause of all their sufferings, and therefore they often adopt violent methods of solution. For example, twenty-eight years ago, seeing themselves reduced to misery by the brutalities of the large landholders, they refused to pay their land rents and obtained from Gladstone remedies and reforms. Today, seeing pastures full of well fed cattle while an eighth of the population lacks means of subsistence, they drive the cattle from the farms. In irritation, the Liberal government arranges to refurbish the coercive tactics of the Conservatives, and for several weeks the London press dedicates innumerable articles to the agrarian crisis, which, it says, is very serious. It publishes alarming news of agrarian revolts, which is then reproduced by journalists abroad.

I do not propose to make an exegesis of the Irish agrarian question nor to relate what goes on behind the scene in the two-faced politics of the government. But I think it useful to make a modest correction of facts. Anyone who has read the telegrams launched from London is sure that Ireland is undergoing a period of unusual crime. An erroneous judgment, very erroneous. There is less crime in Ireland than in any other country in Europe. In Ireland there is no organized underworld. When one of those events which the Parisian journalists, with atrocious irony, call 'red idylls' occurs, the whole country is shaken by it. It is true that in recent months there were two violent deaths in Ireland, but at the hands of British troops in Belfast, where the soldiers fired without warning on an unarmed crowd and killed a man and woman. There were attacks on cattle; but not even these were in Ireland, where the crowd was content to open the stalls and chase the cattle through several miles of streets, but at Great Wyrley in England, where for six years bestial, maddened criminals have ravaged the cattle to such an extent that the English companies will no longer insure them. Five years ago an innocent man, now at liberty, was condemned to forced labour to appease public indignation. But even while he was in prison the crimes continued. And last week two horses were found dead with the usual slashes in their lower abdomen and their bowels scattered in the grass.

See also: Aurobindo; Blyden; Casely Hayford; Plaatje; Schreiner; Woolf.

EDMUND CANDLER
(1874–1926)

from Káshi (1910)

[. . .] From the balcony of a flower-shop one can look down straight
on the gate of Vishéshwar* without being observed, and note from a
few yards the expression of every face that goes in and out. In the
narrow compass between the lintels one may see the epitome of
Hindustan, and to any one who knows enough of its dark worship to
divine even vaguely the impulses that move the people, there is no
more illuminating sight in India. In the morning the gate is thronged.
Pilgrims are entering four abreast, while others are trying to thrust
their way out, holding their brass vessels of Ganges water over their
heads, lest they should be jostled and spill it,—for there are other
shrines to visit and other libations to pour. It is a heterogeneous
crowd. A group of unveiled Dekhani women* come along in dark
blue and green, and colour all the street. They are pilgrims from the
south. There is peace in their faces. Beside them, equally devout if
less picturesque, are women of the city. Many of them carry infants,
whose short frocks are often in brilliant contrast to the maternal *sarhi*.
A bundle of deep red velvet glows on a bosom of puce. There is no
room for disharmony. An orange babe and a magenta mother are not
amiss. And these naked coal-eyed infants in arms are strangely
unimpressed. Held in a fold of the *sarhi*, they sport with their
mother's ear-rings, dreamily chew sugar-cane, or profanely tap the
gate and walls of the shrine with a lacquer stick.

As the Dekhani women leave the shrine and flood the passage
again with indigo tints, they meet a contrary wave of orange. The
blue is thrust to the wall, and the orange sweeps imperiously through.
It is the Mahunt of Ajodhya,* a heavy, square-faced, bull-throated
man, arch-priest of Siva, who rides proudly in his lacquered palanquin, wreathed in marigolds, attended by his chelas*—Brahmins all,
and only less proud than himself. A dozen precede, and a score or
more follow, deep-browed, sunken-eyed, bald-pated, orange-robed
ecclesiastics, who need no lictors, so eminent and palpable is their
authority. The troop passes without an obeisance to the shrine.

The parted crowd meet again and surge towards the gate. A stout Bilaspuri, with his short beard, ear-rings, and pail of brass, forges perfunctorily through. A shock-headed Bengali slips in behind and gains the courtyard in his wake. A dainty Sikh lady, her pink veil tilted forward at the mouth, is thrust against the wall unheeded, while her skirted Punjabi sister is held up by a crowd of drab-coloured pilgrims from Dinapur. Into this packed throng intrudes the sacred bull of Siva. I watched the privileged beast saunter down the passage, nosing the ground in front of every niche that contained a shrine. From Ganesh he stole a sour berry or two; from Sinaichar, the Saturday god, a bunch of fallen leaves. As he turned the corner the vendor of flowers by Anapurna's* temple lifted his basket uneasily; but he passed, hesitated at the gate of Vishéshwar, and elected to enter, thrusting his nose and shoulders into the mob. Soon after, a sturdy up-country vagabond tried to arrogate to himself the same licence and hustle a path through. Cries of dismay and protest met him, as vessels were upset and holy water spilled to the ground, and the clamour brought in three policemen from the street,—turbaned, khaki-clad servants of the Raj,—who ejected him with more cuffs than ceremony.

The commotion roused a lean mendicant who had been waiting by the gate for at least an hour, as still as a moth on a wall. Hunger, or the sight of his empty bowl, transformed him. He awoke, like an insect, from dead passivity into flight, and began to skim among the crowd as a bee among flowers, touching this one on the shoulder, the other on the arm, and stroking another on the nape of the neck, offering his empty bowl, always in vain. For some reason or other the pious would have none of him, and he flitted down the alley to Gyan Kup* without a dole.

Many who pass through the gate have the air of merchants and brokers. The Marwari* seems to have made his bargain with God. It is a case of definite gift and definite reward: he has bought so much security and paid the price. So he strides out briskly, without the least awe, for he is a busy man and feels that this is possibly the least remunerative of his deals during the day.

But the measure and intensity of faith are best observed in the evening, before the second tide of worshippers is full, when the pious may make the *Sashtangam*, or prostration of the eight members, without fear of being trampled under-foot. A sad-eyed cowled

Brahmin widow, who has been carried to the gate in a palanquin, floats through ecstatically. A Saddhu* follows, and presses his forehead in the mire. One may wait ten minutes before one sees another such expression of intense faith. The martial Sikh merely stoops to rub his hand in a puddle of votive water and rub it on his brow. Others are content to throw a flower at Ganesh over the door. One feels that if one could have stood here fifty or a hundred years ago, one would have seen less casual worship and more prostrations. The ritual is intact, but the idolaters decadent. They wear shoes, and generally defile themselves with leather, omit the salute to the ten winds of the body, let the shadow of pariahs cross their food, herd with people of lower caste in packed railway carriages, carry over the threshold the dead who have passed late in the orbit of the moon, and let rude little boys throw stones at Siva's bull and go to school without an offering to Ganesh. In morals, perhaps, they are no better or worse, but that has nothing to do with their faith.

What makes the Hindu so complex and inscrutable is that there is no custom so bound up with his tradition but some sect or family will be privileged to violate it. Practices which are abhorrent at one time are prescribed at another. There are seasons when he is bidden to eat flesh, drink intoxicating drinks, and defy principles the infringement of which, at ordinary times, would lose him his caste. In every district, too, there are folk who have peculiar rites and customs contradictory to the general ideal. So when all these castes and sects are drawn together to Benares for common worship from the ends of Hindustan, it is not to be wondered at that one comes across many drifting atoms which must remain mysterious. My last impression of Vishéshwar is a Punjabi mendicant with a turban of pale saffron gauze, abundance of fine clothes, a saffron scarf swung over his shoulders, and wreaths of marigold round his neck. He strode up jauntily to the gate, took from the folds of his dress a penny English flute and played little snatches of music with the careless finish of a master. He asked no alms and received none; but once an oddity in an orange shift gave him a wreath of marigolds, which he added to those round his neck,—a simple but to me inscrutable action, and one of the many hundred things I saw by the gate of Vishéshwar and did not understand. Why did he stand there and play the flute? It and his staff proclaimed the man a beggar, but I never saw any person less like one in my life than this lusty Punjabi with his quizzical patronising mien, his roguish assertiveness, and general air of wellbeing. And what tie of sympathy, fraternity, duty, love, or fear could there be between him and the apparently infirm little body in the orange shift whom he followed twenty paces up the street?

The mob of religious mendicants perplexes, attracts, and repels. The wild-eyed Bairagi, smeared all over with ashes of cow-dung, and wearing coils of rope matted in his coarse dyed hair; the Yogi on his bed of spikes; the Sannyasi, naked or dressed like a clown; the gentle Saddhu in his salmon-coloured robe; the Dandi with the wand that must not touch the ground; the Talingi* with his staff and gourd and antelope's skin,—are at first-sight elements of drama, but one soon tires of them and their harlequin gear, and finds the true romance in the simple devotee. Yet one in ten thousand may be the genuine anchorite dear to the romancist, the man who has weighed the fat years with their cares and obligations and found them lean and light as thistledown in the scale against the emancipation of the spirit. One likes to think that if one waits long enough a familiar figure will pass through the gate wearing the *rudraksha*,* and a votary make obeisance to the lingam who could find his way blindfold from Petty Cury to Magdalen Bridge.*

To understand the spirit in which the Saddhu is received one must readjust all one's ideas of almsgiving. The Hindu mendicant is honoured, he demands, gratitude is out of the question; alms are his birthright. When refused, he has been known to enter the house of the offender and break his cooking-vessels. In seasons of pilgrimage flocks of Sannyasis scour the land like locusts. At Benares there must be many thousands of them. Twice in a day I saw the house of the Maharajah of D—— invaded. First, in the morning, I was sitting in the verandah overlooking the river when four Saddhus entered by the corkscrew stairs, passed the Sikh guard by the door and the rifle-rack, and gained the balcony unchallenged. Four staffs were planted in four flower-pots, each with a little salmon-coloured rag attached, Saddhu colour, to proclaim that the staff was all they possessed in the world. They waited patiently, and were fed. These were casual visitors. But in the evening of the same day, when I was again a guest in the house, the licensed pensioners came. These were twenty Saddhus, who squatted in a corner turret set apart for their use, and soon raised such a clamour of abuse and indignant protest that one of the Maharajah's servants was sent to ask what was the matter. Their grievance was that they had been given inferior, or insufficient, tobacco.

It was good fortune to be admitted into the house of such an orthodox Hindu as the Maharajah of D——. the building is one of the finest on the river front, equally beautiful and massive. The balcony, where guests are received, is supported by two immense corbelled pilasters, and projects over the ghât, or, as it seems from within, over the Ganges. The face of the house may be described as sixty feet of solid foundation and breastwork, supporting fifty feet of palace. Add the flags descending from the base to the stream, and the whole pile from the topmost parapet to the water measures, when Gunga is not in flood, a good hundred-and-fifty feet.

From the balcony one looks down on the house of the Maharana of X., an ancient neglected mansion, but inveterately Hindu. On the roof is a garden which the Maharana's sacred bull shares with the monkey and the peacock. From the shade of a tamarind tree squat Hanuman surveys Gunga, the silted sand beyond, and the packed city spreading out towards the east. A sacred prospect, but to the god's eyes no doubt imperfect. For seen like this, in a bird's-eye view from the roof of a house overlooking the river or from the railway bridge as the train rolls into Káshi, Benares is as deceptive as the ordinary Hindu. Two alien things dominate the city, the great minarets of Aurungzeb's mosque and the massive girders of the Dufferin Bridge. That is to say, the two most prominent features of Benares are merely casual and uncharacteristic, as distant from the heart of the place as any expression of the human mind can be. They obtrude incongruously, mere surface excrescences, while underneath hidden world-old influences which have outlasted change and revolution course through the body like sap in the bough. The Hindus were throwing marigolds at the feet of Siva when our ancestors were dressed in woad; they performed the sacrifice of the *Hom** with precisely the same rites hundreds of years before Attila swept over Europe. Conquest does not impress them; the motor and the locomotive are not half so wonderful as Vishnu's footprints. And our modern engines give impetus, rather than check, to the cause of the priests, for every year pilgrims flock to Benares in greater numbers. The sum of devotion may be less, but the devotees are more. We span the Ganges for them with iron, and the faithful use our road to approach their gods without sparing any of their awe for the new miracle. To the devout we and our railways are a passing accident, to be used or ignored as indifferently as stepping-stones across a brook. The city is too old in spirit to resent those iron girders, that stucco mission church; they are merely another wrinkle on her brow. The parable is repeated from Rameswaram to Peshawar, —India is too old to resent us. Yet who can doubt that she will survive us?

The secret of her permanence lies, I think, in her passivity and her power to assimilate. The faith that will not fight cannot yield. Before I left Káshi I met a strictly orthodox Hindu B.A., one of those elusive unsatisfactory beings who is ready to explain Karma by heredity, the Sankhya philosophy* by evolution, and yet stand by the laws of Manu and his gods.

'Why, of course,' he said, 'I believe that any one who dies within the Panch Kosi road* at Benares will attain salvation, *eef* he has faith enough to believe that by so dying he will be saved.'

Thus the wretched man stripped his gods of their divinely capricious power. I felt that the terrific arm of Siva had fallen limp, the Trimurti* become impotent and dishonoured, the effulgence of Brahma's godhead dimmed, and Káshi 'splendid' and miraculous no more, but the mother of quibbles wholly rational, trite, and dull.

See also: Arnold; Bird; Clifford; Kingsley; Sorabji; Steel; Trevelyan.

STEPHEN LEACOCK
(1869–1944)

Back to the Bush (1910)

I have a friend called Billy who has the Bush Mania. By trade he is a doctor, but I do not think that he needs to sleep out of doors. In ordinary things his mind appears sound. Over the tops of his gold-rimmed spectacles, as he bends forward to speak to you, there gleams nothing but amiability and kindliness. Like all the rest of us he is, or was until he forgot it all, an extremely well-educated man.

I am aware of no criminal strain in his blood. Yet Billy is in reality hopelessly unbalanced. He has the Mania of the Open Woods.

Worse than that, he is haunted with the desire to drag his friends with him into the depths of the Bush.

Whenever we meet he starts to talk about it.

Not long ago I met him in the club.

'I wish,' he said, 'you'd let me take you clear away up the Gatineau.'*

'Yes, I wish I would, I don't think,' I murmured to myself, but I humoured him and said:

'How do we go, Billy, in a motor-car or by train?'

'No, we paddle.'

'And is it up-stream all the way?'

'Oh, yes,' Billy said enthusiastically.

'And how many days do we paddle all day to get up?'

'Six.'

'Couldn't we do it in less?'

'Yes,' Billy answered, feeling that I was entering into the spirit of the thing, 'if we start each morning just before daylight and paddle hard till moonlight, we could do it in five days and a half.'

'Glorious! and are there portages?'

'Lots of them.'

'And at each of these do I carry two hundred pounds of stuff up a hill on my back?'

'Yes.'

'And will there be a guide, a genuine, dirty-looking Indian guide?'

'Yes.'

'And can I sleep next to him?'

'Oh, yes, if you want to.'

'And when we get to the top, what is there?'

'Well, we go over the height of land.'

'Oh, we do, do we? And is the height of land all rock and about three hundred yards up-hill? And do I carry a barrel of flour up it? And does it roll down and crush me on the other side? Look here, Billy, this trip is a great thing, but it is too luxurious for me. If you will have me paddled up the river in a large iron canoe with an awning, carried over the portages in a sedan-chair, taken across the height of land in a palanquin or a howdah, and lowered down the other side in a derrick, I'll go. Short of that, the thing would be too fattening.'

Billy was discouraged and left me. But he has since returned repeatedly to the attack.

He offers to take me to the head-waters of the Batiscan.* I am content at the foot.

He wants us to go to the sources of the Attahwapiscat. I don't.

He says I ought to see the grand chutes of the Kewakasis. Why should I?

I have made Billy a counter-proposition that he strike through the Adirondacks (in the train) to New York, from there portage to Atlantic City, then to Washington, carrying our own grub (in the dining-car), camp there a few days (at the Willard), and then back, I to return by train and Billy on foot with the outfit.

The thing is still unsettled.

Billy, of course, is only one of thousands that have got this mania. And the autumn is the time when it rages at its worst.

Every day there move northward trains, packed full of lawyers, bankers, and brokers, headed for the bush. They are dressed up to look like pirates. They wear slouch hats, flannel shirts, and leather breeches with belts. They could afford much better clothes than these, but they won't use them. I don't know where they get these clothes. I think the railroad lends them out. They have guns between their knees and big knives at their hips. They smoke the worst tobacco they can find, and they carry ten gallons of alcohol per man in the baggage car.

In the intervals of telling lies to one another they read the railroad pamphlets about hunting. This kind of literature is deliberately and fiendishly contrived to infuriate their mania. I know all about these pamphlets because I write them. I once, for instance, wrote up, from imagination, a little place called Dog Lake at the end of a branch line. The place had failed as a settlement, and the railroad had decided to turn it into a hunting resort. I did the turning. I think I did it rather well, rechristening the lake and stocking the place with suitable varieties of game. The pamphlet ran like this.

'The limpid waters of Lake Owatawetness (the name, according to the old Indian legends of the place, signifies, The Mirror of the Almighty) abound with every known variety of fish. Near to its surface, so close that the angler may reach out his hand and stroke them, schools of pike, pickerel, mackerel, doggerel, and chickerel jostle one another in the water. They rise instantaneously to the bait and swim gratefully ashore holding it in their mouths. In the middle depth of the waters of the lake, the sardine, the lobster, the kippered herring, the anchovy and other tinned varieties of fish disport themselves with evident gratification, while even lower in the pellucid depths the dog-fish, the hog-fish, the log-fish, and the sword-fish whirl about in never-ending circles.

'Nor is Lake Owatawetness merely an Angler's Paradise. Vast forests of primeval pine slope to the very shores of the lake, to which descend great droves of bears—brown, green, and bear-coloured—while as the shades of evening fall, the air is loud with the lowing of moose, cariboo, antelope, cantelope, musk-oxes, musk-rats, and other graminivorous mammalia of the forest. These enormous quadrumana generally move off about 10.30 p.m., from which hour until 11.45 p.m. the whole shore is reserved for bison and buffalo.

'After midnight hunters who so desire it can be chased through the woods, for any distance and at any speed they select, by jaguars, panthers, cougars, tigers, and jackals whose ferocity is reputed to be such that they will tear the breeches off a man with their teeth in their eagerness to sink their fangs in his palpitating flesh. Hunters, attention! Do not miss such attractions as these!'

I have seen men—quiet, reputable, well-shaved men—reading that pamphlet of mine in the rotundas of hotels, with their eyes blazing with excitement. I think it is the jaguar attraction that hits them the hardest, because I notice them rub themselves sympathetically with their hands while they read.

Of course, you can imagine the effect of this sort of literature on the brains of men fresh from their offices, and dressed out as pirates.

They just go crazy and stay crazy.

Just watch them when they get into the bush.

Notice that well-to-do stockbroker crawling about on his stomach in the underbrush, with his spectacles shining like gig-lamps. What is he doing? He is after a cariboo that isn't there. He is 'stalking' it. With his stomach. Of course, away down in his heart he knows that the cariboo isn't there and never was; but that man read my pamphlet and went crazy. He can't help it: he's *got* to stalk something. Mark him as he crawls along; see him crawl through a thimbleberry bush (very quietly so that the cariboo won't hear the noise of the prickles going into him), then through a bee's nest, gently and slowly, so that the cariboo will not take fright when the bees are stinging him. Sheer woodcraft! Yes, mark him. Mark him in any way you like. Go up behind him and paint a blue cross on the seat of his pants as he crawls. He'll never notice. He thinks he's a hunting-dog. Yet this is the man who laughs at his little son of ten for crawling round under the dining-room table with a mat over his shoulders, and pretending to be a bear.

Now see these other men in camp.

Someone has told them—I think I first started the idea in my pamphlet—that the thing is to sleep on a pile of hemlock branches. I think I told them to listen to the wind sowing (you know the word I mean), sowing and crooning in the giant pines. So there they are upside down, doubled up on a couch of green spikes that would have killed St Sebastian. They stare up at the sky with blood-shot, restless eyes, waiting for the crooning to begin. And there isn't a sow in sight.

Here is another man, ragged and with a six days' growth of beard, frying a piece of bacon on a stick over a little fire. Now what does he think he is? The *chef* of the Waldorf Astoria? Yes, he does, and what's more he thinks that that miserable bit of bacon, cut with a tobacco knife from a chunk of meat that lay six days in the rain, is fit to eat. What's more, he'll eat it. So will the rest. They're all crazy together.

There's another man, the Lord help him, who thinks he has the 'knack' of being a carpenter. He is hammering up shelves to a tree. Till the shelves fall down he thinks he is a wizard. Yet this is the same man who swore at his wife for asking him to put up a shelf in the back kitchen. 'How the blazes,' he asked, 'could he nail the damn thing up? Did she think he was a plumber?'

After all, never mind.

Provided they are happy up there, let them stay.

Personally, I wouldn't mind if they didn't come back and lie about it. They get back to the city dead fagged for want of sleep, sogged with alcohol, bitten brown by the bush-flies, trampled on by the moose, and chased through the brush by bears and skunks—and they have the nerve to say that they like it.

Sometimes I think they do.

Men are only animals anyway. They like to get out into the woods and growl round at night and feel something bite them.

Only why haven't they the imagination to be able to do the same thing with less fuss? Why not take their coats and collars off in the office and crawl round on the floor and growl at one another. It would be just as good.

See also: 1880s and 1890s Canadian Poetry; Duncan; Fairbridge; Haggard; Henty; Lawson; Paterson.

DOROTHEA FAIRBRIDGE
(1862–1931)

Pamela (1911)

Over the whispering brown grasses and pink gladioli that carpet the flat top of Table Mountain strode two men. The stillness of the air was unbroken save for the scrunch of little white pebbles under their feet and the chip-chip of small brown birds which scurried away at their approach, melting into the scrubby tussocks of reed and low tufts of heath.

As they came near the edge of the sheer wall of grey rock that rises behind the City of Cape Town a hum of sound floated up to their ears—that ollapodrida of faint noises which only he may hear who stands three or four thousand feet above a busy town. Through the hum distinct notes were audible in the crystal clearness of the atmosphere—the throaty crowings of laggard roosters, the shriek of the long train crawling out of Cape Town on its way to the Zambesi, the hooter from the tobacco-factory, the clang and rumble of the electric trams. And on a ledge two thousand feet below them perched a brown-skinned boy thrumming on a banjo one of the queer oriental melodies, so unmelodious in European ears, which have come down to the coloured people of the Cape from their Batavian forbears.*

Harrison—stock broker in the city of London, pillar of St Hilda's, South Kensington, owner of a yacht in which he never had time to sail, and a moor in Scotland over which his friends shot each August and September—drew in a long breath of the diamond air.

'It's worth it,' he said unexpansively.

The other man lowered himself on to a grey boulder and stared at the view as though he had never seen it before. 'The climb?' he said at last. 'I am glad that you are pleased.'

At the dull apathy in his voice Harrison turned and looked at him in surprise. Wilfred Hayes paid no attention to the movement, but continued to stare at the wonderful picture that lay unrolled at his feet; but with eyes that, as Harrison now saw, marked nothing of blue mountains touched with snow, of the calm waters of the Bay, of wooded kloofs down which tinkled clear brown streamlets, of the red-roofed houses and straight streets of the city at the foot of the mountain. His gaze, with all his soul in it, was fixed on the little flat island that is at the entrance to Table Bay—the low sweep of sand over which the winds moan and the sea-birds wail and the Angel of Affliction spreads his wings.

'What's the matter?' Harrison felt genuine distress as he looked at Hayes and saw the grey dreariness in his face.

They had been friends at Winchester, but had drifted out of each other's ken in the years that had intervened, to meet again unexpectedly on the deck of a Union-Castle steamer. Harrison, of whom the great modern god that men called overstrain had taken heavy toll, was on his way southward with two alternatives confronting him—three months' complete rest from business or——. He didn't care to think of the other alternative, so had taken a taxi from the doctor's door to Fenchurch Street and booked a cabin in the 'Saxon.' Within an hour of sailing, profoundly bored with the prospect of a solitary voyage, he had thankfully hailed his old schoolfellow, returning to a sugar-plantation in Natal after a brief visit to England, ending in a briefer honeymoon.

The bride was one of those pleasant, healthy girls whom you know to be English at a glance, whether you meet them in the Rue de Rivoli or in Adderley Street, Cape Town. Not aggressively English, you understand, but unmistakably the output of the little island which moulds them in their thousands—and might do worse work. You would never have paused to ask Mrs Hayes whether she played hockey and golf, skated, danced, or swam, ate a solid afternoon tea and rode to hounds—all these accomplishments were apparent at sight, as apparent as her robust good looks and evident common sense. And there was nothing pedantic about her vocabulary. Everything that wasn't 'rippin'' or 'simply lovely' was '*rather* nice'—from Salome to Tariff Reform.*

If there were moments when Hayes, after the whirl and excitement of a hurried courtship, wondered whether the frank, cheerful young woman who had consented to go back with him to Natal and set his rambling bungalow and uncontrolled Indian servants in order were in truth the mate of his soul. Marjorie's pleasant, sunny nature made her an agreeable companion and satisfied almost every craving of his nature. And those that she didn't satisfy could be laid to rest, he thought with an unexpected throb of pain. Who was he, to ask more of life than the full measure, pressed down and running over, which had been laid at his feet?

'Hayes?'

The sharp note of interrogation in Harrison's voice roused him. 'Yes?' he said, withdrawing his eyes with an effort. 'I beg your pardon, old chap, but I wasn't listening.'

'So I saw. Nothing wrong, I hope: you look rather queer? Heart all right?' Harrison sat down with his back against a rock and stared reflectively at Hayes.

The latter shook his head: 'I am as fit as a fiddle,' he said with a concentrated bitterness which seemed oddly inappropriate to the words.

The Stock Exchange is not a school for diplomatists, but there are moments when even the least penetrating amongst us knows that it is better to keep silence than to speak. So Harrison lit a pipe and puffed at it, waiting for the confidence if it should come; equally prepared to discuss the weather and Home Rule if Hayes preferred doing so.

But the sympathy in his kindly soul seemed to reach out and touch the other man.

'I want to tell someone,' he said without any preamble.

Harrison nodded gravely, and moved his position slightly, so that he could look out to the African hills instead of into his friend's face.

'I shall go mad if I sit here and look at that island,' Hayes added hoarsely. He turned away sharply and threw himself full length on the ground next to Harrison, and a strong pungent odour floated up into the air from the crushed geranium leaves beneath him.

'It was during the war.* I came out with the Imperial Yeomanry, and for a time my troop was stationed over amongst those mountains.' He jerked his head towards the Drakenstein—steel-blue under the hard light of the midday sun.

'We found it precious hard work to get fresh vegetables for the men. The Cape Town market was out of the question—the trains were too busy carrying troops and ammunition and comforts for the sick and wounded to be utilised for our provisions. I should like to have seen K. of K.'s face* if anyone had suggested it to him,' he added, with the grim ghost of a smile.

'Well—so we had to depend on what we could buy from the neighbouring farmers, few of whom were over anxious to supply us. It was poor work riding from farm to farm only to be told that none of the cabbages and turnips were for sale, all being required for the family. The entire population must have been on a strict vegetarian regimen or have had some secret system of conveyance to our friend the enemy. At last the men grew mutinous and threatened a raid—with which South Africa would have rung to this day, of course.'

His eyes were fixed on the island again, staring passionately at its flat, unlovely surface.

'What did you do?' asked Harrison a little absent-mindedly. He was watching three spreeuws* floating in the abyss below him, the sun gleaming on their polished black bodies and chestnut wings. It is never safe to deduce any man's hobbies from his occupation, and when Harrison wasn't stockbroking he was an ardent ornithologist.

'I had noticed a farm, tucked away in a fold of the hills, farther from the camp than those to which we had applied in vain. So I asked the Colonel for an afternoon's leave, and rode across the veld towards the mountains. A wonderful country! If Providence and a benevolent uncle hadn't made me a tea-planter in Victoria County* I should have turned fruit-farmer at the Cape. I never saw anything like the stately peace of some of the old homesteads I passed on that ride. I wonder how many English people realise that there were great houses and wide cultivated lands at the Cape—Constantia for instance—when James the Second was King. The present generation is doing its best to ruin the old places by pulling down the gables and thatched roofs and clapping on corrugated iron, but there are a good many still unspoiled.*

'Well, I found my homestead at last—a little gem of a house under the shade of giant oaks. The place looked extraordinarily neat and well-kept: it was an agreeable shock to find tubs of blue hydrangeas and pots of azaleas on the stoep, after the eternal paraffin tins of the country.

'I checked my horse, with the sensation of the impossibility of riding up to what was obviously the front door of a gentleman's house and asking him to sell me a cartload of vegetables. As I hesitated, the upper half of the teak door was thrown open and an unmistakably English parlourmaid looked out. At the sight of a stranger she came out on to the stoep and down the flight of rounded steps, in all the incongruity of her neat cap and white apron and her well-trained domestic air.

'"You wish to see Miss North, sir?"

'I didn't: I only wanted to get away more quickly than I had come; but how could I explain that to the immaculate being who stood with impassive face waiting for me to dismount? Under her directions I tied my horse to a ring in one of the oaks and followed her up the steps, brushing off some of the dust that I had acquired during the ride, pulling my khaki jacket into place, and vainly endeavouring to smooth my hair.

'"Mr Hayes, Miss."

'A girl turned, with a look of surprise, from a high old-fashioned bureau at which she sat writing.

'"I heard a horse, and I thought it was Mr Hugo—a neighbour."

'She came forward holding out her hand in a pretty, friendly way. A slip of a girl in a clinging black gown, with grey eyes and dark hair and a soft, low voice. And the grace of her! She was of Huguenot descent on her mother's side, as I found afterwards, and all French in her supple movements as she was all English in her heart and mind.

'"You are at the Yeomanry Camp," she said, glancing at my khaki-clad form, which had never felt so shabby or dust-sodden before. "Jack, my brother, will be sorry to find that he has missed you. He has gone up to Cape Town for a few days to see a doctor."

'A shadow flickered over her face as she spoke. "Nothing serious, I hope," I said, as I laid down my cap and riding-whip on an old brass-bound chest that stood near the door. "Oh, no—only touches of fever every now and then. But old Mr Hugo—our nearest neighbour —gave him no peace until he promised to consult someone. So he went off this morning, leaving me in charge of the house, with my aunt—my father's sister—who has lived with us ever since my mother died, when I was three years old."

'"You haven't always lived on this farm?"

'I was conscious of the note of surprise in my voice, but she only laughed.

'"Why not? There was nothing Miss Henley, my governess, couldn't teach me as thoroughly as I could have learned it in Cape Town. And next year I am going to England to see my father's people. Oh!"

'She drew in her breath with a catch of delight, then her grey eyes filled with tears. "He had always meant to take me himself, but he had important business which often took him away from home and prevented his leaving the Cape. And six months ago—he died."

'Her voice broke on the last words, as she bent over the tea table which the impeccable parlourmaid had placed at her elbow while we were talking. She poured out the tea in silence—then she roused herself.

'"About England"——

'A warm flush crept into her cheeks.

'"Sometimes I lie awake at night and think about it for hours and ache with longing. I have never seen a lily of the valley or heard a rook or a cuckoo. How I shall love it all!"

'"You'll be glad enough to get away when winter comes," I said.

'Then I reviled myself for an idiot as I saw the look of pain in her face.

'"Oh no! It would be wonderful—that white pure world, when the snow is like velvet under your feet and every tree sparkles with diamonds."

'Clearly if her father had told her nothing of November fogs and east winds it was none of my business to do so. So I sat silent and corroborative while she told me of an island of romance which did in very truth bear some distant resemblance to my dear native land—with a difference.

'It was easy to see how all the disadvantages had faded out of the mind of the man who had not seen it for twenty years, leaving only an idealised realm of faery—the England of his waking and sleeping dreams.

'And as she talked I wondered how I should explain myself and my quest for vegetables. Otherwise I didn't see how I should be able to explain myself and my presence in her house at all.

'When she paused, to pour out a second cup of the tea that tasted so good and was served with what seemed such incredible luxury and daintiness after months of camp life, I blurted out my errand. Could she tell me where to get cabbages and onions? None of the neighbouring farmers would sell us any, and I thought—I thought—— At this point I gulped down my tea with great haste and prayed inwardly that she would come to my rescue.

'She did.

'"I will send for our manager," she said at once. "He worked the farm during my father's lifetime, and Jack is keeping him on until the end of the year. He generally sends everything up to the Cape Town market, and will probably be enchanted to find buyers closer at hand."

'Half an hour later I rode away from the farm, the richer by a cartload of sweet potatoes and onions which were to follow me to the camp in the morning, and with the whole world transfigured for me by the light in Pamela North's eyes.

'She asked me to come again, and I went day after day. Sometimes it was ostensibly to interview the Manager on the relative merits and prices of cabbages and knol-kohl.* Sometimes it was brazenly to call on Pamela and her Aunt, Miss Helena North—that dear, deaf woman who must have accomplished miles of crochet while we talked on every subject in heaven and earth.

'Sometimes we rode together between hedges of white Macartney roses and vermilion kafir-honeysuckle or over the open veld in the intoxicating clearness of the air. Or she would take me to farms in the neighbourhood and introduce me to the farmers—good kindly souls with hazily dim ideas as to the genesis of the war, taught by their predikants that all rooineks were "verdoemde,"* but prepared to receive me courteously in my private capacity as Pamela's friend. There were other farmers—life-long friends, now hostile and sullen towards everyone bearing an English name—but of these she never spoke with bitterness.

'"They do not know the truth," she said once. "Many of them honestly believe all that those who have stirred up this war tell them, so we must not judge them as if they knew."

'For England—her father's land—she had a love that was almost a passion. It never clashed with her love for South Africa, any more than my affection for my native Westmorland dales interferes with my part and lot in the Empire. The two things were distinct elements, and it was their fusion that gave her a width of outlook beside which mine was narrow and parochial.

'And of England she never wearied of talking and asking questions. It was absurd, but I sometimes found myself wishing that the lovely dream-structure she had reared on her father's memories need never be shaken. If I could but transport her on a wishing-carpet to my own country! I thought of the wide sweep of Windermere under the silver moon, of the banks of Grasmere yellow with daffodils, of the grey stone cottages covered with scarlet tropæolum, of the harebells on Helvellyn. But of the want and misery in the great towns, of the sin and sorrow that follow in their wake, of chill grey days, of overcrowding and squalor and unloveliness, we never spoke. Would the reality have disappointed her, I wonder? I hardly think so: her love for the England of her daily dreams was so real that it would have embraced everything—shortcomings and wonderful reality alike.

'"I don't believe I shall be able to bear the first sight of it," she said once. "Think! England—England—England!" She sang the words aloud in a rapturous chant, throwing her riding whip into the air and catching it again—as Taillefer sang the song of Roland.*

'"Oh, how much you have missed, you who have always lived there!" she cried laughing—but there were tears in her grey eyes—"you can never see it for the *first* time, as I can!"

'We rode on in silence for a few minutes, spattered by the white petals from an avenue of ancient pear-trees that sheltered us from the sun.

'"And yet I know that I shall always want to come back to South Africa," she said, after a while. "This was my mother's country, and I am part of it. We ought to turn now. Aunt Helena would perish of thirst before she ordered in tea for herself, and it is a quarter past four."

'A week after my first visit I rode away from the camp one afternoon with a new book under my arm. I was eager for Pamela to read it, so that we might discuss it; for she had become the point upon which my every thought was focussed—the One Woman in the whole world for me.'

Hayes lapsed into silence, and the dreariness in his eyes deepened to a look of anguish. After a moment he went on speaking:—

'Half a mile from the farm I met old Hugo—who owned Nacht-wacht, farther up the valley. I had often found him at the farm on my visits to Pamela, and had blessed the kindliness that had moved him to sit near Aunt Helena and shout into her ear while we talked.

'When he saw me he rode forward quickly and, taking hold of the bridle, turned my horse's head towards the direction from which I had come.

'"Go back—go back," he muttered hoarsely. I stared at the old man in amazement. His usually ruddy, cheery face was drawn and shrunken: he mumbled in his speech; and his shoulders were as bowed as if he had been ninety, instead of a hale sixty-eight.

'"Why?" I asked—too alarmed by his appearance to be indignant.

'"It is her wish—Pamela's."

'I felt as though I had been turned to ice—under the vivid South

African sun, with the trill of the cicadas in my ears and the smell of the hot vine-leaves in my nostrils.

'"Last night came back her brother from Cape Town. Oh, my poor boy—my poor boy! Almachtig!"*

'A sensation that was almost relief set my blood free to course through the veins once more. Evidently the doctor's verdict had been unfavourable. But if so, and sorrow had fallen on Pamela, my place was at her side.

'I wrenched the bridle free and turned towards the farm. But, as the angel stood before Balaam's ass,* the old man barred the road.

'"If you go on you will but bring her fresh trouble," he said. "It is by her wish that I ask you to go back."

'A chill of despair crept over me again at his dogged reiteration.

'"If I go back to-day, at her desire, I may come again?"

'For a moment he looked at me with eyes in which pity and misery fought for mastery. He bowed his head.

'"If you wish it—yes; but it is better not."

'In hot indignation I flamed out at him.

'"You have never loved a woman if you can say that to me!"

'He did not speak for a moment. Then:—

'"For forty years I loved one woman—my Letty; and I stood by her grave last year. And now I shall marry Helena—it is all I can do for my children."

'He turned abruptly from me and rode back towards the farm, leaving me to the mercy of the most soul-filling anxiety a man can know.

'On the way home my horse put his foot into a mole-hole and threw me over his shoulder, so that it was not until a week later that—with an arm in splints, and in flagrant defiance of the doctor's orders—I rode up to the steps of the farm.

'I had written to Pamela—my right hand was uninjured—pouring out my love for her and imploring her to write to me, but no answer had reached me.

'Somehow the sight of the closely shuttered windows and locked doors of the homestead awakened no surprise. I think I had known all the time that I should not find her there.

'I sat on my horse, staring like an idiot at the hydrangeas drooping in the heat. They had never flagged when Pamela was at home, I thought idly—as one fiddles with trifles in the face of despair. She would have called Cupido, the gardener, to water them.

'I dismounted slowly and painfully, and tied my horse to the ring in the oak. Then I hunted about for a bucket, filled it at the little brown stream that spluttered past the homestead, and watered her thirsty flowers.

'Taking Bingo's bridle over my uninjured arm I followed a little oak avenue that led to Hugo's farm up the valley. Half an hour's walk brought me out on to a wide werf,* flanked by a fine old white-gabled house. On the stoep sat the farmer, and my heart—heavy enough before—sank like a plummet as I saw his attitude of dejection.

'He looked up wearily.

'"You have come, then?"

'"I broke my arm. They would not give me leave earlier. Where is she?"

'My voice sounded harsh and discordant as I forced my frozen lips to speak.

'He got up from the rustbank* on which he had been seated and went into the house, returning with a letter which he held out to me.

'"For you—from her."

'He walked slowly down the steps and crossed the werf to the guava orchard, leaving me alone with my letter.

'It was very short.

'"Dear—my dear: I shall never see you again, but I take your letter with me into the darkness and I thank God for one week of utter happiness. There is nothing left to me but to care for my brother, for an angel with a flaming sword stands between me and the life of the living. And England—my England—I shall never see. If——"

'The pen had fallen from her hand and blotted the page.

'The envelope was blank.

'An hour—two hours—passed. I was roused by hearing old Hugo's heavy footsteps behind me.

'I sprang to my feet.

'"Where is she?" I gasped.

'"I may not tell you."

'"Why not?"

'"It is her wish."

'"I don't believe it. I love her, and she loves me. What right have you to stand between us?"

'"It is her wish," he repeated drearily, looking at me with pity in his eyes.

' "For God's sake explain. There is no one else?"

' "There is no one else. There can never be anyone else for her, she says. Only—only Jack."

' "Her brother?"

' "Yes. He is very ill."

'Light began to break.

' "She is gone away with him?"

' "Yes. To a place where he may be cared for by doctors who understand his—his sickness."

' "But where is it?"

' "I don't know."

' "What is the matter with him?"

' "I don't know."

'He looked me full in the face as he spoke and we both knew that he lied, for Pamela—for Pamela.

' "Will he get better?"

' "God knows," he said evasively. "But her mother died of it—in the place to which he has gone. The cottage still stands in which she lived—apart from the other patients, who are, for the most part, poor folk. Her husband used to spend all the time he could spare from his children with her, and I hold money in trust to keep it in order and the little garden filled with the flowers that she loved best. Her father died of the sickness before her. He took it from a native who doctored him for a thorn in his foot, and bound up the wound with a strip torn from his own rags. So he drew the poison* into his blood for a legacy to his children's children. God help them!"

'I stood trembling in every limb. What unnameable horror lay behind his words? With shaking lips I whispered "Pamela?"

'As a man in a hideous trance he answered: "She never knew until Jack came home and told her what the doctor had said to him—he knew the family history himself, and his mind was almost unhinged. She has gone with him. She said that she must never see you again." And then, quite suddenly, the old man put his head down on his arms and sobbed.

'I don't know how I got back to the camp that night, but I have a confused recollection of finding it in a state of joyous uproar, consequent on an order to entrain for the North having arrived while I was away at the farm.

'We left next morning, and during the year that followed I never went into action without hoping that I shouldn't come out of it. They said I was brave and gave me the V.C.! God knows I was only utterly indifferent; and if another man thought life worth having I didn't see why I shouldn't risk mine, which was valueless to me, in order to oblige him. And an old uncle who had large sugar-plantations in Natal bequeathed them to me—on account of my pluck, he said.'

Hayes laughed drearily.

'Well the war came to an end at last, and we all went to our own places, and have been busily forgetting ever since that we were once soldiers of the King. My sugar-plantations bring me in as much as I can spend, and—I am married.'

'Did you ever get any news?'

Harrison's pipe had gone out as he listened.

'Never. I inquired in every probable and improbable direction. I addressed letters to old Hugo's care and they were returned, marked "address not known." For eight years the darkness of which she spoke has closed over her head—until to-day.'

He drew a crumpled newspaper from his coat pocket and held it out to Harrison with a hand that shook.

'I found this at luncheon-time, stuffed in between the plates, and I saw her name.'

Harrison's eyes followed the pointing finger and read: 'Died, on Robben Island,* December 1st, 1908. Pamela Mary North.'

'Why Robben Island?' he asked in a hushed voice.

The grey tint in Hayes's face spread to his lips.

'Robben Island,' he said quietly, 'is the leper settlement.'

See also: Barker; Curzon; Duncan; Leacock; Plaatje; Schreiner; Stephens.

J. E. CASELY HAYFORD
(1866–1930)

from *Ethiopia Unbound* (1911)

Ethiopia Unbound, *a loosely constructed autobiographical novel, brings together sketches, dialogues, and meditations on African nationalist and anti-colonial themes. Other chapters deal with religious issues, such as the African origins of Christianity, and the universality of spiritual belief, and present arguments for the regeneration of African cultural traditions.* Ethiopia Unbound *is dedicated to 'the Sons of Ethiopia the World Wide Over'. The parable and essay below give a sense of the variety of forms the novel embraces.*

As in a Glass Darkly*

Not so very long ago in the age of the world, the Nations were gathered in council upon Mount Atlas, even at the point which is nearest the ancient city of Constantine, and there were no people that were not represented, save the Ethiopians, whose kingdoms stretch from the shores of the Mediterranean, where it washes the Lybian coast, across the great desert, taking in the arms of the mighty waste from ocean to ocean, thence sweeping down to the remotest parts of the provinces inhabited by the Kaffirs, a race of mighty men.

It was like the meeting of the gods, the gathering of the Nations, for they had mastered all knowledge and gotten themselves such power as to make men forget the Power beyond, before whom the Nations of the Earth are as grasshoppers.

These Nations, who, in the old pagan days, struggled the one against the other in true manly fashion, had learnt a new method of warfare, which they labelled 'Diplomacy'; and when the uninitiated asked the reason for the change, it was explained that it was dictated by the spirit of their common religion which inculcated universal brotherhood, and the beating of swords into plough-shares. Wherefore it came to pass, that at this universal conference* the Nations said smooth things to one another which no one believed.

But there was one thing concerning which these mighty men were in earnest, and that was the capture of the soul of Ethiopia. Said they, 'We have all increased in knowledge and power, and, being brothers, we can no longer devour one another. Yet must we live. Taught by the instinct of self-preservation, we must have elbow-room* wherein our children and our children's children may thrive. Now, before our hosts lieth the whole stretch of Ethiopia from sea to sea. Come, let us partition it among ourselves.' They were well agreed upon this matter, but not upon the way of encompassing it.

One Nation said, 'How shall we do this thing, seeing we are Christians?' Another said, 'Thou that doubtest, thou art merely slow of counsel. This thing is easily done. We shall go to the Ethiopians, and shall teach them our religion, and that will make them ours, body and soul—lands, goods, and all, for all time.' And the saying pleased them all.*

It came to pass upon the third year after the meeting of the Nations that a mighty prince, sailing from the setting sun, dropped anchor in that portion of Ethiopia which is washed by the waters of the Gulf of Guinea. Retinue he had none, nor arms, nor any outward sign of power. In his hand he held a simple cross, and gifts besides. The Sons of Night gathered around him in great awe, and took the coming of the stranger for the visit of a god. But the gifts set them easy, and the drink of the white man was like nectar unto them.*

There were discerning men among the Ethiopians who would shake their heads and say, This thing will bring us no good. But the crowd submitted to the worship of the new god, and greedily devoured the good things found upon his altars. And soon the discerning ones formed themselves into a group, and the crowd in another camp; and the thing pleased the strange visitor. And now he sent over the seas, and brought yet other teachers, who apparently taught the self-same doctrine, and the more they taught the more the people broke into smaller groups, each denouncing the other heartily. And so it came to pass, that children who had suckled at the same breast and had played with the same toy gods were, as men, feign to slay one another. And the thing seemed to please the new comers, and, being men of knowledge, they winked at one another and said the rest would follow.

By this time the unthinking crowd were beside themselves in emulation of the white man's ways, and when they bowed the knee in the House of Mammon, they thought they worshipped the true God, and seemed to forget that once they were Ethiopians.

The gods met in the ethereal heights of Mount Atlas to undo the work of mortals. Said they, 'The Nations are as a dream before us, and they know not what they do. Are not the Ethiopians a peculiar people, destined for a peculiar part in the world's work? An end to the machinations of men!'

In the self-same era a god descended upon earth to teach the Ethiopians anew the *way of life*. He came not in thunder, or with great sound, but in the garb of a humble teacher, a John the Baptist* among his brethren, preaching racial and national salvation. From land to land, and from shore to shore, his message was the self-same one, which, interpreted in the language of the Christ, was: *What shall it profit a race if it shall gain the whole world and lose its own soul?*

African Nationality

In the name of African nationality the thinker would, through the medium of *Ethiopia Unbound*, greet members of the race everywhere throughout the world. Whether in the east, south, or west of the African Continent, or yet among the teeming millions of Ethiopia's sons in America, the cry of the African, in its last analysis, is for scope and freedom in the struggle for existence, and it would seem as if the care of the leaders of the race has been to discover those avenues of right and natural endeavour which would, in the end, ensure for the race due recognition of its individuality.

The race problem is probably most intense in the United States of America, but there are indications that on the African Continent itself it is fast assuming concrete form. Sir Arthur Lawley, the present Governor of Madras, before leaving the Governorship of the Transvaal, is reported in a public address to have said that the 'black peril' is a reality, and to have advised the whites to consolidate their forces in presence of the potential foe. The leaders of the race have hitherto exercised sound discretion and shown considerable wisdom in advising the African to follow the line of least resistance in meeting any combination of forces against him. The African's way to proper recognition lies not at present so much in the exhibition of material force and power, as in the gentler art of persuasion by the logic of facts and of achievements before which all reasonable men must bow.

A two-fold danger threatens the African everywhere. It is the outcome of certain economic conditions whose method is the exploitation of the Ethiopian for all he is worth. He is said to be pressed into the service of man, in reality, the service of the Caucasian. That being so, he never reaps the full meed of his work as a *man*. He materially contributes to the building of pavements on which he may not walk—take it as a metaphor, or as a fact, which way you please. He helps to work up revenues and to fill up exchequers over which, in most cases, he has no effective control, if any at all. In brief, he is labelled as belonging to a class apart among the races, and any attempt to rise above his station is terribly resented by the aristocracy of the races. Indeed, he is reminded at every turn that he is only intended to be a hewer of wood and a drawer of water. And so it happens that those among the favoured sons of men who occasionally consider the lot of the Ethiopian are met with jeers and taunts. Is it any wonder, then, that even in the Twentieth Century, the African finds it terribly difficult to make headway even in his own country? The African may turn socialist, may preach and cry for reform until the day of judgment; but the experience of mankind shows this, that reform never comes to a class or a people unless and until those concerned have worked out their own salvation. And the lesson we have yet to learn is that we cannot depart from Nature's way and hope for real success.

And yet, it would seem as if in some notable instances the black man is bent upon following the line of greatest resistance in coping with the difficulties before him. Knowledge is the common property of mankind, and the philosophy which seeks for the Ethiopian the highest culture and efficiency in industrial and technical training is a sound one. It is well to arrest in favour of the race public opinion as to its capability in this direction. But that is not all, since there are certain distinctive qualities of race, of country, and of peoples which cannot be ignored without detriment to the particular race, country, or people. Knowledge, deprived of the assimilating element which makes it natural to the one taught, renders that person but a bare imitator. The Japanese, adopting and assimilating Western culture, of necessity commands the respect of Western nations, because there is something distinctly Eastern about him. He commands, to begin with, the uses of his native tongue, and has a literature of his own, enriched by translations from standard authors of other lands. He respects the institutions and customs of his ancestors, and there is an intelligent past which inspires him. He does not discard his national costume, and if, now and again, he dons Western attire, he does so as a matter of convenience, much as the Scotch, across the border, puts away, when the occasion demands it, his Highland costume. It is not the fault of the black man in America, for example, that he suffers to-day from the effects of a wrong that was inflicted upon him years ago by the forefathers of the very ones who now despise him. But he can see to it that as the years go by it becomes a matter of necessity for the American whites to respect and admire his manhood; and the surest way to the one or the other lies not so much in imitation as in originality and natural initiative. Not only must the Ethiopian acquire proficiency in the arts and sciences, in technical and industrial training, but he must pursue a course of scientific enquiry which would reveal to him the good things of the treasure house of his own nationality.

There are probably but a few men of African descent in America who, if they took the trouble by dipping into family tradition, would not be able to trace their connection and relationship with one or other of the great tribes of West Africa; and now that careful enquiry has shown that the institutions of the Aborigines of Africa are capable of scientific handling, what would be easier than for the great centres of culture and learning in the hands of Africans in the United States to found professorships in this relation? In the order of Providence, some of our brethren aforetime were suffered to be enslaved in America for a wise purpose. That event in the history of the race has made it possible for the speedier dissemination and adoption of the better part of Western culture; and to-day Afric's sons in the East and in the West can do peculiar service unto one another in the common cause of uplifting Ethiopia and placing her upon her feet among the nations. The East, for example, can take lessons from the West in the adoption of a sound educational policy, the kind of industrial and technical training which would enable aboriginals to make the best use of their hands and natural resources. And, surely, the West ought not to be averse to taking hints from the East as regards the preservation of national institutions, and the adoption of distinctive garbs and names, much as obtains among our friends the

Japanese. While a student in London, a thrill of Oriental pride used to run through the writer when he brushed against an Asiatic in a garb distinctively Eastern. They aped no one. They were content to remain Eastern. For even when climatic conditions necessitated the adoption of European habiliments, they had sense enough to preserve some symbol of nationality. On the contrary, Africans would seem never to be content unless and until they make it possible for the European to write of them thus:

'How extraordinary is the spectacle of this huge race—millions of men—without land or language of their own, without traditions of the country they came from, bearing the very names of the men that enslaved them! . . .

'The black element is one which cannot be "boiled down" into the great cosmopolitan American nation—the black man must always be tragically apart from the white man'—*

and so on and so forth.

Now, if there is aught in the foregoing which is true to life, it bears but one meaning, namely, this, that the average Afro-American citizen of the United States has lost absolute touch with the past of his race, and is helplessly and hopelessly groping in the dark for affinities that are not natural, and for effects for which there are neither national nor natural causes. That being so, the African in America is in a worse plight than the Hebrew in Egypt. The one preserved his language, his manners and customs, his religion and household gods; the other has committed national suicide, and at present it seems as if the dry bones of the vision have no life in them. Looking at the matter closely, it is not so much *Afro-Americans* that we want as *Africans* or *Ethiopians*, sojourning in a strange land, who, out of a full heart and a full knowledge can say: If I forget thee, Ethiopia, let my right hand forget its cunning! Let us look at the other side of the picture. How extraordinary would be the spectacle of this huge Ethiopian race—some millions of men—having imbibed all that is best in Western culture in the land of their oppressors, yet remaining true to racial instincts and inspiration, customs and institutions, much as did the Israelites of old in captivity! When this more pleasant picture will have become possible of realisation, then, and only then, will it be possible for our people in bondage 'metaphorically to walk out of Egypt in the near future with a great and a real spoil.'*

Someone may say, but, surely, you don't mean to suggest that questions of dress and habits of life matter in the least. I reply emphatically, they do. They go to the root of the Ethiopian's self-respect. Without servile imitation of our teachers in their get-up and manner of life, it stands to reason that the average white man would regard the average black man far more seriously than he does at present. The adoption of a distinctive dress for the cultured African, therefore, would be a distinct step forward, and a gain to the cause of Ethiopian progress and advancement. Pray listen to the greatest authority on national life upon this matter, 'Behold, I have taught you statutes and judgments even as the Lord God commanded me that ye should do in the land whither ye go to possess it. Keep, therefore, and do them: for this is your wisdom and your understanding in the sight of the nations which shall hear these statutes and say, surely, this great nation is a wise and understanding people.'* Yes, my people are pursuing knowledge as for a hidden treasure, and have neglected wisdom and true understanding, and hence are they daily a laughing stock in the sight of the nations.

Here, then, is work for cultured West Africans to start a reform which will be world-wide in its effects among Ethiopians, remembering as a basis that we, as a people, have our own statutes, the customs and institutions of our fore-fathers, which we cannot neglect and live. We on the Gold Coast are making a huge effort in this direction, and though European habits will die hard with some of our people, the effort is worth making; and, if we don't succeed quite with this generation, we shall succeed with the next. That the movement is gaining ground may well be gathered from the following extract from the *Gold Coast Leader* of 24th February, 1907, reporting the coronation of Ababio IV, *Mantse*, that is King, of 'British Accra.' Says the correspondent: 'For the first time I realised that the Gold Coast would be more exhilarating and enjoyable indeed if the educated inhabitants in it would hark back to the times of old and take a few lessons in the art and grace of the sartorial simplicity and elegance of their forebears. The "scholars" looked quite noble and full of dignity in the native dress. There was not one ignoble or mean person among them, and so for the matter of that did the ladies.'

Then I should like to see *Ethiopian Leagues* formed throughout the United States much in the same way as the *Gaelic League* in Ireland for the purpose of studying and employing Fanti, Yoruba, Hausa, or other standard African language, in daily use. The idea may seem extraordinary on the first view, but if you are inclined to regard it thus, I can only point to the examples of Ireland and Denmark, who have found the vehicle of a national language much the safest and most natural way of national conservancy and evolution. If the Dane and Irish find it expedient in Europe, surely the matter is worthy of consideration by the Ethiopian in the United States, in Sierra Leone, in the West Indies, and in Liberia.

A distinguished writer, dwelling upon the advantages of culture in a people's own language, said: 'These are important considerations of a highly practical kind. Ten years ago, we had in Ireland a people divorced, by half a century of education conducted along alien lines, from their own proper language and culture. We had also in Ireland a people seemingly incapable of rational action, sunk in hopeless poverty, apparently doomed to disappear. We have in Ireland to-day the beginnings of a system of education in the national language and along national lines; and we have at the same time, and in the places where this kind of education has been operative, an unmistakable advance in intellectual capacity and material prosperity.'* Now, if the soul that is in the Ethiopian, even in the United States, remains Ethiopian, which it does, to judge from the coon songs which have enriched the sentiment of mankind by their pathos, then, I say, the foregoing words, true as everyone must admit they are, point distinctly to the impossibility of departing from *nature's* way with any hope of lasting good to African nationality. I do sincerely trust these thoughts will catch the eye of such distinguished educationists as Mr Booker T. Washington and others of the United States and in the West Indies as also the attention of similar workers in West Africa who have the materials ready at hand. It is a great work, but I do believe that my countrymen have the heart and the intelligence to grapple with it successfully.

See also: Aurobindo; Blyden; Joyce; Kingsley; McKay; Vivekananda.

CLAUDE McKAY
(1889–1948)

To give some impression of the rich Creole background from which McKay emerged, or as he himself said, of the 'legendary vitality' of the Jamaican vernacular, the selection from his early dialect poetry of 1912 is preceded by three anonymous songs, all of them dancing tunes, collected by McKay's patron Walter Jekyll, in Jamaican Song and Story *(1907). McKay's own adaptation of Creole, even if literary, and annotated by Jekyll, marks a distinct new departure in self-expression by native colonials, a manifestation of what Casely Hayford (q.v.) called cultural 'individuality' as opposed to the 'servile imitation' of the imperial language, English.*

Oh General Jackson! (1907)

Oh General Jackson! Oh General Jackson!*
Oh General Jackson! Oh you kill all the black man them!
Oh what a wrongful judgement! Oh what a wrongful judgement!
Oh what a wrongful judgement! You kill all the black man them.
Oh what a awful mourning! Oh what a awful mourning!
Oh what a awful mourning! You bring on St Thomas people.

The Other Day

The other day me waistcoat cut,*
The other day me waistcoat cut,
The other day me waistcoat cut,
What a pain an' grief to me.

I spend me money but the beggar don't dead,
I spend me money but the beggar don't dead,
I spend me money but the beggar don't dead,
What a pain an' grief to me.

All me money gone like butter 'gainst sun,
All me money gone like butter 'gainst sun,
All me money gone like butter 'gainst sun,
What a pain an' grief to me!

Sake of the man me live 'pon tree,*
Sake of the man me live 'pon tree,
Sake of the man me live 'pon tree,
What a pain an' grief to me!

I Have a News

I have a news* to tell you all about the Mowitahl men;
Time is harder ev'ry day an harder yet to come.
They made a dance on Friday night an failed to pay the drummer,
Say that they all was need of money to buy up their August pork.*
Don't let them go free, drummer! Don't let them go free, drummer!
For your finger cost money to tickle the poor goat-'kin.
Not if the pork even purchase self,* take it away for your labour,
For your finger cost money to tickle the poor goat-'kin.

Cudjoe* Fresh From de Lecture (1912)

'Top *one* minute, Cous' Jarge, an' sit do'n 'pon de grass,
An' mek a¹ tell you 'bout de news I hear at las',
How de buccra* te-day tek time an' bégin teach
All of us dat was deh² in a clear open speech.

You miss somet'ing fe true, but a wi' mek you know,
As much as how a can, how de business a go:
Him tell us 'bout we self, an' mek we fresh³ again,
An' talk about de wul' from commencement to en'.

---

¹ Make I = let me.   ² There.
³ Over: meaning, 'He gave us a new view of our origin, and explained that we did not come from Adam and Eve, but by evolution.'

Me look 'pon me black 'kin, an' so me head grow big,
Aldough me heaby han' dem hab fe plug[1] an' dig;
For ebery single man, no car'[2] about dem rank,
Him bring us ebery one an' put 'pon de same plank.

Say, parson do de same?[3] Yes, in a diff'ren' way,
For parson tell us how de whole o' we are clay;
An' lookin' close at t'ings, we hab to pray quite hard
Fe swaller wha' him say an' don't t'ink bad o' Gahd.

But dis man tell us 'traight 'bout how de whole t'ing came,
An' show us widout doubt how Gahd was not fe blame;
How change cause eberyt'ing fe mix up 'pon de eart',
An' dat most hardship come t'rough accident o' birt'.

Him show us all a sort[4] o' funny 'keleton,
Wid names I won't remember under dis ya sun;
Animals queer to deat',[5] dem bone, teet', an' head-skull,
All dem so dat did live in a de ole-time wul'.

No 'cos say we get cuss mek fe we 'kin come so,
But fe all t'ings come 'quare, same so it was to go:[6]
Seems our lan'[7] must ha' been a bery low-do'n place,
Mek it tek such long time in tu'ning out a race.

Yes, from monkey we spring: I believe ebery wud;
It long time better dan f'go say we come from mud:
No need me keep back part, me hab not'in' fe gain;
It's ebery man dat born—de buccra mek it plain.

It really strange how some o' de lan' dem advance;
Man power in some ways is nummo soso chance;[8]
But suppose eberyt'ing could tu'n right upside down,
Den p'raps we'd be on top an' givin' some one houn'.[9]

---

[1] Plough, *i.e.*, pick up the ground with a pickaxe.
[2] Care: no matter what their rank.   [3] Do you say that parson does the same?
[4] All sorts.   [5] The queerest animals.
[6] It is not because we were cursed (Gen. ix. 25) that our skin is dark; but so that things might come square, there had to be black and white.
[7] Africa.   [8] No more than pure chance.
[9] Hound: equivalent to the English slang phrase 'giving some one beans.'

Yes, Cous' Jarge, slabery hot fe dem dat gone befo':
We gettin' better times, for those days we no know;[1]
But I t'ink it do good, tek we from Africa
An' lan' us in a blessed place as dis a ya.[2]

Talk 'bouten Africa, we would be deh till now,
Maybe same half-naked—all day dribe buccra cow,
An' tearin' t'rough de bush wid all de monkey dem,
Wile an' uncibilise',[3] an' neber comin' tame.

I lef' quite 'way from wha' we be'n deh talk about,[4]
Yet still a couldn' help—de wuds come to me mout';
Just like how yeas' get strong an' sometimes fly de cark,[5]
Same way me feelings grow, so I was boun' fe talk.

Yet both horse partly[6] runnin' in de selfsame gallop,
For it is nearly so de way de buccra pull up:*
Him say, how de wul' stan', dat right will neber be,
But wrong will eber gwon[7] till dis wul' en' fe we.

Old England

I've a longin' in me dept's of heart dat I can conquer not,
'Tis a wish dat I've been havin' from since I could form a t'o't,[8]
'Tis to sail athwart the ocean an' to hear de billows roar,
When dem ride aroun' de steamer, when dem beat on England's
    shore.

Just to view de homeland England, in de streets of London walk,
An' to see de famous sights dem 'bouten which dere's so much talk,
An' to watch de fact'ry chimneys pourin' smoke up to de sky,
An' to see de matches-children, dat I hear 'bout, passin' by.

---

[1] Do not know: have no experience of.   [2] This here.
[3] Wild and uncivilised.
[4] I have run right away from what we were talking about.
[5] Makes the cork fly.   [6] Almost.   [7] Go on.
[8] Thought.

I would see Saint Paul's Cathedral, an' would hear some of de great
Learnin' comin' from de bishops, preachin' relics of old fait';
I would ope me mout' wid wonder at de massive organ soun',
An' would 'train me eyes to see de beauty lyin' all aroun'.

I'd go to de City Temple, where de old fait' is a wreck,
An' de parson is a-preachin' views dat most folks will not tek;
I'd go where de men of science meet togeder in deir hall,
To give light unto de real truths, to obey king Reason's call.

I would view Westminster Abbey, where de great of England sleep,
An' de solemn marble statues o'er deir ashes vigil keep;
I would see immortal Milton an' de wul'-famous Shakespeare,
Past'ral Wordswort', gentle Gray, an' all de great souls buried dere.

I would see de ancient chair where England's kings deir crowns put
  on,
Soon to lay dem by again when all de vanity is done;
An' I'd go to view de lone spot where in peaceful solitude
Rests de body of our Missis Queen,[1] Victoria de Good.

An' dese places dat I sing of now shall afterwards impart
All deir solemn sacred beauty to a weary searchin' heart;
So I'll rest glad an' contented in me min'[2] for evermore,
When I sail across de ocean back to my own native shore.

My Native Land, My Home

Dere is no land dat can compare
  Wid you where'er I roam;
In all de wul' none like you fair,
  My native land, my home.

[1] Always so called in Jamaica.   [2] Mind.

Jamaica is de nigger's place,
  No mind whe' some declare;
Although dem call we 'no-land race,'
  I know we home is here.

You give me life an' nourishment,
  No udder land I know;
My lub* I neber can repent,
  For all to you I owe.

E'en ef you mek me beggar die,
  I'll trust you all de same,
An' none de less on you rely,
  Nor saddle you wid blame.

Though you may cas'' me from your breas'
  An' trample me to deat',
My heart will trus' you none de less,
  My land I won't feget.

An' I hope none o' your sons would
  Refuse deir strengt' to lend,
An' drain de last drop o' deir blood
  Their country to defend.

You draw de t'ousan' from deir shore,
  An' all 'long keep dem please';[2]
De invalid come here fe cure,
  You heal all deir disease.

Your fertile soil grow all o' t'ings[3]
  To full de naygur's* wants,
'Tis seamed wid neber-failing springs[4]
  To give dew to de plants.[5]

---

[1] Cast.
[2] And keep them amused and happy all along (all the time of their stay).
[3] All of (the) things.   [4] Brooks.
[5] The dew falls heavily in the valley-bottoms.

You hab all t'ings fe mek life bles',
  But buccra 'poil de whole
Wid gove'mint[1] an' all de res',
  Fe worry naygur soul.

Still all dem little chupidness[2]
  Caan' tek away me lub;
De time when I'll tu'n 'gains' you is
  When you can't give me grub.

The Apple-Woman's Complaint (1912)

While me deh walk 'long in de street,
Policeman's yawnin' on his beat;
An' dis de wud him chiefta'n say—
Me mus'n' car' me apple-tray.

Ef me no wuk, me boun' fe tief;
S'pose dat will please de pólice chief!
De prison dem mus' be wan' full,[3]
Mek dem's 'pon we like ravin' bull.

Black nigger wukin' laka cow
An' wipin' sweat-drops from him brow,
Dough him is dyin' sake o' need,
P'lice an' dem headman boun' fe feed.

P'lice an' dem headman gamble too,
Dey shuffle card an' bet fe true;
Yet ef me Charlie gamble,—well,
Dem try fe 'queeze him laka hell.

De headman fe de town police
Mind[4] neber know a little peace,
'Cep' when him an' him heartless ban'
Hab sufferin' nigger in dem han'.

---

[1] Government.   [2] Those little stupidnesses.
[3] The prisons must want occupants, and that is why they are down upon us like angry bulls.
[4] The mind of the chief of the town police is never happy, except, etc.

Ah son-son! dough you're bastard, yah,
An' dere's no one you can call pa,
Jes' try to ha' you' mudder's min'
An' Police Force you'll neber jine.

But how judge bélieve pólicemen,
Dem dutty mout' wid lyin' stain'?
While we go batterin' along
Dem doin' we all sort o' wrong.

We hab fe barter-out we soul
To lib t'rough dis ungodly wul';—
O massa Jesus! don't you see
How pólice is oppressin' we?

Dem wan' fe see we in de street
Dah foller dem all 'pon dem beat;
An' after, 'dout a drop o' shame,
Say we be'n dah solicit dem.

Ah massa Jesus! in you' love
Jes' look do'n from you' t'rone above,
An' show me how a poo' weak gal
Can lib good life in dis ya wul'.

If We Must Die (1918)

If we must die, let it not be like hogs
Hunted and penned in an inglorious spot,
While round us bark the mad and hungry dogs,
Making their mock at our accursed lot.
If we must die, Oh let us nobly die,
So that our precious blood may not be shed
In vain; then even the monsters we defy
Shall be constrained to honor us though dead!

Oh, kinsmen! we must meet the common foe!
Though far outnumbered let us show us brave,
And for their thousand blows deal one death-blow!
What though before us lies the open grave?
Like men we'll face the murderous cowardly pack,
Pressed to the wall, dying, but fighting back!

See also: Blyden; Casely Hayford; Fairbridge; Joyce; Naidu; Thomas.

RABINDRANATH TAGORE
(1861–1941)

Tagore's collection Gitanjali *is made up of translations (and subsequent
transmutations into prose-poems) of some of the complicated rhymed
Bengali poetry which he had published under three separate covers in
Calcutta (the very different* Gitanjali *of 1910, and* Naivedya *and*
Kheya*). The transformative reworking of different traditions that marks
much of Tagore's writing, was here taken a significant step further
towards cross-cultural interchange. The translations in the final form of
the English* Gitanjali *bear the mark of, in particular, W. B. Yeats's
editing and emendations, to which Tagore consented. They also won for
the Bengali poet a rapturous reception in the West, culminating in the
award of the Nobel Prize for Literature in 1913, the first time this honour
was bestowed on an Asian writer. Yeats's 'Introduction to* Gitanjali',
*which appeared with the first publication of the poems, and in this
anthology follows them, captures the spirited promotion of Tagore by the
Irish poet and other friends. Yet though Ezra Pound may not unfairly
have called this promotion a piece of 'wise imperialism', it involved more
than simple charity (and misreading) on the part of the European artists.
It was no accident that some of Tagore's supporters were also key
modernist innovators who, even if only passingly, found in Tagore's
devotional cadences and ceremonious poetic the resonances of an integrated tradition which they too sought to retrieve.*

Poems from *Gitanjali (Song Offerings)* (1912)

I

When thou commandest me to sing, it seems that my heart would break with pride; and I look to thy face, and tears come to my eyes.

All that is harsh and dissonant in my life melts into one sweet harmony—and my adoration spreads wings like a glad bird on its flight across the sea.

I know thou takest pleasure in my singing. I know that only as a singer I come before thy presence.

I touch by the edge of the far-spreading wing of my song thy feet which I could never aspire to reach.

Drunk with the joy of singing I forget myself and call thee friend who art my lord.

II

Leave this chanting and singing and telling of beads! Whom dost thou worship in this lonely dark corner of a temple with doors all shut? Open thine eyes and see thy God is not before thee!

He is there where the tiller is tilling the hard ground and where the pathmaker is breaking stones. He is with them in sun and in shower, and his garment is covered with dust. Put off thy holy mantle and even like him come down on the dusty soil!

Deliverance? Where is this deliverance to be found? Our master himself has joyfully taken upon him the bonds of creation; he is bound with us all for ever.

Come out of thy meditations and leave aside thy flowers and incense! What harm is there if thy clothes become tattered and stained? Meet him and stand by him in toil and in sweat of thy brow.

III

Light, oh, where is the light? Kindle it with the burning fire of desire!

There is the lamp but never a flicker of a flame,—is such thy fate, my heart? Ah, death were better by far for thee!

Misery knocks at thy door, and her message is that thy lord is wakeful, and he calls thee to the love-tryst through the darkness of night.

The sky is overcast with clouds and the rain is ceaseless. I know not what this is that stirs in me,—I know not its meaning.

A moment's flash of lightning drags down a deeper gloom on my sight, and my heart gropes for the path to where the music of the night calls me.

Light, oh, where is the light? Kindle it with the burning fire of desire! It thunders and the wind rushes screaming through the void. The night is black as a black stone. Let not the hours pass by in the dark. Kindle the lamp of love with thy life.

IV

Obstinate are the trammels, but my heart aches when I try to break them.

Freedom is all I want, but to hope for it I feel ashamed.

I am certain that priceless wealth is in thee, and that thou art my best friend, but I have not the heart to sweep away the tinsel that fills my room.

The shroud that covers me is a shroud of dust and death; I hate it, yet hug it in love.

My debts are large, my failures great, my shame secret and heavy; yet when I come to ask for my good, I quake in fear lest my prayer be granted.

V

Where the mind is without fear and the head is held high;

Where knowledge is free;

Where the world has not been broken up into fragments by narrow domestic walls;

Where words come out from the depth of truth;

Where tireless striving stretches its arms towards perfection;

Where the clear stream of reason has not lost its way into the dreary desert sand of dead habit;

Where the mind is led forward by thee into ever-widening thought and action—

Into that heaven of freedom, my Father, let my country awake.

VI

I thought that my voyage had come to its end at the last limit of my power—that the path before me was closed, that provisions were exhausted and the time come to take shelter in a silent obscurity.

But I find that thy will knows no end in me. And when old words die out on the tongue, new melodies break forth from the heart; and where the old tracks are lost, new country is revealed with its wonders.

VII

Where dost thou stand behind them all, my lover, hiding thyself in the shadows? They push thee and pass thee by on the dusty road, taking thee for naught. I wait here weary hours spreading my offerings for thee, while passers-by come and take my flowers, one by one, and my basket is nearly empty.

The morning time is past, and the noon. In the shade of evening my eyes are drowsy with sleep. Men going home glance at me and smile and fill me with shame. I sit like a beggar maid, drawing my skirt over my face, and when they ask me what it is I want, I drop my eyes and answer them not.

Oh, how, indeed, could I tell them that for thee I wait, and that thou hast promised to come? How could I utter for shame that I keep for my dowry this poverty? Ah, I hug this pride in the secret of my heart.

I sit on the grass and gaze upon the sky and dream of the sudden splendour of thy coming—all the lights ablaze, golden pennons flying over thy car, and they at the roadside standing agape, when they see thee come down from thy seat to raise me from the dust, and set at thy side this ragged beggar girl a-tremble with shame and pride, like a creeper in a summer breeze.

But time glides on and still no sound of the wheels of thy chariot. Many a procession passes by with noise and shouts and glamour of glory. Is it only thou who wouldst stand in the shadow silent and behind them all? And only I who would wait and weep and wear out my heart in vain longing?

VIII

Have you not heard his silent steps? He comes, comes, ever comes.

Every moment and every age, every day and every night he comes, comes, ever comes.

Many a song have I sung in many a mood of mind, but all their notes have always proclaimed, 'He comes, comes, ever comes.'

In the fragrant days of sunny April through the forest path he comes, comes, ever comes.

In the rainy gloom of July nights on the thundering chariot of clouds he comes, comes, ever comes.

In sorrow after sorrow it is his steps that press upon my heart, and it is the golden touch of his feet that makes my joy to shine.

IX

Thou hast made me known to friends whom I knew not. Thou hast given me seats in homes not my own. Thou hast brought the distant near and made a brother of the stranger.

I am uneasy at heart when I have to leave my accustomed shelter; I forget that there abides the old in the new, and that there also thou abidest.

Through birth and death, in this world or in others, wherever thou leadest me it is thou, the same, the one companion of my endless life who ever linkest my heart with bonds of joy to the unfamiliar.

When one knows thee, then alien there is none, then no door is shut. Oh, grant me my prayer that I may never lose the bliss of the touch of the one in the play of the many.

X

I boasted among men that I had known you. They see your pictures in all works of mine. They come and ask me, 'Who is he?' I know not how to answer them. I say, 'Indeed, I cannot tell.' They blame me and they go away in scorn. And you sit there smiling.

I put my tales of you into lasting songs. The secret gushes out from my heart. They come and ask me, 'Tell me all your meanings.' I know not how to answer them. I say, 'Ah, who knows what they mean!' They smile and go away in utter scorn. And you sit there smiling.

See also: Aurobindo; Dutt; Naidu; Steel, 'In the Permanent Way'; Vivekananda.

WILLIAM BUTLER YEATS
(1865–1939)

Introduction to *Gitanjali* (1912)

A few days ago I said to a distinguished Bengali doctor of medicine, 'I know no German, yet if a translation of a German poet had moved me, I would go to the British Museum and find books in English that would tell me something of his life, and of the history of his thought. But though these prose translations from Rabindranath Tagore have stirred my blood as nothing has for years, I shall not know anything of his life, and of the movements of thought that have made them possible, if some Indian traveller will not tell me.' It seemed to him natural that I should be moved, for he said, 'I read Rabindranath every day, to read one line of his is to forget all the troubles of the world.' I said, 'An Englishman living in London in the reign of Richard the Second had he been shown translations from Petrarch or from Dante, would have found no books to answer his questions, but would have questioned some Florentine banker or Lombard merchant as I question you. For all I know, so abundant and simple is this poetry, the new Renaissance has been born in your country and I shall never know of it except by hearsay.' He answered, 'We have other poets, but none that are his equal; we call this the epoch of Rabindranath. No poet seems to me as famous in Europe as he is among us. He is as great in music as in poetry, and his songs are sung from the west of India into Burmah wherever Bengali is spoken. He was already famous at nineteen when he wrote his first novel; and plays, written when he was but little older, are still played in Calcutta. I so much admire the completeness of his life; when he was very young he wrote much of natural objects, he would sit all day in his garden; from his twenty-fifth year or so to his thirty-fifth perhaps, when he had a great sorrow, he wrote the most beautiful love poetry in our language'; and then he said with deep emotion, 'words can never express what I owed at seventeen to his love poetry. After that his art grew deeper, it became religious and philosophical; all the aspirations of mankind are in his hymns. He is the first among our saints who has not refused to live, but has spoken out of Life itself, and that is why we give him our love.' I may have changed his well-chosen words in my memory but not his thought. 'A little while ago he was to read divine service in one of our churches—we of the Brahma Samaj* use your word "church" in English—it was the largest in Calcutta and not only was it crowded, people even standing in the windows, but the streets were all but impassable because of the people.'

Other Indians came to see me and their reverence for this man sounded strange in our world, where we hide great and little things under the same veil of obvious comedy and half-serious depreciation. When we were making the cathedrals had we a like reverence for our great men? 'Every morning at three—I know, for I have seen it'—one said to me, 'he sits immovable in contemplation, and for two hours does not awake from his reverie upon the nature of God. His father, the Maha Rishi, would sometimes sit there all through the next day; once, upon a river, he fell into contemplation because of the beauty of the landscape, and the rowers waited for eight hours before they could continue their journey.' He then told me of Mr Tagore's family and how for generations great men have come out of its cradles. 'Today,' he said, 'there are Gogonendranath and Abanindranath Tagore, who are artists; and Dwijendranath, Rabindranath's brother,* who is a great philosopher. The squirrels come from the boughs and climb on to his knees and the birds alight upon his hands.' I notice in these men's thought a sense of visible beauty and meaning as though they held that doctrine of Nietzsche that we must not believe in the moral or intellectual beauty which does not sooner or later impress itself upon physical things. I said, 'In the East you know how to keep a family illustrious. The other day the curator of a Museum pointed out to me a little dark-skinned man who was arranging their Chinese prints and said, "That is the hereditary connoisseur of the Mikado, he is the fourteenth of his family to hold the post."' He answered. 'When Rabindranath was a boy he had all round him in his home literature and music.' I thought of the abundance, of the simplicity of the poems, and said, 'In your country is there much propagandist writing, much criticism? We have to do so much, especially in my own country, that our minds gradually cease to be creative, and yet we cannot help it. If our life was not a continual warfare, we would not have taste, we would not know what is good, we would not find hearers and readers. Four-fifths of our energy is spent in the quarrel with bad taste, whether in our own minds or in the minds of others.' 'I understand,' he replied, 'we too have our propagandist writing. In the villages they recite long mythological poems adapted from the Sanscrit in the Middle Ages, and they often insert passages telling the people that they must do their duties.'

II

I have carried the manuscript of these translations about with me for days, reading it in railway trains, or on the top of omnibuses and in restaurants, and I have often had to close it lest some stranger would see how much it moved me. These lyrics—which are in the original, my Indians tell me, full of subtlety of rhythm, of untranslatable delicacies of colour, of metrical invention—display in their thought a world I have dreamed of all my life long. The work of a supreme culture, they yet appear as much the growth of the common soil as the grass and the rushes. A tradition, where poetry and religion are the same thing, has passed through the centuries, gathering from learned and unlearned metaphor and emotion, and carried back again to the multitude the thought of the scholar and of the noble. If the civilization of Bengal remains unbroken, if that common mind which—as one divines—runs through all, is not, as with us, broken into a dozen minds that know nothing of each other, something even of what is most subtle in these verses will have come, in a few generations, to the beggar on the roads. When there was but one mind in England Chaucer wrote his *Troilus and Cressida*,* and though he had written to be read, or to be read out—for our time was coming on apace—he was sung by minstrels for a while. Rabindranath Tagore, like Chaucer's forerunners, writes music for his words, and one understands at every moment that he is so abundant, so spontaneous, so daring in his passion, so full of surprise, because he is doing something which has never seemed strange, unnatural, or in need of defence. These verses will not lie in little well-printed books upon ladies' tables, who turn the pages with indolent hands that they may sigh over a life without meaning, which is yet all they can know of life, or be carried about by students at the university to be laid aside when the work of life begins, but as the generations pass, travellers will hum them on the highway and men rowing upon rivers. Lovers, while they await one another, shall find, in murmuring them, this love of God a magic gulf wherein their own more bitter passion may bathe and renew its youth. At every moment the heart of this poet flows outward to these without derogation or condescension, for it has known that they will understand; and it has filled itself with the circumstance of their lives. The traveller in the red-brown clothes that he wears that dust may not show upon him, the girl searching in her bed for the petals fallen from the wreath of her royal lover, the servant or the bride awaiting the master's home-coming in the empty house, are images of the heart turning to God. Flowers and rivers, the blowing of conch shells, the heavy rain of the Indian July, or the parching heat, are images of the moods of that heart in union or in separation; and a man sitting in a boat upon a river playing upon a lute, like one of those figures full of mysterious meaning in a Chinese picture, is God Himself. A whole people, a whole civilization, immeasurably strange to us, seems to have been taken up into this imagination; and yet we are not moved because of its strangeness, but because we have met our own image, as though we had walked in Rossetti's willow wood,* or heard, perhaps for the first time in literature, our voice as in a dream.

Since the Renaissance the writing of European saints—however familiar their metaphor and the general structure of their thought—has ceased to hold our attention. We know that we must at last forsake the world, and we are accustomed in moments of weariness or exaltation to consider a voluntary forsaking; but how can we, who have read so much poetry, seen so many paintings, listened to so much music, where the cry of the flesh and the cry of the soul seem one, forsake it harshly and rudely? What have we in common with St Bernard covering his eyes that they may not dwell upon the beauty of the lakes of Switzerland, or with the violent rhetoric of the Book of Revelation? We would, if we might, find, as in this book, words full of courtesy. 'I have got my leave. Bid me farewell, my brothers! I bow to you all and take my departure. Here I give back the keys of my door—and I give up all claims to my house. I only ask for last kind words from you. We were neighbours for long, but I received more than I could give. Now the day has dawned and the lamp that lit my dark corner is out. A summons has come and I am ready for my journey.'* And it is our own mood, when it is furthest from À Kempis or John of the Cross,* that cries, 'And because I love this life, I know I shall love death as well.' Yet it is not only in our thoughts of the parting that this book fathoms all. We had not known that we loved God, hardly it may be that we believed in Him; yet looking backward upon our life we discover, in our exploration of the pathways of woods, in our delight in the lonely places of hills, in that mysterious claim that we have made, unavailingly, on the women that we have loved, the emotion that created this insidious sweetness. 'Entering my heart unbidden even as one of the common crowd, unknown to me, my king, thou didst press the signet of eternity upon many a fleeting moment.' This is no longer the sanctity of the cell and of the scourge; being but a lifting up, as it were, into a greater intensity of the mood of the painter, painting the dust and the sunlight, and we go for a like voice to St Francis and to William Blake who have seemed so alien in our violent history.

III

We write long books where no page perhaps has any quality to make writing a pleasure, being confident in some general design, just as we fight and make money and fill our heads with politics—all dull things in the doing—while Mr Tagore, like the Indian civilization itself, has been content to discover the soul and surrender himself to its spontaneity. He often seems to contrast his life with that of those who have lived more after our fashion, and have more seeming weight in the world, and always humbly as though he were only sure his way is best for him: 'Men going home glance at me and smile and fill me with shame. I sit like a beggar maid, drawing my skirt over my face, and when they ask me, what it is I want, I drop my eyes and answer them not.' At another time, remembering how his life had once a different shape, he will say, 'Many an hour have I spent in the strife of the good and the evil, but now it is the pleasure of my playmate of the empty days to draw my heart on to him; and I know not why is this sudden call to what useless inconsequence.' An innocence, a simplicity that one does not find elsewhere in literature makes the birds and the leaves seem as near to him as they are near to children, and the changes of the seasons great events as before our thoughts had arisen between them and us. At times I wonder if he has it from the literature of Bengal or from religion, and at other times, remembering the birds alighting on his brother's hands, I find pleasure in thinking it hereditary, a mystery that was growing through the centuries like the courtesy of a Tristan or a Pelanore.* Indeed, when he is speaking of children, so much a part of himself this quality seems, one is not certain that he is not also speaking of the saints, 'They build their houses with sand and they play with empty shells. With withered leaves they weave their boats and smilingly float them on the vast deep. Children have their play on the seashore of worlds. They know not how to swim, they know not how to cast nets. Pearl fishers dive for pearls, merchants sail in their ships, while children gather pebbles and scatter them again. They seek not for hidden treasures, they know not how to cast nets.'

See also: Candler; Clifford; Joyce; Mansfield; Naidu; Vivekananda.

B. E. BAUGHAN
(1870–1958)

Pipi on the Prowl (1913)

Pipi was very happy. To an indifferent observer, it is true, the little mummy-like old Maori woman, bundled about with a curious muddle of rag-bag jackets and petticoats, and hobbling along the highroad on crippled bare brown feet, might have presented a spectacle more forlorn than otherwise. But then, what does the indifferent observer ever really see? That grotesque and pitiful exterior was nothing but an exterior; and it covered an escaping captive: it clothed incarnate Mirth. For Miria had gone to town, and Pipi, one whole long afternoon, was free!

She chuckled as she thought of Miria—Miria the decorous, Miria the *pakeha** coachman's wife, Miria, who wore tan shoes. Miria did not like her grandmother to go roaming at her own sweet will along the roads; she did not even like her to smoke; what she did like was to have her squatted safe at the *whare** door, holding on to little Hana, whose kicking really began to be painful, and looking out that little Himi did not get hold of the axe and chop himself to bits. She had left her like that half an hour ago; probably she imagined her to be still like that—submissive, stationed, and oh, how lack-lustre, how dull! Well, Pipi might perhaps be a little *porangi* (crazy) at times, but she was never anything like so *porangi* as that. How lucky that Ropata's wife was a trustworthy crony! How fortunate that the babies could neither of them speak! Pipi smiled, and showed her perfect teeth; she took out, from deep recesses of her raiment, her treasured pipe, and stuck it in her mouth. *E! Ka pai te paipa!*—a good thing, the pipe! There was no *topeka* (tobacco) in it, to be sure; but who could say whence *topeka* might not come, this golden afternoon? To those newly at liberty all the world belongs. And, like stolen waters, stolen sport is sweet. No urchin who, having safely conveyed himself away at last out of earshot of mother or teacher, bounds breathless to the beloved creek where 'bullies' wait the hook, knows more of the mingled raptures of lawlessness and expectation than this old great-grandmother Pipi did, out upon the high-road, out upon the hunt!

Although it was midwinter, the afternoon was warm—there is never really cold weather upon that sheltered northern coast. The road ran right round the head of the league-long harbour, and showed a splendid view; for the tide was in; every cove and inlet was full, and the sinuous, satin-blue sheen of the water reflected with the utmost fidelity every one of the little long, low spits, emerald-turfed and darkly crowned with trees, that fringed, as with a succession of piers, the left-hand shore; while the low, orange-coloured cliffs of the fern-flats opposite burned in the brilliant sun like buttresses of gold. But what was a view to Pipi? Her rheumy old brown eyes sought but the one spot, where, far down the glittering water-way, and close to the short, straight sapphire line that parted the purple Heads and meant the open sea, the glass of the township windows sent sparkles to the sun. The township—seven miles away, and Miria not there yet! *Ka pai*! Pipi was ready for whatever fish Tangaroa might kindly send her on dry land, but meanwhile freedom, simple freedom, mere lack of supervision, was in itself enough; and happily, happily she trudged along, nodding, smiling, and sucking vigorously at her empty pipe.

Before very long she came to the river—the sinister-looking river, black and sluggish, that drains the valley-head. In the swamp on the other side of the long white bridge, dark *manuka*-bushes with crooked stems and shaggy boles, like a company of uncanny crones under a spell, stood knee-deep in thick ooze; some withered *raupo* desolately lined the bank above. Even on that bright day, this was a dismal place, and the *raupo*, with its spindly shanks and discoloured leaves fluttering about them, looked lamentably like poor Pipi. *Poor Pipi*, indeed? Dismal place? Huh! what does a fool know?

With brightened eyes, with uncouth gestures of delighted haste, out across the bridge scurried Pipi, slithered down into the swamp, clutched with eager claws at a muddy lump upon the margin, and emitted a deep low grunt of joy. Old snags, quite black with decay, lay rotting round her, and the stagnant water gave forth a most unpleasant smell. But what is foulness when glory beckons through it? Squatting in the slime, her tags and trails of raiment dabbling in and out of the black water, Pipi washed and scraped, scraped and washed, and finally lifted up and out into the sunshine with a grin of delight, a great golden pumpkin, richly streaked with green. The glint of its rind had caught her eye from the other side of the bridge. Evidently it had fallen from some passing cart, and rolled down into the swamp. It was big; it was heavy; it was sound. The goodness of this pumpkin! the triumph of this find! Pipi untied one of her most extra garments, tied the treasure securely in it, slung the bundle on her back as though it had been a baby, and went on.

From the river, the road runs straight uphill, through a cutting between high banks of fern and gorse, with a crumbly crest of *papa* clay boldly yellow on the full blue sky. The road is of yellow *papa* also, and unmetalled, and rather heavy. Pipi grunted a good deal as she toiled up it; and about halfway up stood still to get her breath, for the pumpkin, precious as it was, lay like lead upon her frail old shoulders. Why! at the very top of the bank, glaring in the sunshine against the yellow *papa*, what was that? A white paper only, with nothing in it— or a white paper parcel? Steep as the bank was, go she must, of course, and see; and up, pumpkin and all, she climbed. Aha! Something inside. What? . . . Bread; and, inside the bread? Jam; thick, sweet, deep-red jam, very thick, very sweet, *very* good!

Next to tobacco, Pipi loved sweet things. She did not expend much pity upon the school-child that, heedlessly running along the top edge of the bank that morning, had lost its lunch and spent a hungry dinner-hour; neither did the somewhat travelled appearance of the sandwich trouble her. She scrambled down again on to the firmer footing of the road, and there she stood, and licked and licked at the jam. Miria's face, if she had caught her at it! Oho, that face!—the very fancy of its sourness made the tit-bit sweeter. The bread itself she

threw away. Her stomach was not hungry, Miria saw to that; but her
imagination was, and that was why this chance-come, wayside dainty
had a relish that no good, dull dinner in the *whare* ever had. Sport was
good to-day. First that pumpkin, now this jam! *Ka pai* the catch!
What next?

She resumed her journey up-hill, but had no sooner reached the
top than she suddenly squatted down on the bank by the roadside, as
if at a word of command, with next to no breath left in her lungs, but
hope once more lively in her heart—for here, surely, advancing to
meet her, was the Next—a tall young *pakeha* woman, with a basket on
her arm. Only a woman. That was a pity, for there was the less chance
of *topeka*; still, what had that kit got in it?

Pipi knew all about strategical advantages by instinct. She sat still
and waited on her hill-top as her forefathers had sat still on theirs,
and waited for the prey. Soon it came; a little breathless, and with
footsteps slackening naturally as they neared the brow, just as Pipi
had foreseen. Yes, she would do, this *pakeha*, this pigeon; she would
pay to be plucked. She was nicely dark and stout; she smiled to
herself as she walked; and such good clothes upon the back denoted
certainly a comfortable supply of *hikapeni* (sixpences) in the pocket.

'*Tenakoe! Tenakoe!*' (greeting!) cried Pipi, skipping up from her
bank with a splendid assumption of agility, as the stranger came alongside; and extending her hand, expanding her smile, and wagging her
wily old head, as if this strange young *pakeha* were her very dearest
friend in all the world. And the bait took! The *pakeha*, too, stretched
forth her hand, she, also, smiled. A catch, a catch to Pipi the fisher! Let
us, though, find out first how much she knows, this fish . . . Not to
speak the Maori tongue means not to read the Maori mind, so:

'*E hoa!*' says Pipi leisurely, '*E haere ana koe i whaea?*'

Good! it is all right. The *pakeha* stands still, laughs, and says, 'Oh,
please say it in English!'

She is ignorant, she is affable, she is not in a hurry. She will do, this
nice young *pakeha*! Pipi translates.

'Where you goin'?'

'I am going—oh, just along this road for a bit,' says the girl
vaguely.

Pipi considers. 'Along the road,' in the stranger's present direction, means back towards home for Pipi; it would surely be a pity to
turn back so soon? A fish on the line, however, is worth two in the

water; also, after the feast is eaten, cannot the empty basket be thrown away? in other words, as soon as ever it suits her, cannot she pretend to be tired and let the stranger go on alone? Of course she can! So Pipi says, 'Me, too,' and, turning her back, for the time being, upon the enticement of the open road ahead, goes shambling back, hoppity-hop, down the hill again, at the side of her prey. She shambles slowly, too, by way of a further test, and, see, the girl instinctively adapts her pace. Excellent! Oh, the pleasantness, the complaisance, of this interesting young friend! Pipi takes hold of her sleeve, and strokes it.

'Ah, the good coat,' she cries, with an admiration that she does not need to assume. 'He keep you warm, my word! My coat, see how thin!' and she holds out for inspection a corner of her topmost covering, an old blouse of faded pinkish print, phenomenally spotted with purple roses. It is true that she has the misfortune to hold out also, quite by mistake, a little bit of the layer next beneath, which happens to be a thick tweed coat; but this she drops immediately, without an instant's delay, and it is well known that *pakehas* have as a rule only pebbles in their eye-sockets—they see nothing; while their ears, on the other hand, are as *kokota*-shells, to hold whatever you please to put in. 'I cold, plenty, plenty,' says Pipi accordingly, with a very well-feigned shiver. 'How much he cost, your good, warm coat?'

'Why, I don't quite know,' replies the *pakeha*. 'You see, it was a present; somebody gave it me.'

'Ah, nobody give poor Pipi,' sighs Pipi, very naughtily. Is it a good thing or not, that two of the Colonel's old flannel shirts, Mrs Cameron's knitted petticoat, and Miria's thickest dress, all of them upon her person at that moment, have no tongues? 'Nobody give *kai* (food) even. What you got in your big kit?' she asks coaxingly. '*Plenty* big kit!'

'Ah, nothing at all. Only air. It's just cramful of emptiness,' says the girl, sadly shaking her head. 'What you got on your back in the bundle there? Plenty big bundle!'

It is useless, of course, to deny the existence of so plain a fact as that pumpkin. Why had not Pipi had the wit to hide it in the fern?

'On'y punkin,' she says, with a singular grimace, expressive at first of the contemptibility of all the pumpkin tribe, then changing instantly to a radiant recognition of their priceless worth, for her mind has been

'Stung with the splendour of a sudden thought.'*

'He *fine* punkin, big, *big* punkin,' she cries, and then, munificently, 'You give me coat, I give you this big, big punkin!' She exhibits her treasure as one astounded at her own generosity.

The *pakeha*, however, seems astounded at it, too.

'Why!' says she, 'my coat is worth at least three thousand pumpkins.'

Perhaps it is? Pipi tries to imagine three thousand pumpkins lying spread before her, with a view to assessing their value; but, not unnaturally, fails. Ah well! Bold bargaining is one weapon, but tactful yielding is another.

'*E!* You give me *hikapeni*, then, I give you punkin.' She concedes, with an air of reckless kindness, and a hope of sixpence-worth of *topeka* to be purchased presently on the sly from Wirimu, the gardener.

But 'I don't care much for pumpkins,' says the stupid *pakeha*. 'And I haven't any *hikapeni*,' she adds. The stingy thing! A fish? why, the creature is nothing at all but an empty cockle-shell not worth the digging. And Pipi is just thinking that she shall soon feel too tired to walk a single step farther, when, suddenly producing a small, sweetly-familiar-looking packet from her coat, 'You like cigarettes?' inquires the *pakeha*.

'*Ai! Homai te hikarete! Ka pai te hikarete!* ('Yes! Give me a cigarette! I do like cigarettes),' cries Pipi, enraptured, and the *pakeha* holds out the packet. Alas! there are only two cigarettes left in it, and manners will permit of Pipi's taking only one. This is very trying. 'You smoke?' she asks innocently. The girl denies it, of course, as Pipi knew she would: these *pakeha* women always do, and Miria, their slavish advocate and copyist, declares they speak the truth. Vain words; for, in the hotel at Rotorua, has not Pipi seen the very best attired of them at it? Moreover, why should this girl trouble to carry cigarettes if she does not smoke, herself? Plenty stupid, these *pakeha* women! Plenty good, however, their cigarettes, and greed (oh Miria!) overcoming manners, '*E!* You not smoke; you give me other *hikaret*', then,' she says boldly.

This miserable *pakeha*, however, proves to be as a pig, that, full of feed, yet stands with both feet in the trough—she only shakes her head, laughs sillily, and mutters some foolish remark about keeping the other for somebody else she might meet. Ah, well, never mind; Pipi has at least the one, and she would like to smoke it at once and make sure of it, but 'No right!' she says plaintively—she means 'no light'; she has no matches, and no more, it appears, has the *pakeha*. Boiled-headed slave! How, without matches, can she expect anybody to smoke her cigarettes?

'Perhaps this man has some,' suggests the *pakeha*, pointing to the solitary driver of a wagon coming down the hill behind them. She explains the predicament, and the man, with a good-natured smile, pours out half a boxful into Pipi's upstretched palms, and drives on. Ah, and perhaps he had *topeka* with him, too, real, good, dark, strong *topeka* in a stick; and, had Pipi only been wise enough to wait for him, and let this miserable person go by, she might by now, perhaps, have been having a real smoke. As for this *hikarete*, by the smell of it, Hana, aged thirteen months, could smoke it with impunity. No coat, no *kai*, no *hikapeni*, one *hikarete* of hay—Huh! the unprofitableness of this *pakeha*!

'You go on!' says Pipi, with an authoritative gesture. They have got as far as the bridge, and she squats down by her swamp. All that long hill to toil up again, too!

But behold, the black-hearted one at her side says, actually, 'Oh, I'm in no particular hurry. I think I'll sit down a bit, too,' and does so. Now, who that has found the *riwai* (potato) rotten wants to look at the rind?

Worse and worse—who can grow melons in mid-air, drink water without a mouth, or strike a match without something to strike it on? . . . What now? Here is the *pakeha*, in reply to this reproach, sticking out her thick leather boot right into Pipi's hand—an insult? She would kick the *hikaret'* out of it? Not so, for her eyes are soft. . . . Swift as a weather-cock, round whirl Pipi's mobile wits.

'*E hoa!*' she cries with glee. 'You give me the *hu* (shoe)? Poor Pipi no *hu*, see! I think *ka pai*, you give me the *hu*.'

But the *pakeha* only shakes her head vigorously and laughs out loud. Is she *porangi* quite? No, not quite, it seems, for, taking a match from Pipi's hand, she strikes it on the clumsy sole, and lo! a flame bursts out. Pipi can light her *hikaret'* now, and does so, coolly using the *pakeha's* skirt the while, as a breakwind, for she may as well get out of her all the little good she can. And now, how to get rid of this disappointment, this addled egg, this little, little cockle with the big thick shell? Aha, Pipi knows. She will do what she has done so often with the prying Mrs Colonel Cameron—she will suddenly forget all her English, and hear and speak nothing but Maori any more. That will soon scrape off this *piri-piri* (burr). What shall she start by saying? Anything will do; and accordingly she mechanically asks again in Maori her first question, the question she asks every one. 'You are going, where?' But, O calamity! This time, the *pakeha*, the ignorant one, not only understands, but answers—and in the same tongue—and to alarming purpose!

'*E haere ana ahau ki a Huria* (I am going to Judaea),' she says. And Judaea is the name of Pipi's own *kainga*!*

'*Kia Huria*! and you know to speak the Maori!' she exclaims, startled into consternation.

'Only a very little as yet,' replies the girl. 'But Miria is teaching me.'

'Miria! which Miria?' cries Pipi, in an agony of foreboding.

'Why, Miria Piripi, Colonel Cameron's coachman's wife—*your* Miria, isn't she?' says this monster, with a sudden smile. 'She has told me about you, often.'

The truant who should suddenly see his captured 'bully' pull the hook out of its jaws in order to plunge it in his own, might very well feel as Pipi felt at this frightful moment. True enough, she had often heard Miria speak of the *pakeha* lady who came to visit Mrs Cameron and was 'always so interested in the natives;' and with the greatest care she had always kept out of her way, for Pipi had her pride—she resented being made into a show. And now——!

'Yes, and I have often seen you, too, though you may not have seen me,' pursued the relentless *pakeha*. 'You, and little Hana and Himi. Where are Hana and Himi now? I shall be sure to tell Miria I've met you,' she finished brightly.

Alas, alas for Pipi's sport! The fish had caught the fisher, and with a vengeance. She collected her scattering wits, and met the *pakeha's* eye with a stony stare, for she came of a princely race; but cold, too, as a stone, lay the heart within her breast.

The heart of the *pakeha*, however, had also its peculiarities. For all she was a *pakeha*, clad in a fine coat, wearing boots, and carrying cigarettes about with her only by way of Maori mouth-openers: for all this, her heart was the heart of a fellow-vagabond. It understood. She *had* heard Miria, and Mrs Cameron too, talk of Pipi; but with a result of which those superior speakers were not conscious. How often she had silently sympathised with the poor old free-lance kept so straitly to the beaten track of respectability; how often she had wished for a peep at Pipi *au naturel*! And now she had got it; and she meant to get it again. She could not help a little mischievous enjoyment of the confusion so heroically concealed, but she took quick steps to relieve it.

'Well, I must go on,' she said briskly, rising as she spoke. 'Take the other cigarette, Pipi, and here's a shilling for some *topeka*. *E noho koe* (goodbye)! Oh, and, Pipi, don't let's tell Miria yet that we've met, shall we? It will be so nice for her to introduce us properly some day, you know!'

Pipi was game. '*Haere ra*' (good-bye) was all she answered, unemotionally. But she could not help one gleam of joy shooting out of her deep old eyes, and Lucy Willett saw it, and went on with a kindly laughter in her own.

That night, when she had rolled herself up in her blanket, and lain down on the *whare* floor (she disdained the foppishness of beds), Pipi glowed all through with satisfaction. Miria, on coming home, had found her seated, patient, pipeless, before the fire, Hana and Himi one upon each knee, both intact, both peacefully asleep; and had been so pleased with this model picture, as well as with the size of Pipi's pumpkin, that she had indulged her grandmother with schnapper for supper. And Pipi had found that pumpkin; she had harvested red jam from a fern-bank; she had had one cigarette to smoke, and with another had been able to encourage Ropata's wife to future friendly offices. More than that, she had had time for one blessed pipeful of real Derby, richly odorous, and in her most intimate garment of all could feel now, as she lay, safely knotted up, the rest of a whole stick. Nor was even that all. By some extraordinary good management that she herself did not quite understand, she had eluded the hook as it dangled at her very lips while yet she had secured the bait; and she had an instinctive, shrewd suspicion that, in cleverly causing the eye of the *pakeha* to wink at guilt, she had made sure of more patronage in the future. Who could tell? Perhaps, some fine day, that good thick coat, even, might find its way to Pipi's back. *Taihoa* (just wait)! Meanwhile, what a good day's sport!

See also: Barker; Fairbridge; Mansfield; Perrin; Steel; Trollope.

KATHERINE MANSFIELD
(1888–1923)

How Pearl Button was Kidnapped (1912)

Pearl Button swung on the little gate in front of the House of Boxes. It was the early afternoon of a sunshiny day with little winds playing hide-and-seek in it. They blew Pearl Button's pinafore frill into her mouth, and they blew the street dust all over the House of Boxes. Pearl watched it—like a cloud—like when mother peppered her fish and the top of the pepper-pot came off. She swung on the little gate, all alone, and she sang a small song. Two big women came walking down the street. One was dressed in red and the other was dressed in yellow and green. They had pink handkerchiefs over their heads, and both of them carried a big flax basket of ferns. They had no shoes and stockings on, and they came walking along, slowly, because they were so fat, and talking to each other and always smiling. Pearl stopped swinging, and when they saw her they stopped walking. They looked and looked at her and then they talked to each other, waving their arms and clapping their hands together. Pearl began to laugh.

The two women came up to her, keeping close to the hedge and looking in a frightened way towards the House of Boxes.

'Hallo, little girl!' said one.

Pearl said, 'Hallo!'

'You all alone by yourself?'

Pearl nodded.

'Where's your mother?'

'In the kitching, ironing-because-its-Tuesday.'

The women smiled at her and Pearl smiled back. 'Oh,' she said, 'haven't you got very white teeth indeed! Do it again.'

The dark women laughed, and again they talked to each other with funny words and wavings of the hands. 'What's your name?' they asked her.

'Pearl Button.'

'You coming with us, Pearl Button? We got beautiful things to show you,' whispered one of the women. So Pearl got down from the gate and she slipped out into the road. And she walked between the two dark women down the windy road, taking little running steps to keep up, and wondering what they had in their House of Boxes.

They walked a long way. 'You tired?' asked one of the women, bending down to Pearl. Pearl shook her head. They walked much further. 'You not tired?' asked the other woman. And Pearl shook her head again, but tears shook from her eyes at the same time and her lips trembled. One of the women gave over her flax basket of ferns and caught Pearl Button up in her arms, and walked with Pearl Button's head against her shoulder and her dusty little legs dangling. She was softer than a bed and she had a nice smell—a smell that made you bury your head and breathe and breathe it. . . .

They set Pearl Button down in a log room full of other people the same colour as they were—and all these people came close to her and looked at her, nodding and laughing and throwing up their eyes. The woman who had carried Pearl took off her hair ribbon and shook her curls loose. There was a cry from the other women, and they crowded close and some of them ran a finger through Pearl's yellow curls, very gently, and one of them, a young one, lifted all Pearl's hair and kissed the back of her little white neck. Pearl felt shy but happy at the same time. There were some men on the floor, smoking, with rugs and feather mats round their shoulders. One of them made a funny face at her and he pulled a great big peach out of his pocket and set it on the floor, and flicked it with his finger as though it were a marble. It rolled right over to her. Pearl picked it up. 'Please can I eat it?' she asked. At that they all laughed and clapped their hands, and the man with the funny face made another at her and pulled a pear out of his pocket and sent it bobbling over the floor. Pearl laughed. The women sat on the floor and Pearl sat down too. The floor was very dusty. She carefully pulled up her pinafore and dress and sat on her petticoat as she had been taught to sit in dusty places, and she ate the fruit, the juice running all down her front.

'Oh!' she said in a very frightened voice to one of the women, 'I've spilt all the juice!'

'That doesn't matter at all,' said the woman, patting her cheek. A man came into the room with a long whip in his hand. He shouted something. They all got up, shouting, laughing, wrapping themselves up in rugs and blankets and feather mats. Pearl was carried again, this time into a great cart, and she sat on the lap of one of her women with the driver beside her. It was a green cart with a red pony and a black pony. It went very fast out of the town. The driver stood up and waved the whip round his head. Pearl peered over the shoulder of her woman. Other carts were behind like a procession. She waved at them. Then the country came. First fields of short grass with sheep on them and little bushes of white flowers and pink briar rose baskets—then big trees on both sides of the road—and nothing to be seen except big trees. Pearl tried to look through them but it was quite dark. Birds were singing. She nestled closer in the big lap. The woman was warm as a cat, and she moved up and down when she breathed, just like purring. Pearl played with a green ornament* round her neck, and the woman took the little hand and kissed each of her fingers and then turned it over and kissed the dimples. Pearl had never been happy like this before. On the top of a big hill they stopped. The driving man turned to Pearl and said, 'Look, look!' and pointed with his whip.

And down at the bottom of the hill was something perfectly different—a great big piece of blue water was creeping over the land. She screamed and clutched at the big woman. 'What is it, what is it?'

'Why,' said the woman, 'it's the sea.'

'Will it hurt us—is it coming?'

'Ai-e, no, it doesn't come to us. It's very beautiful. You look again.'

Pearl looked. 'You're sure it can't come,' she said.

'Ai-e, no. It stays in its place,' said the big woman. Waves with white tops came leaping over the blue. Pearl watched them break on a long piece of land covered with garden-path shells. They drove round a corner.

There were some little houses down close to the sea, with wood fences round them and gardens inside. They comforted her. Pink and red and blue washing hung over the fences, and as they came near more people came out, and five yellow dogs with long thin tails. All the people were fat and laughing, with little naked babies holding on to them or rolling about in the gardens like puppies. Pearl was lifted down and taken into a tiny house with only one room and a veranda. There was a girl there with two pieces of black hair down to her feet. She was setting the dinner on the floor. 'It *is* a funny place,' said Pearl, watching the pretty girl while the woman unbuttoned her little drawers for her. She was very hungry. She ate meat and vegetables and fruit and the woman gave her milk out of a green cup. And it was quite silent except for the sea outside and the laughs of the two women watching her. 'Haven't you got any Houses of Boxes?' she said. 'Don't you all live in a row? Don't the men go to offices? Aren't there any nasty things?'

They took off her shoes and stockings, her pinafore and dress. She walked about in her petticoat and then she walked outside with the grass pushing between her toes. The two women came out with different sorts of baskets. They took her hands. Over a little paddock, through a fence, and then on warm sand with brown grass in it they went down to the sea. Pearl held back when the sand grew wet, but the women coaxed, 'Nothing to hurt, very beautiful. You come.' They dug in the sand and found some shells which they threw into the baskets. The sand was wet as mud pies. Pearl forgot her fright and began digging too. She got hot and wet, and suddenly over her feet broke a little line of foam. 'Oo, oo!' she shrieked, dabbling with her feet. 'Lovely, lovely!' She paddled in the shallow water. It was warm. She made a cup of her hands and caught some of it. But it stopped being blue in her hands. She was so excited that she rushed over to her woman and flung her little thin arms round the woman's neck, hugging her, kissing . . .

Suddenly the girl gave a frightful scream. The woman raised herself and Pearl slipped down on the sand and looked towards the land. Little men in blue coats—little blue men came running, running towards her with shouts and whistlings—a crowd of little blue men to carry her back to the House of Boxes.

To Stanislaw Wyspianski (1910)

From the other side of the world,
From a little island cradled in the giant sea bosom,
From a little land with no history,
(Making its own history, slowly and clumsily
Piecing together this and that, finding the pattern, solving the
    problem,
Like a child with a box of bricks),
I, a woman, with the taint of the pioneer in my blood,
Full of a youthful strength that wars with itself and is lawless,
I sing your praises, magnificent warrior; I proclaim your triumphant
    battle.

My people have had nought to contend with;
They have worked in the broad light of day and handled the clay with
　　rude fingers
Life—a thing of blood and muscle; Death—a shovelling under-
　　ground of waste material.
What would they know of ghosts and unseen presences,
Of shadows that blot out reality, of darkness that stultifies morn?
Fine and sweet the water that runs from their mountains;
How could they know of poisonous weed, of rotted and clogging
　　tendrils?
And the tapestry woven from dreams of your tragic childhood
They would tear in their stupid hands,
The sad, pale light of your soul blow out with their childish laughter.

But the dead—the old—Oh Master, we belong to you there;
Oh Master, there we are children and awed by the strength of a giant;
How alive you leapt into the grave and wrestled with Death
And found in the veins of Death the red blood flowing
And raised Death up in your arms and showed him to all the people.
Yours a more personal labor than the Nazarene's miracles,
Yours a more forceful encounter than the Nazarene's gentle com-
　　mands.

Stanislaw Wyspianski—Oh man with the name of a fighter,*
Across these thousands of sea-shattered miles we cry and proclaim
　　you;
We say 'He is lying in Poland, and Poland thinks he is dead;
But he gave the denial to Death—he is lying there, wakeful;
The blood in his giant heart pulls red through his veins.'

The Wind Blows (1915)

Suddenly—dreadfully—she wakes up. What has happened? Something dreadful has happened. No—nothing has happened. It is only
the wind shaking the house, rattling the windows, banging a piece of
iron on the roof and making her bed tremble. Leaves flutter past the
window, up and away; down in the avenue a whole newspaper wags
in the air like a lost kite and falls, spiked on a pine tree. It is cold.
Summer is over—it is autumn—everything is ugly. The carts rattle
by, swinging from side to side; two Chinamen lollop along under

their wooden yokes with the straining vegetable baskets—their pigtails and blue blouses fly out in the wind. A white dog on three legs yelps past the gate. It is all over! What is? Oh, everything! And she begins to plait her hair with shaking fingers, not daring to look in the glass. Mother is talking to grandmother in the hall.

'A perfect idiot! Imagine leaving anything out on the line in weather like this . . . Now my best little Teneriffe-work teacloth is simply in ribbons. *What* is that extraordinary smell? It's the porridge burning. Oh, heavens—this wind!'

She has a music lesson at ten o'clock. At the thought the minor movement of the Beethoven begins to play in her head, the trills long and terrible like little rolling drums. . . . Marie Swainson runs into the garden next door to pick the 'chrysanths' before they are ruined. Her skirt flies up above her waist; she tries to beat it down, to tuck it between her legs while she stoops, but it is no use—up it flies. All the trees and bushes beat about her. She picks as quickly as she can, but she is quite distracted. She doesn't mind what she does—she pulls the plants up by the roots and bends and twists them, stamping her foot and swearing.

'For heaven's sake keep the front door shut! Go round to the back,' shouts someone. And then she hears Bogey:

'Mother, you're wanted on the telephone. Telephone, Mother. It's the butcher.'

How hideous life is—revolting, simply revolting . . . And now her hat-elastic's snapped. Of course it would. She'll wear her old tam and slip out the back way. But Mother has seen.

'Matilda. Matilda. Come back im-me-diately! What on earth have you got on your head? It looks like a tea cosy. And why have you got that mane of hair on your forehead.'

'I can't come back, Mother. I'll be late for my lesson.'

'Come back immediately!'

She won't. She won't. She hates Mother. 'Go to hell,' she shouts, running down the road.

In waves, in clouds, in big round whirls the dust comes stinging, and with it little bits of straw and chaff and manure. There is a loud roaring sound from the trees in the gardens, and standing at the bottom of the road outside Mr Bullen's gate she can hear the sea sob: 'Ah! . . . Ah! . . . Ah-h!' But Mr Bullen's drawing-room is as quiet as a cave. The windows are closed, the blinds half-pulled, and she is not late. The-girl-before-her has just started playing MacDowell's 'To an Iceberg'.* Mr Bullen looks over at her and half smiles.

'Sit down,' he says. 'Sit over there in the sofa corner, little lady.'

How funny he is. He doesn't exactly laugh at you . . . but there is just something. . . . Oh, how peaceful it is here. She likes this room. It smells of art serge and stale smoke and chrysanthemums . . . there is a big vase of them on the mantelpiece behind the pale photograph of Rubinstein* . . . *à mon ami Robert Bullen*. . . . Over the black glittering piano hangs 'Solitude'—a dark tragic woman draped in white, sitting on a rock, her knees crossed, her chin on her hands.

'No, no!' says Mr Bullen, and he leans over the other girl, puts his arms over her shoulders and plays the passage for her. The stupid—she's blushing! How ridiculous!

Now the-girl-before-her has gone; the front door slams. Mr Bullen comes back and walks up and down, very softly, waiting for her. What an extraordinary thing. Her fingers tremble so that she can't undo the knot in the music satchel. It's the wind. . . . And her heart beats so hard she feels it must lift her blouse up and down. Mr Bullen does not say a word. The shabby red piano seat is long enough for two people to sit side by side. Mr Bullen sits down by her.

'Shall I begin with scales?' she asks, squeezing her hands together. 'I had some arpeggios, too.'

But he does not answer. She doesn't believe he even hears . . . and then suddenly his fresh hand with the ring on it reaches over and opens Beethoven.

'Let's have a little of the old master,' he says.

But why does he speak so kindly—so awfully kindly—and as though they had known each other for years and years and knew everything about each other.

He turns the page slowly. She watches his hand—it is a very nice hand and always looks as though it had just been washed.

'Here we are,' says Mr Bullen.

Oh, that kind voice—Oh, that minor movement. Here come the little drums. . . .

'Shall I take the repeat?'

'Yes, dear child.'

His voice is far, far too kind. The crotchets and quavers are dancing up and down the stave like little black boys on a fence. Why is he so . . . She will not cry—she has nothing to cry about. . . .

'What is it, dear child?'

Mr Bullen takes her hands. His shoulder is there—just by her head. She leans on it ever so little, her cheek against the springy tweed.

'Life is so dreadful,' she murmurs, but she does not feel it's dreadful at all. He says something about 'waiting' and 'marking time' and 'that rare thing, a woman', but she does not hear. It is so comfortable . . . for ever . . .

Suddenly the door opens and in pops Marie Swainson, hours before her time.

'Take the allegretto a little faster,' says Mr Bullen, and gets up and begins to walk up and down again.

'Sit in the sofa corner, little lady,' he says to Marie.

The wind, the wind. It's frightening to be here in her room by herself. The bed, the mirror, the white jug and basin gleam like the sky outside. It's the bed that is frightening. There it lies, sound asleep. . . . Does Mother imagine for one moment that she is going to darn all those stockings knotted up on the quilt like a coil of snakes? She's not. No, Mother. I do not see why I should. . . . The wind—the wind! There's a funny smell of soot blowing down the chimney. Hasn't anyone written poems to the wind? . . . 'I bring fresh flowers to the leaves and showers.'* . . . What nonsense.

'Is that you, Bogey?'

'Come for a walk round the esplanade, Matilda. I can't stand this any longer.'

'Right-o. I'll put on my ulster. Isn't it an awful day!' Bogey's ulster is just like hers. Hooking the collar she looks at herself in the glass. Her face is white, they have the same excited eyes and hot lips. Ah, they know those two in the glass. Good-bye, dears; we shall be back soon.

'This is better, isn't it?'

'Hook on,' says Bogey.

They cannot walk fast enough. Their heads bent, their legs just touching, they stride like one eager person through the town, down the asphalt zigzag where the fennel grows wild, and on to the esplanade. It is dusky—just getting dusky. The wind is so strong that they have to fight their way through it, rocking like two old drunkards. All the poor little pohutukawas* on the esplanade are bent to the ground.

'Come on! Come on! Let's get near.'

Over by the breakwater the sea is very high. They pull off their hats and her hair blows across her mouth, tasting of salt. The sea is so high that the waves do not break at all; they thump against the rough stone wall and suck up the weedy, dripping steps. A fine spray skims from the water right across the esplanade. They are covered with drops; the inside of her mouth tastes wet and cold.

Bogey's voice is breaking. When he speaks he rushes up and down the scale. It's funny—it makes you laugh—and yet it just suits the day. The wind carries their voices—away fly the sentences like narrow ribbons.

'Quicker! Quicker!'

It is getting very dark. In the harbour the coal hulks show two lights—one high on a mast, and one from the stern.

'Look, Bogey. Look over there.'

A big black steamer with a long loop of smoke streaming, with the portholes lighted, with lights everywhere, is putting out to sea. The wind does not stop her; she cuts through the waves, making for the open gate between the pointed rocks that leads to . . . It's the light that makes her look so awfully beautiful and mysterious. . . . *They* are on board leaning over the rail arm in arm.

'. . . Who are they?'

'. . . Brother and sister.'

'Look, Bogey, there's the town. Doesn't it look small? There's the post office clock chiming for the last time. There's the esplanade where we walked that windy day. Do you remember? I cried at my music lesson that day—how many years ago! Good-bye, little island, good-bye . . .'

Now the dark stretches a wing over the tumbling water. They can't see those two any more. Good-bye, good-bye. Don't forget. . . . But the ship is gone, now.

The wind—the wind.

See also: Baughan; Baynton; Lawson; Stevenson; Yeats.

SOLOMON T. PLAATJE
(1876–1932)

Plaatje's bitter indictment of South African race law, Native Life in
South Africa *(1916), contains two chapters, of which this is the first,
evoking the privations of Africans rendered homeless as a result of the
Natives' Land Act of 1913. This legislation, a 'plague' Act in Plaatje's
terms, aimed to create a landless black labour force. The first of many laws
of explicit segregation, the Act laid the groundwork of a divisive
geography of state apartheid, confining African landholding to about
one-tenth of the surface area of South Africa.* Native Life in South
Africa *also contains detailed legal commentary and an account of an
extended campaign of opposition waged by Plaatje and his colleagues both
in South Africa and Britain. Unfortunately for their campaign, the
appearance of the book, and the mounting movement of protest of which it
formed a part, coincided with time of the First World War.*

One Night with the Fugitives (1916)

> *Es ist unköniglich zu weinen—ach,*
> *Und hier nicht weinen ist unväterlich.**
> Schiller

'Pray that your flight be not in winter,'* said Jesus Christ; but it was
only during the winter of 1913 that the full significance of this New
Testament passage was revealed to us. We left Kimberley by the
early morning train during the first week in July, on a tour of
observation regarding the operation of the Natives' Land Act; and we
arrived at Bloemhof, in the Transvaal, at about noon. On the river
diggings there were no actual cases representing the effects of the
Act, but traces of these effects were everywhere manifest. Some
fugitives of the Natives' Land Act had crossed the river in full flight.
The fact that they reached the diggings a fortnight before our visit
would seem to show that while the debates were proceeding in
Parliament some farmers already viewed with eager eyes the impend-
ing opportunity for at once making slaves of their tenants and
appropriating their stock; for, acting on the powers conferred on
them by an Act signed by Lord Gladstone,* so lately as June 16, they

had during that very week (probably a couple of days after, and in some cases, it would seem, a couple of days before the actual signing of the Bill) approached their tenants with stories about a new Act which makes it criminal for anyone to have black tenants and lawful to have black servants. Few of these natives, of course, would object to be servants, especially if the white man is worth working for, but this is where the shoe pinches: one of the conditions is that the black man's (that is, the servant's) cattle shall henceforth work for the landlord free of charge. Then the natives would decide to leave the farm rather than make the landlord a present of all their life's savings, and some of them had passed through the diggings in search of a place in the Transvaal. But the higher up they went the more gloomy was their prospect as the news about the new law was now penetrating every part of the country.

One farmer met a wandering native family in the town of Bloemhof a week before our visit. He was willing to employ the native and many more homeless families as follows: A monthly wage of £2 10s. for each such family, the husband working in the fields, the wife in the house, with an additional 10s. a month for each son, and 5s. for each daughter, but on condition that the native's cattle were also handed over to work for him. It must be clearly understood, we are told that the Dutchman added, that occasionally the native would have to leave his family at work on the farm, and go out with his wagon and his oxen to earn money whenever and wherever he was told to go, in order that the master may be enabled to pay the stipulated wage. The natives were at first inclined to laugh at the idea of working for a master with their families and goods and chattels, and then to have the additional pleasure of paying their own small wages, besides bringing money to pay the 'Baas'* for employing them. But the Dutchman's serious demeanour told them that his suggestion was 'no joke'. He himself had for some time been in need of a native cattle-owner, to assist him as transport rider between Bloemhof, Mooifontein, London, and other diggings, in return for the occupation and cultivation of some of his waste lands in the district, but that was now illegal. He could only 'employ' them; but, as he had no money to pay wages, their cattle would have to go out and earn it for him. 'Had they not heard of the law before?' he inquired. Of course they had; in fact that is why they left the other place, but as they thought that it was but a 'Free' State law,* they took the anomalous situation for one of the multifarious aspects of the freedom of the 'Free' State whence they came; they had scarcely thought that the Transvaal was similarly afflicted.

Needless to say the natives did not see their way to agree with such a one-sided bargain. They moved up-country, but only to find the next farmer offering the same terms, however, with a good many more disturbing details—and the next farmer and the next—so that after this native farmer had wandered from farm to farm, occasionally getting into trouble for travelling with unknown stock, 'across my ground without my permission', and at times escaping arrest for he knew not what, and further, being abused for the crimes of having a black skin and no master, he sold some of his stock along the way, beside losing many which died of cold and starvation; and after thus having lost much of his substance, he eventually worked his way back to Bloemhof with the remainder, sold them for anything they could fetch, and went to work for a digger.

The experience of another native sufferer was similar to the above, except that instead of working for a digger he sold his stock for a mere bagatelle, and left with his family by the Johannesburg night train for an unknown destination. More native families crossed the river and went inland during the previous week and as nothing had since been heard of them, it would seem that they were still wandering somewhere, and incidentally becoming well versed in the law that was responsible for their compulsory unsettlement.

Well, we knew that this law was as harsh as its instigators were callous, and we knew that it would, if passed, render many poor people homeless, but it must be confessed that we were scarcely prepared for such a rapid and widespread crash as it caused in the lives of the natives in this neighbourhood. We left our luggage the next morning with the local mission school teacher, and crossed the river to find out some more about this wonderful law of extermination. It was about 10 a.m. when we landed on the south bank of the Vaal River—the picturesque Vaal River, upon whose banks a hundred miles farther west we spent the best and happiest days of our boyhood. It was interesting to walk on one portion of the banks of that beautiful river—a portion which we had never traversed except as an infant in mother's arms more than thirty years before. How the subsequent happy days at Barkly West, so long past, came crowding upon our memory!—days when there were no railways, no bridges, and no system of irrigation. In rainy seasons, which at that time were far more regular and certain, the river used to overflow its high banks and flood the surrounding valleys to such an extent, that no punt could carry the wagons across. Thereby the transport service used to be hung up, and numbers of wagons would congregate for weeks on both sides of the river until the floods subsided. At such times the price of fresh milk used to mount up to 1s. per pint. There being next to no competition, we boys had a monopoly over the milk trade. We recalled the number of haversacks full of bottles of milk we young-sters often carried to those wagons, how we returned with empty bottles and with just that number of shillings. Mother and our elder brothers had leather bags full of gold and did not care for the 'boy's money'; and unlike the boys of the neighbouring village, having no sisters of our own, we gave away some of our money to fair cousins, and jingled the rest in our pockets. We had been told from boyhood that sweets were injurious to the teeth, and so spurning these delights we had hardly any use for money, for all we wanted to eat, drink and wear was at hand in plenty. We could then get six or eight shillings every morning from the pastime of washing that number of bottles, filling them with fresh milk and carrying them down to the wagons; there was always such an abundance of the liquid that our shepherd's hunting dog could not possibly miss what we took, for while the flocks were feeding on the luscious buds of the haak-doorns* and the blossoms of the rich mimosa and other wild vegetation that abounded on the banks of the Vaal River, the cows, similarly engaged, were gathering more and more milk.

The gods are cruel, and one of their cruellest acts of omission was that of giving us no hint that in very much less than a quarter of a century all those hundreds of heads of cattle, and sheep and horses belonging to the family would vanish like a morning mist, and that we ourselves would live to pay 30s. per month for a daily supply of this same precious fluid, and in very limited quantities. They might have warned us that Englishmen would agree with Dutchmen* to make it unlawful for black men to keep milk cows of their own on the banks of that river, and gradually have prepared us for the shock.

Crossing the river from the Transvaal side brings one into the province of the Orange 'Free' State, in which, in the adjoining division of Boshof, we were born thirty-six years back. We remember the name of the farm, but not having been in this neighbourhood since infancy, we could not tell its whereabouts, nor could we say whether the present owner was a Dutchman, his lawyer, or a Hebrew merchant; one thing we do know, however: it is that even if we had the money and the owner was willing to sell the spot upon which we first saw the light of day and breathed the pure air of heaven, the sale would be followed with a fine of one hundred pounds. The law of the country forbids the sale of land to a native. Russia is one of the most abused countries in the world, but it is extremely doubtful if the statute book of that empire contains a law debarring the peasant from purchasing the land whereon he was born, or from building a home wherein he might end his days.

At this time we felt something rising from our heels along our back, gripping us in a spasm, as we were cycling along; a needlelike pang, too, pierced our heart with a sharp thrill. What was it? We remembered feeling something nearly like it when our father died eighteen years ago; but at that time our physical organs were fresh and grief was easily thrown off in tears, but then we lived in a happy South Africa that was full of pleasant anticipations, and now—what changes for the worse have we undergone! For to crown all our calamities, South Africa has by law ceased to be the home of any of her native children whose skins are dyed with a pigment that does not conform with the regulation hue.

We are told to forgive our enemies and not to let the sun go down upon our wrath, so we breathe the prayer that peace may be to the white races, and that they, including our present persecutors of the Union Parliament, may never live to find themselves deprived of all occupation and property rights in their native country as is now the case with the native. History does not tell us of any other continent where the Bantu lived besides Africa, and if this systematic ill treatment of the natives by the colonists is to be the guiding principle of Europe's scramble for Africa, slavery is our only alternative; for now it is only as serfs that the natives are legally entitled to live here. Is it to be thought that God is using the South African Parliament to hound us out of our ancestral homes in order to quicken our pace heavenward? But go from where to heaven? In the beginning, we are told, God created heaven and earth, and peopled the earth, for people do not shoot up to heaven from nowhere. They must have had an earthly home. Enoch, Melchizedek, Elijah, and other saints, came to heaven from earth. God did not say to the Israelites in their bondage:

'Cheer up, boys; bear it all in good part for I have bright mansions on high awaiting you all.' But he said: 'I have surely seen the affliction of my people which are in Egypt, and have heard their cry by reason of their taskmasters; for I know their sorrows, and I am come down to bring them out of the hands of the Egyptians, and to bring them up out of that land unto a good land and a large, unto a land flowing with milk and honey.' And He used Moses to carry out the promise He made to their ancestor Abraham in Canaan, that 'unto thy seed will I give this land.'* It is to be hoped that in the Boer churches, entrance to which is barred against coloured people during divine service, they also read the Pentateuch.

It is doubtful if we ever thought so much on a single bicycle ride as we did on this journey; however, the sight of a policeman ahead of us disturbed these meditations and gave place to thoughts of quite another kind, for—we had no pass. Dutchmen, Englishmen, Jews, Germans and other foreigners may roam the 'Free' State without permission—but not natives. To us it would mean a fine and imprisonment to be without a pass. The 'pass' law was first instituted to check the movement of livestock over sparsely populated areas. In a sense it was a wise provision, in that it served to identify the livestock which one happened to be driving along the high road, to prove the bona fides of the driver and his title to the stock. Although white men still steal large droves of horses in Basutoland and sell them in Natal or in East Griqualand, they, of course, are not required to carry any passes. These white horse-thieves, to escape the clutches of the police, employ natives to go and sell the stolen stock and write the passes for these natives, forging the names of magistrates and justices of the peace. Such native thieves in some instances ceasing to be hirelings in the criminal business, trade on their own, but it is not clear what purpose it is intended to serve by subjecting native pedestrians to the degrading requirement of carrying passes when they are not in charge of any stock.

In a few moments the policeman was before us and we alighted in presence of the representative of the law, with our feet on the accursed soil of the district in which we were born. The policeman stopped. By his looks and his familiar 'Dag jong'* we noticed that the policeman was Dutch, and the embodiment of affability. He spoke and we were glad to notice that he had no intention of dragging an innocent man to prison. We were many miles from the nearest police station, and in such a case one is generally able to gather the real views of the man on patrol, as distinct from the written code of his office, but our friend was becoming very companionable. Naturally we asked him about the operation of the plague law. He was a Transvaler, he said, and he knew that Kaffirs were inferior beings, but they had rights, and were always left in undisturbed possession of their property when Paul Kruger was alive. 'The poor devils must be sorry now', he said, 'that they ever sang "God save the Queen" when the British troops came into the Transvaal, for I have seen, in the course of my duties, that a Kaffir's life nowadays was not worth a —, and I believed that no man regretted the change of flags now more than the Kaffirs of Transvaal.' This information was superfluous, for personal contact with the natives of Transvaal had convinced us of the fact. They say it is only the criminal who has any reason to rejoice over the presence of the Union Jack, because in his case the cat-o'-nine-tails, except for very serious crimes, has been abolished.

'Some of the poor creatures,' continued the policeman, 'I knew to be fairly comfortable, if not rich, and they enjoyed the possession of their stock, living in many instances just like Dutchmen. Many of these are now being forced to leave their homes. Cycling along this road you will meet several of them in search of new homes, and if ever there was a fool's errand, it is that of a Kaffir trying to find a new home for his stock and family just now.'

'And what do you think, Baas Officer, must eventually be the lot of a people under such unfortunate circumstances?' we asked.

'I think,' said the policeman, 'that it must serve them right. They had no business to hanker after British rule, to cheat and plot with the enemies of their Republic for the overthrow of their Government. Why did they not assist the forces of their Republic during the war* instead of supplying the English with scouts and intelligence? Oom Paul* would not have died of a broken heart and he would still be there to protect them. Serve them right, I say.'

So saying he spurred his horse, which showed a clean pair of hoofs. He left us rather abruptly, for we were about to ask why we, too, of Natal and the Cape were suffering, for we, being originally British subjects, never 'cheated and plotted with the enemies of our Colonies,' but he was gone and left us still cogitating by the roadside.

Proceeding on our journey we next came upon a native trek and heard the same old story of prosperity on a Dutch farm: they had raised an average eight hundred bags of grain each season, which, with the increased stock and sale of wool, gave a steady income of about £150 per year after the farmer had taken his share. There were gossipy rumours about somebody having met someone who said that someone else had overheard a conversation between the Baas and somebody else, to the effect that the Kaffirs were getting too rich on his property. This much involved tale incidentally conveys the idea that the Baas was himself getting too rich on his farm. For the native provides his own seed, his own cattle, his own labour for the ploughing, the weeding and the reaping, and after bagging his grain he calls in the landlord to receive his share, which is fifty per cent of the entire crop.

All had gone well till the previous week when the Baas came to the native tenants with the story that a new law had been passed under which 'all my oxen and cows must belong to him, and my family to work for £2 a month, failing which he gave me four days to leave the farm.'

We passed several farmhouses along the road, where all appeared pretty tranquil as we went along, until the evening which we spent in the open country, somewhere near the boundaries of the Hoopstad and Boshof Districts; here a regular circus had gathered. By a 'circus' we mean the meeting of groups of families, moving to every point of the compass, and all bivouacked at this point in the open country where we were passing. It was heartrending to listen to the tales of their cruel experiences derived from the rigour of the Natives' Land Act. Some of their cattle had perished on the journey, from poverty and lack of fodder, and the native owners ran a serious risk of imprisonment for travelling with dying stock. The experience of one of these evicted tenants is typical of the rest, and illustrates the cases of several we met in other parts of the country.

Kgobadi, for instance, had received a message describing the eviction of his father-in-law in the Transvaal Province, without notice, because he had refused to place his stock, his family, and his person at the disposal of his former landlord, who now refuses to let him remain on his farm except on these conditions. The father-in-law asked that Kgobadi should try and secure a place for him in the much dreaded 'Free' State as the Transvaal had suddenly become uninhabitable to natives who cannot become servants; but 'greedy folk hae lang airms', and Kgobadi himself was proceeding with his family and his belongings in a wagon, to inform his people-in-law of his own eviction, without notice, in the 'Free' State, for a similar reason to that which sent his father-in-law adrift. The Baas had exacted from him the services of himself, his wife and his oxen, for wages of 30s. a month, whereas Kgobadi had been making over £100 a year, besides retaining the services of his wife and of his cattle for himself. When he refused the extortionate terms, the Baas retaliated with a Dutch note, dated the 30th day of June 1913, which ordered him to 'betake himself from the farm of the undersigned, by sunset of the same day, failing which his stock would be seized and impounded, and himself handed over to the authorities for trespassing on the farm.'

A drowning man catches at every straw, and so we were again and again appealed to for advice by these sorely afflicted people. To those who were not yet evicted we counselled patience and submission to the absurd terms, pending an appeal to a higher authority than the South African Parliament and finally to His Majesty the King who, we believed, would certainly disapprove of all that we saw on that day had it been brought to his notice. As for those who were already evicted, as a Bechuana we could not help thanking God that Bechuanaland (on the western boundary of this quasi-British Republic) was still entirely British. In the early days it was the base of David Livingstone's activities and peaceful mission against the Portuguese and Arab slave trade. We suggested that they might negotiate the numerous restrictions against the transfer of cattle from the Western Transvaal and seek an asylum in Bechuanaland. We wondered what consolation we could give to these roving wanderers if the whole of Bechuanaland were under the jurisdiction of the relentless Union Parliament.

It was cold that afternoon as we cycled into the 'Free' State from Transvaal, and towards evening the southern winds rose. A cutting blizzard raged during the night, and native mothers evicted from their homes shivered with their babies by their sides. When we saw on that night the teeth of the little children clattering through the cold, we thought of our own little ones in their Kimberley home of an evening after gambolling in their winter frocks with their school-mates, and we wondered what these little mites had done that a home should suddenly become to them a thing of the past.

Kgobadi's goats had been to kid when he trekked from his farm;

but the kids, which in halcyon times represented the interest on his capital, were now one by one dying as fast as they were born and left by the roadside for the jackals and vultures to feast upon.

This visitation was not confined to Kgobadi's stock. Mrs Kgobadi carried a sick baby when the eviction took place, and she had to transfer her darling from the cottage to the jolting ox-wagon in which they left the farm. Two days out the little one began to sink as the result of privation and exposure on the road, and the night before we met them its little soul was released from its earthly bonds. The death of the child added a fresh perplexity to the stricken parents. They had no right or title to the farmlands through which they trekked: they must keep to the public roads—the only places in the country open to the outcasts if they are possessed of travelling permit. The deceased child had to be buried, but where, when, and how?

This young wandering family decided to dig a grave under cover of the darkness of that night, when no one was looking, and in that crude manner the dead child was interred—and interred amid fear and trembling, as well as the throbs of a torturing anguish, in a stolen grave, lest the proprietor of the spot, or any of his servants, should surprise them in the act. Even criminals dropping straight from the gallows have an undisputed claim to six feet of ground on which to rest their criminal remains, but under the cruel operation of the Natives' Land Act little children, whose only crime is that God did not make them white, are sometimes denied that right in their ancestral home.

Numerous details narrated by these victims of an Act of Parliament kept us awake all that night, and by next morning we were glad enough to hear no more of the sickening procedure of extermination voluntarily instituted by the South African Parliament. We had spent a hideous night under a bitterly cold sky, conditions to which hundreds of our unfortunate countrymen and countrywomen in various parts of the country are condemned by the provisions of this Parliamentary land plague. At five o'clock in the morning the cold seemed to redouble its energies; and never before did we so fully appreciate the Master's saying: 'But pray ye that your flight be not in the winter.'

See also: Aurobindo; Blyden; Casely Hayford; Joyce; Livingstone and Stanley; McKay; Naidu; Schreiner; Woolf.

AFTERWORD

LEONARD WOOLF
(1880–1969)

Pearls and Swine (composed *c.* 1912; 1921)

I had finished my hundred up—or rather he had—with the Colonel and we strolled into the smoking-room for a smoke and a drink round the fire before turning in. There were three other men already round the fire and they widened their circle to take us in. I didn't know them, hadn't spoken to them or indeed to anyone except the Colonel in the large gaudy uncomfortably comfortable hotel. I was run down, out of sorts generally, and—like a fool, I thought now—had taken a week off to eat, or rather to read the menus of interminable table d'hôte dinners, to play golf and to walk on the 'front' at Torquay.

I had only arrived the day before, but the Colonel (retired), a jolly tubby little man—with white moustaches like two S's lying side by side on the top of his stupid red lips and his kind choleric eyes bulging out on a life which he was quite content never for a moment to understand—made it a point, my dear Sir, to know every new arrival within one hour after he arrived.

We got our drinks and as, rather forgetting that I was in England, I murmured the Eastern formula, I noticed vaguely one of the other three glance at me over his shoulder for a moment. The Colonel stuck out his fat little legs in front of him, turning up his neatly shoed toes before the blaze. Two of the others were talking, talking as men so often do in the comfortable chairs of smoking rooms between ten and eleven at night, earnestly, seriously, of what they call affairs, or politics, or questions. I listened to their fat, full-fed, assured voices in that heavy room which smelt of solidity, safety, horsehair furniture, tobacco smoke, and the faint civilised aroma of whisky and soda. It came as a shock to me in that atmosphere that they were discussing India and the East: it does, you know, every now and again.

Sentimental? Well, I expect one is sentimental about it, having lived there. It doesn't seem to go with solidity and horsehair furniture: the fifteen years come back to one in one moment, all in a heap. How one hated it and how one loved it!

I suppose they had started on the Durbar* and the King's visit. They had got on to Indian unrest, to our position in India, its duties, responsibilities, to the problem of East and West. They hadn't been there of course, they hadn't even seen the brothel and *café chantant* at Port Said suddenly open out into that pink and blue desert that leads you through Africa and Asia into the heart of the East. But they knew all about it, they had solved, with their fat voices and in their fat heads, riddles, older than the Sphinx, of peoples remote and ancient and mysterious whom they had never seen and could never understand. One was, I imagine, a stock jobber, plump and comfortable with a greasy forehead and a high colour in his cheeks, smooth shiny brown hair and a carefully grown small moustache: a good dealer in the market: sharp and confident, with a loud voice and shifty eyes. The other was a clergyman: need I say more? Except that he was more of a clergyman even than most clergymen. I mean that he wore tight things—leggings don't they call them? or breeches?—round his calves. I never know what it means: whether they are bishops or rural deans or archdeacons or archimandrites. In any case I mistrust them even more than the black trousers: they seem to close the last door for anything human to get in through the black clothes. The dog collar closes up the armour above, and below, as long as they *were* trousers, at any rate some whiff of humanity might have eddied up the legs of them and touched bare flesh. But the gaiters button them up finally, irremediably, for ever.

I expect he was an archdeacon; he was saying:

'You can't impose Western civilisation upon an Eastern people—I believe I'm right in saying that there are over two hundred millions in our Indian Empire—without a little disturbance. I'm a Liberal, you know. I've been a Liberal my whole life—family tradition—though I grieve to say I could *not* follow Mr Gladstone on the Home Rule question. It seems to me a good sign, this movement, an awakening among the people. But don't misunderstand me, my dear Sir, I am not making any excuses for the methods of the extremists. Apart from my calling—I have a natural horror of violence. Nothing can condone violence, the taking of human life, it's savagery, terrible, terrible.'

'They don't put it down with a strong enough hand,' the stock-jobber was saying almost fiercely. 'There's too much Liberalism in the East, too much namby-pambyism. It is all right here, of course, but it's not suited to the East. They want a strong hand. After all they owe us something: we aren't going to take all the kicks and leave them all the halfpence. Rule 'em, I say, rule 'em, if you're going to rule 'em. Look after 'em, of course: give 'em schools, if they want education—schools, hospitals, roads, and railways. Stamp out the plague, fever, famine. But let 'em know you are top dog. That's the way to run an eastern country. I am a white man, you're black; I'll treat you well, give you courts and justice; but I'm the superior race, I'm master here.'

The man who had looked round at me when I said 'Here's luck!' was fidgeting about in his chair uneasily. I examined him more carefully. There was no mistaking the cause of his irritation. It was written on his face, the small close-cut white moustache, the smooth firm cheeks with the deep red-and-brown glow on them, the innumerable wrinkles round the eyes, and above all the eyes themselves, that had grown slow and steady and unastonished, watching that inexplicable, meaningless march of life under blazing suns. He had seen it, he knew. 'Ah,' I thought, 'he is beginning to feel his liver. If he would only begin to speak, we might have some fun.'

'H'm, h'm,' said the Archdeacon. 'Of course there's something in what you say. Slow and sure. Things may be going too fast, and, as I say, I'm entirely for putting down violence and illegality with a strong hand. And after all, my dear Sir, when you say we're the superior race you imply a duty. Even in secular matters we must spread the light. I believe—devoutly—I am not ashamed to say so—that we are. We're reaching the people there, it's the cause of the unrest, we set them an example. They desire to follow. Surely, surely we should help to guide their feet. I don't speak without a certain knowledge. I take a great interest, I may even say that I play my small part, in the work of one of our great missionary societies. I see our young men, many of them risen from the people, educated often, and highly educated (I venture to think), in Board Schools. I see them go out full of high ideals to live among those poor people. And I see them when they come back and tell me their tales honestly, unostentatiously. It is always the same, a message of hope and comfort. We are getting at the people, by example, by our lives, by our conduct. They respect us.'

I heard a sort of groan, and then, quite loud, these strange words:
'*Kasimutal Rameswaramvaraiyil terintavan*'.

'I beg your pardon,' said the Archdeacon, turning to the inter-
rupter.

'I beg yours. Tamil, Tamil proverb. Came into my mind. Spoke
without thinking. Beg yours.'

'Not at all. Very interesting. You've lived in India? Would you
mind my asking you for a translation?'

'It means "he knows everything between Benares and
Rameswaram". Last time I heard it, an old Tamil, seventy or eighty
years old, perhaps—he looked a hundred—used it of one of your
young men. The young man, by the bye, had been a year and a half in
India. D'you understand?'

'Well, I'm not sure I do: I've heard, of course, of Benares, but
Rameswaram, I don't seem to remember the name.'

I laughed; I could not help it; the little Anglo-Indian looked so
fierce. 'Ah!' he said, 'you don't recollect the name. Well, it's pretty
famous out there. Great temple—Hindu—right at the southern tip
of India. Benares, you know, is up north. The old Tamil meant that
your friend knew everything in India after a year and a half: *he* didn't,
you know, after seventy, after seven thousand years. Perhaps you also
don't recollect that the Tamils are Dravidians? They've been there
since the beginning of time, before we came, or the Dutch or
Portuguese or the Muhammadans, or our cousins, the other Aryans.
Uncivilised, black? Perhaps, but, if they're black, after all it's *their*
suns, through thousands of years, that have blackened them. They
ought to know, if anyone does: but they don't, they don't pretend to.
But you two gentlemen, you seem to know everything between
Kasimutal—that's Benares—and Rameswaram, without having seen
the sun at all.'

'My dear sir,' began the Archdeacon pompously, but the jobber
interrupted him. He had had a number of whiskies and sodas, and
was quite heated. 'It's very easy to sneer: it doesn't mean because
you've lived a few years in a place . . .'

'I? Thirty. But they—seven thousand at least.'

'I say, it doesn't mean because you've lived thirty years in a place
that you know all about it. Ramisram, or whatever the damned place
is called, I've never heard of it and don't want to. You do, that's part
of your job, I expect. But I read the papers, I've read books too, mind

you, about India. I know what's going on. One knows enough —enough—data: East and West and the difference: I can form an opinion—I've a right to it even if I've never heard of Ramis what d'you call it. You've lived there and you can't see the wood for the trees. We see it because we're out of it—see it at a distance.'

'Perhaps,' said the Archdeacon, 'there's a little misunderstanding. The discussion—if I may say so—is getting a little heated— unnecessarily, I think. We hold our views. This gentleman has lived in the country. He holds others. I'm sure it would be most interesting to hear them. But I confess I didn't quite gather them from what he said.'

The little man was silent: he sat back, his eyes fixed on the ceiling. Then he smiled:

'I won't give you views,' he said. 'But if you like I'll give you what you call details, things seen, facts.* Then you can give me *your* views on 'em.'

They murmured approval.

'Let's see, it's fifteen, seventeen years ago. I had a district then about as big as England. There may have been twenty Europeans in it, counting the missionaries, and twenty million Tamils and Tele- gus. I expect nineteen million of the Tamils and Telegus never saw a white man from one year's end to the other, or if they did, they caught a glimpse of me under a sun helmet riding through their village on a flea-bitten grey Indian mare. Well, Providence had so designed it that there was a stretch of coast in that district which was a barren wilderness of sand and scrubby thorn jungle—and nothing else—for three hundred miles; no towns, no villages, no water, just sand and trees for three hundred miles. Oh, and sun, I forget that, blazing sun. And in the water off the shore at one place there were oysters, millions of them lying and breeding at the bottom, four or five fathoms down. And in the oysters, or some of them, were pearls.

'Well, we rule India and the sea, so the sea belongs to us, and the oysters are in the sea and the pearls are in the oysters. Therefore of course the pearls belong to us. But they lie in five fathoms. How to get 'em up, that's the question. You'd think being progressive we'd dredge for them or send down divers in diving dresses. But we don't, not in India. They've been fishing up the oysters and the pearls there ever since the beginning of time, naked brown men diving feet first out of long wooden boats into the blue sea and sweeping the oysters off the bottom of the sea into baskets slung to their sides. They were doing it centuries and centuries before we came, when—as someone said—our ancestors were herding swine on the plains of Norway.* the Arabs of the Persian Gulf came down in dhows and fished up pearls which found their way to Solomon and the Queen of Sheba. They still come, and the Tamils and Moormen of the district come, and they fish 'em up in the same way, diving out of long wooden boats shaped and rigged as in Solomon's time, as they were centuries before him and the Queen of Sheba. No difference, you see, except that we—Government I mean—take two-thirds of all the oysters fished up: the other third we give to the diver, Arab or Tamil or Moorman, for his trouble in fishing 'em up.

'We used to have a Pearl Fishery about once in three years, it lasted six weeks or two months just between the two monsoons, the only time the sea is calm there. And I had, of course, to go and superintend it, to take Government's share of oysters, to sell them, to keep order, to keep out K.D.'s—that means Known Depredators—and smallpox and cholera. We had what we called a camp, in the wilderness remember, on the hot sand down there by the sea: it sprang up in a night, a town, a big town of thirty or forty thousand people, a little India, Asia almost, even a bit of Africa. They came from all districts: Tamils, Telegus, fat Chetties, Parsees, Bombay merchants, Sinhalese from Ceylon, the Arabs and their Negroes, Somalis probably, who used to be their slaves. It was an immense gamble; everyone bought oysters for the chance of the prizes in them: it would have taken fifty white men to superintend that camp properly: they gave me one, a little boy of twenty-four fresh-cheeked from England, just joined the service. He had views, he had been educated in a Board School, won prizes, scholarships, passed the Civil Service "Exam". Yes, he had views; he used to explain them to me when he first arrived. He got some new ones, I think, before he got out of that camp. You'd say he only saw details, things happen, facts, data. Well, he did that too. He saw men die—he hadn't seen that in his Board School—die of plague or cholera, like flies, all over the place, under the trees, in the boats, outside the little door of his own little hut. And he saw flies, too, millions, billions of them all day long buzzing, crawling over everything, his hands, his little fresh face, his food. And he smelt the smell of millions of decaying oysters all day long and all night long for six weeks. He was sick four or five times a day for six weeks; the smell did that. Insanitary? Yes, very. Why is it allowed? The pearls, you see, the pearls: you must get them out of the oysters as you must get the oysters out of the sea. And the pearls are very often small and embedded in the oyster's body. So you put all the oysters, millions of them, in dug-out canoes in the sun to rot. They rot very well in that sun, and the flies come and lay eggs in them, and maggots come out of the eggs and more flies come out of the maggots; and between them all, the maggots and the sun, the oysters' bodies disappear, leaving the pearls and a little sand at the bottom of the canoe. Unscientific? Yes, perhaps; but after all it's our camp, our fishery—just as it was in Solomon's time. At any rate, you see, it's the East. But whatever it is, and whatever the reason, the result involves flies, millions of them and a smell, a stench—Lord! I can smell it now.

'There was one other white man there. He was a planter, so he said, and he had come to "deal" in pearls. He dropped in on us out of a native boat at sunset on the second day. He had a red face and red nose, he was unhealthily fat for the East: the whites of his eyes were rather blue and rather red: they were also watery. I noticed that his hand shook, and that he first refused and then took a whisky and soda—a bad sign in the East.* He wore very dirty white clothes and a vest instead of a shirt: he apparently had no baggage of any sort. But he was a white man, and so he ate with us that night and a good many nights afterwards.

'In the second week he had his first attack of D.T. We pulled him through, Robson and I, in the intervals of watching over the oysters. When he hadn't got D.T., he talked: he was a great talker, he also had views. I used to sit in the evenings—they were rare—when the fleet of boats had got in early and the oysters had been divided, in front of my hut and listen to him and Robson settling India and Asia, Africa too probably. We sat there in our long chairs on the sand looking out over the purple sea, towards a sunset like blood shot with gold. Nothing moved or stirred except the flies which were going to sleep in a mustard tree close by; they hung in buzzing clusters, billions of them on the smooth leaves and little twigs: literally it was black with them. It looked as if the whole tree had suddenly broken out all over into some disease of living black currants. Even the sea seemed to move with an effort in the hot, still air; only now and again a little wave would lift itself up very slowly, very wearily, poise itself for a moment, and then fall with a weary little thud on the sand.

'I used to watch them, I say, in the hot still air and the smell of dead oysters—it pushed up against your face like something solid—talking, talking in their long chairs, while the sweat stood out in little drops on their foreheads and trickled from time to time down their noses. There wasn't, I suppose, anything wrong with Robson, he was all right at bottom, but he annoyed me, irritated me in that smell. He was too cocksure altogether, of himself, of his Board School education, of life, of his "views". He was going to run India on new lines, laid down in some damned Manual of Political Science out of which they learn life in Board Schools and extension lectures. He would run his own life, I dare say, on the same lines, laid down in some other text book or primer. He hadn't seen anything, but he knew exactly what it was all like. There was nothing curious, astonishing, unexpected, in life, he was ready for any emergency. And we were all wrong, all on the wrong tack in dealing with natives! He annoyed me a little, you know, when the thermometer stood at 99, at 6 p.m., but what annoyed me still more was that they—the natives!—were all wrong too. They too had to be taught how to live—and die, too, I gathered.

'But his views were interesting, very interesting—especially in the long chairs there under the immense Indian sky, with the camp at our hands—just as it had been in the time of Moses and Abraham—and behind us the jungle for miles, and behind that India, three hundred millions of them listening to the piping voice of a Board School boy. They are the inferior race, these three hundred millions—mark race, though there are more races in India than people in Peckham—and we, of course, are superior. They've stopped somehow on the bottom rung of the ladder of which we've very nearly, if not quite, reached the top. They've stopped there hundreds, thousands of years: but it won't take any time to lead 'em up by the hand to our rung. It's to be done like this: by showing them that they're our brothers, inferior brothers; by reason, arguing them out of their superstitions, false beliefs; by education, by science, by example, yes, even he did not forget example, and White, sitting by his side with his red nose and watery eyes, nodded approval. And all this must be done scientifically, logically, systematically: if it were, a Commissioner could revolutionise a province in five years, turn it into a Japanese India,

with all the *ryots** as well as all the *vakils** and students running up
the ladder of European civilisation to become, I suppose, glorified
Board School angels at the top. "But you've none of you got clear
plans out here," he piped, "you never work on any system: you've got
no point of view. The result is"—here, I think, he was inspired, by
the dead oysters, perhaps—"instead of getting hold of the East, it's
the East which gets hold of you."

'And White agreed with him, solemnly, at any rate when he was
sane and sober. And I couldn't complain of his inexperience. He was
rather reticent at first, but afterwards we heard much—too much—
of his experiences—one does, when a man gets D.T. He said he was
a gentleman, and I believe it was true; he had been to a public school;
Cheltenham or Repton. He hadn't, I gathered, succeeded as a
gentleman at home, so they sent him to travel in the East. He liked it,
it suited him. So he became a planter in Assam. That was fifteen years
ago, but he didn't like Assam: the luck was against him—it always
was—and he began to roll; and when a man starts rolling in India,
well—He had been a clerk in merchants' offices; he had served in a
draper's shop in Calcutta; but the luck was always against him. Then
he tramped up and down India, through Ceylon, Burma; he had got
at one time or another to the Malay States, and when he was very bad
one day, he talked of cultivating camphor in Java. He had been a sailor
on a coasting tramp; he had sold horses (which didn't belong to him)
in the Deccan somewhere; he had tramped day after day begging his
way for months in native bazaars; he had lived for six months with,
and on, a Tamil woman in some little village down in the south. Now
he was "dealing in" pearls. "India's got hold of me," he'd say,
"India's got hold of me, and the East."

'He had views too, very much like Robson's, with additions. "The
strong hand" came in, and "rule". We ought to govern India more;
we didn't now. Why, he had been in hundreds of places where he was
the first Englishman that the people had ever seen. (Lord! think of
that!) He talked a great deal about the hidden wealth of India and
exploitation. He knew places where there was gold—workable too
—only one wanted a little capital—coal probably and iron—and then
there was this new stuff, radium. But we weren't go-ahead, progressive, the Government always put difficulties in his way. They made
"the native" their stalking-horse against European enterprise. He
would work for the good of the native, he'd treat him firmly but

kindly—especially, I thought, the native women, for his teeth were sharp and pointed and there were spaces between each, and there was something about his chin and jaw—*you* know the type, I expect.

'As the fishing went on we had less time to talk. We had to work. The divers go out in the fleet of three hundred or four hundred boats every night and dive until midday. Then they sail back from the pearl banks and bring all their oysters into an immense Government enclosure where the Government share is taken. If the wind is favourable all the boats go back by 6 p.m. and the work is over at 7. But if the wind starts blowing off shore, the fleet gets scattered and boats drop in one by one all night long. Robson and I had to be in the enclosures as long as there was a boat out, ready to see that, as soon as it did get in, the oysters were brought to the enclosure and Government got its share.

'Well, the wind never did blow favourably that year. I sat in that enclosure sometimes for forty-eight hours on end. Robson found managing it rather difficult, so he didn't like to be left there alone. If you get two thousand Arabs, Tamils, Negroes, the Moormen, each with a bag or two of oysters, into an enclosure a hundred and fifty yards by a hundred and fifty yards, and you only have thirty timid native "subordinates" and twelve native policemen to control them —well, somehow or other he found a difficulty in applying his system of reasoning to them. The first time he tried it, we very nearly had a riot; it arose from a dispute between some Arabs and Tamils over the ownership of three oysters which fell out of a bag. The Arabs didn't understand Tamil and the Tamils didn't understand Arabic, and, when I got down there, fetched by a frightened constable, there were sixty or seventy men fighting with great poles—they had pulled up the fence of the enclosure for weapons—and on the outskirts was Robson running round like a distracted hen with a white face and tears in his blue eyes. When we got the combatants separated, they had only killed one Tamil and broken nine or ten heads. Robson was very upset by that dead Tamil, he broke down utterly for a minute or two, I'm afraid.

'Then White got his second attack. He was very bad: he wanted to kill himself, but what was worse than that, before killing himself, he wanted to kill other people. I hadn't been to bed for two nights and I knew I should have to sit up another night in that enclosure as the wind was all wrong again. I had given White a bed in my hut: it wasn't good to let him wander in the bazaar. Robson came down with a white face to tell me he had "gone mad up there again". I had to knock him down with the butt end of a rifle; he was a big man and I hadn't slept for forty-eight hours, and then there were the flies and the smell of those dead oysters.

'It sounds unreal, perhaps a nightmare, all this told here to you behind blinds and windows in this—' he sniffed—'in this smell of—of—horsehair furniture and paint and varnish.* The curious thing is it didn't seem a nightmare out there. It was too real. Things happened, anything might happen, without shocking or astonishing. One just did one's work, hour after hour, keeping things going in that sun which stung one's bare hands, took the skin off even my face, among the flies and the smell. It wasn't a nightmare, it was just a few thousand Arabs and Indians fishing up oysters from the bottom of the sea. It wasn't even new, one felt; it was old, old as the Bible, old as Adam, so the Arabs said. One hadn't much time to think, but one felt it and watched it, watched the things happen quietly, unastonished, as men do in the East. One does one's work—forty-eight hours at a stretch doesn't leave one much time or inclination for thinking —waiting for things to happen. If you can prevent people from killing one another or robbing one another, or burning down the camp, or getting cholera or plague or smallpox, and if one can manage to get one night's sleep in three, one is fairly satisfied; one doesn't much worry about having to knock a mad gentleman from Repton on the head with the butt end of a rifle between-whiles.

'I expect that's just what Robson would call not getting hold of India but letting India get hold of you. Well, I said I wouldn't give you views and I won't: I'm giving you facts: what I want, you know, too is to give you the feeling of facts out there. After all that is data for your views, isn't it? Things here *feel* so different; you seem so far from life, with windows and blinds and curtains always in between, and then nothing ever happens, you never wait for things to happen, never watch things happening here. You are always doing things somehow—Lord knows what they are—according, I suppose, to systems, views, opinions. But out there you live so near to life, every morning you smell damp earth if you splash too much in your tin bath. And things happen slowly, inexorably by fate, and you—you don't do things, you watch with the three hundred millions. You feel it there in everything, even in the sunrise and sunset, every day, the immensity, inexorableness, mystery of things happening. You feel the whole earth waking up or going to sleep in a great arch of sky; you feel small, not very powerful. But who ever felt the sun set or rise in London or Torquay either? It doesn't: you just turn on or turn off the electric light.

'White was very bad that night. When he recovered from being knocked down by the rifle, I had to tie him down to the bed. And then Robson broke down—nerves, you know. I had to go back to the enclosure and I wanted him to stay and look after White in the hut— it wasn't safe to leave him alone even tied down with cord to the camp bed. But this was apparently another emergency to which the manual system did not apply. He couldn't face it alone in the hut with that man tied to the bed. White was certainly not a pretty sight writhing about there, and his face—have you ever seen a man in the last stages of D.T.? I beg your pardon. I suppose you haven't. It isn't nice, and White was also seeing things, not nice either: not snakes, you know, as people do in novels when they get D.T., but things which had happened to him, and things which he had done—they weren't nice either—and curious ordinary things distorted in a most unpleasant way. He was very much troubled by snipe: hundreds of them kept on rising out of the bed from beside him with that shrill "cheep! cheep!" of theirs: he felt their soft little feathered bodies against his bare skin as they fluttered up from under him somewhere and flew out of the window. It threw him into paroxysms of fear, agonies. It made one, I admit, feel chilly round the heart to hear him pray one to stop it.

'And Robson was also not a nice sight. I hate seeing a sane man break down with fear, mere abject fear. He just sat down at last on a cane-bottomed chair and cried like a baby. Well, that did him some good, but he wasn't fit to be left alone with White. I had to take White down to the enclosure, and I tied him to a post with coir rope near the table at which I sat there. There was nothing else to do. And Robson came too and sat there at my side through the night watching White, terrified but fascinated.

'Can you picture that enclosure to yourself down on the sandy shore with its great fence of rough poles cut in the jungle, lighted by a few flares, torches dipped in cocoanut oil: and the white man tied to a pole raving, writhing in the flickering light which just showed too Robson's white scared little face? And in the intervals of taking over oysters and settling disputes between Arabs and Somalis and Tamils and Moormen, I sat at the table writing a report (which had to go by runner next morning) on a proposal to introduce the teaching of French in "English schools" in towns. That wasn't a very good report. White gave us the whole history of his life between ten p.m. and four a.m. in the morning. He didn't leave much to the imagination; a parson would have said that in that hour the memory of his sins came upon him—Oh, I beg your pardon. But really I think they did. I thought I had lived long enough out there to have heard without a shock anything that men can do and do—especially white men who have "gone under". But I hadn't: I couldn't stomach the story of White's life told by himself. It wasn't only that he had robbed and swindled himself through India up and down for fifteen years. That was bad enough for there wasn't a station where he hadn't swindled and bamboozled his fellow white men. But it was what he had done when he got away "among the natives"—to men, and women too, away from "civilisation", in the jungle villages and high up in the mountains. God! the cold, civilised, corrupted cruelty of it. I told you, I think, that his teeth were pointed and spaced out in his mouth.

'And his remorse was the most horrible thing, tied to that post there, writhing under the flickering light of the flare: the remorse of fear—fear of punishment, of what was coming, of death, of the horrors, real horrors and the phantom horrors of madness.

'Often during the night there was nothing to be heard in the enclosure but his screams, curses, hoarse whispers of fear. We seemed alone there in the vast stillness of the sky: only now and then a little splash from the sea down on the shore. And then would come a confused murmur from the sea and a little later perhaps the wailing voice of one man calling to another from boat to boat across the water "Abdulla! Abdulla!" And I would go out on to the shore. There were boats, ten, fifteen, twenty, perhaps, coming in from the banks, sad, mysterious, in the moonlight, gliding in with the little splashings of the great round oars. Except for the slow moving of the oars one would have thought they were full of the dead, there was not a movement on board, until the boats touched the sand. Then the dark shadows, which lay like dead men about the boats, would leap into life—there would rise a sudden din of hoarse voices, shouting, calling, quarrelling. The boats swarmed with shadows running about, gesticulating, staggering under sacks of oysters, dropping one after the other over the boats' sides into the sea. The sea was full of them and soon the shore too, Arabs, Negroes, Tamils, bowed under the weight of the sacks. They came up dripping from the sea. They burst with a roar into the enclosure: they flung down their sacks of oysters with a crash. The place was full of swaying, struggling forms: of men calling to one another in their different tongues: of the smell of the sea.

'And above everything one could hear the screams and prayers of the madman writhing at the post. They gathered about him, stared at him. The light of the flares fell on their dark faces, shining and dripping from the sea. They looked calm, impassive, stern. It shone too on the circle of eyes: one saw the whites of them all round him: they seemed to be judging him, weighing him: calm patient eyes of men who watched unastonished the procession of things. The Tamils' squat black figures, nearly naked, watched him silently, almost carelessly. The Arabs in their long dirty night-shirts, black-bearded, discussed him earnestly together with their guttural voices. Only an enormous Negro, towering up to six feet six at least above the crowd, dressed in sacks and an enormous ulster, with ten copper coffee pots slung over his back and a pipe made of a whole cocoanut with an iron tube stuck in it in his hand, stood smiling mysteriously.

'And White thought they weren't real, that they were devils of Hell sent to plague and torture him. He cursed them, whispered at them, howled with fear. I had to explain to them that the Sahib was not well, that the sun had touched him, that they must move away. They understood. They salaamed quietly, and moved away slowly, dignified.

'I don't know how many times this didn't happen during the night. But towards morning White began to grow very weak. He moaned perpetually. Then he began to be troubled by the flesh. As dawn showed grey in the east, he was suddenly shaken by convulsions horrible to see. He screamed for someone to bring him a woman, and, as he screamed, his head fell back: he was dead. I cut the cords quickly in a terror of haste, and covered the horror of the face. Robson was sitting in a heap in his chair: he was sobbing, his face in his hands.

'At that moment I was told I was wanted on the shore. I went quickly. The sea looked cold and grey under the faint light from the East. A cold little wind just ruffled the surface of the water. A solitary boat stood out black against the sky, just throbbing slowly up and down on the water close in shore. They had a dead Arab on board, he had died suddenly while diving, they wanted my permission to bring the body ashore. Four men waded out to the boat: the corpse was lifted out and placed upon their shoulders. They waded back slowly: the feet of the dead man stuck out, toes pointing up, very stark over the shoulders of the men in front. The body was laid on the sand. The bearded face of the dead man looked very calm, very dignified in the faint light. An Arab, his brother, sat down upon the sand near his head. He covered himself with sackcloth. I heard him weeping. It was very silent, very cold and still on the shore in the early dawn.

'A tall figure stepped forward, it was the Arab sheik, the leader of the boat. He laid his hand on the head of the weeping man and spoke to him calmly, eloquently, compassionately. I didn't understand Arabic, but I could understand what he was saying. The dead man had lived, had worked, had died. He had died working, without suffering, as men should desire to die. He had left a son behind him. The speech went on calmly, eloquently, I heard continually the word *Khallas*—all is over, finished. I watched the figures outlined against the grey sky—the long lean outline of the corpse with the toes sticking up so straight and stark, the crouching huddled figure of the weeping man and the tall upright sheik standing by his side. They were motionless, sombre, mysterious, part of the grey sea, of the grey sky.

'Suddenly the dawn broke red in the sky. The sheik stopped, motioned silently to the four men. They lifted the dead man on to their shoulders. They moved away down the shore by the side of the sea which began to stir under the cold wind. By their side walked the sheik, his hand laid gently on the brother's arm. I watched them move away, silent, dignified. And over the shoulders of the men I saw the feet of the dead man with the toes sticking up straight and stark.

'Then I moved away too, to make arrangements for White's burial: it had to be done at once.'

There was silence in the smoking-room. I looked round. The Colonel had fallen asleep with his mouth open. The jobber tried to look bored. The Archdeacon was, apparently, rather put out.

'It's too late, I think,' said the Archdeacon, 'to—Dear me, dear me, past one o'clock.' He got up. 'Don't you think you've chosen rather exceptional circumstances, out of the ordinary case?'

The Commissioner was looking into the few red coals that were all that was left of the fire.

'There's another Tamil proverb,' he said: 'When the cat puts his head into a pot, he thinks all is darkness.'

See also: Beames; Clifford; Conrad; Joyce; Kipling; Plaatje; Schreiner; Trevelyan; Yeats.

APPENDIX

'L'Irlanda alla sbarra'

the original Italian text of Joyce's
'Ireland at the Bar' (pp. 336–8)

Parecchi anni or sono si tenne in Irlanda un processo sensazionale. Nella provincia occidentale, in un luogo romito, che si chiama Maamtrasna, era stato commesso un eccidio. Furono arrestati quattro o cinque villici del paese, appartenenti tutti all'antica tribù dei Joyce. Il più anziano di loro, tale Milesio Joyce, vecchio di sessant'anni, era particolarmente sospetto alla gendarmeria. L'opinione pubblica lo giudicava allora innocente ed oggi lo stima un martire. Tanto il vecchio quanto gli altri accusati ignoravano l'inglese. La Corte dovette ricorrere ai servizi di un interprete. L'interrogatorio svoltosi col tramite di costui ebbe a volta del comico e a volta del tragico. Dall'un lato vi era l'interprete formalista e dall'altro il patriarca della misera tribù, il quale, poco avvezzo alle usanze civili, sembrava istupidito da tutte quelle cerimonie giudiziarie.

Il magistrato diceva:

—Chieda all'imputato se vide la donna quella mattina.

La domanda gli era riferita in irlandese e il vecchio prorompeva in spiegazioni intricate, gesticolando, facendo appello agli altri accusati, al cielo. Poi, sfinito dallo sforzo, taceva e l'interprete, volgendosi al magistrato, diceva:

—Afferma di no, 'your worship'.

—Gli chieda se era in quei pressi a quell'ora.

Il vecchio si rimetteva a parlare, a protestare, a gridare, quasi fuori di sé dall'angoscia di non capire e di non farsi capire, piangendo d'ira e di terrore. E l'interprete, di nuovo, secco:

—Dice di no, 'your worship'. Ad interrogatorio finito si dichiarò provata la colpabilità del povero vecchio, che fu rinviato al tribunale superiore, il quale lo condannò al capestro. Il giorno dell'esecuzione della sentenza, !a piazza davanti al carcere era gremita di gente che, in ginocchio, ululava in irlandese preghiere pel riposo dell'anima di Milesio Joyce. La leggenda vuole che neppure il carnefice potesse farsi comprendere dalla vittima e, indignato, desse un calcio alla testa dell'infelice per cacciarla nel nodo.

La figura di questo vecchio inebetito, avanzo di una civiltà non nostra, sordomuto dianzi il suo giudice, è la figura simbolica della nazione irlandese alla sbarra dell'opinione pubblica. Essa al pari di lui, non può fare appello alla coscienza moderna dell'Inghilterra e dell'estero. I giornali inglesi fanno da interpreti, fra l'Irlanda e la democrazia inglese, la quale pur dando loro di tratto in tratto ascolto, finisce coll'essere seccata dalle eterne lagnanze dei deputati nazionalisti venuti in casa sua, come ella crede, a turbarne l'ordine e a estorcere denari. All'estero non si parla dell'Irlanda se non quando scoppiano colà tumulti come quelli che fecero sussultare il telegrafo in questi ultimi giorni. Il pubblico sfiorando i dispacci giunti da Londra, che pur mancando di acredine, hanno qualche cosa della laconicità dell'interprete suddetto, si figura allora gli irlandesi come malandrini, dai visi asimmetrici, scorazzanti nella notte con lo scopo di fare la pelle ad ogni unionista. E al vero sovrano dell'Irlanda, il papa, tali notizie giungono come tanti cani in chiesa; le grida, infiacchite dal viaggio lungo, sono già quasi spente quando arrivano alla porta di bronzo: i messi del popolo che non rinnegò mai nel passato la Santa Sede, l'unico popolo cattolico pel quale la fede vuol dire anche l'esercizio della fede, vengono respinti in favore dei messi di un monarca, il quale, discendente di apostati, s'apostatizzò solennemente nel giorno della sua consacrazione, dichiarando in presenza dei suoi nobili e comuni che i riti della chiesa romano-cattolica sono 'superstizione ed idolatria'.

Gli irlandesi sparsi in tutto il mondo sono venti milioni. L'isola di smeraldo ne raccoglie solo una piccola parte. Pure l'osservatore, pensando come l'Inghilterra imperni tutta la sua politica interna sulla questione irlandese, mentre procede con ampiezza di criteri nello sbrigare le questioni più complesse della politica coloniale, non può fare a meno di chiedersi se il canale di San Giorgio non getti un abisso più profondo dell'Oceano fra l'Irlanda e la superba dominatrice.

La questione irlandese difatti non è risolta ancora oggi, dopo sei secoli di occupazione armata e più di cento anni di quella legislazione inglese che ridusse la popolazione dell'isola infelice da otto a quattro milioni, quadruplicò le imposte, aggrovigliò il problema agrario di molti nodi di più.

Invero, non vi è problema più arruffato di questo. Gli irlandesi stessi ne capiscono poco; gli inglesi ancor meno, per gli altri popoli è buio pesto. Ma gli irlandesi sanno invece come esso sia la causa di tutte le loro sofferenze e perciò adottano sovente metodi di soluzione violentissimi. Per esempio, ventotto anni fa, vedendosi ridotti alla miseria dalle angherie dei latifondisti, ricusarono di pagare gli affitti ed ottennero dal Gladstone provvedimenti e riforme. Oggi, vedendo i pascoli pieni di buoi ben pasciuti, mentre un ottavo della popolazione è registrata come priva di mezzi di sussistenza, scacciano i buoi dai poderi. Il Governo liberale, irritato, divisa di ripristinare la tattica coercitiva dei conservatori e la stampa londinese consacra da parecchie settimane innumerevoli articoli alla crisi agraria che dice gravissima e pubblica notizie allarmanti di rivolte agrarie, riprodotte poi dai giornali dell'estero.

Non mi propongo di fare l'esegesi della questione agraria irlandese né di narrare il retroscena della politica bifronte del Governo, ma credo utile fare una modesta rettifica. Chi abbia letto i telegrammi lanciati da Londra credeva certo che l'Irlanda attraversi un periodo di delinquenza eccezionale. Criterio erroneo, quanto mai. La delinquenza in Irlanda è inferiore a quella di qualsiasi altro paese di Europa; in Irlanda non vi è la malavita organizzata; quando avviene uno di quei fatti che i giornalisti parigini chiamano, con atroce ironia, un idillio rosso, tutto il paese ne è scosso. Ci furono, è vero, in questi ultimi mesi due morti violente in Irlanda: ma per opera delle truppe inglesi: a Belfast, dove i soldati caricarono la folla inerme, senza pare le intimazioni, e uccisero un uomo e una donna. Ci furono attentati contro il bestiame, ma neppur questi in Irlanda, dove la folla si appagò di aprire le stalle e di scacciare il bestiame per qualche miglio di strada: ma a Great Wyrley, in Inghilterra, ove da sei anni delinquenti bestiali e pazzeschi infuriano contro il bestiame, tanto che le società inglesi non vogliono più assicurarlo.

Cinque anni fa un innocente, ora in libertà, fu condannato ai lavori forzati per appagare l'indignazione pubblica. Ma anche quando egli si trovava in carcere i delitti continuavano. E la settimana scorsa due cavalle furono trovate morte con i soliti tagli nel basso ventre e con le budella sparse sull'erba.

EXPLANATORY NOTES

To pay some recognition to the specificities of the geographic and cultural contexts represented by the anthology, the notes below aim to offer sufficient background detail to situate individual texts, while not overburdening the reader with annotations. Where relevant, modern spellings of key place names have been given. Writers' own notes appear as footnotes to individual texts. Reference works are included in the Select Bibliography. Unless otherwise indicated, place of publication is London.

GEORGE OTTO TREVELYAN

'An Indian Railway' and 'The Gulf Between Us' are from 'Letter II: An Indian Railway' and 'Letter XII. And Last', respectively, of *The Competition Wallah*. They first appeared in *Macmillan's Magazine*, July 1863–May 1865; the full letter series was published as *The Competition Wallah* (Macmillan and Co., 1864).

3 *my two languages*: the Indian languages a civil servant was expected to learn.

4 *Mofussilpore*: *mofussil* means the hinterland or provinces.

the great river: the Ganges.

Arrian: Flavius Arrian, a Greek historian of the second century AD, author of the *Anabasis* dealing with Alexander the Great's military conquests. The eighth volume describes Indian customs.

5 *Saint Simeon*: or Simon Stylites (*c.* 390–459), known for his ascetic practices.

pice: a quarter of an anna, which was one sixty-fourth of a rupee, hence a coin of very small value.

dacoits: armed robbers.

7 *tiffins*: luncheon parties.

8 *the Indigo question*: this question, which Trevelyan discusses in later letters, dominated colonial Bengal debate in the early 1860s, polarizing settlers and civilians. It emerged out of a proposed contract law whereby planters might coerce contracted small farmers or *ryots* to produce a certain amount of indigo. The price was so low, however, that there was little incentive for *ryots* to do so. Trevelyan's liberal view of the situation earned him the opprobrium of the Indian planter class.

9 *Darius and Artaxerxes*: both kings of Persia involved in campaigns against the Greeks. Darius (550–486 BC) was defeated at the Battle of Marathon in 490 BC.

11 *John Kumpani*: a standard personification of the East India Company.

Lord Steyne . . . Wenhams and Waggs: high-society characters in Thackeray's *Vanity Fair* (1847).

crore . . . lacs: a crore is 10 million and a lac one hundred-thousand.

12 *Sir John Lawrence or Sir Herbert Edwardes*: Lawrence (1811–68) was the Chief Commissioner of the Punjab before becoming Viceroy (1864–9) following Lord Canning (see note below). He shifted the summer residence of the Government of India from Calcutta to Simla. Edwardes (1819–68), a commissioner in the Punjab (1848–9), and later in Peshawar, wrote a book (1850) about his time on the North-West frontier in which he defended 'benevolent despotism'.

Gunduck: the Gandak River.

Haileybury and Addiscombe: the college centred in Hertfordshire where Indian civil servants were trained prior to the introduction of the competitive examination.

Boglipore . . . Gya: Bhagalpur on the Ganges in Bengal, and Gaya in Bihar.

13 *Chupra*: Chapra.

14 *Lord Canning*: Lord Charles Canning (1812–62), the East India Company's last Governor-General and, after 1858 and the creation of the Indian empire, the first Viceroy. At the time of the outbreak of the Indian Mutiny or Uprising, 'Clemency' Canning showed some understanding for sepoy grievances. See Christopher Hibbert, *The Great Indian Mutiny: India 1857* (1978), 165–7.

JOHN RUSKIN

The Inaugural Lecture was delivered on 8 February 1870, and the text first published in *Lectures on Art* (Oxford: Clarendon Press, 1870); it appears in vol. 20, *Lectures on Art and Aratra Pentelici*, *The Works of John Ruskin*, Library edition, eds. E. T. Cook and Alexander Wedderburn (George Allen, 1905). The notes following are to an extent adaptations of their exhaustive annotations.

16 *. . . political virtues*: in his 1887 Preface to *Lectures on Art* Ruskin writes, 'passages that the student will find generally applicable and in all their bearings useful' he will mark either in capitals or italics.

17 *the Cherwell*: a river that flows through Oxford, a tributary of the Thames.

18 *the most offending souls alive*: as Cook and Wedderburn point out, this is an echo of Shakespeare's *Henry V*, IV. iii. 28.

do that which is right in his own eyes: Deuteronomy 12: 8 and Proverbs 12: 15.

a sceptred isle: Shakespeare, *Richard II*, II. i.

goodwill towards men: Luke 2: 14.

'Vexilla Regis prodeunt': 'The Royal banners forward go', an early medieval hymn by Venantius Fortunatus (*c*.530–?609).

18 *Fece per viltate, il gran rifiuto*: 'Who from cowardice made the great refusal.' Dante, *Inferno*, iii. 60 (trans. John D. Sinclair).

19 *pilots on the Galilean lake*: John Milton, *Lycidas* (1638).

   expect every man to do his duty: Nelson's instruction at the Battle of Trafalgar (1805). Ruskin saw Nelson as the epitome of national duty.

   every herb that sips the dew: Milton, *Il Penseroso* (1645), ll. 170–2.

   Circe: as is implied, the goddess associated with natural, especially herbal, knowledge.

20 *... PROSPERABUNTUR*: Ruskin begins this quotation from Psalm 1: 3 at 'man's life', and continues in Latin, 'his leaf also shall not wither; and whatsoever he doeth shall prosper'. The psalm contrasts the ungodly with those who delight in the Lord's Law.

ANTHONY TROLLOPE

'Aboriginals' is Chapter 4 of the 'Queensland' section of *Australia and New Zealand* (Chapman and Hall, 1873); first published as part of ten letters written to the London *Daily Telegraph*, 23 December 1871–28 December 1872; excised from the 1876 third edition; reprinted in *Australia*, eds. P. D. Edwards and R. B. Joyce (St Lucia: University of Queensland Press, 1967).

20 *Rockhampton ... to Brisbane*: towns and settlements in Queensland.

21 *Aboriginal Boney*: in a previous chapter Trollope describes 'Boney's' very summary trial for theft in Brisbane.

22 *savages*: Edwards and Joyce attribute these references to William Dampier, *A New Voyage Around the World*, 7th edn. (1729) and *A Voyage to New Holland, etc in the year 1699*, 3rd edn. (1729).

   ... to take away: paraphrase of Cook's journal observations. See Edwards and Joyce, p. 102.

23 *Bennet's history*: Samuel Bennett, *The History of Australian Discovery and Colonisation* (Sydney, 1865), 138–9.

24 *of the Jedburgh kind*: signifying summary justice, the phrase refers to an execution at Jedburgh in the Scottish borders during the reign of James I (1566–1625).

   the authority I have quoted before: that is, Bennett, p. 213, and, in the following pages, 229 and 268–9.

26 *cannibalism ... among the Australian blacks*: Edwards and Joyce stress that there appears to be no evidence for cannibalism in Aboriginal or Koori cultures.

27 *some years ... that matter*: in Trollope's *The West Indies and the Spanish Main* (1860).

32 *he has to go*: hastily written while Trollope was on the move, *Australia* is often repetitive, most visibly on this point.

JOHN BEAMES

From Chapter 17, 'Cuttack, 1873', of *Memoirs of a Bengal Civilian* (Chatto and Windus, 1961; Eland, 1984). Beames's memoirs of the thirty-five years (1858–93) he worked as a civil servant in India, which he called *The Story of My Life*, were written during 1875–8 and 1896–1900, specifically for his family's perusal. The memoirs were published by a grandson, Christopher Cook.

33 *Cuttack*: head station of the province of Orissa, on the east coast of India.

chota haziri: little breakfast.

'Comparative Grammar': Beames's three-volume *Comparative Grammar of the Modern Languages of India* (1872–9).

cutcherry: office.

34 *tiffin*: lunch.

35 *Ravenshaw*: Thomas Ravenshaw, the 'patriarchal' Commissioner of Cuttack.

38 *Nasmyth's steam hammer*: the powerful steam hammer patented by James Nasmyth (1808–90).

DAVID LIVINGSTONE

From Horace Waller (ed.), *The Last Journals of David Livingstone in Central Africa from 1865 to his Death (Continued by a Narrative of his Last Moments and Sufferings obtained from his faithful servants Chuma and Susi by Horace Waller)*, vol. 2 (John Murray, 1874), 153–7.

39 *Loñgumba*: now Lugamba.

Nyañgwe: in present-day Zaire or the Congo Republic, on the banks of the Lualaba River.

the end towards which I strained: the source of the Nile, the 'biblical' river.

Speke: John Hanning Speke (1827–64), a British explorer of Central Africa and author of *Journal of the Discovery of the Nile* (1863). On his third trip to the continent he established that Lake Victoria Nyanza was the source of the White Nile.

islet Kasengé: in Lake Tanganyika.

40 *dotis*: or *dhotis*, the Indian loincloth.

Shereef: Sherif bin Ahmed, who had brought Livingstone's reinforcements from Zanzibar.

41 *28th October . . . Henry Moreland Stanley*: Livingstone gets the date and the name wrong. His miscalculation of the dates of his travels was due to fever and faulty instruments used in bad weather. Stanley too lost days in his calculation of the date.

terrible fate that had befallen France: defeat in the Franco-Prussian War (1870–1).

the election of General Grant: to his first term as American president (1868–72).

Lord Clarendon: the British Foreign Secretary who had offered Livingstone official assistance on his Zambezi expedition.

41 *Sir Roderick*: Sir Roderick Murchison (1792–1871), the President of the Royal Geographic Society. Livingstone himself was interested in mapping the rivers flowing into and out of Lake Tanganyika to see whether the lake might form one of the sources of the Nile.

HENRY MORTON STANLEY

From the published lecture, *Trans-African Explorations, Adventures and Work 1870–84* (Spottiswoode and Co., 1886). The exchange corresponds closely to that related in *How I Found Livingstone: Travels, Adventures and Discoveries in Central Africa* (Sampson and Low, 1872), 406–19, but is not a word-for-word rendition. Whereas in the lecture the build-up to the meeting is to the fore, the book spends more time on what Stanley calls 'geographical and ethnographic remarks'. Both book and lecture are based on the dispatches Stanley sent to the *New York Herald* in 1871 and 1872.

42 *that date*: 6 January 1871, when Stanley arrived in Zanzibar.

Nyassa Lake: also spelt Nyasa Lake, now Lake Malawi.

44 *the porters . . . deserted*: Relations between Stanley's men were not improved by the ruthlessness with which he drove them at record speeds across Africa. Within six months of setting out several black porters had died, as had his two white assistants, having first tried to assassinate him. See Frank McLynn, *Hearts of Darkness* (1992), 89.

Unyanyembe: Tabora in present-day Tanzania.

48 *Wekotani*: Livingstone's Swahili name, probably meaning 'carried on the back'.

MARCUS CLARKE

This Preface first appeared with Gordon's posthumously reissued *Sea Spray and Smoke Drift* (1867; Melbourne: Clarson Massina, 1876); and was printed in all ensuing editions of his collected *Poems*. Clarke's comments on Australian scenery were originally written for a series *Photographs of Pictures in the National Gallery, Melbourne*, on work by the artists Louis Buvelot and Nicholas Chevalier (serialized October 1873–September 1874; published by F. F. Bailliere, Melbourne, 1875). Adam Lindsay Gordon was an English-educated Australian bush balladeer and steeplechase-rider (1833–70).

51 *'L'Allegro'*: by John Milton (1632), the companion poem to *'Il Penseroso'*. See note to Ruskin, p. 436.

the Bunyip: a monster in Aboriginal myth, inhabiting swampy places.

gracious with temperate air: probably a quotation from Gordon's own work, this might carry a passing allusion to Gonzalo's comment in Shakespeare's *The Tempest*, II. i, that Prospero's island is blessed with 'temperate' air. In the late-eighteenth-century poem 'The Slyph of Summer' by W. L. Bowles it is England which is said to be a place of 'temperate airs': 'not rude | Nor soft, voluptuous, nor effeminate'.

52 *Upas-poison*: in an invented legend of the late eighteenth century, popularized by Erasmus Darwin and frequently referred to in Romantic literature, the Upas was a deadly poisonous tree found in Java and surrounding islands. Clarke's expression is therefore tautologous.

'AUSTRALIE' (EMILY MANNING)

From *The Balance of Pain and Other Poems* (George Bell and Sons, 1877). The setting is the southern reaches of the Australian Great Dividing Range, New South Wales, about fifty miles inland from Nowra.

54 *zamia palms*: a type of cycad or dwarf palm, native to southern Africa and the West Indies, not Australia.

kennedea: an Australian climbing plant.

55 *sassafras*: a small densely green tree, not native to Australia.

EDWIN ARNOLD

Extracted from the concluding paragraphs of Book 7 of *The Light of Asia, or The Great Renunciation: Being the Life and Teaching of Gautama* (Trubner and Co., 1879), a verse translation based on the Pali Canon of the Buddha's teaching, and said by Arnold to be told through 'medium of an imaginary Buddhist votary to depict the life and character and indicate the philosophy of that noble hero and reformer Prince Gautama of India, founder of Buddhism'.

58 *she*: Princess Yasodhara, Siddhartha's wife.

59 *the treasure*: his wisdom.

ALFRED, LORD TENNYSON

'The Defence of Lucknow' was first published in the *Nineteenth Century* (April 1879); reprinted in *Ballads and Other Poems* (1880).

59 *siege of Lucknow*: the siege of the British residency at Lucknow by sepoys during the Indian Mutiny or Uprising lasted three months (till 25 September 1857), and became in imperial mythology a trans-historical symbol of national resilience.

Lawrence: Sir Henry Lawrence (1806–57), the Chief Commissioner and military commander in the province of Oudh, was noted for his far-sighted fortification of the city of Lucknow prior to the uprising. Wounded by sepoy fire in his own exposed bedroom during the early days of the siege, he is said to have died with the instruction never to surrender on his lips.

61 *the tigers*: see note to Henty, p. 448.

62 *Havelock*: Sir Henry Havelock (1795–1857), the gifted military planner and hero of the Mutiny who went to the rescue of Cawnpore (July 1857) and died soon after relieving Lucknow. He was delayed in getting to Lucknow by a lack of reinforcements.

'Opening of the Indian and Colonial Exhibition by the Queen' was first published in *Locksley Hall Sixty Years After* (1886). The exhibition was opened on 4 May 1886.

63 *Britons, hold your own*: a reprise of Tennyson's anti-Napoleon III poem 'Britons, Guard Your Own' (1852), supporting the formation of a militia. See note to Henley, p. 457.

EDWARD WILMOT BLYDEN

Inaugural Address as President of Liberia College, Monrovia, given on 5 January 1881; published a year later (Cambridge, Mass.: John Wilson and Son, 1882).

66 *saepe cadendo*: as it often happens.

which Mr Herbert Spencer describes as difference: in *First Principles* (1862), Herbert Spencer, the English sociologist and evolutionist, argued that difference and variety are fundamental laws of matter; where a force acts on anything homogeneous it will affect one part differently from others.

67 *Longfellow's Iagoo*: the storyteller in Longfellow's *Song of Hiawatha* (1855).

68 *Livingstone . . . and Cameron*: in his book *African Life and Customs* (1908) Blyden again cites these white explorers, in this case as authorities on African communalism.

Non ragionam di lor, ma guarda, e passa: 'Let us not talk of them, but look thou and pass.' Virgil in Dante, *Inferno*, iii. 60 (trans. John D. Sinclair).

Pre-Adamite Man, p. 265 (Blyden's footnote): Alexander Winchell's books on the existence of man before Adam were *Adamites and Preadamites* (1878) and *Preadamites* (1880). Blyden is probably referring to the latter.

69 *Dover's powders*: the Victorian household remedy, a mixture of opium and ipecacuanha.

TORU DUTT

'À mon père' is the concluding sonnet to Dutt's translations of French poetry, *A Sheaf Gleaned in French Fields* (Bhowanipur: Saptahik Sambad Press, 1876). 'Discovered' by Edmund Gosse, the book appeared in a new edition from C. Kegan Paul and Co. (1880), with a Prefatory Memoir dated 1877 by her father Govin Chunder Dutt. Both editions end with an acknowledgement in the form of a note to this poem saying that Dutt's late sister Aru supplied some (relatively few) of the translations or 'flowers': 'Had she lived this book with her help might have been better.'

'Sonnet—Baugmaree', 'Sonnet—The Lotus', and 'Our Casuarina Tree' appeared in the Miscellaneous Poems section of the posthumously published *Ancient Ballads and Legends of Hindustan* (Kegan Paul, Trench and Co., 1882), with an introductory memoir by Edmund Gosse.

70 *Baugmaree*: the name of the Dutts' garden in Calcutta.

seemul: the cotton-tree.

Flora: the Roman deity of fertility and flowers.

Juno: Jupiter's counterpart in Roman religion.

Psyche: the mortal beloved of Cupid.

71 *Casuarina Tree*: a tall coniferous tree, native to Malaya, and adopted as an ornamental tree in Bengal and elsewhere in the tropical empire.

my casement is wide open thrown: perhaps the clearest echo from John Keats's 'Ode to a Nightingale' (1820) though there are others: 'darkling', the ten-line stanza form (but with a different rhyme scheme), the elegiac recollections of dead siblings, and (again a prominent borrowing) the linking of stanzas through repetition in the last and first lines. Towards the end the poem is pervaded by whispers also from Matthew Arnold's 'Dover Beach' (1867) and P. B. Shelley's 'Ode to the West Wind' (1819), as well as from William Wordsworth.

kokilas: the koel bird, the South Asian nightingale.

O sweet companions: Dutt's sister Aru (1854–74) and brother Abju (1851–65).

72 *Borrowdale*: the Derwent valley in the Lake District.

Fear . . . Time the shadow: lacking the words 'Silence and Foresight', following the line ending on 'Hope', the lines are from Wordsworth's poem, 'Ewtrees' (*Poems*, 1815), which contrasts a solitary and gloomy yew in 'Lorton's pleasant vale' with a grove of 'Fraternal' yews in Borrowdale.

JOHN SEELEY

The second half of the opening lecture to two courses of lectures given as Regius Professor of Modern History at Cambridge; published as *The Expansion of England* (Macmillan, 1883); reprinted within three months. The idea of an expanded Britain across the seas is indebted to Charles Dilke's book *Greater Britain* (1869).

78 *Turgot*: Anne Robert Jacques Turgot (1727–81), the French statesman and economist who influenced Adam Smith.

ISABELLA BIRD

Letter II of *The Golden Chersonese and the way thither* (John Murray, 1883). 'Golden Chersonese', derived from the Greek for peninsula, was Milton's term in *Paradise Lost* for this part of the world.

80 *Sungei Ujong*: one of the three protected Malay states (the other two were Selangor and Perak), which along with the Straits Settlements of Singapore, Malacca (Melaka), and Penang (Pinang), comprised British colonial territory on the Malay Peninsula at this time.

81 *palandok or chevrotin*: the South-East Asian musk-deer.

82 *the security and justice of her rule*: in a later letter, from Penang, Bird comments further that all Asiatics enjoy 'absolute security of life and prosperity' and 'even-handed justice' under the British flag (pp. 255–6).

amok: Bird herself describes this as a frenzy attributable either to opium or to an obscure Malay tradition (*The Golden Chersonese*, pp. 356–7). The practice is also frequently commented on by Clifford (q.v.) in his Malay memoirs.

Syed Abdulrahman: the hereditary ruler of Sungei Ujong.

the Governor's daughters: the daughters of General Shaw, the Governor of Malacca.

83 *Babu*: the head servant, also called Hadji. See note to Kipling, p. 443.

84 *gharrie*: Hindi for cart or carriage.

'The best laid schemes of men and mice gang aft agee': Bird's version of lines from Robert Burns, 'To a Mouse' (1786).

krises: Malayan swords.

a 'Sam Slick' clock: Sam Slick is the shrewd Yankee clockmaker in the work of the Nova Scotian writer Thomas Haliburton (1796–1865).

H. RIDER HAGGARD

Chapter 2 of *King Solomon's Mines* (Cassell and Co., 1885). The following notes are indebted to the World's Classics edition by Dennis Butts (1989).

86 *Bamangwato*: in the north of what is now Botswana, where Allan Quatermain last sighted Sir Henry Curtis's estranged brother.

Solomon's Mines: in 1871 a German geologist Karl Mauch advanced the theory that Great Zimbabwe, the complex of stone ruins in the south of present-day Zimbabwe, had been built by Phoenicians. This reawakened long-standing speculation that King Solomon's mines were to be located somewhere in Africa. Recent history in fact tells us that Great Zimbabwe was built by Shona peoples in the fourteenth or fifteenth century.

Kafirs: this Arabic term for unbeliever came to be applied offensively to all black Africans.

87 *koodoo*: or kudu, an antelope.

the Ophir of the Bible: the fabled source of King Solomon's gold, as recorded in *1 Kings* 9: 28 and 10: 11.

an old Isanusi: a diviner, usually female.

88 *Delagoa Portugee*: from the Delagoa Bay area of East Africa, or Mozambique, infiltrated by the Portuguese since the sixteenth century.

89 *rimpi*: or *riempie*, Afrikaans for thong.

93 *disselboom*: shaft.

SARA JEANNETTE DUNCAN

From the Ontario cultural journal *The Week*, 30 September 1886 (not under this title).

97 *sport with Amaryllis . . . the tangles of Neraea's hair*: Milton, *Lycidas* (1638), ll. 64–6.

98 *their Frechette and their Garneau*: the Quebeçois poet Louis Frechette (1839–1908), and the historian François-Xavier Garneau (1809–66).

99 *our chirping poets*: the publication of Charles G. D. Roberts's first book *Orion and Other Poems* (1880) had encouraged other poets like Carman and Lampman (qq.v.) to begin writing.

Faith without works is dead: James 2: 20.

RUDYARD KIPLING

'His Chance in Life' was first published in the Lahore *Civil and Military Gazette*, 2 April 1887, as No. XXIV of the 'Plain Tales' series; collected in *Plain Tales from the Hills* (Calcutta: Thacker, Spink and Co., 1888) with verse headings added; first English edition published by Macmillan, 1890.

99 *Kafir*: in this case from Kafiristan in Afghanistan. On the more standard and notorious meaning of the word, see note to Haggard, p. 442.

100 *Derozio*: Henry Louis Vivian Derozio (1809–31), the Calcutta Romantic poet and reforming Hindu College teacher, who came from the same literary milieu as later fostered Toru Dutt (q.v.). His *Poems* (1827) and the melancholic *The Fakir of Jungheera* (1828) made him, along with Kashi Prasad Ghosh, one of the first Indian writers to use English. When Kipling says that the Borderline folk are 'lower' than Derozio's class, he means that relative to the 'half-European' or Eurasian Derozio, the 'White blood' of the Vezzises or the D'Cruzes is significantly more dilute.

tussur-silk: a rough silk.

101 *huqa*: or hookah (water-pipe), the use of which would have been seen as too native.

Cochin: in the south-west of India, where a Jewish settlement existed since about the third or fourth century AD, the Black Jews having arrived first and the White Jews at a later date, as Andrew Rutherford points out in his Oxford World's Classics edition of *Plain Tales from the Hills* (1987). The Portuguese established a settlement in Cochin in the sixteenth century. Salman Rushdie weaves this strand of the Jewish Diaspora into *The Moor's Last Sigh* (1995), in the history of Abraham Zogoiby.

In nomine Sanctissimae: in the name of the most holy.

102 *'Intermediate'*: lower than Second, the Class of Eurasians and Natives. See Trevelyan's account of class distinctions on the Indian Railway.

Berhampur to Chicacola: a portion of East Indian coastline between Calcutta and Madras.

a Bengali Babu: an educated Bengali, many of whom were employed as clerks in the Civil Service. Though once meaning learned man and signifying respect, 'babu' became a pejorative term. As Kipling illustrates in his story 'The Head of the District' (1891), the babu was seen in Anglo-Indian circles as an Indian aspiring too far above his station in life, on the shaky basis of bogus qualifications and weak character.

102 *Orissa*: on the east coast of India, where John Beames (q.v.) worked as a civil officer.

Mohurrum: a Muslim mourning festival for the martyrs Hasan and Hussain, involving processions through city streets. See Kipling, 'On the City Wall' (1888).

Donnybrook: the expression, derived from the name of an Irish fair town, signifies a rowdy event.

'Christmas in India' was first published in the *Pioneer*, 24 December 1886, and the *Pioneer Mail*, 29 December 1886, with the title, 'Latter Day Carols. The Dyspeptic in India'; collected in the third edition of *Departmental Ditties and Other Verses* (1886; Thacker and Co., 1888).

105 *Heimweh*: (German) homesickness.

O the black dividing Sea: Kipling adapts the Hindu idea of the sea or 'black water' as an alienating and forbidding (and indeed forbidden) medium to cross. See note to Sorabji, p. 459.

'Giffen's Debt' first appeared in *Departmental Ditties and Other Verses* (Lahore: Civil and Military Press, 1886).

105 *Imprimis*: in the first place.

'Went Fantee': went native. The colloquial phrase obviously bears derogatory reference to the Fante people of the then Gold Coast, now Ghana, in West Africa. J. E. Casely Hayford (q.v.) was of the Fante people.

Gauri: in north-western India, Gauri was also the ancient Hindu capital of Bengal.

107 *a Solar Myth*: a tongue-in-cheek acknowledgement of Giffen's deification by reference to the work on sun-myths of the orientalist mythographer F. Max Müller (1823–1900). In addition, as Kipling explains in the poem 'Pagett, M.P.', and in the paragraphs on the Supreme Government in 'On the City Wall' (1888), 'Solar Myths' in the context of the Raj referred to those unfounded beliefs held by the uninitiated English about India being more endurable than Anglo-Indians made out.

'Mandalay' was published in the *Scot's Observer*, 21 June 1890, on W. E. Henley's (q.v.) recommendation; collected in *Barrack-Room Ballads* (Methuen, 1892).

107 *Moulmein*: a Burmese port on the Gulf of Martanban, the chief town of British Burma till 1852. The Kyaikthamlan Pagoda in Moulmein is renowned for its sweeping views.

Mandalay: city and region at the heart of Burma, on the Irrawaddy River, the last area of Burma to be taken over by the British (in 1885).

108 *Theebaw's Queen*: Thibaw was the last independent Burmese king (1878–85) before Burma became a province of Anglo-India.

hathis: elephants.

'What the People Said' was first published in the *Civil and Military Gazette*, 4 May 1887, with the title, 'A Jubilee Ode. Punjab Peasant's Point of View'; collected in the third edition of *Departmental Ditties and Other Verses* (1888). Housman's poem following, written in commemoration of the same mass imperial event, Victoria's Golden Jubilee, provides an interesting point of comparison, as does William Watson's 'Jubilee Night in Westmorland' (below), and, though differently, Hardy's First World War poem, 'In Time of "The Breaking of Nations" ' (1915). 'What the People Said' shares the latter poem's mood of resignation and endurance. Compare also the contemporary Indian writer Nayantara Sahgal's words: 'now [the British are] gone, and their residue is simply one more layer added to the layer upon layer of Indian consciousness. Just *one* more' ('The Schizophrenic Imagination', 1989).

A. E. HOUSMAN

Composed between 1887 and 1895; published in *The Shropshire Lad* (Kegan Paul, Trench, Trubner and Co., 1896). For the significance of the title, see note to Kipling immediately above.

J. A. FROUDE

Extracted from Chapter 5 of *The English in the West Indies; or, the Bow of Ulysses* (Longmans, Green, and Co., 1888). As well as suggesting the shape of the Caribbean archipelago, the subtitle compares Ulysses' bow of Homer's *Odyssey*, which none of Penelope's suitors can bend (and which, Froude notes in his Introduction to the book, is at present 'unstrung' (p. 15)), to the situation of the British race, as represented by its West Indian empire. Penelope's suitors are the neglectful Colonial Office and all those unproductively living on the Empire's substance.

113 *West Indians*: he means white West Indians.

114 *Caffres*: or Kafirs. See note to Haggard, p. 442.

115 *'nigger'*: As Clifford, Haggard, and Trevelyan (qq.v.) make clear in their various accounts of colonial experience, the word 'nigger' was in many circles perceived as derogatory and ignorantly inappropriate. Froude's awareness of this fact is (here but not elsewhere) signalled by the quotation marks. For the biographer of Carlyle the term would have carried an echo of his notorious essay, 'Occasional Discourse on the [West Indian] Nigger Question' (1849).

   Sir Ralph Abercrombie: General Ralph Abercromby helped subdue French-supported rebellions on Grenada, St Lucia, and St Vincent in 1796.

116 *Mr S——*: Henry Scholes, the Administrator of Grenada (1887–8).

   Père Labat: Jean-Baptiste Labat (1663–1738), author of *Nouveau voyage aux îles de l'Amerique* (1722). This book constituted Froude's principal reading for the trip.

117 *paisans aisez*: well-established peasants.

   scarlet rocou: a dye prepared from the South American roucou tree.

   Rodney's peace: George Brydges Rodney (1718–92), the English admiral
   who won several important naval battles against French, Dutch, and
   Spanish forces during the Seven Years War, and secured French-
   occupied St Lucia and Grenada for Britain.

119 *Hayti*: Froude refers throughout to the bad example of Haiti where, he
   claims, revolution brought anarchy and murderous devil-worship. To J. J.
   Thomas (q.v.) this largely inaccurate reference to a very different society
   and historical moment represented 'perversity gone wild in the manufac-
   ture of analogies' (*Froudacity*, p. 10). The Haitian Rebellion began in 1793;
   its leader, Toussaint l'Ouverture, was captured by the French in 1802.

120 '*En un mot, la vie y est délicieuse.*': 'in a word, life there is delightful.'

J. J. THOMAS

The extracts form the first paragraphs of the Introduction, and the last sections
of Book I, about the Windward Islands, of *Froudacity: West Indian Fables by
James Anthony Froude* (T. Fisher Unwin, 1889), published by subscription list.
The fifteen articles that became the book *Froudacity* were first published in the
West Indian *St George's Chronicle and Grenada Gazette*, March–July 1888.

121 *nil admirari*: wondering at nothing.

122 *the citation*: Thomas quotes from Chapter 4, *The Bow of Ulysses*, pp. 42–5.

125 *à vol d'oiseau*: from a 'bird's flight' perspective.

FLORA ANNIE STEEL

'The Duties of the Mistress' forms Chapter 1 of *The Complete Indian Housekeeper and Cook*, revised edition (Edinburgh: Frank Murray, 1890), written
with Grace Gardiner, named as another 'twenty years' resident'. The first
edition appeared in India in 1889. The book contained a Table of Wages and
chapters on such subjects as 'Hints on Outfits' and 'Dressed Vegetables'. In
India the Cookery Section was published separately, and the chapter, 'The
Duties of Servants', appeared in Urdu and Hindi as well as English.

126 *St Giles*: slum area in Soho, London.

   khitmatghar: table servant or waiter.

   pagri: a turban or headscarf.

127 *. . . nobody can't see 'e*: possibly a music-hall reference.

   the Medes and Persians: linked nations distinguished for their military
   discipline (708–331 BC).

130 *khansamah*: butler.

131 *chit*: any brief message exchanged between officials in the Indian Colonial
   Service; also a job-reference.

'Bopolûchî' is one of the Punjabi oral tales collected and transcribed by Steel and her collaborator R. C. Temple; first published, without editorial apparatus, in the *Indian Antiquary*, pp. 9–12 (1879–84); collected in *Wide-Awake Stories: A Collection of Tales told by little children between sunset and sunrise in the Panjab and Kashmir* (Bombay: Education Society's Press; Trubner and Co., 1884), Steel being responsible for the literary reworking, and Temple for the folkloric analysis included in an appendix. 'Bopolûchî' is Steel's story—her work makes up the bulk of the book. In the Preface the transcribers acknowledge the help of a 'coadjutrix', Bakhtawar, a zemindar's (landowner's) daughter, who, they emphasize, has been subjected to 'no foreign influence' even though educated by Steel. The stories were reissued in England under Steel's name alone as *Tales of the Punjab Told by the People* (Macmillan and Co., 1894), with illustrations by J. Lockwood Kipling, the writer's father. The notes which appear with the text are Steel's own.

'In the Permanent Way' first appeared in *In the Permanent Way and Other Stories* (William Heinemann, 1898).

138 *an R.E. man*: of the Royal Engineers.

    Simla: the hot-weather seat of the Indian government.

    Wilson's 'Hindu sects': Horace Hayman Wilson, *Sketches of the Religious Sects of the Hindus* (1846).

    Shiva: the destroyer god, one of the three chief gods of the *trimurti*, Hinduism's tripartite concept of the Divine, dating back to the medieval period of Indian history.

    Vishnu: the preserver of the world, another of the three chief gods representing the Supreme.

    the Vaishnavas and the Saivas: followers of devotional cults dedicated to Vishnu and to Shiva.

139 *byragi or jogi, or gosain or sunyasi*: Hindu holy men. Like King Bharata of Puranic legend, a *bairagi* withdraws from the world to devote himself to Yoga and selfless practice. A *gosain* is a devotee of the erotic theology featuring Krishna and Radha. A *sanyasi* is a Hindu monk.

    a Cooper's Hill joke: Cooper's Hill was the location of the Royal Indian Engineering College. Interestingly, John Denham's 'Cooper's Hill' (1642) is a topographical poem.

140 *serai*: lodgings for travellers.

    Om mi pudmi houm (Steel's footnote): *Om* is the core Vedic mantra. See note to Candler, p. 463.

141 *Mata Devi* (Steel's footnote): the world-mother goddess.

    Vishnu Lukshmi (Steel's footnote): or Lakshmi, the goddess of wealth and happiness, associated with Vishnu.

    Holi, the Indian Saturnalia (Steel's footnote): in fact the Hindu spring festival, when coloured powder is thrown.

144 *sútáras*: strings (usually mnemonic strings of words).

145 *ten minutes to ten*: for the narrator's calculation to be correct this, and the earlier time to which he refers, should probably read, ten minutes *past* ten.

   Vishnu in his various Avatars (Steel's footnote): Krishna, for example, is one of the eight incarnations of Vishnu. Radha is Krishna's companion, the favourite among his *gopi* or milkmaid attendants.

147 *lingam*: Shiva's phallus symbol. See note to Vivekananda, p. 451.

   this arrangement: the mark of Vishnu is an open triangle and a large black dot.

G. A. HENTY

'A Pipe of Mystery' appeared in *Tales of Daring and Danger* (Blackie and Son, 1890). The story is loosely based on an actual incident which took place at Meerut in May 1857, the time of the first outbreak of the Sepoy Rebellion, when two fellow officers and their female companions hid in a stone-built Hindu shrine for several hours, then made a getaway (see Christopher Hibbert, *The Great Mutiny*, 87–9).

147 *snapdragon*: a game in which the players attempt to catch up and eat raisins floating in burning brandy.

148 *Jubbalpore*: now Jubbulpur.

149 *out after tigers*: the man-eating tiger served as a capacious motif in colonial writing, signifying the fear and danger of the unknown, and, of course, as Tennyson makes clear in 'The Defence of Lucknow' (above), the so-called treachery and ferocity of the rebel native as manifested in the Indian Mutiny. For many years after 1857 tiger images continued to shadow the pages of Anglo-Indian stories. Consider, for example, Flora Annie Steel, 'The King's Well' (*The Permanent Way*, 1898); Alice Perrin, 'The Tiger Charm' and 'The White Tiger' (*East of Suez*, 1901), and her novel, *The Spell of the Jungle* (1902); and Henty's own *The Tiger of Mysore* (1896). See also Jim Corbett, *Man-Eaters of Kumaon* (1960).

150 *shekarry*: a hunting guide.

152 *dhoolie*: a palaquin or sedan chair.

153 *Siva*: or Shiva, the Hindu god of destruction, and the lord of the dance of creation. See note to Steel, p. 447.

154 *mussuk*: leather water-bag.

158 *sowar*: a native cavalry soldier.

160 *Lord Clyde*: Sir Colin Campbell, Baron Clyde, Commander-in-Chief in India (1857–60), led the second relief of Lucknow in September 1857, Havelock having entered the besieged residency with few reinforcements. See note to Tennyson, p. 439.

I. V. CRAWFORD

'War' was first published in the Toronto *Evening Telegram*, 4 August 1879, at the time of the conflict between Britain and the Zulus in South Africa, as well as of hostilities between the Empire and the Boers. The annexation of the Transvaal that sparked off the First Boer War (1880–1) had taken place in 1877.

'Said the Canoe' was collected and published posthumously along with 'War' in *The Collected Poems of Isabella Valancy Crawford*, ed. J. W. Garvin (Toronto: William Briggs, 1905). 'Said the Canoe' may well have been part of a longer narrative poem, now lost. See W. H. New, *A History of Canadian Literature* (1989), 120.

BLISS CARMAN

'Low Tide on Grand Pré', the poem that launched Carman, was first published in the *Atlantic Monthly*, March 1887; it appeared in the eponymous *Low Tide on Grand Pré: A Book of Lyrics* (David Nutt/Elkin Mathews) in 1893. Grand Pré is an inlet of the Bay of Fundy, Nova Scotia, the chief settlement of French Acadia before the Expulsion of 1755. Acadia had several times been a French colonial possession but was given to Britain by the Treaty of Utrecht. In 1755, expecting war with France, Britain expelled many Acadians as their loyalties were believed to be in doubt.

'A Vagabond Song' was first published in *More Songs from Vagabondia*, written with Richard Hovey (Boston: Copeland and Day; Elkin Mathews, 1896).

CHARLES G. D. ROBERTS

'The Pea-Fields' and 'My Trees' first appeared in volume form in *Songs of the Common Day and Ave!* (Longmans, Green and Co., 1893). 'The Pea-Fields' formed part of an opening sequence of thirty-seven sonnets.

169 *fields of Tantramar*: the tidal flats of the Tantramar Marshes, New Brunswick, near where both Bliss Carman and Roberts grew up.

ARCHIBALD LAMPMAN

'Late November' was called 'In November' in the collection in which it first appeared, *Among the Millet* (Ottawa: John Durie and Son, 1888); it was retitled by Duncan Campbell Scott, at a remembered suggestion of Lampman's, in his edition of Lampman's *Poems* (1925) in order to distinguish the poem from 'In November', *Lyrics of Earth* (1895).

'Among the Orchards' first appeared in the Toronto *Week*, 1888; published in *Alcyone* (Edinburgh: T. and A. Constable, 1899).

DUNCAN CAMPBELL SCOTT

'The Onondaga Madonna' was first published in volume form in *Labor and the Angel* (Boston: Copeland and Day, 1898). The Onondaga were a branch of the Iroquois people who, divided by rivalries between different white powers, were settled along the St Lawrence River in Ontario, and also in what is now New York State, where they originated.

A. B. ('BANJO') PATERSON

'Clancy of the Overflow' and 'The Travelling Post Office' were first published in the *Bulletin*, 21 December 1889 and 10 March 1894 respectively; collected in *The Man from Snowy River and Other Verses* (Sydney: Angus and Robertson, 1895). 'Old Australian Ways' first appeared in *Rio Grande's Last Race and Other Verses* (Sydney: Angus and Robertson, 1902).

176 *Rejoicing at the Spring*: as in Stephens's Introductory (see below), this scene, suffused in colour, perfume, and joyous birdsong, is clearly intended as a corrective to Marcus Clarke's (q.v.) view of Australian Melancholy.

   oh, lucky elf: possibly an echo of Keats's 'Ode to a Nightingale' (1820): 'the fancy cannot cheat so well | As she is famed to do, deceiving elf.'

HENRY LAWSON

'The Drover's Wife' was first published in the *Bulletin*, 23 July 1892; collected in *Short Stories in Prose and Verse*, privately printed by Louisa Lawson in 1894. The story was subsequently revised for *While the Billy Boils* (1896) and (usually taken as the definitive version) *The Country I Come From* (Edinburgh and London: Blackwood and Sons, 1901).

179 *ex-squatter*: the once-pejorative term 'squatter', which described those who, after the 1836 Squatting Act, settled on pastoral Crown land, later came to define large landowners and stock-raisers. See S. H. Roberts, *The Squatting Age in Australia* (1964).

BARBARA BAYNTON

'The Tramp' was published in the Sydney *Bulletin*, 12 December 1896; collected in *The Bulletin Story Book*, ed. A. G. Stephens (Sydney: Bulletin Newspaper Co., 1901). A revised version, entitled 'The Chosen Vessel', appeared as the final story in Baynton's own *Bush Studies* (Duckworth, 1902). This version includes a penultimate scene in which a Catholic voter meets the stricken woman and child moments before her death and believes them to be a blessed vision. It is not clear whether Baynton cut this final incident for *Bulletin* publication, or whether she later added it. The *Bulletin* version has been preserved here as it is the more coherent and maintains the overriding atmosphere of stifling siege and imprisonment.

A. G. STEPHENS

The Bulletin Story Book was a selection of two decades of *Bulletin* stories, 1881–1901 (Sydney: Bulletin Newspaper Co., 1901).

189 *the local sense of local beauty*: much of the criticism here is directed specifically at Marcus Clarke's widely known descriptions of Australian scenery as 'funereal' in the Preface to Adam Lindsay Gordon's *Poems* (see above).

Henry Kingsley suggests: an English author (1830–76), brother of Charles Kingsley, who spent time in Australia and wrote Australia-based family chronicles.

SWAMI VIVEKANANDA

'The Ideal of a Universal Religion' was a lecture given in New York, 12 January 1896, and again in London, 14 June 1896.

194 *Phallus symbol*: associated with the Hindu god Shiva. See note to Steel, p. 448.

195 *Sir John Lubbock*: the first Baron Avebury (1834–1913), a politician and natural scientist, the author of *The Origin of Civilisation and the Primitive Condition of Man* (1870) and *The Use of Life* (1894).

196 *'I am . . . pearls'*: an aphorism from the *Bhagavadgita*.

ROBERT LOUIS STEVENSON

Chapter 1 of Part 5 of *In the South Seas: Being an Account of Experiences and Observations in the Marquesas, Paumotus and Gilbert Islands*, first published in the New York *Sun*, February–December 1891, and partially in *Black and White* in England during the same period; appeared in the Edinburgh Edition of Stevenson's writing (Chatto and Windus, 1896) and as a separate volume in 1900. Planned as part of a larger South Seas series, the Gilbert Islands chapters, including this one, formed the section of *In the South Seas* with which Stevenson was eventually the most satisfied.

199 *Mainana . . . Nonuti*: Gilbert Islands in the Western Pacific (present-day Kiribati). The group includes Mariki, Tapituea, and Peru, and Apemama (or Abemama) itself.

   the Calendar's pilot: in the *Arabian Nights*.

200 *September 1st*: 1889.

   maniap's: Polynesian dwellings.

201 *Sir Charles Grandison . . . to his own heart*: a reference to the eponymous novel by Samuel Richardson (1754).

   a figure out of Hoffmann: E. T. A. Hoffmann (1776–1822), the German Romantic writer of fantastic and supernatural tales.

   taro: a Polynesian food plant.

202 *ridis*: skirts, made of raffia or similar material.

HUGH CLIFFORD

'Up Country' appeared as the final sketch of *In Court and Kampong: Being Tales and Sketches of Native life in the Malay Peninsula* (Grant Richards, 1897). A *kampong* is a Malay village. The title suggests an alliterative homology with Henty's *Tales of Daring and Danger* or *In Battle and Breeze* (1896), for example.

205 *A Parody (epigraph)*: this is a reworking, if not exactly a parody, of the refrain of Kipling's poem, 'The Long Trail' or 'L'Envoi' (1892), about leaving grey England for the 'shouting seas'.

206 *I sent . . . Heaven or Hell*: quatrain 71 of Edward Fitzgerald, *The Rubaiyat of Omar Khayyam*, 2nd ed. (1868).

208 *Frankenstein's monster*: but in *Saleh* (1908), Clifford uses the same image from Mary Shelley's novel (1818) to describe the denationalized, English-educated Malay: 'miscreated' and therefore potentially unmanageable.

209 *It is not good . . . to hustle the East*: the epigraph to Chapter 4 of Kipling's novel *The Naulahka* (with Walter Balestier, 1892).

210 *Browning's Grammarian*: who 'decided not to live but know' ('The Grammarian's Funeral', *Men and Women*, 1855).

a sounding brass . . . a tinkling cymbal: 1 Corinthians 13: 12.

211 *Regained . . . with a sigh*: Byron, 'The Prisoner of Chillon' (1816). In the Foreword to *Sally: A Study* (1904), Clifford expands on these sentiments: 'Now at last, when the bitter hour of separation has come, a full realisation of all that the East has taught to me . . . of all that the East stands for in my heart and in my memory, is upon me with overpowering force.' *In Court and Kampong* ends with an 'Envoi' summarizing the stories and expressing similar feelings.

JOSEPH CHAMBERLAIN

A speech delivered at the Royal Colonial Institute dinner at the Hotel Metropole, London, 31 March 1897; published in *Foreign and Colonial Speeches* (George Routledge and Sons, 1897), in which the texts of speeches are punctuated by interjections of 'hear, hear' and 'laughter'. The extract begins immediately after the brief toast to the 'Imperial patriotism' which, Chamberlain says, has been demonstrated by the Institute since its founding (1868).

213 *Prempeh and Lobengula*: Prempeh was the King of the Asante in the Gold Coast (now Ghana) whom Chamberlain deposed in 1896. Lobengula, the King of Matabeleland (in present-day Zimbabwe), baulked Cecil John Rhodes's expansionist plans by his persistent efforts to maintain peace. In 1889 the Rudd Concession had duped him into handing over mining rights in his kingdom to Rhodes's company. Four years later Lobengula died by taking poison, having finally submitted to waging war on the company.

214 *Mr Selous*: Frederick Selous (1851–1917), the big-game hunter, folk hero, and author of *A Hunter's Wanderings in Africa* (1881), one of the texts that had a significant influence on Haggard's *King Solomon's Mines* (above).

omelettes without breaking eggs: a favourite saying of Chamberlain's.

Janus: ever-wakeful, the twin-faced Roman god Janus looks to the past and the future, the morning and the night.

215 *the New Zealander . . . ruins of a great dead city*: in Letter XII of *The Competition Wallah*, Trevelyan (q.v.) had written that Macaulay's prose

would still be familiar to 'the New Zealander who from that broken arch of London Bridge contemplates the ruins of St Paul's'—the image of the New Zealander was one of Macaulay's own. Trevelyan and Chamberlain parted company over Tariff Reform in 1886.

OLIVE SCHREINER

From the first part of the two-part 'allegory-story', *Trooper Peter Halket of Mashonaland*, in fact a long political pamphlet, published by T. Fisher Unwin, 1897.

218 *koppje*: in *The Story of an African Farm* (1883), Schreiner describes this southern African hill formation as 'a heap of round iron stones piled upon one another, as over some giant's grave'.

219 ... *dark hair*: the motif of Christ visiting the country to comment on injustice has cropped up since in South African writing, most notably in the play by Percy Mtwa and Mbongeni Ngema, *Woza Albert!* (Rise Up, Albert!, 1983).

Cecil Rhodes: as she makes clear further into *Trooper Peter*, Schreiner saw the imperialist Cecil Rhodes (1853–1902) as 'the only man of genius South Africa possesses', but became convinced he was using his powers for ill after the Jameson Raid (29 December 1895–2 January 1896), which was soon followed by the violent 'pacification' of what became Rhodesia. Masterminded by Rhodes's Chartered Company, the Jameson Raid was intended as a double takeover—from within and without—of the gold-rich Boer Republic of the Transvaal. It failed due to bad management. Schreiner's indignation over this and subsequent events sparked off the writing of *Trooper Peter*.

220 *Barnato and Beit*: the Kimberley diamond magnate 'Barney Barnato' (Barnett Isaacs, 1852–97), and the South African financier and mining magnate Alfred Beit (1853–1906).

the Chartered Company: Rhodes's British South Africa Company, created in 1889 for the conquest of Mashonaland (now part of Zimbabwe).

223 *Martini-Henry*: a brand of rifle.

226 *the Colony*: the Cape Colony.

the British Government here: at this point Mashonaland and Matabeleland were under the control of the Company.

229 *the other who conquered them*: Christ is referring to the 1895–7 massacre of Armenian Christians.

233 *the sons of one mother*: the British and the Boers, pitted against one another by vulture-magnates like Rhodes.

MARY KINGSLEY

'Black Ghosts' appeared in the *Cornhill Magazine*, July 1897. This and two other contemporaneous articles on West African cultures introduce material elaborated in *Travels in West Africa* (1897), in particular in the five chapters (19 to 23) on fetish.

235 *aphaniptera and acanthia lectularia*: brown-coloured butterflies and shield-bugs.

237 *with-thick-fog-overhung mind*: in *Travels in West Africa* Kingsley speaks of the difficulty of penetrating the African 'mind-forest'. She is in part remarking on widely experienced problems in cross-cultural communication.

negroes, and . . . Bantu: Kingsley distinguishes between southern and east African peoples, the Bantu, and darker skinned West Africans, or 'negroes'.

238 *M. Pichault*: possibly an anthropological contact of Kingsley's in the French Congo.

239 *twin children*: as Chinua Achebe records in *Things Fall Apart* (1958), twins were forbidden in Niger Delta cultures.

242 *Srahmandazi*: here Kingsley gives some background to the concept of the West African afterlife, which Newbolt adapted for his poem 'Srámandázi' (below).

243 *'the cat and banjo'*: that is, crazy havoc, possibly with echoes of the children's rhyme 'The Cat and the Fiddle'. The banjo in Kipling's 'The Song of the Banjo' (1896) is the 'prophet of the Utterly Absurd'.

. . . and then it dies: what Achebe in *Things Fall Apart* calls the *ogbanje* child, and Ben Okri in *The Famished Road* (1991), the *abiku*.

245 *1874*: the 1873–4 Asante Expedition which led to the formation of the Gold Coast Crown Colony.

246 *factory*: trading depot.

247 *E. B. Tylor*: in *Primitive Culture* (1871).

248 *'In Memoriam'*: from section 47 of Tennyson's poem (1850).

JOSEPH CONRAD

'An Outpost of Progress' was composed in the first half of 1896; first published in *Cosmopolis* 6–7 (June–July 1897); collected in *Tales of Unrest* (T. Fisher Unwin, 1898).

248 *Loanda*: Luanda in Angola. The story itself is set in the vast Congo Free State, 'the land of darkness and sorrow', on the banks of the Kasai River, a tributary of the Congo.

250 *. . . its opinion*: Conrad develops this thought in Part 2 of 'Heart of Darkness' (1899), as Marlow reflects on Kurtz's possession by the 'powers of darkness': 'stepping delicately between the butcher and the policeman . . . how can you imagine what particular region of the first ages a man's untrammelled feet may take him by way of solitude?'

252 . . . *great emptiness*: the description of the forest shades over into images of the 'impenetrable' forest in 'Heart of Darkness', which severs all connection white men have with the world that is familiar to them.

253 *fetish*: in *Travels in West Africa* (1897), Mary Kingsley (q.v.) describes fetish as images which are seen to harbour or embody spirit.

254 *d'Artagnan . . . Hawk's Eye . . . Father Goriot*: the references are all to early nineteenth-century novels, respectively, *The Three Musketeers* (1844) by Alexander Dumas the elder; (probably) James Fenimore Cooper's *The Last of the Mohicans* (1826) (the character Hawkeye was one of the incarnations of Natty Bumppo who appears in the novel); and Honoré de Balzac, *Le Père Goriot* (1834).

263 . . . *familiar, and disgusting*: a similar idea reverberates through Marlow's observation in 'Heart of Darkness': 'The wilderness had patted [Kurtz] on the head . . . it had taken him, loved him, embraced him, got into his veins, consumed his flesh.'

WILLIAM WATSON

'Jubilee Night in Westmorland' was published in *The Hope of the World and Other Poems* (Bodley Head, 1898). Queen Victoria's Diamond Jubilee of 1897 was a self-glorifying celebration of British imperial greatness on an even grander scale than the 1887 Jubilee (see above). See also Kipling's 'Recessional', which follows.

RUDYARD KIPLING

'Recessional' first appeared in *The Times*, 17 July 1897; collected in *The Five Nations* (Methuen and Co., 1903). Though hardly optimistic in tone, the poem, like Watson's, was written to mark Victoria's Diamond Jubilee.

'The White Man's Burden' appeared in *The Times*, *The New York Times*, and *McClure's Magazine*, February 1899; collected in *The Five Nations* (1903).

273 *United States . . . Philippine Islands*: the historical incident which lay behind the poem was local resistance to the 1898 American annexation of the Philippines following Admiral Dewey's victory over the Spanish at Manila.

ALGERNON CHARLES SWINBURNE

'The Transvaal' was first published in *The Times*, 11 October 1899, the day after war was declared.

275 *Blake*: Robert Blake (1599–1657), the Commander of Cromwell's navy, defeated the Royalists under Prince Rupert of Spain (1650), and destroyed the Spanish treasure fleet off the Canaries seven years later.

ALFRED AUSTIN

'To Arms!' was the fifth of eight warlike poems written in response to the Boer

War; first published in *The Times*, 23 December 1899; added to *Songs of England*, 3rd edn. (1898; Macmillan, 1900).

277 *England's Flag*: in the explanatory preface to *Songs of England*, Austin makes clear that England is anywhere where men feel 'an instantaneous thrill of kinship' at the sound of Queen Victoria's name.

MRS ERNEST AMES

An ABC, for Baby Patriots was published by Dean and Son, 1899; the text is given here in full, without the full-page illustrations.

279 *K . . . naughty*: the illustration for K shows three African chiefs chained together crown-to-crown.

L . . . frown: as for U, the reference is to the nursery rhyme about the Lion and the Unicorn who fought for the Crown.

N . . . dead: it is worth bearing in mind here that in the latter years of the nineteenth century Britain was striving to maintain her naval supremacy in the face of competition from Germany and the USA.

280 *T . . . wakes*: Alice Perrin (q.v.) writes: 'there's something about a bath that raises a Briton's spirits and makes him give tongue' (*East of Suez* (1902), 251). At the end of *The Water-Babies* (1863) Charles Kingsley advises that the child learn his lessons and wash in 'plenty of cold water' 'like a true English man'. In the same book, roast beef is said to prevent degeneration.

W . . . do: in the illustration an African chief holds up a paper labelled 'treaty'. An explorer figure in a topee is explaining its meaning to him.

X . . . peace: the 'x' was the crossed-baton symbol of the London police.

THOMAS HARDY

'Departure' is the second of the 'War Poems' sequence (comprising eleven poems, in which 'A Christmas Ghost-Story' and 'Drummer Hodge' were fourth and fifth) of *Poems of the Past and the Present* (Macmillan, 1901); this was the first appearance of 'Departure'.

'A Christmas Ghost-Story' was first published in the *Westminster Gazette*, 23 December 1899, the same day as Austin's 'To Arms!' (see above). Hardy had been disturbed at the expressions of aggression which Britain's several defeats at the hands of the Boers during December had unleashed. On 24 December the *Daily Chronicle* criticized Hardy's portrayal of what it took to be one of the Dublin Fusiliers in the battle of the Tugela, Natal, who was said to have cried out amid a fury of bullets, 'Let us make a name for ourselves!'

'Drummer Hodge' was first published in *Literature*, 25 November 1899, with the title, 'The Dead Drummer', and headnote: 'One of the Drummers killed was a native of a village near Casterbridge'.

282 *kopje-crest*: see note to Schreiner, p. 453.

veldt: traditional spelling of the Afrikaans word *veld*.

W. E. HENLEY

'Remonstrance' was composed in December 1899, a black month of repeated defeats for Britain; published as the first poem in *For England's Sake: Verses and Songs in Time of War* (David Nutt, 1900), which also includes the two poems below. The collection comprised poems that had appeared in earlier collections, differently ordered.

283 *Strike, England, and strike home!*: borrows (and endorses the, to some, controversial tone of) the last line of Swinburne's sonnet 'The Transvaal' (see above). The line also resonates with Tennyson's refrain 'Britons, hold your own' in 'Opening of the Indian and Colonial Exhibition' (above). Both injunctions may carry an echo of Henry Purcell's 'Britons, strike home' (1695).

'*Pro Rege Nostro*' (For Our Kingdom) was published in the *National Observer*, January 1892, as 'England, my England'; collected in *The Song of the Sword and Other Verses* (David Nutt, 1892; revised edn., *London Voluntaries, The Song of the Sword and Other Verses*, 1893); retitled *For England's Sake*.

'The Choice of the Will' was first published in the *National Observer*, July 1891.

286 *round and round*: images of British power girdling the globe—the Empire on which the sun never set—are a staple of Henley's 1890s poetry.

A. E. HOUSMAN

'Grenadier' is one of Housman's six or so poems about, and composed around the time of, the Boer War; published in *Last Poems* (Richards, 1922).

HENRY NEWBOLT

'*Vitaï Lampada*' (The Lamp of Life) is the earliest-written of Newbolt's poems; first published in *Admirals All and Other Verses* (Elkin Mathews, 1897). This and his poem 'Clifton Chapel' pay a debt to Matthew Arnold's 'Rugby Chapel' (1867).

287 '*dust and smoke*': the scene is that of a much-publicized British Army battle fought in January 1885 at Abu Klea in the Sudan against Mahdist forces—a vain attempt to relieve General Charles Gordon at Khartoum.

'Peace' is dated 21 June 1902, not long after the Boer War peace (31 May); first published in *The Sailing of the Long-Ships and Other Poems* (John Murray, 1902). 'Peace' was sparked off by a comment made to the poet by Virginia Woolf (then Stephen). He sent the verse to her on a postcard, in reply to which she expressed 'great pleasure—and pride', adding that his poetry was pervasive in her life. Leslie Stephen, she wrote, was involved in getting Newbolt's war poems by heart. See Henry Newbolt, *My World as in My Time* (1932), 250.

'April on Waggon Hill' was published in a later edition of *The Sailing of the Long-Ships* (1903). Compare Hardy's 'Drummer Hodge' (above). Waggon (or Wagon) Hill was a crucial position defended by the Devonshire Regiment on

6 January 1900 in an attempt to break the Boers' siege-grip on Ladysmith. At a time of bruising setbacks on the British side, this success was roundly celebrated.

288 *ling*: heather

'Sráhmandázi' was first published in the *Monthly Review*, 7 (June 1902); collected in *The Sailing of the Long-Ships* (1902). Newbolt would include new poems, like these of 1902, in later editions of *Admirals All* and *The Island Race* (1898). The title refers to the West African concept of the afterlife which, as his note makes clear, Newbolt had taken from Mary Kingsley's ethnographic writings. See Mary Kingsley, 'Black Ghosts' (above). The affirmation of a robust life set off by a fascination with death is characteristic of Newbolt's imperialist poems.

WILLIAM WATSON

'Rome and Another', 'The Inexorable Law', and 'The True Imperialism' appeared in *For England: Poems Written During Estrangement* (The Bodley Head, 1903).

RUDYARD KIPLING

'The Lesson' was published in *The Times*, 29 July 1901; collected in *The Five Nations* (1903).

293 *higher than Gilderoy's kite*: very high, an American expression derived from the name of a Scottish criminal who in a ballad was said to have been strung up so high he resembled a kite.

J. A. HOBSON

Chapter 1, Part 2 of *Imperialism: A Study* (James Nisbet and Co., 1902).

295 *Nabob*: an extravagantly rich returnee from India. Derived from Persian, this term had particular currency in the late eighteenth century.

'Life of Cobden,' vol. ii, p. 361 (Hobson's note): John Morley, *The Life of Cobden* (1881).

296 *the South African millionaire*: visiting South Africa to collect material for his book, Hobson was influenced in his analysis of the situation both by meeting Olive Schreiner and Samuel Cronwright-Schreiner, and by their book, *The Political Situation* (1895), which argued that monopoly capitalists were undermining South African economic and political structures. For further details of the named millionaires, see note to Schreiner, p. 453.

297 *poison*: the language of poisoning and contamination here and elsewhere in *Imperialism* is significant, sometimes betraying Hobson's own racial bigotry. While he often qualifies terms like 'the lower races', his thesis is informed by anti-Semitic conspiracy theories current at the turn of the century. International capitalism, he believed, is controlled by a 'single

and peculiar race', the Jews, who are corrupting the rest of the world (*Imperialism*, 64).

. . . *thus summarised*: though his main concern is with Britain, Hobson's anti-imperial economics generalizes from the experience of all the imperial powers.

CORNELIA SORABJI

'Love and Death' appeared as the third sketch in *Love and Life Behind the Purdah* (Freemantle and Co., 1901). The plague of which Sorabji writes continued to sweep through India in the early years of the century, the annual mortality figures exceeding 1 million in 1904.

300 *a lady-doctor and a nurse*: would be able to gain access to women in purdah.

maidan: an open space or common, earthen rather than grassed, which first developed to separate native from Anglo-Indian living quarters.

301 *cross the waters*: go abroad, by sea, forbidden to orthodox Brahmins. In this, the fourth and last age of the present cosmic aeon, the *Kali-yuga*, which is marked by decline and chaos, Hindu practice recommended that Brahmins keep strictly to caste laws, which precluded travel to foreign lands across the 'black water'. See note to Kipling, p. 444.

fire-god: Agni.

302 . . . *equipages*: Sorabji is contrasting hill cultures and cultures of the plain.

cave: (Latin) Beware.

303 . . . *treading the flames*: the imagery of fire-sacrifice carries reflections of *sati* or widow-burning, which had been outlawed by Britain in 1829.

Peste!: an expression of anger, from the French *pester* ('plague').

LADY MARY ANNE BARKER

'Colonial Servants' first appeared in the *Cornhill Magazine*, December 1900; collected in *Colonial Memoirs* (Smith, Elder and Co., 1904). The chapter goes on to describe catering confusions in Mauritius, Western Australian servant problems, and an alcoholic cook in Trinidad.

306 *hathi*: elephant

307 *dhooly*: a palaquin or sedan chair.

308 *sea-change*: Shakespeare, *The Tempest*, I. ii. 403.

SAROJINI NAIDU

'Village Song', 'Humayun to Zobeida', 'Ode to H.H. the Nizam of Hyderabad', and 'To India' were composed between 1896 and 1904; published in *The Golden Threshold*, introduction by Arthur Symons (William Heinemann, 1905). Notes to these poems have been grouped together.

311 *champa buds*: or *champak*, small, fragrant white flowers used in devotional offerings.

köil-haunted: see note to Dutt, p. 441.

'*Humayun to Zobeida*': Humayan was the second Mughal emperor (1530–40; 1555–6).

312 *. . . my tribute to receive*: Naidu takes up the Mughal tradition of the royal ode marking a ruler's achievements.

. . . Galilee: this celebration of religious and cultural diversity, embracing Muslim, Hindu, Parsi, and Christian faiths, outlines Naidu's ideal of a non-sectarian India.

ghazal: a Persian verse-form based on internal rhyme in which the second line of every couplet generally carries a repeated phrase.

313 *Firdusi*: the great Persian poet (*c*.935–*c*.1020), whose epic *Shah-nameh* gives an account of Persian rule up to Muslim invasion in 652.

Rise, Mother: the invocation of the nation as mother, *Bharat*, as also in 'An Anthem of Love', subscribes to the convention of patriotic song strongly influenced by Bankim Chandra Chatterjee's 'Bande Mataram' (Hail Mother) (see Aurobindo's version below). The poem was read at the 1904 Indian National Congress.

'Songs of My City', 'Song of Radha the Milkmaid', and 'An Anthem of Love' were published in *The Bird of Time: Songs of Life, Death and the Spring*, introduction by Edmund Gosse (William Heinemann, 1912).

314 *keora*: a waxy scented flower.

315 '*Song of Radha the Milkmaid*': Radha is Krishna's beloved, the favourite among his *gopi* or milkmaid attendants.

GEORGE NATHANIEL, MARQUESS CURZON

'The British Empire' is a speech, in effect a toast, given at a dinner in honour of Lord Milner, in London, 24 May 1906 (or 'Empire Day'); published in *Subjects of the Day: Being a Selection of the Speeches and Writing by Earl Curzon of Kedleston*, ed. Desmond H. Chapman-Huston (George Allen and Unwin Ltd., 1915). Empire Day was introduced as a day of special imperial observance in 1904.

317 *Milner*: Alfred Milner (1854–1925), 'new imperialist' Governor of the Cape and High Commissioner (1897–1905), who sought the federation and Anglicization of South Africa, and helped to engineer the outbreak of hostilities in 1899.

our Chairman: Joseph Chamberlain (q.v.) presided over the dinner.

Crown Colonies: as in the West Indies, where government by the Crown stood in place of constitutional government.

318 *echoes round the world*: see Henley, 'The Choice of the Will' (above).

SRI AUROBINDO

'The Object of Passive Resistance' is from the second in a series of articles on passive resistance, entitled 'Its Object'; published in the nationalist Calcutta paper *Bande Mataram* (which Aurobindo edited) between 9 and 23 April 1907; published as *The Doctrine of Passive Resistance* (Calcutta: Arya Publishing House, 1948).

321 *Permanent Settlement*: the Permanent Settlement of 1793, engineered by Lord Cornwallis, confirmed the hereditary ownership of Indian estates, especially in Bengal, and formalized the system of land revenue collection.

Simultaneous Examinations: the parallel system of entry to the Indian Civil Service for Indians alongside Europeans.

322 *Home Charges*: in effect the cost to India of being ruled by Britain, reaped mainly in the form of taxes, but also as tariffs and interest on debts. Especially after the 1857 Uprising, the Government of India was almost continuously involved in budgetary crises caused by military campaigns, famine relief, interest on capital investment, the growing cost of land revenue collection, and the falling value of the rupee relative to sterling. It is this that Aurobindo refers to when speaking of 'murderous drain'. The 'drain' theory concerning the extraction of wealth from India by Britain was first developed in the late nineteenth century by the Indian nationalist Dadabhai Naoroji.

324 *Asiatic nations*: in particular, Japan. Elsewhere in the series, resistance in Ireland and Russia is taken as exemplary.

the lessons of English history: in this attack on 'English books', Aurobindo is clearly repudiating the 'civilizing' effects of the liberal English education put in place by Macaulay's Minute on Indian Education (1835).

the new school: the nationalist mass movement manifested in the Swadeshi outburst against Partition, as Aurobindo goes on to describe. Swadeshi, meaning self-help or self-development, involved the boycott of salt, sugar, cloth, alcohol, and other British imports, with the object of achieving independent government.

'Charles Stuart Parnell, 1891' appeared in *Songs to Myrtilla and Other Poems*, printed for private circulation by the Lakshmi Vilas Press, Baroda, 1895, its subject being Charles Parnell (1846–91), the Irish nationalist and leader of the struggle for Irish Home Rule. In the late 1880s he was ruined by revelations concerning his affair with a married woman, Kitty O'Shea.

'*Transiit, Non Periit*' ('he has passed on (crossed over to the other side), not died') first appeared in the Bengali autobiography of Rajnarayan Bose (Calcutta: Kuntaline Press, 1909); reprinted in *Songs to Myrtilla*, 2nd edn. (1923).

'Hymn to the Mother: Bandemataram' was published in *Karmayogin*, 1:20 (November 1909); republished in the Chandernagore pamphlet, *Rishi Bunkim Chandra*, February 1923. The poem is a free translation of Bankim Chandra Chatterjee's patriotic Bengali hymn ('Bande Mataram' or 'Hail Mother', 1882) that gave inspiration to the 1905 Swadeshi resistance movement against Bengal Partition in which Aurobindo was involved.

326 *Mother*: compare Sarojini Naidu's 'To India' and 'An Anthem of Love' (above).

327 *Durga*: a fiercely powerful yet benevolent goddess, and a form of Devi, the world-mother. Durga has featured prominently in Indian nationalist discourse since the late nineteenth century.

'Revelation' and 'Rebirth' were written in the period 1902–10; published in *Ahana and Other Poems* (Pondicherry: The Modern Press, 1915).

ALICE PERRIN

'The Rise of Ram Din' was first published in *Red Records* (Chatto and Windus, 1906).

329 *the Mathura district*: in northern India, present-day Uttar Pradesh. See also Naidu's own note to 'Song of Radha the Milkmaid', p. 315.

Feringhees: foreigners, from Persian, derived from *frank*, meaning European.

330 *khansamah*: see Steel's explanation in 'The Duties of the Mistress' of how the butler might accrue a small private income.

serai: government travel-lodgings.

331 *puggaree*: turban.

ekka: small one-horse carriage.

332 *go-down*: storeroom or cupboard.

333 *syce*: groom.

JAMES JOYCE

'Ireland at the Bar' was first published in Italian as 'L'Irlanda alla sbarra' in the Trieste paper *Il piccolo della serra*, 16 September 1907; reprinted in *The Critical Writings of James Joyce*, ed. Ellsworth Mason and Richard Ellmann (New York: Viking Press, 1959).

336 *a murder was committed*: on 17 August 1882 members of a family named Joyce, believed to be government informers, were murdered in County Galway. In December of the same year three men were hanged by the English authorities for the murders, one of them Myles Joyce. He was generally considered to be innocent. See Mason and Ellman, 197 n.

337 *these last few days*: August 1907 disturbances in Ireland connected with peasant evictions.

EDMUND CANDLER

'Káshi' was first published in *Blackwood's Magazine*, 181 (February 1907); reprinted in *The Mantle of the East* (Edinburgh and London: William Blackwood and Sons, 1910). 'Káshi' (or Kási), meaning splendid, is another name for Varanasi or Benares, the sacred city known for its ghats (broad flagstone banks) along the Ganges off which pilgrims bathe and bodies are cremated. In Hindu cosmology Benares, sacred to Shiva, is the centre of all things. It is also the earthly destination to which Kim and the Lama are headed in Kipling's *Kim* (1901).

339 *Vishéshwar*: the shrine to this early religious leader and follower of Shiva.

Dekhani women: from the Deccan, the plateau region of Southern India.

the Mahunt of Ajodhya: as this means the false prophet of Ayodya, the name may signify a private joke of Candler's. 'Mahound' was a medieval form of the name Muhammed whom, Europeans believed, Muslims worshipped as God.

chelas: young assistants.

340 *Anapurna*: she who is the giver of food, the Hindu goddess of fertility and harvest.

Gyan Kup: Shiva's well.

Marwari: from the Rajasthan area, in the north-west of India.

341 *Saddhu*: a holy man.

342 *Bairagi . . . Yogi . . . Sannyasi . . . Dandi . . . Talingi*: holy men associated with different sects and philosophies. See note to Steel, p. 447.

rudraksha: the symbol of Rudra, the god of storm and destruction linked to Shiva.

Magdalen Bridge: in Cambridge. Candler appears to cast in a positive light this vision of the Hindu colonial 'hybrid', Cambridge-educated yet devout.

343 *Hom*: according to the Vedas, *Om* or *Aum* is the core mantra and sound of the absolute.

344 *Sankhya philosophy*: based on the dualism of spirit and substance.

Panch Kosi road: the Benares boundary road.

Trimurti: the three figures of the Supreme: Shiva, Vishnu, and Brahma. See note to Steel, p. 447.

STEPHEN LEACOCK

'Back to the Bush' was first published as one of the final sketches in *Literary Lapses* (Montreal: Gazette Printing Co., 1910); reprinted by John Lane, 1911.

345 *Gatineau*: river in northern Quebec.

346 *Batiscan*: this and the rivers following lie in northern Ontario.

DOROTHEA FAIRBRIDGE

'Pamela' was published in the pro-South African Union Cape paper *The State*, September 1911.

349 *Batavian forbears*: his Malay ancestors, from Batavia or the Dutch East Indies.

350 *from Salome to Tariff Reform*: subjects extending from the aesthetic, as in Oscar Wilde's play *Salome* (1894), to the political. Opposition to Colonial Tariff Reform swept the British Liberal Party to victory in 1906.

351 *the war*: the South African War.

   K. of K.'s face: Kitchener of Khartoum (1850–1916), the Commander-in-Chief of the imperial forces during the South African War.

352 *spreeuws*: starlings.

   Victoria County: as Hayes farms sugar in Natal, this is an inconsistency.

   unspoiled: Fairbridge supported the restoration of old Cape buildings.

355 *knol-kohl*: Cape Afrikaans for a bulb cabbage, literally translated.

   rooineks were 'verdoemde': Englishmen (literally, rednecks) were damned.

356 *as Taillefer sang the song of Roland*: Taillefer (d. 1066), the Norman minstrel who sang war songs at the Battle of Hastings. The *Chanson de Roland* is the great medieval epic.

357 *Almachtig!*: Afrikaans for Almighty or Almighty God.

   Balaam's ass: Numbers 22: 21–35.

358 *werf*: yard.

   rustbank: bench, for resting upon.

359 *poison*: the image of leprosy (and other diseases) as a contamination associated with native contact, travelled through many colonial writings, including Stevenson's (q.v.) reports on a leper colony in Hawaii. The denouement of Conan Doyle's story 'The Adventure of the Blanched Soldier', in *The Case-Book of Sherlock Holmes* (1927), turns on an assumed case of exposure to leprosy during the Boer War. Leprosy, seen as the fragmentation and corruption of the body, became a particular focus for anxieties about degeneration through contact with 'savages'. For contamination anxieties, compare also Rudyard Kipling, 'The Mark of the Beast' and 'Without Benefit of Clergy', in *Life's Handicap* (1891).

360 *Robben Island*: a leper colony 1846–1931, Robben Island then passed to the South African Ministry of Defence.

J. E. CASELY HAYFORD

'As in a Glass Darkly' and 'African Nationality' are Chapters 15 and 17 of *Ethiopia Unbound* (C. M. Phillips, 1911).

361 *'As in a Glass Darkly'*: 1 Corinthians 13: 12.

   universal conference: Hayford had in mind, in particular, the Berlin Conference of 1885 where Africa was divided up between the European 'Great Powers', and also, more generally, the conferences, alliances, and ententes between these nations at the height of empire, which led up to the Great War.

362 *elbow-room*: a phrase also used in Solomon Plaatje's (q.v.) accounts of white justifications for land appropriation.

   . . . pleased them all: the hypocrisy of a colonizing Christianity has been commented on by African and other postcolonial writers since. In the Aboriginal Sally Morgan's collective autobiography, *My Place* (1986),

Arthur Corunna comments: 'the white people . . . brought the religion here with them and the Commandment, Thou Shalt Not Steal, and yet they stole this country' (p. 213). See also Schreiner, *Trooper Peter* (p. 230, above).

nectar unto them: elsewhere in *Ethiopia Unbound* Casely Hayford expounds on the destructive effects of colonial gin importation.

363 *a John the Baptist*: Edward Wilmot Blyden, according to Casely Hayford 'the foremost thinker of the race' (*Ethiopia Unbound*, 162).

lose its own soul: Mark 8: 36.

'African Nationality' is the second of three consecutive chapters in *Ethiopia Unbound* on 'Race Emancipation': the first profiles Blyden (q.v.); the third further discusses African self-realization and emancipation from foreign ideas.

366 *. . . the white man*: unattributed white American pronouncements of the time.

a real spoil: possibly a citation from an African American pan-nationalist, most likely from Blyden. See Exodus 12: 36.

367 *a wise and understanding people*: Deuteronomy 4: 5–6.

368 *material prosperity*: James O'Hannay in the *Independent Review*, November 1905. The preservation of cultural identity through language has much in common with late twentieth-century post-colonial ideas. Compare in particular the Kenyan writer Ngugi wa Thiong'o's *Decolonising the Mind* (1986).

CLAUDE MCKAY

'Oh General Jackson!', 'The Other Day', and 'I Have a News' were transcribed by Walter Jekyll; published in *Jamaican Song and Story: Annancy Stories, Digging Sings, Ring Tunes, and Dancing Tunes* (The Folk-Lore Society/David Nutt, 1907). In the Preface, in which he offers the book as 'a tribute to my love for Jamaica and its dusky inhabitants', McKay's patron Jekyll notes that the songs and stories were 'taken down from the mouths of men and boys in my employ' (p. xxxviii). It would not be until Louise Bennett came into prominence in the 1940s that the oral artistry of Jamaican women would become more widely recognized. To supplement the words of the songs, Jekyll gives musical notation in each case. Even so, as in any written transcription of oral verse, little sense can be gained of the context of audience participation so vital to the appreciation of orature.

369 *Oh General Jackson!*: refers to the Morant Bay Rebellion in Jamaica in late 1865 led by Reverend George Gordon and severely repressed by Governor Eyre. He proclaimed martial law and sent out troops under General Jackson, amongst others, in order to impose it. The parish of St Thomas was where the rebellion was concentrated. As a result of 1865 the white planter class sought Crown Colony government in order to prevent black West Indians from receiving any form of representation. Froude (q.v.) would later give support to these moves.

369 *waistcoat cut*: the singer's waistcoat is torn because he has unsuccessfully tried to put Obeah or voodoo on to another man.

370 *live 'pon tree*: as the matter has been reported to the police, the singer has to shelter in the bush until the trouble passes (Jekyll, 241).

I have a news: the news concerns travelling professional musicians associated with Mowatt Hall ('Mowitahl') in Jamaica.

August pork: 1 August, Emancipation Day, was celebrated with feasting and dance.

Not if the pork even purchase self: not if the pork itself has already been bought.

Claude McKay's 'Cudjoe Fresh From de Lecture', 'Old England', and 'My Native Land, My Home' were first published in *Songs of Jamaica*, introduction and notes by Walter Jekyll (Kingston: A. W. Gardner and Co., 1912). Notes to these poems have been grouped together.

370 *Cudjoe*: a local name for a male child born on a Monday (from the Fante *kodwo*); also a chief of the Maroon rebel slaves in the eighteenth century.

buccra: white man.

372 *pull up*: ends his talk.

374 *lub*: love

naygur: black people (a version of 'nigger').

'The Apple-Woman's Complaint' was first published in *Constab Ballads* (Kingston: A. W. Gardner and Co., 1912).

'If We Must Die' was first published in the New York *Liberator*, 1918, after the end of the First World War; reprinted in *Harlem Shadows* (New York: Harcourt, Brace and Co., 1922). The poem is a reflection on US interracial conflicts of the period. Black audiences were responsive to the poem's anger, which was uncharacteristic in McKay's work at this time.

RABINDRANATH TAGORE

Gitanjali (Song Offerings) was first issued in a limited edition by the Indian Society (London, November 1912), with the Introduction by Yeats which follows; reprinted by Macmillan, 1913. The poems which appear here are II, XI, XXVII, XVIII, XXXV, XXXVII, XLI, XLV, LXIII, and CII, of the 103 poems. LXIII also appeared as one of six *Gitanjali* poems in Harriet Munro's *Poetry* 1:3 (December 1912). In reading these translations of Tagore's Bengali poetry it is helpful to remember that, like his other lyric poetry, the work is powerfully informed by the influential and highly stylized Vaishnava tradition in Bengali poetry, in which human love (for a beloved, or, more rarely, as expressed within a family or the nation) becomes a metaphor for the yearning of the human for the Divine. In Vaishnava doctrine this relationship often takes the form of the love of Radha for Krishna, one of the incarnations of Vishnu.

W. B. YEATS

For first publication of this Introduction see previous note.

383 *Brahma Samaj*: or Brahmo Samaj, 'the Society of God', a monotheistic Hindu Reform group formed in 1828 by the social reformer Rammohan Roy, supported by Rabindranath Tagore's father, amongst others.

Gogonendranath ... Dwijendranath, Rabindranath's brother: Gaganendranath and his brother were Tagore's nephews; Dijendranath Tagore was the founder of the literary family journal *Bharati*.

384 *Troilus and Cressida*: or *Troylus and Criseyde* (*c.*1380). Yeats uses Shakespeare's spelling.

385 *Rossetti's willow wood*: D. G. Rossetti's 'Willow Wood' sequence of sonnets first appeared in the *Fortnightly Review*, March 1869.

I am ready for my journey: this, and the next four quotations from *Gitanjali*, are taken from poems XCIII, XCV, XLII, XLI, and LXXXIX, respectively. The concluding quotation is from the poem 'On the Seashore' from *The Crescent Moon* (1913), Tagore's second English collection.

À Kempis or John of the Cross: Thomas à Kempis (1380–1471) and St John of the Cross (1542–91), mystics who concentrated on the soul's detachment from the world in its approach to God.

386 *a Tristan or a Pelanore*: or Tristram and Pellinore, the hero and the king from Malory's 'Morte Darthur' (1485).

B. E. BAUGHAN

'Pipi on the Prowl' was first published in *Brown Bread from a Colonial Oven: Being Sketches of Up-Country Life in New Zealand* (Whitcombe and Tombs, 1912).

387 *pakeha*: Maori word for white person.

whare: Maori dwelling.

391 '*Stung with the splendour of a sudden thought*': Robert Browning, 'A Death in the Desert' (1864). The original has 'stung by'.

394 *kainga*: settlement or village.

KATHERINE MANSFIELD

'How Pearl Button was Kidnapped' was first published in *Rhythm*' 8 (September 1912), signed Lili Heron, with a woodcut by Henri Gaudier-Brzeska; reprinted by John Middleton Murry in the posthumous *Something Childish and Other Stories* (Constable, 1924). Whereas Murry gives 1910, Ian Gordon (ed.), *Undiscovered Country* (1974), suggests 1912 as the time of composition. As in her other early colonial stories, like 'The Woman at the Store' and 'Ole Underwood', it is noticeable that Mansfield is here drawing on melodramatic techniques characteristic of antipodean writers such as Henry Lawson (q.v.).

390 *a green ornament*: the Maori greenstone *tiki*.

'To Stanislaw Wyspianski' was composed in 1909; first published in Polish, freely translated in parts by Floryan Sobieniowski with a commentary, under the title 'In Memory, ie. To Stanislaw Wyspianski (From the other side of the world)', in the Warsaw paper *Gazeta poniedzialkowa* 36 (26 December 1910), with the first verse only published in English; reprinted in a limited edition by the London bookseller Bernard Rota, 1938; reprinted in full in *The Penguin Book of New Zealand Verse*, ed. Allen Curnow (1960). Stanislaw Wyspianski (1868–1907) was a Polish playwright and nationalist.

400 *the name of a fighter*: in fact Stanislaw means 'the glory of the land', and Wyspianski, 'of the island'.

'The Wind Blows' was first published as 'Autumns II', *Signature* 1:4 (October 1915), signed Matilda Berry; revised and retitled for *Bliss* (Constable, 1920). The time of first publication coincided with Leslie, her brother's, death in the Great War.

402 *MacDowell's 'To an Iceberg'*: Edward MacDowell (1861–1906), an American composer of piano music marked by literary and pictorial associations.

Rubinstein: Anton Rubinstein (1829–94), a Russian pianist and composer.

403 *leaves and showers*: doggerelized version of the first line of P. B. Shelley's poem 'The Cloud' (1820): 'I bring fresh showers for the thirsting flowers.'

pohutukawas: New Zealand evergreen tree bearing clusters of red flowers.

SOLOMON T. PLAATJE

'One Night with the Fugitives' is Chapter 4 of *Native Life in South Africa* (P. S. King and Son, 1916). The book was based on notes made on a tour around South Africa to investigate the effects of the 1913 Natives' Land Act. Plaatje began writing the book on board ship to England, where he and his deputation were to appeal to the imperial government to overturn the Act.

405 *Es ist . . . unväterlich*: 'It is not kingly to weep—but oh, not to weep here is unfatherly.' The lines spoken by Agamemnon are from Schiller's *Iphigenie in Aulis*, II. iv (1789), a translation from Euripides.

. . . not in winter: Matthew 24: 20 and Mark 13: 18.

Lord Gladstone: Herbert John Gladstone, the first Governor-General of the new Union of South Africa, and the fourth son of the Victorian Prime Minister.

406 *Baas*: Master.

'Free' State law: the Orange Free State, one of the four provinces of the Union of South Africa (1910), and a former Boer Republic (to the former independence of which 'Free' refers).

408 *haak-doorns*: hooked-thorn trees.

Englishmen would agree with Dutchmen: theirs would therefore be the greater betrayal. Plaatje is caught within the contradictions of his role as a conciliatory middleman in *Native Life*, on the one hand referring to the empty promise represented by the Union Jack, on the other appealing to the British sense of justice.

410 *this land*: Exodus 3: 7–8. The biblical tale of the Israelites delivered from Egypt has figured large in black liberation rhetoric. See note to Casely Hayford, p. 465.

Dag jong: Good-day boy.

411 *war*: the Anglo-Boer War (1899–1902).

Oom Paul: Uncle Paul (Kruger), President of the former Transvaal Republic during the war.

LEONARD WOOLF

'Pearls and Swine' was probably composed around 1912 or 1913, when Woolf was working on his Ceylonese novel, *The Village in the Jungle* (1913), and the story 'The Two Brahmans' (see Frederic Spotts (ed.), *The Letters of Leonard Woolf* (Weidenfeld and Nicolson, 1989), p. xxx, and J. H. Willis, Jr., *The Hogarth Press 1917–1941* (University of Virginia Press, 1992), 57); it was not published until *Stories of the East* (Hogarth Press, 1921), which included 'A Tale told by Moonlight' and 'The Two Brahmans'); reprinted in *Stories of the East and Diaries in Ceylon, 1904–11* (Hogarth Press, 1963). For the material of the story Woolf leaned heavily on two letters to Lytton Strachey of 4 and 21 March 1906 (Spotts (ed.), pp. 113–16). The title is a reference to Matthew 7: 6: 'Neither cast ye your pearls before swine.'

416 *Durbar*: the Delhi Durbar of December 1911, at which George V revoked the 1905 Partition of Bengal. The reunion of Bengal was linked to a transfer of the Raj capital from Calcutta to Delhi. See Aurobindo, 'The Object of Passive Resistance' (above).

419 *facts*: the stress on the irrefutable 'facts' of everyday reality in places far from Europe, as opposed to grossly inappropriate theories imported from Europe, forms one of the unmistakable echoes from Conrad's 'Heart of Darkness' (1899).

420 *. . . the plains of Norway*: the idea of the unbroken historical continuity of life in India is central also to Kipling's conception of the subcontinent, as it is to the vision of the contemporary Indian writer, Nayantara Sahgal. See note to Kipling, p. 445.

421 *. . . a bad sign in the East*: White shares many features with the dissolute characters of the Eastern seaboard in Stevenson and Conrad, in particular with the skipper and the chief engineer of the *Patna* in Conrad's *Lord Jim* (1900).

423 *ryots*: tenant farmers.

vakils: attorneys or authorized agents.

425 *paint and varnish*: again a reflection of Conrad's idea that the regulated life of Europe allows no understanding of less secure, alternative forms of reality.

BIOGRAPHIES

Together with her husband Ernest Ames, a railway engineer, Mrs Ernest AMES (born Mary Frances Leslie Miller, probably in Canada, dates unknown) wrote and illustrated jingoistic children's books around the turn of the century. *An ABC, for Baby Patriots* (1899) was the work of Mrs Ames alone. *The Tremendous Twins, or How the Boers were Beaten* (1900), written by Ernest and illustrated by Mary Ames, tells the story of belligerent twins whose exploits in the Boer War show up the inefficiency of the British military leadership.

(Sir) Edwin ARNOLD (1832–1904), the poet, translator, and journalist, worked in India as the principal of the Government College at Pune (1856–61). Thereafter he joined the staff of the London *Daily Telegraph*, becoming chief editor in 1873. As well as his *History of Dalhousie's Administration* (1862–5), he produced several volumes of verse and translation from Sanscrit and Pali, the most notable of which is *The Light of Asia, or The Great Renunciation* (1879), recognized as a respectful and competent 'depiction of the life and character . . . of the founder of Buddhism'. *India Revisited* (1886) is a reflective account of a return visit to Pune.

The 'saint of Pondicherry', Sri AUROBINDO (the honorific title of Aravinda Ackroyd Ghosh, 1872–1950), and his poet-brother Manmohan Ghosh (1869–1924), were from a prominent Victorian Bengali family belonging to the progressive, English-educated Calcutta intelligentsia (like Toru Dutt (q.v.)). Aurobindo was educated in England for fourteen years from 1879, distinguishing himself at Cambridge as a classics scholar. Like later postcolonial nationalists, he kept a close eye on developments in Irish politics as showing one way towards colonial self-determination. He passed the Indian Civil Service examination with distinction, but took up an appointment at Baroda College, India, in 1893. In the early 1890s he began to write prolifically, generally using English, producing journalism and poetry which bears the distinctive mark of his classical training and knowledge of English literature. In addition to the European languages learned in England, he now also studied Sanscrit, Marathi, and Gujerati. After *Songs to Myrtilla and Other Poems* (1895), his first publication, he wrote narrative poems based on Indian legends, *Urvasie* (1896) and *Love and Death* (1899). At around the same time, in a series of articles *New Lamps for Old* (1893–4), he began a sustained critique of the conciliatory politics of the Indian National Congress, instead advocating anti-constitutionalism and solidarity between classes and castes as the only policies that bore any hope of ousting the British. Already at this stage, however, he was seeking the means for such social and political bonding through a revivalist Hinduism. Swadeshi or self-help protests against the Partition of Bengal (1905–8) fired his growing political interests. He became Principal of the National College, Calcutta, and editor of the nationalist paper, *Bande Mataram*, in which he attacked colonial occupation and Congress gradualism. In a hard-hitting series of articles (the second of which appears here), he espoused uncompromising organized resistance at all levels, in particular universal boycott, in order to achieve *swaraj*—this was an unprecedented outburst in the Indian newspaper world. If necessary, he argued, violent repression should be met with violent opposition, and here he parted company with Tagore (q.v.), who termed his political approach 'self-hatred'. (In this he also differed from Gandhi's later passive-resistance programme.) He was believed to be behind several extremist Hindu revivalist groups (also reputedly influenced by the Kali-inspired energies of Vivekananda (q.v.)). He was arrested in connection with a bombing at Muzaffarpur. During his year in solitary confinement he became increasingly more absorbed in spiritual matters and, on his release after a highly publicized trial, retired to Pondicherry, a French enclave in South India, to found an ashram. He remained here for the next four decades, writing and studying religious texts, practising yoga, and developing a system of 'integral' as opposed to foreign education. The French political radical, spiritualist, and feminist Mirra Richard (1878–1973), one of his disciples, became in the 1920s the *de facto* leader of the ashram, its 'Mother'. Though now best known as the founder of a worldwide system of spiritual philosophy, Aurobindo is also recognized as one of the foremost Indian writers in English of his time. Even after moving into deeper retreat from 1926, he continued to write poetry, experimenting intensively with the quantitative metre with which his name is often associated. He produced numbers of devotional lyrics and the epic *Savitri* (1954), as well as spiritual writings, criticism, translations of Indian classical texts, and five full-length plays which, along with his *Collected Poems* (1972), were published posthumously.

The fulsome patriotism that brought Alfred AUSTIN (1835–1913) the poet-laureateship in 1896, a year before Queen Victoria's Diamond Jubilee, today accounts for the oblivion into which his work has fallen. He left the legal profession in order to write prose and verse (twenty volumes in all), and to edit the *National Review*. In a stilted but hectic sub-Tennysonian manner, his poetry communicates admiration for new imperialism, and bellicose belief in the 'English' virtues of liberty and justice. He celebrated the widely condemned Jameson Raid in an ode published in *The Times*, January 1896.

'AUSTRALIE', the pseudonym of Emily Manning (1845–90), suggests her self-conscious connection with the Australian scenery which she painted in her verse. A member of the Sydney elite of her day, she contributed to several local newspapers and worked on the staff of the *Illustrated Sydney News*. *The Balance of Pain and Other Poems* appeared in 1877.

The geographically wide-ranging colonial memoirs of Lady Mary Anne BARKER (born Stewart, Lady Broome after 1884, 1831–1911) are noted for their blend of the whimsical and the practical, of spirited activity and a careful regard for social decorum. She was born in Spanish Town, Jamaica (her father was Colonial Secretary), and educated in England. As she recounts in *Colonial Memories* (1904), she followed her first husband, Colonel Sir George Barker, a veteran of the Indian Mutiny, to India not long after the relief of Lucknow. After his death she took up journalism in order to support herself and her two sons back in England. In 1865 she was married a second time, to Frederick Napier Broome, and accompanied him on an unsuccessful three-year sheep-farming venture in New Zealand. Back in England, she edited *Evening Hours*, wrote children's stories and a housekeeping book, and worked as Lady Superintendent of the National School of Cookery. Further episodes of colonial life followed as Broome became, successively, Colonial Secretary of Natal (in 1875), Lieutenant-Governor of Mauritius, Governor of Western Australia, and then of Barbados and Trinidad (in 1891). As is clear from such books as *Station Life in New Zealand* (1870), a collection of reworked letters home, and *A Year's Housekeeping in South Africa* (1877), as well as *Colonial Memories*, Barker was concerned to offer a feminine ('lady's') perspective on the 'brighter' (that is, domestic) activities of the world-straddling elite to which she belonged.

B. E. (Blanche Edith) BAUGHAN (1870–1958), the New Zealand poet, essayist, and social reformer, was born in England and obtained a degree in classics from the University of London. In England she published *Verses* (1898), dominated by English scenes and seasons, and then, following emigration to Akaroa, New Zealand, in 1900 to work as a housekeeper, she brought out *Reuben and Other Poems* (1903) and *Shingle-Short and Other Verses* (1908). The latter book in particular is distinguished by its rendition, in dramatic monologues, of a variety of New Zealand voices. This ability to 'do voices' is carried over into the prose sketches of *Brown Bread from a Colonial Oven* (1912). A supporter of women's suffrage, Baughan spent the later years of her life working for prison reform in New Zealand. After a period of illness (1909–10) she turned from verse to animated scenic description of the pastoral beauties of her adopted homeland, collected as *Studies in New Zealand Scenery* (1916).

Barbara BAYNTON (born Lawrence, or, she claimed, Kilpatrick, 1857–1929) began to write fairly late in life, in the 1890s, a period marked in Australia by the emergence of a muscular nationalist literature. At the time, therefore, she did not attain to the reputation of more prolific fellow *Bulletin* writers such as Lawson or Paterson (qq.v.). However, her portraits of bush life as enervated rather than energizing, malevolent and crippling rather than heroic and sustaining, have since been recognized as representing a strong if hard-bitten alternative woman-centred tradition. Her stories, collected in *Bush Studies* (1902), were written during the period of her second marriage, to the retired Sydney surgeon Thomas Baynton, yet emerge out of her bush life experiences during her first marriage, to a free selector in the Castlereagh and Scone districts, New South Wales. After Baynton's death in 1904 she divided her time between Australia and England, where she married an English baron and established herself as an antiquarian. Apart from *Bush Studies* she published only one other book, *Human Toll* (1907). If few, her stories are nearly all extremely powerful, first in their combination of colloquial detail and Gothic darkness, but even more in their uncompromising reversal of the images of 'mateship' so central to Australian national identity at the time. While cutting across some of his themes, however, Baynton also shared affinities with Lawson, especially in her grim realism and emphasis on human vulnerability.

John BEAMES (1837–1902) worked in British India as a civil servant and part-time grammarian and philologist for thirty-five years (1858–93), broken only by two periods of leave in England. His *Memoirs of a Bengal Civilian* (published posthumously, 1961), are valuable for the picture they give of a district officer's life, one which corresponds to Leonard Woolf's (q.v.) account of the punishing duties of a civil servant in Ceylon. In Beames's *Memoirs* we see how abstract notions of duty and responsibility articulated in official circles, such as in the speeches of Chamberlain or Curzon (qq.v.), were translated into work on the ground. Training for the Indian Civil Service at Haileybury College in Hertfordshire during the time of the Indian Mutiny, he was one of the last group of Civil Service cadets to be appointed through nomination by the East India Company and not to proceed by the new competitive examination (which produced the 'competition wallah' of Trevelyan (q.v.)). His career in India took him from Calcutta to the Punjab, where he married Ellen Geary (1860), and then to the provinces of Bihar and Orissa. Between 1873 and 1877 he was Magistrate and Collector in Cuttack, the head station of Orissa. For the last fourteen or so years of his service he worked mainly as a commissioner in different parts of Bengal. A determined and outspoken man with a strong sense of administrative work as 'a sacred trust delivered to me by the Government', Beames was denied promotion on several occasions. In 1887 his opposition to Indian education policy again plunged him into controversy, now with respect to Indians. He was a linguist of some note, the author of *Outlines of Indian Philology* (1867), a *Comparative Grammar of the Modern Aryan Languages of India*, 3 vols. (1872–79), and a *Grammar of the Bengali Language* (1891).

An indefatigable wanderer and writer, Isabella BIRD (1831–1904) is probably one of the best-known Victorian women travellers. Apart from a trip to North America in the 1850s, her peripatetic existence began fairly late in life, in her early forties, with a trip through the United States to Hawaii, described in *The Hawaiian Archipelago* (1875) and *A Lady's Life in the Rocky Mountains* (1879). She had been prescribed a course of travel as an antidote to the illnesses she developed fulfilling the archetypal role of the Victorian spinster, looking after the family home. *Unbeaten Tracks in Japan* (1880) and *The Golden Chersonese* (1883) record her first travels in Asia. After the death of her sister Henrietta, the recipient of her travel letters, she married John Bishop (1881). Following Bishop's death there were further long trips to the Middle East and Asia, which produced, among other books, *Among the Tibetans* (1894) and *The Yangtze Valley and Beyond* (1899). She had done some medical missionary work earlier in her life, but neither her Christianity nor her belief in British security and justice weighed too heavily on her depiction of other cultures. Throughout her writing she remains relentlessly open to new impressions, her interest in her surroundings and eagerness to 'rough it' always overcoming apprehension. In 1892 she became the first woman to address the Royal Scottish Geographical Society and was appointed its first woman fellow.

Along with J. Africanus Horton (1835–83), the author of *A Vindication of the African Race* (1868), Edward Wilmot BLYDEN (1832–1912) was probably the foremost African nationalist of the nineteenth century. His follower J. E. Casely Hayford (q.v.) called him 'the greatest living exponent of the true spirit of African nationality'. He was also, variously, theologian, politician, political commentator, and educator. Born in St Thomas in the West Indies, in 1850 he emigrated to Liberia, the African state set aside for slave repatriation, his attempt to gain entry to theological colleges in the United States having failed on racial grounds. In 1858 he was ordained a Presbyterian minister and became principal of Alexander High School, Monrovia, where he had studied. He also became editor of the *Liberia Herald* (and later of the *Negro* in Sierra Leone). During this period he produced many pamphlets and articles on the present oppression and future progress of African people. As is clear from *African Life and Customs* (1908), he sought to refute theories of African inferiority through a till-then unprecedented sociological analysis—showing how the communalism of African society was adapted to conditions on the continent. With the European partition of Africa (from 1885) his pleas that African social systems be respected and understood became particularly insistent. However, while he criticized colonization and Christianization for the social dislocation they produced, he also believed that imperial expansion was a necessary step towards the regeneration of Africa. Throughout his stress was on cultural self-assertion: the 'Negro' must develop according to his own distinctive attributes, or, as he says in his Inaugural Address as president of Liberia College, must 'advance by methods of his own'. Influenced by Irish cultural nationalism, he supported education in the vernacular and the establishment of an African-controlled university in the Liberian hinterland. Blyden twice served as president of Liberia College, the first secular English-speaking institution of higher learning in tropical Africa (1880–4 and 1900–1), and several times acted as Liberian representative to Britain and the United States. He corresponded with the Prime Minister Gladstone (1809–98) and found an ally in Mary Kingsley (q.v.) who agreed with him that imperialism, while necessary, should not destroy African laws and institutions. Alongside *African Life*, his other important publication is *Christianity, Islam and the Negro Race* (1887), in which he supports the spread of Islam for its accommodation of African culture. A visionary rather than a political pragmatist, his thought fed into twentieth-century Pan-Africanism, Negritude, and various African nationalisms.

Edmund CANDLER (1874–1926) was a writer of Anglo-India in the mould of Kipling but with marked descriptive powers of his own. He studied classics at Cambridge and thereafter worked in India on and off for the next twenty-five years, not as a civil servant like so many Englishmen, but, as he called it, a 'free-lance': a schoolmaster in Darjeeling (1896–8), a professor of English in a Native State in Madras Presidency (1900–3), as the *Daily Mail* correspondent on the Francis Younghusband Expedition to Tibet (1903–4), and then as the Principal of Mohindra College, Patiala (1906–14). After serving as a war correspondent during the First World War, he held the post of Director of Publicity for the Punjab (1919–21). He began to publish during his first years in India, in the *Pioneer*, the *Civil and Military Gazette*, and then also in *Blackwood's*, the *Cornhill*, and *Macmillan's Magazine*, journal titles closely linked with the names of Kipling and Conrad (qq.v.), writers whom he knew. In addition to his best-known book, *The Unveiling of Lhasa* (1905), and *The Mantle of the East* (1910), a collection of travel writings, he also published *The General Plan* (1911), *The Long Road to Baghdad* (1919), the autobiography *Youth and the East* (1932), and two novels, *Siri Ram, Revolutionist* (1912) and *Abdication* (1922).

Bliss CARMAN (1861–1929), popularly called the Canadian 'poet laureate' in his old age, was brought up in Fredericton, New Brunswick, like his cousin Charles G. D. Roberts (q.v.). He was educated first at the University of New Brunswick, and then, after an unsuccessful period at Oxford and Edinburgh, entered Harvard (1886), but did not complete his doctorate. He held a number of editorial positions, on the New York *Independent, Current Literature*, and *Cosmopolitan*, amongst other papers. Throughout a life of intensive travel he would maintain New England as well as Canadian Maritime connections. His first book, *Low Tide on Grand Pré* (1893), launched his career as a poet and was welcomed as introducing a new 'American' voice. He was distantly related to Ralph Waldo Emerson (1803–82), whose ideas about natural joy impinged on his own. A mystic and a loner, he went a considerable distance further than his Canadian contemporaries (all of whom were using borrowed forms) in exploring the spiritual dimensions of a late Romantic's—the wandering 'vagabond's' —identification with nature, as is clear from his critical essays, *The Kinship of Nature* (1903). In his reliance on nineteenth-century British models, *fin-de-siècle* as well as Romantic and Victorian, there appears to be much of the colonial chameleon about Carman. However, this should not be allowed to obscure the searching and the versatility that animates his work—as in the contrast between the vigour of the early *Vagabondia* collections (1894 and 1896) and the more meditative *Low Tide on Grand Pré*. In the early years of the new century he adopted Unitrinitarianism, a sub-Theosophical doctrine based on the oneness of nature, mind, and spirit, propagated by Mary Perry King who became his companion. In addition to the work mentioned, his best-regarded poetry is probably *Sappho* (1905).

J. E. (Joseph Ephraim) CASELY HAYFORD (1866–1930), who also called himself by his own rendition of his Fante name, Ekra-Agiman, was one of the foremost African intellectuals of his time. He was educated at Wesleyan Boys' High School and Fourah Bay College, Freetown, in Sierra Leone, where he met his mentor, Edward Wilmot Blyden (q.v.). He worked as a teacher and head teacher in Cape Coast and in Accra, Gold Coast. From 1893 he studied law in London and was called to the Bar in 1896. On his return to the Gold Coast to work as a barrister defending Africans' rights, he wrote on the cultural development of the 'Ethiopian' and the value of the African way of life, publishing in the *Wesleyan Methodist Times* and the *Gold Coast Leader*. He founded the Gold Coast Aborigines' Rights Protection Society in 1897 in response to Crown moves to administer public lands. In 1903 *Gold Coast Native Institutions* was published, and in 1911 his other important book, *Ethiopia Unbound*. As he argued in *Ethiopia Unbound*, Casely Hayford believed strongly, like Blyden, that the African should develop according to his own intellectual lights, that he be 'revealed unto himself'. From the first decade of the new century he began to move into the forefront of Gold Coast politics, seeking constitutional advancement for the West African Dependencies within the British Empire. He became unofficial member of the Gold Coast Legislative Council (1916), and, responding to the impetus for non-white self-determination awakened at Versailles in 1919, was instrumental in founding the Congress of British West Africa, an organization which pressed for local government and educational reforms. He was President of the Congress at the time of his death.

Joseph CHAMBERLAIN (1836–1914), 'Pushful Joe', the Unitarian Birmingham businessman and radical politician, was to change his political stripes several times during his career. In his heyday as Colonial Secretary, however, the time when the empire was at its height, his support for imperial federation and tariff reform—'a commercial Union of the Empire'—and for imperialism in general, was energetic, vehement, and unflagging. He was elected as a Liberal MP (1876), but parted company with Gladstone over Irish Home Rule. In 1895 he was made Colonial Secretary in Lord Salisbury's government, a position which he had much desired. His imperialist convictions, even positive delight in the fact of an expanding and interconnected empire, are undisguised in his speeches of the period. Although he frequently emphasized his antipathy to jingoism, he was intent on promoting imperialism as a worldwide popular movement. Within the 'Greater Britain' of the empire, he urged, imperial Britain should boldly recognize her responsibilities to her 'kinsmen' and to 'subject races'. The development of 'the Imperial estate', boldly lording it in 'splendid isolation', was 'a wise, a far-sighted and a spirited policy'. His years as Colonial Secretary were marked by involvements in South Africa. In his quest to unite the region under the British flag, he was probably passively complicit in the Jameson Raid against the Transvaal Republic (1895–6), and helped engineer the provocations which culminated in the Anglo-Boer War (1899–1902). He resigned from the government over Tariff Reform (1903), and a few years later left politics following a stroke.

Family misfortunes in England brought Marcus CLARKE (1846–81) to Australia at the age of 16. He was first employed by a Melbourne bank, then worked on a sheep station in Victoria while also beginning as a journalist on the *Australasian*. Later he worked for a time at the Melbourne library. Through stints of poverty, procrastination, and bad debts, it was journalism, and in particular the Melbourne writers' café milieu, which was to dominate the rest of his life. He formed the Yorick Club with fellow writers Henry Kendall and Adam Lindsay Gordon. His first novel, *Long Odds*, was serialized in the *Australian Monthly Magazine* (1868–9). Work on *For the Term of his Natural Life* (1874), the much-admired classic of nineteenth-century Australia, was forced by bankruptcy. Based on research into convict records in Tasmania, the novel was serialized in fits and starts in the *Australian Journal* (1871–2). Two collections of short stories were published in his lifetime, *Holiday Peak and Other Tales* (1873) and *Four Stories High* (1877). The strain of financial difficulties contributed to his collapse and relatively early death. In the nationalist 1930s and 1940s in Australia his reputation was downgraded relative to the republican writing clustered round the *Bulletin* and the names of Lawson and Paterson (qq.v.). Yet while he did not manage to develop an involved narrative voice matched to the bush life he represented, Clarke did pioneer the outback story and a naturalist focus on the detail of outback life. He was seen by his contemporaries as 'essentially Australian', exploring the new opportunities offered by a 'new country' for delineating scene and character. Richly talented, he wrote history, light journalism, Gothic and fantastic short stories, social satire, cultural commentary, and literary criticism, and, in *His Natural Life*, went some way toward establishing an Australian tradition of historical fiction which he had learned from American writers like Hawthorn, and refracted through his reading of Dickens and Balzac.

Hugh CLIFFORD (1866–1941) spent what he called 'the best years of my life' working as a colonial officer in remote and recently 'pacified' districts on the Malay Peninsula, often as the single European, as he records in 'Up Country' (1897). More sympathetically and intensely even than Kipling (q.v.), whom he read and had met, or Conrad (q.v.), his correspondent, who dedicated his novel *Chance* (1913) to him, Clifford tried in his stories not only to record incidents from Malay lives but to view those lives 'from the inside', 'to judge the people and their actions by their own standards' and not by those of 'a White Man living in their midst'. Yet mixed up with this strong identification, he held firm imperialist beliefs in the superiority of British culture, the 'Pax Britannica', and the 'spread of modern ideas, progress and civilisation'. He arrived in Malaya in 1883 as a young cadet in the Civil Service of what were then called the Protected Malay States, and was centrally involved in setting up British consular influence in the state of Pahang, a process which included waging wars against Malay rajas (1887–95). Pahang, where he remained as British Resident until leaving Malaya, became the setting for most of his stories and reflections on colonial life. He was first published in the *Straits Times*, and then, with increasing success, in *Macmillan's Magazine*, *Blackwood's*, the *Cornhill*, and the *Living Age*. His first collection of stories and sketches, *East Coast Etchings* (1896), was followed by a flood of work, including the collections *In Court and Kampong* (1897), *Studies in Brown Humanity* (1898), and *Bush-whacking and Other Sketches* (1901), and the novels *A Freelance of Today* (1903) and *Saleh* (1908). He saw much of his work as performing an act of conservation, recording ways of life that colonial 'innovation' was destroying. In 1903 he left Malaya to become Colonial Secretary of Trinidad, and thereafter Governor of Ceylon (where he twice had dealings with Leonard Woolf (q.v.)), of the Gold Coast (where he met Casely Hayford (q.v.)), of Nigeria, and again of Ceylon. His writing, however, retained its strong connection with the Peninsula interior and began to tail off the longer he spent away from Malaya. In 1927 he was appointed Governor of the Straits Settlements and High Commissioner for the Malay States, but did not remain long in post due to the onset of mental illness. It is a signal mark of the contradictions that striate Clifford's work that one who spoke so warmly of matching himself to Malay life, regarded that involvement as representing a racial and moral descent.

A Polish-born émigré to Britain, who cultivated the tone and manner of the

English pragmatist, of being 'one of us', Joseph CONRAD (Josef Konrad Korzeniowski, 1857–1924) also became one of the first and most eloquent *fin-de-siècle* critics of European colonialism. Now, nearly a century on, his novella 'Heart of Darkness' (1899), in which he exposes the vile 'scramble for loot' that was the 'civilizing mission', is probably one of the most intensively analysed of colonial texts. The bitter satire of the short story 'An Outpost of Progress' (1898), also set in the Congo, is an overture to that longer tale, but also a powerful indictment in its own right. The majority of his best-known works are pessimistic reworkings of the imperial seafaring and adventure tale popularized by Henty (q.v.), R. M. Ballantyne, and others. Conrad was born in the Russian-occupied Ukraine; his family background was land-owning and nationalist. Following a long-held dream to go to sea, he left for Marseilles in 1874 to work on trading vessels, and in 1880 passed his third-mate examination in London. For the next thirteen years he served as an officer on a variety of ships and many seas, experiences which filtered into his tales. He was naturalized as a British citizen in 1886. In 1890 he commanded a river steamer *Le Roi des Belges* for a short time in the Congo Free State (see entry on Stanley) and there witnessed the colonial atrocities which he exposed in his writing about Africa, even while continuing to speak of Africans as 'savages'. The publication of his first novel, *Almayer's Folly* (1895), set in the Indonesian archipelago, marked the end of his time at sea and the beginning of his always troubled and often blocked life as a writer. He began to win critical acclaim in the 1900s with novels such as *Lord Jim* (1900), *Nostromo* (1904), and *The Secret Agent* (1907), but it was not until *Chance* (1913), in part promoted by another Far Eastern sojourner, Hugh Clifford (q.v.), that he achieved popular success.

Canada's first prominent women poet, Isabella Valancy CRAWFORD (1850–87), is also seen as having produced the country's first distinctively Canadian poetry, in particular because of her descriptions of the northern wild. She was born into an Anglo-Irish family in Dublin and emigrated to Canada when she was 8. Marked by phases of pioneering and family hardship, and by repeated movements from small to larger towns in Upper Canada, her life can be seen to reflect some of the key moments in Canada's nineteenth-century history of nation-formation. Her doctor father tended local Ojibways in Paisley, a connection which may have turned Isabella towards the interest in native Canadian legend expressed in some of her nature poetry. Educated at home in the classics, she was fortunate to have contact with the writer Catherine Parr Traill and her prominent pioneer family, the Stricklands. She submitted work for publication at a fairly early age, but it was when her family fell into reduced circumstances that she began to rely on her writing for such Toronto publications as the *Mail* and the *Evening Telegram* as a financial support. Her need to write for money accounts for the overtly patriotic, floral, and clichéd style of a great deal of her poetry. However, the contrasts between this gift-book work and, for example, her dialect poetry, such as 'Old Spookses' Pass', the longer narrative poems, and her more severe cynical newspaper verse like 'War' (1879), shows that this was not her own or only poetic voice. In her lifetime Crawford saw only one collection into print, *Old Spookses' Pass, Malcolm's Katie and Other Poems* (1884), which was well received critically, especially in England.

George Nathaniel, Earl (later Marquess) CURZON of Kedleston (1859–1925), was one of the most controversial and brilliant, and certainly the youngest man to hold the prestigious office of Viceroy of India (1898–1905). In the 1890s he made a name for himself as an authority on Eastern affairs with three books based on travel observations, in particular the much-admired *Persia and the Persian Question* (1892), and also *Russia in Central Asia* (1889) and *Problems of the Far East* (1894). His viceregency was noted for bureaucratic, educational, and fiscal reforms, his taste for pomp and ostentatious ceremony, the attention he paid to the restoration of ancient buildings, and his attempts to palliate the Indian peasantry, whom he played off against 'political' middle-class Indians. Efficiency was his self-professed watchword. He won some regard amongst Indians for disciplining English soldiers following a racially motivated rape and a murder. However, it is the part he played in setting in train the Partition of Bengal (1905) for which he remains notorious, and for which he is still frequently criticized. The initial aim of the measure was allegedly administrative efficiency, but he soon perceived that Partition would also help control political dissent in the region by weakening the powerful Bengali nationalists in the Indian Congress (on the principle of 'divide and rule'). The Swadeshi agitation with which Aurobindo (q.v.) was associated was ignited by this move. Curzon resigned early during his second term as Viceroy, not because of these protests so much as because of the (by him) unanticipated military intriguing led by Lord Kitchener (1850–1916) in the Viceroy's Council. In several valedictory addresses he repeated that the Raj should always mean imperial duty and justice to Britons: it was a testing-ground for imperial character. A year later, in his Empire Day speech, this conception of devotion and duty is projected across the entire empire. Curzon served as Foreign Secretary for four years in the Liberal coalition government after the First World War, a crucial time during which Britain was renegotiating and also expanding its imperialist responsibilities.

Thanks to a peripatetic existence, Sara Jeannette DUNCAN (1861–1922) distinguished herself both as a Canadian woman of letters and as a novelist of Anglo-India. A self-declared 'feminine democrat' and 'modern' woman, she ambitiously forged a path for herself in the male-dominated world of journalism in 1880s Canada, contributing to the Toronto *Globe*, the literary journal *The Week*, the Montreal *Star*, and the Washington *Post*. She became known for her lively, straight-talking style, and in 1888 was sent around the world as correspondent for the *Star* and other newspapers. Her vivid observations on the variety and bedazzlement of Japan, Ceylon, India, and Egypt were collected as *A Social Departure* (1889), her first book. In Calcutta she met her husband, Edward Cotes, and spent most of the rest of her writing life in India. Her Indian journalism and novels, including *The Simple Adventures of a Memsahib* (1893) and *Set in Authority* (1906), are noted for her exploration of Anglo-Indian social façades and her increasing interest in Indian political life. (In *A Social Departure* she had described the native masses as at once 'problematical' and 'soulless'.) Duncan's analysis of Canadian life, especially her representation of small-town Ontario in *The Imperialist* (1904), is both sympathetic and dry in a way reminiscent of Stephen Leacock (q.v.). She believed that, post-Confederation, Canadians should foster a non-parochial pride in their nation, though within the context of close imperial links.

The brilliant daughter of a Christianized Calcutta family of high standing, Toru DUTT (1856–77) was educated both in France and England. On her return from Europe she began to study Sansckrit intensively with her father, while also expressing in letters a deep nostalgia for England. In 1874 she published her first writing in the *Bengal Magazine*, including a critical essay in English on the Eurasian Calcutta poet Henry Vivian Derozio (1809–31). (The magazine attributed her writing to an Anglo-Indian pen.) Dutt was unmistakably one of 'Macaulay's children', a member of that 'class' of English-educated interpreters between the ruler and the ruled the creation of which he had supported in his famous Minute on Indian Education (1835). She was fluent in both French and English, which she knew before she could write Bengali, and adapted English verse forms and poetic influences to tell tales from Hindu tradition. Her first book, *A Sheaf Gleaned in French Fields* (1876), was a collection of nearly one hundred translations of French poets, predominantly Victor Hugo. In the mid-1870s she wrote a novella in French, *Le Journal de Mlle d'Arvers* (1879), and an unfinished romance, *Bianca*. The book that was to make her name, however, was *Ancient Ballads and Legends of Hindustan* (1882), one of the first works of Indian poetry in English to be published, and certainly the first such work by a woman, a remarkable achievement for its time. It appeared posthumously, sifted from her fragmentary papers by her father, and was introduced as poetry of 'Vedic solemnity and simplicity' by the Victorian critic Edmund Gosse. The bulk of *Ancient Ballads and Legends* is made up of renditions, mainly in rhymed octosyllabic ballad stanzas, of tales from the Puranas and the Indian epic the *Mahabharata*, such as 'Savitri', 'Lakshman', and 'Buttoo'. In its preoccupation with memory and solitude, the strong influence on Dutt's work of the Romantic poets, in particular Keats, is evident. Like Keats, she died in her early twenties of tuberculosis. Gosse concluded his introductory review of *Ancient Ballads and Legends*: 'when the history of the literature of our country comes to be written, there is sure to be a page in it dedicated to this fragile exotic blossom of song.'

Though now largely forgotten, the work of the Edwardian South African writer Dorothea FAIRBRIDGE (1862–1931) is exemplary for its concern with forging a united white colonial identity within the framework of empire in the years after the South African War (1899–1902). Born into an eminent Cape Town family, she became an important member in her own right of a closely linked Cape elite that included artists, the architect Herbert Baker, writers, and various associates of the Governor Lord Milner (collectively known as his 'Kindergarten'). In the years before and after the Union of South Africa (1910), their aim was to promote a reconciliatory South African identity integrating white cultural traditions but bearing the dominant imprint of England. This concern with national, though still colonial identity, which is crystallized in the symbolism of Fairbridge's story 'Pamela' (1911), brings her work into parallel with settler writing by, for example, the Canadian Sara Jeannette Duncan (q.v.). She produced a history of South Africa, travelogues and works on architecture, short stories for the Cape paper the *State*, and five novels, including *Piet of Italy* (1913). In the context of post-apartheid national reconstruction in South Africa Fairbridge's work has again become topical.

A historian, prose stylist, and memoirist of the Carlyles, James Anthony FROUDE (1818–94) is now perhaps better known as the supporter in his later life of closer white colonial ties—'a single commonwealth' or 'Oceana' of Anglo-Saxons 'embraced in the arms of Neptune'—than for his many historical works. The accuracy of these was called into doubt even during his lifetime. The early and middle portions of his career, during which he published the twelve-volume *History of England from the Fall of Wolsey to the Defeat of the Spanish Armada* (1856–70), were spent as the editor of *Fraser's Magazine* (1860–74) and rector of St Andrew's University. In later life his view of English history as a tale of national and potentially supranational glory led him to express strong imperial interests, most notably in *Oceana, or England and her Colonies* (1886) and in *The English in the West Indies; or, the Bow of Ulysses* (1888), a travelogue and openly racist political commentary. On a trip to South Africa (1874–5), Froude had campaigned for federation. Two years before his death he was appointed Regius Professor of History at Oxford.

In his more than forty romances, but especially in the archetypal imperial adventure tales, *King Solomon's Mines* (1885) and *She* (1887), Henry Rider HAGGARD (1856–1925) developed a symbolism of heroic quest and an exoticized primitive which resonated powerfully with popular imperialist consciousness in Britain. The youngest and apparently undertalented son of a large Norfolk family, Haggard did not receive the elite education of his brothers. In 1875 he embarked on probably the most formative experience of his life when he went out to Natal as personal aide to the new Lieutenant-Governor, Sir Henry Bulwer. Here he came into contact with Zulu culture, and read Frederick Selous's account of big-game hunting (1881)—these, along with the *Arabian Nights*, European oral tales, and *Robinson Crusoe*, would provide important sources in the creation of his adventure tales. Haggard's two visits to South Africa (the first until 1879; the second 1880–1) coincided with such crucial developments as the Zulu War and the First Boer War. In 1877 he accompanied Sir Theophilus Shepstone in the annexation of the Boer Transvaal. In the 1880s the spectacular success of *King Solomon's Mines*, *She*, and *Allan Quatermain* (1887) enabled him to give up practising as a lawyer. His preoccupation with mythic tradition and especially Zulu ritual also encouraged a friendship and collaboration (on *The World's Desire*, 1890) with the mythographer Andrew Lang. As editor of the English edition of *Harper's Magazine*, Lang, and W. E. Henley (q.v.), had acted as enthusiastic readers for *King Solomon's Mines*. Haggard's other works, such as *Eric Brighteyes* (1891) and *Cleopatra* (1889), also draw on myth and the heroic traditions of different cultures. He had a distinguished career as a public servant: he worked on several Royal Commissions on agricultural and imperial affairs, and was knighted for his efforts. Like Kipling (q.v.), who became a close friend around the time of the First World War, Haggard retained a strong sense of binding imperial responsibility throughout his life, though his pessimism meant that he held out little hope for the permanence of the empire. Like his romances, his work on agriculture, such as *Rural England* (1902), demonstrates a concern with loss and decline, and the yearning for a more integrated, hieratic cultural past.

After 1897, his reputation secured by his Wessex novels—including *Far from the Madding Crowd* (1871), *Tess of the D'Urbervilles* (1891), and *Jude the Obscure* (1896)—Thomas HARDY (1840–1928) turned to his first love, poetry, and continued to write almost nothing else for the rest of his life. With the 'War Poems' sequence of *Poems of the Past and the Present* (1901), his second collection, he was one of several poets to respond to the Boer War hostilities, though his grim opposition to the militarism and jingoism of the time was not widely shared. Other collections include *Time's Laughingstocks* (1909), *Satires of Circumstance* (1914), and *Moments of Vision* (1917). In the aftermath of the Boer War he also wrote his great epic-drama of the Napoleonic Wars, *The Dynasts* (1904–8).

'Boisterous and piratic', according to his friend Robert Louis Stevenson (q.v.), W. E. (William Ernest) HENLEY (1849–1903) cuts a contradictory figure in late Victorian letters—at once energetic jingoist and iconoclastic art critic, uncompromising and far-seeing editor, and hysterically patriotic poet. In his first book of poetry, the respected *Hospital Verses* (1875), he gives an account of time spent recovering from tubercular arthritis, an illness that led to the amputation of his left foot. It may be that the frustration resulting from this condition informed some of his later, more belligerent rhymes. In the 1880s Henley and Stevenson collaborated on four unsuccessful plays. Thereafter he turned to editing (of the Tory *National Observer*, 1888–94) and the work of producing and encouraging the production of imperialist poetry (while also, launching the literary careers of Conrad, Kipling, and Yeats (qq.v.)). He edited *Lyra Heroica* (1892), a verse primer of patriotic sentiment popular in public schools, later editions of which included his own strenuous verses. When the Boer War broke out Henley welcomed it as the opening of a magnificent new stage in the realization of British world supremacy, and a conclusive end to the effete decadence of the 1890s. *For England's Sake* (1900), published in the first bleak period of the conflict to whip up fervour and silence quailing voices, was a selection of his most jingoist pieces.

G. A. (George Alfred) HENTY (1832–1902), the quintessential *Boy's Own* story writer, worked first as a hospital orderly in the Crimea and Italy, and then as a war correspondent. He reported on several colonial wars in India and Abyssinia, and against the Asante in West Africa, where he travelled with Stanley (q.v.). He tried his hand unsuccessfully at fiction for adults before becoming one of the chief, and certainly the most prolific, practitioners of the imperial adventure story for boys—'My Dear Lads'—for which his name is now a byword. In 1882 he set up a famous three-books-a-year contract with the educational publishers Blackie and Son, and by 1917 his total sales had topped 1 million. The titles of his many adventure stories—*With Clive in India* (1884), *By Sheer Pluck: A Tale of the Ashanti* (1884), *With Wolfe in Canada* (1887), *Through the Sikh War* (1894), *With Roberts to Pretoria* (1902), *With Kitchener in the Soudan* (1903)—emblazon the heroic episodes in a highly mythologized history of British conquest that spans the time of expansive colonization.

J. A. (John Atkinson) HOBSON (1858–1940), the British liberal pragmatist and economist, was educated at Oxford. His thesis of national under-consumption was first developed in the book he wrote with A. F. Mummery, *The Physiology of Industry* (1889). This argument formed one of the main planks of the critique of new imperialism in *Imperialism* (1902), his most influential and still widely referenced book. Published in the year the Boer War ended, *Imperialism* mounts a systematic attack on the standard economic, social, and political justifications given for empire. It is fuelled by severe disillusionment at the 'muddled' thinking, self-important puffery, and outright jingoism encouraged by the war. In a later book, *The Industrial System* (1909), he set out more explicitly policies that would counter the social and economic inequality that imperialism appeared to remedy, yet in fact exacerbated: high taxation for the rich, a broad range of social services, and the nationalization of monopolies. His work influenced V. I. Lenin's ideas about imperialism.

The poetic reputation of the distinguished classicist A. E. (Alfred Edward) HOUSMAN (1859–1936) is based on the two structurally exacting and subversively sensual volumes of lyrics he published in his lifetime, *A Shropshire Lad* (1896) and *Last Poems* (1922). Despite leaving Oxford without a degree, Housman worked intensively and brilliantly on Greek and Latin authors during time spent in the Civil Service in London, and as a result became Professor of Latin at, successively, University College, London, and Cambridge (1892–1911, 1911–36). The imperial interest of Housman's few poems on national events, including the Anglo-Boer War, lies in their often distinctly homoerotic emphasis on bodily and emotional detail, and on regional connections, 'heartstring' ties, as against the great blank abstracts of honour and duty. *More Poems*, edited by Laurence Housman, appeared after his death.

James JOYCE (1882–1941) was the author of a number of the definitive novels of high European modernism, *Portrait of the Artist as a Young Man* (1914–15), *Ulysses* (1922), and *Finnegans Wake* (1939). Cosmopolitan and iconoclastic, and highly sceptical of Irish nationalism, he left Ireland for good to live in Trieste (1904), and then later Zurich and Paris. However, he continued to reflect upon the occupied status of his country and the downtrodden condition of the people in ways that are insightfully anti-colonial. As his journalism and essays and the short-story collection, *Dubliners* (1914), show, he oscillated between a sincere recognition of the colonial injustices suffered in Ireland, and untiring criticism of Irish Catholic narrowness and hypocrisy, and of the cultural paralysis of Irish society as he saw it. Yet if he was harsh in his judgements, he laid the blame for conditions in Ireland squarely at the feet of English 'tyranny'—its 'incurable ignobility'. He also acutely perceived the insecurity the Irish as a colonized people experienced about the loss of their language, yet saw too what was to be gained by making English their own. Joyce himself was adept at manipulating the colonial tongue to sing his own songs.

Like Isabella Bird (q.v.), Mary KINGSLEY (1862–1900) found in travel release from the gloomy domestic round of an unmarried woman's life in

Victorian Britain. After her parents' death she set out to continue her physician father George Henry Kingsley's work as an amateur ethnographer by going to Africa, one of the few regions where he had not travelled. Endowed with discernment and luck in equal measures, she became a well-regarded specialist in 'raw fetish and fresh-water fishes' in her own right. Because of her respect for native West African cultures she was also a determined opponent of the cultural diminishment inflicted by Christian missionary work. She believed in empire, but an empire based not on proselytizing but on trade, protected by the British flag. Her exuberance, courage, and down-to-earth humour, as captured in her writing, became an example to the numbers of other Englishwomen, such as the cross-Africa traveller Mary Hall, who set out on the escape routes offered by empire. Kingsley's ethnological travelogues, *Travels in West Africa* (1897) and *West African Studies* (1899), describe two African journeys (1893–5) on which she studied religion in the Niger Delta and Calabar and in what is now Gabon, shot the rapids of the Ogowe River with a group of 'Fan' people, and climbed the Great Peak of the Cameroons. The energy of her African writings can seem to move the reader rapidly across its ramifying fault-lines: in particular, belief in the fundamental coherence of African society criss-crossed by condescending descriptions of 'savagery'. In 1900 she edited her father's writings, *Notes on Sport and Travel*, and published *Story of West Africa*. Kingsley died near Cape Town, South Africa, in the same year, on her way to nurse Boer prisoners of war in the South African War.

Bombay-born Rudyard KIPLING (1865–1936) was the Anglo-Indian writer above all others who honed an imaginative vocabulary for imperial experience under the Raj. His stories and poems represent empire in India from diverse perspectives directed from both sides of the colonial divide. While informed by presumptions concerning the superiority of English authority, his work also gives memorable expression to the anxieties of colonial rule, and the interleaved aversions and attractions for the native that were involved. As has often been recognized, he represented in many ways the mood of his time, the period of high empire. He intuited its central cultural archetypes—the triumphs of technological progress, the British fear of losing world supremacy. The clearest sign of how deeply he tapped into people's experience, both in Britain and across the colonies, was his broad-based popularity: for about thirty years from the time his first work appeared—*Departmental Ditties* (1886), *Plain Tales from the Hills* (1888), *Life's Handicap* (1891)—he was the most widely read writer in English. However, so tightly were his own fortunes as a writer bound to the wheel of empire that, as its progress began to falter, so his reputation waned. Nowadays, paradoxically, it is as much for his symptomatic insecurities about empire as well as for his vivid certainties that he continues to demand attention from colonial discourse critics. Educated in England, Kipling returned to India aged 17 to work as assistant-editor on the Lahore *Civil and Military Gazette*, and thereafter as the special correspondent for the *Pioneer* in Allahabad, and as the editor of the *Week's News*. His first publications, based on this early journalism, made his name in Anglo-India. When he arrived in England in 1889 his reputation had preceded him: excited acclaim and personal breakdown followed, which are reflected in the hectic pessimism of *The Light that Failed* (1890). After a cross-empire tour and marriage, he settled for a time in the United States. These years saw the publication of *Barrack-Room Ballads* (1892), *The Jungle Book* (1894), and later, having returned to England, *The Day's Work* (1898), *Stalky & Co.* (1899), and *Kim* (1901), his charming, richly iconographic, and only novel-length study of the Raj. During the Boer War he worked for a time as a correspondent: several poems express monitory responses to this watershed imperial conflict. From 1898 he spent English winters in Cape Town, where he befriended the imperial statesmen Cecil John Rhodes (1853–1902) and Alfred Milner (1854–1925). In the years running up to the award of the Nobel Prize (1907), he published, amongst other books, *Just So Stories* (1902), *The Five Nations* (1903), and *Puck of Pook's Hill* (1906). The coming of the First World War confirmed for him the dark historical vision he had for years been warning of. With the death of his only son, John, in action in 1915, the disaster of the war irrupted into Kipling's own life: from this time his creative output lessened and grew markedly more melancholic. His deeply withdrawn autobiography, *Something of Myself*, appeared in 1937, after his death.

Archibald LAMPMAN (1861–99) was one of the 1890s Canadian poets who identified themselves with the emerging national vision of the new Confederation. He came from Morpeth, Upper Canada, and was educated at Trinity College, Toronto. He was inspired to write by Charles G. D. Roberts's (q.v.) first book, *Orion and Other Poems* (1880), which proved to him that poetry could be written from within Canada, by Canadians. He was employed by the Post Office Department of the Canadian Civil Service in Ottawa from 1883 until his relatively early death. The position was suffocating because of its tedium, but enabling for giving him time for poetry. During the Ottawa years Duncan Campbell Scott (q.v.), another 1890s poet, became a friend (he later edited Lampman's work). Lampman played an active part in Canadian intellectual life, contributing to a weekly column of cultural commentary for the Toronto *Globe*. In his lifetime he produced only two collections, *Among the Millet* (1888) and *Lyrics of Earth* (1895); *Alcyone* (1899) appeared posthumously. Lampman skilfully imported Romantic forms and conventions into the Ontario landscape, and is recognized as one of Canada's finest nineteenth-century practitioners of the sonnet. Even so his Keatsian rhetoric can come across as acquired and artificial, and his stance as alienated.

Paradoxically for a writer who believed that Australian society was inimical to the making of literature, Henry LAWSON (1867–1922) was instrumental in scoring narrative colour and the beginnings of a Europe-derived balladic line into the perceived emptiness of Australia. The Australian writers he encountered as a boy were alienated colonials like Marcus Clarke (q.v.); at the time of his death a self-conscious Australian settler literature had emerged, a development in which his contribution was fundamental. With his naturalist interest in the life of the bush, and heartfelt though circumspect ethos of mateship, Lawson has now long been critically regarded as the representative figure within a predominantly masculine nationalist tradition in 1890s Australian writing. He was born on the Grenfell goldfields; his mother was Louisa Lawson, later an important figure in Sydney publishing and the women's movement. His youth was hard, as his parents struggled to make a living, finally separating in 1883. From this time he was based mainly in Sydney, writing for the *Republican* and the prominent republican paper, the *Bulletin*, which became synonymous with the 1890s writing which it fostered. He first established himself as a poet; especially after his famous staged debate with A. B. Paterson (q.v.) in the *Bulletin* concerning how to represent the outback, he would always be associated with the catchy verse he produced about bush life, such as 'The Roaring Days' and 'The Teams' (1889). Yet it was in the sharply observed, concentrated short stories that he began to hone out of his observations of the 'tramping' life in the Bourke region of New South Wales, that Lawson found his surest, most accomplished voice. Stories such as 'The Bush Undertaker' (1892), 'The Drover's Wife' (1892), and the pessimistic 'The Union Buries Its Dead' (1893) show his growing expertise at the realist sketch, told in flat Australian vernacular by an involved though wry and unsurprised narrator. After a trip to New Zealand he published *Short Stories in Prose and Verse* (1894), a collection of stories and sketches, most of which had first appeared in the *Bulletin*. *While the Billy Boils* and *In the Days When the World Was Wide*, two 1896 collections (of prose and verse respectively), and two 1900 volumes of short fiction, *On the Track* and *Over the Sliprails*, so grounded his reputation that he was able to set out with his family to seek wider recognition and, he believed, a more congenial literary climate in London. Here he produced some of his best prose, collected in particular in *Joe Wilson and His Mates* (1901) and *Children of the Bush* (1902), but signs of artistic sclerosis and self-repetition were already in evidence. After his return from England, his marriage broken, he sank into alcoholic decline. Lawson is now seen as one of the chief pioneers of the Australian short story, sketchy, fragmentary, often dystopic, and marked by a self-aware authorial voice. He was the first Australian writer to be given a state funeral.

Stephen LEACOCK (1869–1944) was born in Hampshire, in England, and moved when young to Orillia, Ontario, where his parents attempted to make a living. After studying at the University of Toronto he obtained his doctorate in political science at the University of Chicago (1903). He taught until his retirement at McGill University in Montreal, eventually becoming Professor of Political Economy. His published work in economics always earned him more money than his literary sketches, which he began to write quite late, first publishing in journals like *Punch* and the Toronto *Saturday Night*. His first collection, *Literary Lapses* (1910), produced at his own expense, was followed by the *Nonsense Novels* parodies (1911), *Sunshine Sketches of a Little Town* (1912), *Behind the Beyond* (1914), and *Arcadian Adventures with the Idle Rich* (1915), which together won him a wide reputation. He was also known as a lecturer, speaking on topics such as the benefits of British Empire (which were 'decent government and fair play', as he said in *Our British Empire* (1940)), and imperial federation, which he supported. His elitism and conservatism, however, coexisted with his interest in locale and the colloquial—the rhythms of Canadian conversation reflected in his stories.

Though celebrated in his time as a missionary explorer who sought to promote Christianity, Commerce, and Civilization in Africa, the Scotsman David LIVINGSTONE (1813–73) was probably less interested in spreading the gospel than he was in mapping the 'blank' spaces at the continent's heart. Especially in his later years, his explorer's zeal fused with religious idealism as he pursued the eventually unfulfilled mission—'to Thy honour'—of locating the headwaters of the Nile, the 'holy river'. A discovery such as this would have carried particular significance at a time when the literal truth of the Bible was being called into question. After several years spent training part-time as a medical missionary in Glasgow while also working in a cotton factory, Livingstone set out for Africa in 1840. In northern South Africa, under the well-known Scottish missionary Robert Moffat, he made the one convert of his entire career, who later lapsed. He also married Moffat's daughter Mary. He persuaded Moffat to support him in making trips into the interior in the name of native improvement. In 1856 he accomplished the first of his three major expeditions, trekking to the African west coast (1853), and then crossing the continent west to east, during which he saw Mosi-oa-Tunga, the Smoke that Thunders, and named it Victoria Falls. Like the next two expeditions, this trip was marked by severe suffering due to fever and other tropical illnesses, and by perhaps unavoidable but also destructive interference in the lives of villagers encountered *en route* (often in an attempt to counter slavery). The expedition was, however, also the most successful of his three and formed the basis of the acclaim with which Livingstone and his book *Missionary Travels* were welcomed in England in 1857. His next two expeditions were to explore the Zambezi River region in quest of habitable land for whites (1861–5), and to map the area of Lake Tanganyika (1865–73). On this longest and finally fatal journey he sought evidence for his own theory plotting the source of the Nile at Lake Mweru, the southernmost and, as it turned out, most off-course point advanced by any of the current theories. Despite, yet also because of his misfortunes, Livingstone alive or dead was for Victorians the embodiment of key imperial virtues—fortitude, faith, the desire to 'uplift'. His already heroic stature in England was further elevated by the remarkable story of the trip made by his helpers Susi and Chuma carrying his embalmed body across Africa to Zanzibar for burial in Westminster Abbey.

Claude MCKAY (1889–1948), the Jamaican poet, holds the distinction of being the first writer to take up West Indian Creole—the vernacular that has become such a powerful vehicle of black self-expression in the second half of this century. It was while he was working as a constable in Kingston (and known as Jamaica's Bobbie Burns) that his work came to the attention of the English folklorist Walter Jekyll who heard in it the 'articulate consciousness of the people'. Recognizing that Jamaican culture lay embedded in local oral traditions, Jekyll had in 1907 published a pioneering collection of Jamaican field and yard songs. (Three songs are included in this anthology, alongside McKay's work.) Under Jekyll's patronage, McKay published two collections in the same year, *Songs of Jamaica* and *Constab Ballads* (1912). The poems, especially those in the latter collection, express his growing awareness of the contradictions manifested in a racialized, elite-run system of colonial oppression. This was also the year when he left Jamaica for good, initially to study agronomy at Tuskegee College, in the United States. The struggle to get by as a black person in America rapidly matured his understanding of social and political injustice. Within a few years of arriving in America he became involved in left-wing political and artistic circles based in New York. Paradoxically, however, though his anger was occasionally expressed in single poems, from this time on his poetry—published as *Spring in New Hampshire* (1920) and *Harlem Shadows* (1922)—became increasingly more literary, more noticeably inflected by Keats and other English Romantic poets. Yet he retained a live connection with the locale of his youth. In the acclaimed novel *Banana Bottom* (1933), in which a Jamaican girl returns from England to her home village, he continues to revel in the 'necromancy' of the black vernacular. He spent the 1920s living and travelling in Western Europe, Russia, and North Africa, coming into his own as a cosmopolitan artist yet at the same time concentrating ever more closely on the importance and the implications of his blackness. *Harlem Shadows* is now recognized as one of the inaugural works of the Harlem Renaissance, the cultural revival movement in African-American arts. McKay lived in the United States from 1934 until his death and was naturalized as an American (1940). As well as poetry and four novels (published 1928–33), he wrote an autobiography, *A Long Way from Home* (1937), and a study of Harlem.

The New Zealand-born Katherine MANSFIELD (the assumed name of Kathleen Mansfield Beauchamp, 1888–1923), who described herself as a woman 'with the taint of the pioneer in my blood', established herself within avant-garde and cosmopolitan circles in London in the 1910s. Yet throughout her writing life she was preoccupied with the dreamlike reconstruction of her 'mysterious' South Pacific homeland. Her work, therefore, emerges at the charged point of intersection between European modernist and symbolist experimentation, and a colonial expatriate longing to recreate in her fiction her distant native land. Paradoxically in a sense, yet also typically, her modernist efforts to move away from, as she said, the intricate plots and 'resolutions' of Victorian writing also testified to uncertainties about identity and cultural displacement which are now regarded as postcolonial. Mansfield's childhood was spent in Wellington: many of her finest short stories, like 'Prelude', 'At the Bay', and 'The Garden Party', outline defining moments from this period of her life. The final year of her education was spent in London where she formed a strong attachment to the city's New Woman freedoms and creative possibilities. During a troubled time back in New Zealand in 1907 she began to publish sketches or 'vignettes' in the Australian *Native Companion* and, on a camping trip on North Island, came into fascinated contact with Maori ways of life. In 1908 she left New Zealand for good with the intention of making her way as a writer in London. *In a German Pension* (1911), her first collection, was written out of a period spent in Bavaria recovering from a miscarriage. She connected herself to the literary circles associated with A. R. Orage's *New Age* and John Middleton Murry's *Rhythm*. Murry became her admirer, supporter, and lover, and later her husband, and after her death the overprotective guardian of her reputation. After 1915, with the death of her brother Leslie ('Bogey') in the Great War and her own increasing ill health, Mansfield's writing became more elegiac, symbolic, and retrospective. Two collections of short stories were published towards the end of her life, *Bliss* (1920) and *The Garden-Party* (1922). *Prelude* (1917) appeared as an individual publication from the Woolfs' Hogarth Press. Her longer short stories may have been destined for an extended New Zealand family chronicle which she planned but never completed. After her death from tuberculosis Murry published two more collections of her short stories, *The Doves' Nest* and *Something Childish* (1924), a selection of her poems in 1923, her *Journal* (1927), and two volumes of her letters (1928, 1929).

(Sir) Henry NEWBOLT (1862–1938) was, like Alfred Austin (q.v.), a patriotic barrister-poet, though kindlier and far more liberal than the Laureate. He wrote fiction and in later life *A Naval History of the War* (1920), but his reputation was made as a balladeer of British maritime history. *Admirals All and Other Verses* (1897, multiply reissued) was his first and best-known collection in this vein. *An Island Race* (1898) and *The Sailing of the Long-Ships* (1902) were also popular. He depicted important British sea-battles as emblematic manifestations of 'a race high-handed, strong of heart, sea-rovers, conquerors, builders in the waste'. A lifelong devotee of Clifton College, he participated in the imperialist conflation of the public school values of patriotism, manliness, and sportsmanship. The poem 'Sráhmandázi' (1902), however, which draws on Mary Kingsley's (q.v.) African anthropology, presents a different side to Newbolt. Of *Admirals All* Yeats (q.v.) said that Newbolt's was a patriotism that 'lays burdens on a man, and not the patriotism that takes burdens off'. As well as being a Devonshire regionalist and a Liberal, he was also a perceptive literary critic: he admired Conrad (q.v.), and included poems by Eliot, Pound, and Lawrence in his anthology *New Paths on the Helicon* (1927). He edited the *Monthly Review* (1900–4).

At first it may be difficult to see in the intensely lyrical poetry of Sarojini NAIDU (born Chattopadhyay, 1876–1949) much that is aslant a European tradition. In the 1890s, following advice given by the Victorian critic Edmund Gosse, she began to concentrate on, in his words, becoming 'a genuine Indian poet of the Deccan' instead of offering cunning imitations of English Romantic poetry. This decision, however, led to reproductions of another kind—images of an exoticized India, for which, in Europe, she was acclaimed as 'the most accomplished living poet of India . . . in English'. Sarojini Chattopadhyay was born in the native state of Hyderabad into a prominent family of Bengali intellectuals. Exposed early on to Muslim and European as well as Hindu cultures, she was brought up, she herself stressed, an 'Indian', believing in the 'brotherhood of diverse creeds'. Like Toru Dutt (q.v.), whose Western interpreter Gosse also was, Naidu as a girl showed an extraordinary precocity in writing poetry. Matriculating at the age of 12 from Madras University, she was sent to England, to King's College, London, and to Cambridge, for her education in an (eventually unsuccessful) attempt to discourage her from marrying a non-Brahmin, Govindaraju Naidu. While in England she met Gosse and Arthur Symons, the Symbolist critic, and other prominent artists and writers. Her poetry appeared in four collections published between 1895 and 1917: *Songs*, *The Golden Threshold* (1905) dedicated to Gosse, *The Bird of Time* (1912), and *The Broken Wing*. The smooth textures of her verse may seem far removed from harsh economic and political realities in India, yet she was intensely committed to the movement for Indian independence, working closely with Gandhi in the Indian National Congress for many years. Her political involvements are captured in her occasional nationalist poems, but may also be unravelled from those implicitly feminist verses which reject child-marriage and express sorrow at purdah-confinement. Throughout her career, as a woman writer striving for poetic recognition, and as an Indian patriot, Naidu continued to perform complicated manoeuvres around the range of strictures imposed by Orientalist preconception, Western paternalism, colonialist racism, and censorship, as well as masculinist nationalism. After 1917 she became increasingly more involved in the public at the expense of the poetic sphere. She was one of the few women to participate in the Salt March of 1930. She also helped establish the All India Women's Conference and, while depressed by Partition, became the Governor of Uttar Pradesh after Indian independence (1947).

Over one hundred years after the publication of his first and enduringly popular collection, *The Man from Snowy River* (1895), A. B. (Andrew Barton, 'Banjo' after his *Bulletin* pseudonym, 'The Banjo') PATERSON (1864–1941) remains Australia's foremost balladeer. In his heyday he was probably more widely read than any poet other than Kipling, whose interest in the demotic he shared, and whom he to some extent imitated, though differing in his strong commitment to democratic and republican values. Illalong Station, near Yass, New South Wales, where he grew up, provided him with the material for the ballads which began to appear in the *Bulletin* from 1889. In 1892–3 Paterson entered into a verse debate with Henry Lawson (q.v.) in the *Bulletin* defending his (to Lawson) over-idealized portrayal of droving life in the Australian outback. This region had already gained near-mythic status in Paterson's poems. Though he worked for a while as a solicitor, the fame which attended him after *The Man from Snowy River* opened the way to a high-profile life of travel, hunting, and pearl-diving (during which time he wrote 'Waltzing Matilda'). He went to South Africa as war correspondent for the *Sydney Morning Herald* and was later sent to cover the Boxer Rebellion in China. *Rio Grande's Last Race and Other Verses* (1902) included verse about the Boer War and his chief passion, horse racing. During the First World War he worked for a limited time as a war correspondent, and thereafter in the Remount Service in Egypt. He edited, in succession, the Sydney *Evening News* and the *Australian Town and Country Journal*. Other work includes *Saltbush Bill J.P. and Other Poems* (1917), two novels, short stories, and the travel memoirs *Happy Dispatches* (1934).

Alice PERRIN (1867–1934) was India-born but educated in England according to the common practice for Anglo-Indian children. As an adult she lived in India for over twenty years and was married to a medical officer in the Indian Civil Service. Her first publications were romantic fictions, including *Into Temptation* (1894) and *The Spell of the Jungle* (1902), but her most accomplished writing, much of it set in India, appears in two collections of short stories, *East of Suez* (1901) and *Red Records* (1906). Focusing almost exclusively on the romantic and cultural complications of Anglo-Indian life, many of her narratives take a line from Kipling tales like 'The Mark of the Beast' (1890) in their heavy dependence on the supernatural and sensational. At the same time, in certain of her stories Perrin draws on her knowledge of folk-ways and local sayings in order to reflect Indian points of view. Reviews of the time praised her Kiplingesque ability to capture the 'weird atmosphere of the East'.

Solomon Tshekisho PLAATJE (1876–1932), the South African nationalist, worked as a journalist, court interpreter (in Mafeking, during the Boer War siege), politician, and novelist, and was a founding member and the first secretary of the African National Congress (then the South African Natives National Congress). Born into a Christian Barolong family and growing up on a German mission station in the Orange Free State, he devoted his life to opposing black dispossession and white injustice. The passionate commitment and anger of this opposition is distilled into the work for which, along with his novel *Mhudi* (1930), he is now best known, *Native Life in South Africa* (1916). His political campaigns took him to London during the First World War, and later to the United States, where he met African American activists like Marcus Garvey and W. E. B. Du Bois. He devoted the later part of his life to moulding his native tongue, Setswana, into a written language, to recording Tswana folk tales, and to translation.

(Sir) Charles G. D. ROBERTS (1860–1943) was, if not the leader then certainly one of the foremost members of the so-called Confederation group of Canadian poets which included Bliss Carman, Archibald Lampman, and Duncan Campbell Scott (qq.v.). Born in the early 1860s, the decade of Canadian federation, these poets were not linked by a common cause or shared style (there is debate as to whether they formed a recognized 'group' at all). Yet, appearing in the aftermath of Canadian federation, their work is distinguished by its concern to give expression to an emerging national spirit in the country. It was symptomatic of a characteristic colonial conflict of values, however, that they continued to embrace British, especially Romantic and late Victorian, poetic values and forms as the vessels in which to create this native tradition. Like his cousin Bliss Carman, Roberts came from Fredericton, New Brunswick, and attended university there. The excitement created by his first book of poems, *Orion and Other Poems* (1880), elevated him at a relatively young age to the editorship of the Toronto literary magazine the *Week*, with which Sara Jeannette Duncan (q.v.) was also associated. In this position he was able to go a considerable distance towards realizing his nationalist ideals, both in fostering critical discussion and in publishing early poems by Lampman and Carman. In 1884 he resigned over his support for Canadian independence (as against imperial federation or American annexation), and became a teacher in Nova Scotia. The next ten years represented his most prolific period as a Canadian nature poet. A highpoint came with *Songs of the Common Day* (1893), which explores the poetic possibilities of the New Brunswick landscape, and *The Book of the Native* (1896). His departure to the United States in 1897 coincided with a late-1890s depression in the national idealism which had so animated young writers. During the years away from Canada Roberts wrote little poetry but remained active as a writer, especially of journalism and the animal stories for which he is also well known, such as *Earth's Enigmas* (1896) and *The Kindred of the Wild* (1902).

John RUSKIN (1819–1900), the Victorian art critic, visionary, and castigator of the mechanized, 'deathfully selfish' society of his time, also offered that society ideals of social reform and images of a time-tried 'noble' Englishness which filtered into and also reflected imperialist self-conceptions. This is evident, for example, in Cecil John Rhodes's enthusiastic response to his *Lectures on Art*, in particular the Inaugural. Ruskin was educated at home and through extensive travel on the European continent. He became known as the interpreter of English landscape painting, most notably Turner's, with the first volume of *Modern Painters* (1843). Four more volumes of *Modern Painters* followed, the last published in 1860, after *The Seven Lamps of Architecture* (1849) and the three-volume *The Stones of Venice* (1851–3). In the latter he set out his belief that the arts, which elevate human life, require as their first condition a favourable working environment and due respect for labour. As an extension of his beliefs he promoted Pre-Raphaelite painting and sought to foster a home-grown national art. He taught at the Working Men's College in London and, in his many lectures, denounced the profit-oriented, narrowly scientific spirit of his time. As Slade Professor at Oxford (1870–9 and again 1883–5) he set up a drawing school and famously encouraged his students to work at making a road just outside the city. In *Fors Clavigera* (1871–84), his letters on political economy, he further developed his ideas about the interaction between art and social practice. From 1879 Ruskin was afflicted by mental illness and spent the last years of his long life in virtual silence, at Brantwood in the Lake District, where he began an autobiography, *Praeterita*.

Olive SCHREINER (1855–1920), the South African novelist, pioneering feminist, and anti-imperial polemicist, was probably the first colonial writer to be widely read and acclaimed in literary London. A courageous reviser of her own thinking, she was noticed in particular for the acuity of her social and political insights. She is seen now as one of the foremost Victorian analysts of material and power relations in a settler society. Her understanding of gender inequities too was ahead of her time. The ninth child of a German Lutheran missionary and an English mother, Schreiner early on lost her faith in Christianity. However, she would continue to draw on the Bible in the creation of her own allegorical stories. Like other free-thinkers of the day (for example Vivekananda (q.v.)), she continued throughout her life to search for some universal moral ideal explaining the disparate phenomena of the physical world. Her adolescence was spent as an itinerant governess in isolated eastern regions of the then Cape Colony, her thinking strongly influenced by Herbert Spencer's *First Principles* (1862), as well as by J. S. Mill and Ralph Waldo Emerson. During these years she began three novels: *From Man to Man* (1926) and the melodrama *Undine* (1928), both of which were obsessively reworked throughout her life, and *The Story of an African Farm* (1883). This last novel, a part-allegorical portrait in microcosm of repressive colonial society, she took with her to England on an unsuccessful mission to train as a doctor (1881). In the century since its first publication, *African Farm* has many times been singled out for its path-breaking attempt to find an imaginative language to fit an alien colonized land. Its appearance brought her into contact with a group of like-minded thinkers including Havelock Ellis and Karl Pearson. In the 1890s she branched into allegory and idealist fantasy in *Dream Life and Real Life* (1893), as well as political writing, such as *Trooper Peter* (1897) and *An English South African's View of the Situation* (1898), a pre-war critique of British treatment of the Boers. A later political essay, *A Letter on the South African Union* (1909), warned against the black dispossession on which the new white South African state was to be built, as too would Solomon Plaatje (q.v.). *Woman and Labour* (1911) was an important analysis of the material bases of gender inequality. In 1913 she resigned her presidency of the Cape Women's Enfranchisement League because it rejected black women's suffrage. Her later years were spent in England, dogged by ill-health. Other publications (brought out posthumously) were *Thoughts on South Africa* (1923) and *Stories, Dreams and Allegories* (1923).

Like his close friend Archibald Lampman (q.v.), Duncan Campbell SCOTT (1862–1947) is seen as one of the Confederation group of Canadian poets, the 'Group of '61'. *The Magic House and Other Poems*, his first collection, was published in 1893, also a debut year for some of his associates. He was born in Ottawa, his lifetime's home. From the late 1880s he published in *Scribner's Magazine*, and until 1893 wrote a column with Lampman for the *Toronto Globe*. His work as Secretary to the Department of Indian Affairs from 1896, and later as Commissioner to Indian tribes, sent him on trips into the Canadian north, providing him with the material on native life which was to mark his work. This influence is especially clear from the time of his second collection, *Labor and the Angel* (1898). Of his contemporaries writing in English, he was probably the most exploratory with regard to form, and was also, in *The Village of Viger* (1896) and *The Witching of Elspie* (1923), Canada's chief experimental short-story writer.

Along with J. A. Froude (q.v.), the historian (Sir) John SEELEY (1834–95) was one of the main Victorian proponents of imperial federation. Influenced by Charles Dilke, he advocated the creation of a 'Greater Britain' beyond the seas, modelled on the federal system of the United States. He was the author of the idea that England had acquired her vast nineteenth-century empire almost inadvertently, accidentally, 'in a fit of absence of mind'. However, this was a tendency, he believed, that called for greater organization and control. In 1857 he became a Fellow and Lecturer in Classics at Christ's College, Cambridge, where he was himself educated. He was later Professor of Latin at University College, London, and from 1869 Regius Professor of Modern History at Cambridge. He first came into prominence with *Ecce Homo* (1865), but it was his two courses of lectures on the lessons offered by early British imperial history that drew wide attention, including in the Colonial Office. *The*

Expansion of England (1883), the published lectures, became a source-book for the 'new imperialism'. In 1895 he published *Lectures on Political Science*.

The first woman to graduate from Bombay University (in first place), and also the first woman to take the BCL degree at Oxford, Cornelia SORABJI (1866–1954) spent her life in a long battle to open public institutions to women in India. Born into a large Christianized Parsi family, she was 'brought up English'. Like so many native colonials of her time, she would inhabit mediatory positions between cultures for most of her life. As a woman trained in an entirely male-dominated profession, she was for many years locked into a contradiction whereby she was unable to practise formally because she could not be called to the Bar. She was eventually called in 1923. As she records in her evocative autobiography, *India Calling* (1932), between 1894, the date of her return to India, and 1923 she worked as the legal representative of propertied women in purdah ('my purdahnashins'). These women were operating at a severe disadvantage because their legal affairs were traditionally conducted by men. *Love and Life Behind the Purdah* (1901) is based on her sympathetic but at times condescending observations of these women's lives. During this period she also wrote *Between the Twilights* (1908), a collection of stories based on Hindu myths featuring women, *Sun-Babies: Studies in the Child-Life of India* (1904), and *The Purdahnashin* (1917). She published in the *Nineteenth Century* and the *National Review*. Like Sarojini Naidu, she knew and was fêted by many eminent Victorians during her time in England, including Benjamin Jowett and F. Max Müller. Though she strongly opposed discrimination against women, and herself suffered from it, Sorabji held back from radicalism. She condemned the Indian nationalist movement for the social upheavals it caused, comparing it unfavourably with the more gradual amelioration which she believed imperialism could effect. In the 1920s these beliefs trapped her in a difficult position when she was seen to give support to Katherine Mayo's highly prejudiced account of gender relations in India, *Mother India* (1927). Her last work was *India Recalled* (1936).

A resolute and notoriously ruthless traverser of Africa, Henry Morton STANLEY (born John Rowlands, 1841–1904) first became known to the world as the influential hagiographer of Livingstone (q.v.)—as the intrepid journalist who discovered the lost discoverer. At 15 he left behind illegitimate origins in north Wales for America, where he took the name of his mentor, a New Orleans plantation owner, fought on both sides in the American Civil War, and then became a roving 'special' for the *New York Herald*. It was the *Herald* proprietor James Gordon Bennett who in 1870 sent him into Africa on a mission to find Livingstone. Stanley's account of the famous meeting was first published in *How I Found Livingstone* (1872) and then repeated in condensed form in fund-raising journalism and lectures. The myth of the stalwart Christian explorer, which he did so much to promote, encouraged British colonial designs on the region, or so Stanley was convinced. Allegedly inspired by the older man's vision of Christianized commerce, and directed by geographical questions he had left unresolved, he set out on a second African expedition in 1874, as he records in *Through the Dark Continent* (1878). His

999-day record African crossing from east to west, which established that the Lualaba River was the beginning of the Congo (and not the Nile— Livingstone's surmise), became well known both for the achievement it represented and its terrible human cost. Between 1879 and 1884 he was employed by the Belgian King Leopold III to set up what was in effect the monarch's own personal colony, the ironically named Congo Free State. He represented Leopold's interests at the Berlin Conference of 1885. Two years later he led the notorious Emin Pasha Relief Expedition through the Free State, a trip which was to claim the highest fatalities of any recorded African expedition. Emin Pasha, the German-born Governor of Equatoria Province, refused to leave his African domain, much like Conrad's Kurtz for whom he, like Stanley himself, was a model. In the last ten years of his life Stanley became a British MP, though his reputation never recovered from the rumours of excessive cruelty surrounding his final exploits.

A writer of many vividly observed short stories and novels about the Indian Empire, Flora Annie STEEL (1847–1929) was regarded in her day as second only to Kipling as a commentator on Indian and Anglo-Indian life. Mainly self-educated, Flora Annie Webster married an Indian civil servant, Henry Steel, in 1867, and went with him to the Punjab, the land of 'the five rivers', where most of her fiction is set. Despite bouts of fever she crammed a phenomenal amount of work into the twenty-two years she lived in India, combining teaching and school inspection with the conservation of traditional handicrafts and collecting oral literature. Folk-tales reorganized into 'literary sequences', though not, Steel stressed, 'orientalised', gave her the material for her first publication, *Wide-Awake Stories* (1884). On return to England she began writing more seriously, first publishing in *Macmillan's Magazine*. *Miss Stuart's Legacy* (1893), her first novel, appeared in the same year as *From the Five Rivers*, a collection of long short stories which reflect her central preoccupation with the persistence of life-threatening customs in native culture in spite of colonization. Her Indian Mutiny novel, *On the Face of the Waters* (1896), for which she returned to India to do research, established her reputation as a key Anglo-Indian writer. *In the Permanent Way* (1898), probably her most varied and skilful collection of stories, appeared two years later. Steel worked at her writing as she did at everything else, indefatigably, efficiently, and productively, publishing several short-story collections and twenty novels, including *The Potter's Thumb* (1894) and *Voices in the Night* (1900); the vast historical compilation *India Through the Ages* (1908); an autobiography, *The Garden of Fidelity* (1929); and the very successful Anglo-Indian 'Mrs Beeton's', *The Complete Indian Housekeeper and Cook* (1889).

A. G. (Alfred George) STEPHENS (1865–1933) was the influential literary editor and critic of the Sydney nationalist paper the *Bulletin* (1894–1906). Stephens was passionately concerned about the formation of a native Australian literature. His taste at once for the local and also for what he called universality is reflected in his selections for the anthologies *The Bulletin Reciter* and *The Bulletin Story Book* (both 1901), though it is his nationalist commitment which is to the fore in the Introduction which appears in this anthology.

He oversaw the 'Red Page', the literary section of the *Bulletin*, and also guided a number of writers, such as Joseph Furphy and Miles Franklin, into book publication. Before his time on the *Bulletin* he worked as editor on a number of journals, mainly based in Queensland, and later produced the literary magazine, the *Bookfellow*. He was also a poet in his own right.

The author of the quintessential nineteenth-century boy's adventure story, *Treasure Island* (1883), Robert Louis STEVENSON (1850–94) was also a short-story and travel writer and an essayist, and, in *Dr Jekyll and Mr Hyde* (1886), a keen-eyed explorer of the dark underside of the Victorian psyche. In the last years of his life these varied interests intersected in his tales and travel notes about the South Seas, where he journeyed from 1888 and eventually settled, in Samoa, pursued by the ill-health that plagued him all his life. The son of an Edinburgh lighthouse-engineer, Stevenson received a strictly Calvinist upbringing. Having taken up first engineering and then the law, he went on to lay down a lifetime's commitment to wandering and writing when, in *An Inland Voyage* (1878) and *Travels with a Donkey* (1879), he recorded his first travels in search of a better climate, on the continent of Europe. In California he met his wife, Fanny Osbourne (1879). In the 1880s, first *Treasure Island*, and then such work as *Kidnapped* (1886), *Catriona* (1893), and *The Master of Ballantrae* (1889), brought him increasing fame as a writer of adventure romances. Admired by Leslie Stephen and Rider Haggard (q.v.), he was in regular contact with Henry James and Andrew Lang, and had also been W. E. Henley's (q.v.) long-standing writing mate. The next six years of criss-crossing the south Pacific Ocean, however, would seriously revise his reputation as *romancier*. Readers expected more adventure from him—the kind of writing associated with exotic places and imperialist expansion. However, not only in the part-anthropological travel writings later collected as *In the South Seas* (1896), and the polemical commentary on the Samoan situation, *A Footnote to History* (1892), but also in the novella *The Ebb-Tide* (1894) and the long short story 'The Beach of Falesá' (published together with the Polynesian-style tales 'The Bottle-Imp' and 'The Isle of Voices' in *Island Nights' Entertainments* (1893)), what they got was a disturbingly realist indictment of the social collapse brought about by empire. Like Hugh Clifford (q.v.), Stevenson lamented the disappearance of local customs, and of whole peoples, due to European interference. Yet, as we see in his portrait of 'the King of Apemama', he was also fascinated by the incongruous mixes that cultural contacts in the region had thrown up, both by the 'stir-about of epochs and races, barbarisms and civilizations, virtues and crimes' created by colonization on the South Pacific islands, and by the complexity of island cultures themselves. In his awareness of the damage done by white incursion, his response to his South Seas experience looks ahead to Conrad's (q.v.) indictments of imperialism.

A poet not usually given to discoursing explicitly on imperial themes, Algernon Charles SWINBURNE (1837–1909) was fired by the outbreak of the South African War to write his notorious, almost inchoately belligerent sonnet 'The Transvaal'. The younger Swinburne had written, very differently, in defiance of social convention, in *Poems and Ballads* (1866), and in *A Song of Italy* and

Songs before Sunrise (1871), which gave support to Italian independence. He was the author of romantic dramas on Mary, Queen of Scots, of many poems of the sea, and of the acclaimed Pre-Raphaelite poem *Tristram of Lyonesse* (1882).

In Bengali literature the stature of Rabindranath TAGORE (1861–1941) is monumental and legendary. Dramatist, essayist, novelist, short-story writer, visionary, and, perhaps above all, poet, Tagore presided magisterially over the vast matrix of cultural interconnections between West and East, tradition and modernity, that marked Bengali society of his day. Forging these diverse and sometimes conflicting influences into new forms (the prose poem, the verse drama), he is also seen as having more or less single-handedly brought into being a modern Bengali poetic. While rejecting Sri Aurobindo's (q.v.) style of assertive nationalist resistance as spiritually destructive, he was a lucid observer of the traumatic experience of colonial assimilation. He promoted the Bengali language, and believed that Indians should work on every front to rebuild cultural self-confidence. Rabindranath was the fourteenth and youngest child of an eminent Calcutta family of Pirili Brahmins (a tabooed sub-caste). His grandfather, Dwarkanath, was a well-connected merchant-prince, his father, Debendranath, one of the founders of the monotheistic Hindu reform group Brahmo Samaj. Rabindranath began early on to devote himself to poetry and resisted institutionalized education, repeatedly abandoning his studies both in Calcutta, and in England (1878–80). In response to these experiences he later founded the experimental school at Santiniketan which became the 'world university', Visva-Bharati. In 1877 his first publications appeared in the family journal *Bharati* (which he edited from 1898). The year 1881, an *annus mirabilis*, saw the appearance of his first devotional songs, a musical play, *Valmiki-Pratibha*, and political writing (on England's opium trade). *Sandhya Sangit* and *Prabhat Sangit* (1882 and 1883, evening and morning songs respectively) appeared at the time he married Mrinalini Devi. Following his move in 1890 to the Tagore estates, Shelaidaha, East Bengal, he began to write short stories inspired by his new pastoral context. Resistance to the Bengal Partition (1905–8) promoted by Curzon (q.v.), inspired him openly to espouse—for a limited time—the politics of non-violent protest. In this role he became an important nationalist figure, though his rejection of extremism later led to repudiation by political activists. In 1912 he set out with members of his family for his third, and life-changing, trip to Europe and America. The highlight of the trip was the appearance of *Gitanjali (Song Offerings)* (1912) which catapulted him into the literary attention of Europe and America, and won him the Nobel Prize (1913). Nine more trips abroad followed, many aimed at raising money for Visva-Bharati. In 1919, after the Amritsar Massacre, he resigned his knighthood (awarded 1915). He was elected to the University Chair in Bengali at Calcutta University (1932), and received an honorary doctorate from Oxford University (1940). Tagore's great and sudden fame probably trammelled his later creativity. Certainly his reputation in the West waned almost as quickly as it had arisen, due to a decline in the vogue for mysticism, and, even more so, to the difficulty of capturing Bengali devotional verse traditions in English. His belief in the close interfusion of the earthly and the divine, as expressed in the *Gitanjali* poems, led him to a conviction of the unity of all human life despite social divisions. Though often ambivalently expressed, this conviction motivated his ceaseless resistance to what he saw as political fanaticism. During an intensely productive life Tagore brought out around one hundred short stories, fifty-four volumes of verse, thirty-nine books of essays, two thousand songs set to music, fifty-two plays in verse and prose, forty collections of essays, ten novels and novellas, and, as an old man, paintings and drawings. Other poetry collections in English translation include *The Crescent Moon* (1913), *Fruit-Gathering* (1916), and *The Fugitive* (1921); and plays, *The Post Office* (1914; from *Dakghar*, 1912), *The Cycle of Spring* (1917; from *Falgani*, 1916), and *The Curse at Farewell* (1924). His most celebrated novel is *Ghare-baire* (1916; translated as *The Home and the World*, 1919).

In the later decades of his almost century-long life, the Victorian Poet Laureate, Alfred, Lord TENNYSON (1809–92), became identified with Britain's triumphal, though always still uneasy, world expansionism. Yet his character as a poet was fundamentally split, divided between his public role, speaking from within the centre of empire, providing it with gilded pictures of national achievement, and the pessimism that shadows his early poems, such as his long elegy *In Memoriam* (1850). His career too was symbolically divided almost exactly in half by his accession to the Poet-Laureateship (1850). While his early work, including *Poems, Chiefly Lyrical* (1830), was unfavourably reviewed, he found success with *Poems* (1842). A prolific period followed, during which *The Princess* (1847), *In Memoriam, Maud and Other Poems* (1855), and the first *Idylls of the King* (1859, completed 1872–3) appeared. But his melancholia still made itself felt in the foreboding and misgivings of his later work. He could speak strenuously of Britain's superiority as a moral culture—in the epilogue to *Idylls of the King*, of the 'faith that made us rulers'. Yet in other poems, like his famously pessimistic 'Locksley Hall Sixty Years After' (1887), the age is 'cramped with menace': 'Progress halts on palsied feet.' However, as in 'The Defence of Lucknow' (1879), it is as the mythologizer of a glorious past of courage and fortitude that Tennyson played his most important role in sustaining Britain's imperial self-image. In the 1880s he eventually agreed to a title—a mark of the extent to which he had become identified as the voice of his times. He was the first poet to be rewarded in such a way for his poetry alone.

(Sir) G. O. (George Otto) TREVELYAN (1838–1928) was a politician, historian, and man of letters and, crucially for his writing about India, the nephew of Thomas Babington Macaulay (1800–59), author of the influential Minute on Indian Education (1835). Educated at Trinity College, Cambridge, he spent only a year in India (1862), working as a private secretary to his father, Sir Charles Trevelyan, the Financial Minister of the Governing Council. This meant that the title of the book based on his Indian experiences, *The Competition Wallah* (1864), was not in fact applicable to him. Having experienced a 'gradual but complete' loss of faith in autocratic empire in India, his liberalism was further radicalized under the influence of John Bright when he entered Parliament (1865). In the 1880s he eventually became a supporter of Irish Home Rule. His rejection of the race prejudices generated by imperialism, as expressed in *Competition Wallah*, largely determined this decision. Trevelyan's other writings include the verse satires *Horace in Athens* (1861) and *Ladies in Parliament* (1886); *Cawnpore* (1865), an expansion of the Mutiny episode in *Competition Wallah*; a *Life of Macaulay* (1876); and *The American Revolution* (in three volumes, 1899–1907).

As well as being a prolific novelist and a superactive post office official, Anthony TROLLOPE (1815–82) travelled globally and wrote extensively about his travels in letters and the books *The West Indies and the Spanish Main* (1860), *North America* (1862), *South Africa* (1878), and *Australia and New Zealand* (1873). As these upfront titles suggest, he was interested in investigating the practical and political aspects of colonial situations. *Australia and New Zealand* is based on the first of two visits (1871–2 and 1875), both made with the object of visiting his agriculturalist son Frederic. Though controversial for its frank opinions, the book was praised as a social history of a country till then not much written up. His politics—the 'advanced . . . conservative' liberalism which is to the fore in his travel writing—was in step with establishment ideology of the time: a belief in unavoidable class- and race inequality, and hope for very gradual amelioration. While he took account of the shift towards a more expansionist imperialism, as advocated by Froude (q.v.), he was broadly in sympathy with white colonial nationalism, emphasizing that colonial well-being depended on political autonomy. He produced two widely acclaimed series of novels, the regionalist Barchester Towers series, including the eponymous *Barchester Towers* (1857) and *The Last Chronicle of Barset* (1866–7), and the Palliser novels which deal with parliamentary politics. He wrote biographies of Thackeray, Cicero, and Lord Palmerston, and his own autobiography.

His name has now undeservedly fallen into obscurity, yet with his work on West Indian Creole and his book *Froudacity* (1889), a testing reply to J. A. Froude's (q.v.) misrepresentations of his islands, J. J. (John Jacob) THOMAS (1840–89) stands as the precursor of a long line of respected anti-colonial West Indian intellectuals – Marcus Garvey, Claude McKay (q.v.), Aimé Césaire, C. L. R. James, Frantz Fanon, Stuart Hall. A self-trained linguist, he was born in Trinidad two years after slave apprenticeship ended in the British West Indies. Growing up, he was therefore influentially surrounded by people whose memories went back to Africa. During time spent teaching and in the Civil Service, his interest in local West Indian ways was expressed in particular by his work on formalizing Creole dialect structures, till then not written down. He published the highly regarded book *The Theory and Practice of Creole Grammar* (1869), on the strength of which he was elected a member of the Philological Society in London, a high honour at this time for a West Indian of African descent. During the 1880s ill-health forced his resignation from the Civil Service, yet he continued to work for short periods as a headmaster, journalist, and linguist. The publication of *The English in the West Indies* (1888), which scandalized local opinion, found Thomas in Grenada, where he wrote in protest to the *Grenada Gazette*. These articles formed the first draft of *Froudacity* which he took with him to London in 1888 to be published. As with other early postcolonial intellectuals, like Solomon Plaatje (q.v.), the target audience for his protest was 'Englishmen' who combined 'conscience with judgement'. He also planned to complete in England an enlarged *Creole Grammar*, but was prevented by illness. He died of tuberculosis in 1889, the same year that *Froudacity* was published to generally approving reviews.

Swami VIVEKANANDA (born Narendranath Datta, 1863–1902) rose out of a middle-class Bengali family to become the disciple and then successor (after 1886) of the Swami Ramakrishna Paramahamsa of the Kali temple, Calcutta. Based on the elder Swami's message of the universalism of religion, his own world influence was in part the result of and to some extent helped mould the 1890s wave of Western interest in alternative beliefs, as reflected in the vogue for spiritualism and theosophy. Growing interest in worldwide religious interaction was crystallized at the World Parliament of Religions, held in Chicago, 1893. Here Vivekananda's theme of the Unity of the Divine beyond sectarianism was recognized as representing an important spiritual force. His talks at the Parliament, as well as speeches given in London and New York (1895 and 1896), were significant for pointing a way beyond the social and cultural borderlines which colonial times embedded and naturalized, and for insisting on the unity of humankind despite cultural and religious differences. His belief in the attainment of the Divine through the four Yogas is set out in *Raja Yoga* (1896). While a universalist abroad, he also expounded an assertive Hinduism with a particular local and nationalist agenda. The anti-Partition protests in Bengal (1905–8; see Aurobindo, Curzon) were stimulated by the religious revivalism which he promoted. He called for spiritual energy in India to be directed towards scientific and technical modernization in order to raise the 'Motherland' out of the stagnation of poverty and to achieve national self-respect. Far from being 'old and effete', as imperial stereotypes suggested, India was full of potential. He attracted many Western followers, including the Irish radical Margaret Noble (Sister Nivedita), his disciple-companion and author of *Kali, the Mother* (1900) and *The Master as I Saw Him* (1910).

(Sir) William WATSON (1858–1935) began as a pessimistic but patriotic English poet of the *fin-de-siècle*, a wistful belated Romantic of an age in which England, 'mine own Ancestral land', had bewilderingly if also fruitfully outgrown her beloved pastoral bounds. What he saw as his country's ignoble treatment of the Boers in South Africa (1899–1902) changed him into a sceptic with regard to imperial enterprise: the 'tramp of Power, and its long trail of pain'. His doubt about empire as a disinterested force for good had already set in during the 1895–7 Armenian massacre in Turkey. Love of country, he wrote in the Preface to *For England* (1903), should not consist in hatred of mankind. Other work includes *Lyric Love* (1892), *The Year of Shame* (1896), *The Heralds of the Dawn* (1906), and his *Collected Poems* (1906). It is probably the case that Watson would have become Poet Laureate after Tennyson, instead of Austin (qq.v.), had it not been for his anti-imperial doubts.

In addition to many other labours and achievements, Leonard WOOLF (1880–1969) is prominent in the history of early twentieth-century literature as the co-founder, with his wife Virginia Woolf, of the Hogarth Press (1917), which published T. S. Eliot and Katherine Mansfield (q.v.), E. M. Forster and Freud. He was also an influential political thinker and organizer on the British Left. His work *International Government* (1916), which laid stress on arbitration and arms controls, contributed to the formation of the League of Nations. Of Jewish origin, Woolf joined the Apostles at Cambridge, like so many other members of the Bloomsbury Group, and was strongly influenced by the thinking of the philosopher G. E. Moore. In 1904 he took up a position in the Ceylon Colonial Service. By eventually turning him into an anti-imperialist this was to be the crucible of his later identity as a political theorist. During the six-odd years he spent in Ceylon he demonstrated an indefatigable, even maniacal capacity for work (by his own admission). In 1908 he was appointed the government agent over the entire district of Hambantota in southern Ceylon, a significant promotion. However, while faultlessly performing as a civil servant, Woolf also experienced a growing 'political schizophrenia', becoming increasingly disillusioned with the charade of European power. Even so, the primary reason for his resignation in 1911 was to marry Virginia Stephen. Thereafter he turned his hand to fiction, producing several short stories and two autobiographical novels, *The Wise Virgins* (1914) and *The Village in the Jungle* (1913), the second of which explores the remoteness of the imperial government apparatus to native lives. Within a few years his increasing political involvements and his own recognition of his wife's greater novelistic brilliance deflected his literary ambitions. He became involved in the Co-operative Movement, the Fabian Society, and the Labour Party, and began writing political journalism. During the First World War Woolf produced a withering critique of imperialist expansionism, *Empire and Commerce in Africa* (1920). Later books—including *Imperialism and Civilisation* (1928), *Barbarians at the Gate* (1939), and *After the Deluge* (1931, 1939)—further elaborated his socialist political philosophy. Up until the early 1960s Woolf worked as an editor for the *International Review*, the *Contemporary Review*, and the *Nation*.

William Butler YEATS (1865–1939) was the son of two prominent though declining Anglo-Irish families. Inspired by conversations with the ageing nationalist John O'Leary, his early poetry of the so-called 'Celtic Twilight' period sought to establish an Irish writing of literary worth, founded upon national myth yet distinct from what he saw as the crude propagandism of his nineteenth-century forebears. This early work also contains strong elements of English Romanticism and of the spiritualism of the period (in 1890 he joined the Hermetic Order of the Golden Dawn). In the first decade of the twentieth century he poured his artistic and political energies into 'theatre business' and the establishment of the Irish National Theatre (1899). Throughout this time he sought to establish and nourish a self-respecting Irish culture, based on its own traditions, distinct from those of England. His own nationalistic play, *Cathleen Ni Houlihan*, written with Lady Gregory, was produced in 1902, with his long-time love the revolutionary Maud Gonne in the title role. Later Yeats became disillusioned with the prudery and materialism of the Theatre's largely middle-class audiences and returned to his own writing, producing a new, stripped style and a developing personal mythology from *Responsibilities* (1914) onwards. This did not prevent, however, a continuing engagement with Irish political events—his great elegy 'Easter 1916' brings together his aesthetic sense with reflections on the 'terrible beauty' of political sacrifice. He served as a senator in the Upper House of the new Irish Free State (1922), but again became depressed by materialism and political factionalism. In his late writing he continued his pursuit of a personal symbolic language. His interests in eastern religion, an integrated culture, and hierarchical social forms, which figured in his readiness to promote Tagore (q.v.), are manifested in his own mystical book *A Vision* (1925, 1937), in his late essays, and in the collaboration with Shri Purohit Swami on a translation of the *Upanishads*. Tagore's repudiation of nationalist fanaticism, and belief in the separation of politics and art, had also appealed to Yeats's uneasiness at the restrictions imposed by political activity. Yeats's hugely energetic, eclectic, metamorphic, and contradictory character and writing led T. S. Eliot to declare that 'he was one of those few whose history is the history of their own time'.

PUBLISHER'S ACKNOWLEDGEMENTS

The editor and publisher are grateful for permission to include the following copyright material:

Candler, Edmund, 'Káshi' from *The Mantle of the East* (Edinburgh and London: William Blackwood and Sons, 1910), repr. by kind permission of Mrs Rachael Corkill.

Hardy, Thomas, 'A Christmas Ghost Story', 'Drummer Hodge', 'War Poems II: Departure', originally published *Poems of the Past and Present* (1901), repr. in *The Collected Poems of Thomas Hardy*, ed. James Gibson (Macmillan 1976, copyright Papermac, London).

Housman, A. E., 'From Clee to Heaven the Beacon Burns' and 'Grenadier' from *The Collected Poems of A. E. Housman* (copyright 1939, 1940, © 1965 by Henry Holt and Company, Inc., © 1967 by Robert E. Symons; repr. by permission of Henry Holt and Company, Inc.). UK rights copyright The Society of Authors as the Literary Representative of the Estate of A. E. Housman.

Joyce, James, 'Ireland at the Bar' from *Il piccolo della serra* (16 Sept. 1907), copyright the Estate of James Joyce.

Kipling, Rudyard, 'His Chance in Life' from *Plain Tales from the Hills*, 1888; 'Recessional', 'The White Man's Burden', and 'The Lesson' from *Rudyard Kipling's Verse: Definitive Edition*. 1941 repr. by permission of A. P. Watt Ltd. on behalf of The National Trust.

Leacock, Stephen, 'Back to the Bush' from *Literary Lapses* (Gazette Printing Company, Montreal, 1910), repr. by John Lane in London, 1911, repr. by kind permission of the author's estate.

McKay, Claude, 'Cudjoe Fresh from de Lecture', 'Old England', and 'My Native Land, My Home' from *Songs of Jamaica*, introduction and notes by Walter Jekyll (A. W. Gardner and Co., Kingston, 1912), repr. by kind permission of the author's estate.

McKay, Claude, 'Apple Woman's Complaint' from *Constab Ballads* (A. W. Gardner & Co., Kingston, 1912), repr. by kind permission of the author's estate; 'If We Must Die', first published in *Liberator* (New York, 1918), after the end of the First World War; repr. in *Harlem Shadows* (Harcourt, Brace, and Co., 1922), repr. by kind permission of the author's estate; 'Oh General Jackson', 'The Other Day' and 'I Have a News', transcribed by Walter Jekyll from *Jamaican Song and Story: Annancy Stories, Digging Sings, Ring Tunes, and Dancing Tunes* (David Nutt/The Folk-Lore Society, 1907).

Naidu, Sarojini, 'Village Song', 'Humajan to Zobeida', 'Ode to H.H. The Nizam of Hyderabad', and 'To India' from *The Golden Threshold*, introd. by Arthur Symons (William Heinemann, London, 1905).

Sorabji, Cornelia, 'Love and Death' from *Love and Life Behind the Purdah* (Freemantle and Co., London, 1901), repr. by kind permission of Mr Richard Sorabji.

Steel, Flora Annie, 'The Duties of the Mistress', chapter 1 of *The Complete Indian Housekeeper and Cook*, revised edn. (Frank Murray, Edinburgh, 1890), repr. by kind permission of Joss Pearson. Copyright holder Flora Annie Steel works; 'Bopoluchi' from *Tales of the Punjab Told by the People*, with R. C. Temple (Macmillan and Co., London 1894), repr. by kind permission of Joss Pearson. Copyright holder Flora Annie Steel works; 'In the Permanent Way' from *In the Permanent Way and Other Stories* (William Heinemann, London, 1898), repr. by kind permission of Joss Pearson. Copyright holder Flora Annie Steel works.

Tagore, Rabindranath, Poems II, XI, XXVII, XVIII, XXV, XXXVII, XLI, XLV, LXIII, CII, from *Gitanjali* (Macmillan, London, 1913), repr. by kind permission of Upachanya, West Bengal.

Woolf, Leonard Sidney, 'Pearls and Swine' from *Stories of the East* (Hogarth Press, 1921), repr. by kind permission of copyright holders, Manuscripts Section, the University Library, University of Sussex at Brighton.

Yeats, William Butler, 'Introduction' from *Gitanjali* (Song Offerings), Macmillan, London, 1913, repr. by permission of A. P. Watt Ltd. on behalf of Michael Yeats.

Every effort has been made to contact copyright holders and obtain permission prior to publication. If notified, the publisher undertakes to rectify any inadvertent omissions at the earliest opportunity.

INDEX

GEORGE ELIOT	Adam Bede
	Daniel Deronda
	Middlemarch
	The Mill on the Floss
	Silas Marner
ELIZABETH GASKELL	Cranford
	The Life of Charlotte Brontë
	Mary Barton
	North and South
	Wives and Daughters
THOMAS HARDY	Far from the Madding Crowd
	Jude the Obscure
	The Mayor of Casterbridge
	A Pair of Blue Eyes
	The Return of the Native
	Tess of the d'Urbervilles
	The Woodlanders
WALTER SCOTT	Ivanhoe
	Rob Roy
	Waverley
MARY SHELLEY	Frankenstein
	The Last Man
ROBERT LOUIS STEVENSON	Kidnapped and Catriona
	The Strange Case of Dr Jekyll and Mr Hyde and Weir of Hermiston
	Treasure Island
BRAM STOKER	Dracula
WILLIAM MAKEPEACE THACKERAY	Barry Lyndon
	Vanity Fair
OSCAR WILDE	Complete Shorter Fiction
	The Picture of Dorian Gray

ANTHONY TROLLOPE

An Autobiography

Ayala's Angel

Barchester Towers

The Belton Estate

The Bertrams

Can You Forgive Her?

The Claverings

Cousin Henry

Doctor Thorne

Doctor Wortle's School

The Duke's Children

Early Short Stories

The Eustace Diamonds

An Eye for an Eye

Framley Parsonage

He Knew He Was Right

Lady Anna

The Last Chronicle of Barset

Later Short Stories

Miss Mackenzie

Mr Scarborough's Family

Orley Farm

Phineas Finn

Phineas Redux

The Prime Minister

Rachel Ray

The Small House at Allington

La Vendée

The Warden

The Way We Live Now

HANS CHRISTIAN ANDERSEN	**Fairy Tales**
J. M. BARRIE	**Peter Pan in Kensington Gardens** and **Peter and Wendy**
L. FRANK BAUM	**The Wonderful Wizard of Oz**
FRANCES HODGSON BURNETT	**The Secret Garden**
LEWIS CARROLL	**Alice's Adventures in Wonderland** and **Through the Looking-Glass**
CARLO COLLODI	**The Adventures of Pinocchio**
KENNETH GRAHAME	**The Wind in the Willows**
THOMAS HUGHES	**Tom Brown's Schooldays**
CHARLES KINGSLEY	**The Water-Babies**
GEORGE MACDONALD	**The Princess and the Goblin** and **The Princess and Curdie**
EDITH NESBIT	**Five Children and It** **The Railway Children**
ANNA SEWELL	**Black Beauty**
JOHANN DAVID WYSS	**The Swiss Family Robinson**

THE OXFORD SHERLOCK HOLMES

ARTHUR CONAN DOYLE

The Adventures of Sherlock Holmes
The Case-Book of Sherlock Holmes
His Last Bow
The Hound of the Baskervilles
The Memoirs of Sherlock Holmes
The Return of Sherlock Holmes
The Valley of Fear
Sherlock Holmes Stories
The Sign of the Four
A Study in Scarlet

The Oxford World's Classics Website

www.worldsclassics.co.uk

- Information about new titles
- Explore the full range of Oxford World's Classics
- Links to other literary sites and the main OUP webpage
- Imaginative competitions, with bookish prizes
- Peruse *Compass*, the Oxford World's Classics magazine
- Articles by editors
- Extracts from Introductions
- A forum for discussion and feedback on the series
- Special information for teachers and lecturers

www.worldsclassics.co.uk

American Literature

British and Irish Literature

Children's Literature

Classics and Ancient Literature

Colonial Literature

Eastern Literature

European Literature

History

Medieval Literature

Oxford English Drama

Poetry

Philosophy

Politics

Religion

The Oxford Shakespeare